LEAD, FOLLOW, OR MOVE OUT OF THE WAY!

global perspectives in literature and film

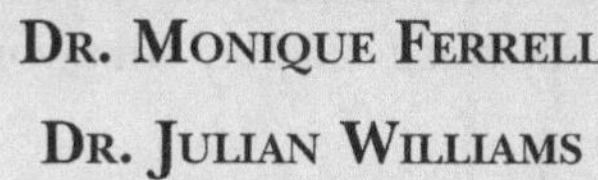
DR. MONIQUE FERRELL

DR. JULIAN WILLIAMS

NYCCT, City University of New York (CUNY)

Kendall Hunt
publishing company

Kendall Hunt
publishing company
www.kendallhunt.com
Send all inquiries to:
4050 Westmark Drive
Dubuque, IA 52004-1840

ISBN 978-1-4652-6894-5

Printed in the United States of America

Contents

FILMS ix
FOREWORD xxxix
PREFACE xli

CHAPTER 1 *Social Responsibility*

RALPH WALDO EMERSON ▶ Self-Reliance 3
Emerson's essay presents the timeless call for individuals to reflect upon, study, and pursue the inner workings of their own minds, as opposed to conforming to the well-trod path of the villainous "society."

KHALED HOSSEINI ▶ From the Novel *The Kite Runner* 19
Hosseini examines how childhood friends, two Afghan boys separated by Class and religion, make devastating choices that alter their lives forever.

BIDPAI ▶ The Camel and His Friends 39
This parable asks us to consider the importance of sacrificing the self for others.

MARGARET SANGER ▶ The Turbid Ebb and Flow of Misery. 41
During the 1920s, a nurse describes the frustration of visiting and treating impoverished women with large families and how she agonizes over the ethics of palliative care during this conservative point in American history.

TODD CRAIG ▶ "Open Season 2014": The Birth of Civil Rights Lost. 47
Focusing on Hip Hop culture and music as it relates to gender, race, Class, and social responsibility, the author determines whether or not current trends in the genre are becoming counterintuitive.

JL WILLIAMS ▶ The Ride From the Novel *Legacies* 57
On a crowded NYC train, a man with a troubled past struggles while observing his fellow passengers being harassed by two offensive and aggressive individuals.

CHAPTER 2 *Death and Violence*

TONI MORRISON ▶ From the Novel *Paradise* 69
This selection from Morrison's novel explores how acts of violence are perpetrated by men in an effort to cleanse their community of "wayward" women.

MARK TWAIN ▶ From the Novel *Adventures of Huckleberry Finn* 75
This selection from Twain's most controversial work asks us to examine the "mob mentality" and its impact on the collective voice of a community.

IDA B. WELLS-BARNETT ▶ Lynch Law in America 80
Given in 1900, this speech discusses the misinformation disseminated about lynching in the United States and provides the real motivations behind the gruesome practice.

WILLIAM SHAKESPEARE ▶ *The Tragedy of Macbeth* 87
A Scottish general is convinced that ultimate power is within his grasp. Spurred on by his cunning wife, who has ambitions of her own, Macbeth chooses evil and violence in order to snatch the crown.

MICHAEL WALSH ▶ Three Californian Teens Arrested for Rape That Allegedly Drove Teen Girl to Suicide, Parents Demand Justice. 137
This article takes a look at social media, bullying, sexual violence, and today's growing acceptance of our so-called "rape culture."

H.G. WELLS ▶ From the Novel *The War of the Worlds* 140
This excerpt focuses on the inevitable decline of human kindness and social graces once mankind is confronted with the end of civilization at the hands of an alien invasion.

CHAPTER 3 *Religion, Faith, and Spirituality*

ADAM WEYMOUTH ▶ When Global Warming Kills Your God 157
A dispute over the fishing practices of an indigenous Alaskan tribe becomes a battle over American law verses tribal faith, customs, and spirituality.

MOHAMMED NASEEHU ALI ▶ Mallam Sile 162
A Muslim man allows his faith to fight his battles and the cruelty he suffers at the hands of his community.

THOMAS PAINE ▶ Age of Reason 171
The British radical and American revolutionary stresses a deistic treatise while critiquing institutionalized religion and the inerrancy of the Bible.

TIERNEY SNEED ▶ When It Comes to Same-Sex Marriage, Both Sides Claim Pope Francis 206
LGBTQ activists and church officials both contend that the new Pope supports their respective agendas.

THE BOOK OF GENESIS ▶ The Great Flood 210
A disgruntled and angered God determines to cleanse humanity of its wickedness by sending a great flood to Earth and, as a result, Noah is charged with collecting those deemed worthy of saving.

RALPH WALDO EMERSON ▶ Divinity School Address 215
When the former Unitarian minister addressed the senior class at Cambridge in 1838, he stressed the need for moral intuition and discounted the necessity of beliefs rooted in miracles.

CHAPTER 4 Fork in the Road

SIR ARTHUR CONAN DOYLE ▶ From the Novel *A Study in Scarlet*............ 229
A broken and battered Dr. Watson, weary from the pangs of war, wallows in despair until he determines to make life worthwhile by dedicating himself to working with the great Sherlock Holmes.

FREDERICK DOUGLASS ▶ From the autobiography *Narrative of the Life of Frederick Douglass, An American Slave* 265
This excerpt from Douglass's memoir introduces one of the greatest orators and abolitionists in American history as he looks at his early years: a brutalized slave making candid observations about what human beings can both inflict and endure.

BHARATI MUKHERJEE ▶ A Father.. 272
A father, who is a practicing Hindi, feels that the women in his family are "too" American and that their behavior will ultimately bring about disastrous consequences.

DAVID SEDARIS ▶ Go Carolina 280
A man reflects on the speech therapy lessons he was forced to take as a young child; in doing so, he shares the hilarious battle he waged against being "normalized."

MONIQUE FERRELL ▶ Go Brooklyn! 287
Dire consequences abound when a half-Black, half-Hispanic female reporter decides to destroy Hip Hop Music and advance the cause of women by humiliating a rap artist on live television.

MARY SHELLEY ▶ From the Novel *Frankenstein* 306
Having taken it upon himself to create life, scientist Victor Frankenstein learns firsthand from his "monster" that he has helped to contribute to the prejudice, violence, and elitism of his society.

CHAPTER 5 Class and the Culture of Power

NAOMI WOLF ▶ The Making of a Slut.................................. 317
The author examines the "bad girl" and positions her as a social construct for "good girls"—those females who, by separating themselves, maintain their reputations while endangering those upon whom the negative title falls.

MARK TWAIN ▶ The Lowest Animal 323
Twain's "experiments" provide cynical views of mankind that, interestingly enough, are just as distressing today as they have ever been.

JHUMPA LAHIRI ▶ Interpreter of Maladies............................ 328
A poor taxi driver, who works part-time at a doctor's office, picks up a wealthy Indian-American family having an obnoxious and, as he soon learns, revealing visit.

HENRY DAVID THOREAU ▶ On The Duty of Civil Disobedience............. 343
Thoreau argues that it is incumbent upon the average citizen to resist a controlling government.

FYODOR DOSTOYEVSKY ▶ From the Novel *Notes from the Underground* 350
A disgruntled and disenchanted man battles his perceived invisibility to the larger society.

AESOP ▶ A Lion and Other Animals Go Hunting 358
Aesop's timeless and seemingly simple tale is a poignant look at power and respect.

AL ANGELORO ▶ Comic Books: How I Learned to Love Reading and Hate the Censors 360
Now an adult, the author looks back on his childhood. In doing so, he remembers how he developed a love for reading, in spite of those who sought to destroy it.

CHAPTER 6 *Race and Racial Matters*

DEAN OBEIDALLAH ▶ Do Palestinians Really Exist? 367
A Palestinian man provides the reader with a detailed historical and cultural look at who he and his people are.

WOODEN LEG ▶ Young Men, Go Out and Fight Them. 371
Confronted with impending colonialism, a warrior challenges the men of his tribe to engage in an act of war.

TAHIRA NAQVI ▶ Brave We Are. 376
While preparing a routine dinner, a mother finds herself attempting to explain the complexities of racial mixing and how people perceive biracial children.

STEVEN ERLANGER ▶ Amid Tears, Flickering Candles and Flowers, a Shaken Norway Mourns 381
People of Norway attempt to understand how and why one of its very own citizens committed an act of racially motivated mass murder.

CHARLES CHESNUT ▶ An Evening Visit From the Novel *The House Behind the Cedars* 385
After successfully "passing" in the White world, a man returns home to visit the women he left behind.

CHAPTER 7 *Gender, Sex, and Sexuality*

JAMES BALDWIN ▶ From the Novel *Giovanni's Room* 397
Excerpt looks at a man, conflicted with his sexuality, having sex with a woman and, throughout the entire process, feeling a great sense of sadness and regret.

JUNOT DIAZ ▶ Fiesta 1980. 402
A son recalls what it meant to discover that his father had an affair throughout his childhood.

FRANCES A. ALTHAUS ▶ Female Circumcision: Rite of Passage or Violation of Rights? 412
A detailed look at the culture, politics, and practice of the tradition.

CARA DORRIS ▶ My Fake Levatine Romance 420
While visiting family in Jerusalem, a young Jewish woman falls in love with an Arab man, only to learn that he is hiding a secret that alters their relationship.

ELIZA HAYWOOD ▶ Fantomina: Or, Love in a Maze. 423
A supposed member of the weaker sex sets out to determine whether or not she can manipulate a man into thinking she is several different women.

CHAPTER 8 *Manmade and Natural Disasters*

SIMON ROMERO ▶ Quake Accentuated Chasm That Has Defined Haiti 443
In the wake of the horrific natural disaster that all but decimated the already impoverished nation, a reporter finds that the divide between the rich and poor has widened with devastating effects.

JEEVAN VASAGAR ▶ The Nightwalkers 447
40,000 Ugandan children attempt to avoid being kidnapped and turned into murderous soldiers by walking to safe houses each night.

RICHARD LLOYD PARRY ▶ Ghosts of the Tsunami 451
A heartbreaking account of what happened to the families and communities that survived the 2011 earthquake and subsequent tsunami that struck Japan and killed an estimated 20,000 people.

ELI SASLOW ▶ After Newtown Shooting, Mourning Parents Enter into the Lonely Quiet 463
Following the devastating aftermath of twenty children and six adults massacred by a lone gunman, this article slowly walks the reader through the subsequent politicizing of the tragedy and its impact on those left behind.

NICHOLAS KRISTOF ▶ "Bring Back Our Girls" 475
An impassioned plea for world involvement occurs after 273 Nigerian school girls are kidnapped from their beds–bringing to light the need for civil rights protection and freedom for girls everywhere.

INDEX 479

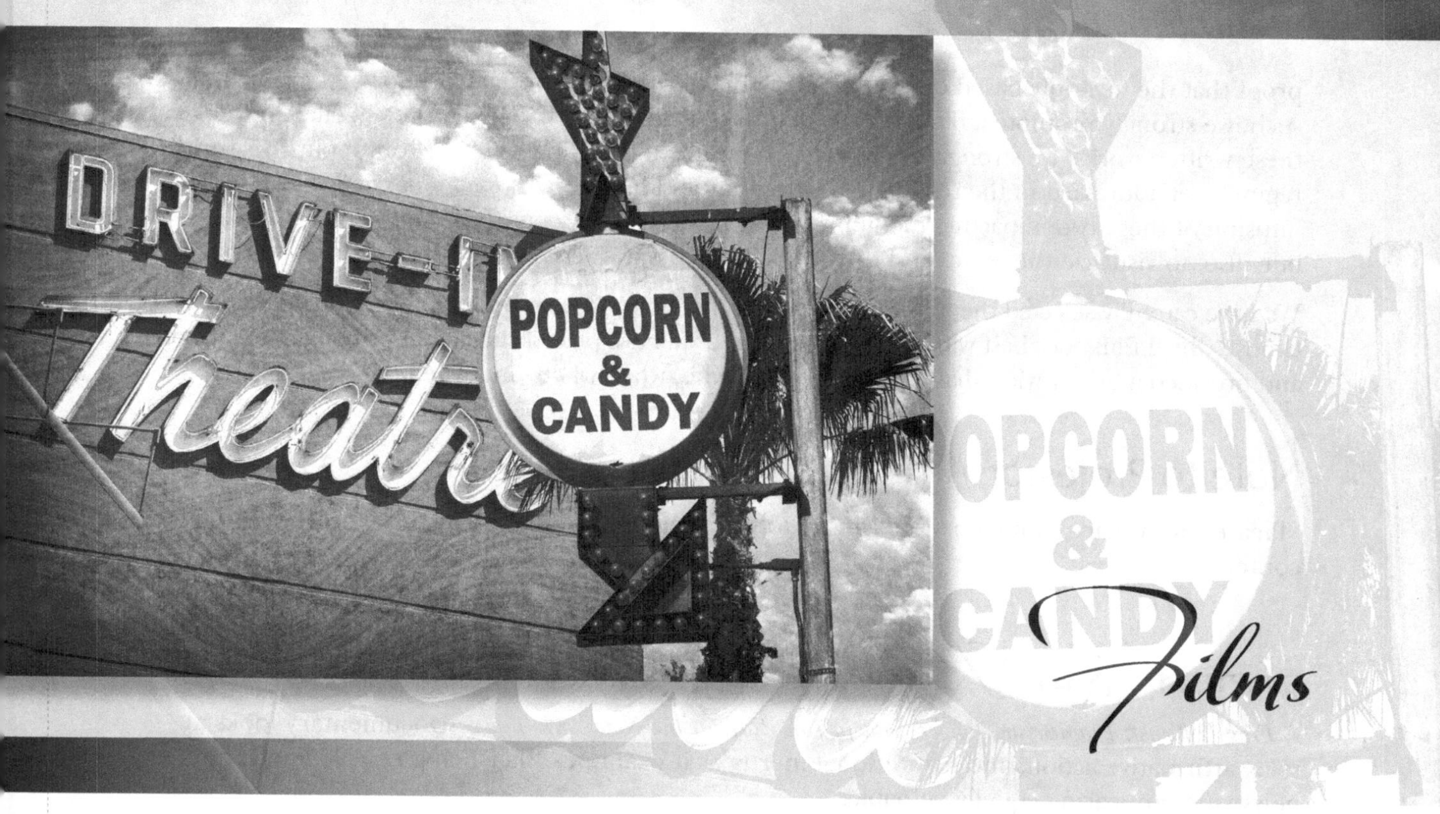

Films

Now, more than ever, we need to talk to each other, to listen to each other, and understand how we see the world, and cinema is the best medium for doing this.
—Martin Scorsese

We live in a visual world. Every day, our senses are stimulated by what we wear and how we wear it. In a flash, thanks to Twitter and Instagram, we can send out a picture of where we are, what we're eating, and who we are with. The old adage about "seeing is believing" holds more truth than ever before. For many of us, what we see helps us to know something or believe an idea to be true or false. And so it is with film. A good film, a brilliant one, can bring home to the viewer a perspective that was once elusive. It can inspire. It can also make real and more relevant an equally brilliant piece of writing. For educators, film can and should be an important tool.

Our students, like the majority of the world's population, love movies. Whether it's drama or action/adventure or mystery or comedy or the love story or, with ever increasing audiences, the documentary, film has proven that it is arguably the main vehicle used to both express sentiment and entertain viewers. Even though this point is virtually inarguable, literary materials still remain the core for most classrooms. However, books are now, more than ever, forced to compete with our growing technological societies. Let's be honest: today's students relate more readily to wireless communication devices and the internet than they do with paper texts. With the advent of wireless portable reading devices–such as the Kindle, Nook, Galaxy Note, and IPad–there is now further proof that the text-only based classroom must adjust to this new visual world or be left behind. As such, we strongly promote a blending of what the students love with what they need. Alongside these written works, we strongly encourage that selected films–movies that round out the world's regions not addressed in the readings–be incorporated into the classroom curriculum. The infusion of these two impacting mediums allows the students to not only read and discuss texts but, also, to visualize the topics and themes that come out of classroom examinations.

We have carefully selected the following films. In an attempt to help both professor and students choose which film goes best with what written work, we have placed specific films in chapter sections and provided a brief review that gives insight into who, what, when, and where for each film.

Note to Professors/Instructors

*Please review each film before showing it to your students. Some films contain serious, adult content.

CHAPTER 1 *Social Responsibility*

A Fragile Trust: Plagiarism, Power, and Jayson Blair at the New York Times: Documentary looks at race, affirmative action, and institutional inertia as it examines Blair being revealed and the newspaper appearing equally culpable.

The Agronomist: A documentary on the assassination of Haitian political activist Jean Dominique.

All You Need Is Love: This documentary focuses on the lives and dreams of the children of Good Morning School in the district of Mae Sot, Thailand. Mae Sot is one of the many towns along the Thai-Burma border where hundreds of thousands of Burmese nationals have chosen to live as a result of the repressive actions taken by Burma's military junta. The film highlights not just their plight, but also the positive way these children go about their lives under circumstances that are, to many, unimaginable.

The Armstrong Lie: Documentary looks at one of the world's most famous athletes and the unapologetic lies about doping he told.

August: Osage County: Mouth cancer and a missing husband are what inspire family members to return to the matriarch's hot Oklahoma home and endure her insults.

Aunt Diane: Exploration of the mystery surrounding the tragic 2009 wrong-way crash that killed a mother and seven others on NY's Taconic Parkway.

The Business of Being Born: Documentary that explores issues surrounding child birthing, noting that the U.S. spends twice as much per birth than any other industrialized country, while, interestingly, having the second worst mortality rate for both mothers and infants.

Dallas Buyers Club: Given an HIV death sentence, a bottom scarping drug addict survives, becomes a drug importer, and a provider of hope.

Dead Poet's Society: In the spirit of Emerson, a prep-school teacher challenges his male students to be nonconformists and tap into their inner genius.

Death Metal Angola: Touching documentary chronicles the lives and mission of a couple, Sonja and Wilker, whose love for death metal music is bringing hope to both the town and children of Huambo and Angola as a country–a land with a history of wars and civil unrest that has left the people torn, broken, and starving for something to give them peace.

The Devil's Miner: Chronicling the daily ordeal of a 14-year-old who works in the Bolivian silver mines, this somber documentary captures the hellish realities of fear.

Fight Club: Looking at the duality that resides within men–males who prove themselves by fighting bare knuckled–the film examines a specific question: Does a man belong to himself or is maleness a societal construct to which he inevitably falls prey?

Flowers of Evil: A love story between Gecko, an Algerian-French hotel bellman and parkourer, and Anahita, an Iranian student forced to leave her country for her own safety after the controversial elections in 2009. Via Youtube and Twitter, the film explores the power of social networking for change.

Gun Fight: An eye-opening documentary that looks at the complicated issues surrounding private gun ownership in America.

Hot Coffee: Documentary that looks at the real story behind the infamous McDonald's coffee scalding and three other cases that impacted the tort-reform movement.

Hotel Rwanda: An examination of a man who stands up to be counted when the "new" norm in his African homeland is violence and warfare.

I Am Because We Are: Writer-producer Madonna exposes the tragic stories of the millions of Malawi children orphaned by AIDS.

In the Year of the Pig: Emile de Antonio's ground breaking 1968 protest documentary against the Vietnam War, where he reveals the American government's lies, and calls into question all versions of the war released to the public.

Jump Tomorrow: A Nigerian pledged in an arranged marriage questions "his situation."

Juno: Two adolescent outcasts find themselves expecting a child in a reserved Minnesota community. Film examines abortion, adoption, and the growing pains of the protagonists and everyone around them.

Keane: A film dedicated to unearthing the reality of what it means to live with mental illness.

Kill the Messenger: Movie looks at journalist Gary Webb's real life during and after he wrote the series "Dark Alliance" for the *San Jose Mercury News*–an uncompromising expose on the CIA's complicity in the early years of the cocaine trade; as a result, he was destroyed by other journalists at powerful newspapers and left disgraced and ruined for writing about something we would all eventually learn was indeed true.

The Kite Runner: The subtitled film adaptation of Khalid Hosseini's best selling novel on Afghanistan, lost childhoods, betrayal, and redemption.

Koch: Documentary looks at Mayor Ed Koch and his catch-phrase question, "How'm I doing?" As he led New York City for twelve years, the film looks at how he saved the city from bankruptcy and became a national celebrity, alongside his failures–government scandals, alienation of the black community, and ignoring the AIDS epidemic.

The Last Supper: Five midwestern graduate students decide to rid the world of those who hold opposing political ideas, by offering them dinners and a very special glass of wine.

Lincoln: Biographical drama that focuses largely on the iconic president trying to pass the Thirteenth Amendment, and how he learned to fight and compromise for the good of a nation.

Mama Africa: Documentary is packed with five decades of rare archival footage that examine the history and music of Miriam Makeba, whose songs exposed the world to the injustices of Apartheid in South Africa and resulted in a thirty year exile from her home country.

Men, Women, and Children: Timely film follows the story of a group of high school teenagers and their parents as they attempt to navigate the many ways the internet has changed their relationships, communication, self-image, and their love lives.

Moolaadé: A mother who experienced female circumcision as a child attempts to prevent her daughter from being forced to take part in the ceremony.

Norma Rae: In spite of conspiring forces, a factory worker in a small North Carolina town fights to establish a union.

Red Army: Documentary about the Soviet Union and the most successful dynasty in sports history: the Red Army hockey team. Looking at former team captain Slava Fetisov, a hero turned political enemy, the film looks at how a man stood up to a powerful system and paved the way for change for generations of Russians.

Reportero: Following the rise in attacks and threats against journalists, this documentary looks at veteran reporter Sergio Haro and his colleagues at *Zeta*, a Tijuana, Mexico–based weekly paper. Since the paper's founding in 1980, two of the paper's editors have been murdered and the founder viciously attacked.

School Ties: In the 1950s, an all-male school is challenged to open the prejudiced minds and hearts of its privileged students after one of their own admits he is Jewish.

Silenced Voices: Documentary looks at one of the champions of journalism in Sri Lanka, Lasantha Wickrematunge, who was gunned down by eight men in broad daylight in the country's capital, Colombo. Since 1992, twenty-five journalist have been killed by suspected government forces.

The Tillman Story: Government turns former professional football player turned Army Ranger Pat Tillman's death into propaganda.

Twilight Zone: Eye of the Beholder: A woman struggles to change her face so that she can look like everyone else in order to avoid being evicted from her community.

Walk Away Renee: This documentary is a sequel to 2003's *Tarnation*, and it returns to look at Jonathon Caouette's struggles with his mentally deteriorating mother, Renee. Film examines the son's battles with his volatile mother and, oftentimes, reticent prescription-filling doctors.

Weatherman: Local weatherman's convoluted journey to find his place in the world while dealing with the disintegration of his family.

Without the King: This lively documentary looks at the tiny African nation of Swaziland, one of the last existing absolute monarchies. This look at the African kingdom exposes a life expectancy that is one of the shortest in the world—the rate of HIV infection is the globe's highest—as well as thousands of citizens who subsist on some of the most revolting food imaginable.

Words of Witness: Defying cultural norms and family expectations, this documentary looks at 22-year-old Heba Afify as she takes to the streets to report on an Egypt in turmoil, using tweets, texts, and Facebook posts.

Young Rebels: A documentary on young Cuban revolutionaries who use Hip-Hop music as a forum to discuss race and class issues in their native Cuba.

CHAPTER 2 Death and Violence

96 Minutes: This thriller tells the story of a violent carjacking from the perspective of both the perpetrators and their unsuspecting victims.

After Kony: Staging Hope: This documentary follows a team of activists in Uganda who use theater to help former child soldiers and sex slaves cope with traumatic experiences.

Ai Weiwei: Never Sorry: Following the artist for three years, Ai questioned the deaths of more than 5,000 students in the 2008 Sichuan earthquake.

American Gun: Vignettes on gun violence and how this epidemic is devastating American families.

American Sniper: Movie about the life of Chris Kyle, the most lethal sniper in U.S. military history, who, before being killed by a former veteran at a shooting range, served four tours in the Iraq War.

An Omar Broadway Film: Using a contraband video camera inside the gang unit at Newark's Northern State Prison, a jailed Bloods member puts his life on the line to document guards' corruption and excessive force. Documentary exposes the often corrupt and violent world behind bars.

An Unreal Dream: The Michael Morton Story: Documentary examines the 1986 murder of Morton's wife in front of their only child—a crime that led to Michael's wrongful conviction.

Apocalypse Now: Francis Ford Coppola's surrealistic and symbolic film details the confusion, violence, fear, and madness that encompassed the Vietnam War.

Beautiful Boy: A school shooting rampage is viewed from the perspective of the killer's bewildered parents.

Better this World: Film looks at the "Texas Two," David McKay and Bradley Crowder, two teens who, at the volatile Republican Convention, cross a line that results in high-stakes entrapment. The result is a movie that presents a story of loyalty, betrayal, and the world of civil liberties post-9/11.

Blue Caprice: Intense drama that looks at the scary season in 2002, when the Beltway Snipers brought a sense of domestic terrorism to the nation.

Bowling for Columbine: Documentary filmmaker Michael Moore examines how the culture of fear, class, racism, and violence may have led to America's most horrific school shooting.

Camp 14–Total Control Zone: Documentary provides a fascinating portrait of a young man born inside a prison in North Korea–an individual who grew up imprisoned by dehumanizing violence yet still found the will to escape.

Crips: Strapped 'n' Strong: Documentary follows Dutch Crips Main C and Santos, who both yearn to escape gang life, but hardened leader Keylow holds the keys to their fates.

Crying Ladies: Comedy that follows the lives of three women who cry at funerals–professionally.

Dormant Beauty: Poignant dramatization around the final days of Italy's Eluana Englaro, a woman who spent 17 years in a coma, the end result of a car accident.

El Sicario, Room 164: Sitting in a motel room in Mexico, a hooded former hit man for the Ciudad Juarez drug cartel recounts his troubled adolescence, his entry into a corrupt police academy, and the many kidnappings and murders he committed.

Family Affair: Chico Colvard's documentary film explores a history of abuse that went on inside his house as a child, including his own accidental shooting of his sister when he was nine years old.

Freak: Told with seamless comic flare, comedian John Leguizamo's stand-up show explores what it means to grow up in a house of domestic abuse.

Give up Tomorrow: Documentary that re-examines the 1997 murder of two sisters on a provincial island in the Phillipines. For the next thirteen years, Paco Larranaga's case received the highest profile in the nation's history. The film seems to be a murder mystery and a courtroom drama, but evolves into a powerful indictment of national corruption.

Half of a Yellow Sun: Film adaptation of Chimamanda Ngozi Adichie's novel follows two sisters–English- educated twins–who return to Nigeria to play a part in nation building, only to be swept into conflict.

How I Killed a Saint: A woman living abroad in America returns to her native war-torn Balkans and discovers that both her family and country are in utter turmoil.

Into the Abyss: This compelling documentary examines the emotional aftermath of a triple murder in Texas, interviewing the two killers and victim's relatives.

The Invisible War: Investigative documentary about the shameful and underreported epidemic of rape within the U.S. military, and the institutions that perpetuate it, as well as its profound and social consequences.

Kassim the Dream: Documentary that follows Kassim "The Dream" Ouma, who went from Ugandan child soldier to world champion boxer.

Love Story: Harvard rich kid meets Radcliffe musician. They fall in love and then discover that she is terminally ill. (Original, 1970)

The Missing Picture: Documentary examines 1970s Cambodia and their mass starvation and workcamp despair under the Khmer Rouge.

Munyurangabo: Following the relationship between two boys traveling on a vengeance mission across Rwanda's countryside, the film, which has a completely nonprofessional cast, takes a potent look at genocide, as it depicts friendships and familial betrayals.

My Afghanistan: Documentary follows Nagieb Khaja, a Danish journalist of Afghan origin, as he travels to Lashkar Gah, capital Helmand province in Afghanistan. Film examines 35 years of armed conflict, and the ordinary citizens and their struggles to live in the constant shadow of violence.

Mystic River: Boston community implodes as the death of a teenage girl puts her father at odds with his childhood friends–men bonded through a horrible childhood experience.

Nanking: Powerful documentary that provides first person recollections of the near-total destruction of the Chinese city and its inhabitants by imperial Japanese troops in 1937.

Narco Cultura: Documentary looks at how Mexican drug cartels are having a major escalation in the region's murders over the past few years, specifically the influence of Americans who make money writing narcoscorridos–songs dedicated to lionizing Mexican drug lords.

Nothing but a Man: Classic drama presents a blue-collar worker struggling to retain his dignity in an age of southern inhospitality.

Only God Can Save Us: Documentary on Heidegger's philosophy and his relationship to Nazism.

Ordinary People: The accidental death of an older son from an affluent family deeply strains the relationships between the bitter mother, the good-natured father, and the guilt-ridden son. (Original, 1980)

Paradise Now: After a horrific experience, two Palestinian friends decide to become suicide bombers in Tel Aviv.

Parkland: Movie looks at the events that occurred on November 22, 1963, the day John F. Kennedy was transported to Parkland Hospital after being shot and killed.

The Passion of the Christ: An exploration of the violence Christ endured during his last days.

Raging Bull: The story details the main stages of temperamental, paranoid, and abusive boxer Jake Lamotta: his rise, fall, and in-between life.

Saving Face: Oscar-winning documentary about women disfigured by acid attacks in Pakistan.

Series 7: The Contenders: Movie looks at how far reality television can go, as well as presenting a sobering look at what we consider entertainment. The violent "series" has contestants actually winning and moving forward in the game by killing each other.

Sleepers: Supposedly based on a true crime, four teenage pranksters are sent to a juvenile detention center where they are physically and sexually abused by the guards. Ten years later, two of the boys murder the ringleader, leading to a highly publicized trial.

State of Fear: Documentary that offers a balanced view of the atrocities occurring during Peru's sordid twenty-year cycle of violence and corruption.

Taxi Driver: The quintessential average man is compelled to seek social validation through the only means available: violence.

Terms of Endearment: Movie traces the lives of mother and daughter, women always trying to find happiness, who march to the beat of different drummers–women reunited when one becomes stricken with cancer.

The Undocumented: Film examines the life of Marcos Hernandez, an undocumented Mexican living and working in Chicago. Chronicled over the course of Arizona's deadly summer months, the film weaves Marco's search for his father with the efforts of humanitarians and Border Patrol agents who try to prevent migrant deaths.

United 93: Reenactment of the final hours of the doomed flight that plunged out of the Pennsylvania sky on September 11, 2001.

The War of the Roses: A married couple turns to horrendous acts of violence after the collapse of their "ideal" marriage.

We Were Soldiers: Story of the first major battle of the American phase of the Vietnam War and the soldiers on both sides who fought.

The Whistleblower: Based on true events, this political thriller follows Kathryn, a UN peacekeeper who arrives in post-war Bosnia. There, she is met with chaos and disorder and unearths an underworld of human trafficking.

Whitey: United States of America v. James J. Bulger: Second only to Osama bin Laden on the FBI's most wanted, this documentary examines Bulger's rage and the evolution of a killer. It also looks at the relatives of murdered victims seeking closure and local journalists hoping for more than a confession.

Winter Soldier: True-life accounts from actual soldiers who returned from Vietnam–men physically and mentally left too scarred to rejoin society.

Wit: Literary scholar faced with cancer discovers human kindness.

CHAPTER 3 Religion, Faith, and Spirituality

Agnes of God: When a nun is discovered in her quarters with a dead newborn, a court-appointed psychiatrist investigates.

Amazing Love: When a confrontation occurs between two teens on a youth group camping trip, their leader shares the Old Testament story about the prophet Hosea.

Ana Arabia: Drama depicts a small community of Jews and Arabs living together near Jaffa in a forgotten enclave surrounded by mass public housing.

Believe Me: In debt, a smart and handsome college student convinces his three roommates they can make a killing exploiting the gullible church crowd. They take their message on the road, raising funds for a cause as fake as their message.

Camp: An investment banker gets more than he bargained for when he spends a week as a counselor at a camp for troubled kids and bonds with an abused boy.

Constantine's Sword: Based on the 2001 book of the same name, this documentary follows James Carroll–a former Catholic priest whose faith was rocked by Christianity's militancy and anti-Semitism–as he examines the Crusades, the infamous treaty between Pope Pius XII and Adolf Hitler, and the rise of Mega Churches and evangelical fervor.

The Dali Lama: Peace and Prosperity: A visual record of the Dali Lama's sold out Radio City Music Hall visit and presentation.

Destiny: Examines the historic battle between Islamic fundamentalists and liberals through the story of the enlightened 12th-century Andalusian philosopher and Quranic scholar Averroes.

The Dhamma Brothers: Documentary looks at a group of inmates sentenced to Alabama's maximum-security prison who began practicing meditation following a ten-day course in the Buddhist technique of vipassana.

Dogma: Two renegade angels try to exploit a religious loophole that could bring an end to humanity.

A Door to the Sky: Father's death forces Moroccan woman to return from her expatriate life in Paris to the constrained Muslim customs of her homeland.

The Encounter: When five strangers come together at an eatery, they meet the owner, who seems to know everything about them and is reminiscent of Jesus Christ.

The Excorcist: Teen is possessed by the devil, and priests are forced to perform a dangerous religious ceremony. (Original, 1973)

Faith Like Potatoes: Weary of the conflict in Zambia, a white farmer moves his family to South Africa, where they try to transform a bare plot of land into a working farm.

Guyana Tragedy–The Story of Jim Jones: This made for TV film is based on the cult-like world of charismatic leader Jim Jones and the 1978 mass suicide of the People's Temple in Jonestown, Guyana. Not only does this real life event–one that took the lives of over 900 people–serve as one of the largest mass suicides in world history, it also serves as the greatest single loss of American civilian life in a non-natural disaster until the events of September 11th, 2001. (Original, 1980)

History of the World: Mel Brooks's satire where we learn what "really happened" at the last supper.

The Jewish Cardinal (Le Metis de Dieu): Amazing true story of Jean-Marie Lustiger, who maintained his cultural identity as a Jew, even after converting to Catholicism and rising through the ranks of the priesthood.

The Journey of L.A. Mass: Documentary explores Donald Taylor and his vision that changed Gospel music through his success with the L.A. Mass Choir.

The Kid with a Bike: Eleven-year-old foster kid, Cyril, clings to his bicycle, which is stolen repeatedly throughout the movie. This movie has a religious parable undertone, as the boy is seen as a puerile Christ figure surrounded by saintly characters who all hope to find redemption.

Koran by Heart: The world's preeminent Koran-recitation competition that takes place each year in Cairo is captured in this documentary that follows diverse children as the undergo intense preparation before performing in front of prominent judges.

The Last Temptation of Christ: At his execution, Jesus is tempted by an alluring image of a blissful life with Mary Magdelene–a temptation that tries to sway him from the sacrifice he must make.

Life of Pi: Indian teen survives a shipwreck that kills his entire family, only to be stranded in a boat in the middle of the ocean with a ferocious Bengal tiger.

LoveCrimesKabul: Inside look documentary that examines Afghanistan's Badam Baugh Women's Prison, where half of the inmates are locked up for "moral crimes."

Maidentrip: Dutch teenager Laura Dekker's battle to be allowed to circumnavigate the globe in a 38-foot ketch is the platform for this beautiful documentary. With cameras in tow, she filmed her two-year odyssey, one that reveals a child's spiritual growth while sailing alone with nature.

Manakamana: Nepal-set documentary follows a cable car that travels to the Manakamana Temple, a shrine to the Hindu Goddess.

Mooz-Lum: Strict Muslim student goes to college and is transformed. Then 9/11 terrorist attacks occur and he experiences distrust from angry classmates.

The Omen: Diplomat learns that his son is the literal anti-Christ. (Original, 1976)

Orthodox Stance: Documentary that looks at 25-year old Orthodox Jewish prizefighter Dmitry Salita who literally won't fight after Sundown of Friday.

Pur: A documentary featuring rare archival footage of Purim plays staged by small groups of Jewish dissidents during the Soviet regime.

Religulous: Bill Mahr's hilarious documentary on the current state of world religion.

Rosemary's Baby: Woman learns that her pregnancy is actually part of a satanic ritual. (Original, 1968)

Saint Ralph: A young man is forced to join his Catholic school track team after it is discovered that he has committed twenty-two sins against the flesh–his own flesh.

Saved: This satire looks at how religious beliefs can lead to extreme intolerance when a girl finds herself pregnant at a Baptist high school.

Saving Faith: A man whose life is crumbling after surviving a car accident that killed his daughter finds faith after clashing with a rebellious gang member.

The Song: Inspired by the Song of Solomon: Aspiring singer-songwriter struggles to catch a break while trying to escape the shadow of his famous father. He falls in love, writes a hit, and finds himself thrust into the trappings of stardom–rewards that begin to unravel his life and marriage.

Take Shelter: Ohio man plagued by visions builds a backyard storm shelter that he insists is essential to survive the impending apocalypse.

Twist of Faith: Documentary that looks at a man who confronts his past sexual abuse at the hands of a Catholic priest, only to discover how this shatters his relationships with his family, community, and faith.

West Beirut: Follows two teenagers during the beginning of the civil war between Christians and Muslims that devastated Lebanon between 1975 and 1990 and turned cosmopolitan Beirut into a bombed-out ruin.

Witness to Jonestown: A powerful and extremely revealing documentary that explores the social and political worlds that allowed Jim Jones to successfully seduce the city of San Francisco. The film interviews survivors and family members on the thirty year anniversary of the Jones Town massacre–tracing Jones' unstoppable rise as reverend and community activist to this tragic last days in the jungle of Guyana.

CHAPTER 4 Fork in the Road

12 Angry Lebanese: For nearly a year and a half, forty-five prison inmates in Lebanon's largest prison found themselves working together to present their version of Reginald Rose's play *12 Angry Men,* which they rename in this powerful documentary.

26 Years: The Dewey Bozella Story: Tragic and uplifting documentary that looks at a horrible injustice. After spending time in prison for a crime he didn't commit, a former boxer hopes to fulfill his dream to fight a professional bout as a free man.

50/50: After being diagnosed with cancer, Adam receives distractions from his friend, Kyle, who shows him how to turn the corner regarding his illness and, as such, strengthen his personal resolve.

Angels Crest: In the working class town of Angels Crest, a young father tries to raise his son. This is made more difficult because the child's mother is an alcoholic. When tragedy strikes, the tight knit community splinters as it attempts to decide where the blame lies.

The Announcement: In 1991, basketball's "Magic" Johnson suddenly retired, announcing that he was HIV positive. This film chronicles the 20 years that followed.

The Arbor: Documentary that looks at a poor housing project in England's Yorkshire where real life ravages of alcohol and drug abuse become the centerpiece of playwright Andrea Dunbar's life.

Beats, Rhymes, & Life: The Travels of a Tribe Called Quest: Documentary that explores one of the most ground breaking Hip-Hop groups of the early 90s.

Bhutto: This documentary examines the life of Pakistani Prime Minister Benazir Bhutto, whose assassination sent her nation's political system into a tailspin.

Bigger, Stronger, Faster: Documentary that examines America's fascination–athletes and amateurs–with being the biggest, strongest, and the fastest.

The Big One: On his book tour, Michael Moore exposes wrongdoings by greedy big businesses and callous politicians.

Billy the Kid: Documentary on teenager Billy Price and his dignified coping with Asperger's syndrome.

Boli Zhi Cheng (City of Glass): Twenty years after a college couple's break-up and marriage to other people, their children–from respective marriages–meet and join forces to help them live out a dream.

Boyhood: Filmed over the course of 12 years with the same cast, this film follows a boy and his dysfunctional family as they grow and change.

Changing Lanes: Road rage spirals into a all-consuming feud between two men who both find they are at crossroads in their lives.

Chef: L.A. eatery wunderkind has taken to passionless, crow-baiting cooking. He hates his boss, who only wants to fill seats. When a critic notes his complacency and his career derails, he returns to Miami and finds love again in a junky Cubano food truck.

City of God: Poor Brazilian youth decides to pick up a camera and abandon his life of crime and embrace his new hobby: recording the violence and disparity of his world on film.

Dorian Blues: One night, a closeted high school senior–saddled with a domineering father, an athletic brother, and a loopy mother–challenges his father's conservative views and, during their argument, has an epiphany: he is gay.

The English Sheik and the Yemeni Gentleman: Follows a British filmmaker who returns to Yemen–the home of his father–and meets a British expatriate. Together they roam the land and discover a true sense of belonging.

Entre Nos: Abandoned by her husband in a country foreign to her, a Colombian struggles to take care of herself and her two children on the streets of New York.

Fame: Students at NYC's School for the Performing Arts attempt to overcome social and personal barriers and fulfill their artistic dreams. (Original, 1980)

Flight of the Red Balloon: Film deals with a Parisian summer filled with uncertainty, with each of the characters–mother, son, and Chinese au pair–expressing loss and pain.

Footnote: Dueling Talmudic scholars–the wizened father who has been overlooked in academia, and his middle aged son who reaps the rewards of success–seek their homeland's Israel Prize. When the father mistakenly thinks the prize is for him, the world of academia and its approval seeking recognition becomes the focus for this comedy's scrutiny.

The Girl: While transporting illegal immigrants across the Texas border, a cash-strapped single mother finds herself caring for a young Mexican girl.

Go For Sisters: A parole officer, ex-con, and a former cop head to Mexico to find answers about a missing Iraq veteran.

The Good Life: Timely documentary that looks at a mother and daughter in costal Portuguese who, once rich, now live off a small pension. The film is a character study of the women's struggle to adapt to their new situation during uncertain financial times.

Ida: Driven by the historical catastrophe of the Holocaust, this Polish film about an apprentice nun who, on the eve of taking her final vows, leaves the convent to track down her last surviving relative, is an intense look at life's cruelty.

Imitation of Life: Explores the practice of passing by a young Black woman attempting to prosper in segregated America. (Original, 1934 and 1959 remake)

The Journals of Musan: Story of a North Korean defector forging a new life in capitalist South Korea. This film is a vision of loneliness, disconnect, and ethical ambiguity.

Khodorkovsky: Documentary that unpacks the biographical rise and current imprisonment of Mikhail Khodorkovsky–a Russian oligarch who, a victim of Vladimir Putin's enmity, was imprisoned after fabricated tax-evasion charges.

A Late Quartet: Cellist is diagnosed with Parkinson's, leading to a host of resentments among the other members of the group who harbor resentment and hostility and aspirations–emotions that boil over in Manhattan.

Lilting: This film is a moving study of love, grief, and cultural differences that looks at a fragile young gay man mourning the death of his partner and the uneasy bond he forges with his lover's mother—an elderly woman living in a retirement home who speaks no English and may not have known her son was gay.

Little Fugitive: Classic film that shows what happens when a boy is tricked into believing he's killed his older brother. Spending two guilt-filled days on the run, little Joey hangs out at Coney Island experiencing the glory and terror of childhood.

Little Heaven: Documentary examines Lydia, a 13-year-old Ethiopian girl, and her diary entries, her daily routines at the Little Heaven Orphanage for Children with HIV, her conversations with other children there, her doctor's appointments, and her exercise, study, and prayer.

Look at Me: A Parisian choral student lives in a world of disconnectedness. Notably, there is a subplot on weight obsession after the father marries a rail-thin trophy wife, leaving his heavyset daughter feeling threatened.

Marathon Boy: Documentary that looks at the rags-to-riches story of an Indian boy who rose to fame as a long-distance runner before his coach was caught up in a damaging scandal.

Mildred Pierce: After her cheating husband leaves her, title character proves she can thrive independently. (Original, 1945)

My Brother is an Only Child: A coming of age story that chronicles the political awakening of a rural Italian boy in the 1960s and 70s. The film follows the contentious protagonist as he drifts from a seminary stint to Fascist party membership to Communist activism in search of a purpose.

Nas: TIME IS illMATIC: Twenty years after the release of the rapper's famous *Illmatic* album, this documentary follows Nas back to Queensbridge, where he shares stories about his upbringing, his influences, and the countless obstacles he faced.

Obvious Child: Woman contemplates abortion in this often hilarious movie about a Jewish standup comedian who makes fun of her life and finds an unlikely love interest.

The Punk Singer: While dealing with late-stage Lyme disease in 2010, riot-grrrl icon Kathleen Hanna is shown dealing with the disease, while, at the same time, remaining an artist and feminist firebrand. Documentary addresses her abusive childhood, medical struggles, and the torment she encountered as the face of a movement.

Rafea: Solar Mama: When she is selected for an intriguing program called the Barefoot College solar program in India, Rafea, a Jordanian Bedouin, travels to join 30 illiterate women from other countries to train to become solar engineers over the course of six months.

The Reception: A french woman, her daughter, and new son-in-law, along with a gay African American painter, drink and unleash a torrent of frank talk about sex, race, class, and hopelessly damaged family relationships.

Sister: Young boy's worlds collide—the home he shares with his deadbeat older sister and the mountaintop Swiss ski resort where he steals from the vacationing rich—when carelessness and encroaching adolescence change his life.

A Teacher: A high school teacher in Austin, Texas, has an affair with one of her students. Her life begins to unravel as their controversial relationship comes to an end.

Thumbsucker: Once the teenage protagonist feels overwhelmed, he indulges in the infantile oral fixation of sucking his thumb. Once the teen discovers Ritalin, he goes from vulnerable to being overly aggressive.

To Be Heard: For students at the Power Writers program at East Harlem's Renaissance Charter High School for Innovation, poetry is an essential part of their survival. In this documentary that spans four years, the kids come from various challenging backgrounds that expose personal tribulations as they try to develop a positive mode of self-expression.

Trudell: Documentary that examines Native American activist, actor, and poet John Trudell's political life, which changed drastically and tragically twelve hours after he burned an American flag on the steps of FBI's Washington, D.C., headquarters in 1979.

Tsotsi: Set in postapartheid Johannesburg, film follows the moral rehabilitation of a street thug who, after carjacking an affluent woman, decides to nurture her baby as his own.

Two for the Road: Couple drives across Europe at three different, precarious points in their relationship. Film focuses on specific questions: Are they a happy twosome facing a rough road, or a mismatch finally realizing their mutual error; or, is marriage just about the journey itself? (Original, 1967)

Viola: Delightful comedy, featuring a mainly female cast, about a group of Argentines who engage in a romantic roundelay reminiscent of Shakespeare's *Twelfth Night.*

Where in the World is Osama bin Laden?: Morgan Spurlock, the director of the documentary *Super Size Me,* chronicles his search for Osama bin Laden and other high ranking Al Qaeda officials. Film travels through Egypt, Morocco, Israel, Jordan, Saudi Arabia, Afghanistan, and Pakistan. While comedic in many ways, the film reveals rampant poverty and people who would love to have some semblance of justice and peace.

Winter Passing: East Village young woman, eventually joined by other lost souls desperately trying to stay numb by any means necessary, attempts to heal.

CHAPTER 5 *Class and the Culture of Power*

4 Months, 3 Weeks and 2 Days: Set in 1980s Bucharest, while still behind the Iron Curtain, movie concerns two friends–one pregnant, one supportive–as they attempt to have an illegal procedure with a black-market abortionist. The film is centered mainly in the hotel room where the negotiations are discussed, revealing to the audience the hellish dynamics of economics, power games, and sex.

99%–The Occupy Wall Street Collaborative Film: Documentary–featuring supporters, participants, and critics–goes behind the scenes of the movement, revealing what happened and why.

After the Dark: Philosophy students at an international school in Indonesia must decide who among them would survive a hypothetical nuclear apocalypse.

Alexandra: Story of an elderly woman who visits a remote military outpost in implied Chechnya and observes various degrees of soldiering: banality of barrack life and machinery placement over human beings. This moving film also provides a face and voice to the enemy, as well as the difficulties of politics and the bond of the woman and her ward.

American Promise: Parents film their kids for 14 years as they progress through largely White schools. Life challenges–learning disabilities and deaths–alongside national conversations on race, surrounding both Barack Obama and Trayvon Martin, shape the background of these young boys becoming young men.

Amores Perros: Three interconnected stories about the different strata of life in Mexico City, revolving around a fatal car crash.

Arbitrage: Smooth-talking hedge-fund giant embezzles millions and attempts to cover up the accidental killing of his mistress.

Ballast: A cryptic and intimate tale of three people dealing with a tragedy in the Deep South. Film brilliantly handles people living below the poverty line with poetic sensitivity.

Bastards: A working-class mariner is out for revenge against the big businessman who ruined his family.

Beaufort: Well crafted movie that looks at various soldiers in Lebanon guarding the highly symbolic Beaufort Castle from Hezbollah forces in the last remaining days of Israel's occupation.

Bitter Seeds: Manjusha Amberwar, a young journalist, examines the causes of an epidemic of farmer suicides in India–approximately one every 30 minutes–that includes her own father.

Blue Jasmine: A rich Manhattan socialite falls into poverty and homelessness.

Boy: Coming-of-age story about a 10-year-old boy and his family as they trek across Japan, stopping in each location to fake traffic accidents and extort money from stunned drivers.

A Bronx Tale: The protagonist struggles to come to terms with his growing affinity for a neighborhood gangster, who treats him like a son, and his father, a working-class bus driver.

Bubble: Set in small-town Ohio and West Virginia, the movie examines the lives of three paycheck-to-paycheck wage earners–individuals who have lived this way for so long they have forgotten how to imagine a future. Film also contains a murder mystery twist.

The Central Park Five: In the late 1980s, the rape of a White jogger, and the subsequent trial and conviction of five Black and Hispanic teenagers in New York City, shocked the nation. This documentary examines corruption, racial division, and a countrywide social divide.

Claudine: A classic "dramadey" that examines America's welfare system and the ways in which it forces a wedge between a mother and her garbage-man boyfriend in 1970s New York.

The Colors of the Mountain: This film exposes us to warfare through the eyes of children as we meet nine-year old Manuel, who lives in the rural mountains of Columbia. He has friends, plays soccer, and is learning how to read thanks to a new teacher. Unfortunately, his village just happens to be the headquarters for a rebel group taking on the country's military power.

The Constant Gardner: In an attempt to expose the corporate and political AIDS drug racket in Kenya, a couple risks their lives.

Detropia: As the focus of the sobering documentary, the decline of Detroit also reflects the nation's larger failure to keep up in a modern global economy.

Duck Season: Adolescents spend a lazy Sunday afternoon together. Melancholy film that examines loneliness, togetherness, and the end of family in a small Mexico City apartment.

El Inmortal: Mercedes Moncarda Rodriguez follows the plight of a woman and her four children living in Nicaragua.

Enron: The Smartest Guys in the Room: Based on the 2003 investigative digest, this documentary is a methodical look at the men who became known as the largest white-collar crooks ever taken to trial in American history.

Escape Fire: The Fight to Rescue American Healthcare: Documentary tackles the American healthcare crisis, which has a trillion dollar and rising cost, where patients pay more, yet health outcomes are worse.

Fire in Babylon: Using the backdrops of the national liberation movements of the 70s and 80s, this documentary pays tribute to the golden age of cricket in the West Indies. Film shows how players set out to triumph over their former colonial masters while, simultaneously, making a name for themselves on the world stage.

The First Grader: In 2003, when the Kenyan government offered free education to all citizens, 84year-old villager Kimai N'gan'ga Maruge showed up at the gates of the local primary school. This movie looks at how the international media attention turns the main character into a poster boy and social pariah, as well as a celebrity and pupil.

Goodwill Hunting: The main character, a poor street kid from Boston's low-end–who just happens to be genius–attempts to work out his issues about who he is in relation to where he lives and the expectations of those around him.

Hustle and Flow: Sympathetic southern pimp attempts to better his station in life–involving everyone in his limited world–through Hip-Hop.

The Immigrant: From Ellis Island to the big city, a young Polish woman seeking a better life finds herself involved in prostitution and a bitter love triangle.

In America: Irish immigrants struggle to survive and maintain their sanity in New York City's Hell's Kitchen.

The Inheritors: Haunting documentary that, over the course of two years, examines children working long and hard in dirt-poor rural regions of Mexico.

Ivory Tower: Documentary looks at the real costs of crippling debt against the transformative power of learning while examining Harvard and party school Arizona State.

The Joy Luck Club: Chinese mothers and daughters reflect on the roles they played in the culture clash between the mothers' traditional Chinese values and their Americanized children.

Lenny Cooke: Thought to be the next big thing in basketball, Cooke instead became a cautionary tale about what happens when a student athlete makes the wrong choices, resulting in unfulfilled regret.

Like Father, Like Son: Heart-wrenching drama about two Japanese families from vastly different economic circumstances who learn that their six-year-old boys were switched at birth.

Lost Angels: Skid Row Is My Home: This compelling documentary about skid row in Los Angeles finds both desperation and inspiration reflected in the area's indigent population.

Mardi Gras: Made in China: Conscience-stirring documentary examines the life cycle of the bead necklaces used during this New Orleans' event, alongside the millionaires who own the Tai Kuen bead factory in China and their employees–individuals who work fourteen hour days, six days a week under horrendous conditions.

Mother India: Life Through the Eyes of the Orphan: This documentary tells the stories of 25 orphaned children, just a handful of India's 31 million orphans who wrestle with poverty and abandonment.

Nebraska: Modern-day black-and-white film that shows a cantankerous old man and his son determined to cash in a sweepstakes prize in bleak Americana.

Norte, the End of History: Filipino film is a regional riff on *Crime and Punishment*. This movie is a study of fractured morality–a louche law student and a farmer's son are connected when one commits a double murder and the other takes the fall. Brilliantly done, the film brings together politics, nationalism, Class, capitalism, and history–all wrapped in the context of social injustice.

Pray the Devil Back to Hell: After more than a decade of civil wars leading to more than 250,000 deaths and one million refugees, the documentary looks at a group of courageous Liberian women who rose up and propelled to victory the first female head of state on the African continent.

A Raisin in the Sun: Desperate to be seen as the breadwinner in his family, a Black man–a son, husband, and father–blames himself, his mother, and his wife for what he sees as his personal failure with regard to not being able to provide as a "man." (Original, 1961)

Return to the Land of Wonders: Documentary where the filmmaker–having lived thirty-five years abroad–walks the streets in Iraq, her homeland, and interviews everyday citizens about what they have been through–both under Saddam Hussein's regime and during U.S. occupation.

Rocky: In this classic "underdog" tale, the self-titled main character boxes his way out of Philadelphia's underbelly, training his way to a heavyweight championship fight.

Sarafina: A young girl struggles to break the racial and Class barriers while living in apartheid South Africa.

A Separation: In modern day Iran, we see a mother who hopes to take her child abroad for a better life and a bank clerk who feels trapped because he has to care for his ailing father. This powerful movie is filled with twists that reveal catastrophic consequences between seemingly unlikely people battling Class, social responsibility, and religious devotion.

Sicko: Michael Moore's compelling documentary is a scathing indictment of America's failing health care system. He travels to Canada, England, France, and Cuba–where free universal health care is the norm–and finds himself asking, "Why can't this happen in America?"

Skid Row: Hip-hop artist Pras goes undercover on the Los Angeles Skid Row and documents his experiences living as a homeless person on the violent streets.

SlumDog Millionaire: While consistently winning India's most popular game show, an impoverished teen who has no desire for fame comes face to face with the social pressures associated with instant wealth; at the same time, the police suspect him of cheating because they cannot figure out how he, a street kid, continues to do so well.

Snowpiercer: Set in the future, this film looks at an experiment to counteract global warming that goes horribly wrong and causes an ice age that kills nearly all life on earth. The only survivors live on a massive train, where a class system is installed, with the elites inhabiting the front of the train and the poor inhabiting the tail.

Special Flight: Fernand Melgar's intimate and emotionally charged portrait of the rejected asylum seekers and illegal migrants in Switzerland's Frambois Detention Centre'.

The Squid and the Whale: A failed novelist and his successful-writer wife split and the ugliness of divorce forces their sons to choose sides.

Terri: More than a teen misfit movie, this film introduces us to 17 year-old Terri and his hell that is high school. This movie is a genuinely touching character study, one that refuses to glamorize its hopeless hero as hip or treat him with mockery.

Twenty-Four Eyes: Released in 1954, this award winning Japanese film traces the close relationship between a young teacher and her twelve students over the course of twenty years, spanning the period of world-wide economic collapse and World War II.

Wadjda: A young girl in the Saudi Arabian capital of Riyadh wants nothing more than to bicycle, but she encounters plenty of obstacles; namely, the equality lines between men and women are especially stark, but headstrong Wadjda—who dresses different and is defiant at school—will not be stopped, which causes tension everywhere.

A Walk to Beautiful: This documentary follows five Ethiopian women from isolated rural communities who developed obstetric fistulas after prolonged obstructed deliveries. These women are ostracized and abandoned, even though a simple surgery can correct their condition. This film is an unabashed humanitarian call to action, as it examines how superstition, poverty, and hundreds of miles to medical care all stand in the way of these women's survival.

Wal-Mart: The High Cost of Low Price: Documentary that chronicles the corporation's ruthless policies.

The Weeping Meadow: A romantic Greek tragedy. Film tracks two runaway lovers from the 1919 incursion of Bolshevism to the bitter end of World War II.

Where Soldiers Come From: Documentary follows three small-town friends in the National Guard who are deployed to Afghanistan in 2008.

Young and Restless in China: Documentary follows the lives of nine youngish Chinese citizens over the course of a few years, ranging from a Western-educated entrepreneur struggling with the ethical challenges of doing business in his home country, to a young factory worker contemplating breaking off the engagement arranged by her rural family. Film illustrates the profound changes that China's double-digit economic growth has instigated in every area of life.

CHAPTER 6 Race and Racial Matters

12 Years a Slave: The powerful story of a free Black man, Solomon Northrup, and his fight for survival and dignity after he is enslaved in pre-Civil War America.

Arranged: Movie revolves around the friendship of two young teachers in Brooklyn—one Muslim, one an Orthodox Jew—who meet at a racially and culturally diverse Brooklyn grade school. The film tackles arranged marriages, faith, secular Americanism, and the boundaries of family tolerance.

Big Words: Three friends, once a promising hip-hop group but now nearing middle age, reunite on the evening of Barack Obama's first presidential win.

Blind Faith: In this powerful and historically centered film, a Black Lawyer's nephew is accused of murdering a White man.

Booker's Place: A Mississippi Story: Documentary explores a Black waiter's bold and fateful decision to expose the reality of race relations in 1960s Mississippi.

The Boy Who Played on the Buddhas of Bamiyan: Family of Afghani refugees lives among the ruins of a tourist attraction that was destroyed by the Taliban.

Cairo Exit: A look into the collapsing world of an eighteen year-old unwed mother in Egypt who struggles with choices that become more complicated after she is robbed and fired from her job.

Champs: Fascinating documentary that looks at Mike Tyson, Evander Holyfield, and Bernard Hopkins. Examining the fascination we have with boxing, they give praise to the sport where they found fame and salvation, while pointing out the dubious practices like mismanagement and racial bias.

The Citizen: An Arab immigrant arrives in the United States a day before the September 11 attacks, which will forever change his life.

Color of the Cross: An examination of the last forty-eight hours of Jesus Christ as a Black man.

Crime after Crime: Two novice attorneys take on the case of a woman who was convicted of killing her brutally abusive boyfriend and languished in prison for 20 years.

C.S.A.: The Confederate States of America: An alternate historical society where the South won the Revolutionary War and America has embraced racism as a part of life.

Dark Girls: This fascinating and controversial documentary goes underneath the surface to explore the prejudices dark-skinned women face throughout the world.

The Day the Earth Stood Still: In this 1951 classic, an envoy from another world warns Earth's people to cease their violent behavior. But panic erupts when a nervous soldier shoots the messenger.

Dear White People: Hilarious satire that looks at exploding racial tensions within a university's student body as a group of African-American students navigate campus life and racial politics at a predominantly White college.

The Defiant Ones: Two escaped convicts–one White, the other Black–must overcome their own prejudices in an attempt to evade their pursuers, survive in a racist society, and, most of all, overcome their own social conditioning. (Original, 1958)

Donkey in Lahore: An unusual love story style documentary of an Australian puppeteer who falls in love with a Muslim woman he met in Pakistan. Can this unlikely couple survive the challenges they are about to face?

Freedomland: A portrait of a White mother who claims her child was abducted by a Black male and how this accusation fuels negative race relations in a segregated, racially charged community.

The Grey Zone: Based on actual events, this is the staggeringly powerful story of Auschwitz's 12th Sonderkommando–one of 13 "special squads" of Jewish prisoners forced by the Nazis to help exterminate fellow Jews in exchange for a few more months of life.

The Help: Film follows the lives of two maids and best friends who live in Jackson, Mississippi during the Jim Crow era. They meet and open up to a budding White writer who wants to write an explosive tell-all book about their subservient existence.

The Interrupters: Powerful documentary that chronicles a year spent with Chicago's antiviolence crusaders CeaseFire and their attempts to intervene in gang warfare.

In the Heat of the Night: Black Philadelphia police detective reluctantly becomes embroiled in a murder investigation in racially hostile 1960s Mississippi. (Original, 1967)

Kippur: Portrait of the 1973 Yom Kippur between Syria and Israel, told from the perspective of a skeptical soldier.

The Last White Knight: Paul Saltzman's documentary follows the filmmaker as he returns to Mississippi to talk with the Ku Klux Klan member who assaulted him in 1965 for helping Blacks register to vote.

La Vita e Bella (Life Is Beautiful): Man uses humor and fantasy to protect his son in a Nazi death camp.

The Loving Story: This documentary profiles Mildred and Richard Loving, who were arrested in 1958 for breaking Virginia's laws against interracial marriage.

Mandela: Long Walk to Freedom: Biopic that attempts to tell the whole story of the famed civil rights icon's life.

Michael Collins: Leader fights to establish Irish Free State in the 1920s while becoming vilified by those hoping to create a completely independent Irish Republic.

Mississippi Burning: Two FBI agents are sent to Mississippi to investigate the disappearance of missing civil rights workers. The film is an exploration of one of the ugliest chapters in American history, examining White supremacy, corruption, and extreme conflicts of social conscience.

My Life Inside: Film follows the tragic life of Rosa Jimenez who, at seventeen, came to the U.S. to provide a better life for her family back in Mexico. This heartbreaking documentary examines how she came to stand accused of murder in a Texas courtroom.

Occupation: Dreamland: Documentary filmmakers record soldiers who are stationed in Iraq and gain insight about how and why they are perceived as invaders.

The Order of Myths: Based on Alabama's 2007 Mardi Gras, an annual event that has existed since the 1700s, this documentary examines Mobile's first ethnically blended events, where the African-American community's regents attended their White counterparts' coronation and vice-versa. The result is a microcosmic look at race relations that proves how largely divided this nation still remains.

The Other Son: Two Middle Eastern teens–one raised as an Israeli and the other as a Palestinian–discover they were switched at birth and have to decide to keep their old lives and beliefs, or abandon them for new ones.

Planet of the Apes: An astronaut crew crash-lands on a planet in the distant future where talking apes are the dominant species and humans are oppressed and enslaved. (Original, 1968)

The Price of the Ticket: Documentary on the life and literary career of one of America's most prolific writers, James Baldwin. This is an American Masters Series.

Protocols of Zion: Documentary about anti-Semitism in America and the rise of anti-Jewish sentiment after 9/11.

The Retrieval: Black adolescent and his uncle are tasked to track down an escaped runaway slave by a white bounty hunter.

Rosewood: Based on the actual massacre of Black townspeople in Rosewood Florida, this film gives an account of the events that led to White town's people attacking the Black community over several days.

Sandra: Woman returns to her family's provincial Tuscan estate with her new American husband. Issues around her mother remarrying after her father's murder at Auschwitz arise and cause drama for the whole family.

Scenes of a Crime: Troy, NY resident Adrian Thomas was interrogated for ten hours before confessing to throwing his infant son against a bed. When the child died, Thomas was convicted of second-degree murder. When the evidence exonerates him, the documentary questions legally sanctioned coercion, race, Class and the effects all have on this tragic tale.

SEC Storied: Croom: Compelling documentary chronicles Sylvester Croom's journey to become the first African-American head football coach in the Southeastern Conference.

Some Mother's Son: Based on the true story of IRA prisoner Bobby Sands' 1981 hunger strike in a British prison.

Spies of Mississippi: Documentary that looks at 1960s Mississippi, and the formation of a secret agency that employed black spies to infiltrate and dismantle civil rights organizations.

Street Fight: Documentary that chronicles the racist overtones involved in the 2002 mayoral race in Newark, New Jersey, between Sharpe James–the "average-Joe," darker skinned incumbent–and Cory Booker–the fair-skinned, Yale Law School graduate.

The Suspect: Two African-American academics travel to a small southern town to impersonate bank robbers as a way of examining the role of race in law enforcement.

Twilight Zone: Maple Street: After the power goes out in a small middle-America neighborhood, all hell breaks loose as neighbors and friends turn against one another.

Ukraine Brides: Mystifying, often heartbreaking, documentary that covers 13 years of footage covering Ukrainian women who married Israeli men.

Undefeated: Academy award winning documentary that follows a White Memphis football coach and his 100% Black football team. Race and Class and learning to communicate become the prevailing themes of this heart wrenching film.

Venus and Serena: Compton born, these sisters have become the most dominant force in women's tennis. To do this, they have overcome a sport's image that often sees the sisters and their family as villains because of their ethnicity and attitudes.

What's Cooking?: Tensions mount amidst four families of different ethnic and economic backgrounds living in contemporary Los Angeles as they prepare dinner for family and guests.

Which Way Home: This documentary follows three children who make a dangerous trek through Mexico en route to the U.S. border, hoping to reunite with their parents.

White Man's Burden: The film takes an alternative view on Black/White race relations by constructing a world where Blacks hold all of the power.

Winnie Mandela: This movie is a different look at the noble proponent of the antiapartheid movement, one that shows the stances she took against her famous husband, as well as being implicated in a murder.

Zoned In: Filmed over the course of nine years, this documentary traces the remarkable journey of sixteen-year-old Daniel who, beginning at a Bronx high school, goes to an Ivy League university. At the same time, this film explores the role of race and Class in the American educational system.

CHAPTER 7 Gender, Sex, and Sexuality

12 Angry Men: This 1957 classic introduces viewers to a jury of various male personalities who, during deliberation, are prevented from sentencing a Latino male when one of the men refuses to vote guilty. The result is a tense contrast in racist, bullying, often apathetic personas that boil to a head, leading to the film's dramatic conclusion. (Original, 1957)

American Beauty: A depressed suburban father in the midst of a midlife crisis decides to change his life–most notably through the pursuit of his teenage daughter's friend.

ANITA: *Speaking Truth to Power*: Documentary that explores Anita Hill and the sexist power dynamic that revealed itself during the Senate Judiciary Committee when she testified on the lewd behavior of Supreme Court nominee Clarence Thomas.

Antwone Fisher: An abused societal outcast attempts to understand what it means to be a man by exploring the institutions and determining factors that shaped him as a boy.

The Ballad of Genesis and Lady Jaye: Gender identity documentary that explores the mesmerizing love story between pioneering musician and performance artist Genesis P-Orridge and soul mate Lady Jaye.

Beneath the Veil: Examines women rebelling against the treatment they receive under the Taliban in Afghanistan.

Born into Brothels: Documentary that focuses on the children existing in Calcutta's inherently abusive red-light district.

Born This Way: Four young gay Cameroonians are followed in a day-to-day portrait that follows them in the country that prosecutes homosexuality more than in any other country in the world.

Boys Don't Cry: The true story of Teena Brandon, who chose to live her short life as her male alter-ego, Brandon Teena.

Boys in the Hood: Coming-of-age tale about three friends–young males trying to grasp manhood in various ways–living in violent South Central, Los Angeles.

A Boy's Life: Documentary that follows a Mississippi family's struggle–according to the obviously disturbed grandmother–with an increasingly violent and erratic child.

Bridget Jones' Diary: A thirty-something woman struggles with the notion of becoming a spinster.

Brokeback Mountain: Love story that examines the forbidden love between two modern-day cowboys.

The Business of Fancy Dancing: Gay Indian poet from Spokane confronts his past when he returns to his childhood home, on the reservation, to attend a friend's funeral.

Call Me Kuchu: Frightening documentary examines David Kato, Uganda's first openly gay man, as he labors to repeal Uganda's homophobic laws and liberate his fellow lesbian, gay, bisexual, and transgender men and women, also known as "kuchus."

The Carrier: Documentary that follows a pregnant Zamibian mother who is a subsistence farmer in a polygamous marriage who has just learned she is HIV positive.

The Case Against 8: On the eve of Barack Obama's 2008 election, Proposition 8 was passed, banning same-sex marriage in California. The documentary charts five years of testimony, appeals, cheers, and tears, as it shows how Californians organized, found money, and put on a brilliant legal show.

The Circle: Tracks the hopeless situation of a half-dozen Iranian women, including three who have escaped from jail.

The Day I Became a Woman: A trio of tales that simply, yet evocatively, lays out the problems of being a woman in Iran.

Deep South: Documentary examines the layers of history, poverty, and now soaring HIV infections amongst the lives of families in Alabama, Louisiana, and Mississippi.

Disney's Beauty and the Beast: Young maiden offers herself to the beast–a raging and abusive male–and eventually discovers the prince inside.

Eat Drink Man Woman: Living in Tai Pei, a senior chef lives with his three unmarried adult daughters. Film revolves around everyone's relationships and the elaborate Sunday dinners.

Fading Gigolo: Comedy introduces an impish bookstore owner facing financial ruin who finds himself negotiating sexual encounters for desperate well-to-do women with his reticent florist friend.

Geraldine Ferraro: Paving the Way: In this documentary, the subject's daughter looks at Ferraro's 1984 VP run, a historical moment for female political representation.

Gloria: An older divorcee samples the singles scene in Santiago, Chile.

Going Up the Stairs: Portrait of an Unlikely Iranian Artist: A grandmother living with her husband in Tehran finds sudden success painting. The film examines the journey of a woman who was married at age nine to a man in his thirties–one who was so fearful of displeasing her husband that she left school before learning to read–finding a new lease on life.

Gun Hill Road: Man returns home from three years in prison to find that his wife is a virtual stranger and his son is in the throes of a sexual identity crisis.

How to Murder Your Wife: When a nationally syndicated cartoonist–one so successful he lives in a luxurious penthouse with his man-servant, Charles–attends a stag party and awakens the next day married to a young woman who barely speaks English, he finds that this mistake turns his life upside down. The end result is as complex as it is hilarious when he begins to plot his wife's murder within the pages of his cartoon. When she suddenly disappears, the cartoon is used as evidence at his trial. (Original, 1965)

In the Family: Heart-wrenching drama about a gay Tennessee contractor who fights for custody of his nonbiological son after his lover, the boy's father, is killed in a car crash.

The Law in These Parts: This documentary examines Israel's rule of law in its post-1967-occupied territories. Retired judges and legal experts discuss how they helped establish a parallel set of statues for Palestinian citizens–"temporary" laws that would allow for land to be seized and colonized, and for an Arabic suspect to be told that he must defend himself against crimes which are classified.

A League of Their Own: Women grow and stand up to oppression when they start their own baseball league.

Like Water for Chocolate: Living in Mexico, a woman, prevented from marrying the man she loves, discovers she can do amazing things through her cooking.

Love Actually: Follows the lives of eight very different London couples dealing with their love lives in various interrelated tales.

Love Free or Die: Gene Robinson, the first openly gay Episcopal Church bishop, is chronicled as he champions the rights of LGBT worshippers in a faith still grappling with homophobia.

Love Is Strange: After four decades, a gay couple marries and then finds themselves broke and forced to live with family and friends. This sensitive domestic tragedy examines the finite nature of being together.

Mona Lisa Smile: Feminist-thinking art professor challenges the conditioned lives of her students at an all-female college.

Mother of George: Nigerian immigrants in Brooklyn marry, and soon after the wife is pressured to produce a male heir–a path that leaves the heroine ever more isolated and powerless.

My Beautiful Laundrette: Omar, a young gay man of Pakistani background, opens a launderette in London and hires his former classmate, Johnny. Their developing relationship is much to the chagrin of Johnny's skinhead pals and Omar's successful immigrant family.

The New Black: Documentary looks at how the African-American community is grappling with lesbian, gay, and transgender (LGBT) rights in light of the marriage equality movement and over civil rights.

No Secret Anymore: Documentary that tackles–through the attempts of the filmmakers to develop a coalition–the prevailing belief that lesbians are illegal, immoral, and sick.

On the Outs: Three different Latinas and their crack-laced lives face the horrors and ravages of inner-city life.

The Parade: A comedic look at Serbia through the lens of a group fighting to hold a Gay Pride parade in Belgrade.

Pariah: Closeted Brooklyn teen spends her nights sucking up the lesbian subculture she so desperately wants to embrace, all the while trying to escape the confines of her feminine days and the scrutiny of a religious mother.

Paris Is Burning: Documentary on "drag nights" among New York's underclass.

Pretty Woman: Prostitute elevates her social standing when a wealthy businessman decides to teach her how to be a proper woman.

*The Price of Sex: F*eature-length documentary about young Eastern European women who have been drawn into a world of sex trafficking and abuse.

Pride: Movie recalls how a small group of gay activists took a trip from London to blue-collar South Wales in 1984 to lend support to a miners' strike—a struggle they believed was not unlike their own.

Pussy Riot–A Punk Prayer: After Putin returned to power in Russia, a group of young, radical-feminist punk rockers known as Pussy Riot took a stand against the direction Putin was taking Russia and attracted global attention.

Real Women Have Curves: Young L.A. Mexican butts heads with her matriarchal mother after expressing that she wants more out of life—namely a quality education—than simply being supportive of her family.

Salaam Dunk: Documentary delivers a tale of hope and inspiration, courtesy of one winning group of Iraqi women basketball players at the American University in Sulaimani, Iraq.

Salma: Now a published poet, Salma, a young Muslim woman, once a girl in India, was pushed into seclusion once she reached puberty, was forbidden to study, and forced into marriage. Eventually, she discovered an intricate smuggling system to get her words, a scrap of paper at a time, out to the world.

Same Sex in America: Documentary looks at same-sex marriage, as seen through several couples experiencing dilemmas.

Second Hand Lions: Two set-in-their-ways veterans, men who have lived full and active lives, reluctantly teach their young nephew what manhood is all about.

The Sisterhood of the Traveling Pants: A group of teenage friends from different backgrounds separate for the summer and have life-changing experiences—but not before discovering that they all can share a very special pair of jeans.

The Strange History of Don't Ask, Don't Tell: Documentary examines the legacy of gays in the military.

Streets of Shame: Set at a brothel named Dreamland, this classic film, with a mostly female ensemble, examines Japan's red-light district. The movie is an incisive portrait of a life that provides for and punishes these women in equal measure.

Tall as the Baobab Tree: Film depicts sisters who are the first to leave their African village to attend in the city. When an accident threatens the family's survival, the family decides to sell the younger daughter into an arranged marriage, while her sister plots to save her from a life not of her choosing.

Thelma & Louise: Two women take a road trip and become wanted fugitives, all while embracing life, womanhood, and friendship.

Thirteen: A thirteen-year-old girl's relationship with her mother is put to the test as she discovers drugs, petty crime, and sex.

The Three Burials of Melquiades Estrada: Ranch hand attempts to fulfill two promises: bury his friend in his home in Mexico and punish the man who killed him.

Turning: Gender, sexuality, identity, and empowerment are the themes addressed in this documentary that looks at the British-American androgyny Antony Hegarty and the 13 women who appeared on stage with him.

Very Good Girls: During the summer, two friends make a pact to lose their virginity. This results in secrets and a test of their lifelong bond.

Water: Set in 1938, the movie is a dark introspect into the tales of rural Indian widows, covering controversial subjects such as misogyny and ostracism.

We Are the Best!: Feel-good movie examines three bullied 13-year-old girls who start a punk band in early-1980s Stockholm.

The Woman Pioneers: The stories of feminist pioneers who emigrated from Europe to Palestine a hundred years ago are brought to life through fascinating archival footage and first-person accounts.

The World According the Garp: Young man, who sees himself as a serious writer, is overwhelmed by his famous feminist mother and the variously distressed women that come into his life.

Y Tu Mama Tambien: In Mexico, two teenage boys and an attractive older woman embark on a road trip and learn about life, friendship, sex, and each other.

CHAPTER 8 Manmade and Natural Disaters

The Act of Killing: A documentary explores prideful reenactments performed by former killers, including Indonesian paramilitary leader Anwar Congo—men who participated in the mass murder of more than 1 million alleged communists.

Bermuda Triangle Exposed: Discovery Channel documentary dives deep to explore the 440,000 square miles of ocean below the deadly marine graveyard known as the Bermuda triangle.

Blackfish: A troubling look at Sea World's hazardous and dangerous entertainment trade. Netting orcas, stunts gone wrong, and a history of whale-on-human violence is examined in this frightening documentary.

Brother Number One: New Zealander Rob Hamill's story of his brother's death at the hands of the Khmer Rouge and how the regime and its followers killed nearly 2 million Cambodians between 1975 and 1979.

Bully: Socially awkward twelve-year-old Alex is tormented daily in Sioux City, Iowa. This documentary looks closely at several stories of victimization, none more so than Alex, in an attempt to shine a light on the spiraling bullying epidemic that is impacting Middle America.

Children of Men: Futuristic thriller in which humankind is facing extinction because women have become infertile.

City of Life and Death: Filmed in black-and-white, this movie is a sobering depiction of Japan's 1937 three-day siege of Nanking and its bloody aftermath.

Contagion: In this epidemic thriller, an airborne virus kills millions.

Countdown to Zero: This documentary takes an unblinking look at the threats posed by a growing list of nuclear-armed states and weighs the prospects of global disarmament.

Dawn of the Planet of the Apes: This is the sequel to the popular *Rise of the Planet of the Apes*. Here, mankind is on the cusp of extinction and human domination after a pandemic that results in a world of burgeoning ape civilization.

Deep Impact: Meteors are going to destroy the planet and the government starts a raffle to determine who is worthy of survival.

Dirty Wars: Documentary exposes recent foreign conflict and the branches that engage in conflict in Afghanistan, Somalia, and Yemen.

Dr. Strangelove or: How I Learned to Stop Worrying and Love the Bomb: This classic movie, often called a "vicious comedy," looks at a madman and the threat of nuclear annihilation.

Evacuate Earth: This intriguing "what if?" documentary explores the possibility of transporting Earth's population to a new planet if the world faced impending doom.

Extremely Loud and Incredibly Close: After 9/11, the "worst day" in American history, a son, whose father dies when the Towers collapse, attempts to discover said parent's final message while traveling through the shaken city and meeting others in need of healing.

The Gatekeepers: Built around six candid interviews with former agency chiefs from Israel's ultra-secret intelligence group Shin Bet, this documentary presents men who admit to years of orchestrating the alienation of millions in the West Bank and Gaza.

Goodbye World: After the world's energy grid suddenly fails, some longtime friends find their way to a self-sufficient compound in Northern California.

Gravity: Lone astronaut struggles to survive after a Russian missile strike destroys a defunct satellite, which causes a chain reaction forming a cloud of debris in space.

The Great Flood: Documentary focuses on the Mississippi River deluge of 1926-27, which caused widespread devastation. An interesting twist is the connection the film makes to how this resulted in the jumpstart of the electric blues and rock and roll eras after Black southern migrants left the area to go to Chicago and other northern cities.

Hiroshima: BBC History of World War II: Blending archival film, dramatizations, and special effects, this documentary recounts the world's first nuclear attack and examines the repercussions.

The House I Live In: Examining the War on Drugs, this documentary interviews convicts, addicts, and cops; throughout, the film examines America's unbalanced federally funded attack on those who have been systematically targeted, as well as the industries who have become War on Drugs profiteers.

How to Survive a Plague: Archival video tells this heroic story of AIDS during the hysteria of the Reagan administration, focusing on the activists who fought to generate compassion while battling shame and hatred.

If God is Willing and Da Creek Don't Rise: A post Hurricane Katrina documentary by Spike Lee that examines 2010 New Orleans. Included within the film is an examination of the BP oil spill.

I'm Carolyn Parker: Heartbreaking documentary continues to revisit the aforementioned Lower Ninth Ward resident, whose home was gutted by the storm but remained standing, between 2006 and 2010.

The Island President: Looking at the Maldives, off the coast of India, this documentary examines the island paradise alongside former President Mohamed Nasheed as he prepared to discuss the devastating impact Global Warming is having on his nation at the Copenhagen climate summit.

Lazarus Effect: A documentary look at the HIV/AIDS pandemic in East Africa and the impact drug treatments can have on a person's chances for survival.

Let the Fire Burn: Documentary looks at the African-American collective known as MOVE and how they were labeled a terrorist organization, allowing the City of Brotherly Love's police to start a campaign of harassment and shootouts that eventually escalated to the bombing from a helicopter in 1985 onto MOVE's headquarters. This resulted in the death of 11 members barricaded inside.

Mugabe: Villain or Hero?: Zimbabwean president Robert Mugabe is put under the lens in this documentary, which looks at him as rebel leader, political prisoner, hero, killer, and hateful homophobe.

New York Says Thank You: New Yorkers impacted by the events of 911 travel the country helping communities rebuild after disasters in this moving documentary.

Outbreak: Film follows scientist as they try to stop the spread of the Motaba virus that has infected a town and is wiping out the population, as well as examines the extreme military response to the threat.

Panic in the Streets: Shot on location in New Orleans 1950, the manhunt is on after a waterfront murder victim is discovered to carry pneumonic plague.

Pompeii: Back from the Dead: This documentary uncovers long-buried secrets of the Italian city of Pompeii, which was preserved by volcanic pumice and ash 2,000 years ago.

Semper Fi: Always Faithful: After Marine Master Sergeant Jerry Ensminger's daughter dies of a rare leukemia, he relentlessly searches for answers. This documentary shows how he uncovers one of the largest water contamination sites in U.S. history and struggles for justice on behalf of his family and fellow soldiers.

Twister: Tornado chasers follow the deadly funnels' paths of destruction across the Midwest.

War Witch: Drama shot in the Democratic Republic of Congo, Komona's life is turned upside down when rebels come and force her to kill her parents. Spared by a warlord who believes she is a witch, Komona eventually realizes she must return to her home and lay her parents' souls to rest.

When the Levees Broke: Spike Lee's investigative documentary explores the most devastating natural disaster in American history.

When the Mountains Tremble: Documentary looks at Guatemalan death squads in the early 1980s that roamed the countryside in a war against the unarmed indigenous population.

Which Way From the Front Line Here? The Life and Time of Tim Herrington: Photojournalist Tim Hetherington, killed by a mortar blast in 2011, is examined during his travels to hellish war zones, a period that reveals him as a man seeking truth rather than adventure.

World War Z: Action movie that introduces a zombie pandemic and the global search to discover its origin.

You Don't Like the Truth: 4 Days Inside Guantanamo: Guantanamo Bay Prison interrogation footage of Canadian citizen Omar Khadr, who is grilled about his possible terrorist ties in Afghanistan. The documentary brilliantly explores–through interviews with Khadr's lawyers, family members, and former cell mates– the debate over ends justifying the means during an era of endless war.

Foreword

We don't write writing—we write about, because, in order to. We write to say something—something best expressed in a medium with permanency—to someone—readers who want to understand our proclamations and questions, who want to engage with us. Oftentimes, other people's texts play an essential role in inspiring, provoking, even inciting writing. Here, then, we have a collection of provocative, insightful, opinionated, and sometimes thoroughly disturbing pieces. What better way to launch authentic communication through writing?

Beyond that, *Lead, Follow or Move Out of the Way* amply demonstrates that there are public purposes for education and schooling, that learning to write well is not just a matter of accumulating skills but, rather, an occasion for examining the real and pressing issues of the social and political context in which we live. Education has moral dimensions. Thus, educators have a responsibility to build a citizenry that is not only competent but informed, not only informed but willing and able to participate in our emerging democracy. Education ought to produce participants, not bystanders.

There are several riffs on Thomas Paine here. One is, of course, the title, but the content and structure of this text instantiates another deeply held belief of Paine. In the same text from which the title comes (*The American Crisis,* 1776), Paine asserts, "Moderation in temper is always a virtue; but moderation in principle is always a vice." This anthology provides multiple opportunities to be informed and provoked, and thereby to develop strong commitments, grounded in reason and tested through deliberation.

The pieces contained in the collection are, however, not mere polemic. Their strength lies in how varied they are in genre, historical and geographical location, and authorial voice. Moreover, unlike the customary organization of anthologies—by genre, geography, or historical period—the thematic organization here creates a truly global perspective, one which is both timeless and timely, as the reader can see how the most perplexing socio-political issues know no bounds. Man-made and Natural Disasters, a theme new to this edition, enhances the global and social justice perspectives. Readers are helped to see that even the seemingly neutral acts of Mother Nature impact the poor and the voiceless disproportionately.

This text is a rich resource for teachers and students alike as its thoughtful selection and organization encourage what Short, Harste& Burke (1995) call "wondering and wandering," the central impulses of self-directed exploration and investigation. The films provide another means to access the texts and themes and are particularly useful for struggling readers. They enhance each theme and the editors' thoughtful commentary provides an orientation for both teachers and students so that they might make informed choices about where to wander and what to wonder about.

Of particular note is that *Lead, Follow, Move Out of the Way* can be used within a wide range of pedagogies, from student directed to teacher directed. Instructors can create curricula that invite students to inquire into a theme, or a particular incident, time period, author, or geographic location. Students can work alone or collaboratively. They may explore their own points of view, compare perspectives and even construct ways to put their new knowledge to use outside of the classroom. They can turn their school knowledge into action knowledge through social justice and service learning projects that emerge from their readings and viewing. Alternatively, assignments can be created that ask students to create their own mimetic texts or to construct critical reflections, analyses, and arguments.

This anthology waits for students and teachers to bring it to life. In every instance, the discussions, writing and actions that result will be purposeful, passionate, and informed. And that's what we want novice writers to learn about writing—that it serves genuine purposes and is meant for real audiences, and can make things happen in the world. Beyond that, this collection opens up a space to understand how text and film can serve social and political purposes, purposes beyond information or aesthetic delights. Readers will have a hard time maintaining moderate positions. Rather, they can develop informed and passionate principles, just as Thomas Paine would wish.

Dr. Cynthia Onore
Emeritus Professor of Education
Montclair State University

Preface

It seems that every time we set about creating a new edition of *Lead, Follow, Or Move Out of the Way*, we are stunned by the amount of change the world has undergone. With the aid of social media and other forms of technology, these changes no longer happen in small, private pockets of the world; instead, these events are shared and viewed by curious eyes, and they become events open to global scrutiny, bewilderment, and, more and more, shared calls for action. Indeed, we are no longer little islands unto ourselves. Instead, we share, feel, and witness everything together.

All of us awoke one morning to find that hundreds of young girls were stolen from their beds in Nigeria. Immediately after, the men who kidnapped them asserted on camera that God willed this action. We all witnessed a category 3 super storm shake New York and New Jersey, traumatizing the East Coast in unimaginable ways. Today, the world understands that al-Qaeda has been replaced by ISIS. We all sat dumbfounded as two Malaysian planes flew into tragedy, devastating surviving family members and stunning onlookers into believing that metaphorical lightening could in fact strike in the same place twice. Israel and Palestine went to war. Russia and Ukraine are locked in a heated battle. The name Trayvon Martin has now been replaced by Michael Brown, whose death led to a small community in Missouri resembling the streets of a war-torn country, reigniting the heated debate about race, police, community, and violence. The much-beloved comedian Robin Williams committed suicide, bringing much needed global attention to depression and mental illness. On a brighter note, a doctor performed the most extensive transplant any surgeon ever attempted, giving Richard Norris a whole new face. And, reinforcing the impact of social media and new technology, the "ice bucket challenge" raised record-breaking funds for Amyotrophic Lateral Sclerosis (ALS).

Clearly, what has been happening reveals something about us–that we are all, simultaneously, both different and the same. We do not all hail from the same places or share a cultural understanding; we can, however, empathize and sympathize as human beings. We do not all share the same skin color or economic background, but we all know what it means to yearn for freedom and equality. We don't share the same geography and language, which sometimes stands as a barrier to understanding, but we know what it means to love, experience joy and pain, or shed tears. Whether a story of war or one about a Good Samaritan, we have come to know that these are ALL our stories, and they belong to us and we to them. And because we are so connected, to quote our 2012 preface, "now, more than ever, knowledge and critical thought are so very important to whom we will all become." Twitter, Facebook, Instagram, and 24-hour news reporting, among other things, have made it almost impossible to say "I didn't know that" or "I don't really have an opinion about that." And because we know so much, and know it as soon as it happens, we are obligated to have informed discussions about the world we live in. Neglecting to do so, to have no opinion or feeling about the circumstances that guide and govern us all, is almost sacrilegious–an insult to the gifts we've been given.

As usual, this book is our offering to the global conversation. It has been designed to inspire thought, critical ideas, passionate debate, and true feeling. Once again, we welcome you.

Dr. Monique Ferrell and Dr. Julian Williams, Editors
NYCCT, City University of New York (CUNY)

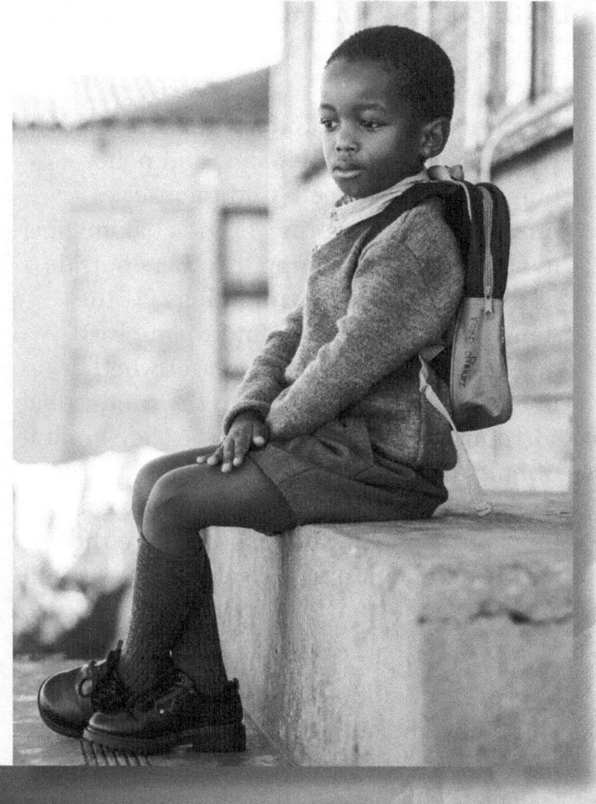

Social Responsibility

History will have to record that the greatest tragedy of this period of social transition was not the strident clamor of the bad people, but the appalling silence of the good people.
Martin Luther King Jr.

We have the Bill of Rights. What we need is a Bill of Responsibilities.
Bill Maher

"I didn't do it." Outside of "yes," "no," "me," and "mine," this declarative sentence offers quite a bit of power to the learning child. It is the instant when the child discovers the opportunity to either engage in or back away from a definitive moment. As we grow older, making a decision to engage, accept responsibility, or become involved becomes less and less easy because every adult decision usually comes with consequences, and, let's be honest, who wants to deal with those?

Perhaps it would behoove us to listen to the words of our well-meaning parents: "Show me who your friends are, and I'll tell you who you are" or "If you don't stand for something, you will fall for everything." In essence, our world does not lend itself easily to the bystander. At some point, some cause or question will beg for our time, attention, or input. Whether we move constantly or stand still, choices must inevitably be made.

Today's world is one in which the threat of war and natural disasters looms over the heads of all persons everywhere. The ravages of a world involved in manmade combat have now been equaled by nature's vengeful forces affecting our ocean shores–issues that must be watched closely. With worry and fear becoming the call of the day, our need to be more socially conscious has become insistent. No longer can the citizens of the world ignore or exclude their brethren, no matter where they reside or what their ethnic, Class, or religious backgrounds may be. The world has awoken in peril, and we, as a world community, must demonstrate an unprecedented sense of communal responsibility. And, for those who ask, "what is my role to be?" the reality is that social responsibility in our world community might be more than just a little perplexing.

Because our human role is ever evolving–a result of culture, technology, and policy–human beings, indeed, find themselves puzzled as to where they fit in, let alone how to accommodate or support others outside of their immediate surroundings. At the same time, citizens may find themselves questioning the ethical weight of whether or not their first allegiance is to their individual surroundings as opposed to the wide embrace of humankind. On the other hand, a large section of our population recognizes that humanity's plights and responses are the clearly defined moral obligations of everyone.

The texts in this section explore the various ways that people from all walks of life interpret the notion of social responsibility. Hopefully, the authors and their writings provide us with ways to examine and articulate these ideas to their communities, their families, their enemies, and themselves.

RALPH WALDO EMERSON

SELF-RELIANCE

(1841)

"Ne te quaesiveris extra."

"Man is his own star; and the soul that can
Render an honest and a perfect man,
Commands all light, all influence, all fate;
Nothing to him falls early or too late.
Our acts our angels are, or good or ill,
Our fatal shadows that walk by us still."
Epilogue to Beaumont and
Fletcher's *Honest Man's Fortune*

Cast the bantling on the rocks,
Suckle him with the she-wolf's teat;
Wintered with the hawk and fox,
Power and speed be hands and feet.

I read the other day some verses written by an eminent painter which were original and not conventional. The soul always hears an admonition in such lines, let the subject be what it may. The sentiment they instill is of more value than any thought they may contain. To believe your own thought, to believe that what is true for you in your private heart is true for all men,–that is genius. Speak your latent conviction, and it shall be the universal sense; for the inmost in due time becomes the outmost,–and our first thought is rendered back to us by the trumpets of the Last Judgment. Familiar as the voice of the mind is to each, the highest merit we ascribe to Moses, Plato, and Milton is, that they set at naught books and traditions, and spoke not what men but what they thought. A man should learn to detect and watch that gleam of light which flashes across his mind from within, more than the lustre of the firmament of bards and sages. Yet he dismisses without notice his thought, because it is his. In every work of genius we recognize our own rejected thoughts: they come back to us with a certain alienated majesty. Great works of art have no more affecting lesson for us than this. They teach us to abide by our spontaneous impression with good-humored inflexibility then most when the whole cry of voices is on the other side. Else, to-morrow a stranger will say with masterly good sense precisely what we have thought and felt all the time, and we shall be forced to take with shame our own opinion from another.

There is a time in every man's education when he arrives at the conviction that envy is ignorance; that imitation is suicide; that he must take himself for better, for worse, as his portion; that though the wide universe is full of good, no kernel of nourishing corn can come to him but through his toil bestowed on that plot of ground which is given to him to till. The power which resides in him is new in nature, and none but he knows what that is which he can do, nor does he know until he has tried. Not for nothing one face, one character, one fact, makes much impression on him, and another none. This sculpture in the memory is not without preestablished harmony. The eye was placed where one ray should fall, that it might testify of that particular ray. We but half express ourselves, and are ashamed of that divine idea which each of us represents. It may be safely trusted as proportionate and of good issues, so it be faithfully imparted, but God will not have his work made manifest by cowards. A man is relieved and gay when he has put his heart into his work and done his best; but what he has said or done otherwise, shall give him no peace. It is a deliverance which does not deliver. In the attempt his genius deserts him; no muse befriends; no invention, no hope.

Trust thyself: every heart vibrates to that iron string. Accept the place the divine providence has found for you, the society of your contemporaries, the connection of events. Great men have always done so, and confided themselves childlike to the genius of their age, betraying their perception that the absolutely trustworthy was seated at their heart, working through their hands, predominating in all their being. And we are now men, and must accept in the highest mind the same transcendent destiny; and not minors and invalids in a protected corner, not cowards fleeing before a revolution, but guides, redeemers, and benefactors, obeying the Almighty effort, and advancing on Chaos and the Dark.

What pretty oracles nature yields us on this text, in the face and behaviour of children, babes, and even brutes! That divided and rebel mind, that distrust of a sentiment because our arithmetic has computed the strength and means opposed to our purpose, these have not. Their mind being whole, their eye is as yet unconquered, and when we look in their faces, we are disconcerted. Infancy conforms to nobody: all conform to it, so that one babe commonly makes four or five out of the adults who prattle and play to it. So God has armed youth and puberty and manhood no less with its own piquancy and charm, and made it enviable and gracious and its claims not to be put by, if it will stand by itself. Do not think the youth has no force, because he cannot speak to you and me. Hark! in the next room his voice is sufficiently clear and emphatic. It seems he knows how to speak to his contemporaries. Bashful or bold, then, he will know how to make us seniors very unnecessary.

The nonchalance of boys who are sure of a dinner, and would disdain as much as a lord to do or say aught to conciliate one, is the healthy attitude of human nature. A boy is in the parlour what the pit is in the playhouse; independent, irresponsible, looking out from his corner on such people and facts as pass by, he tries and sentences them on their merits, in the swift, summary way of boys, as good, bad, interesting, silly, eloquent, troublesome. He cumbers himself never about consequences, about interests: he gives an independent, genuine verdict. You must court him: he does not court you. But the man is, as it were, clapped into jail by his consciousness. As soon as he has once acted or spoken with eclat, he is a committed person, watched by the sympathy or the hatred of hundreds, whose affections must now enter into his account. There is no Lethe for this. Ah, that he could pass again into his neutrality! Who can thus avoid all pledges, and having observed, observe again from the same unaffected, unbiased, unbribable, unaffrighted innocence, must always be formidable. He would utter opinions on all passing affairs, which being seen to be not private, but necessary, would sink like darts into the ear of men, and put them in fear.

These are the voices which we hear in solitude, but they grow faint and inaudible as we enter into the world. Society everywhere is in conspiracy against the manhood of every one of its members. Society is a joint-stock company, in which the members agree, for the better securing of his bread to each shareholder, to surrender the liberty and culture of the eater. The virtue in most request is conformity. Self-reliance is its aversion. It loves not realities and creators, but names and customs.

Whoso would be a man must be a nonconformist. He who would gather immortal palms must not be hindered by the name of goodness, but must explore if it be goodness. Nothing is at last sacred but the integrity of your own mind. Absolve you to yourself, and you shall have the suffrage of the world. I remember an answer which when quite young I was prompted to make to a valued adviser, who was wont to importune me with the dear old doctrines of the church. On my saying, What have I to do with the sacredness of traditions, if I live wholly from within? my friend suggested,—"But these impulses may be from below, not from above." I replied, "They do not seem to me to be such; but if I am the Devil's child, I will live then from the Devil." No law can be sacred to me but that of my nature. Good and bad are but names very readily transferable to that or this; the only right is what is after my constitution, the only wrong what is against it. A man is to carry himself in the presence of all opposition, as if every thing were titular and ephemeral but he. I am ashamed to think how easily we capitulate to badges and names, to large societies and dead institutions. Every decent and well-spoken individual affects and sways me more than is right. I ought to go upright and vital, and speak the rude truth in all ways. If malice and vanity wear the coat of philanthropy, shall that pass? If an angry bigot assumes this bountiful cause of Abolition, and comes to me with his last news from Barbadoes, why should I not say to him, 'Go love thy infant; love thy wood-chopper: be good-natured and modest: have that grace; and never varnish your hard, uncharitable ambition with this incredible tenderness for black folk a thousand miles off. Thy love afar is spite at home.' Rough and graceless would be such greeting, but truth is handsomer than the affectation of love. Your goodness must have some edge to it,—else it is none. The doctrine of hatred must be preached as the counteraction of the doctrine of love when that pules and whines. I shun father and mother and wife and brother, when my genius calls me. I would write on the lintels of the door-post, Whim. I hope it is somewhat better than whim at last, but we cannot spend the day in explanation. Expect me not to show cause why I seek or why I exclude company. Then, again, do not tell me, as a good man did to-day, of my obligation to put all poor men in good situations. Are they my poor? I tell thee, thou foolish philanthropist, that I grudge the dollar, the dime, the cent, I give to such men as do not belong to me and to whom I do not belong. There is a class of persons to whom by all spiritual affinity I am bought and sold; for them I will go to prison, if need be; but your miscellaneous popular charities; the education at college of fools; the building of meeting-houses to the vain end to which many now stand; alms to sots; and the thousandfold Relief Societies;—though I confess with shame I sometimes succumb and give the dollar, it is a wicked dollar which by and by I shall have the manhood to withhold.

Virtues are, in the popular estimate, rather the exception than the rule. There is the man *and* his virtues. Men do what is called a good action, as some piece of courage or charity, much as they would pay a fine in expiation of daily non-appearance on parade. Their works are done as an apology or extenuation of their living in the world,—as invalids and the insane pay a high board. Their virtues are penances. I do not wish to expiate, but to live. My life is for itself and not for a spectacle. I much prefer that it should be of a lower strain, so it be genuine and equal, than that it should be glittering and unsteady. I wish it to be sound and sweet, and not to need diet and bleeding. I ask primary evidence that you are a man, and refuse this appeal from the man to his actions. I know that for myself it makes no difference whether I do or forbear those actions which are reckoned excellent. I cannot consent to pay for a privilege where I have intrinsic right. Few and mean as my gifts may be, I actually am, and do not need for my own assurance or the assurance of my fellows any secondary testimony.

What I must do is all that concerns me, not what the people think. This rule, equally arduous in actual and in intellectual life, may serve for the whole distinction between greatness and meanness. It is the harder, because you will always find those who think they know what is your duty better than you know it. It is easy in the world to live after the world's opinion; it is easy in solitude to live after our own; but the great man is he who in the midst of the crowd keeps with perfect sweetness the independence of solitude.

The objection to conforming to usages that have become dead to you is, that it scatters your force. It loses your time and blurs the impression of your character. If you maintain a dead church, contribute to a dead Bible-society, vote with a great party either for the government or against it, spread your table like base housekeepers,–under all these screens I have difficulty to detect the precise man you are. And, of course, so much force is withdrawn from your proper life. But do your work, and I shall know you. Do your work, and you shall reinforce yourself. A man must consider what a blindman's-buff is this game of conformity. If I know your sect, I anticipate your argument. I hear a preacher announce for his text and topic the expediency of one of the institutions of his church. Do I not know beforehand that not possibly can he say a new and spontaneous word? Do I not know that, with all this ostentation of examining the grounds of the institution, he will do no such thing? Do I not know that he is pledged to himself not to look but at one side,–the permitted side, not as a man, but as a parish minister? He is a retained attorney, and these airs of the bench are the emptiest affectation. Well, most men have bound their eyes with one or another handkerchief, and attached themselves to some one of these communities of opinion. This conformity makes them not false in a few particulars, authors of a few lies, but false in all particulars. Their every truth is not quite true. Their two is not the real two, their four not the real four; so that every word they say chagrins us, and we know not where to begin to set them right. Meantime nature is not slow to equip us in the prison-uniform of the party to which we adhere. We come to wear one cut of lace and figure, and acquire by degrees the gentlest asinine expression. There is a mortifying experience in particular, which does not fail to wreak itself also in the general history; I mean "the foolish face of praise," the forced smile which we put on in company where we do not feel at ease in answer to conversation which does not interest us. The muscles, not spontaneously moved, but moved by a low usurping wilfulness, grow tight about the outline of the face with the most disagreeable sensation.

For nonconformity the world whips you with its displeasure. And therefore a man must know how to estimate a sour face. The by-standers look askance on him in the public street or in the friend's parlour. If this aversation had its origin in contempt and resistance like his own, he might well go home with a sad countenance; but the sour faces of the multitude, like their sweet faces, have no deep cause, but are put on and off as the wind blows and a newspaper directs. Yet is the discontent of the multitude more formidable than that of the senate and the college. It is easy enough for a firm man who knows the world to brook the rage of the cultivated classes. Their rage is decorous and prudent, for they are timid as being very vulnerable themselves. But when to their feminine rage the indignation of the people is added, when the ignorant and the poor are aroused, when the unintelligent brute force that lies at the bottom of society is made to growl and mow, it needs the habit of magnanimity and religion to treat it godlike as a trifle of no concernment.

The other terror that scares us from self-trust is our consistency; a reverence for our past act or word, because the eyes of others have no other data for computing our orbit than our past acts, and we are loath to disappoint them.

But why should you keep your head over your shoulder? Why drag about this corpse of your memory, lest you contradict somewhat you have stated in this or that public place? Suppose you should contradict yourself; what then? It seems to be a rule of wisdom never to rely on your memory alone, scarcely even in acts of pure memory, but to bring the past for judgment into the thousand-eyed present, and live ever in a new day. In your metaphysics you have denied personality to the Deity: yet when the devout motions of the soul come, yield to them heart and life, though they should clothe God with shape and color. Leave your theory, as Joseph his coat in the hand of the harlot, and flee.

A foolish consistency is the hobgoblin of little minds, adored by little statesmen and philosophers and divines. With consistency a great soul has simply nothing to do. He may as well concern himself with his shadow on the wall. Speak what you think now in hard words, and to-morrow speak what to-morrow thinks in hard words again, though it contradict every thing you said to-day.—'Ah, so you shall be sure to be misunderstood.'—Is it so bad, then, to be misunderstood? Pythagoras was misunderstood, and Socrates, and Jesus, and Luther, and Copernicus, and Galileo, and Newton, and every pure and wise spirit that ever took flesh. To be great is to be misunderstood.

I suppose no man can violate his nature. All the sallies of his will are rounded in by the law of his being, as the inequalities of Andes and Himmaleh are insignificant to the curve of the sphere. Nor does it matter how you gauge and try him. A character is like an acrostic or Alexandrian stanza;—read it forward, backward, or across, it still spells the same thing. In this pleasing, contrite wood-life which God allows me, let me record day by day my honest thought without prospect or retrospect, and, I cannot doubt, it will be found symmetrical, though I mean it not, and see it not. My book should smell of pines and resound with the hum of insects. The swallow over my window should interweave that thread or straw he carries in his bill into my web also. We pass for what we are. Character teaches above our wills. Men imagine that they communicate their virtue or vice only by overt actions, and do not see that virtue or vice emit a breath every moment.

There will be an agreement in whatever variety of actions, so they be each honest and natural in their hour. For of one will, the actions will be harmonious, however unlike they seem. These varieties are lost sight of at a little distance, at a little height of thought. One tendency unites them all. The voyage of the best ship is a zigzag line of a hundred tacks. See the line from a sufficient distance, and it straightens itself to the average tendency. Your genuine action will explain itself, and will explain your other genuine actions. Your conformity explains nothing. Act singly, and what you have already done singly will justify you now. Greatness appeals to the future. If I can be firm enough to-day to do right, and scorn eyes, I must have done so much right before as to defend me now. Be it how it will, do right now. Always scorn appearances, and you always may. The force of character is cumulative. All the foregone days of virtue work their health into this. What makes the majesty of the heroes of the senate and the field, which so fills the imagination? The consciousness of a train of great days and victories behind. They shed an united light on the advancing actor. He is attended as by a visible escort of angels. That is it which throws thunder into Chatham's voice, and dignity into Washington's port, and America into Adams's eye. Honor is venerable to us because it is no ephemeris. It is always ancient virtue. We worship it to-day because it is not of to-day. We love it and pay it homage, because it is not a trap for our love and homage, but is self-dependent, self-derived, and therefore of an old immaculate pedigree, even if shown in a young person.

I hope in these days we have heard the last of conformity and consistency. Let the words be gazetted and ridiculous henceforward. Instead of the gong for dinner, let us hear a whistle from the Spartan fife. Let us never bow and apologize more. A great man is coming to eat at my house. I do not wish to please him; I wish that he should wish to please me. I will stand here for humanity, and though I would make it kind, I would make it true. Let us affront and reprimand the smooth mediocrity and squalid contentment of the times, and hurl in the face of custom, and trade, and office, the fact which is the upshot of all history, that there is a great responsible Thinker and Actor working wherever a man works; that a true man belongs to no other time or place, but is the centre of things. Where he is, there is nature. He measures you, and all men, and all events. Ordinarily, every body in society reminds us of somewhat else, or of some other person. Character, reality, reminds you of nothing else; it takes place of the whole creation. The man must be so much, that he must make all circumstances indifferent. Every true man is a cause, a country, and an age; requires infinite spaces and numbers and time fully to accomplish his design;–and posterity seem to follow his steps as a train of clients. A man Caesar is born, and for ages after we have a Roman Empire. Christ is born, and millions of minds so grow and cleave to his genius, that he is confounded with virtue and the possible of man. An institution is the lengthened shadow of one man; as, Monachism, of the Hermit Antony; the Reformation, of Luther; Quakerism, of Fox; Methodism, of Wesley; Abolition, of Clarkson. Scipio, Milton called "the height of Rome"; and all history resolves itself very easily into the biography of a few stout and earnest persons.

Let a man then know his worth, and keep things under his feet. Let him not peep or steal, or skulk up and down with the air of a charity-boy, a bastard, or an interloper, in the world which exists for him. But the man in the street, finding no worth in himself which corresponds to the force which built a tower or sculptured a marble god, feels poor when he looks on these. To him a palace, a statue, or a costly book have an alien and forbidding air, much like a gay equipage, and seem to say like that, 'Who are you, Sir?' Yet they all are his, suitors for his notice, petitioners to his faculties that they will come out and take possession. The picture waits for my verdict: it is not to command me, but I am to settle its claims to praise. That popular fable of the sot who was picked up dead drunk in the street, carried to the duke's house, washed and dressed and laid in the duke's bed, and, on his waking, treated with all obsequious ceremony like the duke, and assured that he had been insane, owes its popularity to the fact, that it symbolizes so well the state of man, who is in the world a sort of sot, but now and then wakes up, exercises his reason, and finds himself a true prince.

Our reading is mendicant and sycophantic. In history, our imagination plays us false. Kingdom and lordship, power and estate, are a gaudier vocabulary than private John and Edward in a small house and common day's work; but the things of life are the same to both; the sum total of both is the same. Why all this deference to Alfred, and Scanderbeg, and Gustavus? Suppose they were virtuous; did they wear out virtue? As great a stake depends on your private act to-day, as followed their public and renowned steps. When private men shall act with original views, the lustre will be transferred from the actions of kings to those of gentlemen.

The world has been instructed by its kings, who have so magnetized the eyes of nations. It has been taught by this colossal symbol the mutual reverence that is due from man to man. The joyful loyalty with which men have everywhere suffered the king, the noble, or the great proprietor to walk among them by a law of his own, make his own scale of men and things, and reverse theirs, pay for benefits not with money but with honor, and represent the law in his person, was the hieroglyphic by which they obscurely signified their consciousness of their own right and comeliness, the right of every man.

The magnetism which all original action exerts is explained when we inquire the reason of self-trust. Who is the Trustee? What is the aboriginal Self, on which a universal reliance may be grounded? What is the nature and power of that science-baffling star, without parallax, without calculable elements, which shoots a ray of beauty even into trivial and impure actions, if the least mark of independence appear? The inquiry leads us to that source, at once the essence of genius, of virtue, and of life, which we call Spontaneity or Instinct. We denote this primary wisdom as Intuition, whilst all later teachings are tuitions. In that deep force, the last fact behind which analysis cannot go, all things find their common origin. For, the sense of being which in calm hours rises, we know not how, in the soul, is not diverse from things, from space, from light, from time, from man, but one with them, and proceeds obviously from the same source whence their life and being also proceed. We first share the life by which things exist, and afterwards see them as appearances in nature, and forget that we have shared their cause. Here is the fountain of action and of thought. Here are the lungs of that inspiration which giveth man wisdom, and which cannot be denied without impiety and atheism. We lie in the lap of immense intelligence, which makes us receivers of its truth and organs of its activity. When we discern justice, when we discern truth, we do nothing of ourselves, but allow a passage to its beams. If we ask whence this comes, if we seek to pry into the soul that causes, all philosophy is at fault. Its presence or its absence is all we can affirm. Every man discriminates between the voluntary acts of his mind, and his involuntary perceptions, and knows that to his involuntary perceptions a perfect faith is due. He may err in the expression of them, but he knows that these things are so, like day and night, not to be disputed. My wilful actions and acquisitions are but roving;—the idlest reverie, the faintest native emotion, command my curiosity and respect. Thoughtless people contradict as readily the statement of perceptions as of opinions, or rather much more readily; for, they do not distinguish between perception and notion. They fancy that I choose to see this or that thing. But perception is not whimsical, but fatal. If I see a trait, my children will see it after me, and in course of time, all mankind,—although it may chance that no one has seen it before me. For my perception of it is as much a fact as the sun.

The relations of the soul to the divine spirit are so pure, that it is profane to seek to interpose helps. It must be that when God speaketh he should communicate, not one thing, but all things; should fill the world with his voice; should scatter forth light, nature, time, souls, from the centre of the present thought; and new date and new create the whole. Whenever a mind is simple, and receives a divine wisdom, old things pass away,—means, teachers, texts, temples fall; it lives now, and absorbs past and future into the present hour. All things are made sacred by relation to it,—one as much as another. All things are dissolved to their centre by their cause, and, in the universal miracle, petty and particular miracles disappear. If, therefore, a man claims to know and speak of God, and carries you backward to the phraseology of some old mouldered nation in another country, in another world, believe him not. Is the acorn better than the oak which is its fulness and completion? Is the parent better than the child into whom he has cast his ripened being? Whence, then, this worship of the past? The centuries are conspirators against the sanity and authority of the soul. Time and space are but physiological colors which the eye makes, but the soul is light; where it is, is day; where it was, is night; and history is an impertinence and an injury, if it be any thing more than a cheerful apologue or parable of my being and becoming.

Man is timid and apologetic; he is no longer upright; he dares not say 'I think,' 'I am,' but quotes some saint or sage. He is ashamed before the blade of grass or the blowing rose. These roses under my window make no reference to former roses or to better ones; they are for what they are; they exist with God to-day. There is no time to them. There is simply the rose; it is perfect in every moment of its existence. Before a leaf-bud has burst, its whole life acts; in the full-blown flower there is no more; in the leafless root there is no less. Its nature is satisfied, and it satisfies nature, in all moments alike. But man postpones or remembers; he does not live in the present, but with reverted eye laments the past, or, heedless of the riches that surround him, stands on tiptoe to foresee the future. He cannot be happy and strong until he too lives with nature in the present, above time.

This should be plain enough. Yet see what strong intellects dare not yet hear God himself, unless he speak the phraseology of I know not what David, or Jeremiah, or Paul. We shall not always set so great a price on a few texts, on a few lives. We are like children who repeat by rote the sentences of grandames and tutors, and, as they grow older, of the men of talents and character they chance to see,—painfully recollecting the exact words they spoke; afterwards, when they come into the point of view which those had who uttered these sayings, they understand them, and are willing to let the words go; for, at any time, they can use words as good when occasion comes. If we live truly, we shall see truly. It is as easy for the strong man to be strong, as it is for the weak to be weak. When we have new perception, we shall gladly disburden the memory of its hoarded treasures as old rubbish. When a man lives with God, his voice shall be as sweet as the murmur of the brook and the rustle of the corn.

And now at last the highest truth on this subject remains unsaid; probably cannot be said; for all that we say is the far-off remembering of the intuition. That thought, by what I can now nearest approach to say it, is this. When good is near you, when you have life in yourself, it is not by any known or accustomed way; you shall not discern the foot-prints of any other; you shall not see the face of man; you shall not hear any name;—the way, the thought, the good, shall be wholly strange and new. It shall exclude example and experience. You take the way from man, not to man. All persons that ever existed are its forgotten ministers. Fear and hope are alike beneath it. There is somewhat low even in hope. In the hour of vision, there is nothing that can be called gratitude, nor properly joy. The soul raised over passion beholds identity and eternal causation, perceives the self-existence of Truth and Right, and calms itself with knowing that all things go well.

Vast spaces of nature, the Atlantic Ocean, the South Sea,–long intervals of time, years, centuries,–are of no account. This which I think and feel underlay every former state of life and circumstances, as it does underlie my present, and what is called life, and what is called death.

Life only avails, not the having lived. Power ceases in the instant of repose; it resides in the moment of transition from a past to a new state, in the shooting of the gulf, in the darting to an aim. This one fact the world hates, that the soul becomes; for that for ever degrades the past, turns all riches to poverty, all reputation to a shame, confounds the saint with the rogue, shoves Jesus and Judas equally aside. Why, then, do we prate of self-reliance? Inasmuch as the soul is present, there will be power not confident but agent. To talk of reliance is a poor external way of speaking. Speak rather of that which relies, because it works and is. Who has more obedience than I masters me, though he should not raise his finger. Round him I must revolve by the gravitation of spirits. We fancy it rhetoric, when we speak of eminent virtue. We do not yet see that virtue is Height, and that a man or a company of men, plastic and permeable to principles, by the law of nature must overpower and ride all cities, nations, kings, rich men, poets, who are not.

This is the ultimate fact which we so quickly reach on this, as on every topic, the resolution of all into the ever-blessed ONE. Self-existence is the attribute of the Supreme Cause, and it constitutes the measure of good by the degree in which it enters into all lower forms. All things real are so by so much virtue as they contain. Commerce, husbandry, hunting, whaling, war, eloquence, personal weight, are somewhat, and engage my respect as examples of its presence and impure action. I see the same law working in nature for conservation and growth. Power is in nature the essential measure of right. Nature suffers nothing to remain in her kingdoms which cannot help itself. The genesis and maturation of a planet, its poise and orbit, the bended tree recovering itself from the strong wind, the vital resources of every animal and vegetable, are demonstrations of the self-sufficing, and therefore self-relying soul.

Thus all concentrates: let us not rove; let us sit at home with the cause. Let us stun and astonish the intruding rabble of men and books and institutions, by a simple declaration of the divine fact. Bid the invaders take the shoes from off their feet, for God is here within. Let our simplicity judge them, and our docility to our own law demonstrate the poverty of nature and fortune beside our native riches.

But now we are a mob. Man does not stand in awe of man, nor is his genius admonished to stay at home, to put itself in communication with the internal ocean, but it goes abroad to beg a cup of water of the urns of other men. We must go alone. I like the silent church before the service begins, better than any preaching. How far off, how cool, how chaste the persons look, begirt each one with a precinct or sanctuary! So let us always sit. Why should we assume the faults of our friend, or wife, or father, or child, because they sit around our hearth, or are said to have the same blood? All men have my blood, and I have all men's. Not for that will I adopt their petulance or folly, even to the extent of being ashamed of it. But your isolation must not be mechanical, but spiritual, that is, must be elevation. At times the whole world seems to be in conspiracy to importune you with emphatic trifles. Friend, client, child, sickness, fear, want, charity, all knock at once at thy closet door, and say,–'Come out unto us.' But keep thy state; come not into their confusion. The power men possess to annoy me, I give them by a weak curiosity. No man can come near me but through my act. "What we love that we have, but by desire we bereave ourselves of the love."

If we cannot at once rise to the sanctities of obedience and faith, let us at least resist our temptations; let us enter into the state of war, and wake Thor and Woden, courage and constancy, in our Saxon breasts. This is to be done in our smooth times by speaking the truth. Check this lying hospitality and lying affection. Live no longer to the expectation of these deceived and deceiving people with whom we converse. Say to them, O father, O mother, O wife, O brother, O friend, I have lived with you after appearances hitherto. Henceforward I am the truth's. Be it known unto you that henceforward I obey no law less than the eternal law. I will have no covenants but proximities. I shall endeavour to nourish my parents, to support my family, to be the chaste husband of one wife,—but these relations I must fill after a new and unprecedented way. I appeal from your customs. I must be myself. I cannot break myself any longer for you, or you. If you can love me for what I am, we shall be the happier. If you cannot, I will still seek to deserve that you should. I will not hide my tastes or aversions. I will so trust that what is deep is holy, that I will do strongly before the sun and moon whatever inly rejoices me, and the heart appoints. If you are noble, I will love you; if you are not, I will not hurt you and myself by hypocritical attentions. If you are true, but not in the same truth with me, cleave to your companions; I will seek my own. I do this not selfishly, but humbly and truly. It is alike your interest, and mine, and all men's, however long we have dwelt in lies, to live in truth. Does this sound harsh today? You will soon love what is dictated by your nature as well as mine, and, if we follow the truth, it will bring us out safe at last.—But so you may give these friends pain. Yes, but I cannot sell my liberty and my power, to save their sensibility. Besides, all persons have their moments of reason, when they look out into the region of absolute truth; then will they justify me, and do the same thing.

The populace think that your rejection of popular standards is a rejection of all standard, and mere antinomianism; and the bold sensualist will use the name of philosophy to gild his crimes. But the law of consciousness abides. There are two confessionals, in one or the other of which we must be shriven. You may fulfil your round of duties by clearing yourself in the *direct*, or in the *reflex* way. Consider whether you have satisfied your relations to father, mother, cousin, neighbour, town, cat, and dog; whether any of these can upbraid you. But I may also neglect this reflex standard, and absolve me to myself. I have my own stern claims and perfect circle. It denies the name of duty to many offices that are called duties. But if I can discharge its debts, it enables me to dispense with the popular code. If any one imagines that this law is lax, let him keep its commandment one day.

And truly it demands something godlike in him who has cast off the common motives of humanity, and has ventured to trust himself for a taskmaster. High be his heart, faithful his will, clear his sight, that he may in good earnest be doctrine, society, law, to himself, that a simple purpose may be to him as strong as iron necessity is to others!

If any man consider the present aspects of what is called by distinction *society,* he will see the need of these ethics. The sinew and heart of man seem to be drawn out, and we are become timorous, desponding whimperers. We are afraid of truth, afraid of fortune, afraid of death, and afraid of each other. Our age yields no great and perfect persons. We want men and women who shall renovate life and our social state, but we see that most natures are insolvent, cannot satisfy their own wants, have an ambition out of all proportion to their practical force, and do lean and beg day and night continually. Our housekeeping is mendicant, our arts, our occupations, our marriages, our religion, we have not chosen, but society has chosen for us. We are parlour soldiers. We shun the rugged battle of fate, where strength is born.

If our young men miscarry in their first enterprises, they lose all heart. If the young merchant fails, men say he is *ruined.* If the finest genius studies at one of our colleges, and is not installed in an office within one year afterwards in the cities or suburbs of Boston or New York, it seems to his friends and to himself that he is right in being disheartened, and in complaining the rest of his life. A sturdy lad from New Hampshire or Vermont, who in turn tries all the professions, who *teams it, farms it, peddles,* keeps a school, preaches, edits a newspaper, goes to Congress, buys a township, and so forth, in successive years, and always, like a cat, falls on his feet, is worth a hundred of these city dolls. He walks abreast with his days, and feels no shame in not 'studying a profession,' for he does not postpone his life, but lives already. He has not one chance, but a hundred chances. Let a Stoic open the resources of man, and tell men they are not leaning willows, but can and must detach themselves; that with the exercise of self-trust, new powers shall appear; that a man is the word made flesh, born to shed healing to the nations, that he should be ashamed of our compassion, and that the moment he acts from himself, tossing the laws, the books, idolatries, and customs out of the window, we pity him no more, but thank and revere him,— and that teacher shall restore the life of man to splendor, and make his name dear to all history.

It is easy to see that a greater self-reliance must work a revolution in all the offices and relations of men; in their religion; in their education; in their pursuits; their modes of living; their association; in their property; in their speculative views.

1. In what prayers do men allow themselves! That which they call a holy office is not so much as brave and manly. Prayer looks abroad and asks for some foreign addition to come through some foreign virtue, and loses itself in endless mazes of natural and supernatural, and mediatorial and miraculous. Prayer that craves a particular commodity,— any thing less than all good,—is vicious. Prayer is the contemplation of the facts of life from the highest point of view. It is the soliloquy of a beholding and jubilant soul. It is the spirit of God pronouncing his works good. But prayer as a means to effect a private end is meanness and theft. It supposes dualism and not unity in nature and consciousness. As soon as the man is at one with God, he will not beg. He will then see prayer in all action. The prayer of the farmer kneeling in his field to weed it, the prayer of the rower kneeling with the stroke of his oar, are true prayers heard throughout nature, though for cheap ends. Caratach, in Fletcher's Bonduca, when admonished to inquire the mind of the god Audate, replies,—

> "His hidden meaning lies in our
> endeavours;
> Our valors are our best gods."

Another sort of false prayers are our regrets. Discontent is the want of self-reliance: it is infirmity of will. Regret calamities, if you can thereby help the sufferer; if not, attend your own work, and already the evil begins to be repaired. Our sympathy is just as base. We come to them who weep foolishly, and sit down and cry for company, instead of imparting to them truth and health in rough electric shocks, putting them once more in communication with their own reason. The secret of fortune is joy in our hands. Welcome evermore to gods and men is the self-helping man. For him all doors are flung wide: him all tongues greet, all honors crown, all eyes follow with desire. Our love goes out to him and embraces him, because he did not need it. We solicitously and apologetically caress and celebrate him, because he held on his way and scorned our disapprobation. The gods love him because men hated him. "To the persevering mortal," said Zoroaster, "the blessed Immortals are swift."

As men's prayers are a disease of the will, so are their creeds a disease of the intellect. They say with those foolish Israelites, 'Let not God speak to us, lest we die. Speak thou, speak any man with us, and we will obey.' Everywhere I am hindered of meeting God in my brother, because he has shut his own temple doors, and recites fables merely of his brother's, or his brother's brother's God. Every new mind is a new classification. If it prove a mind of uncommon activity and power, a Locke, a Lavoisier, a Hutton, a Bentham, a Fourier, it imposes its classification on other men, and lo! a new system. In proportion to the depth of the thought, and so to the number of the objects it touches and brings within reach of the pupil, is his complacency. But chiefly is this apparent in creeds and churches, which are also classifications of some powerful mind acting on the elemental thought of duty, and man's relation to the Highest. Such is Calvinism, Quakerism, Swedenborgism. The pupil takes the same delight in subordinating every thing to the new terminology, as a girl who has just learned botany in seeing a new earth and new seasons thereby. It will happen for a time, that the pupil will find his intellectual power has grown by the study of his master's mind. But in all unbalanced minds, the classification is idolized, passes for the end, and not for a speedily exhaustible means, so that the walls of the system blend to their eye in the remote horizon with the walls of the universe; the luminaries of heaven seem to them hung on the arch their master built. They cannot imagine how you aliens have any right to see,—how you can see; 'It must be somehow that you stole the light from us.' They do not yet perceive, that light, unsystematic, indomitable, will break into any cabin, even into theirs. Let them chirp awhile and call it their own. If they are honest and do well, presently their neat new pinfold will be too strait and low, will crack, will lean, will rot and vanish, and the immortal light, all young and joyful, million-orbed, million-colored, will beam over the universe as on the first morning.

2. It is for want of self-culture that the superstition of Travelling, whose idols are Italy, England, Egypt, retains its fascination for all educated Americans. They who made England, Italy, or Greece venerable in the imagination did so by sticking fast where they were, like an axis of the earth. In manly hours, we feel that duty is our place. The soul is no traveller; the wise man stays at home, and when his necessities, his duties, on any occasion call him from his house, or into foreign lands, he is at home still, and shall make men sensible by the expression of his countenance, that he goes the missionary of wisdom and virtue, and visits cities and men like a sovereign, and not like an interloper or a valet.

I have no churlish objection to the circumnavigation of the globe, for the purposes of art, of study, and benevolence, so that the man is first domesticated, or does not go abroad with the hope of finding somewhat greater than he knows. He who travels to be amused, or to get somewhat which he does not carry, travels away from himself, and grows old even in youth among old things. In Thebes, in Palmyra, his will and mind have become old and dilapidated as they. He carries ruins to ruins.

Travelling is a fool's paradise. Our first journeys discover to us the indifference of places. At home I dream that at Naples, at

Rome, I can be intoxicated with beauty, and lose my sadness. I pack my trunk, embrace my friends, embark on the sea, and at last wake up in Naples, and there beside me is the stern fact, the sad self, unrelenting, identical, that I fled from. I seek the Vatican, and the palaces. I affect to be intoxicated with sights and suggestions, but I am not intoxicated. My giant goes with me wherever I go.

3. But the rage of travelling is a symptom of a deeper unsoundness affecting the whole intellectual action. The intellect is vagabond, and our system of education fosters restlessness. Our minds travel when our bodies are forced to stay at home. We imitate; and what is imitation but the travelling of the mind? Our houses are built with foreign taste; our shelves are garnished with foreign ornaments; our opinions, our tastes, our faculties, lean, and follow the Past and the Distant. The soul created the arts wherever they have flourished. It was in his own mind that the artist sought his model. It was an application of his own thought to the thing to be done and the conditions to be observed. And why need we copy the Doric or the Gothic model? Beauty, convenience, grandeur of thought, and quaint expression are as near to us as to any, and if the American artist will study with hope and love the precise thing to be done by him, considering the climate, the soil, the length of the day, the wants of the people, the habit and form of the government, he will create a house in which all these will find themselves fitted, and taste and sentiment will be satisfied also.

Insist on yourself; never imitate. Your own gift you can present every moment with the cumulative force of a whole life's cultivation; but of the adopted talent of another, you have only an extemporaneous, half possession. That which each can do best, none but his Maker can teach him. No man yet knows what it is, nor can, till that person has exhibited it. Where is the master who could have taught Shakspeare? Where is the master who could have instructed Franklin, or Washington, or Bacon, or Newton? Every great man is a unique. The Scipionism of Scipio is precisely that part he could not borrow. Shakspeare will never be made by the study of Shakspeare. Do that which is assigned you, and you cannot hope too much or dare too much. There is at this moment for you an utterance brave and grand as that of the colossal chisel of Phidias, or trowel of the Egyptians, or the pen of Moses, or Dante, but different from all these. Not possibly will the soul all rich, all eloquent, with thousand-cloven tongue, deign to repeat itself; but if you can hear what these patriarchs say, surely you can reply to them in the same pitch of voice; for the ear and the tongue are two organs of one nature. Abide in the simple and noble regions of thy life, obey thy heart, and thou shalt reproduce the Foreworld again.

4. As our Religion, our Education, our Art look abroad, so does our spirit of society. All men plume themselves on the improvement of society, and no man improves.

Society never advances. It recedes as fast on one side as it gains on the other. It undergoes continual changes; it is barbarous, it is civilized, it is christianized, it is rich, it is scientific; but this change is not amelioration. For every thing that is given, something is taken. Society acquires new arts, and loses old instincts. What a contrast between the well-clad, reading, writing, thinking American, with a watch, a pencil, and a bill of exchange in his pocket, and the naked New Zealander, whose property is a club, a spear, a mat, and an undivided twentieth of a shed to sleep under! But compare the health of the two men, and you shall see that the white man has lost his aboriginal strength. If the traveller tell us truly, strike the savage with a broad axe, and in a day or two the flesh shall unite and heal as if you struck the blow into soft pitch, and the same blow shall send the white to his grave.

The civilized man has built a coach, but has lost the use of his feet. He is supported on crutches, but lacks so much support of muscle. He has a fine Geneva watch, but he fails of the skill to tell the hour by the sun. A Greenwich nautical almanac he has, and so being sure of the information when he wants it, the man in the street does not know a star in the sky. The solstice he does not observe; the equinox he knows as little; and the whole bright calendar of the year is without a dial in his mind. His note-books impair his memory; his libraries overload his wit; the insurance-office increases the number of accidents; and it may be a question whether machinery does not encumber; whether we have not lost by refinement some energy, by a Christianity entrenched in establishments and forms, some vigor of wild virtue. For every Stoic was a Stoic; but in Christendom where is the Christian?

There is no more deviation in the moral standard than in the standard of height or bulk. No greater men are now than ever were. A singular equality may be observed between the great men of the first and of the last ages; nor can all the science, art, religion, and philosophy of the nineteenth century avail to educate greater men than Plutarch's heroes, three or four and twenty centuries ago. Not in time is the race progressive. Phocion, Socrates, Anaxagoras, Diogenes, are great men, but they leave no class. He who is really of their class will not be called by their name, but will be his own man, and, in his turn, the founder of a sect. The arts and inventions of each period are only its costume, and do not invigorate men. The harm of the improved machinery may compensate its good. Hudson and Behring accomplished so much in their fishing-boats, as to astonish Parry and Franklin, whose equipment exhausted the resources of science and art. Galileo, with an opera-glass, discovered a more splendid series of celestial phenomena than any one since. Columbus found the New World in an undecked boat. It is curious to see the periodical disuse and perishing of means and machinery, which were introduced with loud laudation a few years or centuries before. The great genius returns to essential man. We reckoned the improvements of the art of war among the triumphs of science, and yet Napoleon conquered Europe by the bivouac, which consisted of falling back on naked valor, and disencumbering it of all aids. The Emperor held it impossible to make a perfect army, says Las Casas, "without abolishing our arms, magazines, commissaries, and carriages, until, in imitation of the Roman custom, the soldier should receive his supply of corn, grind it in his hand-mill, and bake his bread himself."

Society is a wave. The wave moves onward, but the water of which it is composed does not. The same particle does not rise from the valley to the ridge. Its unity is only phenomenal. The persons who make up a nation to-day, next year die, and their experience with them.

And so the reliance on Property, including the reliance on governments which protect it, is the want of self-reliance. Men have looked away from themselves and at things so long, that they have come to esteem the religious, learned, and civil institutions as guards of property, and they deprecate assaults on these, because they feel them to be assaults on property. They measure their esteem of each other by what each has, and not by what each is. But a cultivated man becomes ashamed of his property, out of new respect for his nature. Especially he hates what he has, if he see that it is accidental,—came to him by inheritance, or gift, or crime; then he feels that it is not having; it does not belong to him, has no root in him, and merely lies there, because no revolution or no robber takes it away. But that which a man is does always by necessity acquire, and what the man acquires is living property, which does not wait the beck of rulers, or mobs, or revolutions, or fire, or storm, or bankruptcies, but perpetually renews itself wherever the man breathes. "Thy lot or portion of life," said the Caliph Ali, "is seeking after thee; therefore be at rest from seeking after it." Our dependence on these foreign goods leads us to our slavish respect for numbers. The political parties meet in numerous conventions; the greater the concourse, and with each new uproar of announcement, The delegation from Essex! The Democrats from New Hampshire! The Whigs of Maine! the young patriot feels himself stronger than before by a new thousand of eyes and arms. In like manner the reformers summon conventions, and vote and resolve in multitude. Not so, O friends! will the God deign to enter and inhabit you, but by a method precisely the reverse. It is only as a man puts off all foreign support, and stands alone, that I see him to be strong and to prevail. He is weaker by every recruit to his banner. Is not a man better than a town? Ask nothing of men, and in the endless mutation, thou only firm column must presently appear the upholder of all that surrounds thee. He who knows that power is inborn, that he is weak because he has looked for good out of him and elsewhere, and so perceiving, throws himself unhesitatingly on his thought, instantly rights himself, stands in the erect position, commands his limbs, works miracles; just as a man who stands on his feet is stronger than a man who stands on his head.

So use all that is called Fortune. Most men gamble with her, and gain all, and lose all, as her wheel rolls. But do thou leave as unlawful these winnings, and deal with Cause and Effect, the chancellors of God. In the Will work and acquire, and thou hast chained the wheel of Chance, and shalt sit hereafter out of fear from her rotations. A political victory, a rise of rents, the recovery of your sick, or the return of your absent friend, or some other favorable event, raises your spirits, and you think good days are preparing for you. Do not believe it. Nothing can bring you peace but yourself. Nothing can bring you peace but the triumph of principles.

CRITICAL EYE

For Discussion

a. Emerson asserts that every individual has an inner genius and that it is our responsibility to honor it. Do you agree with this sentiment?

b. According to Emerson, we have all become conformists because we refuse to speak "the rude truth." In your opinion, is his assessment accurate?

Re-approaching the Reading

Rap music has been called a kind of poetry that speaks to the youth of today. Are rap artists following their "inner genius" or are they conformists?

Writing Assignment

Why is conformity dangerous? How does this conformity speak to Emerson's notions of "self-trust" and "foolish consistency"?

KHALED HOSSEINI

From the Novel *THE KITE RUNNER*

Five

Something roared like thunder. The earth shook a little and we heard the *rat-a-tat-tat* of gunfire. "Father!" Hassan cried. We sprung to our feet and raced out of the living room. We found Ali hobbling frantically across the foyer.

"Father! What's that sound?" Hassan yelped, his hands out-stretched toward Ali. Ali wrapped his arms around us. A white light flashed, lit the sky in silver. It flashed again and was followed by a rapid staccato of gunfire.

"They're hunting ducks," Ali said in a hoarse voice. "They hunt ducks at night, you know. Don't be afraid."

A siren went off in the distance. Somewhere glass shattered and someone shouted. I heard people on the street, jolted from sleep and probably still in their pajamas, with ruffled hair and puffy eyes. Hassan was crying. Ali pulled him close, clutched him with tenderness. Later, I would tell myself I hadn't felt envious of Hassan. Not at all.

We stayed huddled that way until the early hours of the morning. The shootings and explosions had lasted less than an hour, but they had frightened us badly, because none of us had ever heard gunshots in the streets. They were foreign sounds to us then. The generation of Afghan children whose ears would know nothing but the sounds of bombs and gunfire was not yet born. Huddled together in the dining room and waiting for the sun to rise, none of us had any notion that a way of life had ended. *Our* way of life. If not quite yet, then at least it was the beginning of the end. The end, the *official* end, would come first in April 1978 with the communist coup d'état, and then in December 1979, when Russian tanks would roll into the very same streets where Hassan and I played, bringing the death of the Afghanistan I knew and marking the start of a still ongoing era of bloodletting.

Just before sunrise, Baba's car peeled into the driveway. His door slammed shut and his running footsteps pounded the stairs. Then he appeared in the doorway and I saw something on his face. Something I didn't recognize right away because I'd never seen it before: fear. "Amir! Hassan!" he exclaimed as he ran to us, opening his arms wide. "They blocked all the roads and the telephone didn't work. I was so worried!"

We let him wrap us in his arms and, for a brief insane moment, I was glad about whatever had happened that night.

They weren't shooting ducks after all. As it turned out, they hadn't shot much of anything that night of July 17, 1973. Kabul awoke the next morning to find that the monarchy was a thing of the past. The king, Zahir Shah, was away in Italy. In his absence, his cousin Daoud

Khan had ended the king's forty-year reign with a bloodless coup.

I remember Hassan and I crouching that next morning outside my father's study, as Baba and Rahim Khan sipped black tea and listened to breaking news of the coup on Radio Kabul.

"Amir agha?" Hassan whispered.

"What?"

"What's a 'republic'?"

I shrugged. "I don't know." On Baba's radio, they were saying that word, "republic," over and over again.

"Amir agha?"

"What?"

"Does 'republic' mean Father and I will have to move away?"

"I don't think so," I whispered back.

Hassan considered this. "Amir agha?"

"What?"

"I don't want them to send me and Father away."

I smiled. "*Bas,* you donkey. No one's sending you away."

"Amir agha?"

"What?"

"Do you want to go climb our tree?"

My smile broadened. That was another thing about Hassan. He always knew when to say the right thing–the news on the radio was getting pretty boring. Hassan went to his shack to get ready and I ran upstairs to grab a book. Then I went to the kitchen, stuffed my pockets with handfuls of pine nuts, and ran outside to find Hassan waiting for me. We burst through the front gates and headed for the hill.

We crossed the residential street and were trekking through a barren patch of rough land that led to the hill when, suddenly, a rock struck Hassan in the back. We whirled around and my heart dropped. Assef and two of his friends, Wali and Kamal, were approaching us.

Assef was the son of one of my father's friends, Mahmood, an airline pilot. His family lived a few streets south of our home, in a posh, high-walled compound with palm trees. If you were a kid living in the Wazir Akbar Khan section of Kabul, you knew about Assef and his famous stainless-steel brass knuckles, hopefully not through personal experience. Born to a German mother and Afghan father, the blond, blue-eyed Assef towered over the other kids. His well-earned reputation for savagery preceded him on the streets. Flanked by his obeying friends, he walked the neighborhood like a Khan strolling through his land with his eager-to-please entourage. His word was law, and if you needed a little legal education, then those brass knuckles were just the right teaching tool. I saw him use those knuckles once on a kid from the Karteh-Char district. I will never forget how Assef's blue eyes glinted with a light not entirely sane and how he grinned, how he *grinned,* as he pummeled that poor kid unconscious. Some of the boys in Wazir Akbar Khan had nicknamed him Assef *Goshkhor,* or Assef "the Ear Eater." Of course, none of them dared utter it to his face unless they wished to suffer the same fate as the poor kid who had unwittingly inspired that nickname when he had fought Assef over a kite and ended up fishing his right ear from a muddy gutter. Years later, I learned an English word for the creature that Assef was, a word for which a good Farsi equivalent does not exist: "sociopath."

Of all the neighborhood boys who tortured Ali, Assef was by far the most relentless. He was, in fact, the originator of the Babalu jeer, *Hey, Babalu, who did you eat today? Huh? Come on, Babalu, give us a smile!* And on days when he felt particularly inspired, he spiced up his badgering a little, *Hey, you flat-nosed Babalu, who did you eat today? Tell us, you slant-eyed donkey!*

Now he was walking toward us, hands on his hips, his sneakers kicking up little puffs of dust.

"Good morning, *kunis!*" Assef exclaimed, waving. "Fag," that was another of his favorite insults. Hassan retreated behind me as the three older boys closed in. They stood before us, three tall boys dressed in jeans and T-shirts. Towering over us all, Assef crossed his thick arms on his chest, a savage sort of grin on his lips. Not for the first time, it occurred to me that Assef might not be entirely sane. It also occurred to me how lucky I was to have Baba as my father, the sole reason, I believe, Assef had mostly refrained from harassing me too much.

He tipped his chin to Hassan. "Hey, Flat-Nose," he said. "How is Babalu?"

Hassan said nothing and crept another step behind me.

"Have you heard the news, boys?" Assef said, his grin never faltering. "The king is gone. Good riddance. Long live the president! My father knows Daoud Khan, did you know that, Amir?"

"So does my father," I said. In reality, I had no idea if that was true or not.

"'So does my father,'" Assef mimicked me in a whining voice. Kamal and Wali cackled in unison. I wished Baba were here.

"Well, Daoud Khan dined at our house last year," Assef went on. "How do you like that, Amir?"

I wondered if anyone would hear us scream in this remote patch of land. Baba's house was a good kilometer away, I wished we'd stayed at the house.

"Do you know what I will tell Daoud Khan the next time he comes to our house for dinner?" Assef said. "I'm going to have a little chat with him, man to man, *mard* to *mard.* Tell him what I told my mother. About Hitler. Now, there was a leader. A great leader. A man with vision. I'll tell Daoud Khan to remember that if they had let Hitter finish what he had started, the world would be a better place now."

"Baba says Hitler was crazy, that he ordered a lot of innocent people killed," I heard myself say before I could clamp a hand on my mouth.

Assef snickered. "He sounds like my mother, and she's German; she should know better. But then they want you to believe that, don't they? They don't want you to know the truth."

I didn't know who "they" were, or what truth they were hiding, and I didn't want to find out. I wished I hadn't said anything. I wished again I'd look up and see Baba coming up the hill.

"But you have to read books they don't give out in school," Assef said. "I have. And my eyes have been opened. Now I have a vision, and I'm going to share it with our new president. Do you know what it is?"

I shook my head. He'd tell me anyway; Assef always answered his own questions.

His blue eyes flicked to Hassan. "Afghanistan is the land of Pashtuns. It always has been, always will be. We are the true Afghans, the pure Afghans, not this Flat-Nose here. His people pollute our homeland, our *watan.* They dirty our blood." He made a sweeping, grandiose gesture with his hands. "Afghanistan for Pashtuns, I say. That's my vision."

Assef shifted his gaze to me again. He looked like someone coming out of a good dream. "Too late for Hitler," he said. "But not for us."

He reached for something from the back pocket of his jeans. "I'll ask the president to do what the king didn't have the *quwat* to do. To rid Afghanistan of all the dirty, *kasseef* Hazaras."

"Just let us go, Assef", I said, hating the way my voice trembled. "We're not bothering you."

"Oh, you're bothering me," Assef said. And I saw with a sinking heart what he had fished out of his pocket. Of course. His stainless-steel brass knuckles sparkled in the sun. "You're bothering me very much. In fact, you bother me more than this Hazara here. How can you talk to him, play with him, let him touch you?" he said, his voice dripping with disgust. Wali and Kamal nodded and grunted in agreement. Assef narrowed his eyes. Shook his head. When he spoke again, he sounded as baffled as he looked. "How can you call him your 'friend'?"

But he's not my friend! I almost blurted. *He's my servant!* Had I really thought that? Of course I hadn't. I hadn't. I treated Hassan well, just like a friend, better even, more like a brother. But if so, then why, when Baba's friends came to visit with their kids, didn't I ever include Hassan in our games? Why did I play with Hassan only when no one else was around?

Assef slipped on the brass knuckles. Gave me an icy look. "You're part of the problem, Amir. If idiots like you and your father didn't take these people in, we'd be rid of them by now. They'd all just go rot in Hazarajat where they belong. You're a disgrace to Afghanistan."

I looked in his crazy eyes and saw that he meant it. He *really* meant to hurt me. Assef raised his fist and came for me.

There was a flurry of rapid movement behind me. Out of the corner of my eye, I saw Hassan bend down and stand up quickly. Assef's eyes flicked to something behind me and widened with surprise. I saw that same look of astonishment on Kamal and Wali's faces as they too saw what had happened behind me.

I turned and came face to face with Hassan's slingshot. Hassan had pulled the wide elastic band all the way back. In the cup was a rock the size of a walnut. Hassan held the slingshot pointed directly at Assef's face. His hand trembled with the strain of the pulled elastic band and beads of sweat had erupted on his brow.

"Please leave us alone, Agha," Hassan said in a flat tone. He'd referred to Assef as "Agha," and I wondered briefly what it must be like to live with such an ingrained sense of one's place in a hierarchy.

Assef gritted his teeth. "Put it down, you motherless Hazara."

"Please leave us be, Agha," Hassan said.

Assef smiled. "Maybe you didn't notice, but there are three of us and two of you."

Hassan shrugged. To an outsider, he didn't look scared. But Hassan's face was my earliest memory and I knew all of its subtle nuances, knew each and every twitch and flicker that ever rippled across it. And I saw that he was scared. He was scared plenty.

"You are right, Agha. But perhaps you didn't notice that I'm the one holding the slingshot. If you make a move, they'll have to change your nickname from Assef 'the Ear Eater' to 'One-Eyed Assef,' because I have this rock pointed at your left eye." He said this so flatly that even I had to strain to hear the fear that I knew hid under that calm voice.

Assef's mouth twitched. Wali and Kamal watched this exchange with something akin to fascination. Someone had challenged their god. Humiliated him. And, worst of all, that someone was a skinny Hazara. Assef looked from the rock to Hassan. He searched Hassan's face intently. What he found in it must have convinced him of the seriousness of Hassan's intentions, because he lowered his fist.

"You should know something about me, Hazara," Assef said gravely. "I'm a very patient person. This doesn't end today, believe me." He turned to me. "This isn't the end for you either, Amir. Someday, I'll make you face me one on one." Assef retreated a step. His disciples followed.

"Your Hazara made a big mistake today, Amir," he said. They then turned around, walked away. I watched them walk down the hill and disappear behind a wall.

Hassan was trying to tuck the slingshot in his waist with a pair of trembling hands. His mouth curled up into something that was supposed to be a reassuring smile. It took him five tries to tie the string of his trousers. Neither one of us said much of anything as we walked home in trepidation, certain that Assef and his friends would ambush us every time we turned a corner. They didn't and that should have comforted us a little. But it didn't. Not at all.

Six

Winter.

Here is what I do on the first day of snowfall every year: I step out of the house early in the morning, still in my pajamas, hugging my arms against the chill. I find the driveway, my father's car, the walls, the trees, the rooftops, and the hills buried under a foot of snow. I smile. The sky is seamless and blue, the snow so white my eyes burn. I shovel a handful of the fresh snow into my mouth, listen to the muffled stillness broken only by the cawing of crows. I walk down the front steps, barefoot, and call for Hassan to come out and see.

Winter was every kid's favorite season in Kabul, at least those whose fathers could afford to buy a good iron stove. The reason was simple: They shut down school for the icy season. Winter to me was the end of long division and naming the capital of Bulgaria, and the start of three months of playing cards by the stove with Hassan, free Russian movies on Tuesday mornings at Cinema Park, sweet turnip *qurma* over rice for a lunch after a morning of build-ing snowmen.

And kites, of course. Flying kites. And running them.

For a few unfortunate kids, winter did not spell the end of the school year. There were the so-called voluntary winter courses. No kid I knew ever volunteered to go to these classes; parents, of course, did the volunteering for them. Fortunately for me, Baba was not one of them. I remember one kid, Ahmad, who lived across the street from us. His father was some kind of doctor, I think. Ahmad had epilepsy and always wore a wool vest and thick black-rimmed glasses–he was one of Assef's regular victims. Every morning, I watched from my bedroom window as their Hazara servant shoveled snow from the driveway, cleared the way for the black Opel. I made a point of watching Ahmad and his father get into the car, Ahmad in his wool vest and winter coat, his schoolbag filled with books and pencils. I waited until they pulled away, turned the corner, then I slipped back into bed in my flannel pajamas. I pulled the blanket to my chin and watched the snowcapped hills in the north through the window. Watched them until I drifted back to sleep.

I loved wintertime in Kabul. I loved it for the soft pattering of snow against my window at night, for the way fresh snow crunched under my black rubber boots, for the warmth of the cast-iron stove as the wind screeched through the yards, the streets. But mostly because, as the trees froze and ice sheathed the roads, the chill between Baba and me thawed a little. And the reason for that was the kites. Baba and I lived in the same house, but in different spheres of existence. Kites were the one paper-thin slice of intersection between those spheres.

Every winter, districts in Kabul held a kite-fighting tournament. And if you were a boy living in Kabul, the day of the tournament was undeniably the highlight of the cold season. I never slept the night before the tournament. I'd roll from side to side, make shadow animals on the wall, even sit on the balcony in the dark, a blanket wrapped around me. I felt like a soldier trying to sleep in the trenches the night before a major battle. And that wasn't so far off. In Kabul, fighting kites was a little like going to war.

As with any war, you had to ready yourself for battle. For a while, Hassan and I used to build our own kites. We saved our weekly allowances in the fall, dropped the money in a little porcelain horse Baba had brought one time from Herat. When the winds of winter began to blow and snow fell in chunks, we undid the snap under the horse's belly. We went to the bazaar and bought bamboo, glue, string, and paper. We spent hours every day shaving bamboo for the center and cross spars, cutting the thin tissue paper which made for easy dipping and recovery. And then, of course, we had to make our own string, or *tar*. If the kite was the gun, then *tar*, the glass-coated cutting line, was the bullet in the chamber. We'd go out in the yard and feed up to five hundred feet of string through a mixture of ground glass and glue. We'd then hang the line between the trees, leave it to dry. The next day, we'd wind the battle-ready line around a wooden spool. By the time the snow melted and the rains of spring swept in, every boy in Kabul bore telltale horizontal gashes on his fingers from a whole winter of fighting kites. I remember how my classmates and I used to huddle, compare our battle scars on the first day of school. The cuts stung and didn't heal for a couple of weeks, but I didn't mind. They were reminders of a beloved season that had once again passed too quickly. Then the class captain would blow his whistle and we'd march in a single file to our classrooms, longing for winter already, greeted instead by the specter of yet another long school year.

But it quickly became apparent that Hassan and I were better kite fighters than kite makers. Some flaw or other in our design always spelled its doom. So Baba started taking us to Saifo's to buy our kites. Saifo was a nearly blind old man who was a *moochi* by profession—a shoe repairman. But he was also the city's most famous kite maker, working out of a tiny hovel on Jadeh Maywand, the crowded street south of the muddy banks of the Kabul River. I remember you had to crouch to enter the prison cell–sized store, and then had to lift a trapdoor to creep down a set of wooden steps to the dank basement where Saifo stored his coveted kites. Baba would buy us each three identical kites and spools of glass string. If I changed my mind and asked for a bigger and fancier kite, Baba would buy it for me—but then he'd buy it for Hassan too. Sometimes I wished he wouldn't do that. Wished he'd let me be the favorite.

The kite-fighting tournament was an old winter tradition in Afghanistan. It started early in the morning on the day of the contest and didn't end until only the winning kite flew in the sky—I remember one year the tournament outlasted daylight. People gathered on sidewalks and roofs to cheer for their kids. The streets filled with kite fighters, jerking and tugging on their lines, squinting up to the sky, trying to gain position to cut the opponent's line. Every kite fighter had an assistant—in my case, Hassan—who held the spool and fed the line.

One time, a bratty Hindi kid whose family had recently moved into the neighborhood told us that in his hometown, kite fighting had strict rules and regulations. "You have to play in a boxed area and you have to stand at a right angle to the wind," he said proudly. "And you can't use aluminum to make your glass string."

Hassan and I looked at each other. Cracked up. The Hindi kid would soon learn what the British learned earlier in the century, and what the Russians would eventually learn by the late 1980s: the Afghans are an independent people. Afghans cherish custom but abhor rules. And so it was with kite fighting. The rules were simple: No rules. Fly your kite. Cut the opponents. Good luck.

Except that wasn't all. The real fun began when a kite was cut. That was where the kite runners came in, those kids who chased the windblown kite drifting through the neighborhoods until it came spiraling down in a field, dropping in someone's yard, on a tree, or a rooftop. The chase got pretty fierce; hordes of kite runners swarmed the streets, shoved past each other like those people from Spain I'd read about once, the ones who ran from the bulls. One year a neighborhood kid climbed a pine tree for a kite. A branch snapped under his weight and he fell thirty feet. Broke his back and never walked again. But he fell with the kite still in his hands. And when a kite runner had his hands on a kite, no one could take it from him. That wasn't a rule. That was custom.

For kite runners, the most coveted prize was the last fallen kite of a winter tournament. It was a trophy of honor, something to be displayed on a mantle for guests to admire. When the sky cleared of kites and only the final two remained, every kite runner readied himself for the chance to land this prize. He positioned himself at a spot that he thought would give him a head start. Tense muscles readied themselves to uncoil. Necks craned. Eyes crinkled. Fights broke out. And when the last kite was cut, all hell broke loose.

Over the years, I had seen a lot of guys run kites. But Hassan was by far the greatest kite runner I'd ever seen. It was downright eerie the way he always got to the spot the kite would land *before* the kite did, as if he had some sort of inner compass.

I remember one overcast winter day, Hassan and I were running a kite. I was chasing him through neighborhoods, hopping gutters, weaving through narrow streets. I was a year older than him, but Hassan ran faster than I did, and I was falling behind.

"Hassan! Wait!" I yelled, my breathing hot and ragged.

He whirled around, motioned with his hand. "This way!" he called before dashing around another corner. I looked up, saw that the direction we were running was opposite to the one the kite was drifting.

"We're losing it! We're going the wrong way!" I cried out.

"Trust me!" I heard him call up ahead. I reached the corner and saw Hassan bolting along, his head down, not even looking at the sky, sweat soaking through the back of his shirt. I tripped over a rock and fell—I wasn't just slower than Hassan but clumsier too; I'd always envied his natural athleticism. When I staggered to my feet, I caught a glimpse of Hassan disappearing around another street corner. I hobbled after him, spikes of pain battering my scraped knees.

I saw we had ended up on a rutted dirt road near Isteqlal Middle School. There was a field on one side where lettuce grew in the summer, and a row of sour cherry trees on the other. I found Hassan sitting cross-legged at the foot of one of the trees, eating from a fistful of dried mulberries.

"What are we doing here?" I panted, my stomach roiling with nausea.

He smiled. "Sit with me, Amir agha."

I dropped next to him, lay on a thin patch of snow, wheezing. "You're wasting our time. It was going the other way, didn't you see?"

Hassan popped a mulberry in his mouth. "It's coming," he said. I could hardly breathe and he didn't even sound tired.

"How do you know?" I said.

"I know."

"How can you *know?*"

He turned to me. A few sweat beads rolled from his bald scalp. "Would I ever lie to you, Amir agha?"

Suddenly I decided to toy with him a little. "I don't know. Would you?"

"I'd sooner eat dirt," he said with a look of indignation.

"Really? You'd do that?"

He threw me a puzzled look. "Do what?"

"Eat dirt if I told you to," I said. I knew I was being cruel, like when I'd taunt him if he didn't know some big word. But there was something fascinating—albeit in a sick way—about teasing Hassan. Kind of like when we used to play insect torture. Except now, he was the ant and I was holding the magnifying glass.

His eyes searched my face for a long time. We sat there, two boys under a sour cherry tree, suddenly looking, *really* looking, at each other. That's when it happened again: Hassan's face changed. Maybe not *changed*, not really, but suddenly I had the feeling I was looking at two faces, the one I knew, the one that was my first memory, and another, a second face, this one lurking just beneath the surface. I'd seen it happen before—it always shook me up a little. It just appeared, this other face, for a fraction of a moment, long enough to leave me with the unsettling feeling that maybe I'd seen it someplace before. Then Hassan blinked and it was just him again. Just Hassan.

"If you asked, I would," he finally said, looking right at me. I dropped my eyes. To this day, I find it hard to gaze directly at people like Hassan, people who mean every word they say.

"But I wonder," he added. "Would you ever ask me to do such a thing, Amir agha?" And, just like that, he had thrown at me his own little test. If I was going to toy with him and challenge his loyalty, then he'd toy with me, test my integrity.

I wished I hadn't started this conversation. I forced a smile. "Don't be stupid, Hassan. You know I wouldn't."

Hassan returned the smile. Except his didn't look forced. "I know," he said. And that's the thing about people who mean everything they say. They think everyone else does too.

"Here it comes," Hassan said, pointing to the sky. He rose to his feet and walked a few paces to his left. I looked up, saw the kite plummeting toward us. I heard footfalls, shouts, an approaching melee of kite runners. But they were wasting their time. Because Hassan stood with his arms wide open, smiling, waiting for the kite. And may God—if He exists, that is—strike me blind if the kite didn't just drop into his outstretched arms.

In the winter of 1975, I saw Hassan run a kite for the last time.

Usually, each neighborhood held its own competition. But that year, the tournament was going to be held in my neighborhood, Wazir Akbar Khan, and several other districts—Karteh-Char, Karteh-Parwan, Mekro-Rayan, and Koteh-Sangi—had been invited. You could hardly go anywhere without hearing talk of the upcoming tournament. Word had it this was going to be the biggest tournament in twenty-five years.

One night that winter, with the big contest only four days away, Baba and I sat in his study in overstuffed leather chairs by the glow of the fireplace. We were sipping tea, talking. Ali had served dinner earlier—potatoes and curried cauliflower over rice—and had retired for the night with Hassan. Baba was fattening his pipe and I was asking him to tell the story about the winter a pack of wolves had descended from the mountains in Herat and forced everyone to stay indoors for a week, when he lit a match and said, casually, "I think maybe you'll win the tournament this year. What do you think?"

I didn't know what to think. Or what to say. Was that what it would take? Had he just slipped me a key? I was a good kite fighter. Actually, a very good one. A few times, I'd even come close to winning the winter tournament—

once, I'd made it to the final three. But coming close wasn't the same as winning, was it? Baba hadn't *come close*. He had won because winners won and everyone else just went home. Baba was used to winning, winning at everything he set his mind to. Didn't he have a right to expect the same from his son? And just imagine. If I did win . . .

Baba smoked his pipe and talked. I pretended to listen. But I couldn't listen, not really, because Baba's casual little comment had planted a seed in my head: the resolution that I would win that winter's tournament. I was going to win. There was no other viable option. I was going to win, and I was going to run that last kite. Then I'd bring it home and show it to Baba. Show him once and for all that his son was worthy. Then maybe my life as a ghost in this house would finally be over. I let myself dream: I imagined conversation and laughter over dinner instead of silence broken only by the clinking of silverware and the occasional grunt. I envisioned us taking a Friday drive in Baba's car to Paghman, stopping on the way at Ghargha Lake for some fried trout and potatoes. We'd go to the zoo to see Marjan the lion, and maybe Baba wouldn't yawn and steal looks at his wristwatch all the time. Maybe Baba would read one of my stories. I'd write him a hundred if I thought he'd read one. Maybe he'd call me Amir jan like Rahim Khan did. And maybe, just maybe, I would finally be pardoned for killing my mother.

Baba was telling me about the time he'd cut fourteen kites on the same day. I smiled, nodded, laughed at all the right places, but I hardly heard a word he said. I had a mission now. And I wasn't going to fail Baba. Not this time.

It snowed heavily the night before the tournament. Hassan and I sat under the *kursi* and played panjpar as wind-rattled tree branches tapped on the window. Earlier that day, I'd asked Ali to set up the kursi for us—which was basically an electric heater under a low table covered with a thick, quilted blanket. Around the table, he arranged mattresses and cushions, so as many as twenty people could sit and slip their legs under. Hassan and I used to spend entire snowy days snug under the *kursi,* playing chess, cards—mostly panjpar.

I killed Hassan's ten of diamonds, played him two jacks and a six. Next door, in Baba's study, Baba and Rahim Khan were discussing business with a couple of other men—one of them I recognized as Assef's father. Through the wall, I could hear the scratchy sound of Radio Kabul News.

Hassan killed the six and picked up the jacks. On the radio, Daoud Khan was announcing something about foreign investments.

"He says someday we'll have television in Kabul," I said.

"Who?"

"Daoud Khan, you ass, the president."

Hassan giggled. "I heard they already have it in Iran," he said.

I sighed. "Those Iranians . . ." For a lot of Hazaras, Iran represented a sanctuary of sorts—I guess because, like Hazaras, most Iranians were Shi'a Muslims. But I remembered something my teacher had said that summer about Iranians, that they were grinning smooth talkers who patted you on the back with one hand and picked your pocket with the other. I told Baba about that and he said my teacher was one of those jealous Afghans, jealous because Iran was a rising power in Asia and most people around the world couldn't even find Afghanistan on a world map. "It hurts to say that," he said, shrugging. "But better to get hurt by the truth than comforted with a lie."

"I'll buy you one someday," I said.

Hassan's face brightened. "A television? In truth?"

"Sure. And not the black-and-white kind either. We'll probably be grown-ups by then, but I'll get us two. One for you and one for me."

"I'll put it on my table, where I keep my drawings," Hassan said.

His saying that made me kind of sad. Sad for who Hassan was, where he lived. For how he'd accepted the fact that he'd grow old in the mud shack in the yard, the way his father had. I drew the last card, played him a pair of queens and a ten.

Hassan picked up the queens. "You know, I think you're going to make Agha sahib very proud tomorrow."

"You think so?"

"*Inshallah,*" he said.

"*Inshallah,*" I echoed, though the "God willing" qualifier didn't sound as sincere coming from my lips. That was the thing with Hassan. He was so goddamn pure, you always felt like a phony around him.

I killed his king and played him my final card, the ace of spades. He had to pick it up, I'd won, but as I shuffled for a new game, I had the distinct suspicion that Hassan had *let* me win.

"Amir agha?"

"What?"

"You know . . . I *like* where I live." He was always doing that, reading my mind. "It's my home."

"Whatever," I said. "Get ready to lose again."

Seven

The next morning, as he brewed black tea for breakfast, Hassan told me he'd had a dream. "We were at Ghargha Lake, you, me, Father, Agha sahib, Rahim Khan, and thousands of other people," he said. "It was warm and sunny, and the lake was clear like a mirror. But no one was swimming because they said a monster had come to the lake. It was swimming at the bottom, waiting."

He poured me a cup and added sugar, blew on it a few times. Put it before me, "So everyone is scared to get in the water, and suddenly you kick off your shoes, Amir agha, and take off your shirt. 'There's no monster,' you say. 'I'll show you all.' And before anyone can stop you, you dive into the water, start swimming away. I follow you in and we're both swimming."

"But you can't swim."

Hassan laughed. "It's a dream, Amir agha, you can do anything. Anyway, everyone is screaming, 'Get out! Get out!' but we just swim in the cold water. We make it way out to the middle of the lake and we stop swimming. We turn toward the shore and wave to the people. They look small like ants, but we can hear them clapping. They see now. There is no monster, just water. They change the name of the lake after that, and call it the 'Lake of Amir and Hassan, Sultans of Kabul,' and we get to charge people money for swimming in it."

"So what does it mean?" I said.

He coated my *naan* with marmalade, placed it on a plate. "I don't know. I was hoping you could tell me."

"Well, it's a dumb dream. Nothing happens in it."

"Father says dreams always mean something."

I sipped some tea. "Why don't you ask him, then? He's so smart," I said, more curtly than I had intended. I hadn't slept all night. My neck and back were like coiled springs, and my eyes stung. Still, I had been mean to Hassan. I almost apologized, then didn't. Hassan understood I was just nervous. Hassan always understood about me.

Upstairs, I could hear the water running in Baba's bathroom.

The streets glistened with fresh snow and the sky was a blameless blue. Snow blanketed every rooftop and weighed on the branches of the stunted mulberry trees that lined our street. Overnight, snow had nudged its way into every crack and gutter. I squinted against the blinding white when Hassan and I stepped through the wrought-iron gates. Ali shut the gates behind us. I heard him mutter a prayer under his breath—he always said a prayer when his son left the house.

I had never seen so many people on our street. Kids were flinging snowballs, squabbling, chasing one another, giggling. Kite fighters were huddling with their spool holders, making last-minute preparations. From adjacent streets, I could hear laughter and chatter. Already, rooftops were jammed with spectators reclining in lawn chairs, hot tea steaming from thermoses, and the music of Ahmad Zahir blaring from cassette players. The immensely popular Ahmad Zahir had revolutionized Afghan music and outraged the purists by adding electric guitars, drums, and horns to the traditional tabla and harmonium; on stage or at parties, he shirked the austere and nearly morose stance of older singers and actually smiled when he sang—sometimes even at women. I turned my gaze to our rooftop, found Baba and Rahim Khan sitting on a bench, both dressed in wool sweaters, sipping tea. Baba waved. I couldn't tell if he was waving at me or Hassan.

"We should get started," Hassan said. He wore black rubber snow boots and a bright green *chapan* over a thick sweater and faded corduroy pants. Sunlight washed over his face, and, in it, I saw how well the pink sear above his lip had healed.

Suddenly I wanted to withdraw. Pack it all in, go back home. What was I thinking? Why was I putting myself through this, when I already knew the outcome? Baba was on the roof, watching me. I felt his glare on me like the heat of a blistering sun. This would be failure on a grand scale, even for me.

"I'm not sure I want to fly a kite today," I said.

"It's a beautiful day," Hassan said.

I shifted on my feet. Tried to peel my gaze away from our rooftop. "I don't know. Maybe we should go home."

Then he stepped toward me and, in a low voice, said something that scared me a little. "Remember, Amir agha. There's no monster, just a beautiful day." How could I be such an open book to him when, half the time, I had no idea what was milling around in his head? I was the one who went to school, the one who could read, write. I was the smart one. Hassan couldn't read a first-grade textbook but he'd read me plenty. That was a little unsettling, but also sort of comfortable to have someone who always knew what you needed.

"No monster," I said, feeling a little better, to my own surprise.

He smiled, "No monster."

"Are you sure?"

He closed his eyes. Nodded.

I looked to the kids scampering down the street, flinging snowballs. "It is a beautiful day, isn't it?"

"Let's fly," he said.

It occurred to me then that maybe Hassan had made up his dream. Was that possible? I decided it wasn't. Hassan wasn't that smart. *I* wasn't that smart. But made up or not, the silly dream had lifted some of my anxiety. Maybe I *should* take off my shirt, take a swim in the lake. Why not?

"Let's do it," I said.

Hassan's face brightened. "Good," he said. He lifted our kite, red with yellow borders, and, just beneath where the central and cross spars met, marked with Saifo's unmistakable signature. He licked his finger and held it up, tested the wind, then ran in its direction—on those rare occasions we flew kites in the summer, he'd kick up dust to see which way the wind blew it. The spool rolled in my hands until Hassan stopped, about fifty feet away. He held the kite high over his head, like an Olympic athlete showing his gold medal. I jerked the string twice, our usual signal, and Hassan tossed the kite.

Caught between Baba and the mullahs at school, I still hadn't made up my mind about God. But when a Koran *ayat* I had learned in my *diniyat* class rose to my lips, I muttered it. I took a deep breath, exhaled, and pulled on the string. Within a minute, my kite was rocketing to the sky. It made a sound like a paper bird flapping its wings. Hassan clapped his hands, whistled, and ran back to me. I handed him the spool, holding on to the string, and he spun it quickly to roll the loose string back on.

At least two dozen kites already hung in the sky, like paper sharks roaming for prey. Within an hour, the number doubled, and red, blue, and yellow kites glided and spun in the sky. A cold breeze wafted through my hair. The wind was perfect for kite flying, blowing just hard enough to give some lift, make the sweeps easier. Next to me, Hassan held the spool, his hands already bloodied by the string.

Soon, the cutting started and the first of the defeated kites whirled out of control. They fell from the sky like shooting stars with brilliant, rippling tails, showering the neighborhoods below with prizes for the kite runners. I could hear the runners now, hollering as they ran the streets. Someone shouted reports of a fight breaking out two streets down.

I kept stealing glances at Baba sitting with Rahim Khan on the roof, wondered what he was thinking. Was he cheering for me? Or did a part of him enjoy watching me fail? That was the thing about kite flying: Your mind drifted with the kite.

They were coming down all over the place now, the kites, and I was still flying. I was still flying. My eyes keep wandering over to Baba, bundled up in his wool sweater. Was he surprised I had lasted as long as I had? *You don't keep your eyes to the sky, you won't last much longer.* I snapped my gaze back to the sky. A red kite was closing in on me—I'd caught it just in time. I tangled a bit with it, ended up besting him when he became impatient and tried to cut me from below.

Up and down the streets, kite runners were returning triumphantly, their captured kites held high. They showed them off to their parents, their friends. But they all knew the best was yet to come. The biggest prize of all was still flying. I sliced a bright yellow kite with a coiled white tail. It cost me another gash on the index finger and blood trickled down into my palm. I had Hassan hold the string and sucked the blood dry, blotted my finger against my jeans.

Within another hour, the number of surviving kites dwindled from maybe fifty to a dozen. I was one of them. I'd made it to the last dozen. I knew this part of the tournament would take a while, because the guys who had lasted this long were good—they wouldn't easily fall into simple traps like the old lift-and-dive, Hassan's favorite trick.

By three o'clock that afternoon, tufts of clouds had drifted in and the sun had slipped behind them. Shadows started to lengthen. The spectators on the roofs bundled up in scarves and thick coats. We were down to a half dozen and I was still flying. My legs ached and my neck was stiff. But with each defeated kite, hope grew in my heart, like snow collecting on a wall, one flake at a time.

My eyes kept returning to a blue kite that had been wreaking havoc for the last hour.

"How many has he cut?" I asked.

"I counted eleven," Hassan said.

"Do you know whose it might be?"

Hassan clucked his tongue and tipped his chin. That was a trademark Hassan gesture, meant he had no idea. The blue kite sliced a big purple one and swept twice in big loops. Ten minutes later, he'd cut another two, sending hordes of kite runners racing after them.

After another thirty minutes, only four kites remained. And I was still flying. It seemed I could hardly make a wrong move, as if every gust of wind blew in my favor. I'd never felt so in command, so lucky. It felt intoxicating. I didn't dare look up to the roof. Didn't dare take my eyes off the sky. I had to concentrate, play it smart. Another fifteen minutes and what had seemed like a laughable dream that morning had suddenly become reality: It was just me and the other guy. The blue kite.

The tension in the air was as taut as the glass string I was tugging with my bloody hands. People were stomping their feet, clapping, whistling, chanting, "*Boboresh! Boboresh!*" *Cut him! Cut him!* I wondered if Baba's voice was one of them. Music blasted. The smell of steamed *mantu* and fried *pakora* drifted from rooftops and open doors.

But all I heard—all I willed myself to hear—was the thudding of blood in my head. All I saw was the blue kite. All I smelled was victory. Salvation. Redemption. If Baba was wrong and there *was* a God like they said in school, then He'd let me win. I didn't know what the other guy was playing for, maybe just bragging rights. But this was my one chance to become someone who was looked at, not seen, listened to, not heard. If there was a God, Heguide the winds, let them blow for me so that, with a tug of my string, I'd cut loose my pain, my longing. I'd endured too much, come too far. And suddenly, just like that, hope became knowledge. I was going to win. It was just a matter of when.

It turned out to be sooner than later. A gust of wind lifted my kite and I took advantage. Fed the string, pulled up. Looped my kite on top of the blue one. I held position. The blue kite knew it was in trouble. It was trying desperately to maneuver out of the jam, but I didn't let go. I held position. The crowd sensed the end was at hand. The chorus of "Cut him! Cut him!" grew louder, like Romans chanting for the gladiators to kill, kill!

"You're almost there, Amir agha! Almost there!" Hassan was panting.

Then the moment came. I closed my eyes and loosened my grip on the string. It sliced my fingers again as the wind dragged it. And then . . . I didn't need to hear the crowd's roar to know. I didn't need to see either. Hassan was screaming and his arm was wrapped around my neck.

"Bravo! Bravo, Amir agha!"

I opened my eyes, saw the blue kite spinning wildly like a tire come loose from a speeding car. I blinked, tried to say something. Nothing came out. Suddenly I was hovering, looking down on myself from above. Black leather coat, red scarf, faded jeans. A thin boy, a little sallow, and a tad short of his twelve years. He had narrow shoulders and a hint of dark circles around his pale hazel eyes. The breeze rustled his light brown hair. He looked up to me and we smiled at each other.

Then I was screaming, and everything was color and sound, everything was alive and good. I was throwing my free arm around Hassan and we were hopping up and down, both of us laughing, both of us weeping. "You won, Amir agha! You won!"

"*We* won! *We* won!" was all I could say. This wasn't happening. In a moment, I'd blink and rouse from this beautiful dream, get out of bed, march down to the kitchen to eat breakfast with no one to talk to but Hassan. Get dressed. Wait for Baba. Give up. Back to my old life. Then I saw Baba on our roof. He was standing on the edge, pumping both of his fists. Hollering and clapping. And that right there was the single greatest moment of my twelve years of life, seeing Baba on that roof, proud of me at last.

But he was doing something now, motioning with his hands in an urgent way. Then I understood. "Hassan, we–"

"I know," he said, breaking our embrace. "*Inshallah,* we'll celebrate later. Right now, I'm going to run that blue kite for you," he said. He dropped the spool and took off running, the hem of his green *chapan* dragging in the snow behind him.

"Hassan!" I called. "Come back with it!"

He was already turning the street corner, his rubber boots kicking up snow. He stopped, turned. He cupped his hands around his mouth. "For you a thousand times over!" he said. Then he smiled his Hassan smile and disappeared around the corner. The next time I saw him smile unabashedly like that was twenty-six years later, in a faded Polaroid photograph.

I began to pull my kite back as people rushed to congratulate me. I shook hands with them, said my thanks. The younger kids looked at me with an awestruck twinkle in their eyes; I was a hero. Hands patted my back and tousled my hair. I pulled on the string and returned every smile, but my mind was on the blue kite.

Finally, I had my kite in hand. I wrapped the loose string that had collected at my feet around the spool, shook a few more hands, and trotted home. When I reached the wrought-iron gates, Ali was waiting on the other side. He stuck his hand through the bars. "Congratulations," he said.

I gave him my kite and spool, shook his hand, "*Tashakor,* Ali jan."

"I was praying for you the whole time."

"Then keep praying. We're not done yet."

I hurried back to the street. I didn't ask Ali about Baba. I didn't want to see him yet. In my head, I had it all planned: I'd make a grand entrance, a hero, prized trophy in my bloodied hands. Heads would turn and eyes would lock. Rostam and Sohrab sizing each other up. A dramatic moment of silence. Then the old warrior would walk to the young one, embrace him, acknowledge his worthiness. Vindication. Salvation. Redemption. And then? Well . . . happily ever after, of course. What else?

The streets of Wazir Akbar Khan were numbered and set at right angles to each other like a grid. It was a new neighborhood then, still developing, with empty lots of land and half-constructed homes on every street between compounds surrounded by eight-foot walls. I ran up and down every street, looking for Hassan. Everywhere, people were busy folding chairs, packing food and utensils after a long day of partying. Some, still sitting on their rooftops, shouted their congratulations to me.

Four streets south of ours, I saw Omar, the son of an engineer who was a friend of Baba's. He was dribbling a soccer ball with his brother on the front lawn of their house. Omar was a pretty good guy. We'd been classmates in fourth grade, and one time he'd given me a fountain pen, the kind you had to load with a cartridge.

"I heard you won, Amir," he said. "Congratulations."

"Thanks. Have you seen Hassan?"

"Your Hazara?"

I nodded.

Omar headed the ball to his brother. "I hear he's a great kite runner." His brother headed the ball back to him. Omar caught it, tossed it up and down. "Although I've always wondered how he manages. I mean, with those tight little eyes, how does he *see* anything?"

His brother laughed, a short burst, and asked for the ball. Omar ignored him.

"Have you seen him?"

Omar flicked a thumb over his shoulder, pointing southwest. "I saw him running toward the bazaar awhile ago."

"Thanks." I scuttled away.

By the time I reached the marketplace, the sun had almost sunk behind the hills and dusk had painted the sky pink and purple. A few blocks away, from the Haji Yaghoub Mosque, the mullah bellowed *azan,* calling for the faithful to unroll their rugs and bow their heads west in prayer. Hassan never missed any of the five daily prayers. Even when we were out playing, he'd excuse himself, draw water from the well in the yard, wash up, and disappear into the hut. He'd come out a few minutes later, smiling, find me sitting against the wall or perched on a tree. He was going to miss prayer tonight, though, because of me.

The bazaar was emptying quickly, the merchants finishing up their haggling for the day. I trotted in the mud between rows of closely packed cubicles where you could buy a freshly slaughtered pheasant in one stand and a calculator from the adjacent one. I picked my way through the dwindling crowd, the lame beggars dressed in layers of tattered rags, the vendors with rugs on their shoulders, the cloth merchants and butchers closing shop for the day. I found no sign of Hassan.

I stopped by a dried fruit stand, described Hassan to an old merchant loading his mule with crates of pine seeds and raisins. He wore a powder blue turban.

He paused to look at me for a long time before answering. "I might have seen him."

"Which way did he go?"

He eyed me up and down. "What is a boy like you doing here at this time of the day looking for a Hazara?" His glance lingered admiringly on my leather coat and my jeans—*cowboy pants,* we used to call them. In Afghanistan, owning anything American, especially if it wasn't secondhand, was a sign of wealth.

"I need to find him, Agha."

"What is he to you" he said. I didn't see the point of his question, but I reminded myself that impatience wasn't going to make him tell me any faster.

"He's our servant's son," I said.

The old man raised a pepper gray eyebrow. "He is? Lucky Hazara, having such a concerned master. His father should get on his knees, sweep the dust at your feet with his eyelashes."

"Are you going to tell me or not?"

He rested an arm on the mule's back, pointed south. "I think I saw the boy you described running that way. He had a kite in his hand. A blue one."

"He did?" I said. *For you a thousand times over,* he'd promised. Good old Hassan. Good old reliable Hassan. He'd kept his promise and run the last kite for me.

"Of course, they've probably caught him by now," the old merchant said, grunting and loading another box on the mule's back.

"Who?"

"The other boys," he said. "The ones chasing him. They were dressed like you." He glanced to the sky and sighed. "Now, run along, you're making me late for *namaz.*"

But I was already scrambling down the lane.

For the next few minutes, I scoured the bazaar in vain. Maybe the old merchant's eyes had betrayed him. Except he'd seen the blue kite. The thought of getting my hands on that kite . . . I poked my head behind every lane, every shop. No sign of Hassan.

I had begun to worry that darkness would fall before I found Hassan when I heard voices from up ahead. I'd reached a secluded, muddy road. It ran perpendicular to the end of the main thoroughfare bisecting the bazaar. I turned onto the rutted track and followed the voices. My boot squished in mud with every step and my breath puffed out in white clouds before me. The narrow path ran parallel on one side to a snow-filled ravine through which a stream may have tumbled in the spring. To my other side stood rows of snow-burdened cypress trees peppered among flat-topped clay houses–no more than mud shacks in most cases–separated by narrow alleys.

I heard the voices again, louder this time, coming from one of the alleys. I crept close to the mouth of the alley. Held my breath. Peeked around the corner.

Hassan was standing at the blind end of the alley in a defiant stance: fists curled, legs slightly apart. Behind him, sitting on piles of scrap and rubble, was the blue kite. My key to Baba's heart.

Blocking Hassan's way out of the alley were three boys, the same three from that day on the hill, the day after Daoud Khan's coup, when Hassan had saved us with his slingshot. Wali was standing on one side, Kamal on the other, and in the middle, Assef. I felt my body clench up, and something cold rippled up my spine. Assef seemed relaxed, confident. He was twirling his brass knuckles. The other two guys shifted nervously on their feet, looking from Assef to Hassan, like they'd cornered some kind of wild animal that only Assef could tame.

"Where is your slingshot, Hazara?" Assef said, turning the brass knuckles in his hand. "What was it you said? 'They'll have to call you One-Eyed Assef.' That's right. One-Eyed Assef. That was clever. Really clever. Then again, it's easy to be clever when you're holding a loaded weapon."

I realized I still hadn't breathed out. I exhaled, slowly, quietly. I felt paralyzed. I watched them close in on the boy I'd grown up with, the boy whose harelipped face had been my first memory.

"But today is your lucky day, Hazara," Assef said. He had his back to me, but I would have bet he was grinning. "I'm in a mood to forgive. What do you say to that, boys?"

"That's generous," Kamal blurted, "Especially after the rude manners he showed us last time." He was trying to sound like Assef, except there was a tremor in his voice. Then I understood: He wasn't afraid of Hassan, not really. He was afraid because he had no idea what Assef had in mind.

Assef waved a dismissive hand. "*Bakhshida.* Forgiven. It's done." His voice dropped a little. "Of course, nothing is free in this world, and my pardon comes with a small price."

"That's fair," Kamal said.

"Nothing is free," Wali added.

"You're a lucky Hazara," Assef said, taking a step toward Hassan. "Because today, it's only going to cost you that blue kite. A fair deal, boys, isn't it?"

"More than fair," Kamal said.

Even from where I was standing, I could see the fear creeping into Hassan's eyes, but he shook his head. "Amir agha won the tournament and I ran this kite for him. I ran it fairly. This is his kite."

"A loyal Hazara. Loyal as a dog," Assef said.

Kamal's laugh was a shrill, nervous sound.

"But before you sacrifice yourself for him, think about this: Would he do the same for you? Have you ever wondered why he never includes you in games when he has guests? Why he only plays with you when no one else is around? I'll tell you why, Hazara. Because to him, you're nothing but an ugly pet. Something he can play with when he's bored, something he can kick when he's angry. Don't ever fool yourself and think you're something more."

"Amir agha and I are friends," Hassan said. He looked flushed.

"Friends?" Assef said, laughing. "You pathetic fool! Someday you'll wake up from your little fantasy and learn just how good of a friend he is. Now, bas! Enough of this. Give us that kite."

Hassan stooped and picked up a rock.

Assef flinched. He began to take a step back, stopped. "Last chance, Hazara."

Hassan's answer was to cock the arm that held the rock.

"Whatever you wish."Assef unbuttoned his winter coat, took it off, folded it slowly and deliberately. He placed it against the wall.

I opened my mouth, almost said something. Almost. The rest of my life might have turned out differently if I had. But I didn't. I just watched. Paralyzed.

Assef motioned with his hand, and the other two boys separated, forming a half circle, trapping Hassan in the alley.

"I've changed my mind," Assef said. "I'm letting you keep the kite, Hazara. I'll let you keep it so it will always remind you of what I'm about to do."

Then he charged. Hassan hurled the rock. It struck Assef in the forehead. Assef yelped as he flung himself at Hassan, knocking him to the ground. Wali and Kamal followed.

I bit on my fist. Shut my eyes.

A memory:

Did you know Hassan and you fed from the same breast? Did you know that, Amir agha? Sakina, her name was. She was a fair, blue-eyed Hazara woman from Bamiyan and she sang you old wedding songs. They say there is a brotherhood between people who've fed from the same breast. Did you know that?

A memory:

"A *rupia* each, children. Just one *rupia* each and I will part the curtain of truth." *The old man sits against a mud wall. His sightless eyes are like molten silver embedded in deep, twin craters. Hunched over his cane, the fortune-teller runs a gnarled hand across the surface of his deflated cheeks. Cups it before us.* "Not much to ask for the truth, is it, a *rupia* each?" *Hassan drops a coin in the leathery palm. I drop mine too.* "In the name of Allah most beneficent, most merciful," *the old fortune-teller whispers. He takes Hassan's hand first, strokes the palm with one hornlike fingernail, round and round, round and round. The finger then floats to Hassan's face and makes a dry, scratchy sound as it slowly traces the curve of his cheeks, the outline of his ears. The calloused pads of his fingers brush against Hassan's eyes. The hand stops there. Lingers. A shadow passes across the old man's face. Hassan and I exchange a glance. The old man takes Hassan's hand and puts the rupia back in Hassan's palm. He turns to me.* "How about you, young friend?" *he says. On the other side of the wall, a rooster crows. The old man reaches for my hand and I withdraw it.*

A dream:

I am lost in a snowstorm. The wind shrieks, blows stinging sheets of snow into my eyes. I stagger through layers of shifting white. I call for help but the wind drowns my cries. I fall and lie panting on the snow, lost in the white, the wind wailing in my ears. I watch the snow erase my fresh footprints. I'm a ghost now, *I think,* a ghost with no footprints. *I cry out again, hope fading like my footprints. But this time, a muffled reply. I shield my eyes and manage to sit up. Out of the swaying curtains of snow, I catch a glimpse of movement, a flurry of color. A familiar shape materializes. A hand reaches out for me. I see deep, parallel gashes across the palm, blood dripping, staining the snow. I take the hand and suddenly the snow is gone. We're standing in a field of apple green grass with soft wisps of clouds drifting above. I look up and see the clear sky is filled with kites, green, yellow, red, orange. They shimmer in the afternoon light.*

A havoc of scrap and rubble littered the alley. Worn bicycle tires, bottles with peeled labels, ripped up magazines, yellowed newspapers, all scattered amid a pile of bricks and slabs of cement. A rusted cast-iron stove with a gaping hole on its side tilted against a wall. But there were two things amid the garbage that I couldn't stop looking at: One was the blue kite resting against the wall, close to the cast-iron stove; the other was Hassan's brown corduroy pants thrown on a heap of eroded bricks.

"I don't know," Wali was saying. "My father says it's sinful." He sounded unsure, excited, scared, all at the same time. Hassan lay with his chest pinned to the ground. Kamal and Wali each gripped an arm, twisted and bent at the elbow so that Hassan's hands were pressed to his back. Assef was standing over them, the heel of his snow boots crushing the back of Hassan's neck.

"Your father won't find out," Assef said. "And there's nothing sinful about teaching a lesson to a disrespectful donkey."

"I don't know," Wali muttered.

"Suit yourself," Assef said. He turned to Kamal. "What about you?"

"I . . . well . . ."

"It's just a Hazara," Assef said. But Kamal kept looking away.

"Fine," Assef snapped. "All I want you weaklings to do is hold him down. Can you manage that?"

Wali and Kamal nodded. They looked relieved.

Assef knelt behind Hassan, put his hands on Hassan's hips and lifted his bare buttocks. He kept one hand on Hassan's back and undid his own belt buckle with his free hand. He unzipped his jeans. Dropped his underwear. He positioned himself behind Hassan. Hassan didn't struggle. Didn't even whimper. He moved his head slightly and I caught a glimpse of his face. Saw the resignation in it. It was a look I had seen before. It was the look of the lamb.

Tomorrow is the tenth day of Dhul-Hijjah, *the last month of the Muslim calendar, and the first of three days of Eid Al-Adha, or* Eid-e-Qorban, as *Afghans call it–a day to celebrate how the prophet Ibrahim almost sacrificed his own son for God. Baba has handpicked the sheep again this year, a powder white one with crooked black ears.*

We all stand in the backyard, Hassan, Ali, Baba, and I. The mullah recites the prayer, rubs his beard. Baba mutters, Get on with it, *under his breath. He sounds annoyed with the endless praying, the ritual of making the meat halal. Baba mocks the story behind this* Eid, *like he mocks everything religious. But he respects the tradition of* Eid-e-Qorban. *The custom is to divide the meat in thirds, one for the family, one for friends, and one for the poor. Every year, Baba gives it all to the poor.* The rich are fat enough already, *he says.*

The mullah finishes the prayer. Ameen. *He picks up the kitchen knife with the long blade. The custom is to not let the sheep see the knife. Ali feeds the animal a cube of sugar–another custom, to make death sweeter. The sheep kicks, but not much. The mullah grabs it under its jaw and places the blade on its neck. Just a second before he slices the throat in one expert motion, I see the sheep's eyes. It is a look that will haunt my dreams for weeks. I don't know why I watch this yearly ritual in our backyard; my nightmares persist long after the bloodstains on the grass have faded. But I always watch. I watch because of that look of acceptance in the animal's eyes. Absurdly, I imagine the animal understands. I imagine the animal sees that its imminent demise is for a higher purpose. This is the look. . .*

I STOPPED WATCHING, turned away from the alley. Something warm was running down my wrist. I blinked, saw I was still biting down on my fist, hard enough to draw blood from the knuckles. I realized something else. I was weeping. From just around the corner, I could hear Assef's quick, rhythmic grunts.

I had one last chance to make a decision. One final opportunity to decide who I was going to be. I could step into that alley, stand up for Hassan—the way he'd stood up for me all those times in the past—and accept whatever would happen to me. Or I could run.

In the end, I ran.

I ran because I was a coward. I was afraid of Assef and what he would do to me. I was afraid of getting hurt. That's what I told myself as I turned my back to the alley, to Hassan. That's what I made myself believe. I actually *aspired* to cowardice, because the alternative, the real reason I was running, was that Assef was right: Nothing was free in this world. Maybe Hassan was the price I had to pay, the lamb I had to slay, to win Baba. Was it a fair price? The answer floated to my conscious mind before I could thwart it: He was just a Hazara, wasn't he?

I ran back the way I'd come. Ran back to the all but deserted bazaar. I lurched to a cubicle and leaned against the padlocked swinging doors. I stood there panting, sweating, wishing things had turned out some other way.

About fifteen minutes later, I heard voices and running footfalls. I crouched behind the cubicle and watched Assef and the other two sprinting by, laughing as they hurried down the deserted lane. I forced myself to wait ten more minutes. Then I walked back to the rutted track that ran along the snow-filled ravine. I squinted in the dimming light and spotted Hassan walking slowly toward me. I met him by a leafless birch tree on the edge of the ravine.

He had the blue kite in his hands; that was the first thing I saw. And I can't lie now and say my eyes didn't scan it for any rips. His *chapan* had mud smudges down the front and his shirt was ripped just below the collar. He stopped. Swayed on his feet like he was going to collapse. Then he steadied himself. Handed me the kite.

"Where were you? I looked for you," I said. Speaking those words was like chewing on a rock.

Hassan dragged a sleeve across his face, wiped snot and tears. I waited for him to say something, but we just stood there in silence, in the fading light. I was grateful for the early-evening shadows that fell on Hassan's face and concealed mine. I was glad I didn't have to return his gaze. Did he know I knew? And if he knew, then what would I see if I *did* look in his eyes? Blame? Indignation? Or, God forbid, what I feared most: guileless devotion? That, most of all, I couldn't bear to see.

He began to say something and his voice cracked. He closed his mouth, opened it, and closed it again. Took a step back. Wiped his face. And that was as close as Hassan and I ever came to discussing what had happened in the alley. I thought he might burst into tears, but, to my relief, he didn't, and I pretended I hadn't heard the crack in his voice. Just like I pretended I hadn't seen the dark stain in the seat of his pants. Or those tiny drops that fell from between his legs and stained the snow black.

"Agha sahib will worry," was all he said. He turned from me and limped away.

It happened just the way I'd imagined. I opened the door to the smoky study and stepped in. Baba and Rahim Khan were drinking tea and listening to the news crackling on the radio. Their heads turned. Then a smile played on my father's lips. He opened his arms. I put the kite down and walked into his thick hairy arms. I buried my face in the warmth of his chest and wept. Baba held me close to him, rocking me back and forth. In his arms, I forgot what I'd done. And that was good.

CRITICAL EYE

For Discussion

a. Are all friendships equal, or is there usually one personality that dominates the relationship?

b. Why is Amir unable/unwilling to help Hassan?

c. Can a friendship survive if the parties are members of different classes?

d. Is Hassan stronger than Amir? Why?

Re-approaching the Reading

Would the story change if Hassan's character were a girl? Would this make the assault even more tragic? If so, why? If not, why?

Writing Assignment

When it comes to being a "man," why is cowardice never an option?

BIDPAI

The Camel and His Friends

c. 4th century

Once a merchant was leading a caravan of heavily-laden camels through a jungle when one of them, overcome by fatigue, collapsed. The merchant decided to leave the camel in the jungle and go on his way. Later, when the camel recovered his strength, he realized that he was alone in a strange jungle. Fortunately there was plenty of grass, and he survived.

One day the king of the jungle, a lion, arrived along with his three friends–a leopard, a fox, and a crow. The king lion wondered what the camel was doing in the jungle! He came near the camel and asked how he, a creature of the desert, had ended up in the hostile jungle. The camel tearfully explained what happened. The lion took pity on him and said, "You have nothing to fear now. Henceforth, you are under my protection and can stay with us." The camel began to live happily in the jungle.

Then one day the lion was wounded in a fight with an elephant. He retired to his cave and stayed there for several days. His friends came to offer their sympathy. They tried to catch prey for the hungry lion but failed. The camel had no problem as he lived on grass while the others were starving.

The fox came up with a plan. He secretly went to the lion and suggested that the camel be sacrificed for the good of the others. The lion got furious, "I can never kill an animal who is under my protection."

The fox humbly said, "But Lord, you have provided us food all the time. If any one of us voluntarily offered himself to save your life, I hope you won't mind!" The hungry lion did not object to that and agreed to take the offer.

The fox went back to his companions and said, "Friends, our king is dying of starvation. Let us go and beg him to eat one of us. It is the least we can do for such a noble soul."

So they went to the king and the crow offered his life. The fox interrupted, and said, "You are a small creature, the master's hunger will hardly be appeased by eating you. May I humbly offer my life to satisfy my master's hunger."

The leopard stepped forward and said, "You are no bigger than the crow, it is me whom our master should eat."

The foolish camel thought, "Everyone has offered to lay down their lives for the king, but he has not hurt any one. It is now my turn to offer myself." So he stepped forward and said, "Stand aside friend leopard, the king and you have close family ties. It is me whom the master must eat."

An ominous silence greeted the camel's offer. Then the king gladly said, "I accept your offer, O noble camel." And in no time he was killed by the three rogues, the false friends.

Moral: Be careful in choosing your friends.

CRITICAL EYE

For Discussion

a. Do we live in a society where people are willing to sacrifice themselves for a greater good or in defense of the weak?

b. Should the leaders of nations expect/demand their citizens to make sacrifices?

c. Does the story suggest that the masses cannot trust those who are in charge?

Re-approaching the Reading

Imagine the animals in the story are people of different races, faiths, and genders. With these new factors in mind, what would the story be saying about human nature?

Writing Assignment

Why should we feel compelled to sacrifice ourselves for strangers when they need our help? What is gained by doing so?

MARGARET SANGER

THE TURBID EBB AND FLOW OF MISERY

Every night and every morn
Some to misery are born.
Every morn and every night
Some are born to sweet delight.
Some are born to sweet delight,
Some are born to endless night.
William Blake

During these years [about 1912] in New York trained nurses were in great demand. Few people wanted to enter hospitals; they were afraid they might be "practiced" upon, and consented to go only in desperate emergencies. Sentiment was especially vehement in the matter of having babies. A woman's own bedroom, no matter how inconveniently arranged, was the usual place for her lying-in. I was not sufficiently free from domestic duties to be a general nurse, but I could ordinarily manage obstetrical cases because I was notified far enough ahead to plan my schedule. And after serving my two weeks I could get home again.

Sometimes I was summoned to small apartments occupied by young clerks, insurance salesmen, or lawyers, just starting out, most of them under thirty and whose wives were having their first or second baby. They were always eager to know the best and latest method in infant care and feeding. In particular, Jewish patients, whose lives centered around the family, welcomed advice and followed it implicitly.

But more and more my calls began to come from the Lower East Side, as though I were being magnetically drawn there by some force outside my control. I hated the wretchedness and hopelessness of the poor, and never experienced that satisfaction in working among them that so many noble women have found. My concern for my patients was now quite different from my earlier hospital attitude. I could see that much was wrong with them which did not appear in the physiological or medical diagnosis. A woman in childbirth was not merely a woman in childbirth. My expanded outlook included a view of her background, her potentialities as a human being, the kind of children she was bearing, and what was going to happen to them.

The wives of small shopkeepers were my most frequent cases, but I had carpenters, truck drivers, dishwashers, and pushcart vendors. I admired intensely the consideration most of these people had for their own. Money to pay doctor and nurse had been carefully saved months in advance–parents-in-law, grandfathers, grandmothers, all contributing.

As soon as the neighbors learned that a nurse was in the building they came in a friendly

Chapter 7 of *An Autobiography* (1938). Sanger has taken her chapter title from a line in Matthew Arnold's poem "Dover Beach" [Editor's note].

way to visit, often carrying fruit, jellies, or gefüllter fish made after a cherished recipe. It was infinitely pathetic to me that they, so poor themselves, should bring me food. Later they drifted in again with the excuse of getting the plate, and sat down for a nice talk; there was no hurry. Always back of the little gift was the question, "I am pregnant (or my daughter, or my sister is). Tell me something to keep from having another baby. We cannot afford another yet."

I tried to explain the only two methods I had ever heard of among the middle classes, both of which were invariably brushed aside as unacceptable. They were of no certain avail to the wife because they placed the burden of responsibility solely upon the husband–a burden which he seldom assumed. What she was seeking was self-protection she could herself use, and there was none.

Below this stratum of society was one in truly desperate circumstances. The men were sullen and unskilled, picking up odd jobs now and then, but more often unemployed, lounging in and out of the house at all hours of the day and night. The women seemed to slink on their way to market and were without neighborliness.

These submerged, untouched classes were beyond the scope of organized charity or religion. No labor union, no church, not even the Salvation Army reached them. They were apprehensive of everyone and rejected help of any kind, ordering all intruders to keep out: both birth and death they considered their own business. Social agents, who were just beginning to appear, were profoundly mistrusted because they pried into homes and lives, asking questions about wages, how many were in the family, had any of them ever been in jail. Often two or three had been there or were now under suspicion of prostitution, shoplifting, purse snatching, petty thievery, and, in consequence, passed furtively by the big blue uniforms on the corner.

The utmost depression came over me as I approached this surreptitious region. Below Fourteenth Street I seemed to be breathing a different air, to be in another world and country where the people had habits and customs alien to anything I had ever heard about.

There were then approximately ten thousand apartments in New York into which no sun ray penetrated directly; such windows as they had opened only on a narrow court from which rose fetid odors. It was seldom cleaned, though garbage and refuse often went down into it. All these dwellings were pervaded by the foul breath of poverty, that moldy, indefinable, indescribable smell which cannot be fumigated out, sickening to me but apparently unnoticed by those who lived there. When I set to work with antiseptics, their pungent sting, at least temporarily, obscured the stench.

I remember one confinement case to which I was called by the doctor of an insurance company. I climbed up the five flights and entered the airless rooms, but the baby had come with too great speed. A boy of ten had been the only assistant. Five flights was a long way; he had wrapped the placenta in a piece of newspaper and dropped it out the window into the court.

Many families took in "boarders," as they were termed, whose small contributions paid the rent. These derelicts, wanderers, alternately working and drinking, were crowded in with the children; a single room sometimes held as many as six sleepers. Little girls were accustomed to dressing and undressing in front of the men, and were often violated, occasionally by their own fathers or brothers, before they reached the age of puberty.

Pregnancy was a chronic condition among the women of this class. Suggestions as to what to do for a girl who was "in trouble" or a married woman who was "caught" passed from mouth to mouth—herb teas, turpentine, steaming, rolling downstairs, inserting slippery elm, knitting needles, shoe-hooks. When they had word of a new remedy they hurried to the drugstore, and if the clerk were inclined to be friendly he might say, "Oh, that won't help you, but here's something that may." The younger druggists usually refused to give advice because, if it were to be known, they would come under the law; midwives were even more fearful. The doomed women implored me to reveal the "secret" rich people had, offering to pay me extra to tell them; many really believed I was holding back information for money. They asked everybody and tried anything, but nothing did them any good. On Saturday nights I have seen groups of from fifty to one hundred with their shawls over their heads waiting outside the office of a five-dollar abortionist.

Each time I returned to this district, which was becoming a recurrent nightmare, I used to hear that Mrs. Cohen "had been carried to a hospital, but had never come back," or that Mrs. Kelly "had sent the children to a neighbor and had put her head into the gas oven." Day after day such tales were poured into my ears—a baby born dead, great relief—the death of an older child, sorrow but again relief of a sort—the story told a thousand times of death from abortion and children going into institutions. I shuddered with horror as I listened to the details and studied the reasons back of them—destitution linked with excessive childbearing. The waste of life seemed utterly senseless. One by one worried, sad, pensive, and aging faces marshaled themselves before me in my dreams, sometimes appealingly, sometimes accusingly.

These were not merely "unfortunate conditions among the poor" such as we read about. I knew the women personally. They were living, breathing, human beings, with hopes, fears, and aspirations like my own, yet the weary, misshapen bodies, "always ailing, never failing," were destined to be thrown on the scrap heap before they were thirty-five. I could not escape from the facts of their wretchedness; neither was I able to see any way out. My own cozy and comfortable family existence was becoming a reproach to me.

Then one stifling mid-July day of 1912 I was summoned to a Grand Street tenement. My patient was a small, slight Russian Jewess, about twenty-eight years old, of the special cast of feature to which suffering lends a madonna-like expression. The cramped three-room apartment was in a sorry state of turmoil. Jake Sachs, a truck driver scarcely older than his wife, had come home to find the three children crying and her unconscious from the effects of a self-induced abortion. He had called the nearest doctor, who in turn had sent for me. Jake's earnings were trifling, and most of them had gone to keep the none-too-strong children clean and properly fed. But his wife's ingenuity had helped them to save a little, and this he was glad to spend on a nurse rather than have her go to a hospital.

The doctor and I settled ourselves to the task of fighting the septicemia. Never had I worked so fast, never so concentratedly. The sultry days and nights were melted into a torpid inferno. It did not seem possible there could be such heat, and every bit of food, ice, and drugs had to be carried up three flights of stairs.

Jake was more kind and thoughtful than many of the husbands I have encountered. He loved his children, and had always helped his wife wash and dress them. He had brought water up and carried garbage down before he left in the morning, and did as much as he could for me while he anxiously watched her progress.

After a fortnight Mrs. Sachs' recovery was in sight. Neighbors, ordinarily fatalistic as to the results of abortion, were genuinely pleased that she had survived. She smiled wanly at all who came to see her and thanked them gently, but she could not respond to their hearty congratulations. She appeared to be more despondent and anxious than she should have been, and spent too much time in meditation.

At the end of three weeks, as I was preparing to leave the fragile patient to take up her difficult life once more, she finally voiced her fears. "Another baby will finish me, I suppose?"

"It's too early to talk about that," I temporized.

But when the doctor came to make his last call, I drew him aside. "Mrs. Sachs is terribly worried about having another baby."

"She well may be," replied the doctor, and then he stood before her and said, "Any more such capers, young woman, and there'll be no need to send for me."

"I know, doctor," she replied timidly, "but," and she hesitated as though it took all her courage to say it, "what can I do to prevent it?"

The doctor was a kindly man, and he had worked hard to save her, but such incidents had become so familiar to him that he had long since lost whatever delicacy he might once have had. He laughed good-naturedly. "You want to have your cake and eat it too, do you? Well, it can't be done."

Then picking up his hat and bag to depart he said, "Tell Jake to sleep on the roof."

I glanced quickly at Mrs. Sachs. Even through my sudden tears I could see stamped on her face an expression of absolute despair. We simply looked at each other, saying no word until the door had closed behind the doctor. Then she lifted her thin, blue-veined hands and clasped them beseechingly. "He can't understand. He's only a man. But you do, don't you? Please tell me the secret, and I'll never breathe it to a soul. *Please!*"

What was I to do? I could not speak the conventionally comforting phrases which would be of no comfort. Instead, I made her as physically easy as I could and promised to come back in a few days to talk with her again. A little later, when she slept, I tiptoed away.

Night after night the wistful image of Mrs. Sachs appeared before me. I made all sorts of excuses to myself for not going back. I was busy on other cases; I really did not know what to say to her or how to convince her of my own ignorance; I was helpless to avert such monstrous atrocities. Time rolled by and I did nothing.

The telephone rang one evening three months later, and Jake Sachs' agitated voice begged me to come at once; his wife was sick again and from the same cause. For a wild moment I thought of sending someone else, but actually, of course, I hurried into my uniform, caught up my bag, and started out. All the way I longed for a subway wreck, an explosion, anything to keep me from having to enter that home again. But nothing happened, even to delay me. I turned into the dingy doorway and climbed the familiar stairs once more. The children were there, young little things.

Mrs. Sachs was in a coma and died within ten minutes. I folded her still hands across her breast, remembering how they had pleaded with me, begging so humbly for the knowledge which was her right. I drew a sheet over her pallid face. Jake was sobbing, running his hands through his hair and pulling it out like an insane person. Over and over again he wailed, "My God! My God! My God!"

I left him pacing desperately back and forth, and for hours I myself walked and walked and walked through the hushed streets. When I finally arrived home and let myself quietly in, all the household was sleeping. I looked out my window and down upon the dimly lighted city. Its pains and griefs crowded in upon me, a moving picture rolled before my eyes with photographic clearness: women writhing in travail to bring forth little babies; the babies themselves naked and hungry, wrapped in newspapers to keep them from the cold; six-year-old children with pinched, pale, wrinkled faces, old in concentrated wretchedness, pushed into gray and fetid cellars, crouching on stone floors, their small scrawny hands scuttling through rags, making lamp shades, artificial flowers; white coffins, black coffins, coffins, coffins interminably passing in never-ending succession. The scenes piled one upon another on another. I could bear it no longer.

As I stood there the darkness faded. The sun came up and threw its reflection over the house tops. It was the dawn of a new day in my life also. The doubt and questioning, the experimenting and trying, were now to be put behind me. I knew I could not go back merely to keeping people alive.

I went to bed, knowing that no matter what it might cost, I was finished with palliatives and superficial cures; I was resolved to seek out the root of evil, to do something to change the destiny of mothers whose reveries were vast as the sky.

CRITICAL EYE

For Discussion

a. What is Sanger arguing regarding the notion of poverty and the lack of opportunities it affords women?

b. Does anyone have the right to determine that a segment of the population is overbreeding?

c. Are marriage and childbearing the best options for women?

Re-approaching the Reading

If Sanger were a man, would her story change? How?

Writing Assignment

What would happen in America if *Roe vs. Wade* were overturned?

TODD CRAIG

"Open Season 2014": The Birth of Civil Rights Lost

Starring the Continuing Saga Called Hip-Hop

We are in a state of emergency, living in the midst of a new day and time that I like to call the 21st-century iteration of "Open Season." This idea becomes quite clear to me when the moving images in the news and the still images across the Web, newspapers, and magazines display Ferguson, Missouri, looking more like Iraq than the Bible Belt. Unfortunately, this isn't anything new, as we've seen and experienced this paradigm with a litany of other names of victims whose lives have been lost.

Hip-hop is in a state of emergency, as well. I remember growing up in the midst of a budding hip-hop culture, hearing records like "Self Destruction" and others from artists like KRS-One, Gangstarr, and the whole Native Tongues Collective and knowing there was a level of socio-cultural and political consciousness I would be responsible for being connected to; it would be blasphemous for me *not* to be in tune and attune with my culture as an African-American male as it related to a larger American society. There are still some moments when I see and feel this connectivity within hip-hop. The most recent example comes from J. Cole and his response to the Michael Brown incident in Ferguson.

An eloquent spitter and lyricist, you can hear the urgency in the cadence of Cole's crackly voice as he croons a distraught and openly honest inquiry about the state of affairs for young black men in America. His words resonate and fester like the pain from alcohol poured atop an open flesh wound as Cole makes the gravity of the situation apparent in his scant song structure: three, eight-bar verses only separated by either the chorus of the song or interspersed clips of an interview from witness Dorian Johnson. There is a sonic quality and clarity to Cole's voice alongside only a synthesized piano that captured the emotion of the moment; and unfortunately, the most compelling part of the song is the hook, which forces a level of introspection—you hear it and have to wonder why in 2014 it sounds like a 1960s Civil Rights mantra or even an old spiritual when Cole begs a larger society to understand that as African-Americans, "all we wanna do is take the chains off/ all we wanna do is break the chains off/ all we wanna do is be free/ all we wanna do is be free" (Cole). It is here where hip-hop artist J. Cole has captured the pulse of the African-American community with the power of a twitter statement containing only three words in the post for his song: "How we feel." One listen and it becomes evident that "Free" fulfills the power, perplexity, and depth of these three words. But it didn't just stop there. Shortly after the record, you could see the media buzz around J. Cole going to visit Ferguson, spending time with the protestors, and then finally visiting the site where Michael

Brown was slain. This is a profound point in praxis: where theory and practice meet in the best of ways.

These moments are critically important because they illuminate the vision many people of Generation X thought would unfold: hip-hop culture—a lens and paradigm originally both of and for African-American culture—becoming a voice of commentary on a larger American popular culture. This is the nexus I always longed for in school, wishing I could utilize hip-hop music and culture as the focal point for my critical thinking. And it took a while, but by the time I was finishing up the last piece of my formal academic education, that time had come.

"Conservatives don't understand slang linguistics": The Contemporary Temperature of Our Trodden Terrain

In his essay "If Black English Isn't a Language, Then Tell Me, What Is?" James Baldwin identifies how African-American culture has always infused, displayed, and dictated the level of "cool" for whites within American culture. He states: "[N]ow, I do not know what white Americans would sound like if there had never been any black people in the United States, but they would not sound the way they sound...[blacks] *were* funky, baby, like *funk* was going out of style" (Baldwin). From language to music, African-Americans have always been at the forefront of dictating the trends in American popular culture. But now, we've shifted very far away from this. We live in the days and times where *Forbes* magazine tells us Iggy Azalea is "running" hip-hop and where no African-Americans are winning Grammy Awards in music categories that were created by blacks (see Kanye West's *Yeezus* nomination comments and Macklemore beating out Kendrick Lamar at the 2014 Grammys, only to later say Kendrick should've won it). The time we live in has shifted so far, in fact, that one could make the argument that as members of hip-hop culture, we are actually moving in ways that are counterintuitive to what we see and what we are being told on a daily basis.

So in this piece entitled, "'Open Season 2014': The Birth of Civil Rights Lost, Starring the Continuing Saga Called Hip-Hop," I will utilize hip-hop as a lens to address and analyze different incidents to speak to where we—members of the hip-hop, African-American, and American communities—are cultural, and then rely on a few different pieces of text to help flesh out this landscape accordingly. And the premise of this piece hinges on the following observation: We, as members of both hip-hop and African-American culture, are writing our history counterintuitive to what the reality of our current situation suggests. It's as if we are engaging in an inverted anarchy, an exercise in chaos with no semblance of reason or functionality. Be very clear that this statement is an observation—and not an indictment. I arrive at this location based on some very strategic thinking about how our experiences are written, documented, and then historicized.

"'Your captions be deep, but you shallow as a puddle…' aka 'Turn Down for me Mommy!?!": When Volume Control Becomes Catastrophic Lifestyle Regimen

I start with this thought: My most memorable moment with the Trayvon Martin incident comes from the CNN Roundtable discussions aka the Anderson Cooper chronicles. In the days after the verdict, there were a number of roundtables on CNN. What I found most insightful were some of the Town Hall meetings hosted by Anderson Cooper. During one of the roundtables, he hosted African-American journalist Charles Blow; at one point, both Blow and Geoffrey Canada discussed the difficulty of having the conversations with their sons about carrying themselves with a body language that telegraphs they are not trying to break the law or engage in any illegal or threatening activity. However, the most poignant instance was when Blow explained: "There is a bigger question here which is—for a lot of black men—it is the moderation of masculinity. That you have to put a dial on your masculinity that nobody else has to have on it. And you have to crank it up when you want it to be at your regular pace and crank it down when you are in the presence of authority. And that is an exhausting exercise, it's a horrible idea, and it is heartbreaking" (Blow). This concept presented by Blow is an issue that transcends the idea of emasculating the black male; it is problematic because the not-guilty verdict in the Trayvon Martin case was truly introducing the idea of having to dial down all elements of black masculinity to nil. It was as if one's manhood could be turned off and on like the dimmer on your living room lights.

The irony of "dialing down" black masculinity is that presently hip-hop culture seems to live in the world of "turn up." Er'ybody telling you to "turn up"! I would listen to the Hot97 Morning Show on my way to work and DJ Cipha Sounds rocked his daily "Turn Up mix".[1] Chris Brown, Weezy, Yeezy, Lil John, Drake—even Chocolate Drop (aka Kevin Hart)—is in rap cyphers telling you to "TURN UP." But there's a more interesting take on this new slogan, which is "turn down for what?"

If you look at these two scenarios in tandem, they really speak to the ways that hip-hop culture is writing its history counterintuitive to what the reality of our situation suggests—and again: observation, not indictment. I mean, one would think that in a post–Trayvon Martin society, in a "Stop and Frisk" era, we wouldn't necessarily be focused on being "turned up." This is not only the text, but also the context and subtext of our present-day reality. But this is a reality that has been captured and chronicled throughout the African-American experience domestically. So my goal is to examine and interrogate how we have seen this reality written throughout history within various forms of text.

"My lips is like an oh-wop as I start to spray it": When Spewing Slurs Goes Dead-Wrong

In Gloria Naylor's essay entitled "The Meanings of a Word," which was originally published in *The New York Times*, she discusses her connection to the word "nigger" based on her family's southern roots, and she characterizes how she heard her family use the word in varying degrees. But it all changed for her when she first experienced discrimination as a third grader who received a higher score on her math test than her classmate behind her. When she commented on it, his backlash came as a response to her intellectual success. Once he snatched his test and called her a "nigger," Naylor began to comprehend how that word manifested itself in the larger American worldview and context:

> I didn't know what a nigger was,
> but I knew that whatever it meant,
> it was something he shouldn't have
> called me. This was verified when I

1. It is important to note that in the beginning of 2014, Cipha Sounds went back to the original name of his morning mix, changing it from the "Turn Up" mix to the "More Fiyah" mix. He spoke one morning to the fact that "turn up" had essentially been "turned up" too much.

> raised my hand, and in a loud voice repeated what he had said and watched the teacher scold him for using a 'bad' word. I was later to go home and ask the inevitable question that every black parent must face—"Mommy, what does nigger mean?"...there must have been dozens of times that the word "nigger" was spoken in front of me before I reached the third grade. But I didn't "hear" it until it was said by a small pair of lips that had already learned it could be a way to humiliate me. That was the word I went home and asked my mother about. And since she knew that I had to grow up in America, she took me in her lap and explained. (Naylor)

It is here where we see this recurring theme in the African-American experience: the theme of denigration and devaluing of African-American life. Here, a young third grader—who couldn't have been much older than 8 or 9—finds out just how invaluable her existence is; and this devaluing comes from her demonstrating academic prowess!

But note that this runs counterintuitive to the parameters of our reality and to our contemporary notions of language, for on any given day, you can hear the word "nigger" used by students walking on many of the CUNY campuses I've taught at more than you might hear the word at a Klan meeting. Again—observation, not indictment. This can clearly be attributed to a contemporary historical disconnect that puts the word into a particular context and framework. Couple this disconnect with the freedom demonstrated in current-day hip-hop song lyrics with using this word and the rabbit hole that is created becomes a deep one. For example, count how many times Lil Wayne and Drake use the word in the song "Believe Me"—there are many more examples, but I feel comfortable resting my case here.

For me, the issue has never necessarily been solely about the usage of the word, but thinking about that word's usage within a historical context and framework. Because frankly, I rock with Drake and Wayne's verses, but when we then see ourselves in 2014 being treated in the same ways our elders were treated during the Civil Rights movement (see the throwback separate but equal "poor door" in the New York City luxury condominium as evidence), one has to ask if we can be mad. After all, we have desensitized and extracted the historical context of that word, claiming its use is now "empowering" and removes the older, more negative meaning. But Naylor shows us when we need that context, that history, and that feeling—especially to mobilize as people—we've deadened it for the sake of making a dope verse or two.

I bet you that Michael Brown really dug that dope-sounding verse.

But that dope-sounding verse is NOT helping the racial climate, attitudes, and perceptions in Ferguson, Missouri, after his shooting.

So we would be remiss to not reposition that language in its rightful historical context, so we can begin to understand how to maneuver with language in our present-day reality.

We are moving counterintuitive to what we see and are being told in society.

The Need for Estrogen, A$AP: When Hip-Hop Turns Total Testosterone

In her collection of published essays entitled *Black Looks: Race and Representation*, bell hooks discusses these same issues in 1994. In her essay entitled "Eating the Other: Desire and Resistance," she writes about an alarming experience that speaks directly to this conversation. One day, she's walking down the street in downtown New Haven; she describes the downtown location as a place where usually white males—primarily jocks—find themselves not only coming into contact with poor blacks of the area, but also using their bodies to "force" black people off the sidewalks. But on this particular day, she overheard a conversation held between a group of young white males, who calculatedly plotted on having sex with various women of color—charting black women on the top of the list and Asian women as "prime targets." When she presented this conversation to her students, she found it was common practice that "one 'shopped' for sexual partners in the same way one 'shopped' for courses at Yale, and that race and ethnicity was a serious category on which selections were based" (hooks). As she continued to process this thinking amongst her students, what became even more alarming to her is that

> unlike racist white men who historically violated the bodies of black women to assert their position as colonizer/conqueror, these young men see themselves as non-racists, who choose to transgress racial boundaries within the sexual realm not to dominate the Other, but rather so that they can be acted, so that they can be changed utterly. Not at all attuned to those aspects of their sexual fantasies that irrevocably link them to collective white racist domination, they believe their desire for contact represents a progressive change in white attitudes towards non-whites. They do not see themselves as perpetuating racism. To them the most potent indication of that change is the frank expression of longing, the open declaration of desire, the need to be intimate with dark Others. (hooks)

With this depiction, bell hooks is describing race relations approximately 20 years ago while teaching at Yale University—an ivy-league school, a bastion of intellectual fortitude. It is also the alma mater of George W. Bush, which should give an indication of the mindset succinctly communicated by Kanye West, but alas I digress. What hooks identifies is the racial sentiment of young white "educated" males at an ivy-league institution. Their desire to be with non-whites, or women of color, has nothing to do with brains, intelligence, sports, hobbies, or even anything that two people may have in common. It has everything to do with skin color—with black women at the top of the list. And they don't see this behavior at all being connected to, say, the racist mentalities of white slave masters who are documented in history as raping black female slaves. No, they see nothing racist at all in wanting to "fuck" as many black girls as possible before graduation. Because after all, the value of African-American life is far greater than a quick jump-off, right?

But alas, we continue to move counterintuitive to what the reality of our situation suggests. Because knowing this is the misogynistic mindset towards African-American women, what slogan do we uphold: "I love bad bitches that's my fuckin' problem/ and yeah I like to fuck, I got a fuckin' problem/ if findin' somebody real is ya fuckin' problem/ bring ya girls to the crib, maybe we can solve'em" (A$AP Rocky).

Observation...not indictment. I'll leave that dichotomy for y'all to think on.

But it's important to recognize that the misogyny goes hand in hand with a specific targeting and emasculation of African-American males as well.

"All these rappers is my sons!?!": When Rap Goes Visual with Viral Media Messages

In his article from *Essence* magazine, entitled "Hollywood: The Dark Side," Sylvester Monroe talks about the difficulty in Hollywood with finding both television shows and movies that depict African-Americans in a positive light–that is, shows and movies that don't merely address African-Americans in roles solely involving comedy or violence. In the article, Monroe quoted the late George Gerbner, who at the time was a professor in the Annenberg School for Communication at the University of Pennsylvania. After a research study uncovered that white males under the age of 40 work more and earn more than any other groups in television, Gerbner shared that "television seems to be frozen in a time warp of obsolete and damaging representations that deprive millions of people of the chance to see themselves growing up with the same opportunities, values and potential as everyone else" (Monroe). Think about this concept in tandem with what we know to be television in 2013. One of the most famous TV slogans in this day and age is "you are NOT the father." Not only did the *Maury Show* reach a landmark 2,500th episode in May 2013, but also in that same week, the show had "hit 100 consecutive weeks of being the number 1 syndicated talk show among Women 18-34... and Adults 18-49" (Kondolojy). Take things one step further in looking at the 2006 *New York Times* article by Erik Eckholm, entitled "Plight Deepens for Black Men, Studies Warn," which examines the decline in social and economic mobility of young black males. In looking at the variety of factors effecting this mobility, as well as the current research on the issue, Eckholm's assessment is "terrible schools, absent parents, racism, the decline in blue collar jobs and a subculture that glorifies swagger over work have all been cited as causes of the deepening ruin of black youths. Scholars–and the young men themselves–agree that all of these issues must be addressed" (Eckholm). Add all these different ingredients in the pot and you can see the stew that bubbles over in the current state of affairs in contemporary America.

Thus, after being bombarded Monday through Friday with either the images of young black dead-beat males turned fathers who don't believe children they've created are their own or lie detector tests and "sexy decoys" in green rooms who prove that young black males are hypersexual incessant cheaters, is it a mystery that the all-female jury sided with George Zimmerman, or as juror B37 would call him, "Georgie"? Television is the 21st-century text that has begun to write "history" based on the fallacy of a movement called "Reality TV." And who are we in these narratives? We ARE the father...or the promiscuous rapper...or the ex-wife of an athlete trying to cash in on ex-dom in order to secure a check.

We are moving counterintuitive to what our reality is. Observation...not indictment.

What incidents like the Trayvon Martin verdict and Michael Brown shooting do is write into existence a new policy. There was a time when it seemed like there was a specific moral code of operation: "no women or children." We see that in many of the blatant examples of the devaluing of African-American life that I didn't mention because they're so obvious. But you all know the names: Akai Gurley, Eric Gardner, Sean Bell, Amadou Diallo, Rodney King, Emmitt Till, Medgar Evers. However, this writing is different. Michael Brown was set to start college 24 hours after he was slain. Trayvon Martin was 17...a young boy, younger than the overwhelming majority of the college student population. Tamir Rice was 12 years old. Couple these experiences with those of

Ersula Ore, Renisha McBride or Marissa Alexander–the woman in Florida who was being abused by her husband, fired a warning shot, and was then sentenced to 20 years–and we can clearly see what is being written into existence for the African-American legacy in the United States is that "all bets are off. Women AND children are now fair game." So in essence, it's officially "Open Season," and black bodies of all shapes and sizes, ages and shades have now become the targets. We haven't seen the likes of such blatant disregard of African-American life since the days of Jim Crow.

"I hope they acknowledge the knowledge cuz yeah, they 'gon need it": The Various Nexuses of Unseen Hope

There are still glimmers of hope that become apparent, like a lighthouse shining a beacon of light for sailors in the midst of the dark and unseen. I found this beacon in a hot-button article by hip-hop artist Homeboy Sandman entitled "Black People Are Cowards." As Sandman scribes a call to action around the events of the Los Angeles Clippers and Donald Sterling's racist remarks, he clearly pinpoints a potential concern for Sterling: "perhaps he recently tuned in to an FM 'hip hop' station and after hearing song after drug, sex, and violence-laden song decided that it might be a good idea to keep some distance" (Sandman). Homeboy Sandman understands the writing on the walls, but he is also clear in thinking that we can collectively change the course we're travelling. He knows it's a moral imperative for both African-American and hip-hop culture to begin to facilitate the change we want to see:

> The problem is, we, us, black people, can't afford to be like everyone else anymore. Not if we want to survive. I don't know how we got here, but everywhere you look we're at the bottom of the global totem pole. We need to make history. We can't be cowards like every one else, not any more. In fact, we need to set a new standard for heroism. For bravery. For courage. Maybe a standard never before seen in the history of humankind. Extreme situations call for extreme measures, and in modern times our inferiority is ingrained in every single aspect of our lives, from our media, to our religion, to our science, to our public education, to our higher education, to Africa appearing to be the same size as Greenland on all of the maps despite the fact that in reality Africa is 14 times larger...let's boycott. Boycott was the foundation of the Civil Rights movement... If we boycotted every night spot that spins music about how much we love killing each other and taking and selling drugs, every single one of them would have new DJs by next week (don't even get me started on these new DJs. The new drug dealers. Admitting that they know what they're giving people is bad for them but caring more about getting paid). (Sandman)

For Sandman, his call to action requires we begin to visualize and enact the necessary change given the climate of contemporary culture, if for no other reason than "survival." He clearly identifies the idea of African-American culture lagging far behind the global culture, but he also indicts hip-hop culture as a culprit in this climate. By evoking the Civil Rights mantra of boycott, Sandman is returning to the narratives of the past with the hope to achieve a similar outcome for our future. But he is very clear in diagnosing hip-hop culture moving counterintuitive to what our reality suggests when he compares "the new DJs" to "drug dealers": deliberately harming the budding listening populace with poison in the form of certain musical choices, all in the name of the almighty dollar. Similar to Eckholm's assessment of "a subculture that glorifies swagger over work," hip-hop culture has gotten away from a moral compass centered on consciousness that we need to revisit in the effort to not only achieve balance, but also reconnect our youth to the socio-cultural and political happenings of the present with a knowledge and awareness of the historical narratives of oppression from the past to guide our contemporary thinking. We need to return to this connectivity between knowledge of African-American historical happenings and hip-hop culture.

"'No doubt I'm stuck and I can't get out of this lifestyle' aka 'I'm in Marty McFly mode, so tell'em that the future's back'": How Can We Revert to Civil Rights Found?

So where do we go from here, and how do we start to change the ending(s)? I have been very clear in distinguishing my commentary as observation and not indictment. My rationale in this is clear: When one is indicted, it is an accusation that immediately puts the accused on the defensive and sets up a dynamic of confrontation. Nothing is amicably solved in this way. However, when one is presented with an "observation"–something that is seen, noticed, and articulated–it lends room for the observed to look inward in order to assess his or her actions. Let's be very clear: I myself have used the word "nigger" in my lifetime... I turn the stereo up in the truck when that Drake and Wayne or A$AP record drops, and nod particularly hard to Drake's flow and Kendrick's wordplay. I too have also found myself at times caught up watching Maury. But I also understand the context from which these things spring forth. I truly believe that moving forward we must make a concerted effort to observe these conditions and connect them to the narratives and experiences of the past. It is only when we individually and collectively do this, that we might be in a position to reshape and rewrite our realities as intuitive to moral consciousness, collective elevation, and freedom. And put an end to open season before our species is extinct...it's evident we are presently an endangered species that won't be put on a preservation list.

I charge you all to observe the writing of our experiences in contemporary America.

Works Cited

A Tribe Called Quest. "Sucka Nigga." *Midnight Marauders*. Jive Records, 1993. Vinyl.

A$AP Rocky featuring Two Chainz, Drake and Kendrick Lamar. "Fuckin' Problem." *Long. Live. ASAP.* Polo Grounds Music/RCA Records/Sony Music Entertainment. 2013. CD.

Baldwin, James. "If Black English Isn't a Language, Then Tell Me, What Is?" *NYTimes.com.* New York Times, 29 July 1979. Web. 13 November 2013.

Eckholm, Erik. "Plight Deepens for Black Men, Studies Warm." *NYTimes.com.* New York Times, 20 March 2006. Web. 3 November 2013.

Fabolous. "Cuffin Season." *S.O.U.L. Tape 3.* My Fabolous Life, 2013. CD/ Web.

Harling, Danielle. "Kanye West Says He's Never Won A Grammy Against A White Artist." *Hiphopdx.com.* 11 December 2013. Web. 1 August 2014.

Homeboy Sandman. "Black People Are Cowards." Gawker.com. 28 April 2014. Web. 29 April 2014.

Homeboy Sandman. "The Plot Thickens." *Peter Rosenberg x Ecko Present: The New York Renaissance.* 2013. MP3 file.

hooks, bell. *Black Looks: Race and Representation.* Boston: South End Press, 1992. Print.

J. Cole. "Free." Roc Nation/Columbia/Dreamville Records. 2014. MP3 file.

Jeru the Damaja. "Can't Stop the Prophet." *The Sun Rises in the East.* PayDay/FFRR/PolyGram Records. 1994. CD.

Joey Bada$$. "Waves." *1999.* 2012. Web.

Joey Bada$$ feat. Capital STEEZ. "Survival Tactics." *1999.* 2012. Web.

Kirkland, Allegra. "Luxury Condo in Manhattan Will Have a 'Poor Door' for Low-Income Tenants." *Alternet.org.* Independent Media Institute, 21 July 2014. Web. 1 August 2014.

Kondolojy, Amanda. "'Maury' Celebrates His 2500th Episode." *TV by the Numbers.* Zap2it, 14 May 2013. Web. 3 November 2013.

Lil Wayne feat. Drake. "Believe Me." *Tha Carter V.* Young Money/Cash Money/Republic Records. 2014. MP3 file.

Mobb Deep. "Start of Your Ending." *The Infamous.* Loud/RCA Records. 1994. Vinyl.

Monroe, Sylvester. "Hollywood: The Dark Side." *Essence Magazine.* March 1994: 82-87. Print.

Nas feat. Mary J. Blige. "Reach Out." *Life Is Good.* Def Jam Records, 2012. CD.

Naylor, Gloria. "The Meanings of a Word." *Models for Writers: Short Essays for Composition.* Boston: Bedford/St. Martins, 2012. Print.

Nikki Minaj. "Did It On 'Em." *Pink Friday.* Young Money/Cash Money/Universal Motown Records, 2010. CD.

"Race and Justice in America." AC 360. Narr. Anderson Cooper. CNN. 19 July 2013. Television.

"Race and Justice in America II." AC 360. Narr. Anderson Cooper. CNN. 23 July 2013. Television.

"Turn Up Mix by DJ Cypher Sounds." HOT 97 Morning Show. WQHT 91.1 FM - Hot 97, New York. 8 November 2013. Radio.

Westcott, Lucy. "New York City Approves 'Poor Door' for Luxury Apartment Building." *Newsweek.com.* Newsweek. 21 July 2014. Web. 1 August 2014.

Wilson, Carl. "The Same Loves: White People Win Again at the Grammys." *Slate.com.* Graham Holdings Company, 27 January 2014. Web. 1 August 2014.

CRITICAL EYE

For Discussion

a. Craig suggests that Hip Hop music–once evocative and socio-political–is now counter intuitive to the needs of the Black community. Considering current trends in Hip Hop, are Craig's assertions true?

b. Weigh Hip Hop culture alongside your understanding of Black culture. Are the two the same thing? If not, what are the distinctions? Use Craig's essay for insight.

Re-approaching the Reading

Ultimately, all music is entertainment. As such, why is our society so concerned about messages present or absent within this particular genre?

Writing Assignment

Choose one contemporary Hip Hop artist whose music does exactly what Craig asserts the genre should. How well-known is the artist? Do they sell albums? Who follows the artist? In the end, if rappers are unwilling to compromise, are they reaching out to an inconsequential audience–one that actually doesn't need convincing? Does this somehow invalidate their message and render it ineffective?

JL WILLIAMS

THE RIDE

From the Novel Legacies

The woman was anywhere between twenty-five and fifty years old. She was dressed in a tight form-fitting white top that struggled to contain breasts so large they seemed to actually fight against the fabric of her shirt. Seated, she appeared to be relatively short, maybe 5'1. Below the waist, she was dressed in a miniskirt with red and black polka dots that, like her top, was begging to escape the uncomfortable confines created by her bulging hips and thighs. And then, of course, there were the four-inch heels that she somehow had squeezed her feet inside of. The way her ankles swelled over the sides of the shoes gave one the impression that she was a woman who probably wore a size eight sneaker but had somehow squeezed into a size six pump.

On every train car, every day, there is at least one person who irritates the rest of us, who makes us feel like we are visitors in their living room, irritants that they feel the need to convey their disdain for while we share a confined space for a limited time. Yesterday, it was a slender Black woman aggressively pushing an oversized baby carriage onto the barely opened car as soon as the doors parted. Bumped and jostled, the white haired gentleman in her path must have said something to her because all the rest of us heard–as she forced the stroller as fast as she could push the sleeping child down to the opposite end–was a loud and repeated, "Suck my dick!" Once seated, she proceeded to sit there and argue with the man who was still standing near the doors where they had initially crossed paths. He said, "All you had to say was excuse me. We're all trying to get on the train." Her response was the same vulgar retort: "Suck my dick!" Well, sometimes she changed it up and said, "Suck my dick, motherfucker!"

That was yesterday's angry show. Today, on this train, at this moment, the woman across from me was *that* person. Collectively, the entire train radiated a passive hatred toward her.

With her legs elevated and her ankles crossed, she sat sideways and took up two seats. She had a large bag next to her, which took up another seat. Without ever acknowledging anyone directly, she wore a look of what might be best described as "combative anticipation" on her face, as if she was hoping someone would ask her to allow them the opportunity to sit and share what she had obviously staked out as her property. On top of that, she was listening to an iPod at max volume, with those cheap white earplugs that Apple should be ashamed to sell, subjecting those of us around her to what sounded like Caribbean techno rifts and cat wails. Her singing aloud was the icing on the proverbial cake.

I put her weight anywhere between 160 and 180 pounds. This was a conservative estimate, but she was very short. What amazed me as she wiggled in her seats, oblivious to the rest of us traveling on the crowded Downtown #1 train, was that if you had tried to explain to this woman that since Halle Berry missed this train she was in turn not the most put together and deservedly entitled woman any of us had ever seen, she would have taken such umbrage she might have removed one of her ill-fitting shoes and clubbed us all to death with it.

In her mind, she was the queen of the MTA and we were merely subjects she was forced to spend limited, annoying time amongst. All around the train car, people cut their eyes and shook their heads at the woman who radiated a royal aloofness that bordered on a blatant resentment for us, the peasants in her court.

Loud music, obesity, and seat dancing on the #1 line–which, for some reason, was one of the few Manhattan train routes that had not upgraded the subway cars and, thus, still has the horribly uncomfortable ride-on-your-neighbor's-lap two-toned orange seats that have no separation for riders–is an assured way to be despised by your fellow commuters. This morning, she was definitely the most despised rider so far.

But that was about to change.

It was at the next stop, 86th Street, that the man got on. Standing approximately 6'1, he was a head taller than me. He was wiry thin, but rippled with lean shredded muscle. His eyes were electric, dancing from side to side, indicating that he was high on a narcotic of some sort and had absolutely no business being around other people. He constantly bounced on his toes, moving and bumping those standing near him.

Everyone gave him as much distance as possible, a trick only real New Yorkers know considering that there were at least fifty people on the single subway car. However, the man seemed determined to make us all as uncomfortable as possible, and no amount of huddling together was going to stop him.

As I sat there reading my book, taking in everything while trying to look like I saw nothing, I felt the tension crawl up my back as the stress of an impending act loomed. What that act was, exactly, I was unsure, but I had spent a lifetime around fools and bad behavior, and this was a bad behaving fool.

The man, reeking of urine and the conspicuous smell of the unwashed, was not a new occurrence to any of us on the subway car. He was, like so many like him, a daily distraction we all had to deal with as we rode the nation's most expansive city rail system. But he seemed to be fighting a battle with whatever drug he was on, or off, and the kinetic energy that crackled around him suggested he was losing. Seated in the cramped corner nearest the crossing doors, I watched him seemingly take pleasure in the discord he was causing. As I looked around, I noticed that in the whole car there were only three people, including myself, who seemed oblivious to the man's antics. Only three who refused to acknowledge his presence.

And then he noticed it, too.

With a wide, toothy grin, he bopped down toward the three of us that had not retreated, who remained seemingly oblivious to his presence. Myself. An overtly effeminate White guy wearing red skinny jeans, silver rings on every finger and both thumbs, way too many colorful wrist bangles, and an old fading yellow t-shirt that said, "Bitch, I am the 99%!" And, of course, Miss Thang.

As he mumbled to himself about how "fucked up" something with something was because of something else, I began to wonder if he was possibly schizophrenic, but his constant nose wiping and the unnatural whiteness covering his lips seemed to suggest long-time drug abuse. Maybe, I thought, he's a schizophrenic crack-head. It was impossible to be sure.

Either way, he continued to approach the three of us, squatting down and doing a slow run, like a football player entering the arena to the cheers of fans and the palm claps of teammates. Once he waddled down to our end of the car—now appearing slow and awkward, imitating a lopsided shuffling movement as if he had a hip injury that prevented him from moving quicker—he proceeded to hover around us, taking his time, giving us that train-crazy-person stare he, and so many like him, had perfected.

I noticed he was giggling to himself, making noises not words, obviously excited by the prospect of mayhem he saw ahead. Talking it over with himself and then looking around as if trying to make a weighty decision, he finally shrugged and, seeming satisfied with his choice, decided where he would begin.

Much to my chagrin, he started with me.

I wasn't sure what he saw in his crazed eyes, so I decided, book slightly lowered, forearms squeezed, to allow him to get a good look.

At 5'10, I had become a specimen that was unnaturally different from what I would have been without weight lifting. Genetically, I should have been slim and lean like my father, as was the look I projected many years ago. Early on in life, I had been a slightly chubby kid during those awkward years of development between eight and thirteen, a fact neither of my parents ever let me forget. "Get yo' fat ass over here!" was a recurring summons from my childhood. However, as a teen, I grew several inches and looked thin with tight sinewy muscles like my father and brother before me. Around the time I turned twenty-three, soon after my world caved in, I decided that a new life, any life, was better than the one I'd led. As such, I knew that to reinvent myself, it had to be just as physical as it was mental.

My new body took years to accomplish, and it was as much of a makeover as plastic surgery would have been. I could not change my face, more than shaving my curly hair as close to my head as a low clipper guard allowed, but I was determined to adjust my look. Thirteen years later, I finally feel like I have achieved my goal. In my beige t-shirt, it was obvious that my shoulders were well-rounded and that my biceps bulged. Because of the revealing top, if I had stood he would have seen that my back was wide and defined with muscle bellies, and that, while much shorter than he, I would have been a problem in a tussle. Even through my jeans, my quads were pressing against the fabric of Levi's denim. After years of eating right and exercising, muscularly, I was now truly the opposite of my father's physical self. Naturally lean, my waist was a tapered 33 inches. Yet, unlike my father, I was broad across my front, having carved out a chest that curved upward, poked outward, and hung downward, all in one bubbled muscle cavity. While not overly-developed, huge in no sense of the word, I was what my girlfriend called "chiseled." Finally, I was what my father had never been. And this distinction was very important to me.

While being scrutinized, I laughed in my head, thinking about all the time in the gym, at all the shakes and vitamins and protein loading and calorie counting it took to achieve my body while here, like so many others I'd seen, stood a drug addict, possibly a homeless guy, who rippled with muscles and physical force. Here before me stood a poster child for lean conditioned bodybuilding. A man who, if he ever had a gym membership, smoked it up a long time ago.

While clearly I presented a picture of one who physically trains on a regular basis, one must keep in mind that this is Manhattan and that muscular men are everywhere. Moreover, most New Yorkers also know that the most extremely developed of these muscular males generally belong to the card carrying gay community.

My mind flashed back to years ago teaching at a community college in Long Island. In my classroom, the simpleminded suburban males, with their waxed arched eyebrows and front-gelled hair, were always talking about going into "the city" as they called it. On this day, one of them, addressing a point I'd made about sodomy laws, felt inclined to say to the room, "Man, if one of those sissies says something to me on the train or down in the West Village, I might have to smack him." When I asked the group why, they explained excitedly with their heavy Long Island accents, "Uh, because they faggots, that's why!"

To this discourteous response, I remember responding, "Well, you should be careful smacking 'sissies' in the village. You manly men out here probably don't know this, but 'sissies' in the village keep steroids in business. When I go to the gym and there are 'sissies' lifting weights, I'm usually one of the smallest people in the room. And, just to help you out, I wouldn't be walking around calling them 'sissies' either, because if one of them grabs you—well, I guess you'll find out who the 'faggot' really is."

This kind of lecture was usually met with a hint of quiet dismissal by some, an assumption that I was verifying their assumptions regarding my own sexuality and, as such, confirming their asinine perceptions of a Black male in academia for a few, or a new thought to process for others. I often prayed these life-limited students would actually go to the West Village and poke fun at some of the gay population. Maybe being pummeled by a group of steroid raging homosexuals would give them life altering lessons that would turn them into better human beings.

As energy man sized me up, I could tell he was trying to decide if I was one of the "sissies" my former students often worried would grab them on the streets of New York City and sodomize them on the sidewalk. And, even though I did not make eye contact—if he was crazy, on or off some kind of drug, eye contact could be seen as a direct challenge, a final stressor—I had the look on my face, the one that simply says, gay man or not, one thing: "Don't."

After jumping around in front of me, he decided I was not the fun he was looking for. Next to get sized-up, the White guy.

I was pretty sure he wouldn't be as lucky.

He, like me, saw this coming and tried his best not to look uncomfortable, let alone afraid. But to a person who probably has never thrown a punch, let alone had an honest to goodness fist fight, energy man was quite intimidating. And he knew it. As soon as he stood in front of the much smaller man, looking in an exaggeratedly slow up and down motion, obviously taking in the bangles dangling on the slight wrist, the super tight skinny jeans, the ridiculous red coloring, energy man literally started to crackle.

He began his awkward attack by gyrating his hips slowly and thrusting his crotch into the seated man's space. I could see now that his penis was flopping around unrestrained in his sweatpants like a mongoose struggling for release inside a burlap bag. He kept dipping lowly and then bouncing back up, and his private area—please, I thought, don't let that thing out—was thrashing about directly in the seated man's face.

Because his prey tried to look unfazed, energy man started holding the train's standing bars with both hands and moving slowly and provocatively like a stripper working hard on stage. He then ran his oversized pink tongue over his graying teeth, doing his best to make the man regret his decision to leave the house. His burlesque performance was as disturbing as it was comical. As I sat there, thinking how funny I might have found this years ago, I was grateful he had moved on from me, yet enraged that this passenger, that any person minding their business, could be subjected to such behavior. I felt myself getting worked up, so I tried to calm down. I tried not to listen to the voice saying that I could take this guy. I tried not to allow my ego to become a part of this. I tried because I'm always trying not to be who I once was.

Just as it seemed he might grab the smaller man, one can only imagine what his fried mind might have done to him after that, our subway hostage taker noticed Miss Thang, sitting in her own world, apparently oblivious to all going on around her, bouncing, singing, enjoying her music. Her ignoring him, her seeming outwardly unfazed by all around that was happening, is what saved the White guy. Because now, energy man no longer seemed to be enjoying himself.

Now, he actually appeared to be angry.

At that moment, almost like an inside joke, I thought maybe, on top of everything else, he is a sexist, too. Being ignored by us males was one thing–but by a woman? Unacceptable.

Moving over into her space, he seemed more amped up and more determined than ever. Again, I started to think that he might unsheathe his dangling manhood. Looking at the woman sing and act blasé, I wondered if he unzipped and swung his phallus in her face, maybe laid it on her forehead, Queen Elizabeth might finally acknowledge that she wasn't on this train alone.

After waving his hands in her face as if her eyes were not closed but, actually, she was merely pretending to be blind, he smiled at the rest of the car, as if to say, "Watch this." As we all prepared to witness some form of assault, the woman, opening her eyes and speaking in a heavy West Indian accent, attacked first. "You dirte' fucka. You get yo' naste' ass back from me. Who de' fuck you dink you are? You must be crazy, you junkie fuck," she hissed.

She met his eyes. Stared at him. Then she bucked her eyes out and jutted her chin in his direction, giving that, "What are you going to do about it?" look.

At first he just stared, as if expecting her to say more. When he realized she was done, that she had no more to say, he just stood there with a look that seemed to reflect a kind of embarrassment. Finally backing away like he had been slapped, he surprised us all and simply stood by the closest doors. Looking around at those of us who were in large part utterly amazed at her bravado, she, with smug satisfaction, closed her eyes and, once again, became the annoyance she was before he came.

Fascinating, I thought. For at least two stops, he was quiet, standing in the doorway, rocking back and forth.

We were stalled in the 72nd street station when I saw the sparks in his eyes reignite. Unfortunately, Miss Thang seemed oblivious to his renewed interest in her. Unlike me, she was now ignoring him completely, as if she had disciplined her own insolent child and that, as such, there was no consequence for her actions.

But she was wrong.

Her first mistake was that she had taken her eyes off the man. You must always keep a predator in sight. Not acknowledging the extent of his mind's problems was her second mistake.

As I sniffed the air, I noticed the distinct smell of nicotine. As I looked around, I saw that energy man had lit a cigarette and was taking deep pulls before blowing the smoke into the enclosed space. As crazy as crazy gets on the train, someone lighting a cigarette is still pretty unheard of. In a city that banned smoking in bars and restaurants in 2003, most of us have gotten pretty comfortable with smoke-free environments where smoking used to be allowed. And, as far as I know, it was never allowed on the subway, making his lighting up all the more unsettling.

As I peeked up and stole a glimpse of the man, I noted that his face had changed. He now had a look in his eyes I knew too well. He didn't look excited. He didn't look angry. Instead, he now had the look of a man reduced to his most primal self, like a rabid dog who can no longer contain his impulses and, quietly, without further warning, attacks. What I saw before me was a man who had made a decision.

Those who entered the train after the initial incident were crowding around until they noticed him smoking. Backing away, the commuters now gave energy man, who, interestingly, appeared more calm than before, a little distance. Room enough that he was able to saddle up next to Miss Thang again.

Opening her eyes, she rolled her pupils upward and stared him right in the face, like a fighter in the presence of a lesser opponent. In response, he blew a stream of smoke that completely enveloped her whole head. Those who had seen her earlier act looked at the woman, wondering what her retort might be. Those who got on after looked around for escape, as if they were considering crossing between the cars or dashing off to change cars at the next stop. Any option besides staying and being silent witnesses.

But I knew what would happen next. I knew when she didn't move. I knew when she did not jump out of her seat immediately. I knew when I looked at her and her eyes shifted to the right, a sense of panic building as her mind tried to process the situation.

I knew because I know.

In a fight you either respond immediately, answer an attack with an attack, or your mind weighs the odds. When the latter happens, you lose. Someone smacks you, you smack them back. Immediately. If not, all is lost.

Miss Thang was reviewing the situation rationally, putting her own socially aggressive disdain for others' comfort alongside his literal craziness. And in that moment, you could tell she knew he was serious and that she, no matter how angry, how right, was no match for him. Blowing another stream of smoke in her face, he spoke for the first time.

"You think you can...you can just say anything you want to me? Like I'm nothing? Like I don't count? You sitting there like yo' ass don't stink, with yo' big titties poking out. You fat hoe," he said. "Bitch, I will piss on you. Don't think I won't!" he yelled.

Please, don't take that thing out! I almost screamed.

In one swift movement he yanked her earplugs out and, in the same movement, fondled the woman's breasts, actually popping several buttons on her shirt. As I felt my pressure rise, the other onlookers in the car made gasping noises and, to our communal shame, looked away. But not me.

The first thing I noticed was that her nipples were now erect. I reflected back to a graduate school course where we learned about how the body still becomes stimulated, even when the brain knows that what it's experiencing is not pleasure. Then I noticed that the woman's eyes had begun filming with tears. Raising my head slightly, I noted that she was looking directly across at me with an expression of pleading I had seen before. I was now looking at someone who thought she was filled with enough animus to combat any person she came in contact with. But that was before she collided with real, raw anger—before she met this man who, spurred by drugs and a sense of social ostracism that ate away at any thoughts of morally acceptable behavior, desired to show her the error of her ways. It wasn't the look of the victim. She was not an innocent person minding her own business who suddenly found herself out-muscled and outgunned. She was not a lamb abducted and hoping until the end to be spared a horrible slaughter. No, she was a hyena, a predator in her own right. But she had finally been cornered by a lion—an animal stronger, faster, whose annoyance with the aggressive lesser creature would be evident in the merciless assault that followed. She was out of her depth.

Looking directly at the two of them, I could see sweat now beading her forehead. Her face trembled, and I noticed that her makeup was beginning to stain the back of her collar. As he loomed over her, there was a sense of fear so visibly pervasive that I thought I could see it float off her in waves. Sucking the inside of my cheeks, I thought how no one should ever feel as helpless as she looked now.

As I sat there and weighed my options—intervene and possibly really hurt this man, followed by arrest or, worse, a trip to the emergency room where I might need some form of reconstructive attention—I felt the enormous heaviness that is shame wash over me. Because I too had made a decision. I wasn't going to help her.

While this woman was a stereotype that I loathed—rude, loud, overweight, angry, a woman who tried as often as possible to tell the world to kiss her swollen feet, always wishing someone would challenge her so she could truly express her rage by lashing out and, as such, convey a taste of the disappointment her own life held—I still believed that no one deserves to have hands laid upon their person. No one deserves to be assaulted on a train in front of dozens upon dozens of cowardly spectators. No one deserves to be harassed and bullied and attacked.

Acts I once reveled in.

A life I once enjoyed too easily.

And, more than anything, this woman's helplessness, her eyes now acting as a faucet for streaming tears, took me back to a hardness in my heart that I had spent years trying to forget. I tried to pump myself up. Maybe it was time to physically act after so many years of trying to perfect invisibility. Part of my brain said, "Do something!" But that was the other side of me, the part I buried long ago. The side that was left, my rational non-reactive side, simply frowned at the thought. No matter what happened, I knew I wouldn't do anything.

Suddenly the doors at the back of the car banged open and two NYPD transit cops came through. Word had probably gotten to the conductor about the smoking, and he'd signaled ahead for assistance. Seeing that the party was over, energy man departed through the connecting doors at the opposite end of the train, but not before committing an act so vile that I, too, found myself forced to look away.

Before he made his escape, smile wide and vindictive, he took several of his own fingers and inserted them deep into his mouth. He then removed the three wet fingers and slowly wiped them down the front of the woman's entire face. Laughing, he bounced away, almost like a child anticipating the chase from playground tag. The cops followed and, just that quickly, our captor and his pursuers were gone. And just that quickly, as things happen in New York, poof, all returned to normal.

The stress of the moment seemed to dissipate like the cigarette smoke that minutes ago consumed the whole car. More people got on the train, many got off. While a few looked through the doors to see if the police arrested the guy, most seemed relieved the incident was out of their sight and returned to their own interests.

As we approached Columbus Circle, my stop, I rose and stood by the door, trying desperately not to look at Miss Thang, who remained seated. But, like a car accident, I could only look away for so long. Turning slightly so as not to be seen looking, I saw that the woman had mascara streaking her chubby cheeks, and that her earplugs remained jumbled in her lap. But mostly I noticed that she was staring at me with a look of such utter disdain that for a brief moment anyone watching would have assumed that I was the one who'd actually violated her.

As I exited and headed toward the turnstile, I stopped and watched as the train departed the station. As the last car disappeared from sight, I thought with much regret that I had indeed, in some way, been part of her assault and, because of that, my mind was now playing tricks on me.

Something was wrong.

I immediately tensed up. Cautiously, I looked down into the subway tunnel, the lights of the next approaching train visible in the distance. I then looked around the narrow walkway with my feet spread shoulder length apart, ready to defend myself.

I waited.

Suddenly, people started to flood the platform, a mid-morning New York station only deserted for as long as it takes the train to depart from sight. When nothing happened, I dismissed the chill that blew over me like a cartoon omen. My nerves were obviously on edge. Shaking my head, I felt frustrated by what I believed the woman saw when she looked at me. She'd stared openly, and what she glimpsed was an image I'd been sculpting for years. When I looked in the mirror, I now saw the same person she had. I wore "disinterested New Yorker" like a pair of comfortable, weathered sneakers. I'd kept my head down and attracted no attention. Once again, I hadn't revealed my true nature. As always, I didn't risk anything.

The strange thing is that, even after all these years, this person I have become still feels unnatural.

Pressing through the turnstile, I stopped again. I turned and looked over my shoulder, just as another train was heading into the station. Weird, I thought. I was suddenly disturbed by the certainty that when the train hit the brakes and sparks flew off the tracks, I heard the high-pitched screeching, as clear as day, whistling the word "soon." I laughed aloud as I headed for the stairs. The thought that ten minutes of excitement had me so shaken that I was hearing things was amusing.

As I walked by the booth that held a single, bored-looking MTA worker, I saw my reflection in the glass. Physically, I looked fine. But how I looked wasn't the issue. When I glanced at myself, I wasn't pleased with who stared back at me. As a matter of fact, I wasn't happy about my life at all. My trance was broken when the booth attendant waved. She probably thought I was staring at her. I gave her a weak smile and waved back before walking up the stairwell and out into the day.

CRITICAL EYE

For Discussion

a. How is this excerpt a representation of "everyday" life in a big city? Why are the passengers unable or unwilling to speak up during the disturbance?

b. Given that the female passenger was being disruptive, determine whether or not, based on the essay's climax, we should actually feel sorry for her? Are you mad at her? Do you believe she deserves to be treated so harshly? If so, why? If not, why?

Re-approaching the Reading

Most of us abhor using physical violence as a response to difficult situations. What would have happened if our narrator or one or more of the onlookers had used violence to address the aggressive male passenger?

Writing Assignment

Advancements in technology are bringing our large world closer together. We can now read books and listen to music on electronic devices. We also communicate on cell phones (talk or text) in the air on planes and underground on trains; as such, is our large world actually getting smaller? Said differently, does the incident on the train foreshadow what our daily interactions with our neighbors will be like someday? Are we becoming less and less inclined to tolerate each other?

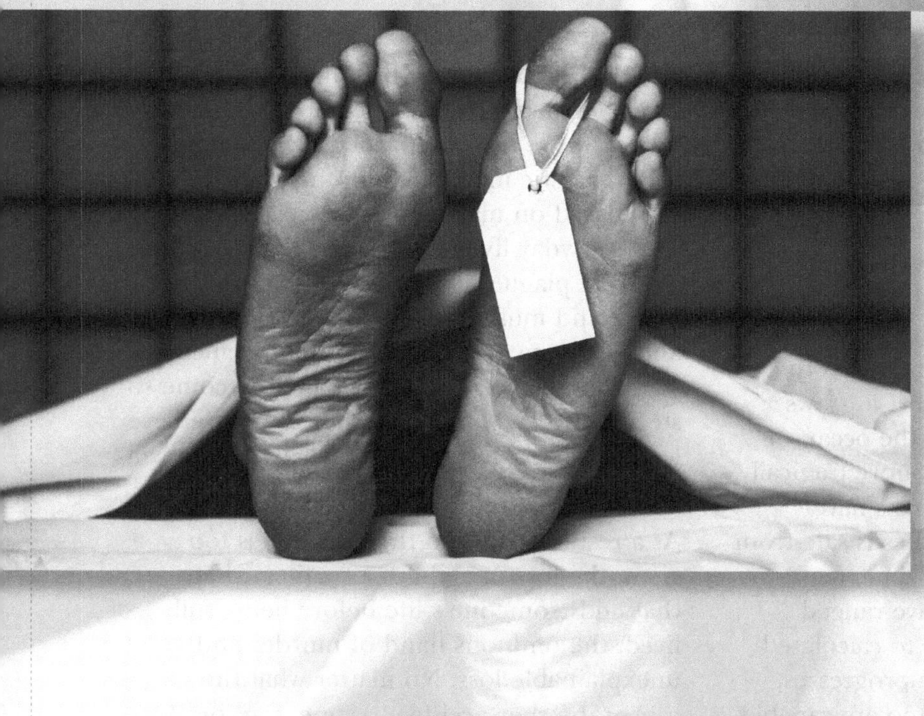

Death and Violence

Since we're all going to die, it's obvious that when and how don't matter.
Albert Camus, *The Stranger*

If I die a violent death, as some fear and a few are plotting, I know that the violence will be the thought and action of the assassins, not in my dying.
Indira Gandhi

Death wouldn't be so frightening if we could live forever. Or perhaps it wouldn't be so terrifying if we could be assured that we would pass gently from this world into the next. While we slept. At a ripe old age. But the world doesn't work that way. We live, and then we die–and only a few of us will never experience pain. We are born into a wondrous world that can be abhorrently violent. As such, although we fear death and loathe acts of violence, we are unable to stem either.

Miracle pills, serums, diets, gym memberships, and plastic surgery cannot change the inevitable waning of a human life, no more than policing, prisons, security systems, and weaponry can fully deter or eliminate whether or not we witness, are part of, or experience acts of violence. On top of that, minute-by-minute coverage makes us uniquely aware of death and violence on an hourly basis. Unquestioningly, ours is a violent world that is engaged in a strange courtship with death.

As the world evolves and mankind pushes forward into this new millennium, there is an understood axiom that seems to be inescapable: earth's species will continue to reproduce, and human beings will, both indiscriminately and discriminately, try to kill them all. It does not matter if it grows out of the ground or swims in the ocean or soars through the sky or, even more tragically, looks just like themselves—humans have proven that nothing that breathes is safe from their wrath. Since the dawn of time, man's reasons for violent behavior have ranged from accidental to self-defense to calculated murder. Unfortunately, as time progresses, women have proven that they too are capable of committing aggressively heinous acts, sometimes at the expense of their children.

Understandably, violence as a mode of preservation is not uncommon. Many would argue that these types of acts are necessary for the very survival of our species. As a matter of fact, few would deny that the defense of one's family—one's way of life, for that matter—is a right of the living. Killing for food actually speaks to the essence of perpetuating the species. Yet, we live in a world where cruelties—not those deeds that speak to survival—have become the norm. Each day, we are bombarded by brutal and often sadistic images: children's games are now based on mayhem; the news, our lens into everyday living, relays the horrendous acts that plague our world; and murder sells books and music more than the idea of love and harmony ever has. This embracement suggests that our social media has become so steeped in the world of violence that we have learned to expect that a destructive hand will one day knock upon our door.

As a result, too often the end comes too soon: the loss of a child; a tragic mishap that ends someone's life before being fully lived; the ominous hand of murder and unexplainable loss. No matter what the causes—be they accident, crime, war, or mental illness—what seems fascinating about death and violence is not only how we die, or who else is involved, but how family and friends—often passersby—are forced to adjust and bereave in the aftermath.

The chosen selections in this chapter can in no way answer the question, "Why must we die?" Instead, they ponder how death and violence—so often joined at the hip—are received and accepted, even measured out, across gender, class, and ethnic boundaries.

TONI MORRISON

From the Novel *PARADISE*

Set in the all Black town of Ruby, Oklahoma during the post-slavery decades of segregation and civil disobedience, ***Paradise*** *focuses on the a puritanical town of patriarchs and their desire to destroy five women beyond their reach. The following excerpt depicts the showdown between these self-proclaimed defenders of decency and the women they've come to massacre.*

This selection opens the novel and begins after the men have invaded this "female" space–a renovated convent previously used as a missionary school designed to "Americanize" young Native American girls. The reader is privy to the internal monologues of each of the men after they have gunned down the five female inhabitants.

They shoot the white girl first. With the rest they can take their time. No need to hurry out here. They are seventeen miles from a town which has ninety miles between it and any other. Hiding places will be plentiful in the Convent, but there is time and the day has just begun.

They are nine, over twice the number of the women they are obliged to stampede or kill and they have the paraphernalia for either requirement: rope, a palm leaf cross, handcuffs, Mace and sunglasses, along with clean, handsome guns.

They have never been this deep in the Convent. Some of them have parked Chevrolets near its porch to pick up a string of peppers or have gone into the kitchen for a gallon of barbecue sauce; but only a few have seen the halls, the chapel, the schoolroom, the bedrooms. Now they all will. And at last they will see the cellar and expose its filth to the light that is soon to scour the Oklahoma sky. Meantime they are startled by the clothes they are wearing–suddenly aware of being ill-dressed. For at the dawn of a July day how could they have guessed the cold that is inside this place? Their T-shirts, work shirts and dashikis soak up cold like fever. Those who have worn work shoes are unnerved by the thunder of their steps on marble floors; those in Pro-Keds by the silence. Then there is the grandeur. Only the two who are wearing ties seem to belong here and one by one each is reminded that before it was a Convent, this house was an embezzler's folly. A mansion where bisque and rose-tone marble floors segue into teak ones. Isinglass holds yesterday's light and patterns walls that were stripped and whitewashed fifty years ago. The ornate bathroom fixtures, which sickened the nuns, were replaced with good plain spigots, but the princely tubs and sinks, which could not be inexpensively removed, remain coolly corrupt. The embezzler's joy that could be demolished was, particularly in the dining room, which the nuns converted to a schoolroom, where stilled Arapaho girls once sat and learned to forget.

Now armed men search rooms where macramé baskets float next to Flemish candelabra; where Christ and His mother glow in niches trimmed in grapevines. The Sisters of the Sacred Cross chipped away all the nymphs, but curves of their marble hair still strangle grape leaves and tease the fruit. The chill intensifies as the men spread deeper into the mansion, taking their time, looking, listening, alert to the female malice that hides here and the yeast-and-butter smell of rising dough.

One of them, the youngest, looks back, forcing himself to see how the dream he is in might go. The shot woman, lying uncomfortably on marble, waves her fingers at him—or seems to. So his dream is doing okay, except for its color. He has never before dreamed in colors such as these: imperial black sporting a wild swipe of red, then thick, feverish yellow. Like the clothes of an easily had woman. The leading man pauses, raising his left hand to halt the silhouettes behind him. They stop, editing their breath, making friendly adjustments in the grip of rifles and handguns. The leading man turns and gestures the separations: you two over there to the kitchen; two more upstairs; two others into the chapel. He saves himself, his brother and the one who thinks he is dreaming for the cellar.

They part gracefully without words or haste. Earlier, when they blew open the Convent door, the nature of their mission made them giddy. But the target, after all, is detritus: throwaway people that sometimes blow back into the room after being swept out the door. So the venom is manageable now. Shooting the first woman (the white one) has clarified it like butter: the pure oil of hatred on top, its hardness stabilized below.

Outside, the mist is waist high. It will turn silver soon and make grass rainbows low enough for children's play before the sun burns it off, exposing acres of bluestem and maybe witch tracks as well.

The kitchen is bigger than the house in which either man was born. The ceiling barn-rafter high. More shelving than Ace's Grocery Store. The table is fourteen feet long if an inch, and it's easy to tell that the women they are hunting have been taken by surprise. At one end a full pitcher of milk stands near four bowls of shredded wheat. At the other end vegetable chopping has been interrupted: scallions piled like a handful of green confetti nestles brilliant disks of carrot, and the potatoes, peeled and whole, are bone white, wet and crisp. Stock simmers on the stove. It is restaurant size with eight burners and on a shelf beneath the great steel hood a dozen loaves of bread swell. A stool is overturned. There are no windows.

One man signals the other to open the pantry while he goes to the back door. It is closed but unlocked. Peering out he sees an old hen, her puffed and bloody hind parts cherished, he supposes, for delivering freaks—double, triple yolks in outsize and misshapen shells. Soft stuttering comes from the coop beyond; fryers padding confidently into the yard's mist disappear, reappear and disappear again, each flat eye indifferent to anything but breakfast. No footprints disturb the mud around the stone steps. This man closes the door and joins his partner at the pantry. Together they scan dusty mason jars and what is left of last year's canning: tomatoes, green beans, peaches. Slack, they think. August just around the corner and these women have not even sorted, let alone washed, the jars.

He turns the fire off under the stockpot. His mother bathed him in a pot no bigger than that. A luxury in the sod house where she was born. The house he lives in is big, comfortable, and this town is resplendent compared to his birthplace, which had gone from feet to belly in fifty years. From Haven, a dreamtown in Oklahoma Territory, to Haven, a ghosttown in Oklahoma State. Freedmen who stood tall in 1889 dropped to their knees in 1934 and were stomach-crawling by 1948. That is why they are here in this Convent. To make sure it never happens again. That nothing inside or out rots the one all-black town worth the pain. All the others he knew about or heard tell of knuckled to or merged with white towns; otherwise, like Haven, they had shriveled into tracery: foundation outlines marked by the way grass grew there, wallpaper turned negative behind missing windowpanes, schoolhouse floors moved aside by elder trees growing toward the bell housing. One thousand citizens in 1905 becoming five hundred by 1934. Then two hundred, then eighty as cotton collapsed or railroad companies laid their tracks elsewhere. Subsistence farming, once the only bounty a large family needed, became just scrap farming as each married son got his bit, which had to be broken up into more pieces for his children, until finally the owners of the bits and pieces who had not walked off in disgust welcomed any offer from a white speculator, so eager were they to get away and try someplace else. A big city this time, or a small town that was already built.

But he and the others, veterans all, had a different idea. Loving what Haven had been—the idea of it and its reach—they carried that devotion, gentling and nursing it from Bataan to Guam, from Iwo Jima to Stuttgart, and they made up their minds to do it again. He touched the stove hood admiring its construction and power. It was the same length as the brick oven that once sat in the middle of his hometown. When they got back to the States, they took it apart, carrying the bricks, the hearthstone and its iron plate two hundred and forty miles west—far far from the old Creek Nation which once upon a time a witty government called "unassigned land." He remembers the ceremony they'd had when the Oven's iron lip was recemented into place and its worn letters polished for all to see. He himself had helped clean off sixty-two years of carbon and animal fat so the words shone as brightly as they did in 1890 when they were new. And if it hurt—pulling asunder what their grandfathers had put together—it was nothing compared to what they had endured and what they might become if they did not begin anew. As new fathers, who had fought the world, they could not (would not) be less than the Old Fathers who had outfoxed it; who had not let danger or natural evil keep them from cutting Haven out of mud and who knew enough to seal their triumph with that priority. An Oven. Round as a head, deep as desire. Living in or near their wagons, boiling meal in the open, cutting sod and mesquite for shelter, the Old Fathers did that first: put most of their strength into constructing the huge, flawlessly designed Oven that both nourished them and monumentalized what they had done. When it was finished—each pale brick perfectly pitched; the chimney wide, lofty; the pegs and grill secure; the draft pulling steadily from the tail hole; the fire door plumb—then the ironmonger did his work. From barrel staves and busted axles, from kettles and bent nails, he fashioned an iron plate five feet by two and set it at the base of the Oven's mouth. It is still not clear where the words came from. Something he heard, invented, or something whispered to him while he slept curled over his tools in a wagon bed. His name was Morgan and who knew if he invented or stole the half-dozen or so words he forged. Words that seemed at first to bless them; later to confound them; finally to announce that they had lost.

The man eyes the kitchen sink. He moves to the long table and lifts the pitcher of milk. He sniffs it first and then, the pistol in his right hand, he uses his left to raise the pitcher to his mouth, taking such long, measured swallows the milk is half gone by the time he smells the wintergreen.

On the floor above two men walk the hall and examine the four bedrooms, each with a name card taped on its door. The first name, written in lipstick, is Seneca. The next, Divine, is inked in capital letters. They exchange knowing looks when they learn that each woman sleeps not in a bed, like normal people, but in a hammock. Other than that, and except for a narrow desk or an end table, there is no additional furniture. No clothes in the closets, of course, since the women wore no-fit dirty dresses and nothing you could honestly call shoes. But there are strange things nailed or taped to the walls or propped in a corner. A 1968 calendar, large X's marking various dates (April 4, July 19): a letter written in blood so smeary its satanic message cannot be deciphered; an astrology chart; a fedora tilted on the plastic neck of a female torso, and, in a place that once housed Christians–well, Catholics anyway–not a cross of Jesus anywhere. But what alarms the two men most is the series of infant booties and shoes ribboned to a cord hanging from a crib in the last bedroom they enter. A teething ring, cracked and stiff, dangles among the tiny shoes. Signaling with his eyes, one man directs his partner to four more bedrooms on the opposite side of the hall. He himself moves closer to the bouquet of baby shoes. Looking for what? More evidence? He isn't sure. Blood? A little toe, maybe, left in a white calfskin shoe? He slides the safety on his gun and joins the search across the hall.

These rooms are normal. Messy–the floor in one of them is covered with food-encrusted dishes, dirty cups, its bed invisible under a hill of clothes; another room sports two rocking chairs full of dolls; a third the debris and smell of a heavy drinker–but normal at least. His saliva is bitter and although he knows this place is diseased, he is startled by the whip of pity flicking in his chest. What, he wonders, could do this to women? How can their plain brains think up such things: revolting sex, deceit and the sly torture of children? Out here in wide-open space tucked away in a mansion–no one to bother or insult them–they managed to call into question the value of almost every woman he knew. The winter coat money for which his father saved in secret for two harvests; the light in his mother's eyes when she stroked its seal collar. The surprise party he and his brothers threw for a sister's sixteenth birthday. Yet here, not twenty miles away from a quiet, orderly community, there were women like none he knew or ever heard tell of. In this place of all places. Unique and isolated, his was a town justifiably pleased with itself. It neither had nor needed a jail. No criminals had ever come from his town. And the one or two people who acted up, humiliated their families or threatened the town's view of itself were taken good care of. Certainly there wasn't a slack or sloven woman anywhere in town and the reasons, he thought, were clear. From the beginning its people were free and protected. A sleepless woman could always rise from her bed, wrap a shawl around her shoulders and sit on the steps in the moonlight. And if she felt like it she could walk out the yard and on down the road. No lamp and no fear. A hiss-crackle from the side of the road would never scare her because whatever it was that made the sound, it wasn't something creeping up on her. Nothing for ninety miles around thought she was prey. She could stroll as slowly as she liked, think of food preparations, war, of family things, or lift her eyes to stars and think of nothing at all. Lampless and without fear she could make her way. And if a light shone from a house up a ways and the cry of a colicky baby caught her attention, she might step over to the house and call out softly to the woman inside trying to soothe the baby.

The two of them might take turns massaging the infant stomach, rocking, or trying to get a little soda water down. When the baby quieted they could sit together for a spell, gossiping, chuckling low so as not to wake anybody else.

The woman could decide to go back to her own house then, refreshed and ready to sleep, or she might keep her direction and walk further down the road, past other houses, past the three churches, past the feedlot. On out, beyond the limits of town, because nothing at the edge thought she was prey.

At each end of the hall is a bathroom. As each man enters one, neither is working his jaws because both believe they are prepared for anything. In one bathroom, the biggest, the taps are too small and dowdy for the wide sink. The bathtub rests on the backs of four mermaids—their tails split wide for the tub's security, their breasts arched for stability. The tile underfoot is bottle green. A Modess box is on the toilet tank and a bucket of soiled things stands nearby. There is no toilet paper. Only one mirror has not been covered with chalky paint and that one the man ignores. He does not want to see himself stalking females or their liquid. With relief he backs out and closes the door. With relief he lets his handgun point down.

CRITICAL EYE

For Discussion

a. What distinctions does the narrator make between what makes a woman good or bad?

b. It is clear that the men who enter the Convent are in conflict with these women and mean to do them harm. For these men, why does violence seem to be the "best" way to handle conflict rather than discussion?

Re-approaching the Reading

The women in the text are seen as "bad" women/girls. Feminist critic Naomi Wolf suggests that there is, in fact, no such thing as a "bad girl," and, moreover, society has created the bad girl persona in order to have someone to mistreat. Taking this idea into consideration, determine whether or not these women are indeed "bad" or are simply living outside of the stereotypical female archetype.

Writing Topic

As human beings, we often deal harshly with those we feel are encroaching upon our territory or are not following our social/cultural mores. Why is this?

MARK TWAIN

From the Novel

ADVENTURES OF HUCKLEBERRY FINN

Chapters 21–22 excerpted

Chapter XXI.

The nearer it got to noon that day the thicker and thicker was the wagons and horses in the streets, and more coming all the time. Families fetched their dinners with them from the country, and eat them in the wagons. There was considerable whisky drinking going on, and I seen three fights. By and by somebody sings out:

"Here comes old Boggs!–in from the country for his little old monthly drunk; here he comes, boys!"

All the loafers looked glad; I reckoned they was used to having fun out of Boggs. One of them says:

"Wonder who he's a-gwyne to chaw up this time. If he'd a-chawed up all the men he's ben a-gwyne to chaw up in the last twenty year he'd have considerable ruputation now."

Another one says, "I wisht old Boggs 'd threaten me, 'cuz then I'd know I warn't gwyne to die for a thousan' year."

Boggs comes a-tearing along on his horse, whooping and yelling like an Injun, and singing out:

"Cler the track, thar. I'm on the waw-path, and the price uv coffins is a-gwyne to raise."

He was drunk, and weaving about in his saddle; he was over fifty year old, and had a very red face. Everybody yelled at him and laughed at him and sassed him, and he sassed back, and said he'd attend to them and lay them out in their regular turns, but he couldn't wait now because he'd come to town to kill old Colonel Sherburn, and his motto was, "Meat first, and spoon vittles to top off on."

He see me, and rode up and says:

"Whar'd you come f'm, boy? You prepared to die?"

Then he rode on. I was scared, but a man says:

"He don't mean nothing; he's always a-carryin' on like that when he's drunk. He's the best naturedest old fool in Arkansaw–never hurt nobody, drunk nor sober."

Boggs rode up before the biggest store in town, and bent his head down so he could see under the curtain of the awning and yells:

"Come out here, Sherburn! Come out and meet the man you've swindled.

You're the houn' I'm after, and I'm a-gwyne to have you, too!"

And so he went on, calling Sherburn everything he could lay his tongue to, and the whole street packed with people listening and laughing and going on. By and by a proud-looking man about fifty-five–and he was a heap the best dressed man in that town, too–steps out of the store, and the crowd drops back on each side to let him come. He says to Boggs, mighty ca'm and slow–he says:

"I'm tired of this, but I'll endure it till one o'clock. Till one o'clock, mind–no longer. If you open your mouth against me only once after that time you can't travel so far but I will find you."

Then he turns and goes in. The crowd looked mighty sober; nobody stirred, and there warn't no more laughing. Boggs rode off blackguarding Sherburn as loud as he could yell, all down the street; and pretty soon back he comes and stops before the store, still keeping it up. Some men crowded around him and tried to get him to shut up, but he wouldn't; they told him it would be one o'clock in about fifteen minutes, and so he MUST go home–he must go right away. But it didn't do no good. He cussed away with all his might, and throwed his hat down in the mud and rode over it, and pretty soon away he went a-raging down the street again, with his gray hair a-flying. Everybody that could get a chance at him tried their best to coax him off of his horse so they could lock him up and get him sober; but it warn't no use–up the street he would tear again, and give Sherburn another cussing. By and by somebody says:

"Go for his daughter!–quick, go for his daughter; sometimes he'll listen to her. If anybody can persuade him, she can."

So somebody started on a run. I walked down street a ways and stopped. In about five or ten minutes here comes Boggs again, but not on his horse. He was a-reeling across the street towards me, bare-headed, with a friend on both sides of him a-holt of his arms and hurrying him along. He was quiet, and looked uneasy; and he warn't hanging back any, but was doing some of the hurrying himself. Somebody sings out:

"Boggs!"

I looked over there to see who said it, and it was that Colonel Sherburn. He was standing perfectly still in the street, and had a pistol raised in his right hand–not aiming it, but holding it out with the barrel tilted up towards the sky. The same second I see a young girl coming on the run, and two men with her. Boggs and the men turned round to see who called him, and when they see the pistol the men jumped to one side, and the pistol-barrel come down slow and steady to a level–both barrels cocked. Boggs throws up both of his hands and says, "O Lord, don't shoot!" Bang! goes the first shot, and he staggers back, clawing at the air–bang! goes the second one, and he tumbles backwards on to the ground, heavy and solid, with his arms spread out. That young girl screamed out and comes rushing, and down she throws herself on her father, crying, and saying, "Oh, he's killed him, he's killed him!" The crowd closed up around them, and shouldered and jammed one another, with their necks stretched, trying to see, and people on the inside trying to shove them back and shouting, "Back, back! give him air, give him air!"

Colonel Sherburn he tossed his pistol on to the ground, and turned around on his heels and walked off.

They took Boggs to a little drug store, the crowd pressing around just the same, and the whole town following, and I rushed and got a good place at the window, where I was close to him and could see in. They laid him on the floor and put one large Bible under his head, and opened another one and spread it on his breast; but they tore open his shirt first, and I seen where one of the bullets went in. He made about a dozen long gasps, his breast lifting the Bible up when he drawed in his breath, and letting it down again when he breathed it out–and after that he laid still; he was dead. Then they pulled his daughter away from him, screaming and crying, and took her off. She was about sixteen, and very sweet and gentle looking, but awful pale and scared.

Well, pretty soon the whole town was there, squirming and scrouging and pushing and shoving to get at the window and have a look, but people that had the places wouldn't give them up, and folks behind them was saying all the time, "Say, now, you've looked enough, you fellows; 'tain't right and 'tain't fair for you to stay thar all the time, and never give nobody a chance; other folks has their rights as well as you."

There was considerable jawing back, so I slid out, thinking maybe there was going to be trouble. The streets was full, and everybody was excited. Everybody that seen the shooting was telling how it happened, and there was a big crowd packed around each one of these fellows, stretching their necks and listening. One long, lanky man, with long hair and a big white fur stovepipe hat on the back of his head, and a crooked-handled cane, marked out the places on the ground where Boggs stood and where Sherburn stood, and the people following him around from one place to t'other and watching everything he done, and bobbing their heads to show they understood, and stooping a little and resting their hands on their thighs to watch him mark the places on the ground with his cane; and then he stood up straight and stiff where Sherburn had stood, frowning and having his hat-brim down over his eyes, and sung out, "Boggs!" and then fetched his cane down slow to a level, and says "Bang!" staggered backwards, says "Bang!" again, and fell down flat on his back. The people that had seen the thing said he done it perfect; said it was just exactly the way it all happened. Then as much as a dozen people got out their bottles and treated him.

Well, by and by somebody said Sherburn ought to be lynched. In about a minute everybody was saying it; so away they went, mad and yelling, and snatching down every clothes-line they come to to do the hanging with.

Chapter XXII.

They swarmed up towards Sherburn's house, a-whooping and raging like Injuns, and everything had to clear the way or get run over and tromped to mush, and it was awful to see. Children was heeling it ahead of the mob, screaming and trying to get out of the way; and every window along the road was full of women's heads, and there was nigger boys in every tree, and bucks and wenches looking over every fence; and as soon as the mob would get nearly to them they would break and skaddle back out of reach. Lots of the women and girls was crying and taking on, scared most to death.

They swarmed up in front of Sherburn's palings as thick as they could jam together, and you couldn't hear yourself think for the noise. It was a little twenty-foot yard. Some sung out "Tear down the fence! tear down the fence!" Then there was a racket of ripping and tearing and smashing, and down she goes, and the front wall of the crowd begins to roll in like a wave.

Just then Sherburn steps out on to the roof of his little front porch, with a double-barrel gun in his hand, and takes his stand, perfectly ca'm and deliberate, not saying a word. The racket stopped, and the wave sucked back.

Sherburn never said a word–just stood there, looking down. The stillness was awful creepy and uncomfortable. Sherburn run his eye slow along the crowd; and wherever it struck the people tried a little to out-gaze him, but they couldn't; they dropped their eyes and looked sneaky. Then pretty soon Sherburn sort of laughed; not the pleasant kind, but the kind that makes you feel like when you are eating bread that's got sand in it.

Then he says, slow and scornful:

"The idea of YOU lynching anybody! It's amusing. The idea of you thinking you had pluck enough to lynch a MAN! Because you're brave enough to tar and feather poor friendless cast-out women that come along here, did that make you think you had grit enough to lay your hands on a MAN? Why, a MAN'S safe in the hands of ten thousand of your kind—as long as it's daytime and you're not behind him.

"Do I know you? I know you clear through was born and raised in the South, and I've lived in the North; so I know the average all around. The average man's a coward. In the North he lets anybody walk over him that wants to, and goes home and prays for a humble spirit to bear it. In the South one man all by himself, has stopped a stage full of men in the daytime, and robbed the lot. Your newspapers call you a brave people so much that you think you are braver than any other people—whereas you're just AS brave, and no braver. Why don't your juries hang murderers? Because they're afraid the man's friends will shoot them in the back, in the dark—and it's just what they WOULD do.

"So they always acquit; and then a MAN goes in the night, with a hundred masked cowards at his back and lynches the rascal. Your mistake is, that you didn't bring a man with you; that's one mistake, and the other is that you didn't come in the dark and fetch your masks. You brought PART of a man—Buck Harkness, there—and if you hadn't had him to start you, you'd a taken it out in blowing.

"You didn't want to come. The average man don't like trouble and danger. YOU don't like trouble and danger. But if only HALF a man—like Buck Harkness, there—shouts 'Lynch him! lynch him!' you're afraid to back down—afraid you'll be found out to be what you are—COWARDS—and so you raise a yell, and hang yourselves on to that half-a-man's coat-tail, and come raging up here, swearing what big things you're going to do. The pitifulest thing out is a mob; that's what an army is—a mob; they don't fight with courage that's born in them, but with courage that's borrowed from their mass, and from their officers. But a mob without any MAN at the head of it is BENEATH pitifulness. Now the thing for YOU to do is to droop your tails and go home and crawl in a hole. If any real lynching's going to be done it will be done in the dark, Southern fashion; and when they come they'll bring their masks, and fetch a MAN along. Now LEAVE—and take your half-a-man with you"—tossing his gun up across his left arm and cocking it when he says this.

The crowd washed back sudden, and then broke all apart, and went tearing off every which way, and Buck Harkness he heeled it after them, looking tolerable cheap. I could a stayed if I wanted to, but I didn't want to.

Critical Eye

For Discussion

a. Why does the mob retreat in the presence of a "real man"?

b. Looking at Twain's "The Lowest Animal," how does this iconic novel figure into the points raised by Twain in this essay?

Re-approaching the Reading

Col. Sherburn has maliciously killed Boggs, yet he is presented to the reader as being wise and heroic–a man of character. What commentary is Twain making on responsibility and keeping one's word?

Writing Assignment

Examine this excerpt alongside of Ida B. Wells' "Lynch Law in America." Note how she describes in her speech the barbarity that Col. Sherburn mentions. Why does the "mob" in both texts lead to the absence of humanity?

IDA B. WELLS-BARNETT

LYNCH LAW IN AMERICA

OUR country's national crime is lynching. It is not the creature of an hour, the sudden outburst of uncontrolled fury, or the unspeakable brutality of an insane mob. It represents the cool, calculating deliberation of intelligent people who openly avow that there is an "unwritten law" that justifies them in putting human beings to death without complaint under oath, without trial by jury, without opportunity to make defense, and without right of appeal. The "unwritten law" first found excuse with the rough, rugged, and determined man who left the civilized centers of eastern States to seek for quick returns in the gold-fields of the far West. Following in uncertain pursuit of continually eluding fortune, they dared the savagery of the Indians, the hardships of mountain travel, and the constant terror of border State outlaws. Naturally, they felt slight toleration for traitors in their own ranks. It was enough to fight the enemies from without; woe to the foe within! Far removed from and entirely without protection of the courts of civilized life, these fortune-seekers made laws to meet their varying emergencies. The thief who stole a horse, the bully who "jumped" a claim, was a common enemy. If caught he was promptly tried, and if found guilty was hanged to the tree under which the court convened.

Those were busy days of busy men. They had no time to give the prisoner a bill of exception or stay of execution. The only way a man had to secure a stay of execution was to behave himself. Judge Lynch was original in methods but exceedingly effective in procedure. He made the charge, impaneled the jurors, and directed the execution. When the court adjourned, the prisoner was dead. Thus lynch law held sway in the far West until civilization spread into the Territories and the orderly processes of law took its place. The emergency no longer existing, lynching gradually disappeared from the West.

But the spirit of mob procedure seemed to have fastened itself upon the lawless classes, and the grim process that at first was invoked to declare justice was made the excuse to wreak vengeance and cover crime. It next appeared in the South, where centuries of Anglo-Saxon civilization had made effective all the safeguards of court procedure. No emergency called for lynch law. It asserted its sway in defiance of law and in favor of anarchy. There it has flourished ever since, marking the thirty years of its existence with the inhuman butchery of more than ten thousand men, women, and children by shooting, drowning, hanging, and burning them alive. Not only this, but so potent is the force of example that the lynching mania has spread throughout the North and middle West. It is now no uncommon thing to read of lynchings north of Mason and Dixon's line, and those most responsible for this fashion gleefully point to these instances and assert that the North is no better than the South.

This is the work of the "unwritten law" about which so much is said, and in whose behest butchery is made a pastime and national savagery condoned. The first statute of this "unwritten law" was written in the blood of thousands of brave men who thought that a government that was good enough to create a citizenship was strong enough to protect it. Under the authority of a national law that gave every citizen the right to vote, the newly-made citizens chose to exercise their suffrage. But the reign of the national law was short-lived and illusionary. Hardly had the sentences dried upon the statute-books before one Southern State after another raised the cry against "negro domination" and proclaimed there was an "unwritten law" that justified any means to resist it.

The method then inaugurated was the outrages by the "red-shirt" bands of Louisiana, South Carolina, and other Southern States, which were succeeded by the Ku-Klux Klans. These advocates of the "unwritten law" boldly avowed their purpose to intimidate, suppress, and nullify the negro's right to vote. In support of its plans the Ku-Klux Klans, the "red-shirt" and similar organizations proceeded to beat, exile, and kill negroes until the purpose of their organization was accomplished and the supremacy of the "unwritten law" was effected. Thus lynchings began in the South, rapidly spreading into the various States until the national law was nullified and the reign of the "unwritten law" was supreme. Men were taken from their homes by "red-shirt" bands and stripped, beaten, and exiled; others were assassinated when their political prominence made them obnoxious to their political opponents; while the Ku-Klux barbarism of election days, reveling in the butchery of thousands of colored voters, furnished records in Congressional investigations that are a disgrace to civilization.

The alleged menace of universal suffrage having been avoided by the absolute suppression of the negro vote, the spirit of mob murder should have been satisfied and the butchery of negroes should have ceased. But men, women, and children were the victims of murder by individuals and murder by mobs, just as they had been when killed at the demands of the "unwritten law" to prevent "negro domination." Negroes were killed for disputing over terms of contracts with their employers. If a few barns were burned some colored man was killed to stop it. If a colored man resented the imposition of a white man and the two came to blows, the colored man had to die, either at the hands of the white man then and there or later at the hands of a mob that speedily gathered. If he showed a spirit of courageous manhood he was hanged for his pains, and the killing was justified by the declaration that he was a "saucy nigger." Colored women have been murdered because they refused to tell the mobs where relatives could be found for "lynching bees." Boys of fourteen years have been lynched by white representatives of American civilization. In fact, for all kinds of offenses–and, for no offenses–from murders to misdemeanors, men and women are put to death without judge or jury; so that, although the political excuse was no longer necessary, the wholesale murder of human beings went on just the same. A new name was given to the killings and a new excuse was invented for so doing.

Again the aid of the "unwritten law" is invoked, and again it comes to the rescue. During the last ten years a new statute has been added to the "unwritten law." This statute proclaims that for certain crimes or alleged crimes no negro shall be allowed a trial; that no white woman shall be compelled to charge an assault under oath or to submit any such charge to the investigation of a court of law. The result is that many men have been put to death whose innocence was afterward established; and to-day, under this reign of the "unwritten law," no colored man, no matter what his reputation, is safe from lynching if a white woman, no matter what her standing or motive, cares to charge him with insult or assault.

It is considered a sufficient excuse and reasonable justification to put a prisoner to death under this "unwritten law" for the frequently repeated charge that these lynching horrors are necessary to prevent crimes against women. The sentiment of the country has been appealed to, in describing the isolated condition of white families in thickly populated negro districts; and the charge is made that these homes are in as great danger as if they were surrounded by wild beasts. And the world has accepted this theory without let or hindrance. In many cases there has been open expression that the fate meted out to the victim was only what he deserved. In many other instances there has been a silence that says more forcibly than words can proclaim it that it is right and proper that a human being should be seized by a mob and burned to death upon the unsworn and the uncorroborated charge of his accuser. No matter that our laws presume every man innocent until he is proved guilty; no matter that it leaves a certain class of individuals completely at the mercy of another class; no matter that it encourages those criminally disposed to blacken their faces and commit any crime in the calendar so long as they can throw suspicion on some negro, as is frequently done, and then lead a mob to take his life; no matter that mobs make a farce of the law and a mockery of justice; no matter that hundreds of boys are being hardened in crime and schooled in vice by the repetition of such scenes before their eyes–if a white woman declares herself insulted or assaulted, some life must pay the penalty, with all the horrors of the Spanish Inquisition and all the barbarism of the Middle Ages. The world looks on and says it is well.

Not only are two hundred men and women put to death annually, on the average, in this country by mobs, but these lives are taken with the greatest publicity. In many instances the leading citizens aid and abet by their presence when they do not participate, and the leading journals inflame the public mind to the lynching point with scare-head articles and offers of rewards. Whenever a burning is advertised to take place, the railroads run excursions, photographs are taken, and the same jubilee is indulged in that characterized the public hangings of one hundred years ago. There is, however, this difference: in those old days the multitude that stood by was permitted only to guy or jeer. The nineteenth century lynching mob cuts off ears, toes, and fingers, strips off flesh, and distributes portions of the body as souvenirs among the crowd. If the leaders of the mob are so minded, coal-oil is poured over the body and the victim is then roasted to death. This has been done in Texarkana and Paris, Tex., in Bardswell, Ky., and in Newman, Ga. In Paris the officers of the law delivered the prisoner to the mob. The mayor gave the school children a holiday and the railroads ran excursion trains so that the people might see a human being burned to death. In Texarkana, the year before, men and boys amused themselves by cutting off strips of flesh and thrusting knives into their helpless victim. At Newman, Ga., of the present year, the mob tried every conceivable torture to compel the victim to cry out and confess, before they set fire to the faggots that burned him. But their trouble was all in vain–he never uttered a cry, and they could not make him confess.

This condition of affairs were brutal enough and horrible enough if it were true that lynchings occurred only because of the commission of crimes against women–as is constantly declared by ministers, editors, lawyers, teachers, statesmen, and even by women themselves. It has been to the interest of those who did the lynching to blacken the good name of the helpless and defenseless victims of their hate. For this reason they publish at every possible opportunity this excuse for lynching, hoping thereby not only to palliate their own crime but at the same time to prove the negro a moral monster and unworthy of the respect and sympathy of the civilized world. But this alleged reason adds to the deliberate injustice of the mob's work. Instead of lynchings being caused by assaults upon women, the statistics show that not one-third of the victims of lynchings are even charged with such crimes. The Chicago Tribune, which publishes annually lynching statistics, is authority for the following:

In 1892, when lynching reached high-water mark, there were 241 persons lynched. The entire number is divided among the following States:

Alabama	22	Montana	4
Arkansas	25	New York	1
California	3	North Carolina	5
Florida	11	North Dakota	1
Georgia	17	Ohio	3
Idaho	8	South Carolina	5
Illinois	1	Tennessee	28
Kansas	3	Texas	15
Kentucky	9	Virginia	7
Louisiana	29	West Virginia	5
Maryland	1	Wyoming	9
Mississippi	16	Arizona Ter	3
Missouri	6	Oklahoma	2

Of this number, 160 were of negro descent. Four of them were lynched in New York, Ohio, and Kansas; the remainder were murdered in the South. Five of this number were females. The charges for which they were lynched cover a wide range. They are as follows:

Rape	46	Attempted rape	11
Murder	58	Suspected robbery	4
Rioting	3	Larceny	1
Race Prejudice	6	Self-defense	1
No cause given	4	Insulting women	2
Incendiarism	6	Desperadoes	6
Robbery	6	Fraud	1
Assault and battery			1
Attempted murder			2
No offense stated, boy and girl			2

In the case of the boy and girl above referred to, their father, named Hastings, was accused of the murder of a white man. His fourteen-year-old daughter and sixteen-year-old son were hanged and their bodies filled with bullets; then the father was also lynched. This occurred in November, 1892, at Jonesville, La.

Indeed, the record for the last twenty years shows exactly the same or a smaller proportion who have been charged with this horrible crime. Quite a number of the one-third alleged cases of assault that have been personally investigated by the writer have shown that there was no foundation in fact for the charges; yet the claim is not made that there were no real culprits among them. The negro has been too long associated with the white man not to have copied his vices as well as his virtues. But the negro resents and utterly repudiates the efforts to blacken his good name by asserting that assaults upon women are peculiar to his race. The negro has suffered far more from the commission of this crime against the women of his race by white men than the white race has ever suffered through *his* crimes. Very scant notice is taken of the matter when this is the condition of affairs. What becomes a crime deserving capital punishment when the tables are turned is a matter of small moment when the negro woman is the accusing party.

But since the world has accepted this false and unjust statement, and the burden of proof has been placed upon the negro to vindicate his race, he is taking steps to do so. The Anti-Lynching Bureau of the National Afro-American Council is arranging to have every lynching investigated and publish the facts to the world, as has been done in the case of Sam Hose, who was burned alive last April at Newman, Ga. The detective's report showed that Hose killed Cranford, his employer, in self-defense, and that, while a mob was organizing to hunt Hose to punish him for killing a white man, not till twenty-four hours after the murder was the charge of rape, embellished with psychological and physical impossibilities, circulated. That gave an impetus to the hunt, and the Atlanta *Constitution's* reward of $500 keyed the mob to the necessary burning and roasting pitch. Of five hundred newspaper clippings of that horrible affair, nine-tenths of them assumed Hose's guilt–simply because his murderers said so, and because it is the fashion to believe the negro peculiarly addicted to this species of crime. All the negro asks is justice–a fair and impartial trial in the courts of the country. That given, he will abide the result.

But this question affects the entire American nation, and from several points of view: First, on the ground of consistency. Our watchword has been "the land of the free and the home of the brave." Brave men do not gather by thousands to torture and murder a single individual, so gagged and bound he cannot make even feeble resistance or defense. Neither do brave men or women stand by and see such things done without compunction of conscience, nor read of them without protest. Our nation has been active and outspoken in its endeavors to right the wrongs of the Armenian Christian, the Russian Jew, the Irish Home Ruler, the native women of India, the Siberian exile, and the Cuban patriot. Surely it should be the nation's duty to correct its own evils!

Second, on the ground of economy. To those who fail to be convinced from any other point of view touching this momentous question, a consideration of the economic phase might not be amiss. It is generally known that mobs in Louisiana, Colorado, Wyoming, and other States have lynched subjects of other countries. When their different governments demanded satisfaction, our country was forced to confess her inability to protect said subjects in the several States because of our State-rights doctrines, or in turn demand punishment of the lynchers. This confession, while humiliating in the extreme, was not satisfactory; and, while the United States cannot protect, she can pay. This she has done, and it is certain will have to do again in the case of the recent lynching of Italians in Louisiana. The United States already has paid in indemnities for lynching nearly a half million dollars, as follows:

Paid China for Rock Springs (Wyo.) massacre $147,748.74

Paid China for outrages on Pacific Coast 276,619.75

Paid Italy for massacre of Italian prisoners at New Orleans 24,330.90

Paid Italy for lynchings at Walsenburg, Col. 10,000.00

Paid Great Britain for outrages on James Bain and Frederick Dawson 2,800.00

Third, for the honor of Anglo-Saxon civilization. No scoffer at our boasted American civilization could say anything more harsh of it than does the American white man himself who says he is unable to protect the honor of his women without resort to such brutal, inhuman, and degrading exhibitions as characterize "lynching bees." The cannibals of the South Sea Islands roast human beings alive to satisfy hunger. The red Indian of the Western plains tied his prisoner to the stake, tortured him, and danced in fiendish glee while his victim writhed in the flames. His savage, untutored mind suggested no better way than that of wreaking vengeance upon those who had wronged him. These people knew nothing about Christianity and did not profess to follow its teachings; but such primary laws as they had they lived up to. No nation, savage or civilized, save only the United States of America, has confessed its inability to protect its women save by hanging, shooting, and burning alleged offenders.

Finally, for love of country. No American travels abroad without blushing for shame for his country on this subject. And whatever the excuse that passes current in the United States, it avails nothing abroad. With all the powers of government in control; with all laws made by white men, administered by white judges, jurors, prosecuting attorneys, and sheriffs; with every office of the executive department filled by white men–no excuse can be offered for exchanging the orderly administration of justice for barbarous lynchings and "unwritten laws." Our country should be placed speedily above the plane of confessing herself a failure at self-government. This cannot be until Americans of every section, of broadest patriotism and best and wisest citizenship, not only see the defect in our country's armor but take the necessary steps to remedy it. Although lynchings have steadily increased in number and barbarity during the last twenty years, there has been no single effort put forth by the many moral and philanthropic forces of the country to put a stop to this wholesale slaughter. Indeed, the silence and seeming condonation grow more marked as the years go by.

A few months ago the conscience of this country was shocked because, after a two-weeks trial, a French judicial tribunal pronounced Captain Dreyfus guilty. And yet, in our own land and under our own flag, the writer can give day and detail of one thousand men, women, and children who during the last six years were put to death without trial before any tribunal on earth. Humiliating indeed, but altogether unanswerable, was the reply of the French press to our protest: "Stop your lynchings at home before you send your protests abroad."

CRITICAL EYE

For Discussion

a. Wells-Barnett is addressing a White audience who exists within a heavily racially charged world. Given the history of race and racial matters, she is unable to make a plea for the cessation of lynching based upon goodness and humanity. Instead, she discusses American law and the biases and abuses suffered by her people due to legal inequality. Is this effective?

Re-approaching the Reading

Compare Wells-Barnett's argument to the one presented by Frederick Douglass about slavery. How are their revelations the same? Given the emancipation of the slaves and the abolishment of slavery, why has very little changed for oppressed Blacks in Wells-Barnett's world?

Writing Assignment

In Todd Craig's essay about Hip Hop music, he argues for a socially and politically responsible music that addresses the needs of the Black community. Based on Wells-Barnett's assertions about the worth of Black life, how is Craig's claim that the most popular genre of music today is desperately in need of a new kind of message–or, based on Wells-Barnett's plea, an "old" message?

WILLIAM SHAKESPEARE

THE TRAGEDY OF MACBETH

ACT I

SCENE I. A desert place.

Thunder and lightning. Enter three Witches

First Witch

When shall we three meet again
In thunder, lightning, or in rain?

Second Witch

When the hurlyburly's done,
When the battle's lost and won.

Third Witch

That will be ere the set of sun.

First Witch

Where the place?

Second Witch

Upon the heath.

Third Witch

There to meet with Macbeth.

First Witch

I come, Graymalkin!

Second Witch

Paddock calls.

Third Witch

Anon.

ALL

Fair is foul, and foul is fair:
Hover through the fog and filthy air.

Exeunt

SCENE II. A camp near Forres.

Alarum within. Enter DUNCAN, MALCOLM, DONALBAIN, LENNOX, with Attendants, meeting a bleeding Sergeant

DUNCAN

What bloody man is that? He can report,
As seemeth by his plight, of the revolt
The newest state.

MALCOLM

This is the sergeant
Who like a good and hardy soldier fought
'Gainst my captivity. Hail, brave friend!
Say to the king the knowledge of the broil
As thou didst leave it.

Sergeant

Doubtful it stood;
As two spent swimmers, that do cling together
And choke their art. The merciless Macdonwald–
Worthy to be a rebel, for to that
The multiplying villanies of nature
Do swarm upon him–from the western isles
Of kerns and gallowglasses is supplied;
And fortune, on his damned quarrel smiling,

Show'd like a rebel's whore: but all's too weak:
For brave Macbeth–well he deserves that name–
Disdaining fortune, with his brandish'd steel,
Which smoked with bloody execution,
Like valour's minion carved out his passage
Till he faced the slave;
Which ne'er shook hands, nor bade farewell to him,
Till he unseam'd him from the nave to the chaps,
And fix'd his head upon our battlements.

DUNCAN

O valiant cousin! worthy gentleman!

Sergeant

As whence the sun 'gins his reflection
Shipwrecking storms and direful thunders break,
So from that spring whence comfort seem'd to come
Discomfort swells. Mark, king of Scotland, mark:
No sooner justice had with valour arm'd
Compell'd these skipping kerns to trust their heels,
But the Norweyan lord surveying vantage,
With furbish'd arms and new supplies of men
Began a fresh assault.

DUNCAN

Dismay'd not this
Our captains, Macbeth and Banquo?

Sergeant

Yes;
As sparrows eagles, or the hare the lion.
If I say sooth, I must report they were
As cannons overcharged with double cracks, so they
Doubly redoubled strokes upon the foe:
Except they meant to bathe in reeking wounds,
Or memorise another Golgotha,
I cannot tell.
But I am faint, my gashes cry for help.

DUNCAN

So well thy words become thee as thy wounds;
They smack of honour both. Go get him surgeons.

Exit Sergeant, attended

Who comes here?

Enter ROSS

MALCOLM

The worthy thane of Ross.

LENNOX

What a haste looks through his eyes! So should he look
That seems to speak things strange.

ROSS

God save the king!

DUNCAN

Whence camest thou, worthy thane?

ROSS

From Fife, great king;
Where the Norweyan banners flout the sky
And fan our people cold. Norway himself,
With terrible numbers,
Assisted by that most disloyal traitor
The thane of Cawdor, began a dismal conflict;
Till that Bellona's bridegroom, lapp'd in proof,
Confronted him with self-comparisons,
Point against point rebellious, arm 'gainst arm.
Curbing his lavish spirit: and, to conclude,
The victory fell on us.

DUNCAN

Great happiness!

ROSS

That now
Sweno, the Norways' king, craves composition:
Nor would we deign him burial of his men
Till he disbursed at Saint Colme's inch
Ten thousand dollars to our general use.

DUNCAN

No more that thane of Cawdor shall deceive
Our bosom interest: go pronounce his present death,
And with his former title greet Macbeth.

ROSS

I'll see it done.

DUNCAN

What he hath lost noble Macbeth hath won.

Exeunt

SCENE III. A heath near Forres.

Thunder. Enter the three Witches

First Witch

Where hast thou been, sister?

Second Witch

Killing swine.

Third Witch

Sister, where thou?

First Witch

A sailor's wife had chestnuts in her lap,
And munch'd, and munch'd, and munch'd:–
'Give me,' quoth I:
'Aroint thee, witch!' the rump-fed ronyon cries.
Her husband's to Aleppo gone, master o' the Tiger:
But in a sieve I'll thither sail,
And, like a rat without a tail,
I'll do, I'll do, and I'll do.

Second Witch

I'll give thee a wind.

First Witch

Thou'rt kind.

Third Witch

And I another.

First Witch

I myself have all the other,
And the very ports they blow,
All the quarters that they know
I' the shipman's card.
I will drain him dry as hay:
Sleep shall neither night nor day
Hang upon his pent-house lid;
He shall live a man forbid:
Weary se'nnights nine times nine
Shall he dwindle, peak and pine:
Though his bark cannot be lost,
Yet it shall be tempest-tost.
Look what I have.

Second Witch

Show me, show me.

First Witch

Here I have a pilot's thumb,
Wreck'd as homeward he did come.

Drum within

Third Witch

A drum, a drum!
Macbeth doth come.

ALL

The weird sisters, hand in hand,
Posters of the sea and land,
Thus do go about, about:
Thrice to thine and thrice to mine
And thrice again, to make up nine.
Peace! the charm's wound up.

Enter MACBETH and BANQUO

MACBETH

So foul and fair a day I have not seen.

BANQUO

How far is't call'd to Forres? What are these
So wither'd and so wild in their attire,
That look not like the inhabitants o' the earth,
And yet are on't? Live you? or are you aught
That man may question? You seem to understand me,
By each at once her chappy finger laying
Upon her skinny lips: you should be women,
And yet your beards forbid me to interpret
That you are so.

MACBETH

Speak, if you can: what are you?

First Witch

All hail, Macbeth! hail to thee, thane of Glamis!

Second Witch

All hail, Macbeth, hail to thee, thane of Cawdor!

Third Witch

All hail, Macbeth, thou shalt be king hereafter!

BANQUO

Good sir, why do you start; and seem to fear
Things that do sound so fair? I' the name of truth,
Are ye fantastical, or that indeed
Which outwardly ye show? My noble partner
You greet with present grace and great prediction
Of noble having and of royal hope,
That he seems rapt withal: to me you speak not.
If you can look into the seeds of time,
And say which grain will grow and which will not,
Speak then to me, who neither beg nor fear
Your favours nor your hate.

First Witch

Hail!

Second Witch

Hail!

Third Witch

Hail!

First Witch

Lesser than Macbeth, and greater.

Second Witch

Not so happy, yet much happier.

Third Witch

Thou shalt get kings, though thou be none:
So all hail, Macbeth and Banquo!

First Witch

Banquo and Macbeth, all hail!

MACBETH

Stay, you imperfect speakers, tell me more:
By Sinel's death I know I am thane of Glamis;
But how of Cawdor? the thane of Cawdor lives,
A prosperous gentleman; and to be king
Stands not within the prospect of belief,
No more than to be Cawdor. Say from whence
You owe this strange intelligence? or why
Upon this blasted heath you stop our way
With such prophetic greeting? Speak, I charge you.

Witches vanish

BANQUO

The earth hath bubbles, as the water has,
And these are of them. Whither are they vanish'd?

MACBETH

Into the air; and what seem'd corporal melted
As breath into the wind. Would they had stay'd!

BANQUO

Were such things here as we do speak about?
Or have we eaten on the insane root

That takes the reason prisoner?

MACBETH

Your children shall be kings.

BANQUO

You shall be king.

MACBETH

And thane of Cawdor too: went it not so?

BANQUO

To the selfsame tune and words. Who's here?

Enter ROSS and ANGUS

ROSS

The king hath happily received, Macbeth,
The news of thy success; and when he reads
Thy personal venture in the rebels' fight,
His wonders and his praises do contend
Which should be thine or his: silenced with that,
In viewing o'er the rest o' the selfsame day,
He finds thee in the stout Norweyan ranks,
Nothing afeard of what thyself didst make,
Strange images of death. As thick as hail
Came post with post; and every one did bear
Thy praises in his kingdom's great defence,
And pour'd them down before him.

ANGUS

We are sent
To give thee from our royal master thanks;
Only to herald thee into his sight,
Not pay thee.

ROSS

And, for an earnest of a greater honour,
He bade me, from him, call thee thane of Cawdor:
In which addition, hail, most worthy thane!
For it is thine.

BANQUO

What, can the devil speak true?

MACBETH

The thane of Cawdor lives: why do you dress me
In borrow'd robes?

ANGUS

Who was the thane lives yet;
But under heavy judgment bears that life
Which he deserves to lose. Whether he was combined
With those of Norway, or did line the rebel
With hidden help and vantage, or that with both
He labour'd in his country's wreck, I know not;
But treasons capital, confess'd and proved,
Have overthrown him.

MACBETH

[Aside] Glamis, and thane of Cawdor!
The greatest is behind.

To ROSS and ANGUS

Thanks for your pains.

To BANQUO

Do you not hope your children shall be kings,
When those that gave the thane of Cawdor to me
Promised no less to them?

BANQUO

That trusted home
Might yet enkindle you unto the crown,
Besides the thane of Cawdor. But 'tis strange:
And oftentimes, to win us to our harm,
The instruments of darkness tell us truths,
Win us with honest trifles, to betray's
In deepest consequence.
Cousins, a word, I pray you.

MACBETH

[Aside] Two truths are told,
As happy prologues to the swelling act
Of the imperial theme.–I thank you, gentlemen.

Aside

Cannot be ill, cannot be good: if ill,
Why hath it given me earnest of success,
Commencing in a truth? I am thane of Cawdor:
If good, why do I yield to that suggestion
Whose horrid image doth unfix my hair
And make my seated heart knock at my ribs,
Against the use of nature? Present fears
Are less than horrible imaginings:
My thought, whose murder yet is but fantastical,
Shakes so my single state of man that function
Is smother'd in surmise, and nothing is
But what is not.

BANQUO

Look, how our partner's rapt.

MACBETH

[Aside] If chance will have me king, why,
chance may crown me,
Without my stir.

BANQUO

New horrors come upon him,
Like our strange garments, cleave not to their
mould
But with the aid of use.

MACBETH

[Aside] Come what come may,
Time and the hour runs through the roughest
day.

BANQUO

Worthy Macbeth, we stay upon your leisure.

MACBETH

Give me your favour: my dull brain was
wrought
With things forgotten. Kind gentlemen, your
pains
Are register'd where every day I turn
The leaf to read them. Let us toward the king.
Think upon what hath chanced, and, at more
time,
The interim having weigh'd it, let us speak
Our free hearts each to other.

BANQUO

Very gladly.

MACBETH

Till then, enough. Come, friends.

Exeunt

SCENE IV. Forres. The palace.

Flourish. Enter DUNCAN, MALCOLM, DONAL-BAIN, LENNOX, and Attendants

DUNCAN

Is execution done on Cawdor? Are not
Those in commission yet return'd?

MALCOLM

My liege,
They are not yet come back. But I have spoke
With one that saw him die: who did report
That very frankly he confess'd his treasons,
Implored your highness' pardon and set forth
A deep repentance: nothing in his life
Became him like the leaving it; he died
As one that had been studied in his death
To throw away the dearest thing he owed,
As 'twere a careless trifle.

DUNCAN

There's no art
To find the mind's construction in the face:
He was a gentleman on whom I built
An absolute trust.

Enter MACBETH, BANQUO, ROSS, and ANGUS

O worthiest cousin!
The sin of my ingratitude even now
Was heavy on me: thou art so far before
That swiftest wing of recompense is slow
To overtake thee. Would thou hadst less
deserved,
That the proportion both of thanks and payment

Might have been mine! only I have left to say,
More is thy due than more than all can pay.

MACBETH

The service and the loyalty I owe,
In doing it, pays itself. Your highness' part
Is to receive our duties; and our duties
Are to your throne and state children and servants,
Which do but what they should, by doing every thing
Safe toward your love and honour.

DUNCAN

Welcome hither:
I have begun to plant thee, and will labour
To make thee full of growing. Noble Banquo,
That hast no less deserved, nor must be known
No less to have done so, let me enfold thee
And hold thee to my heart.

BANQUO

There if I grow,
The harvest is your own.

DUNCAN

My plenteous joys,
Wanton in fulness, seek to hide themselves
In drops of sorrow. Sons, kinsmen, thanes,
And you whose places are the nearest, know
We will establish our estate upon
Our eldest, Malcolm, whom we name hereafter
The Prince of Cumberland; which honour must
Not unaccompanied invest him only,
But signs of nobleness, like stars, shall shine
On all deservers. From hence to Inverness,
And bind us further to you.

MACBETH

The rest is labour, which is not used for you:
I'll be myself the harbinger and make joyful
The hearing of my wife with your approach;
So humbly take my leave.

DUNCAN

My worthy Cawdor!

MACBETH

[Aside] The Prince of Cumberland! that is a step
On which I must fall down, or else o'erleap,
For in my way it lies. Stars, hide your fires;
Let not light see my black and deep desires:
The eye wink at the hand; yet let that be,
Which the eye fears, when it is done, to see.

Exit

DUNCAN

True, worthy Banquo; he is full so valiant,
And in his commendations I am fed;
It is a banquet to me. Let's after him,
Whose care is gone before to bid us welcome:
It is a peerless kinsman.

Flourish. Exeunt

SCENE V. Inverness. Macbeth's castle.

Enter LADY MACBETH, reading a letter

LADY MACBETH

'They met me in the day of success: and I have learned by the perfectest report, they have more in them than mortal knowledge. When I burned in desire to question them further, they made themselves air, into which they vanished. Whiles I stood rapt in the wonder of it, came missives from the king, who all-hailed me 'Thane of Cawdor;' by which title, before, these weird sisters saluted me, and referred me to the coming on of time, with 'Hail, king that shalt be!' This have I thought good to deliver thee, my dearest partner of greatness, that thou mightst not lose the dues of rejoicing, by being ignorant of what greatness is promised thee. Lay it to thy heart, and farewell.'
Glamis thou art, and Cawdor; and shalt be
What thou art promised: yet do I fear thy nature;
It is too full o' the milk of human kindness
To catch the nearest way: thou wouldst be great;
Art not without ambition, but without

The illness should attend it: what thou wouldst highly,
That wouldst thou holily; wouldst not play false,
And yet wouldst wrongly win: thou'ldst have, great Glamis,
That which cries 'Thus thou must do, if thou have it;
And that which rather thou dost fear to do
Than wishest should be undone.' Hie thee hither,
That I may pour my spirits in thine ear;
And chastise with the valour of my tongue
All that impedes thee from the golden round,
Which fate and metaphysical aid doth seem
To have thee crown'd withal.

Enter a Messenger

What is your tidings?

Messenger

The king comes here to-night.

LADY MACBETH

Thou'rt mad to say it:
Is not thy master with him? who, were't so,
Would have inform'd for preparation.

Messenger

So please you, it is true: our thane is coming:
One of my fellows had the speed of him,
Who, almost dead for breath, had scarcely more
Than would make up his message.

LADY MACBETH

Give him tending;
He brings great news.

Exit Messenger

The raven himself is hoarse
That croaks the fatal entrance of Duncan
Under my battlements. Come, you spirits
That tend on mortal thoughts, unsex me here,
And fill me from the crown to the toe top-full
Of direst cruelty! make thick my blood;
Stop up the access and passage to remorse,
That no compunctious visitings of nature
Shake my fell purpose, nor keep peace between
The effect and it! Come to my woman's breasts,
And take my milk for gall, you murdering ministers,
Wherever in your sightless substances
You wait on nature's mischief! Come, thick night,
And pall thee in the dunnest smoke of hell,
That my keen knife see not the wound it makes,
Nor heaven peep through the blanket of the dark,
To cry 'Hold, hold!'

Enter MACBETH

Great Glamis! worthy Cawdor!
Greater than both, by the all-hail hereafter!
Thy letters have transported me beyond
This ignorant present, and I feel now
The future in the instant.

MACBETH

My dearest love,
Duncan comes here to-night.

LADY MACBETH

And when goes hence?

MACBETH

To-morrow, as he purposes.

LADY MACBETH

O, never
Shall sun that morrow see!
Your face, my thane, is as a book where men
May read strange matters. To beguile the time,
Look like the time; bear welcome in your eye,
Your hand, your tongue: look like the innocent flower,
But be the serpent under't. He that's coming
Must be provided for: and you shall put
This night's great business into my dispatch;
Which shall to all our nights and days to come
Give solely sovereign sway and masterdom.

MACBETH

We will speak further.

LADY MACBETH

Only look up clear;
To alter favour ever is to fear:
Leave all the rest to me.

Exeunt

SCENE VI. Before Macbeth's castle.

Hautboys and torches. Enter DUNCAN, MALCOLM, DONALBAIN, BANQUO, LENNOX, MACDUFF, ROSS, ANGUS, and Attendants

DUNCAN

This castle hath a pleasant seat; the air
Nimbly and sweetly recommends itself
Unto our gentle senses.

BANQUO

This guest of summer,
The temple-haunting martlet, does approve,
By his loved mansionry, that the heaven's breath
Smells wooingly here: no jutty, frieze,
Buttress, nor coign of vantage, but this bird
Hath made his pendent bed and procreant cradle:
Where they most breed and haunt, I have observed,
The air is delicate.

Enter LADY MACBETH

DUNCAN

See, see, our honour'd hostess!
The love that follows us sometime is our trouble,
Which still we thank as love. Herein I teach you
How you shall bid God 'ild us for your pains,
And thank us for your trouble.

LADY MACBETH

All our service
In every point twice done and then done double
Were poor and single business to contend
Against those honours deep and broad wherewith
Your majesty loads our house: for those of old,
And the late dignities heap'd up to them,
We rest your hermits.

DUNCAN

Where's the thane of Cawdor?
We coursed him at the heels, and had a purpose
To be his purveyor: but he rides well;
And his great love, sharp as his spur, hath holp him
To his home before us. Fair and noble hostess,
We are your guest to-night.

LADY MACBETH

Your servants ever
Have theirs, themselves and what is theirs, in compt,
To make their audit at your highness' pleasure,
Still to return your own.

DUNCAN

Give me your hand;
Conduct me to mine host: we love him highly,
And shall continue our graces towards him.
By your leave, hostess.

Exeunt

SCENE VII. Macbeth's castle.

Hautboys and torches. Enter a Sewer, and divers Servants with dishes and service, and pass over the stage. Then enter MACBETH

MACBETH

If it were done when 'tis done, then 'twere well
It were done quickly: if the assassination
Could trammel up the consequence, and catch
With his surcease success; that but this blow
Might be the be-all and the end-all here,
But here, upon this bank and shoal of time,
We'ld jump the life to come. But in these cases
We still have judgment here; that we but teach

Bloody instructions, which, being taught, return
To plague the inventor: this even-handed justice
Commends the ingredients of our poison'd chalice
To our own lips. He's here in double trust;
First, as I am his kinsman and his subject,
Strong both against the deed; then, as his host,
Who should against his murderer shut the door,
Not bear the knife myself. Besides, this Duncan
Hath borne his faculties so meek, hath been
So clear in his great office, that his virtues
Will plead like angels, trumpet-tongued, against
The deep damnation of his taking-off;
And pity, like a naked new-born babe,
Striding the blast, or heaven's cherubim, horsed
Upon the sightless couriers of the air,
Shall blow the horrid deed in every eye,
That tears shall drown the wind. I have no spur
To prick the sides of my intent, but only
Vaulting ambition, which o'erleaps itself
And falls on the other.

Enter LADY MACBETH

How now! what news?

LADY MACBETH

He has almost supp'd: why have you left the chamber?

MACBETH

Hath he ask'd for me?

LADY MACBETH

Know you not he has?

MACBETH

We will proceed no further in this business:
He hath honour'd me of late; and I have bought
Golden opinions from all sorts of people,
Which would be worn now in their newest gloss,
Not cast aside so soon.

LADY MACBETH

Was the hope drunk
Wherein you dress'd yourself? hath it slept since?
And wakes it now, to look so green and pale
At what it did so freely? From this time
Such I account thy love. Art thou afeard
To be the same in thine own act and valour
As thou art in desire? Wouldst thou have that
Which thou esteem'st the ornament of life,
And live a coward in thine own esteem,
Letting 'I dare not' wait upon 'I would,'
Like the poor cat i' the adage?

MACBETH

Prithee, peace:
I dare do all that may become a man;
Who dares do more is none.

LADY MACBETH

What beast was't, then,
That made you break this enterprise to me?
When you durst do it, then you were a man;
And, to be more than what you were, you would
Be so much more the man. Nor time nor place
Did then adhere, and yet you would make both:
They have made themselves, and that their fitness now
Does unmake you. I have given suck, and know
How tender 'tis to love the babe that milks me:
I would, while it was smiling in my face,
Have pluck'd my nipple from his boneless gums,
And dash'd the brains out, had I so sworn as you
Have done to this.

MACBETH

If we should fail?

LADY MACBETH

We fail!
But screw your courage to the sticking-place,

And we'll not fail. When Duncan is asleep–
Whereto the rather shall his day's hard journey
Soundly invite him–his two chamberlains
Will I with wine and wassail so convince
That memory, the warder of the brain,
Shall be a fume, and the receipt of reason
A limbeck only: when in swinish sleep
Their drenched natures lie as in a death,
What cannot you and I perform upon
The unguarded Duncan? what not put upon
His spongy officers, who shall bear the guilt
Of our great quell?

MACBETH

Bring forth men-children only;
For thy undaunted mettle should compose
Nothing but males. Will it not be received,
When we have mark'd with blood those sleepy two
Of his own chamber and used their very daggers,
That they have done't?

LADY MACBETH

Who dares receive it other,
As we shall make our griefs and clamour roar
Upon his death?

MACBETH

I am settled, and bend up
Each corporal agent to this terrible feat.
Away, and mock the time with fairest show:
False face must hide what the false heart doth know.

Exeunt

ACT II

SCENE I. Court of Macbeth's castle.

Enter BANQUO, and FLEANCE bearing a torch before him

BANQUO

How goes the night, boy?

FLEANCE

The moon is down; I have not heard the clock.

BANQUO

And she goes down at twelve.

FLEANCE

I take't, 'tis later, sir.

BANQUO

Hold, take my sword. There's husbandry in heaven;
Their candles are all out. Take thee that too.
A heavy summons lies like lead upon me,
And yet I would not sleep: merciful powers,
Restrain in me the cursed thoughts that nature
Gives way to in repose!

Enter MACBETH, and a Servant with a torch

Give me my sword.
Who's there?

MACBETH

A friend.

BANQUO

What, sir, not yet at rest? The king's a-bed:
He hath been in unusual pleasure, and
Sent forth great largess to your offices.
This diamond he greets your wife withal,
By the name of most kind hostess; and shut up
In measureless content.

MACBETH

Being unprepared,
Our will became the servant to defect;
Which else should free have wrought.

BANQUO

All's well.
I dreamt last night of the three weird sisters:
To you they have show'd some truth.

MACBETH

I think not of them:

Yet, when we can entreat an hour to serve,
We would spend it in some words upon that business,
If you would grant the time.

BANQUO

At your kind'st leisure.

MACBETH

If you shall cleave to my consent, when 'tis,
It shall make honour for you.

BANQUO

So I lose none
In seeking to augment it, but still keep
My bosom franchised and allegiance clear,
I shall be counsell'd.

MACBETH

Good repose the while!

BANQUO

Thanks, sir: the like to you!

Exeunt BANQUO and FLEANCE

MACBETH

Go bid thy mistress, when my drink is ready,
She strike upon the bell. Get thee to bed.

Exit Servant

Is this a dagger which I see before me,
The handle toward my hand? Come, let me clutch thee.
I have thee not, and yet I see thee still.
Art thou not, fatal vision, sensible
To feeling as to sight? or art thou but
A dagger of the mind, a false creation,
Proceeding from the heat-oppressed brain?
I see thee yet, in form as palpable
As this which now I draw.
Thou marshall'st me the way that I was going;
And such an instrument I was to use.
Mine eyes are made the fools o' the other senses,
Or else worth all the rest; I see thee still,
And on thy blade and dudgeon gouts of blood,
Which was not so before. There's no such thing:
It is the bloody business which informs
Thus to mine eyes. Now o'er the one half-world
Nature seems dead, and wicked dreams abuse
The curtain'd sleep; witchcraft celebrates
Pale Hecate's offerings, and wither'd murder,
Alarum'd by his sentinel, the wolf,
Whose howl's his watch, thus with his stealthy pace.
With Tarquin's ravishing strides, towards his design
Moves like a ghost. Thou sure and firm-set earth,
Hear not my steps, which way they walk, for fear
Thy very stones prate of my whereabout,
And take the present horror from the time,
Which now suits with it. Whiles I threat, he lives:
Words to the heat of deeds too cold breath gives.

A bell rings

I go, and it is done; the bell invites me.
Hear it not, Duncan; for it is a knell
That summons thee to heaven or to hell.

Exit

SCENE II. The same.

Enter LADY MACBETH

LADY MACBETH

That which hath made them drunk hath made me bold;
What hath quench'd them hath given me fire.
Hark! Peace!
It was the owl that shriek'd, the fatal bellman,
Which gives the stern'st good-night. He is about it:
The doors are open; and the surfeited grooms

Do mock their charge with snores: I have drugg'd their possets,
That death and nature do contend about them,
Whether they live or die.

MACBETH

[Within] Who's there? what, ho!

LADY MACBETH

Alack, I am afraid they have awaked,
And 'tis not done. The attempt and not the deed
Confounds us. Hark! I laid their daggers ready;
He could not miss 'em. Had he not resembled
My father as he slept, I had done't.

Enter MACBETH

My husband!

MACBETH

I have done the deed. Didst thou not hear a noise?

LADY MACBETH

I heard the owl scream and the crickets cry.
Did not you speak?

MACBETH

When?

LADY MACBETH

Now.

MACBETH

As I descended?

LADY MACBETH

Ay.

MACBETH

Hark!
Who lies i' the second chamber?

LADY MACBETH

Donalbain.

MACBETH

This is a sorry sight.

Looking on his hands

LADY MACBETH

A foolish thought, to say a sorry sight.

MACBETH

There's one did laugh in's sleep, and one cried 'Murder!'
That they did wake each other: I stood and heard them:
But they did say their prayers, and address'd them
Again to sleep.

LADY MACBETH

There are two lodged together.

MACBETH

One cried 'God bless us!' and 'Amen' the other;
As they had seen me with these hangman's hands.
Listening their fear, I could not say 'Amen,'
When they did say 'God bless us!'

LADY MACBETH

Consider it not so deeply.

MACBETH

But wherefore could not I pronounce 'Amen'?
I had most need of blessing, and 'Amen'
Stuck in my throat.

LADY MACBETH

These deeds must not be thought
After these ways; so, it will make us mad.

MACBETH

Methought I heard a voice cry 'Sleep no more!
Macbeth does murder sleep', the innocent sleep,
Sleep that knits up the ravell'd sleeve of care,
The death of each day's life, sore labour's bath,

Balm of hurt minds, great nature's second course,
Chief nourisher in life's feast,–

LADY MACBETH

What do you mean?

MACBETH

Still it cried 'Sleep no more!' to all the house:
'Glamis hath murder'd sleep, and therefore Cawdor
Shall sleep no more; Macbeth shall sleep no more.'

LADY MACBETH

Who was it that thus cried? Why, worthy thane,
You do unbend your noble strength, to think
So brainsickly of things. Go get some water,
And wash this filthy witness from your hand.
Why did you bring these daggers from the place?
They must lie there: go carry them; and smear
The sleepy grooms with blood.

MACBETH

I'll go no more:
I am afraid to think what I have done;
Look on't again I dare not.

LADY MACBETH

Infirm of purpose!
Give me the daggers: the sleeping and the dead
Are but as pictures: 'tis the eye of childhood
That fears a painted devil. If he do bleed,
I'll gild the faces of the grooms withal;
For it must seem their guilt.

Exit. Knocking within

MACBETH

Whence is that knocking?
How is't with me, when every noise appals me?
What hands are here? ha! they pluck out mine eyes.
Will all great Neptune's ocean wash this blood
Clean from my hand? No, this my hand will rather
The multitudinous seas in incarnadine,
Making the green one red.

Re-enter LADY MACBETH

LADY MACBETH

My hands are of your colour; but I shame
To wear a heart so white.

Knocking within

I hear a knocking
At the south entry: retire we to our chamber;
A little water clears us of this deed:
How easy is it, then! Your constancy
Hath left you unattended.

Knocking within

Hark! more knocking.
Get on your nightgown, lest occasion call us,
And show us to be watchers. Be not lost
So poorly in your thoughts.

MACBETH

To know my deed, 'twere best not know myself.

Knocking within

Wake Duncan with thy knocking! I would thou couldst!

Exeunt

SCENE III. The same.

Knocking within. Enter a Porter

Porter

Here's a knocking indeed! If a
man were porter of hell-gate, he should have
old turning the key.

Knocking within

Knock,
knock, knock! Who's there, i' the name of

Beelzebub? Here's a farmer, that hanged himself on the expectation of plenty: come in time; have napkins enow about you; here you'll sweat for't.

Knocking within

Knock,
knock! Who's there, in the other devil's name? Faith, here's an equivocator, that could swear in both the scales against either scale; who committed treason enough for God's sake, yet could not equivocate to heaven: O, come in, equivocator.

Knocking within

Knock,
knock, knock! Who's there? Faith, here's an English tailor come hither, for stealing out of a French hose: come in, tailor; here you may roast your goose.

Knocking within

Knock,
knock; never at quiet! What are you? But this place is too cold for hell. I'll devil-porter it no further: I had thought to have let in some of all professions that go the primrose way to the everlasting bonfire.

Knocking within

Anon, anon! I pray you, remember the porter.

Opens the gate

Enter MACDUFF and LENNOX

MACDUFF

Was it so late, friend, ere you went to bed,
That you do lie so late?

Porter

'Faith sir, we were carousing till the second cock: and drink, sir, is a great provoker of three things.

MACDUFF

What three things does drink especially provoke?

Porter

Marry, sir, nose-painting, sleep, and urine. Lechery, sir, it provokes, and unprovokes;
it provokes the desire, but it takes away the performance: therefore, much drink may be said to be an equivocator with lechery: it makes him, and it mars him; it sets him on, and it takes him off; it persuades him, and disheartens him; makes him stand to, and not stand to; in conclusion, equivocates him in a sleep, and, giving him the lie, leaves him.

MACDUFF

I believe drink gave thee the lie last night.

Porter

That it did, sir, i' the very throat on me: but I requited him for his lie; and, I think, being too strong for him, though he took
up my legs sometime, yet I made a shift to cast him.

MACDUFF

Is thy master stirring?

Enter MACBETH

Our knocking has awaked him; here he comes.

LENNOX

Good morrow, noble sir.

MACBETH

Good morrow, both.

MACDUFF

Is the king stirring, worthy thane?

MACBETH

Not yet.

MACDUFF

He did command me to call timely on him:
I have almost slipp'd the hour.

MACBETH

I'll bring you to him.

MACDUFF

I know this is a joyful trouble to you;
But yet 'tis one.

MACBETH

The labour we delight in physics pain.
This is the door.

MACDUFF

I'll make so bold to call,
For 'tis my limited service.

Exit

LENNOX

Goes the king hence to-day?

MACBETH

He does: he did appoint so.

LENNOX

The night has been unruly: where we lay,
Our chimneys were blown down; and, as they say,
Lamentings heard i' the air; strange screams of death,
And prophesying with accents terrible
Of dire combustion and confused events
New hatch'd to the woeful time: the obscure bird
Clamour'd the livelong night: some say, the earth
Was feverous and did shake.

MACBETH

'Twas a rough night.

LENNOX

My young remembrance cannot parallel
A fellow to it.

Re-enter MACDUFF

MACDUFF

O horror, horror, horror! Tongue nor heart
Cannot conceive nor name thee!

MACBETH LENNOX

What's the matter.

MACDUFF

Confusion now hath made his masterpiece!
Most sacrilegious murder hath broke ope
The Lord's anointed temple, and stole thence
The life o' the building!

MACBETH

What is 't you say? the life?

LENNOX

Mean you his majesty?

MACDUFF

Approach the chamber, and destroy your sight
With a new Gorgon: do not bid me speak;
See, and then speak yourselves.

Exeunt MACBETH and LENNOX

Awake, awake!
Ring the alarum-bell. Murder and treason!
Banquo and Donalbain! Malcolm! awake!
Shake off this downy sleep, death's counterfeit,
And look on death itself! up, up, and see
The great doom's image! Malcolm! Banquo!
As from your graves rise up, and walk like sprites,
To countenance this horror! Ring the bell.

Bell rings

Enter LADY MACBETH

LADY MACBETH

What's the business,
That such a hideous trumpet calls to parley
The sleepers of the house? speak, speak!

MACDUFF

O gentle lady,
'Tis not for you to hear what I can speak:
The repetition, in a woman's ear,
Would murder as it fell.

Enter BANQUO

O Banquo, Banquo,
Our royal master 's murder'd!

LADY MACBETH

Woe, alas!
What, in our house?

BANQUO

Too cruel any where.
Dear Duff, I prithee, contradict thyself,
And say it is not so.

Re-enter MACBETH and LENNOX, with ROSS

MACBETH

Had I but died an hour before this chance,
I had lived a blessed time; for, from this instant,
There 's nothing serious in mortality:
All is but toys: renown and grace is dead;
The wine of life is drawn, and the mere lees
Is left this vault to brag of.

Enter MALCOLM and DONALBAIN

DONALBAIN

What is amiss?

MACBETH

You are, and do not know't:
The spring, the head, the fountain of your blood
Is stopp'd; the very source of it is stopp'd.

MACDUFF

Your royal father 's murder'd.

MALCOLM

O, by whom?

LENNOX

Those of his chamber, as it seem'd, had done 't:
Their hands and faces were an badged with blood;
So were their daggers, which unwiped we found
Upon their pillows:
They stared, and were distracted; no man's life
Was to be trusted with them.

MACBETH

O, yet I do repent me of my fury,
That I did kill them.

MACDUFF

Wherefore did you so?

MACBETH

Who can be wise, amazed, temperate and furious,
Loyal and neutral, in a moment? No man:
The expedition my violent love
Outrun the pauser, reason. Here lay Duncan,
His silver skin laced with his golden blood;
And his gash'd stabs look'd like a breach in nature
For ruin's wasteful entrance: there, the murderers,
Steep'd in the colours of their trade, their daggers
Unmannerly breech'd with gore: who could refrain,
That had a heart to love, and in that heart
Courage to make 's love known?

LADY MACBETH

Help me hence, ho!

MACDUFF

Look to the lady.

MALCOLM

[Aside to DONALBAIN] Why do we hold our tongues,
That most may claim this argument for ours?

DONALBAIN

[Aside to MALCOLM] What should be spoken here,
where our fate,
Hid in an auger-hole, may rush, and seize us?
Let 's away;
Our tears are not yet brew'd.

MALCOLM

[Aside to DONALBAIN] Nor our strong sorrow
Upon the foot of motion.

BANQUO

Look to the lady:

LADY MACBETH is carried out

And when we have our naked frailties hid,
That suffer in exposure, let us meet,
And question this most bloody piece of work,
To know it further. Fears and scruples shake us:
In the great hand of God I stand; and thence
Against the undivulged pretence I fight
Of treasonous malice.

MACDUFF

And so do I.

ALL

So all.

MACBETH

Let's briefly put on manly readiness,
And meet i' the hall together.

ALL

Well contented.

Exeunt all but Malcolm and Donalbain.

MALCOLM

What will you do? Let's not consort with them:
To show an unfelt sorrow is an office
Which the false man does easy. I'll to England.

DONALBAIN

To Ireland, I; our separated fortune
Shall keep us both the safer: where we are,
There's daggers in men's smiles: the near in blood,
The nearer bloody.

MALCOLM

This murderous shaft that's shot
Hath not yet lighted, and our safest way
Is to avoid the aim. Therefore, to horse;
And let us not be dainty of leave-taking,
But shift away: there's warrant in that theft
Which steals itself, when there's no mercy left.

Exeunt

SCENE IV. Outside Macbeth's castle.

Enter ROSS and an old Man

Old Man

Threescore and ten I can remember well:
Within the volume of which time I have seen
Hours dreadful and things strange; but this sore night
Hath trifled former knowings.

ROSS

Ah, good father,
Thou seest, the heavens, as troubled with man's act,
Threaten his bloody stage: by the clock, 'tis day,
And yet dark night strangles the travelling lamp:
Is't night's predominance, or the day's shame,
That darkness does the face of earth entomb,
When living light should kiss it?

Old Man

'Tis unnatural,
Even like the deed that's done. On Tuesday last,
A falcon, towering in her pride of place,
Was by a mousing owl hawk'd at and kill'd.

ROSS

And Duncan's horses–a thing most strange and certain–
Beauteous and swift, the minions of their race,
Turn'd wild in nature, broke their stalls, flung out,
Contending 'gainst obedience, as they would make
War with mankind.

Old Man

'Tis said they eat each other.

ROSS

They did so, to the amazement of mine eyes
That look'd upon't. Here comes the good Macduff.

Enter MACDUFF

How goes the world, sir, now?

MACDUFF

Why, see you not?

ROSS

Is't known who did this more than bloody deed?

MACDUFF

Those that Macbeth hath slain.

ROSS

Alas, the day!
What good could they pretend?

MACDUFF

They were suborn'd:
Malcolm and Donalbain, the king's two sons,
Are stol'n away and fled; which puts upon them
Suspicion of the deed.

ROSS

'Gainst nature still!
Thriftless ambition, that wilt ravin up
Thine own life's means! Then 'tis most like
The sovereignty will fall upon Macbeth.

MACDUFF

He is already named, and gone to Scone
To be invested.

ROSS

Where is Duncan's body?

MACDUFF

Carried to Colmekill,
The sacred storehouse of his predecessors,
And guardian of their bones.

ROSS

Will you to Scone?

MACDUFF

No, cousin, I'll to Fife.

ROSS

Well, I will thither.

MACDUFF

Well, may you see things well done there: adieu!
Lest our old robes sit easier than our new!

ROSS

Farewell, father.

Old Man

God's benison go with you; and with those
That would make good of bad, and friends of foes!

Exeunt

ACT III

SCENE I. Forres. The palace.

Enter BANQUO

BANQUO

Thou hast it now: king, Cawdor, Glamis, all,
As the weird women promised, and, I fear,
Thou play'dst most foully for't: yet it was said
It should not stand in thy posterity,

But that myself should be the root and father
Of many kings. If there come truth from them–
As upon thee, Macbeth, their speeches shine–
Why, by the verities on thee made good,
May they not be my oracles as well,
And set me up in hope? But hush! no more.

Sennet sounded. Enter MACBETH, as king, LADY MACBETH, as queen, LENNOX, ROSS, Lords, Ladies, and Attendants

MACBETH

Here's our chief guest.

LADY MACBETH

If he had been forgotten,
It had been as a gap in our great feast,
And all-thing unbecoming.

MACBETH

To-night we hold a solemn supper sir,
And I'll request your presence.

BANQUO

Let your highness
Command upon me; to the which my duties
Are with a most indissoluble tie
Forever knit.

MACBETH

Ride you this afternoon?

BANQUO

Ay, my good lord.

MACBETH

We should have else desired your good advice,
Which still hath been both grave and prosperous,
In this day's council; but we'll take to-morrow.
Is't far you ride?

BANQUO

As far, my lord, as will fill up the time
'Twixt this and supper: go not my horse the better,
I must become a borrower of the night
For a dark hour or twain.

MACBETH

Fail not our feast.

BANQUO

My lord, I will not.

MACBETH

We hear, our bloody cousins are bestow'd
In England and in Ireland, not confessing
Their cruel parricide, filling their hearers
With strange invention: but of that to-morrow,
When therewithal we shall have cause of state
Craving us jointly. Hie you to horse: adieu,
Till you return at night. Goes Fleance with you?

BANQUO

Ay, my good lord: our time does call upon 's.

MACBETH

I wish your horses swift and sure of foot;
And so I do commend you to their backs.
Farewell.

Exit BANQUO

Let every man be master of his time
Till seven at night: to make society
The sweeter welcome, we will keep ourself
Till supper-time alone: while then, God be with you!

Exeunt all but MACBETH, and an attendant

Sirrah, a word with you: attend those men
Our pleasure?

ATTENDANT

They are, my lord, without the palace gate.

MACBETH

Bring them before us.

Exit Attendant

To be thus is nothing;
But to be safely thus.–Our fears in Banquo
Stick deep; and in his royalty of nature
Reigns that which would be fear'd: 'tis much he dares;
And, to that dauntless temper of his mind,
He hath a wisdom that doth guide his valour
To act in safety. There is none but he
Whose being I do fear: and, under him,
My Genius is rebuked; as, it is said,
Mark Antony's was by Caesar. He chid the sisters
When first they put the name of king upon me,
And bade them speak to him: then prophet-like
They hail'd him father to a line of kings:
Upon my head they placed a fruitless crown,
And put a barren sceptre in my gripe,
Thence to be wrench'd with an unlineal hand,
No son of mine succeeding. If 't be so,
For Banquo's issue have I filed my mind;
For them the gracious Duncan have I murder'd;
Put rancours in the vessel of my peace
Only for them; and mine eternal jewel
Given to the common enemy of man,
To make them kings, the seed of Banquo kings!
Rather than so, come fate into the list.
And champion me to the utterance! Who's there!

Re-enter Attendant, with two Murderers

Now go to the door, and stay there till we call.

Exit Attendant

Was it not yesterday we spoke together?

First Murderer

It was, so please your highness.

MACBETH

Well then, now
Have you consider'd of my speeches? Know
That it was he in the times past which held you
So under fortune, which you thought had been
Our innocent self: this I made good to you
In our last conference, pass'd in probation with you,
How you were borne in hand, how cross'd, the instruments,
Who wrought with them, and all things else that might
To half a soul and to a notion crazed
Say 'Thus did Banquo.'

First Murderer

You made it known to us.

MACBETH

I did so, and went further, which is now
Our point of second meeting. Do you find
Your patience so predominant in your nature
That you can let this go? Are you so gospell'd
To pray for this good man and for his issue,
Whose heavy hand hath bow'd you to the grave
And beggar'd yours for ever?

First Murderer

We are men, my liege.

MACBETH

Ay, in the catalogue ye go for men;
As hounds and greyhounds, mongrels, spaniels, curs,
Shoughs, water-rugs and demi-wolves, are clept
All by the name of dogs: the valued file
Distinguishes the swift, the slow, the subtle,
The housekeeper, the hunter, every one
According to the gift which bounteous nature
Hath in him closed; whereby he does receive
Particular addition. from the bill
That writes them all alike: and so of men.
Now, if you have a station in the file,
Not i' the worst rank of manhood, say 't;
And I will put that business in your bosoms,
Whose execution takes your enemy off,
Grapples you to the heart and love of us,
Who wear our health but sickly in his life,
Which in his death were perfect.

Second Murderer

I am one, my liege,
Whom the vile blows and buffets of the world
Have so incensed that I am reckless what
I do to spite the world.

First Murderer

And I another
So weary with disasters, tugg'd with fortune,
That I would set my lie on any chance,
To mend it, or be rid on't.

MACBETH

Both of you
Know Banquo was your enemy.

Both Murderers

True, my lord.

MACBETH

So is he mine; and in such bloody distance,
That every minute of his being thrusts
Against my near'st of life: and though I could
With barefaced power sweep him from my sight
And bid my will avouch it, yet I must not,
For certain friends that are both his and mine,
Whose loves I may not drop, but wail his fall
Who I myself struck down; and thence it is,
That I to your assistance do make love,
Masking the business from the common eye
For sundry weighty reasons.

Second Murderer

We shall, my lord,
Perform what you command us.

First Murderer

Though our lives–

MACBETH

Your spirits shine through you. Within this
hour at most
I will advise you where to plant yourselves;
Acquaint you with the perfect spy o' the time,
The moment on't; for't must be done to-night,
And something from the palace; always thought
That I require a clearness: and with him–
To leave no rubs nor botches in the work–
Fleance his son, that keeps him company,
Whose absence is no less material to me
Than is his father's, must embrace the fate
Of that dark hour. Resolve yourselves apart:
I'll come to you anon.

Both Murderers

We are resolved, my lord.

MACBETH

I'll call upon you straight: abide within.

Exeunt Murderers

It is concluded. Banquo, thy soul's flight,
If it find heaven, must find it out to-night.

Exit

SCENE II. The palace.

Enter LADY MACBETH and a Servant

LADY MACBETH

Is Banquo gone from court?

Servant

Ay, madam, but returns again to-night.

LADY MACBETH

Say to the king, I would attend his leisure
For a few words.

Servant

Madam, I will.

Exit

LADY MACBETH

Nought's had, all's spent,
Where our desire is got without content:
'Tis safer to be that which we destroy
Than by destruction dwell in doubtful joy.

Enter MACBETH

How now, my lord! why do you keep alone,

Of sorriest fancies your companions making,
Using those thoughts which should indeed have died
With them they think on? Things without all remedy
Should be without regard: what's done is done.

MACBETH

We have scotch'd the snake, not kill'd it:
She'll close and be herself, whilst our poor malice
Remains in danger of her former tooth.
But let the frame of things disjoint, both the worlds suffer,
Ere we will eat our meal in fear and sleep
In the affliction of these terrible dreams
That shake us nightly: better be with the dead,
Whom we, to gain our peace, have sent to peace,
Than on the torture of the mind to lie
In restless ecstasy. Duncan is in his grave;
After life's fitful fever he sleeps well;
Treason has done his worst: nor steel, nor poison,
Malice domestic, foreign levy, nothing,
Can touch him further.

LADY MACBETH

Come on;
Gentle my lord, sleek o'er your rugged looks;
Be bright and jovial among your guests to-night.

MACBETH

So shall I, love; and so, I pray, be you:
Let your remembrance apply to Banquo;
Present him eminence, both with eye and tongue:
Unsafe the while, that we
Must lave our honours in these flattering streams,
And make our faces vizards to our hearts,
Disguising what they are.

LADY MACBETH

You must leave this.

MACBETH

O, full of scorpions is my mind, dear wife!
Thou know'st that Banquo, and his Fleance, lives.

LADY MACBETH

But in them nature's copy's not eterne.

MACBETH

There's comfort yet; they are assailable;
Then be thou jocund: ere the bat hath flown
His cloister'd flight, ere to black Hecate's summons
The shard-borne beetle with his drowsy hums
Hath rung night's yawning peal, there shall be done
A deed of dreadful note.

LADY MACBETH

What's to be done?

MACBETH

Be innocent of the knowledge, dearest chuck,
Till thou applaud the deed. Come, seeling night,
Scarf up the tender eye of pitiful day;
And with thy bloody and invisible hand
Cancel and tear to pieces that great bond
Which keeps me pale! Light thickens; and the crow
Makes wing to the rooky wood:
Good things of day begin to droop and drowse;
While night's black agents to their preys do rouse.
Thou marvell'st at my words: but hold thee still;
Things bad begun make strong themselves by ill.
So, prithee, go with me.

Exeunt

SCENE III. A park near the palace.

Enter three Murderers

First Murderer

But who did bid thee join with us?

Third Murderer

Macbeth.

Second Murderer

He needs not our mistrust, since he delivers
Our offices and what we have to do
To the direction just.

First Murderer

Then stand with us.
The west yet glimmers with some streaks of day:
Now spurs the lated traveller apace
To gain the timely inn; and near approaches
The subject of our watch.

Third Murderer

Hark! I hear horses.

BANQUO

[Within] Give us a light there, ho!

Second Murderer

Then 'tis he: the rest
That are within the note of expectation
Already are i' the court.

First Murderer

His horses go about.

Third Murderer

Almost a mile: but he does usually,
So all men do, from hence to the palace gate
Make it their walk.

Second Murderer

A light, a light!

Enter BANQUO, and FLEANCE with a torch

Third Murderer

'Tis he.

First Murderer

Stand to't.

BANQUO

It will be rain to-night.

First Murderer

Let it come down.

They set upon BANQUO

BANQUO

O, treachery! Fly, good Fleance, fly, fly, fly!
Thou mayst revenge. O slave!

Dies. FLEANCE escapes

Third Murderer

Who did strike out the light?

First Murderer

Wast not the way?

Third Murderer

There's but one down; the son is fled.

Second Murderer

We have lost
Best half of our affair.

First Murderer

Well, let's away, and say how much is done.

Exeunt

SCENE IV. The same. Hall in the palace.

A banquet prepared. Enter MACBETH, LADY MACBETH, ROSS, LENNOX, Lords, and Attendants

MACBETH

You know your own degrees; sit down: at first
And last the hearty welcome.

Lords

Thanks to your majesty.

MACBETH

Ourself will mingle with society,
And play the humble host.
Our hostess keeps her state, but in best time
We will require her welcome.

LADY MACBETH

Pronounce it for me, sir, to all our friends;
For my heart speaks they are welcome.

First Murderer appears at the door

MACBETH

See, they encounter thee with their hearts' thanks.
Both sides are even: here I'll sit i' the midst:
Be large in mirth; anon we'll drink a measure
The table round.

Approaching the door

There's blood on thy face.

First Murderer

'Tis Banquo's then.

MACBETH

'Tis better thee without than he within.
Is he dispatch'd?

First Murderer

My lord, his throat is cut; that I did for him.

MACBETH

Thou art the best o' the cut-throats: yet he's good
That did the like for Fleance: if thou didst it,
Thou art the nonpareil.

First Murderer

Most royal sir,
Fleance is 'scaped.

MACBETH

Then comes my fit again: I had else been perfect,
Whole as the marble, founded as the rock,
As broad and general as the casing air:
But now I am cabin'd, cribb'd, confined, bound in
To saucy doubts and fears. But Banquo's safe?

First Murderer

Ay, my good lord: safe in a ditch he bides,
With twenty trenched gashes on his head;
The least a death to nature.

MACBETH

Thanks for that:
There the grown serpent lies; the worm that's fled
Hath nature that in time will venom breed,
No teeth for the present. Get thee gone: to-morrow
We'll hear, ourselves, again.

Exit Murderer

LADY MACBETH

My royal lord,
You do not give the cheer: the feast is sold
That is not often vouch'd, while 'tis a-making,
'Tis given with welcome: to feed were best at home;
From thence the sauce to meat is ceremony;
Meeting were bare without it.

MACBETH

Sweet remembrancer!
Now, good digestion wait on appetite,
And health on both!

LENNOX

May't please your highness sit.

The GHOST OF BANQUO enters, and sits in MACBETH's place

MACBETH

Here had we now our country's honour roof'd,
Were the graced person of our Banquo present;
Who may I rather challenge for unkindness
Than pity for mischance!

ROSS

His absence, sir,

Lays blame upon his promise. Please't your highness
To grace us with your royal company.

MACBETH

The table's full.

LENNOX

Here is a place reserved, sir.

MACBETH

Where?

LENNOX

Here, my good lord. What is't that moves your highness?

MACBETH

Which of you have done this?

Lords

What, my good lord?

MACBETH

Thou canst not say I did it: never shake
Thy gory locks at me.

ROSS

Gentlemen, rise: his highness is not well.

LADY MACBETH

Sit, worthy friends: my lord is often thus,
And hath been from his youth: pray you, keep seat;
The fit is momentary; upon a thought
He will again be well: if much you note him,
You shall offend him and extend his passion:
Feed, and regard him not. Are you a man?

MACBETH

Ay, and a bold one, that dare look on that
Which might appal the devil.

LADY MACBETH

O proper stuff!
This is the very painting of your fear:
This is the air-drawn dagger which, you said,
Led you to Duncan. O, these flaws and starts,
Impostors to true fear, would well become
A woman's story at a winter's fire,
Authorized by her grandam. Shame itself!
Why do you make such faces? When all's done,
You look but on a stool.

MACBETH

Prithee, see there! behold! look! lo!
how say you?
Why, what care I? If thou canst nod, speak too.
If charnel-houses and our graves must send
Those that we bury back, our monuments
Shall be the maws of kites.

GHOST OF BANQUO vanishes

LADY MACBETH

What, quite unmann'd in folly?

MACBETH

If I stand here, I saw him.

LADY MACBETH

Fie, for shame!

MACBETH

Blood hath been shed ere now, i' the olden time,
Ere human statute purged the gentle weal;
Ay, and since too, murders have been perform'd
Too terrible for the ear: the times have been,
That, when the brains were out, the man would die,
And there an end; but now they rise again,
With twenty mortal murders on their crowns,
And push us from our stools: this is more strange
Than such a murder is.

LADY MACBETH

My worthy lord,
Your noble friends do lack you.

MACBETH

I do forget.
Do not muse at me, my most worthy friends,
I have a strange infirmity, which is nothing
To those that know me. Come, love and health to all;
Then I'll sit down. Give me some wine; fill full.
I drink to the general joy o' the whole table,
And to our dear friend Banquo, whom we miss;
Would he were here! to all, and him, we thirst,
And all to all.

Lords

Our duties, and the pledge.

Re-enter GHOST OF BANQUO

MACBETH

Avaunt! and quit my sight! let the earth hide thee!
Thy bones are marrowless, thy blood is cold;
Thou hast no speculation in those eyes
Which thou dost glare with!

LADY MACBETH

Think of this, good peers,
But as a thing of custom: 'tis no other;
Only it spoils the pleasure of the time.

MACBETH

What man dare, I dare:
Approach thou like the rugged Russian bear,
The arm'd rhinoceros, or the Hyrcan tiger;
Take any shape but that, and my firm nerves
Shall never tremble: or be alive again,
And dare me to the desert with thy sword;
If trembling I inhabit then, protest me
The baby of a girl. Hence, horrible shadow!
Unreal mockery, hence!

GHOST OF BANQUO vanishes

Why, so: being gone,
I am a man again. Pray you, sit still.

LADY MACBETH

You have displaced the mirth, broke the good meeting,
With most admired disorder.

MACBETH

Can such things be,
And overcome us like a summer's cloud,
Without our special wonder? You make me strange
Even to the disposition that I owe,
When now I think you can behold such sights,
And keep the natural ruby of your cheeks,
When mine is blanched with fear.

ROSS

What sights, my lord?

LADY MACBETH

I pray you, speak not; he grows worse and worse;
Question enrages him. At once, good night:
Stand not upon the order of your going,
But go at once.

LENNOX

Good night; and better health
Attend his majesty!

LADY MACBETH

A kind good night to all!

Exeunt all but MACBETH and LADY MACBETH

MACBETH

It will have blood; they say, blood will have blood:
Stones have been known to move and trees to speak;
Augurs and understood relations have
By magot-pies and choughs and rooks brought forth
The secret'st man of blood. What is the night?

LADY MACBETH

Almost at odds with morning, which is which.

MACBETH

How say'st thou, that Macduff denies his person
At our great bidding?

LADY MACBETH

Did you send to him, sir?

MACBETH

I hear it by the way; but I will send:
There's not a one of them but in his house
I keep a servant fee'd. I will to-morrow,
And betimes I will, to the weird sisters:
More shall they speak; for now I am bent to know,
By the worst means, the worst. For mine own good,
All causes shall give way: I am in blood
Stepp'd in so far that, should I wade no more,
Returning were as tedious as go o'er:
Strange things I have in head, that will to hand;
Which must be acted ere they may be scann'd.

LADY MACBETH

You lack the season of all natures, sleep.

MACBETH

Come, we'll to sleep. My strange and self-abuse
Is the initiate fear that wants hard use:
We are yet but young in deed.

Exeunt

SCENE V. A Heath.

Thunder. Enter the three Witches meeting HECATE

First Witch

Why, how now, Hecate! you look angerly.

HECATE

Have I not reason, beldams as you are,
Saucy and overbold? How did you dare
To trade and traffic with Macbeth
In riddles and affairs of death;
And I, the mistress of your charms,
The close contriver of all harms,
Was never call'd to bear my part,
Or show the glory of our art?
And, which is worse, all you have done
Hath been but for a wayward son,
Spiteful and wrathful, who, as others do,
Loves for his own ends, not for you.
But make amends now: get you gone,
And at the pit of Acheron
Meet me i' the morning: thither he
Will come to know his destiny:
Your vessels and your spells provide,
Your charms and every thing beside.
I am for the air; this night I'll spend
Unto a dismal and a fatal end:
Great business must be wrought ere noon:
Upon the corner of the moon
There hangs a vaporous drop profound;
I'll catch it ere it come to ground:
And that distill'd by magic sleights
Shall raise such artificial sprites
As by the strength of their illusion
Shall draw him on to his confusion:
He shall spurn fate, scorn death, and bear
He hopes 'bove wisdom, grace and fear:
And you all know, security
Is mortals' chiefest enemy.

Music and a song within: 'Come away, come away,' & c

Hark! I am call'd; my little spirit, see,
Sits in a foggy cloud, and stays for me.

Exit

First Witch

Come, let's make haste; she'll soon be back again.

Exeunt

SCENE VI. Forres. The palace.

Enter LENNOX and another Lord

LENNOX

My former speeches have but hit your thoughts,
Which can interpret further: only, I say,
Things have been strangely borne. The gracious Duncan
Was pitied of Macbeth: marry, he was dead:
And the right-valiant Banquo walk'd too late;
Whom, you may say, if't please you, Fleance kill'd,
For Fleance fled: men must not walk too late.
Who cannot want the thought how monstrous
It was for Malcolm and for Donalbain
To kill their gracious father? damned fact!
How it did grieve Macbeth! did he not straight
In pious rage the two delinquents tear,
That were the slaves of drink and thralls of sleep?
Was not that nobly done? Ay, and wisely too;
For 'twould have anger'd any heart alive
To hear the men deny't. So that, I say,
He has borne all things well: and I do think
That had he Duncan's sons under his key–
As, an't please heaven, he shall not–they should find
What 'twere to kill a father; so should Fleance.
But, peace! for from broad words and 'cause he fail'd
His presence at the tyrant's feast, I hear
Macduff lives in disgrace: sir, can you tell
Where he bestows himself?

Lord

The son of Duncan,
From whom this tyrant holds the due of birth
Lives in the English court, and is received
Of the most pious Edward with such grace
That the malevolence of fortune nothing
Takes from his high respect: thither Macduff
Is gone to pray the holy king, upon his aid
To wake Northumberland and warlike Siward:
That, by the help of these–with Him above
To ratify the work–we may again
Give to our tables meat, sleep to our nights,
Free from our feasts and banquets bloody knives,
Do faithful homage and receive free honours:
All which we pine for now: and this report
Hath so exasperate the king that he
Prepares for some attempt of war.

LENNOX

Sent he to Macduff?

Lord

He did: and with an absolute 'Sir, not I,'
The cloudy messenger turns me his back,
And hums, as who should say 'You'll rue the time
That clogs me with this answer.'

LENNOX

And that well might
Advise him to a caution, to hold what distance
His wisdom can provide. Some holy angel
Fly to the court of England and unfold
His message ere he come, that a swift blessing
May soon return to this our suffering country
Under a hand accursed!

Lord

I'll send my prayers with him.

Exeunt

ACT IV

SCENE I. A cavern. In the middle, a boiling cauldron.

Thunder. Enter the three Witches

First Witch

Thrice the brinded cat hath mew'd.

Second Witch

Thrice and once the hedge-pig whined.

Third Witch

Harpier cries 'Tis time, 'tis time.

First Witch

Round about the cauldron go;

In the poison'd entrails throw.
Toad, that under cold stone
Days and nights has thirty-one
Swelter'd venom sleeping got,
Boil thou first i' the charmed pot.

ALL

Double, double toil and trouble;
Fire burn, and cauldron bubble.

Second Witch

Fillet of a fenny snake,
In the cauldron boil and bake;
Eye of newt and toe of frog,
Wool of bat and tongue of dog,
Adder's fork and blind-worm's sting,
Lizard's leg and owlet's wing,
For a charm of powerful trouble,
Like a hell-broth boil and bubble.

ALL

Double, double toil and trouble;
Fire burn and cauldron bubble.

Third Witch

Scale of dragon, tooth of wolf,
Witches' mummy, maw and gulf
Of the ravin'd salt-sea shark,
Root of hemlock digg'd i' the dark,
Liver of blaspheming Jew,
Gall of goat, and slips of yew
Silver'd in the moon's eclipse,
Nose of Turk and Tartar's lips,
Finger of birth-strangled babe
Ditch-deliver'd by a drab,
Make the gruel thick and slab:
Add thereto a tiger's chaudron,
For the ingredients of our cauldron.

ALL

Double, double toil and trouble;
Fire burn and cauldron bubble.

Second Witch

Cool it with a baboon's blood,
Then the charm is firm and good.

Enter HECATE to the other three Witches

HECATE

O well done! I commend your pains;
And every one shall share i' the gains;
And now about the cauldron sing,
Live elves and fairies in a ring,
Enchanting all that you put in.

Music and a song: 'Black spirits,' & c

HECATE retires

Second Witch

By the pricking of my thumbs,
Something wicked this way comes.
Open, locks,
Whoever knocks!

Enter MACBETH

MACBETH

How now, you secret, black, and midnight hags!
What is't you do?

ALL

A deed without a name.

MACBETH

I conjure you, by that which you profess,
Howe'er you come to know it, answer me:
Though you untie the winds and let them fight
Against the churches; though the yesty waves
Confound and swallow navigation up;
Though bladed corn be lodged and trees blown down;
Though castles topple on their warders' heads;
Though palaces and pyramids do slope
Their heads to their foundations; though the treasure
Of nature's germens tumble all together,
Even till destruction sicken; answer me
To what I ask you.

First Witch

Speak.

Second Witch

Demand.

Third Witch

We'll answer.

First Witch

Say, if thou'dst rather hear it from our mouths,
Or from our masters?

MACBETH

Call 'em; let me see 'em.

First Witch

Pour in sow's blood, that hath eaten
Her nine farrow; grease that's sweaten
From the murderer's gibbet throw
Into the flame.

ALL

Come, high or low;
Thyself and office deftly show!

Thunder. First Apparition: an armed Head

MACBETH

Tell me, thou unknown power,–

First Witch

He knows thy thought:
Hear his speech, but say thou nought.

First Apparition

Macbeth! Macbeth! Macbeth! beware Macduff;
Beware the thane of Fife. Dismiss me.
Enough.

Descends

MACBETH

Whate'er thou art, for thy good caution, thanks;
Thou hast harp'd my fear aright: but one word more,–

First Witch

He will not be commanded: here's another,
More potent than the first.

Thunder. Second Apparition: A bloody Child

Second Apparition

Macbeth! Macbeth! Macbeth!

MACBETH

Had I three ears, I'ld hear thee.

Second Apparition

Be bloody, bold, and resolute; laugh to scorn
The power of man, for none of woman born
Shall harm Macbeth.

Descends

MACBETH

Then live, Macduff: what need I fear of thee?
But yet I'll make assurance double sure,
And take a bond of fate: thou shalt not live;
That I may tell pale-hearted fear it lies,
And sleep in spite of thunder.

Thunder. Third Apparition: a Child crowned, with a tree in his hand

What is this
That rises like the issue of a king,
And wears upon his baby-brow the round
And top of sovereignty?

ALL

Listen, but speak not to't.

Third Apparition

Be lion-mettled, proud; and take no care
Who chafes, who frets, or where conspirers are:
Macbeth shall never vanquish'd be until
Great Birnam wood to high Dunsinane hill
Shall come against him.

Descends

MACBETH

That will never be
Who can impress the forest, bid the tree
Unfix his earth-bound root? Sweet bodements! good!
Rebellion's head, rise never till the wood
Of Birnam rise, and our high-placed Macbeth
Shall live the lease of nature, pay his breath
To time and mortal custom. Yet my heart
Throbs to know one thing: tell me, if your art
Can tell so much: shall Banquo's issue ever
Reign in this kingdom?

ALL

Seek to know no more.

MACBETH

I will be satisfied: deny me this,
And an eternal curse fall on you! Let me know.
Why sinks that cauldron? and what noise is this?

Hautboys

First Witch

Show!

Second Witch

Show!

Third Witch

Show!

ALL

Show his eyes, and grieve his heart;
Come like shadows, so depart!

A show of Eight Kings, the last with a glass in his hand; GHOST OF BANQUO following

MACBETH

Thou art too like the spirit of Banquo: down!
Thy crown does sear mine eye-balls. And thy hair,
Thou other gold-bound brow, is like the first.
A third is like the former. Filthy hags!
Why do you show me this? A fourth! Start, eyes!
What, will the line stretch out to the crack of doom?
Another yet! A seventh! I'll see no more:
And yet the eighth appears, who bears a glass
Which shows me many more; and some I see
That two-fold balls and treble scepters carry:
Horrible sight! Now, I see, 'tis true;
For the blood-bolter'd Banquo smiles upon me,
And points at them for his.

Apparitions vanish

What, is this so?

First Witch

Ay, sir, all this is so: but why
Stands Macbeth thus amazedly?
Come, sisters, cheer we up his sprites,
And show the best of our delights:
I'll charm the air to give a sound,
While you perform your antic round:
That this great king may kindly say,
Our duties did his welcome pay.

Music. The witches dance and then vanish, with HECATE

MACBETH

Where are they? Gone? Let this pernicious hour
Stand aye accursed in the calendar!
Come in, without there!

Enter LENNOX

LENNOX

What's your grace's will?

MACBETH

Saw you the weird sisters?

LENNOX

No, my lord.

MACBETH

Came they not by you?

LENNOX

No, indeed, my lord.

MACBETH

Infected be the air whereon they ride;
And damn'd all those that trust them! I did hear
The galloping of horse: who was't came by?

LENNOX

'Tis two or three, my lord, that bring you word
Macduff is fled to England.

MACBETH

Fled to England!

LENNOX

Ay, my good lord.

MACBETH

Time, thou anticipatest my dread exploits:
The flighty purpose never is o'ertook
Unless the deed go with it; from this moment
The very firstlings of my heart shall be
The firstlings of my hand. And even now,
To crown my thoughts with acts, be it thought and done:
The castle of Macduff I will surprise;
Seize upon Fife; give to the edge o' the sword
His wife, his babes, and all unfortunate souls
That trace him in his line. No boasting like a fool;
This deed I'll do before this purpose cool.
But no more sights!–Where are these gentlemen?
Come, bring me where they are.

Exeunt

SCENE II. Fife. Macduff's castle.

Enter LADY MACDUFF, her Son, and ROSS

LADY MACDUFF

What had he done, to make him fly the land?

ROSS

You must have patience, madam.

LADY MACDUFF

He had none:
His flight was madness: when our actions do not,
Our fears do make us traitors.

ROSS

You know not
Whether it was his wisdom or his fear.

LADY MACDUFF

Wisdom! to leave his wife, to leave his babes,
His mansion and his titles in a place
From whence himself does fly? He loves us not;
He wants the natural touch: for the poor wren,
The most diminutive of birds, will fight,
Her young ones in her nest, against the owl.
All is the fear and nothing is the love;
As little is the wisdom, where the flight
So runs against all reason.

ROSS

My dearest coz,
I pray you, school yourself: but for your husband,
He is noble, wise, judicious, and best knows
The fits o' the season. I dare not speak much further;
But cruel are the times, when we are traitors
And do not know ourselves, when we hold rumour
From what we fear, yet know not what we fear,
But float upon a wild and violent sea
Each way and move. I take my leave of you:
Shall not be long but I'll be here again:
Things at the worst will cease, or else climb upward
To what they were before. My pretty cousin,
Blessing upon you!

LADY MACDUFF

Father'd he is, and yet he's fatherless.

ROSS

I am so much a fool, should I stay longer,
It would be my disgrace and your discomfort:
I take my leave at once.

Exit

LADY MACDUFF

Sirrah, your father's dead;
And what will you do now? How will you live?

Son

As birds do, mother.

LADY MACDUFF

What, with worms and flies?

Son

With what I get, I mean; and so do they.

LADY MACDUFF

Poor bird! thou'ldst never fear the net nor lime,
The pitfall nor the gin.

Son

Why should I, mother? Poor birds they are
not set for.
My father is not dead, for all your saying.

LADY MACDUFF

Yes, he is dead; how wilt thou do for a father?

Son

Nay, how will you do for a husband?

LADY MACDUFF

Why, I can buy me twenty at any market.

Son

Then you'll buy 'em to sell again.

LADY MACDUFF

Thou speak'st with all thy wit: and yet, i' faith,
With wit enough for thee.

Son

Was my father a traitor, mother?

LADY MACDUFF

Ay, that he was.

Son

What is a traitor?

LADY MACDUFF

Why, one that swears and lies.

Son

And be all traitors that do so?

LADY MACDUFF

Every one that does so is a traitor, and must
be hanged.

Son

And must they all be hanged that swear and lie?

LADY MACDUFF

Every one.

Son

Who must hang them?

LADY MACDUFF

Why, the honest men.

Son

Then the liars and swearers are fools,
for there are liars and swearers enow to beat
the honest men and hang up them.

LADY MACDUFF

Now, God help thee, poor monkey!
But how wilt thou do for a father?

Son

If he were dead, you'ld weep for
him: if you would not, it were a good sign
that I should quickly have a new father.

LADY MACDUFF

Poor prattler, how thou talk'st!

Enter a Messenger

Messenger

Bless you, fair dame! I am not to you known,
Though in your state of honour I am perfect.
I doubt some danger does approach you nearly:
If you will take a homely man's advice,
Be not found here; hence, with your little ones.
To fright you thus, methinks, I am too savage;
To do worse to you were fell cruelty,
Which is too nigh your person. Heaven preserve you!
I dare abide no longer.

Exit

LADY MACDUFF

Whither should I fly?
I have done no harm. But I remember now
I am in this earthly world; where to do harm
Is often laudable, to do good sometime
Accounted dangerous folly: why then, alas,
Do I put up that womanly defence,
To say I have done no harm?

Enter Murderers

What are these faces?

First Murderer

Where is your husband?

LADY MACDUFF

I hope, in no place so unsanctified
Where such as thou mayst find him.

First Murderer

He's a traitor.

Son

Thou liest, thou shag-hair'd villain!

First Murderer

What, you egg!

Stabbing him

Young fry of treachery!

Son

He has kill'd me, mother:
Run away, I pray you!

Dies

Exit LADY MACDUFF, crying 'Murder!' Exeunt Murderers, following her

SCENE III. England. Before the King's palace.

Enter MALCOLM and MACDUFF

MALCOLM

Let us seek out some desolate shade, and there
Weep our sad bosoms empty.

MACDUFF

Let us rather
Hold fast the mortal sword, and like good men
Bestride our down-fall'n birthdom: each new morn
New widows howl, new orphans cry, new sorrows
Strike heaven on the face, that it resounds
As if it felt with Scotland and yell'd out
Like syllable of dolour.

MALCOLM

What I believe I'll wail,
What know believe, and what I can redress,
As I shall find the time to friend, I will.
What you have spoke, it may be so perchance.
This tyrant, whose sole name blisters our tongues,
Was once thought honest: you have loved him well.
He hath not touch'd you yet. I am young; but something
You may deserve of him through me, and wisdom
To offer up a weak poor innocent lamb
To appease an angry god.

MACDUFF

I am not treacherous.

MALCOLM

But Macbeth is.
A good and virtuous nature may recoil
In an imperial charge. But I shall crave
your pardon;
That which you are my thoughts cannot
transpose:
Angels are bright still, though the brightest fell;
Though all things foul would wear the brows
of grace,
Yet grace must still look so.

MACDUFF

I have lost my hopes.

MALCOLM

Perchance even there where I did find my
doubts.
Why in that rawness left you wife and child,
Those precious motives, those strong knots of
love,
Without leave-taking? I pray you,
Let not my jealousies be your dishonours,
But mine own safeties. You may be rightly just,
Whatever I shall think.

MACDUFF

Bleed, bleed, poor country!
Great tyranny! lay thou thy basis sure,
For goodness dare not cheque thee: wear thou
thy wrongs;
The title is affeer'd! Fare thee well, lord:
I would not be the villain that thou think'st
For the whole space that's in the tyrant's grasp,
And the rich East to boot.

MALCOLM

Be not offended:
I speak not as in absolute fear of you.
I think our country sinks beneath the yoke;
It weeps, it bleeds; and each new day a gash
Is added to her wounds: I think withal
There would be hands uplifted in my right;
And here from gracious England have I offer
Of goodly thousands: but, for all this,
When I shall tread upon the tyrant's head,
Or wear it on my sword, yet my poor country
Shall have more vices than it had before,
More suffer and more sundry ways than ever,
By him that shall succeed.

MACDUFF

What should he be?

MALCOLM

It is myself I mean: in whom I know
All the particulars of vice so grafted
That, when they shall be open'd, black Macbeth
Will seem as pure as snow, and the poor state
Esteem him as a lamb, being compared
With my confineless harms.

MACDUFF

Not in the legions
Of horrid hell can come a devil more damn'd
In evils to top Macbeth.

MALCOLM

I grant him bloody,
Luxurious, avaricious, false, deceitful,
Sudden, malicious, smacking of every sin
That has a name: but there's no bottom, none,
In my voluptuousness: your wives, your
daughters,
Your matrons and your maids, could not fill up
The cistern of my lust, and my desire
All continent impediments would o'erbear
That did oppose my will: better Macbeth
Than such an one to reign.

MACDUFF

Boundless intemperance
In nature is a tyranny; it hath been
The untimely emptying of the happy throne
And fall of many kings. But fear not yet
To take upon you what is yours: you may
Convey your pleasures in a spacious plenty,
And yet seem cold, the time you may so hood-
wink.

We have willing dames enough: there cannot be
That vulture in you, to devour so many
As will to greatness dedicate themselves,
Finding it so inclined.

MALCOLM

With this there grows
In my most ill-composed affection such
A stanchless avarice that, were I king,
I should cut off the nobles for their lands,
Desire his jewels and this other's house:
And my more-having would be as a sauce
To make me hunger more; that I should forge
Quarrels unjust against the good and loyal,
Destroying them for wealth.

MACDUFF

This avarice
Sticks deeper, grows with more pernicious root
Than summer-seeming lust, and it hath been
The sword of our slain kings: yet do not fear;
Scotland hath foisons to fill up your will.
Of your mere own: all these are portable,
With other graces weigh'd.

MALCOLM

But I have none: the king-becoming graces,
As justice, verity, temperance, stableness,
Bounty, perseverance, mercy, lowliness,
Devotion, patience, courage, fortitude,
I have no relish of them, but abound
In the division of each several crime,
Acting it many ways. Nay, had I power, I should
Pour the sweet milk of concord into hell,
Uproar the universal peace, confound
All unity on earth.

MACDUFF

O Scotland, Scotland!

MALCOLM

If such a one be fit to govern, speak:
I am as I have spoken.

MACDUFF

Fit to govern!
No, not to live. O nation miserable,
With an untitled tyrant bloody-scepter'd,
When shalt thou see thy wholesome days again,
Since that the truest issue of thy throne
By his own interdiction stands accursed,
And does blaspheme his breed? Thy royal father
Was a most sainted king: the queen that bore thee,
Oftener upon her knees than on her feet,
Died every day she lived. Fare thee well!
These evils thou repeat'st upon thyself
Have banish'd me from Scotland. O my breast,
Thy hope ends here!

MALCOLM

Macduff, this noble passion,
Child of integrity, hath from my soul
Wiped the black scruples, reconciled my thoughts
To thy good truth and honour. Devilish Macbeth
By many of these trains hath sought to win me
Into his power, and modest wisdom plucks me
From over-credulous haste: but God above
Deal between thee and me! for even now
I put myself to thy direction, and
Unspeak mine own detraction, here abjure
The taints and blames I laid upon myself,
For strangers to my nature. I am yet
Unknown to woman, never was forsworn,
Scarcely have coveted what was mine own,
At no time broke my faith, would not betray
The devil to his fellow and delight
No less in truth than life: my first false speaking
Was this upon myself: what I am truly,
Is thine and my poor country's to command:
Whither indeed, before thy here-approach,
Old Siward, with ten thousand warlike men,
Already at a point, was setting forth.
Now we'll together; and the chance of goodness

Be like our warranted quarrel! Why are you silent?

MACDUFF

Such welcome and unwelcome things at once
'Tis hard to reconcile.

Enter a Doctor

MALCOLM

Well; more anon.–Comes the king forth, I pray you?

Doctor

Ay, sir; there are a crew of wretched souls
That stay his cure: their malady convinces
The great assay of art; but at his touch–
Such sanctity hath heaven given his hand–
They presently amend.

MALCOLM

I thank you, doctor.

Exit Doctor

MACDUFF

What's the disease he means?

MALCOLM

'Tis call'd the evil:
A most miraculous work in this good king;
Which often, since my here-remain in England,
I have seen him do. How he solicits heaven,
Himself best knows: but strangely-visited people,
All swoln and ulcerous, pitiful to the eye,
The mere despair of surgery, he cures,
Hanging a golden stamp about their necks,
Put on with holy prayers: and 'tis spoken,
To the succeeding royalty he leaves
The healing benediction. With this strange virtue,
He hath a heavenly gift of prophecy,
And sundry blessings hang about his throne,
That speak him full of grace.

Enter ROSS

MACDUFF

See, who comes here?

MALCOLM

My countryman; but yet I know him not.

MACDUFF

My ever-gentle cousin, welcome hither.

MALCOLM

I know him now. Good God, betimes remove
The means that makes us strangers!

ROSS

Sir, amen.

MACDUFF

Stands Scotland where it did?

ROSS

Alas, poor country!
Almost afraid to know itself. It cannot
Be call'd our mother, but our grave; where nothing,
But who knows nothing, is once seen to smile;
Where sighs and groans and shrieks that rend the air
Are made, not mark'd; where violent sorrow seems
A modern ecstasy; the dead man's knell
Is there scarce ask'd for who; and good men's lives
Expire before the flowers in their caps,
Dying or ere they sicken.

MACDUFF

O, relation
Too nice, and yet too true!

MALCOLM

What's the newest grief?

ROSS

That of an hour's age doth hiss the speaker:
Each minute teems a new one.

MACDUFF

How does my wife?

ROSS

Why, well.

MACDUFF

And all my children?

ROSS

Well too.

MACDUFF

The tyrant has not batter'd at their peace?

ROSS

No; they were well at peace when I did leave 'em.

MACDUFF

But not a niggard of your speech: how goes't?

ROSS

When I came hither to transport the tidings,
Which I have heavily borne, there ran a rumour
Of many worthy fellows that were out;
Which was to my belief witness'd the rather,
For that I saw the tyrant's power a-foot:
Now is the time of help; your eye in Scotland
Would create soldiers, make our women fight,
To doff their dire distresses.

MALCOLM

Be't their comfort
We are coming thither: gracious England hath
Lent us good Siward and ten thousand men;
An older and a better soldier none
That Christendom gives out.

ROSS

Would I could answer
This comfort with the like! But I have words
That would be howl'd out in the desert air,
Where hearing should not latch them.

MACDUFF

What concern they?
The general cause? or is it a fee-grief
Due to some single breast?

ROSS

No mind that's honest
But in it shares some woe; though the main part
Pertains to you alone.

MACDUFF

If it be mine,
Keep it not from me, quickly let me have it.

ROSS

Let not your ears despise my tongue for ever,
Which shall possess them with the heaviest sound
That ever yet they heard.

MACDUFF

Hum! I guess at it.

ROSS

Your castle is surprised; your wife and babes
Savagely slaughter'd: to relate the manner,
Were, on the quarry of these murder'd deer,
To add the death of you.

MALCOLM

Merciful heaven!
What, man! ne'er pull your hat upon your brows;
Give sorrow words: the grief that does not speak
Whispers the o'er-fraught heart and bids it break.

MACDUFF

My children too?

ROSS

Wife, children, servants, all
That could be found.

MACDUFF

And I must be from thence!
My wife kill'd too?

ROSS

I have said.

MALCOLM

Be comforted:
Let's make us medicines of our great revenge,
To cure this deadly grief.

MACDUFF

He has no children. All my pretty ones?
Did you say all? O hell-kite! All?
What, all my pretty chickens and their dam
At one fell swoop?

MALCOLM

Dispute it like a man.

MACDUFF

I shall do so;
But I must also feel it as a man:
I cannot but remember such things were,
That were most precious to me. Did heaven
look on,
And would not take their part? Sinful
Macduff,
They were all struck for thee! naught that I am,
Not for their own demerits, but for mine,
Fell slaughter on their souls. Heaven rest
them now!

MALCOLM

Be this the whetstone of your sword: let grief
Convert to anger; blunt not the heart, enrage it.

MACDUFF

O, I could play the woman with mine eyes
And braggart with my tongue! But, gentle
heavens,
Cut short all intermission; front to front
Bring thou this fiend of Scotland and myself;
Within my sword's length set him; if he 'scape,
Heaven forgive him too!

MALCOLM

This tune goes manly.
Come, go we to the king; our power is ready;
Our lack is nothing but our leave; Macbeth
Is ripe for shaking, and the powers above
Put on their instruments. Receive what cheer
you may:
The night is long that never finds the day.

Exeunt

ACT V

SCENE I. Dunsinane. Ante-room in the castle.

Enter a Doctor of Physic and a Waiting-Gentlewoman

Doctor

I have two nights watched with you, but can
perceive
no truth in your report. When was it she last
walked?

Gentlewoman

Since his majesty went into the field, I have
seen
her rise from her bed, throw her night-gown
upon
her, unlock her closet, take forth paper, fold it,
write upon't, read it, afterwards seal it, and
again
return to bed; yet all this while in a most fast
sleep.

Doctor

A great perturbation in nature, to receive at
once
the benefit of sleep, and do the effects of
watching! In this slumbery agitation, besides
her
walking and other actual performances, what,
at any
time, have you heard her say?

Gentlewoman

That, sir, which I will not report after her.

Doctor

You may to me: and 'tis most meet you should.

Gentlewoman

Neither to you nor any one; having no witness to confirm my speech.

Enter LADY MACBETH, with a taper

Lo you, here she comes! This is her very guise; and, upon my life, fast asleep. Observe her; stand close.

Doctor

How came she by that light?

Gentlewoman

Why, it stood by her: she has light by her continually; 'tis her command.

Doctor

You see, her eyes are open.

Gentlewoman

Ay, but their sense is shut.

Doctor

What is it she does now? Look, how she rubs her hands.

Gentlewoman

It is an accustomed action with her, to seem thus
washing her hands: I have known her continue in
this a quarter of an hour.

LADY MACBETH

Yet here's a spot.

Doctor

Hark! she speaks: I will set down what comes from
her, to satisfy my remembrance the more strongly.

LADY MACBETH

Out, damned spot! out, I say!–One: two: why, then, 'tis time to do't.–Hell is murky!–Fie, my lord, fie! a soldier, and afeard? What need we fear who knows it, when none can call our power to
account?–Yet who would have thought the old man
to have had so much blood in him.

Doctor

Do you mark that?

LADY MACBETH

The thane of Fife had a wife: where is she now?–
What, will these hands ne'er be clean?–No more o'
that, my lord, no more o' that: you mar all with this starting.

Doctor

Go to, go to; you have known what you should not.

Gentlewoman

She has spoke what she should not, I am sure of that: heaven knows what she has known.

LADY MACBETH

Here's the smell of the blood still: all the perfumes of Arabia will not sweeten this little hand. Oh, oh, oh!

Doctor

What a sigh is there! The heart is sorely charged.

Gentlewoman

I would not have such a heart in my bosom for the
dignity of the whole body.

Doctor

Well, well, well,–

Gentlewoman

Pray God it be, sir.

Doctor

This disease is beyond my practise: yet I have known
those which have walked in their sleep who have died
holily in their beds.

LADY MACBETH

Wash your hands, put on your nightgown; look not so
pale.–I tell you yet again, Banquo's buried; he cannot come out on's grave.

Doctor

Even so?

LADY MACBETH

To bed, to bed! there's knocking at the gate:
come, come, come, come, give me your hand. What's
done cannot be undone.–To bed, to bed, to bed!

Exit

Doctor

Will she go now to bed?

Gentlewoman

Directly.

Doctor

Foul whisperings are abroad: unnatural deeds
Do breed unnatural troubles: infected minds
To their deaf pillows will discharge their secrets:
More needs she the divine than the physician.
God, God forgive us all! Look after her;
Remove from her the means of all annoyance,
And still keep eyes upon her. So, good night:
My mind she has mated, and amazed my sight.
I think, but dare not speak.

Gentlewoman

Good night, good doctor.

Exeunt

SCENE II. The country near Dunsinane.

Drum and colours. Enter MENTEITH, CAITHNESS, ANGUS, LENNOX, and Soldiers

MENTEITH

The English power is near, led on by Malcolm,
His uncle Siward and the good Macduff:
Revenges burn in them; for their dear causes
Would to the bleeding and the grim alarm
Excite the mortified man.

ANGUS

Near Birnam wood
Shall we well meet them; that way are they coming.

CAITHNESS

Who knows if Donalbain be with his brother?

LENNOX

For certain, sir, he is not: I have a file
Of all the gentry: there is Siward's son,
And many unrough youths that even now
Protest their first of manhood.

MENTEITH

What does the tyrant?

CAITHNESS

Great Dunsinane he strongly fortifies:
Some say he's mad; others that lesser hate him
Do call it valiant fury: but, for certain,
He cannot buckle his distemper'd cause
Within the belt of rule.

ANGUS

Now does he feel
His secret murders sticking on his hands;
Now minutely revolts upbraid his faith-breach;
Those he commands move only in command,
Nothing in love: now does he feel his title

Hang loose about him, like a giant's robe
Upon a dwarfish thief.

MENTEITH

Who then shall blame
His pester'd senses to recoil and start,
When all that is within him does condemn
Itself for being there?

CAITHNESS

Well, march we on,
To give obedience where 'tis truly owed:
Meet we the medicine of the sickly weal,
And with him pour we in our country's purge
Each drop of us.

LENNOX

Or so much as it needs,
To dew the sovereign flower and drown the weeds.
Make we our march towards Birnam.

Exeunt, marching

SCENE III. Dunsinane. A room in the castle.

Enter MACBETH, Doctor, and Attendants

MACBETH

Bring me no more reports; let them fly all:
Till Birnam wood remove to Dunsinane,
I cannot taint with fear. What's the boy Malcolm?
Was he not born of woman? The spirits that know
All mortal consequences have pronounced me thus:
'Fear not, Macbeth; no man that's born of woman
Shall e'er have power upon thee.' Then fly, false thanes,
And mingle with the English epicures:
The mind I sway by and the heart I bear
Shall never sag with doubt nor shake with fear.

Enter a Servant

The devil damn thee black, thou cream-faced loon!
Where got'st thou that goose look?

Servant

There is ten thousand–

MACBETH

Geese, villain!

Servant

Soldiers, sir.

MACBETH

Go prick thy face, and over-red thy fear,
Thou lily-liver'd boy. What soldiers, patch?
Death of thy soul! those linen cheeks of thine
Are counsellors to fear. What soldiers, whey-face?

Servant

The English force, so please you.

MACBETH

Take thy face hence.

Exit Servant

Seyton!–I am sick at heart,
When I behold–Seyton, I say!–This push
Will cheer me ever, or disseat me now.
I have lived long enough: my way of life
Is fall'n into the sear, the yellow leaf;
And that which should accompany old age,
As honour, love, obedience, troops of friends,
I must not look to have; but, in their stead,
Curses, not loud but deep, mouth-honour, breath,
Which the poor heart would fain deny, and dare not. Seyton!

Enter SEYTON

SEYTON

What is your gracious pleasure?

MACBETH

What news more?

SEYTON

All is confirm'd, my lord, which was reported.

MACBETH

I'll fight till from my bones my flesh be hack'd.
Give me my armour.

SEYTON

'Tis not needed yet.

MACBETH

I'll put it on.
Send out more horses; skirr the country round;
Hang those that talk of fear. Give me mine armour.
How does your patient, doctor?

Doctor

Not so sick, my lord,
As she is troubled with thick coming fancies,
That keep her from her rest.

MACBETH

Cure her of that.
Canst thou not minister to a mind diseased,
Pluck from the memory a rooted sorrow,
Raze out the written troubles of the brain
And with some sweet oblivious antidote
Cleanse the stuff'd bosom of that perilous stuff
Which weighs upon the heart?

Doctor

Therein the patient
Must minister to himself.

MACBETH

Throw physic to the dogs; I'll none of it.
Come, put mine armour on; give me my staff.
Seyton, send out. Doctor, the thanes fly from me.
Come, sir, dispatch. If thou couldst, doctor, cast
The water of my land, find her disease,
And purge it to a sound and pristine health,
I would applaud thee to the very echo,
That should applaud again.–Pull't off, I say.–
What rhubarb, cyme, or what purgative drug,
Would scour these English hence? Hear'st thou of them?

Doctor

Ay, my good lord; your royal preparation
Makes us hear something.

MACBETH

Bring it after me.
I will not be afraid of death and bane,
Till Birnam forest come to Dunsinane.

Doctor

[Aside] Were I from Dunsinane away and clear,
Profit again should hardly draw me here.

Exeunt

SCENE IV. Country near Birnam wood.

Drum and colours. Enter MALCOLM, SIWARD and YOUNG SIWARD, MACDUFF, MENTEITH, CAITHNESS, ANGUS, LENNOX, ROSS, and Soldiers, marching

MALCOLM

Cousins, I hope the days are near at hand
That chambers will be safe.

MENTEITH

We doubt it nothing.

SIWARD

What wood is this before us?

MENTEITH

The wood of Birnam.

MALCOLM

Let every soldier hew him down a bough
And bear't before him: thereby shall we shadow

The numbers of our host and make discovery
Err in report of us.

Soldiers

It shall be done.

SIWARD

We learn no other but the confident tyrant
Keeps still in Dunsinane, and will endure
Our setting down before 't.

MALCOLM

'Tis his main hope:
For where there is advantage to be given,
Both more and less have given him the revolt,
And none serve with him but constrained things
Whose hearts are absent too.

MACDUFF

Let our just censures
Attend the true event, and put we on
Industrious soldiership.

SIWARD

The time approaches
That will with due decision make us know
What we shall say we have and what we owe.
Thoughts speculative their unsure hopes relate,
But certain issue strokes must arbitrate:
Towards which advance the war.

Exeunt, marching

SCENE V. Dunsinane. Within the castle.

Enter MACBETH, SEYTON, and Soldiers, with drum and colours

MACBETH

Hang out our banners on the outward walls;
The cry is still 'They come:' our castle's strength
Will laugh a siege to scorn: here let them lie
Till famine and the ague eat them up:
Were they not forced with those that should be ours,
We might have met them dareful, beard to beard,
And beat them backward home.

A cry of women within

What is that noise?

SEYTON

It is the cry of women, my good lord.

Exit

MACBETH

I have almost forgot the taste of fears;
The time has been, my senses would have cool'd
To hear a night-shriek; and my fell of hair
Would at a dismal treatise rouse and stir
As life were in't: I have supp'd full with horrors;
Direness, familiar to my slaughterous thoughts
Cannot once start me.

Re-enter SEYTON

Wherefore was that cry?

SEYTON

The queen, my lord, is dead.

MACBETH

She should have died hereafter;
There would have been a time for such a word.
To-morrow, and to-morrow, and to-morrow,
Creeps in this petty pace from day to day
To the last syllable of recorded time,
And all our yesterdays have lighted fools
The way to dusty death. Out, out, brief candle!
Life's but a walking shadow, a poor player
That struts and frets his hour upon the stage
And then is heard no more: it is a tale
Told by an idiot, full of sound and fury,
Signifying nothing.

Enter a Messenger

Thou comest to use thy tongue; thy story quickly.

Messenger

Gracious my lord,
I should report that which I say I saw,
But know not how to do it.

MACBETH

Well, say, sir.

Messenger

As I did stand my watch upon the hill,
I look'd toward Birnam, and anon, methought,
The wood began to move.

MACBETH

Liar and slave!

Messenger

Let me endure your wrath, if't be not so:
Within this three mile may you see it coming;
I say, a moving grove.

MACBETH

If thou speak'st false,
Upon the next tree shalt thou hang alive,
Till famine cling thee: if thy speech be sooth,
I care not if thou dost for me as much.
I pull in resolution, and begin
To doubt the equivocation of the fiend
That lies like truth: 'Fear not, till Birnam wood
Do come to Dunsinane:' and now a wood
Comes toward Dunsinane. Arm, arm, and out!
If this which he avouches does appear,
There is nor flying hence nor tarrying here.
I gin to be aweary of the sun,
And wish the estate o' the world were now undone.
Ring the alarum-bell! Blow, wind! come, wrack!
At least we'll die with harness on our back.

Exeunt

SCENE VI. Dunsinane. Before the castle.

Drum and colours. Enter MALCOLM, SIWARD, MACDUFF, and their Army, with boughs

MALCOLM

Now near enough: your leafy screens throw down.
And show like those you are. You, worthy uncle,
Shall, with my cousin, your right-noble son,
Lead our first battle: worthy Macduff and we
Shall take upon 's what else remains to do,
According to our order.

SIWARD

Fare you well.
Do we but find the tyrant's power to-night,
Let us be beaten, if we cannot fight.

MACDUFF

Make all our trumpets speak; give them all breath,
Those clamorous harbingers of blood and death.

Exeunt

SCENE VII. Another part of the field.

Alarums. Enter MACBETH

MACBETH

They have tied me to a stake; I cannot fly,
But, bear-like, I must fight the course. What's he
That was not born of woman? Such a one
Am I to fear, or none.

Enter YOUNG SIWARD

YOUNG SIWARD

What is thy name?

MACBETH

Thou'lt be afraid to hear it.

YOUNG SIWARD

No; though thou call'st thyself a hotter name
Than any is in hell.

MACBETH

My name's Macbeth.

YOUNG SIWARD

The devil himself could not pronounce a title
More hateful to mine ear.

MACBETH

No, nor more fearful.

YOUNG SIWARD

Thou liest, abhorred tyrant; with my sword
I'll prove the lie thou speak'st.

They fight and YOUNG SIWARD is slain

MACBETH

Thou wast born of woman
But swords I smile at, weapons laugh to scorn,
Brandish'd by man that's of a woman born.

Exit

Alarums. Enter MACDUFF

MACDUFF

That way the noise is. Tyrant, show thy face!
If thou be'st slain and with no stroke of mine,
My wife and children's ghosts will haunt me still.
I cannot strike at wretched kerns, whose arms
Are hired to bear their staves: either thou, Macbeth,
Or else my sword with an unbatter'd edge
I sheathe again undeeded. There thou shouldst be;
By this great clatter, one of greatest note
Seems bruited. Let me find him, fortune!
And more I beg not.

Exit. Alarums

Enter MALCOLM and SIWARD

SIWARD

This way, my lord; the castle's gently render'd:
The tyrant's people on both sides do fight;
The noble thanes do bravely in the war;
The day almost itself professes yours,
And little is to do.

MALCOLM

We have met with foes
That strike beside us.

SIWARD

Enter, sir, the castle.

Exeunt. Alarums

SCENE VIII. Another part of the field.

Enter MACBETH

MACBETH

Why should I play the Roman fool, and die
On mine own sword? whiles I see lives, the gashes
Do better upon them.

Enter MACDUFF

MACDUFF

Turn, hell-hound, turn!

MACBETH

Of all men else I have avoided thee:
But get thee back; my soul is too much charged
With blood of thine already.

MACDUFF

I have no words:
My voice is in my sword: thou bloodier villain
Than terms can give thee out!

They fight

MACBETH

Thou losest labour:
As easy mayst thou the intrenchant air
With thy keen sword impress as make me bleed:
Let fall thy blade on vulnerable crests;

I bear a charmed life, which must not yield,
To one of woman born.

MACDUFF

Despair thy charm;
And let the angel whom thou still hast served
Tell thee, Macduff was from his mother's womb
Untimely ripp'd.

MACBETH

Accursed be that tongue that tells me so,
For it hath cow'd my better part of man!
And be these juggling fiends no more believed,
That palter with us in a double sense;
That keep the word of promise to our ear,
And break it to our hope. I'll not fight with thee.

MACDUFF

Then yield thee, coward,
And live to be the show and gaze o' the time:
We'll have thee, as our rarer monsters are,
Painted on a pole, and underwrit,
'Here may you see the tyrant.'

MACBETH

I will not yield,
To kiss the ground before young Malcolm's feet,
And to be baited with the rabble's curse.
Though Birnam wood be come to Dunsinane,
And thou opposed, being of no woman born,
Yet I will try the last. Before my body
I throw my warlike shield. Lay on, Macduff,
And damn'd be him that first cries, 'Hold, enough!'

Exeunt, fighting. Alarums

Retreat. Flourish. Enter, with drum and colours, MALCOLM, SIWARD, ROSS, the other Thanes, and Soldiers

MALCOLM

I would the friends we miss were safe arrived.

SIWARD

Some must go off: and yet, by these I see,
So great a day as this is cheaply bought.

MALCOLM

Macduff is missing, and your noble son.

ROSS

Your son, my lord, has paid a soldier's debt:
He only lived but till he was a man;
The which no sooner had his prowess confirm'd
In the unshrinking station where he fought,
But like a man he died.

SIWARD

Then he is dead?

ROSS

Ay, and brought off the field: your cause of sorrow
Must not be measured by his worth, for then
It hath no end.

SIWARD

Had he his hurts before?

ROSS

Ay, on the front.

SIWARD

Why then, God's soldier be he!
Had I as many sons as I have hairs,
I would not wish them to a fairer death:
And so, his knell is knoll'd.

MALCOLM

He's worth more sorrow,
And that I'll spend for him.

SIWARD

He's worth no more
They say he parted well, and paid his score:
And so, God be with him! Here comes newer comfort.

Re-enter MACDUFF, with MACBETH's head

MACDUFF

Hail, king! for so thou art: behold, where stands
The usurper's cursed head: the time is free:
I see thee compass'd with thy kingdom's pearl,
That speak my salutation in their minds;
Whose voices I desire aloud with mine:
Hail, King of Scotland!

ALL

Hail, King of Scotland!

Flourish

MALCOLM

We shall not spend a large expense of time
Before we reckon with your several loves,
And make us even with you. My thanes and kinsmen,
Henceforth be earls, the first that ever Scotland
In such an honour named. What's more to do,
Which would be planted newly with the time,
As calling home our exiled friends abroad
That fled the snares of watchful tyranny;
Producing forth the cruel ministers
Of this dead butcher and his fiend-like queen,
Who, as 'tis thought, by self and violent hands
Took off her life; this, and what needful else
That calls upon us, by the grace of Grace,
We will perform in measure, time and place:
So, thanks to all at once and to each one,
Whom we invite to see us crown'd at Scone.

Flourish. Exeunt

CRITICAL EYE

For Discussion

a. Lady Macbeth is much more than the standard traditional wife. Clearly she has ambitions of her own. As you see it, is her madness a punishment for stepping outside of her social standing as a woman?

b. Although a powerful leader in his own right, Macbeth is not satisfied with his position. Why is this? What more does he need? Why does he crave more?

Re-approaching the Reading

If we examine the play from the perspective of The Witches, they seem to delight in torturing Macbeth. The Witches know all too well that the "prophesies" will lead Macbeth to distraction and destruction, yet they play on his vanity and his feelings of desperation and low self-esteem. Is the play suggesting that mankind lives without the support of Gods and angels; is it saying that we are essentially on our own?

Writing Assignment

Macbeth is not his own man. He is easily swayed by those he comes into contact with. What is this play attempting to reveal about the human ego and male frailty?

MICHAEL WALSH

THREE CALIFORNIA TEENS ARRESTED FOR RAPE THAT ALLEGEDLY DROVE TEEN GIRL TO SUICIDE, PARENTS DEMAND JUSTICE

Audrie Pott hanged herself in September after enduring relentless bullying, which focused on compromising pictures taken by alleged rapists from her San Francisco Bay Area high school. Her parents do not want these boys to get off without being punished as adults, especially since cases like these are woefully all too common.

Another girl's life ended too soon.

Now her parents want the three teen boys who allegedly drove their daughter to suicide through rape and public humiliation – and later tried to cover it up – to be punished as adults.

The California teens, arrested Thursday, are accused of sexually abusing Audrie Pott, 15, while she was passed out drunk at a classmate's house party.

To make matters worse, they allegedly took photos of the reported assault and used cell phones to spread them "like wildfire" through Saratoga High School in the San Francisco Bay Area.

"The whole school knows.... My life is ruined," Audrie wrote on her Facebook page.

Eight days later, on Sept. 10, 2012, she hanged herself.

Her heartbreaking suicide was not unique. Rehtaeh Parsons, a 17-year-old Canadian girl, also endured continuous bullying from classmates after being raped at a party, her mother said. Earlier this month, Rehtaeh hanged herself and died several days later when she was removed from life support.

And in Steubenville, Ohio, two teen football players were convicted of raping a nearly passed-out 16-year-old girl at a party. A teammate testified that he videotaped one of the suspects penetrate the girl with his finger.

In Audrie's case, her parents did not learn about the rape and cyber harassment of their daughter until after her death, said Robert Allard, the attorney for the victim's family.

Allard said Thursday's arrests "reopened a wound" for the family.

"Based on what we know, she was unconscious, there were multiple boys in the room with her," said Allard. "They did unimaginable things to her while she was unconscious."

Two of the teens were arrested at Saratoga High. A third, a former Saratoga High student, was picked up at Christopher High School in Gilroy, authorities said.

The boys face sexual battery charges and might be charged with the dissemination of child pornography because the pictures went viral online, NBC Bay Area reported. Their names were not released because they are minors.

Her parents want the trio to be prosecuted as adults. All three suspects are being held at Juvenile Hall until their detention hearing early next week.

"What these boys did is beyond unconscionable," said Allard. "They should be held to the highest standard of the law to make sure this never ever happens again."

The Santa Clara District Attorney's Office refused to comment on the case because the suspects are minors. The superintendent of the students' school district told San Jose Mercury News that school officials are cooperating with law enforcement as the investigation continues.

Meanwhile, the family started the Audrie Pott Foundation to provide scholarships for students of music and art, two of Audrie's passions. They also intend to promote tragedy prevention by counseling youths through depression.

"She was compassionate about life, her friends, her family, and would never do anything to harm anyone. She was in the process of developing the ability to cope with the cruelty of this world but had not quite figured it all out," the foundation's website reads. "Ultimately, she had not yet acquired the antibiotics to deal with the challenges present for teens in today's society."

The family wants Audrie's name to become well-known so that she puts a face on instances of adolescent sexual assault and subsequent cyber bullying.

They hope to have a law passed in their daughter's name to protect other teens.

CRITICAL EYE

For Discussion

a. In the article, we learn that there is an expected/accepted amount of sexual violence that can be visited upon a girl should she become incapacitated while partying. Given that we are taught right from wrong at an early age, and that we all understand that a sexual assault is illegal, why do the rules seem to no longer apply when alcohol and a party atmosphere, alongside being female, are involved?

Re-approaching the Reading

The article about how the family members struggle to survive after the Newtown shootings walks us through the horror of the event and the aftermath. No less chilling is the aftermath presented here describing how the parents struggle after their daughter's suicide, which was the result of a public sexual assault. The two journalists, however, tell their stories differently. How is this true? Why is the telling of their stories so drastically different even though the tales are equally tragic?

Writing Assignment

Research the outcomes for each of the rape cases mentioned in the article. Was justice served? Or have the victims and their families been violated all over again?

H.G. WELLS

From the Novel

THE WAR OF THE WORLDS

Chapter Sixteen

The Exodus from London

So you understand the roaring wave of fear that swept through the greatest city in the world just as Monday was dawning–the stream of flight rising swiftly to a torrent, lashing in a foaming tumult round the railway stations, banked up into a horrible struggle about the shipping in the Thames, and hurrying by every available channel northward and eastward. By ten o'clock the police organisation, and by midday even the railway organisations, were losing coherency, losing shape and efficiency, guttering, softening, running at last in that swift liquefaction of the social body.

All the railway lines north of the Thames and the South-Eastern people at Cannon Street had been warned by midnight on Sunday, and trains were being filled. People were fighting savagely for standing-room in the carriages even at two o'clock. By three, people were being trampled and crushed even in Bishopsgate Street, a couple of hundred yards or more from Liverpool Street station; revolvers were fired, people stabbed, and the policemen who had been sent to direct the traffic, exhausted and infuriated, were breaking the heads of the people they were called out to protect.

And as the day advanced and the engine drivers and stokers refused to return to London, the pressure of the flight drove the people in an ever-thickening multitude away from the stations and along the northward-running roads. By midday a Martian had been seen at Barnes, and a cloud of slowly sinking black vapour drove along the Thames and across the flats of Lambeth, cutting off all escape over the bridges in its sluggish advance. Another bank drove over Ealing, and surrounded a little island of survivors on Castle Hill, alive, but unable to escape.

After a fruitless struggle to get aboard a North-Western train at Chalk Farm–the engines of the trains that had loaded in the goods yard there ploughed through shrieking people, and a dozen stalwart men fought to keep the crowd from crushing the driver against his furnace–my brother emerged upon the Chalk Farm road, dodged across through a hurrying swarm of vehicles, and had the luck to be foremost in the sack of a cycle shop. The front tire of the machine he got was punctured in dragging it through the window, but he got up and off, notwithstanding, with no further injury than a cut wrist. The steep foot of Haverstock Hill was impassable owing to several overturned horses, and my brother struck into Belsize Road.

So he got out of the fury of the panic, and, skirting the Edgware Road, reached Edgware about seven, fasting and wearied, but well ahead of the crowd. Along the road people were standing in the roadway, curious, wondering. He was passed by a number of cyclists, some horsemen, and two motor cars. A mile from Edgware the rim of the wheel broke, and the machine became unridable. He left it by the roadside and trudged through the village. There were shops half opened in the main street of the place, and people crowded on the pavement and in the doorways and windows, staring astonished at this extraordinary procession of fugitives that was beginning. He succeeded in getting some food at an inn.

For a time he remained in Edgware not knowing what next to do. The flying people increased in number. Many of them, like my brother, seemed inclined to loiter in the place. There was no fresh news of the invaders from Mars.

At that time the road was crowded, but as yet far from congested. Most of the fugitives at that hour were mounted on cycles, but there were soon motor cars, hansom cabs, and carriages hurrying along, and the dust hung in heavy clouds along the road to St. Albans.

It was perhaps a vague idea of making his way to Chelmsford, where some friends of his lived, that at last induced my brother to strike into a quiet lane running eastward. Presently he came upon a stile, and, crossing it, followed a footpath northeastward. He passed near several farmhouses and some little places whose names he did not learn. He saw few fugitives until, in a grass lane towards High Barnet, he happened upon two ladies who became his fellow travellers. He came upon them just in time to save them.

He heard their screams, and, hurrying round the corner, saw a couple of men struggling to drag them out of the little pony-chaise in which they had been driving, while a third with difficulty held the frightened pony's head. One of the ladies, a short woman dressed in white, was simply screaming; the other, a dark, slender figure, slashed at the man who gripped her arm with a whip she held in her disengaged hand.

My brother immediately grasped the situation, shouted, and hurried towards the struggle. One of the men desisted and turned towards him, and my brother, realising from his antagonist's face that a fight was unavoidable, and being an expert boxer, went into him forthwith and sent him down against the wheel of the chaise.

It was no time for pugilistic chivalry and my brother laid him quiet with a kick, and gripped the collar of the man who pulled at the slender lady's arm. He heard the clatter of hoofs, the whip stung across his face, a third antagonist struck him between the eyes, and the man he held wrenched himself free and made off down the lane in the direction from which he had come.

Partly stunned, he found himself facing the man who had held the horse's head, and became aware of the chaise receding from him down the lane, swaying from side to side, and with the women in it looking back. The man before him, a burly rough, tried to close, and he stopped him with a blow in the face. Then, realising that he was deserted, he dodged round and made off down the lane after the chaise, with the sturdy man close behind him, and the fugitive, who had turned now, following remotely.

Suddenly he stumbled and fell; his immediate pursuer went headlong, and he rose to his feet to find himself with a couple of antagonists again. He would have had little chance against them had not the slender lady very pluckily pulled up and returned to his help. It seems she had had a revolver all this time, but it had been under the seat when she and her companion were attacked. She fired at six yards' distance, narrowly missing my brother. The less courageous of the robbers made off, and his companion followed him, cursing his cowardice. They both stopped in sight down the lane, where the third man lay insensible.

"Take this!" said the slender lady, and she gave my brother her revolver.

"Go back to the chaise," said my brother, wiping the blood from his split lip.

She turned without a word–they were both panting–and they went back to where the lady in white struggled to hold back the frightened pony.

The robbers had evidently had enough of it. When my brother looked again they were retreating.

"I'll sit here," said my brother, "if I may"; and he got upon the empty front seat. The lady looked over her shoulder.

"Give me the reins," she said, and laid the whip along the pony's side. In another moment a bend in the road hid the three men from my brother's eyes.

So, quite unexpectedly, my brother found himself, panting, with a cut mouth, a bruised jaw, and bloodstained knuckles, driving along an unknown lane with these two women.

He learned they were the wife and the younger sister of a surgeon living at Stanmore, who had come in the small hours from a dangerous case at Pinner, and heard at some railway station on his way of the Martian advance. He had hurried home, roused the women–their servant had left them two days before–packed some provisions, put his revolver under the seat–luckily for my brother–and told them to drive on to Edgware, with the idea of getting a train there. He stopped behind to tell the neighbours. He would overtake them, he said, at about half past four in the morning, and now it was nearly nine and they had seen nothing of him. They could not stop in Edgware because of the growing traffic through the place, and so they had come into this side lane.

That was the story they told my brother in fragments when presently they stopped again, nearer to New Barnet. He promised to stay with them, at least until they could determine what to do, or until the missing man arrived, and professed to be an expert shot with the revolver–a weapon strange to him–in order to give them confidence.

They made a sort of encampment by the wayside, and the pony became happy in the hedge. He told them of his own escape out of London, and all that he knew of these Martians and their ways. The sun crept higher in the sky, and after a time their talk died out and gave place to an uneasy state of anticipation. Several wayfarers came along the lane, and of these my brother gathered such news as he could. Every broken answer he had deepened his impression of the great disaster that had come on humanity, deepened his persuasion of the immediate necessity for prosecuting this flight. He urged the matter upon them.

"We have money," said the slender woman, and hesitated.

Her eyes met my brother's, and her hesitation ended.

"So have I," said my brother.

She explained that they had as much as thirty pounds in gold, besides a five-pound note, and suggested that with that they might get upon a train at St. Albans or New Barnet. My brother thought that was hopeless, seeing the fury of the Londoners to crowd upon the trains, and broached his own idea of striking across Essex towards Harwich and thence escaping from the country altogether.

Mrs. Elphinstone–that was the name of the woman in white–would listen to no reasoning, and kept calling upon "George"; but her sister-in-law was astonishingly quiet and deliberate, and at last agreed to my brother's suggestion. So, designing to cross the Great North Road, they went on towards Barnet, my brother leading the pony to save it as much as possible.

As the sun crept up the sky the day became excessively hot, and under foot a thick, whitish sand grew burning and blinding, so that they travelled only very slowly. The hedges were grey with dust. And as they advanced towards Barnet a tumultuous murmuring grew stronger.

They began to meet more people. For the most part these were staring before them, murmuring indistinct questions, jaded, haggard, unclean. One man in evening dress passed them on foot, his eyes on the ground. They heard his voice, and, looking back at him, saw one hand clutched in his hair and the other beating invisible things. His paroxysm of rage over, he went on his way without once looking back.

As my brother's party went on towards the crossroads to the south of Barnet they saw a woman approaching the road across some fields on their left, carrying a child and with two other children; and then passed a man in dirty black, with a thick stick in one hand and a small portmanteau in the other. Then round the corner of the lane, from between the villas that guarded it at its confluence with the high road, came a little cart drawn by a sweating black pony and driven by a sallow youth in a bowler hat, grey with dust. There were three girls, East End factory girls, and a couple of little children crowded in the cart.

"This'll tike us rahnd Edgware?" asked the driver, wild-eyed, white-faced; and when my brother told him it would if he turned to the left, he whipped up at once without the formality of thanks.

My brother noticed a pale grey smoke or haze rising among the houses in front of them, and veiling the white facade of a terrace beyond the road that appeared between the backs of the villas. Mrs. Elphinstone suddenly cried out at a number of tongues of smoky red flame leaping up above the houses in front of them against the hot, blue sky. The tumultuous noise resolved itself now into the disorderly mingling of many voices, the gride of many wheels, the creaking of waggons, and the staccato of hoofs. The lane came round sharply not fifty yards from the crossroads.

"Good heavens!" cried Mrs. Elphinstone. "What is this you are driving us into?"

My brother stopped.

For the main road was a boiling stream of people, a torrent of human beings rushing northward, one pressing on another. A great bank of dust, white and luminous in the blaze of the sun, made everything within twenty feet of the ground grey and indistinct and was perpetually renewed by the hurrying feet of a dense crowd of horses and of men and women on foot, and by the wheels of vehicles of every description.

"Way!" my brother heard voices crying. "Make way!"

It was like riding into the smoke of a fire to approach the meeting point of the lane and road; the crowd roared like a fire, and the dust was hot and pungent. And, indeed, a little way up the road a villa was burning and sending rolling masses of black smoke across the road to add to the confusion.

Two men came past them. Then a dirty woman, carrying a heavy bundle and weeping. A lost retriever dog, with hanging tongue, circled dubiously round them, scared and wretched, and fled at my brother's threat.

So much as they could see of the road Londonward between the houses to the right was a tumultuous stream of dirty, hurrying people, pent in between the villas on either side; the black heads, the crowded forms, grew into distinctness as they rushed towards the corner, hurried past, and merged their individuality again in a receding multitude that was swallowed up at last in a cloud of dust.

"Go on! Go on!" cried the voices. "Way! Way!"

One man's hands pressed on the back of another. My brother stood at the pony's head. Irresistibly attracted, he advanced slowly, pace by pace, down the lane.

Edgware had been a scene of confusion, Chalk Farm a riotous tumult, but this was a whole population in movement. It is hard to imagine that host. It had no character of its own. The figures poured out past the corner, and receded with their backs to the group in the lane. Along the margin came those who were on foot threatened by the wheels, stumbling in the ditches, blundering into one another.

The carts and carriages crowded close upon one another, making little way for those swifter and more impatient vehicles that darted forward every now and then when an opportunity showed itself of doing so, sending the people scattering against the fences and gates of the villas.

"Push on!" was the cry. "Push on! They are coming!"

In one cart stood a blind man in the uniform of the Salvation Army, gesticulating with his crooked fingers and bawling, "Eternity! Eternity!" His voice was hoarse and very loud so that my brother could hear him long after he was lost to sight in the dust. Some of the people who crowded in the carts whipped stupidly at their horses and quarrelled with other drivers; some sat motionless, staring at nothing with miserable eyes; some gnawed their hands with thirst, or lay prostrate in the bottoms of their conveyances. The horses' bits were covered with foam, their eyes bloodshot.

There were cabs, carriages, shop cars, waggons, beyond counting; a mail cart, a road-cleaner's cart marked "Vestry of St. Pancras," a huge timber waggon crowded with roughs. A brewer's dray rumbled by with its two near wheels splashed with fresh blood.

"Clear the way!" cried the voices. "Clear the way!"

"Eter-nity! Eter-nity!" came echoing down the road.

There were sad, haggard women tramping by, well dressed, with children that cried and stumbled, their dainty clothes smothered in dust, their weary faces smeared with tears. With many of these came men, sometimes helpful, sometimes lowering and savage. Fighting side by side with them pushed some weary street outcast in faded black rags, wide-eyed, loud-voiced, and foul-mouthed. There were sturdy workmen thrusting their way along, wretched, unkempt men, clothed like clerks or shopmen, struggling spasmodically; a wounded soldier my brother noticed, men dressed in the clothes of railway porters, one wretched creature in a nightshirt with a coat thrown over it.

But varied as its composition was, certain things all that host had in common. There were fear and pain on their faces, and fear behind them. A tumult up the road, a quarrel for a place in a waggon, sent the whole host of them quickening their pace; even a man so scared and broken that his knees bent under him was galvanised for a moment into renewed activity. The heat and dust had already been at work upon this multitude. Their skins were dry, their lips black and cracked. They were all thirsty, weary, and footsore. And amid the various cries one heard disputes, reproaches, groans of weariness and fatigue; the voices of most of them were hoarse and weak. Through it all ran a refrain:

"Way! Way! The Martians are coming!"

Few stopped and came aside from that flood. The lane opened slantingly into the main road with a narrow opening, and had a delusive appearance of coming from the direction of London. Yet a kind of eddy of people drove into its mouth; weaklings elbowed out of the stream, who for the most part rested but a moment before plunging into it again. A little way down the lane, with two friends bending over him, lay a man with a bare leg, wrapped about with bloody rags. He was a lucky man to have friends.

A little old man, with a grey military moustache and a filthy black frock coat, limped out and sat down beside the trap, removed his boot–his sock was blood-stained–shook out a pebble, and hobbled on again; and then a little girl of eight or nine, all alone, threw herself under the hedge close by my brother, weeping.

"I can't go on! I can't go on!"

My brother woke from his torpor of astonishment and lifted her up, speaking gently to her, and carried her to Miss Elphinstone. So soon as my brother touched her she became quite still, as if frightened.

"Ellen!" shrieked a woman in the crowd, with tears in her voice–"Ellen!" And the child suddenly darted away from my brother, crying "Mother!"

"They are coming," said a man on horseback, riding past along the lane.

"Out of the way, there!" bawled a coachman, towering high; and my brother saw a closed carriage turning into the lane.

The people crushed back on one another to avoid the horse. My brother pushed the pony and chaise back into the hedge, and the man drove by and stopped at the turn of the way. It was a carriage, with a pole for a pair of horses, but only one was in the traces. My brother saw dimly through the dust that two men lifted out something on a white stretcher and put it gently on the grass beneath the privet hedge.

One of the men came running to my brother.

"Where is there any water?" he said. "He is dying fast, and very thirsty. It is Lord Garrick."

"Lord Garrick!" said my brother; "the Chief Justice?"

"The water?" he said.

"There may be a tap," said my brother, "in some of the houses. We have no water. I dare not leave my people."

The man pushed against the crowd towards the gate of the corner house.

"Go on!" said the people, thrusting at him. "They are coming! Go on!"

Then my brother's attention was distracted by a bearded, eagle-faced man lugging a small handbag, which split even as my brother's eyes rested on it and disgorged a mass of sovereigns that seemed to break up into separate coins as it struck the ground. They rolled hither and thither among the struggling feet of men and horses. The man stopped and looked stupidly at the heap, and the shaft of a cab struck his shoulder and sent him reeling. He gave a shriek and dodged back, and a cartwheel shaved him narrowly.

"Way!" cried the men all about him. "Make way!"

So soon as the cab had passed, he flung himself, with both hands open, upon the heap of coins, and began thrusting handfuls in his pocket. A horse rose close upon him, and in another moment, half rising, he had been borne down under the horse's hoofs.

"Stop!" screamed my brother, and pushing a woman out of his way, tried to clutch the bit of the horse.

Before he could get to it, he heard a scream under the wheels, and saw through the dust the rim passing over the poor wretch's back. The driver of the cart slashed his whip at my brother, who ran round behind the cart. The multitudinous shouting confused his ears. The man was writhing in the dust among his scattered money, unable to rise, for the wheel had broken his back, and his lower limbs lay limp and dead. My brother stood up and yelled at the next driver, and a man on a black horse came to his assistance.

"Get him out of the road," said he; and, clutching the man's collar with his free hand, my brother lugged him sideways. But he still clutched after his money, and regarded my brother fiercely, hammering at his arm with a handful of gold. "Go on! Go on!" shouted angry voices behind.

"Way! Way!"

There was a smash as the pole of a carriage crashed into the cart that the man on horseback stopped. My brother looked up, and the man with the gold twisted his head round and bit the wrist that held his collar. There was a concussion, and the black horse came staggering sideways, and the carthorse pushed beside it. A hoof missed my brother's foot by a hair's breadth. He released his grip on the fallen man and jumped back. He saw anger change to terror on the face of the poor wretch on the ground, and in a moment he was hidden and my brother was borne backward and carried past the entrance of the lane, and had to fight hard in the torrent to recover it.

He saw Miss Elphinstone covering her eyes, and a little child, with all a child's want of sympathetic imagination, staring with dilated eyes at a dusty something that lay black and still, ground and crushed under the rolling wheels. "Let us go back!" he shouted, and began turning the pony round. "We cannot cross this–hell," he said and they went back a hundred yards the way they had come, until the fighting crowd was hidden. As they passed the bend in the lane my brother saw the face of the dying man in the ditch under the privet, deadly white and drawn, and shining with perspiration. The two women sat silent, crouching in their seat and shivering.

Then beyond the bend my brother stopped again. Miss Elphinstone was white and pale, and her sister-in-law sat weeping, too wretched even to call upon "George." My brother was horrified and perplexed. So soon as they had retreated he realised how urgent and unavoidable it was to attempt this crossing. He turned to Miss Elphinstone, suddenly resolute.

"We must go that way," he said, and led the pony round again.

For the second time that day this girl proved her quality. To force their way into the torrent of people, my brother plunged into the traffic and held back a cab horse, while she drove the pony across its head. A waggon locked wheels for a moment and ripped a long splinter from the chaise. In another moment they were caught and swept forward by the stream. My brother, with the cabman's whip marks red across his face and hands, scrambled into the chaise and took the reins from her.

"Point the revolver at the man behind," he said, giving it to her, "if he presses us too hard. No!–point it at his horse."

Then he began to look out for a chance of edging to the right across the road. But once in the stream he seemed to lose volition, to become a part of that dusty rout. They swept through Chipping Barnet with the torrent; they were nearly a mile beyond the centre of the town before they had fought across to the opposite side of the way. It was din and confusion indescribable; but in and beyond the town the road forks repeatedly, and this to some extent relieved the stress.

They struck eastward through Hadley, and there on either side of the road, and at another place farther on they came upon a great multitude of people drinking at the stream, some fighting to come at the water. And farther on, from a lull near East Barnet, they saw two trains running slowly one after the other without signal or order–trains swarming with people, with men even among the coals behind the engines–going northward along the Great Northern Railway. My brother supposes they must have filled outside London, for at that time the furious terror of the people had rendered the central termini impossible.

Near this place they halted for the rest of the afternoon, for the violence of the day had already utterly exhausted all three of them. They began to suffer the beginnings of hunger; the night was cold, and none of them dared to sleep. And in the evening many people came hurrying along the road nearby their stopping place, fleeing from unknown dangers before them, and going in the direction from which my brother had come.

Chapter Seventeen

The *Thunder Child*

Had the Martians aimed only at destruction, they might on Monday have annihilated the entire population of London, as it spread itself slowly through the home counties. Not only along the road through Barnet, but also through Edgware and Waltham Abbey, and along the roads eastward to Southend and Shoeburyness, and south of the Thames to Deal and Broadstairs, poured the same frantic rout. If one could have hung that June morning in a balloon in the blazing blue above London every northward and eastward road running out of the tangled maze of streets would have seemed stippled black with the streaming fugitives, each dot a human agony of terror and physical distress. I have set forth at length in the last chapter my brother's account of the road through Chipping Barnet, in order that my readers may realise how that swarming of black dots appeared to one of those concerned. Never before in the history of the world had such a mass of human beings moved and suffered together. The legendary hosts of Goths and Huns, the hugest armies Asia has ever seen, would have been but a drop in that current. And this was no disciplined march; it was a stampede–a stampede gigantic and terrible–without order and without a goal, six million people unarmed and unprovisioned, driving headlong. It was the beginning of the rout of civilisation, of the massacre of mankind.

Directly below him the balloonist would have seen the network of streets far and wide, houses, churches, squares, crescents, gardens—already derelict—spread out like a huge map, and in the southward *blotted*. Over Ealing, Richmond, Wimbledon, it would have seemed as if some monstrous pen had flung ink upon the chart. Steadily, incessantly, each black splash grew and spread, shooting out ramifications this way and that, now banking itself against rising ground, now pouring swiftly over a crest into a new-found valley, exactly as a gout of ink would spread itself upon blotting paper.

And beyond, over the blue hills that rise southward of the river, the glittering Martians went to and fro, calmly and methodically spreading their poison cloud over this patch of country and then over that, laying it again with their steam jets when it had served its purpose, and taking possession of the conquered country. They do not seem to have aimed at extermination so much as at complete demoralisation and the destruction of any opposition. They exploded any stores of powder they came upon, cut every telegraph, and wrecked the railways here and there. They were hamstringing mankind. They seemed in no hurry to extend the field of their operations, and did not come beyond the central part of London all that day. It is possible that a very considerable number of people in London stuck to their houses through Monday morning. Certain it is that many died at home suffocated by the Black Smoke.

Until about midday the Pool of London was an astonishing scene. Steamboats and shipping of all sorts lay there, tempted by the enormous sums of money offered by fugitives, and it is said that many who swam out to these vessels were thrust off with boathooks and drowned. About one o'clock in the afternoon the thinning remnant of a cloud of the black vapour appeared between the arches of Blackfriars Bridge. At that the Pool became a scene of mad confusion, fighting, and collision, and for some time a multitude of boats and barges jammed in the northern arch of the Tower Bridge, and the sailors and lightermen had to fight savagely against the people who swarmed upon them from the riverfront. People were actually clambering down the piers of the bridge from above.

When, an hour later, a Martian appeared beyond the Clock Tower and waded down the river, nothing but wreckage floated above Limehouse.

Of the falling of the fifth cylinder I have presently to tell. The sixth star fell at Wimbledon. My brother, keeping watch beside the women in the chaise in a meadow, saw the green flash of it far beyond the hills. On Tuesday the little party, still set upon getting across the sea, made its way through the swarming country towards Colchester. The news that the Martians were now in possession of the whole of London was confirmed. They had been seen at Highgate, and even, it was said, at Neasden. But they did not come into my brother's view until the morrow.

That day the scattered multitudes began to realise the urgent need of provisions. As they grew hungry the rights of property ceased to be regarded. Farmers were out to defend their cattle-sheds, granaries, and ripening root crops with arms in their hands. A number of people now, like my brother, had their faces eastward, and there were some desperate souls even going back towards London to get food. These were chiefly people from the northern suburbs, whose knowledge of the Black Smoke came by hearsay. He heard that about half the members of the government had gathered at Birmingham, and that enormous quantities of high explosives were being prepared to be used in automatic mines across the Midland counties.

He was also told that the Midland Railway Company had replaced the desertions of the first day's panic, had resumed traffic, and was running northward trains from St. Albans to relieve the congestion of the home counties. There was also a placard in Chipping Ongar announcing that large stores of flour were available in the northern towns and that within twenty-four hours bread would be distributed among the starving people in the neighbourhood. But this intelligence did not deter him from the plan of escape he had formed, and the three pressed eastward all day, and heard no more of the bread distribution than this promise. Nor, as a matter of fact, did anyone else hear more of it. That night fell the seventh star, falling upon Primrose Hill. It fell while Miss Elphinstone was watching, for she took that duty alternately with my brother. She saw it.

On Wednesday the three fugitives–they had passed the night in a field of unripe wheat–reached Chelmsford, and there a body of the inhabitants, calling itself the Committee of Public Supply, seized the pony as provisions, and would give nothing in exchange for it but the promise of a share in it the next day. Here there were rumours of Martians at Epping, and news of the destruction of Waltham Abbey Powder Mills in a vain attempt to blow up one of the invaders.

People were watching for Martians here from the church towers. My brother, very luckily for him as it chanced, preferred to push on at once to the coast rather than wait for food, although all three of them were very hungry.

By midday they passed through Tillingham, which, strangely enough, seemed to be quite silent and deserted, save for a few furtive plunderers hunting for food. Near Tillingham they suddenly came in sight of the sea, and the most amazing crowd of shipping of all sorts that it is possible to imagine.

For after the sailors could no longer come up the Thames, they came on to the Essex coast, to Harwich and Walton and Clacton, and afterwards to Foulness and Shoebury, to bring off the people. They lay in a huge sickle-shaped curve that vanished into mist at last towards the Naze. Close inshore was a multitude of fishing smacks–English, Scotch, French, Dutch, and Swedish; steam launches from the Thames, yachts, electric boats; and beyond were ships of large burden, a multitude of filthy colliers, trim merchantmen, cattle ships, passenger boats, petroleum tanks, ocean tramps, an old white transport even, neat white and grey liners from Southampton and Hamburg; and along the blue coast across the Blackwater my brother could make out dimly a dense swarm of boats chaffering with the people on the beach, a swarm which also extended up the Blackwater almost to Maldon.

About a couple of miles out lay an ironclad, very low in the water, almost, to my brother's perception, like a waterlogged ship. This was the ram *Thunder Child*. It was the only warship in sight, but far away to the right over the smooth surface of the sea–for that day there was a dead calm–lay a serpent of black smoke to mark the next ironclads of the Channel Fleet, which hovered in an extended line, steam up and ready for action, across the Thames estuary during the course of the Martian conquest, vigilant and yet powerless to prevent it.

At the sight of the sea, Mrs. Elphinstone, in spite of the assurances of her sister-in-law, gave way to panic. She had never been out of England before, she would rather die than trust herself friendless in a foreign country, and so forth. She seemed, poor woman, to imagine that the French and the Martians might prove very similar. She had been growing increasingly hysterical, fearful, and depressed during the two days' journeyings. Her great idea was to return to Stanmore. Things had been always well and safe at Stanmore. They would find George at Stanmore.

It was with the greatest difficulty they could get her down to the beach, where presently my brother succeeded in attracting the attention of some men on a paddle steamer from the Thames. They sent a boat and drove a bargain for thirty-six pounds for the three. The steamer was going, these men said, to Ostend.

It was about two o'clock when my brother, having paid their fares at the gangway, found himself safely aboard the steamboat with his charges. There was food aboard, albeit at exorbitant prices, and the three of them contrived to eat a meal on one of the seats forward.

There were already a couple of score of passengers aboard, some of whom had expended their last money in securing a passage, but the captain lay off the Blackwater until five in the afternoon, picking up passengers until the seated decks were even dangerously crowded. He would probably have remained longer had it not been for the sound of guns that began about that hour in the south. As if in answer, the ironclad seaward fired a small gun and hoisted a string of flags. A jet of smoke sprang out of her funnels.

Some of the passengers were of opinion that this firing came from Shoeburyness, until it was noticed that it was growing louder. At the same time, far away in the southeast the masts and upperworks of three ironclads rose one after the other out of the sea, beneath clouds of black smoke. But my brother's attention speedily reverted to the distant firing in the south. He fancied he saw a column of smoke rising out of the distant grey haze.

The little steamer was already flapping her way eastward of the big crescent of shipping, and the low Essex coast was growing blue and hazy, when a Martian appeared, small and faint in the remote distance, advancing along the muddy coast from the direction of Foulness. At that the captain on the bridge swore at the top of his voice with fear and anger at his own delay, and the paddles seemed infected with his terror. Every soul aboard stood at the bulwarks or on the seats of the steamer and stared at that distant shape, higher than the trees or church towers inland, and advancing with a leisurely parody of a human stride.

It was the first Martian my brother had seen, and he stood, more amazed than terrified, watching this Titan advancing deliberately towards the shipping, wading farther and farther into the water as the coast fell away. Then, far away beyond the Crouch, came another, striding over some stunted trees, and then yet another, still farther off, wading deeply through a shiny mudflat that seemed to hang halfway up between sea and sky. They were all stalking seaward, as if to intercept the escape of the multitudinous vessels that were crowded between Foulness and the Naze. In spite of the throbbing exertions of the engines of the little paddleboat, and the pouring foam that her wheels flung behind her, she receded with terrifying slowness from this ominous advance.

Glancing northwestward, my brother saw the large crescent of shipping already writhing with the approaching terror; one ship passing behind another, another coming round from broadside to end on, steamships whistling and giving off volumes of steam, sails being let out, launches rushing hither and thither. He was so fascinated by this and by the creeping danger away to the left that he had no eyes for anything seaward. And then a swift movement of the steamboat (she had suddenly come round to avoid being run down) flung him headlong from the seat upon which he was standing. There was a shouting all about him, a trampling of feet, and a cheer that seemed to be answered faintly. The steamboat lurched and rolled him over upon his hands.

He sprang to his feet and saw to starboard, and not a hundred yards from their heeling, pitching boat, a vast iron bulk like the blade of a plough tearing through the water, tossing it on either side in huge waves of foam that leaped towards the steamer, flinging her paddles helplessly in the air, and then sucking her deck down almost to the waterline.

A douche of spray blinded my brother for a moment. When his eyes were clear again he saw the monster had passed and was rushing landward. Big iron upperworks rose out of this headlong structure, and from that twin funnels projected and spat a smoking blast shot with fire. It was the torpedo ram, *Thunder Child*, steaming headlong, coming to the rescue of the threatened shipping.

Keeping his footing on the heaving deck by clutching the bulwarks, my brother looked past this charging leviathan at the Martians again, and he saw the three of them now close together, and standing so far out to sea that their tripod supports were almost entirely submerged. Thus sunken, and seen in remote perspective, they appeared far less formidable than the huge iron bulk in whose wake the steamer was pitching so helplessly. It would seem they were regarding this new antagonist with astonishment. To their intelligence, it may be, the giant was even such another as themselves. The *Thunder Child* fired no gun, but simply drove full speed towards them. It was probably her not firing that enabled her to get so near the enemy as she did. They did not know what to make of her. One shell, and they would have sent her to the bottom forthwith with the Heat-Ray.

She was steaming at such a pace that in a minute she seemed halfway between the steamboat and the Martians–a diminishing black bulk against the receding horizontal expanse of the Essex coast.

Suddenly the foremost Martian lowered his tube and discharged a canister of the black gas at the ironclad. It hit her larboard side and glanced off in an inky jet that rolled away to seaward, an unfolding torrent of Black Smoke, from which the ironclad drove clear. To the watchers from the steamer, low in the water and with the sun in their eyes, it seemed as though she were already among the Martians.

They saw the gaunt figures separating and rising out of the water as they retreated shoreward, and one of them raised the camera-like generator of the Heat-Ray. He held it pointing obliquely downward, and a bank of steam sprang from the water at its touch. It must have driven through the iron of the ship's side like a white-hot iron rod through paper.

A flicker of flame went up through the rising steam, and then the Martian reeled and staggered. In another moment he was cut down, and a great body of water and steam shot high in the air. The guns of the*Thunder Child* sounded through the reek, going off one after the other, and one shot splashed the water high close by the steamer, ricocheted towards the other flying ships to the north, and smashed a smack to matchwood.

But no one heeded that very much. At the sight of the Martian's collapse the captain on the bridge yelled inarticulately, and all the crowding passengers on the steamer's stern shouted together. And then they yelled again. For, surging out beyond the white tumult, drove something long and black, the flames streaming from its middle parts, its ventilators and funnels spouting fire.

She was alive still; the steering gear, it seems, was intact and her engines working. She headed straight for a second Martian, and was within a hundred yards of him when the Heat-Ray came to bear. Then with a violent thud, a blinding flash, her decks, her funnels, leaped upward. The Martian staggered with the violence of her explosion, and in another moment the flaming wreckage, still driving forward with the impetus of its pace, had struck him and crumpled him up like a thing of cardboard. My brother shouted involuntarily. A boiling tumult of steam hid everything again.

"Two!," yelled the captain.

Everyone was shouting. The whole steamer from end to end rang with frantic cheering that was taken up first by one and then by all in the crowding multitude of ships and boats that was driving out to sea.

The steam hung upon the water for many minutes, hiding the third Martian and the coast altogether. And all this time the boat was paddling steadily out to sea and away from the fight; and when at last the confusion cleared, the drifting bank of black vapour intervened, and nothing of the *Thunder Child* could be made out, nor could the third Martian be seen. But the ironclads to seaward were now quite close and standing in towards shore past the steamboat.

The little vessel continued to beat its way seaward, and the ironclads receded slowly towards the coast, which was hidden still by a marbled bank of vapour, part steam, part black gas, eddying and combining in the strangest way. The fleet of refugees was scattering to the northeast; several smacks were sailing between the ironclads and the steamboat. After a time, and before they reached the sinking cloud bank, the warships turned northward, and then abruptly went about and passed into the thickening haze of evening southward. The coast grew faint, and at last indistinguishable amid the low banks of clouds that were gathering about the sinking sun.

Then suddenly out of the golden haze of the sunset came the vibration of guns, and a form of black shadows moving. Everyone struggled to the rail of the steamer and peered into the blinding furnace of the west, but nothing was to be distinguished clearly. A mass of smoke rose slanting and barred the face of the sun. The steamboat throbbed on its way through an interminable suspense.

The sun sank into grey clouds, the sky flushed and darkened, the evening star trembled into sight. It was deep twilight when the captain cried out and pointed. My brother strained his eyes. Something rushed up into the sky out of the greyness–rushed slantingly upward and very swiftly into the luminous clearness above the clouds in the western sky; something flat and broad, and very large, that swept round in a vast curve, grew smaller, sank slowly, and vanished again into the grey mystery of the night. And as it flew it rained down darkness upon the land.

Critical Eye

For Discussion

a. What does this excerpt reveal to us about what happens when civility leaves an otherwise ordered and structured society?

Re-approaching the Reading

From the outside, the alien annihilation of the humans appears cruel and vicious, but is their behavior any different from how human beings have behaved toward each other throughout history?

Writing Assignment

Research the vast and varied interpretations of this literary work. In doing so, you will find that it has been associated with political, racial, and cultural movements throughout history. In short, the story is not solely about an alien invasion; it is instead about colonialism, social Darwinism, and imperialism. How is this so? How does an apocalyptic tale about the end of the world become a text that really speaks to what it means to lose one's personal world–a society that before this provided identity and meaning?

Religion, Faith, and Spirituality

This is my simple religion. There is no need for temples; no need for complicated philosophy. Our own brain, our own heart is our temple; the philosophy is kindness.
Dalai Lama

Pray that your loneliness may spur you into finding something to live for, great enough to die for.
Dag Hammarskjold

In 1996, singer Joan Osborne released her song "One of Us." Using her lyrics, she asked the listener to consider what accepting God really meant in a modern-day world filled with a contemporary understanding of how life works. The song was an immediate success, yet the Catholic Church condemned it in one fell swoop. Now, almost twenty years later, the Catholic Church has a new pope, Francis, who, if not more accepting, is at least less judgmental when it comes to ideals that don't easily mesh with Catholic doctrine. It's amazing how time changes things. And while our ideas about whether or not a God exists are evolving, the fact that most people of all faiths still believe in a God remains a constant. For many of us, knowing that there is a God is not enough. We long for ceremony and order to surround our beliefs. And that's when religion comes into play.

Religion is generally perceived as a belief in and, arguably—maybe more importantly—a reverence for a supernatural power or powers regarded as both the creator and governing body of the universe. A subtler notion of religion is defined as a cause, activity, or principle that is undertaken with conscientious devotion. Almost every person walking the planet has either embraced or been touched by the broad hand of a higher being and the tradition that governs it. While all humans may not believe or follow, none are unaffected by the influence and power of religion. Oddly enough, religion is, like taxes, inescapable.

Historically, religion has appeared in the embracing words and arms of the church; at the same time, at least in some cases, our faiths have harmed as many as they have helped. For some, religion, faith, and spiritual matters provide support for the people. Yet, too often have our faith-based beliefs become blurred with our worldly views on power and dominance. This blending of religion with politics, power, and—as we see as clearly in the 21st century as ever before—"intolerance" demands a converting with the snap of a merciless whip that appears as fanatical as it is blind. Which is accurate? What is the real face of our world's churches, synagogues, mosques, temples, and meeting places where people gather to worship? What happens when the "word" of deities is played out and manipulated by flawed humans who manipulate religious doctrines to fit their own vision of the world? And, moreover, what happens when religious mandates become vexing to the point of oppression? Undoubtedly, the fact that we have various religions is a blessing. But, the judgment that seems to follow—the worldwide bickering that one interpretation of a higher power is better than others—seems as absurd as it is contradictory. Surely the purpose of faith is to bring a sense of reconciliation that humankind cannot explain. As such, if spirituality is an elevation from our secular lives to a higher sense of being, then shouldn't those who so wholeheartedly claim to "believe" denounce the shallow views of politics, financial compensation, rivalry—as well as mores and rules that seem painfully outdated—in an attempt to heal our damaged world?

The selections in this chapter touch different parts of the world and brazenly cross gender lines. For some, faith not only guarantees salvation but also provides the individual with patience and fortitude in a trying world. For others, faith is neither black nor white, but, as we recognize now more than ever before, varied shades of gray that are so very difficult to muddle through.

ADAM WEYMOUTH

When Global Warming Kills Your God

Twenty-three Alaskan tribesmen broke the law when they overfished king salmon, but they claim their faith gave them no other choice.

"So there is a black fish swimming up the river, looking for a fish trap to swim into. Cycle of life, right?"

Grant Kashatok was telling me stories the traditional Yup'ik way—his fingers entwined with string, like a child playing cat's cradle. As he spoke, he looped the string into different shapes: it became a hunter, a mountain, a boat, an oar. "And he came to a fish trap that was broken," he said, "and some of the fish in it were dead. The black fish poked his head out of the river to see who it was that owned the trap, and he saw that the village was dirty, and that the dogs were not tied up, and the woman came out to throw out the scraps of a fish dinner and he watched the dogs fight over the bones. The fish did not want his bones fought over. So he carried on swimming up river."

Kashatok is the principal of the only school in Newtok, Alaska—a town of 354 perched at the mouth of the Ninglick River, just a few miles from the Pacific Ocean. In 2009, it was one of 26 indigenous villages listed by the U.S. Army Corps of Engineers as "priority action communities": The ground beneath it is slipping into the sea at such a rate that the village may only have two more years before the first houses fall away.

"If Yup'ik people do not fish for King Salmon, the King Salmon spirit will be offended and it will not return to the river."

Throughout the state, climate change is intensifying storm surges and thawing the permafrost—land that previously remained frozen throughout the year. Parts of highways are sinking. Trees around Fairbanks have slipped to such rakish angles that they have become known as drunken forests.

But it's not hard to see why the Yukon-Kuskokwim Delta, a watershed the size of Britain, is especially vulnerable. Approaching from the air, it's difficult to determine whether this region is a landmass with many lakes or a body of water with many islands. The Yup'ik never intended to live here year-round: They were a nomadic people forced into settlements by missionaries and the government. The villages where the Yup'ik now live year-round were once their summer fishing and hunting grounds.

I went to the Delta to cover the trial of 23 Yup'ik fishermen who had violated a ban on the fishing of king (or Chinook) salmon. In late June and early July, as many as 40 million of the fish have been known to migrate throughout the state, returning from the sea to spawn on gravel beds. They run so thick that the fish swimming on the outer edges of the river are forced onto the banks. King salmon, I am told, can weigh as much as sled dogs.

But over the past few years, their numbers have dropped dramatically. By the beginning of the 2012 season, the Department of Fish and Game was alarmed enough to gather a panel of fishery scientists and ecologists from across Alaska to determine a response.

They came up with seven hypotheses for the decline. Natural cycles are cited, but the report returns again and again to climate change. Rivers are breaking up earlier along their routes, sending more vulnerable juveniles out into the ocean. Changing ocean currents may be spreading disease. There are shifts in other species in the food chain upon which the salmon depend. Warmer waters are depleting the energy of the fish, causing higher mortality rates along the migration route. The impact of each of these factors is currently unknown.

In June 2012, after Fish and Game announced a ban throughout the Delta, State Trooper Brett Scott Gibbens was sent out to patrol the rivers around Bethel, the central hub of the Yukon-Kuskokwim Delta. He'd learned, through a press release, that a group of Yup'ik fishermen planned to defy the ban, and as he came down the Kuskokwim River, he found a small fleet of boats–somewhere between 12 and 16, he later testified. The gill nets they were using were perhaps 50 fathoms long, which made them illegal under the ban. Many of the fishermen pulled their gear and left as he was identifying and rounding up the others. Some of the fishermen later went on to pay fines. But 23 of them refused, and last summer, they stood trial in a Bethel courtroom.

On the first morning of the trial, the court was standing-room only, crowded with defendants, supporters, families with babies, and a handful of journalists and cops. Behind Judge Bruce Ward, next to the American flag, hung a traditional Yup'ik mask. Someone produced a Ziploc of salmon jerky and passed it down the row. Everyone took a piece and chewed on it, including the two state troopers. The courtroom began to smell like a fish market.

Felix Flynn was the first fisherman to take the stand. "Is it okay if he occasionally breaks into Yup'ik?" asked his lawyer, Jim Davis, pushing back a luxuriant sweep of hair. He is one of the founders of the Northern Justice Project, a private firm that represents low- and middle-income native Alaskans, and had taken this case pro bono.

"We'll cross that bridge when we come to it," replied the judge.

Flynn raised his hand and swore on the Bible. A short man with drooping moustaches and cheeks scarred by frostbite, he began by telling the court how his father took him out herring fishing when he was a boy. "To start with, all I see is ocean," he said. "Then after a while there's glassy water, and there's other water that's not glassy. And that means the herring are here. That's what I learnt from my father. I'm subsistence. I was born and raised an Eskimo. It's in my blood. It's in my family blood."

"And what does that mean to you, subsistence?" prompted Davis, leaning over with his hands on the podium.

"Subsistence is living from the land," said Flynn. "It's what we've always done. We go hunt ducks and seals in the ocean in the springtime. Ptarmigan. Salmon. My great-grandfather and grandfather told us we have to be very careful what we catch. God made them for everyone. I was living subsistence even when I was in the military. My whole life. I make a fish camp every year and dry 30, 40 kings. I set a net last summer but there was too much closure. Things have been rough."

"And how did it feel not to be able to catch enough?" Davis asked him.

"I have a grandchild, 2 years old–" He paused and rubbed his eyes. Several other men in the gallery also began to cry. "My grandson said to me, 'When we gonna go check the net?' And I couldn't say anything."

Michael Cresswell, a state trooper, leaned over and whispered in my ear: "This is momentous. This is climate change on trial."

A few days later, I flew to the small village of Akiak, population 346, to visit Mike Williams, the current chief of the Yupiit nation. Williams is one of Alaska's most outspoken voices on climate change. In 2007, he was invited to testify before a U.S. Representatives Select Committee on Energy Independence and Global Warming. "If global warming is not addressed," he told them, "the impacts on Alaskan Natives and American Indians will be immense." He spoke to Congress about the Iditarod, the thousand-mile sled dog race from Anchorage to Nome. "To keep the dogs cool, since the days are too warm, we have to mostly mush by night now," Williams told the politicians. "And we also mush more on land and less on frozen rivers because of thawing." The Iditarod's sponsors include, among others, ExxonMobil.

Now, Williams was helping to coordinate the fishermen's defense. To get to his Akiak office, you have to enter through a bingo hall. The doors hang from their hinges, the plasterboard sags from the ceiling. The toilet is broken. During our interview, the Internet was down; he spent much of the two hours trying to check his Yahoo account. "This is my war room," he said, gesturing around himself. "This is where I cause trouble. I'm doing better than Gandhi."

In court, the fishermen's civil disobedience has been framed as a First Amendment issue: The Yup'ik believe they have an obligation to continue their ancestral traditions. As Jim Davis summarized it, in a brief submitted before the trial: "If Yup'ik people do not fish for King Salmon, the King Salmon spirit will be offended and it will not return to the river."

An amicus brief filed by the American Civil Liberties Union elaborated further:

> A Yup'ik fisherman who is a sincere believer in his religious role as a steward of nature, believes that he must fulfill his prescribed role to maintain this 'collaborative reciprocity' between hunter and game. Completely barring him from the salmon fishery thwarts the practice of a real religious belief. Under Yup'ik religious belief, this cycle of interplay between humans and animals helped perpetuate the seasons; without the maintaining of that balance, a new year will not follow the old one.

But now the seasons are out of balance, and the Yup'ik can't stop hold the sea back. According to the U.S. Army Corps of Engineers, an estimated 86 percent of indigenous villages in Alaska will need to move within the next 50 years, at a cost of \$200 to \$500 million per village. Newtok is preparing to move to a new site, across the water to Nelson Island, but a struggle against the village leadership has recently stalled the relocation effort.

As Williams drove me back to his house for lunch, he told me how Akiak had lost its graveyard to the water three years earlier. The bones and skulls of their ancestors had started emerging from the banks, drifting down toward Bethel. The community had gathered up what they could and carried the remains to a new mass grave on the other side of town.

Lunch was a soup of whitefront goose, shot by one of Mike's five kids. I sucked at the thin flesh of a boiled head, its eyes cooked to cataracts, its teeth a saw line. Dessert was the local version of ice cream: blueberries, margarine, and sugar, mixed and frozen. The soup was good, the ice cream revolting. The paneled walls were lined with photos of sledding kids bundled up in parkas, dream catchers, graduation portraits, animal hide drums, mushing memorabilia, and a Moravian church calendar. There was a basketball game on the corner–Montana vs. Indiana. A wood-burning stove in the corner heated the room, fueled with driftwood snagged from the river.

Outside, Williams told me he wanted to show me where he had been born. He led me down to his dog yard by the river. His 30-year-old son, Mike Jr.–who ran his first Iditarod last year and came in 22 places ahead of his dad–was putting eight dogs into their traces and tethering them to a quad bike, the only way to exercise them without snow on the ground. About 40 dogs were pacing on their chains, yelping and yammering–a mottled crew of huskies and malamutes, lean, strong, and eager.

"So where were you born?" I asked, looking at the houses around us: cheap rectangular structures raised on stilts. Their yards were full of buoys and outboards, caribou antlers and skulls, snowmobiles and aluminum skiffs awaiting their respective seasons. Williams pointed out toward the middle of the river.

"Out there."

That, he told me, is where the hospital once was–where all of Akiak once was. He waved his hand expansively. "I'm continuously moving my dog yard," he said. I followed him down a dirt track that stopped abruptly at the river. "We lost this whole road last year," he said. "One day I was driving down it. The next day, it was gone."

Shrubs had slipped, pointing horizontally across the water. The detritus of a house lay beside them–twisted sheets of corrugated iron, sodden insulation, pipes and tubes and lumber. It looked like the flotsam from a storm.

"Nobody here knows the weather," said 66-year-old fisherman Noah Okoviak, speaking from the witness stand in the Bethel courtroom. "Nobody here knows how many fish will come. Only the creator."

Judge Ward listened to Okoviak's defense and found his beliefs to be sincere. But as with the other 22 fishermen, he found Okoviak guilty. The state had sufficient reason to impose the ban, the judge explained, and the fishermen had violated it. But the sentences were lenient–a year of probation and a fine of $250 apiece (in one case, $500) to be paid over the course of a year or sometimes two. At times, the judge was openly sympathetic. "When this case goes up for appeal," he said, as Okoviak took his seat, "the cold transcript will not reflect that everyone in the courtroom was standing, and that record will not reflect that there are a number of people in the courtroom with tears in their eyes."

The fishermen's cases have indeed moved on to the Alaska Court of Appeals, where their oral arguments may be heard as early as this summer. There, state-appointed judges will grapple with the same question the court faced in 1979, when an indigenous hunter named Carlos Frank was charged with illegally transporting a newly slain moose. Frank argued that he had needed the animal for a religious ceremony. Two lower courts found him guilty, but the Alaska Supreme Court reversed the verdict, calling moose meat "the sacramental equivalent to the wine and wafer in Christianity."

This, in the end, is what's at stake for the Yup'ik fishermen. Their villages may be swallowed up by the sea, but the people themselves won't float away. They'll relocate en masse or drift into the urban diaspora of Anchorage. But if they stop fishing king salmon, the Yup'ik believe they'll lose something far more fundamental than their homes. Harold Borbridge, an indigenous Fairbanks-based consultant with a wife from Newtok, put it this way: "If they can move the things that are important, the language, the culture, the dancing, if they can move the character, they'll have been successful. Anyone can move a few houses."

CRITICAL EYE

For Discussion

a. The indigenous people of Alaska are speaking about their home and their relationship to the land through a spiritual connection. The American government is assessing the situation in terms of money, laws, and science. Where/what is the "disconnect" between the people and their political representatives? Which of the two interested parties seems more correct? Truthfully, can authority or correctness be measured in this case?

Re-approaching the Reading

Craig's essay on Hip Hop addresses social responsibility and the Black community. This article seeks to explore what is owed to the American indigenous population. What are the similarities between the two pieces as they relate to community, government, and cultural responses to changes within disenfranchised ethnic groups?

Writing Assignment

What, if any, scientific proof exists about the realities that face our planet as a result of global warming? If, in fact, climate change is a real, why have we done little to nothing to combat it?

MOHAMMED NASEEHU ALI

MALLAM SILE

He was popularly known as *mai tea,* or the tea seller. His shop was situated right in the navel of Zongo Street—a stone's throw from the chief's assembly shed and adjacent to the kiosk where Mansa BBC, the town gossip, sold her provisions. Along with fried eggs and white butter bread, Mallam Sile carried all kinds of beverages: regular black tea, Japanese green tea, Milo, Bournvita, cocoa drink, instant coffee. But on Zongo Street all hot beverages were referred to just as tea, and it was common, therefore, to hear people say, "Mallam Sile, may I have a mug of cocoa tea?" or "Sile, may I have a cup of coffee tea?"

The tea shop had no windows. It was built of *wawa,* a cheap wood easily infested by termites. The floor was uncemented, and heaps of dust rose in the air whenever a customer walked in. Sile protected his merchandise from the dust by keeping everything in plastic bags. An enormous wooden "chop box," the top of which he used as a serving table, covered most of the space in the shop. There was a tall chair behind the chop box for Sile, but he never used it, preferring instead to stand on his feet even when the shop was empty. There were also three benches that were meant to be used only by those who bought tea, though the idle gossips who crowded the shop and never spent any money occupied the seats most of the time.

Old Sile had an irrational fear of being electrocuted and so he'd never tapped electricity into his shack, as was usually done on Zongo Street. Instead, he used kerosene lanterns, three of which hung from the low wooden ceiling. Sile kept a small radio in the shop, and whenever he had no customers he listened, in meditative silence, to the English programs on GBC 2, as though he understood what was being said. Mallam Sile was fluent only in his northern Sisaala tongue, though he understood Hausa—the language of the street's inhabitants—and spoke just enough pidgin to be able to conduct his business.

The mornings were usually slow for the tea seller, as a majority of the street folks preferred the traditional breakfast of *kókó da mása,* or corn porridge with rice cake. But, come evening, the shop was crowded with the street's young men and women, who gossiped and talked about the "latest news" in town. Some came to the shop just to meet their loved ones. During the shop's peak hours—from eight in the evening until around midnight—one could hardly hear oneself talk because of the boisterous chattering that went on. But anytime Mallam Sile opened his mouth to add to a conversation people would say, "Shut up, Sile, what do you know about this?" or "Close your beak, Sile, who told you that?" The tea seller learned to swallow his words, and eventually spoke only when he was engaged in a transaction with a customer. But nothing said or even whispered in the shop escaped his sharp ears.

Mallam Sile was a loner, without kin on the street or anywhere else in the city. He was born in Nanpugu, a small border town in the north. He left home at age sixteen, and, all by himself, journeyed more than nine hundred miles in a cow truck to find work down south in Kumasi—the capital city of Ghana's gold-rich Ashanti region.

Within a week of his arrival in the city, Sile landed a job as a house servant. Although his monthly wages were meagre, he sent a portion of them home to his ailing parents, who lived like paupers in their drought-stricken village. Even so, Sile's efforts were not enough to save his parents from the claws of Death, who took them away in their sleep one night. They were found clinging tightly to each other, as if one of them had seen what was coming and had grabbed onto the other so that they could go together.

The young Sile received the news of his parents' death with mixed emotions. He was sad to lose them, of course, but he saw it as a well-deserved rest for them, as they both had been ill and bedridden for many months. Though Sile didn't travel up north to attend their funeral, he sent money for a decent burial. With his parents deceased, Sile suddenly found himself with more money in his hands. He quit his house-servant job and found another, selling iced *kenkey* in Kumasi's central market. Sile kept every pesewa he earned, and two years later he was able to use his savings to open a tea business. It was the first of such establishments on Zongo Street, and would remain the only one for many years to come.

Mallam Sile was short—so short, in fact, that many claimed he was a Pygmy. He stood exactly five feet one inch tall. Although he didn't have the broad, flat nose, poorly developed chin, and round head of the Pygmies, he was stout and hairy all over, as they were. A childhood illness that had caused Sile's vision to deteriorate had continued to plague him throughout his adult life. Yet he refused to go to the hospital and condemned any form of medication, traditional or Western. "God is the one who brings illness, and he is the only true healer"—this was Sile's simple, if rather mystical, explanation.

Sile's small face was covered with a thick, long beard. The wrinkles on his dark forehead and the moistness of his soft, squinted eyes gave him the appearance of a sage, one who had lived through and conquered many adversities in his life. His smile, which stretched from one wrinkled cheek to the other, baring his kola-stained teeth, radiated strength, wisdom, and self-confidence.

Sile wore the same outfit every day: a white polyester djellabah and its matching *wando,* a loose pair of slacks that tied with strings at the waist. He had eight of these suits, and wore a different one each day of the week. Also, his head was perpetually shaved, and he was never without his white embroidered Mecca hat—worn by highly devout Muslims as a reflection of their submission to Allah. Like most of the street's dwellers, Sile owned just one pair of slippers at a time, and replaced them only when they were worn out beyond repair. An unusual birth defect that caused the tea seller to grow an additional toe on each foot had made it impossible for him to find footwear that fit him properly; special slippers were made for him by Anaba the cobbler, who used discarded car tires for the soles of the shoes he made. The rascals of Zongo Street, led by Samadu, the street's most notorious bully, poked at Sile's feet and his slippers, which they called *kalabilwala,* a nonsensical term that no one could understand, let alone translate.

At forty-six, Mallam Sile was still a virgin. He routinely made passes at the divorcées and widows who came to his shop, but none showed any interest in him whatsoever. "What would I do with a dwarf?" the women would ask, feeling ashamed of having had passes made at them by Sile. A couple of them seemed receptive to tea seller Sile's advances, but everyone knew that they were flirting with him only in order to get free tea.

Eventually, Sile resigned himself to his lack of success with women. He was convinced that he would die a virgin. Yet late at night, after all the customers, idlers, and rumormongers had left the shop to seek refuge in their shanties and on their bug-ridden grass mattresses, Sile could be heard singing love songs, hoping that a woman somewhere would respond to his passionate cries:

> A beautiful woman, they say,
> Is like an elephant's meat.
> And only the man with the sharpest knife
> Can cut through.
> That's what they say.
> Young girl, I have no knife,
> I am not a hunter of meat.
> And I am not savage.
> I am only looking for love.
> This is what I say.
> Up north where I am from,
> Young girls are not what they are here.
> Up north where I am from,
> People don't judge you by your knife.
> They look at the size of your heart.
> Young girl, I don't know what you look like.
> I don't know where to look for you.
> I don't even know who you are, young girl.
> All I know is: my heart is aching.
> Oh, oh, oh! My heart is aching for you.

Sile's voice rang with melancholy when he sang his songs. But still the rascals derided him. "When are you going to give up, Sile?" they would say. "Can't you see that no woman would marry you?"

"I have given up on them long, long ago," he would reply. "But I am never going to give up on myself!" "You keep fooling yourself," they told him, laughing.

The rascals' mocking didn't end there. Knowing that Mallam Sile couldn't see properly, they often used fake or banned cedi notes to purchase tea from him at night. The tea seller pinned the useless bills to the walls of his shop as if they were good-luck charms. He believed that it was hunger—and not mischief—that had led the rascals to cheat him. And, since he considered it inhuman to refuse a hungry person food, Mallam Sile allowed them to get away with their frauds.

To cool off the hot tea for his customers, Sile poured the contents of one mug into another, raising one over the other. The rascals would push Sile in the middle of this process, causing the hot liquid to spill all over his arms. The tea seller was never angered by such pranks. He merely grinned and, without saying a word, wiped off the spilled tea and continued to serve his customers. And when the rascals blew out the lanterns in the shop, so as to steal bread and Milo while he was trying to rekindle the light, Sile accepted that, too. He managed to rid his heart of any ill feelings. He would wave his short arms to anyone who walked past his shop, and shout, by way of greeting, "How are the heavens with you, boy?" Sile called everyone "boy," including women and older people, and he hardly ever uttered a sentence without referring to the heavens.

He prided himself on his hard work, and smiled whenever he looked in the mirror and saw his dwarfish body and ailing eyes, two abnormalities that he had learned to love. A few months before the death of his parents, he had come to the conclusion that if Allah had made him any differently he would not have been Mallam Sile—and Mallam Sile was an individual whom Sile's heart, mind, and spirit had come to accept and respect. This created within him a peace that made it possible for him not only to tolerate the rascals' ill treatment but also to forgive them. Though in their eyes Sile was only a buffoon.

One sunny afternoon during the dry season, Mallam Sile was seen atop the roof of his shack with hammers, saws, pliers, and all kinds of building tools. He lingered there all day long like a stray monkey, and by dusk he had dismantled all the aluminum roofing sheets that had once sheltered him and his business. He resumed work early the following morning, and by about one-thirty, before *azafar,* the first of the two afternoon prayers, Sile had no place to call either home or tea shop—he had demolished the shack down to its dusty floor.

At three-thirty, after *la-asar,* the second afternoon worship, Mallam Sile moved his personal belongings and all his tea paraphernalia to a room in the servants' quarters of the chiefs' palace. The room had been arranged for him by the chief's wazir, or right-hand man, who was sympathetic to the tea seller.

During the next two days, Mallam Sile ordered plywood and planks of *odum,* a wood superior to the *wawa* used for the old shop. He also ordered a few bags of cement and truckloads of sand and stones, and immediately began building a new shack, much bigger than the first.

The street folks were shocked by Sile's new building—they wondered where he had got the money to embark on such an enterprise. Sile was rumored to be constructing a mini-market store to compete with Alhaji Saifa, the owner of the street's provision store. (And though the tea seller denied the rumor, it rapidly spread up and down the street, eventually creating bad blood between Sile and Alhaji Saifa.)

It took three days for Mallam Sile to complete work on the new shop's foundation, and an additional three weeks for him to erect the wooden walls and the aluminum roofing sheets. While Sile was busy at work, passersby would call out, "How is the provision store coming?" or "*Mai tea,* how is the mansion coming?" Sile would reply simply, "It is coming well, boy. It will be completed soon, *Inshallah.*" He would grin his usual wide grin and wave his short hairy arms, and then return to his work.

Meanwhile, as the days and weeks passed, the street folks grew impatient and somewhat angry at the closing of Sile's shop. The nearest tea shack was three hundred metres away, on Zerikyi Road—and not only that but the owner of the shack, Abongo, was generally abhorred. And for good reason. Abongo, also a northerner, was quite unfriendly even to his loyal customers. He maintained a rigid no-credit policy, and made customers pay him even before they were served. No one was an exception to this policy—even if he or she was dying of hunger. And, unlike Sile, Abongo didn't tolerate idlers or loud conversation in his shop. If a customer persisted in chatting, Abongo reached for the customer's mug, poured the contents in a plastic basin, and refunded his money. He then chased the customer out of the shop, brandishing his bullwhip and cursing after him, "If your mama and papa never teach you manners, I'll teach you some! I'll sew those careless lips of yours together, you bastard son of a bastard woman!"

As soon as work on the shop was completed, Sile left for his home town. Soon afterward, yet another rumor surfaced: it was said that the tea seller had travelled up north in search of "black medicine" for his bad eyesight.

Sile finally returned one Friday evening, some six weeks after he'd begun work on the shop, flanked by a stern woman who looked to be in her late thirties and was three times larger than the tea seller. The woman, whose name was Abeeba, turned out to be Mallam Sile's wife. She was tall and massive, with a face as gloomy as that of someone mourning a dead relative. Like her husband, Abeeba said very little to people in or out of the shop. She, too, grinned and waved her huge arms whenever she greeted people, though, unlike the tea seller, she seemed to have something harder lurking behind her cheerful smile. Abeeba carried herself with the grace and confidence of a lioness, and covered her head and part of her face with an Islamic veil, a practice that had been dropped by most of the married women on Zongo Street.

The rascals asked Sile, when they ran into him at the market, "From where did you get this elephant? Better not get on her bad side; she'll sit on you till you sink into the ground." To this, the tea seller did not say a word.

Exactly one week after Sile's return from his village, he and his wife opened the doors of the new shop to their customers. Among the most talked-about features were the smooth concrete floor and the bright gas lantern that illuminated every corner. In a small wooden box behind the counter, Sile and his wife burned *tularen mayu,* or witches' lavender, a strong yet sweet-smelling incense that doubled as a jinx repellent–to drive bad spirits away from the establishment.

On the first night, the tea shop was so crowded that some customers couldn't find a seat, even with the twelve new metal folding chairs that Sile had bought. The patrons sang songs of praise to the variety of food on the new menu, which included meat pies, brown bread, custard, and Tom Brown, an imported grain porridge. Some of the patrons even went so far as to thank Sile and his wife for relieving them of "Abongo's nastiness." But wise old Sile, who was as familiar with the street folks' cynicism as he was with the palms of his hands, merely nodded and grinned his sheepish grin. He knew that, despite their praise, and despite the smiles they flashed his way, some customers were at that very moment thinking of ways to cheat him.

While Sile prepared the tea and food, Abeeba served and collected the money. Prior to the shop's reopening, Abeeba had tried to convince her husband that they, too, should adopt Abongo's no-credit policy. Sile had quickly frowned upon the idea, claiming that it was inhumane to do such a thing.

The tea seller and his wife debated the matter for three days before they came to a compromise. They agreed to extend credit, but only in special cases and also on condition that the debtor swear by the Koran to pay on time; if a debtor didn't make a payment, he or she would not be given any credit in the future. But, even with the new policy in place, it wasn't long before some of the customers reverted to their old habits and began skipping payments. Then an encounter between Abeeba and one of the defaulters changed everything.

What took place was this: Samadu, the pugnacious sixteen-year-old whose fame had reached every corner of the city, was the tough guy of Zongo Street. He was of medium height, muscular, and a natural-born athlete. For nine months running, no one in the neighborhood had managed to put Samadu's back to the ground in the haphazard wrestling contests held beside the central market's latrine. Samadu's "power" was such that parents paid him to protect their children from other bullies at school. He was also known for having tortured and even killed the livestock of the adults who denounced him.

If they didn't have pets or domestic animals, he harassed their children for several days until he was appeased with cash or goods. Some parents won Samadu's friendship for their children by bribing him with gifts of money, food, or clothing.

Samadu, of course, was deeply in debt to Mallam Sile—he owed him eighty cedis, about four dollars. Early one Tuesday morning, Mallam Sile's wife showed up at Samadu's house to collect the money. Abeeba had tried to collect the debt amicably, but after her third futile attempt she had suggested to Sile that they use force to persuade the boy to pay. Sile had responded by telling his wife, "Stay out of that boy's way—he is dangerous. If he has decided not to pay, let him keep it. He will be the loser in the end."

"But, Mallam, it is an insult what he is doing," Abeeba argued. "I think people to whom we have been generous should only be generous in return. I am getting fed up with their ways, and the sooner the folks here know that even the toad gets sick of filling his belly with the same dirty pond water every day, the better!" Though Sile wasn't sure what his wife meant, he let the matter drop.

When Abeeba arrived at Samadu's house, a number of housewives and young women were busily doing their morning chores in and around the compound—some sweeping and stirring up dust, others fetching water from the tap in the compound's center or lighting up charcoal pots to warm the food left over from the previous night. Abeeba greeted them politely and asked to be shown to the tough guy's door. The women tried to turn Abeeba away, as they feared that Samadu would humiliate her in some way. But Abeeba insisted that she had important business with him, and so the housewives reluctantly directed her to Samadu's room, which, like all the young men's rooms, was situated just outside the main compound.

The usual tactic that the street's teen-age boys used when fighting girls or women was to strip them of the wrapper around their waist, knowing that they would be reluctant to continue fighting half-naked. But Abeeba had heard young boys in the shop discussing Samadu's bullying ways and had come prepared for anything. She wore a sleeveless shirt and a pair of tight-fitting khaki shorts, and, for the first time ever, she had left her veil at home.

"You rogue! If you call yourself a man, come out and pay your debt!" Abeeba shouted, as she pounded on Samadu's door.

"Who do you think you are, ruining my sleep because of some useless eighty cedis?" Samadu screamed from inside.

"The money may be useless, but it is certainly worthier than you, and that's why you haven't been able to pay, you rubbish heap of a man!" Abeeba's voice was coarse and full of menace. The veins on her neck stood out, like those of the *juju* fighters at the annual wrestling contest. Her eyes moved rapidly inside her head, as though she were having a fit of some sort.

One of the onlookers, a famished-looking housewife, pleaded with the tea seller's wife, "Go back to your house, woman. Don't fight him, he will disgrace you in public." Another woman in the background added, "What kind of a woman thinks she can fight a man? Be careful, oh!"

Abeeba didn't pay any attention to the women's admonitions. Just then, a loud bang was heard inside the room. The door swung open, and Samadu stormed out, his face red with anger. "No one gets away with insulting me. No one!" he shouted. There was a line of dried drool on his right cheek, and whitish mucus had gathered in the corners of his eyes. "You ugly elephant-woman. After I am done with you today, you'll learn a lesson or two about why women don't grow beards!"

"Ha, you teach me a lesson? You?" Abeeba said. "I, too, will educate you about the need to have money in your pocket before you flag the candy man!" With this, she lunged at Samadu.

The women placed their palms on their breasts, and their bodies shook with dread. "Where are the men on the street? Come and separate the fight, oh! Men, come out, oh!" they shouted. The children in the compound, though freshly aroused from sleep, hopped about excitedly, as if they were watching a ritual. Half of them called out, *"Piri pirin-pi!,"* while the other half responded, *"Wein son!,"* as they chanted and cheered for Samadu.

Samadu knew immediately that if he engaged Abeeba in a wrestling match she would use her bulky mass to force him to the ground. His strategy, therefore, was to throw punches and kicks from a safe distance, thereby avoiding close contact. But Abeeba was a lot quicker than he imagined, and she managed to dodge the first five punches he threw. He threw a sixth punch, and missed. He stumbled over his own foot when he tried to connect the seventh, and landed inches from Abeeba. With blinding quickness, she seized him by the sleeping wrapper tied around his neck and began to punch him. The exuberant crowd was hushed by this unexpected turn of events.

But Samadu wasn't heralded as the street's tough guy for nothing. He threw a sharp jab at Abeeba's stomach and succeeded in releasing himself from her grip by deftly undoing the knot of his sleeping cloth. He was topless now, clad only in a pair of corduroy knickers. He danced on his feet, swung his arms, and moved his torso from side to side, the way true boxers do. The crowd got excited again and picked up the fight song, *"Piri pirin-pi, Wein son! Piri pirin-pi, Wein son!"* Some among them shouted "Ali! Ali! Ali!" as Samadu danced and pranced, carefully avoiding Abeeba, who watched his movements with the keenness of a hungry lioness.

The women in the crowd went from holding their breasts to slapping their massive thighs. They jumped about nervously, moving their bodies in rhythm to the chants. The boys booed Abeeba, calling her all sorts of names for the beasts of the jungle. "Destroy that elephant!" they shouted.

The harder the crowd cheered for Samadu, the fancier his footwork became. He finally threw a punch that landed on Abeeba's left shoulder, though she seemed completely unfazed and continued to chase him around the small circle created by the spectators. When Samadu next threw his fist, Abeeba anticipated it. She dodged, then grabbed his wrist and twisted his arm with such force that he let out a high-pitched cry: "*Wayyo* Allah!" The crowd gasped as the tough guy attempted to extricate himself from Abeeba's grip. He tightened all the muscles in his body and craned his neck. But her strength was just too much for him.

The crowd booed, "Wooh, ugly rhinoceros." Then, in a sudden, swift motion, Abeeba lifted the tough guy off the ground, raised him above her head (the crowd booed louder), and dumped him back down like a sack of rice. She then jumped on top of him and began to whack him violently.

The women, now frantic, shouted, "Where are the men in this house?" Men, come out, oh! There is a fight!"

A handful of men came running to the scene, followed by many more a few minutes later.

Meanwhile, with each punch Abeeba asked, "Where is our money?"

"I don't have it, and wouldn't pay even if I did!" Samadu responded. The men drew nearer and tried to pull Abeeba off, but her grip on Samadu's waistband was too firm. The men pleaded with Abeeba to let go. "I will not release him until he pays us back our money!"

she shouted. "And if he doesn't I'll drag his ass all the way to the Zongo police station."

On hearing this, an elderly man who lived in Samadu's compound ran inside the house; he returned a few minutes later with eighty cedis, which he placed in the palm of Abeeba's free hand. With one hand gripping Samadu's waistband, she used the fingers of the other to flip and count the money. Once she was sure the amount was right, she released the boy, giving him a mean, hard look as she left. The crowd watched silently, mouths agape, as though they had just witnessed something from a cinema reel.

Mallam Sile was still engaged in his morning *zikhr,* or meditation, when Abeeba returned to the shack. He, of course, had no inkling of what had taken place. Later, when Abeeba told him that Samadu had paid the money he owed, the tea seller, though surprised, didn't think to ask how this had happened. In his naïveté, he concluded that Samadu had finally been entered by the love and fear of God. Abeeba's news therefore confirmed Mallam Sile's long-standing belief that every man was capable of goodness, just as he was capable of evil.

The tea seller's belief was further solidified when he ran into Samadu a fortnight later. The tough guy greeted him politely, something he had never done before. When Mallam Sile related this to his wife, she restrained herself from telling him the truth. Abeeba knew that Sile would be quite displeased with her methods. Just a week ago, he had spoken to her about the pointlessness of using fire to put out fire, of how it "worsens rather than extinguishes the original flame." Abeeba prayed that no one else would tell her husband about her duel with Samadu, although the entire city seemed to know about it by now. Tough guys from other neighborhoods came to the tea shop just to steal a glance at the woman who had conquered the tough guy of Zongo Street.

Then one night during the fasting month of Ramadan, some two months after the fight, a voice in Mallam Sile's head asked, "Why is everyone calling my wife 'the man checker'? How come people I give credit to suddenly pay me on time? Why am I being treated with such respect, even by the worst and most stubborn rascals on the street?" Sile was lying in bed with his wife when these questions came to him. But, in his usual fashion, he didn't try to answer them. Instead, he drew in a deep breath and began to pray. He smiled and thanked Allahu-Raheemu, the Merciful One, for curing the street folks of the prejudice they had nursed against him for so long. Mallam Sile also thanked Allah for giving his neighbors the will and the courage to finally accept him just as he was created. He flashed a grin in the darkness and moved closer to his slumbering wife. He buried his small body in her massive, protective frame and soon fell into a deep, dreamless sleep.

CRITICAL EYE

For Discussion

a. What commentary is the author making about relying on faith as a means of self-protection?

b. If Mallam had come to know the truth about why everyone's treatment toward him changed so drastically, could/would he still consider himself a man?

c. Indeed, men hold the power throughout many lands worldwide, but why is it that Mallam, although a man by birthright, is treated with so little respect?

Re-approaching the Reading

Considering that, generally, women are not celebrated for aggressive or overly "manish" behavior, make the argument that Mallam's wife has overstepped her boundary as a woman.

Writing Assignment

Is it important for a man to assert himself physically in order to be taken seriously? If so, why? Why are the rules for manhood so specific? What is at stake for them should they fall short?

THOMAS PAINE

THE AGE OF REASON

Part I

Luxembourg, 8th Pluviose, Second Year of the French Republic, one and indivisible. January 27, O. S. 1794.

To My Fellow-Citizens of the United States of America:

I put the following work under your protection. It contains my opinions upon Religion. You will do me the justice to remember, that I have always strenuously supported the Right of every Man to his own opinion, however different that opinion might be to mine. He who denies to another this right, makes a slave of himself to his present opinion, because he precludes himself the right of changing it.

The most formidable weapon against errors of every kind is Reason. I have never used any other, and I trust I never shall.

Your affectionate friend and fellow-citizen,

Thomas Paine

It has been my intention, for several years past, to publish my thoughts upon religion. I am well aware of the difficulties that attend the subject, and from that consideration, had reserved it to a more advanced period of life. I intended it to be the last offering I should make to my fellow-citizens of all nations, and that at a time when the purity of the motive that induced me to it, could not admit of a question, even by those who might disapprove the work.

The circumstance that has now taken place in France, of the total abolition of the whole national order of priesthood, and of everything appertaining to compulsive systems of religion, and compulsive articles of faith, has not only precipitated my intention, but rendered a work of this kind exceedingly necessary, lest in the general wreck of superstition, of false systems of government, and false theology, we lose sight of morality, of humanity, and of the theology that is true.

As several of my colleagues, and others of my fellow-citizens of France have given me the example of making their voluntary and individual profession of faith, I also will make mine; and I do this with all that sincerity and frankness with which the mind of man communicates with itself.

I believe in one God, and no more; and I hope for happiness beyond this life.

I believe in the equality of man; and I believe that religious duties consist in doing justice, loving mercy, and endeavoring to make our fellow-creatures happy.

But, lest it should be supposed that I believe many other things in addition to these, I shall, in the progress of this work, declare the things I do not believe, and my reasons for not believing them.

I do not believe in the creed professed by the Jewish church, by the Roman church, by the Greek church, by the Turkish church, by the Protestant church, nor by any church that I know of. My own mind is my own church.

All national institutions of churches, whether Jewish, Christian or Turkish, appear to me no other than human inventions set up to terrify and enslave mankind, and monopolize power and profit.

I do not mean by this declaration to condemn those who believe otherwise; they have the same right to their belief as I have to mine. But it is necessary to the happiness of man, that he be mentally faithful to himself. Infidelity does not consist in believing, or in disbelieving; it consists in professing to believe what he does not believe.

It is impossible to calculate the moral mischief, if I may so express it, that mental lying has produced in society. When a man has so far corrupted and prostituted the chastity of his mind, as to subscribe his professional belief to things he does not believe, he has prepared himself for the commission of every other crime. He takes up the trade of a priest for the sake of gain, and in order to qualify himself for that trade, he begins with a perjury. Can we conceive any thing more destructive to morality than this?

Soon after I had published the pamphlet Common Sense, in America, I saw the exceeding probability that a revolution in the system of government would be followed by a revolution in the system of religion. The adulterous connection of church and state, wherever it had taken place, whether Jewish, Christian, or Turkish, had so effectually prohibited by pains and penalties, every discussion upon established creeds, and upon first principles of religion, that until the system of government should be changed, those subjects could not be brought fairly and openly before the world; but that whenever this should be done, a revolution in the system of religion would follow. Human inventions and priestcraft would be detected; and man would return to the pure, unmixed and unadulterated belief of one God, and no more.

Every national church or religion has established itself by pretending some special mission from God, communicated to certain individuals. The Jews have their Moses; the Christians their Jesus Christ, their apostles and saints; and the Turks their Mahomet, as if the way to God was not open to every man alike.

Each of those churches shows certain books, which they call revelation, or the word of God. The Jews say that their word of God was given by God to Moses, face to face; the Christians say, that their word of God came by divine inspiration; and the Turks say, that their word of God (the Koran) was brought by an angel from Heaven. Each of those churches accuses the other of unbelief; and for my own part, I disbelieve them all.

As it is necessary to affix right ideas to words, I will, before I proceed further into the subject, offer some observations on the word revelation. Revelation, when applied to religion, means something communicated immediately from God to man.

No one will deny or dispute the power of the Almighty to make such a communication, if he pleases. But admitting, for the sake of a case, that something has been revealed to a certain person, and not revealed to any other person, it is revelation to that person only. When he tells it to a second person, a second to a third, a third to a fourth, and so on, it ceases to be a revelation to all those persons. It is revelation to the first person only, and hearsay to every other, and consequently they are not obliged to believe it.

It is a contradiction in terms and ideas, to call anything a revelation that comes to us at second-hand, either verbally or in writing. Revelation is necessarily limited to the first communication–after this, it is only an account of something which that person says was a revelation made to him; and though he may find himself obliged to believe it, it cannot be incumbent on me to believe it in the same manner; for it was not a revelation made to me, and I have only his word for it that it was made to him.

When Moses told the children of Israel that he received the two tables of the commandments from the hand of God, they were not obliged to believe him, because they had no other authority for it than his telling them so; and I have no other authority for it than some historian telling me so. The commandments carrying no internal evidence of divinity with them; they contain some good moral precepts, such as any man qualified to be a lawgiver, or a legislator, could produce himself, without having recourse to supernatural intervention.*

*It is, however, necessary to accept the declamation which says that God visits the sins of the fathers upon the children; it is contrary to every principle of moral justice.

When I am told that the Koran was written in Heaven, and brought to Mahomet by an angel, the account comes too near the same kind of hearsay evidence and second-hand authority as the former. I did not see the angel myself, and, therefore, I have a right not to believe it.

When also I am told that a woman, called the Virgin Mary, said, or gave out, that she was with child without any cohabitation with a man, and that her betrothed husband, Joseph, said that an angel told him so, I have a right to believe them or not; such a circumstance required a much stronger evidence than their bare word for it; but we have not even this–for neither Joseph nor Mary wrote any such matter themselves–it is only reported by others that they said so–it is hearsay upon hearsay, and I do not chose to rest my belief upon such evidence.

It is, however, not difficult to account for the credit that was given to the story of Jesus Christ being the son of God. He was born when the heathen mythology had still some fashion and repute in the world, and that mythology had prepared the people for the belief of such a story. Almost all the extraordinary men that lived under the heathen mythology were reputed to be the sons of some of their gods. It was not a new thing, at that time, to believe a man to have been celestially begotten; the intercourse of gods with women was then a matter of familiar opinion. Their Jupiter, according to their accounts, had cohabited with hundreds: the story, therefore, had nothing in it either new, wonderful, or obscene; it was conformable to the opinions that then prevailed among the people called Gentiles, or Mythologists, and it was those people only that believed it. The Jews who had kept strictly to the belief of one God, and no more, and who had always rejected the heathen mythology, never credited the story.

It is curious to observe how the theory of what is called the Christian Church sprung out of the tail of the heathen mythology. A direct incorporation took place in the first instance, by making the reputed founder to be celestially begotten. The trinity of gods that then followed was no other than a reduction of the former plurality, which was about twenty or thirty thousand; the statue of Mary succeeded the statue of Diana of Ephesus; the deification of heroes changed into the canonization of saints; the Mythologists had gods for everything; the Christian Mythologists had saints for everything; the church became as crowded with the one, as the Pantheon had been with the other, and Rome was the place of both. The Christian theory is little else than the idolatry of the ancient Mythologists, accommodated to the purposes of power and revenue; and it yet remains to reason and philosophy to abolish the amphibious fraud.

Nothing that is here said can apply, even with the most distant disrespect, to the real character of Jesus Christ. He was a virtuous and an amiable man. The morality that he preached and practiced was of the most benevolent kind; and though similar systems of morality had been preached by Confucius, and by some of the Greek philosophers, many years before; by the Quakers since; and by many good men in all ages, it has not been exceeded by any.

Jesus Christ wrote no account of himself, of his birth, parentage, or anything else; not a line of what is called the New Testament is of his writing. The history of him is altogether the work of other people; and as to the account given of his resurrection and ascension, it was the necessary counterpart to the story of his birth. His historians having brought him into the world in a supernatural manner, were obliged to take him out again in the same manner, or the first part of the story must have fallen to the ground.

The wretched contrivance with which this latter part is told exceeds every thing that went before it. The first part, that of the miraculous conception, was not a thing that admitted of publicity; and therefore the tellers of this part of the story had this advantage, that though they might not be credited, they could not be detected. They could not be expected to prove it, because it was not one of those things that admitted of proof, and it was impossible that the person of whom it was told could prove it himself.

But the resurrection of a dead person from the grave, and his ascension through the air, is a thing very different as to the evidence it admits of, to the invisible conception of a child in the womb. The resurrection and ascension, supposing them to have taken place, admitted of public and ocular demonstration, like that of the ascension of a balloon, or the sun at noon-day, to all Jerusalem at least. A thing which everybody is required to believe, requires that the proof and evidence of it should be equal to all, and universal; and as the public visibility of this last related act was the only evidence that could give sanction to the former part, the whole of it falls to the ground, because that evidence never was given. Instead of this, a small number of persons, not more than eight or nine, are introduced as proxies for the whole world, to say they saw it, and all the rest of the world are called upon to believe it. But it appears that Thomas did not believe the resurrection, and, as they say, would not believe without having ocular and manual demonstration himself. So neither will I, and the reason is equally as good for me, and for every other person, as for Thomas.

It is in vain to attempt to palliate or disguise this matter. The story, so far as relates to the supernatural part, has every mark of fraud and imposition stamped upon the face of it. Who were the authors of it is as impossible for us now to know, as it is for us to be assured that the books in which the account is related were written by the persons whose names they bear; the best surviving evidence we now have respecting this affair is the Jews. They are regularly descended from the people who lived in the times this resurrection and ascension is said to have happened, and they say, it is not true. It has long appeared to me a strange inconsistency to cite the Jews as a proof of the truth of the story. It is just the same as if a man were to say, I will prove the truth of what I have told you, by producing the people who say it is false.

That such a person as Jesus Christ existed, and that he was crucified, which was the mode of execution at that day, are historical relations strictly within the limits of probability. He preached most excellent morality, and the equality of man; but he preached also against the corruptions and avarice of the

Jewish priests, and this brought upon him the hatred and vengeance of the whole order of priesthood. The accusation which those priests brought against him was that of sedition and conspiracy against the Roman government, to which the Jews were then subject and tributary; and it is not improbable that the Roman government might have some secret apprehensions of the effects of his doctrine, as well as the Jewish priests; neither is it improbable that Jesus Christ had in contemplation the delivery of the Jewish nation from the bondage of the Romans. Between the two, however, this virtuous reformer and revolutionist lost his life. It is upon this plain narrative of facts, together with another case I am going to mention, that the Christian Mythologists, calling themselves the Christian Church, have erected their fable, which, for absurdity and extravagance, is not exceeded by anything that is to be found in the mythology of the ancients.

The ancient Mythologists tell us that the race of Giants made war against Jupiter, and that one of them threw a hundred rocks against him at one throw; that Jupiter defeated him with thunder, and confined him afterwards under Mount Etna, and that every time the Giant turns himself Mount Etna belches fire.

It is here easy to see that the circumstance of the mountain, that of its being a volcano, suggested the idea of the fable; and that the fable is made to fit and wind itself up with that circumstance.

The Christian mythologists tell us that their Satan made war against the Almighty, who defeated him, and confined him afterward, not under a mountain, but in a pit. It is here easy to see that the first fable suggested the idea of the second; for the fable of Jupiter and the Giants was told many hundred years before that of Satan. Thus far the ancient and the Christian Mythologists differ very little from each other. But the latter have contrived to carry the matter much farther. They have contrived to connect the fabulous part of the story of Jesus Christ with the fable originating from Mount Etna; and in order to make all the parts of the story tie together, they have taken to their aid the traditions of the Jews; for the Christian mythology is made up partly from the ancient mythology and partly from the Jewish traditions.

The Christian Mythologists, after having confined Satan in a pit, were obliged to let him out again to bring on the sequel of the fable. He is then introduced into the Garden of Eden in the shape of a snake or a serpent, and in that shape he enters into familiar conversation with Eve, who is no way surprised to hear a snake talk; and the issue of this tete-a-tete is that he persuades her to eat an apple, and the eating of that apple damns all mankind.

After giving Satan this triumph over the whole creation, one would have supposed that the Church Mythologists would have been kind enough to send him back again to the pit; or, if they had not done this, that they would have put a mountain upon him (for they say that their faith can remove a mountain), or have put him under a mountain, as the former mythologists had done, to prevent his getting again among the women and doing more mischief. But instead of this they leave him at large, without even obliging him to give his parole—the secret of which is, that they could not do without him; and after being at the trouble of making him, they bribed him to stay. They promised him ALL the Jews, ALL the Turks by anticipation, nine-tenths of the world beside, and Mahomet into the bargain. After this, who can doubt the bountifulness of the Christian Mythology?

Having thus made an insurrection and a battle in Heaven, in which none of the combatants could be either killed or wounded—put Satan into the pit—let him out again—giving him a triumph over the whole creation—damned all mankind by the eating of an apple, these Christian Mythologists bring the two ends of their fable together. They represent this virtuous and amiable man, Jesus Christ, to be at once both God and Man, and also the Son of God, celestially begotten, on purpose to be sacrificed, because they say that Eve in her longing had eaten an apple.

Putting aside everything that might excite laughter by its absurdity, or detestation by its profaneness, and confining ourselves merely to an examination of the parts, it is impossible to conceive a story more derogatory to the Almighty, more inconsistent with his wisdom, more contradictory to his power, than this story is. In order to make for it a foundation to rise upon, the inventors were under the necessity of giving to the being whom they call Satan, a power equally as great, if not greater, than they attribute to the Almighty. They have not only given him the power of liberating himself from the pit, after what they call his fall, but they have made that power increase afterward to infinity. Before this fall they represent him only as an angel of limited existence, as they represent the rest. After his fall, he becomes, by their account, omnipresent. He exists everywhere, and at the same time. He occupies the whole immensity of space.

Not content with this deification of Satan, they represent him as defeating, by stratagem, in the shape of an animal of the creation, all the power and wisdom of the Almighty. They represent him as having compelled the Almighty to the direct necessity either of surrendering the whole of the creation to the government and sovereignty of this Satan, or of capitulating for its redemption by coming down upon earth, and exhibiting himself upon a cross in the shape of a man.

Had the inventors of this story told it the contrary way, that is, had they represented the Almighty as compelling Satan to exhibit himself on a cross, in the shape of a snake, as a punishment for his new transgression, the story would have been less absurd—less contradictory. But instead of this, they make the transgressor triumph, and the Almighty fall.

That many good men have believed this strange fable, and lived very good lives under that belief (for credulity is not a crime), is what I have no doubt of. In the first place, they were educated to believe it, and they would have believed anything else in the same manner. There are also many who have been so enthusiastically enraptured by what they conceived to be the infinite love of God to man, in making a sacrifice of himself, that the vehemence of the idea has forbidden and deterred them from examining into the absurdity and profaneness of the story. The more unnatural anything is, the more is it capable of becoming the object of dismal admiration.

But if objects for gratitude and admiration are our desire, do they not present themselves every hour to our eyes? Do we not see a fair creation prepared to receive us the instant we are born—a world furnished to our hands, that cost us nothing? Is it we that light up the sun, that pour down the rain, and fill the earth with abundance? Whether we sleep or wake, the vast machinery of the universe still goes on. Are these things, and the blessings they indicate in future, nothing to us? Can our gross feelings be excited by no other subjects than tragedy and suicide? Or is the gloomy pride of man become so intolerable, that nothing can flatter it but a sacrifice of the Creator?

I know that this bold investigation will alarm many, but it would be paying too great a compliment to their credulity to forbear it on that account; the times and the subject demand it to be done. The suspicion that the theory of what is called the Christian Church is fabulous is becoming very extensive in all countries; and it will be a consolation to men staggering under that suspicion, and doubting what to believe and what to disbelieve, to see the subject freely investigated. I therefore pass on to an examination of the books called the Old and the New Testament.

These books, beginning with Genesis and ending with Revelation (which, by the by, is a book of riddles that requires a revelation to explain it) are, we are told, the word of God. It is, therefore, proper for us to know who told us so, that we may know what credit to give to the report. The answer to this question is, that nobody can tell, except that we tell one another so. The case, however, historically appears to be as follows:

When the church mythologists established their system, they collected all the writings they could find, and managed them as they pleased. It is a matter altogether of uncertainty to us whether such of the writings as now appear under the name of the Old and New Testament are in the same state in which those collectors say they found them, or whether they added, altered, abridged, or dressed them up.

Be this as it may, they decided by vote which of the books out of the collection they had made should be the WORD OF GOD, and which should not. They rejected several; they voted others to be doubtful, such as the books called the Apocrypha; and those books which had a majority of votes, were voted to be the word of God. Had they voted otherwise, all the people, since calling themselves Christians, had believed otherwise—for the belief of the one comes from the vote of the other. Who the people were that did all this, we know nothing of; they called themselves by the general name of the Church and this is all we know of the matter.

As we have no other external evidence or authority for believing these books to be the word of God than what I have mentioned, which is no evidence or authority at all, I come, in the next place, to examine the internal evidence contained in the books themselves. In the former part of this Essay, I have spoken of revelation; I now proceed further with that subject, for the purpose of applying it to the books in question.

Revelation is a communication of something which the person to whom that thing is revealed did not know before. For if I have done a thing, or seen it done, it needs no revelation to tell me I have done it, or seen it, nor to enable me to tell it, or to write it.

Revelation, therefore, cannot be applied to anything done upon earth, of which man is himself the actor or the witness; and consequently all the historical and anecdotal parts of the Bible, which is almost the whole of it, is not within the meaning and compass of the word revelation, and, therefore, is not the word of God.

When Samson ran off with the gate-posts of Gaza, if he ever did so (and whether he did or not is nothing to us), or when he visited his Delilah, or caught his foxes, or did any thing else, what has revelation to do with these things? If they were facts, he could tell them himself or his secretary, if he kept one, could write them, if they were worth either telling or writing; and if they were fictions, revelation could not make them true; and whether true or not, we are neither the better nor the wiser for knowing them. When we contemplate the immensity of that Being who directs and governs the incomprehensible WHOLE, of which the utmost ken of human sight can discover but a part, we ought to feel shame at calling such paltry stories the word of God.

As to the account of the Creation, with which the Book of Genesis opens, it has all the appearance of being a tradition which the Israelites had among them before they came into Egypt; and after their departure from that country they put it at the head of their history, without telling (as it is most probable) that they did not know how they came by it. The manner in which the account opens, shows it to be traditionary. It begins abruptly; it is nobody that speaks; it is nobody that hears; it is addressed to nobody; it has neither first, second, nor third person; it has every criterion of being a tradition; it has no voucher. Moses does not take it upon himself by introducing it with the formality that he uses on other occasions, such as that of saying, "The Lord spake unto Moses, saying."

Why it has been called the Mosaic account of the Creation, I am at a loss to conceive. Moses, I believe, was too good a judge of such subjects to put his name to that account. He had been educated among the Egyptians, who were a people as well skilled in science, and particularly in astronomy, as any people of their day; and the silence and caution that Moses observes, in not authenticating the account, is a good negative evidence that he neither told it nor believed it. The case is, that every nation of people has been world-makers, and the Israelites had as much right to set up the trade of world-making as any of the rest; and as Moses was not an Israelite, he might not chose to contradict the tradition. The account, however, is harmless; and this is more than can be said for many other parts of the Bible.

Whenever we read the obscene stories, the voluptuous debaucheries, the cruel and torturous executions, the unrelenting vindictiveness, with which more than half the Bible is filled, it would be more consistent that we called it the word of a demon, than the word of God. It is a history of wickedness, that has served to corrupt and brutalize mankind; and, for my own part, I sincerely detest it, as I detest everything that is cruel.

We scarcely meet with anything, a few phrases excepted, but what deserves either our abhorrence or our contempt, till we come to the miscellaneous parts of the Bible. In the anonymous publications, the Psalms, and the Book of Job, more particularly in the latter, we find a great deal of elevated sentiment reverentially expressed of the power and benignity of the Almighty; but they stand on no higher rank than many other compositions on similar subjects, as well before that time as since.

The Proverbs which are said to be Solomon's, though most probably a collection (because they discover a knowledge of life which his situation excluded him from knowing), are an instructive table of ethics. They are inferior in keenness to the proverbs of the Spaniards, and not more wise and economical than those of the American Franklin.

All the remaining parts of the Bible, generally known by the name of the Prophets, are the works of the Jewish poets and itinerant preachers, who mixed poetry,* anecdote, and devotion together–and those works still retain the air and style of poetry, though in translation.

*As there are many readers who do not see that a composition is poetry unless it be in rhyme, it is for their information that I add this note. Poetry consists principally in two things–imagery and composition. The composition of poetry differs from that of prose in the manner of mixing long and short syllables together. Take a long syllable out of a line of poetry, and put a short one in the room of it, or put a long syllable where a short one should be, and that line will lose its poetical harmony. It will have an effect upon the line like that of misplacing a note in a song. The imagery in these books, called the Prophets, appertains altogether to poetry. It is fictitious, and often extravagant, and not admissible in any other kind of writing than poetry. To show that these writings are composed in poetical numbers, I will take ten syllables, as they stand in the book, and make a line of the same number of syllables, (heroic measure) that shall rhyme with the last word. It will then be seen that the composition of those books is poetical measure. The instance I shall first produce is from Isaiah:

"Hear, O ye heavens, and give ear, O earth"
Tis God himself that calls attention forth.

Another instance I shall quote is from the mournful Jeremiah, to which I shall add two other lines, for the purpose of carrying out the figure, and showing the intention of the poet:

"O! that mine head were waters and mine eyes"
Were fountains flowing like the liquid skies;
Then would I give the mighty flood release
And weep a deluge for the human race.

There is not, throughout the whole book called the Bible, any word that describes to us what we call a poet, nor any word that describes what we call poetry. The case is, that the word prophet, to which latter times have affixed a new idea, was the Bible word for poet, and the word 'prophesying' meant the art of making poetry. It also meant the art of playing poetry to a tune upon any instrument of music.

We read of prophesying with pipes, tabrets, and horns–of prophesying with harps, with psalteries, with cymbals, and with every other instrument of music then in fashion. Were we now to speak of prophesying with a fiddle, or with a pipe and tabor, the expression would have no meaning or would appear ridiculous, and to some people contemptuous, because we have changed the meaning of the word.

We are told of Saul being among the prophets, and also that he prophesied; but we are not told what they prophesied, nor what he prophesied. The case is, there was nothing to tell; for these prophets were a company of musicians and poets, and Saul joined in the concert, and this was called prophesying.

The account given of this affair in the book called Samuel is, that Saul met a company of prophets; a whole company of them! coming down with a psaltery, a tabret, a pipe and a harp, and that they prophesied, and that he prophesied with them. But it appears afterwards, that Saul prophesied badly; that is, he performed his part badly; for it is said that an "evil spirit from God"* came upon Saul, and he prophesied.

*As those men who call themselves divines and commentators, are very fond of puzzling one another, I leave them to contest the meaning of the first part of the phrase, that of an evil spirit from God. I keep to my text–I keep to the meaning of the word prophesy.

Now, were there no other passage in the book called the Bible than this, to demonstrate to us that we have lost the original meaning of the word prophesy, and substituted another meaning in its place, this alone would be sufficient; for it is impossible to use and apply the word prophesy, in the place it is here used and applied, if we give to it the sense which latter times have affixed to it. The manner in which it is here used strips it of all religious meaning, and shows that a man might then be a prophet, or he might prophesy, as he may now be a poet or a musician, without any regard to the morality or the immorality of his character. The word was originally a term of science, promiscuously applied to poetry and to music, and not restricted to any subject upon which poetry and music might be exercised.

Deborah and Barak are called prophets, not because they predicted anything, but because they composed the poem or song that bears their name, in celebration of an act already done. David is ranked among the prophets, for he was a musician, and was also reputed to be (though perhaps very erroneously) the author of the Psalms. But Abraham, Isaac, and Jacob are not called prophets; it does not appear from any accounts we have that they could either sing, play music, or make poetry.

We are told of the greater and the lesser prophets. They might as well tell us of the greater and the lesser God; for there cannot be degrees in prophesying consistently with its modern sense. But there are degrees in poetry, and therefore the phrase is reconcilable to the case, when we understand by it the greater and the lesser poets.

It is altogether unnecessary, after this, to offer any observations upon what those men, styled propliets, have written. The axe goes at once to the root, by showing that the original meaning of the word has been mistaken and consequently all the inferences that have been drawn from those books, the devotional respect that has been paid to them, and the labored commentaries that have been written upon them, under that mistaken meaning, are not worth disputing about. In many things, however, the writings of the Jewish poets deserve a better fate than that of being bound up, as they now are with the trash that accompanies them, under the abused name of the word of God.

If we permit ourselves to conceive right ideas of things, we must necessarily affix the idea, not only of unchangeableness, but of the utter impossibility of any change taking place, by any means or accident whatever, in that which we would honor with the name of the word of God; and therefore the word of God cannot exist in any written or human language.

The continually progressive change to which the meaning of words is subject, the want of a universal language which renders translation necessary, the errors to which translations are again subject, the mistakes of copyists and printers, together with the possibility of willful alteration, are of themselves evidences that the human language, whether in speech or in print, cannot be the vehicle of the word of God. The word of God exists in something else.

Did the book called the Bible excel in purity of ideas and expression all the books now extant in the world, I would not take it for my rule of faith, as being the word of God, because the possibility would nevertheless exist of my being imposed upon. But when I see throughout the greatest part of this book scarcely anything but a history of the grossest vices and a collection of the most paltry and contemptible tales, I cannot dishonor my Creator by calling it by his name.

Thus much for the Bible; I now go on to the book called the New Testament. The new Testament! that is, the new will, as if there could be two wills of the Creator.

Had it been the object or the intention of Jesus Christ to establish a new religion, he would undoubtedly have written the system himself, or procured it to be written in his life-time. But there is no publication extant authenticated with his name. All the books called the New Testament were written after his death. He was a Jew by birth and by profession; and he was the son of God in like manner that every other person is–for the Creator is the Father of All.

The first four books, called Matthew, Mark, Luke, and John, do not give a history of the life of Jesus Christ, but only detached anecdotes of him. It appears from these books that the whole time of his being a preacher was not more than eighteen months; and it was only during this short time that these men became acquainted with him. They make mention of him at the age of twelve years, sitting, they say, among the Jewish doctors, asking and answering questions. As this was several years before their acquaintance with him began, it is most probable they had this anecdote from his parents. From this time there is no account of him for about sixteen years. Where he lived, or how he employed himself during this interval, is not known.

Most probably he was working at his father's trade, which was that of a carpenter. It does not appear that he had any school education, and the probability is, that he could not write, for his parents were extremely poor, as appears from their not being able to pay for a bed when he was born.

It is somewhat curious that the three persons whose names are the most universally recorded, were of very obscure parentage. Moses was a foundling; Jesus Christ was born in a stable; and Mahomet was a mule driver. The first and the last of these men were founders of different systems of religion; but Jesus Christ founded no new system. He called men to the practice of moral virtues, and the belief of one God. The great trait in his character is philanthropy.

The manner in which he was apprehended shows that he was not much known at that time; and it shows also, that the meetings he then held with his followers were in secret; and that he had given over or suspended preaching publicly. Judas could no otherwise betray him than by giving information where he was, and pointing him out to the officers that went to arrest him; and the reason for employing and paying Judas to do this could arise only from the causes already mentioned, that of his not being much known and living concealed.

The idea of his concealment, not only agrees very ill with his reputed divinity, but associates with it something of pusillanimity; and his being betrayed, or in other words, his being apprehended, on the information of one of his followers, shows that he did not intend to be apprehended, and consequently that he did not intend to be crucified.

The Christian Mythologists tell us, that Christ died for the sins of the world, and that he came on purpose to die. Would it not then have been the same if he had died of a fever or of the small-pox, of old age, or of anything else?

The declaratory sentence which, they say, was passed upon Adam, in case he eat of the apple, was not, that thou shalt surely be crucified, but thou shalt surely die—the sentence of death, and not the manner of dying. Crucifixion, therefore, or any other particular manner of dying, made no part of the sentence that Adam was to suffer, and consequently, even upon their own tactics, it could make no part of the sentence that Christ was to suffer in the room of Adam. A fever would have done as well as a cross, if there was any occasion for either.

This sentence of death, which they tell us was thus passed upon Adam must either have meant dying naturally, that is, ceasing to live, or have meant what these Mythologists call damnation; and, consequently, the act of dying on the part of Jesus Christ, must, according to their system, apply as a prevention to one or other of these two things happening to Adam and to us.

That it does not prevent our dying is evident, because we all die; and if their accounts of longevity be true, men die faster since the crucifixion than before: and with respect to the second explanation (including with it the natural death of Jesus Christ as a substitute for the eternal death or damnation of all mankind), it is impertinently representing the Creator as coming off, or revoking the sentence, by a pun or a quibble upon the word death. That manufacturer of quibbles, St. Paul, if he wrote the books that bear his name, has helped this quibble on by making another quibble upon the word Adam. He makes there to be two Adams; the one who sins in fact, and suffers by proxy; the other who sins by proxy, and suffers in fact. A religion thus interlarded with quibble, subterfuge, and pun has a tendency to instruct its professors in the practice of these arts. They acquire the habit without being aware of the cause.

If Jesus Christ was the being which those Mythologists tell us he was, and that he came into this world to suffer, which is a word they sometimes use instead of to die, the only real suffering he could have endured would have been to live. His existence here was a state of exilement or transportation from Heaven, and the way back to his original country was to die. In finè, everything in this strange system is the reverse of what it pretends to be. It is the reverse of truth, and I become so tired of examining into its inconsistencies and absurdities, that I hasten to the conclusion of it, in order to proceed to something better.

How much or what parts of the books called the New Testament, were written by the persons whose names they bear, is what we can know nothing of; neither are we certain in what language they were originally written. The matters they now contain may be classed under two heads–anecdote and epistolary correspondence.

The four books already mentioned, Matthew, Mark, Luke, and John, are altogether anecdotal. They relate events after they had taken place. They tell what Jesus Christ did and said, and what others did and said to him; and in several instances they relate the same event differently. Revelation is necessarily out of the question with respect to those books; not only because of the disagreement of the writers, but because revelation cannot be applied to the relating of facts by the person who saw them done, nor to the relating or recording of any discourse or conversation by those who heard it. The book called the Acts of the Apostles (an anonymous work) belongs also to the anecdotal part.

All the other parts of the New Testament, except the book of enigmas, called the Revelations, are a collection of letters under the name of epistles; and the forgery of letters has been such a common practice in the world, that the probability is at least equal, whether they are genuine or forged. One thing, however, is much less equivocal, which is, that out of the matters contained in those books, together with the assistance of some old stories, the Church has set up a system of religion very contradictory to the character of the person whose name it bears. It has set up a religion of pomp and of revenue, in pretended imitation of a person whose life was humility and poverty.

The invention of a purgatory, and of the releasing of souls therefrom by prayers bought of the church with money; the selling of pardons, dispensations, and indulgences, are revenue laws, without bearing that name or carrying that appearance. But the case nevertheless is, that those things derive their origin from the paroxysm of the crucifixion and the theory deduced therefrom, which was that one person could stand in the place of another, and could perform meritorious services for him. The probability, therefore, is, that the whole theory or doctrine of what is called the redemption (which is said to have been accomplished by the act of one person in the room of another) was originally fabricated on purpose to bring forward and build all those secondary and pecuniary redemptions upon; and that the passages in the books, upon which the idea or theory of redemption is built, have been manufactured and fabricated for that purpose. Why are we to give this Church Credit when she tells us that those books are genuine in every part, any more than we give her credit for everything else she has told us, or for the miracles she says she had performed? That she could fabricate writings is certain, because she could write; and the composition of the writings in question, is of that kind that anybody might do it; and that she did fabricate them is not more inconsistent with probability than that she could tell us, as she has done, that she could and did work miracles.

Since, then no external evidence can, at this long distance of time, be produced to prove whether the Church fabricated the doctrines called redemption or not (for such evidence, whether for or against, would be subject to the same suspicion of being fabricated), the case can only be referred to the internal evidence which the thing carries of itself; and this affords a very strong presumption of its being a fabrication. For the internal evidence is that the theory or doctrine of redemption has for its basis an idea of pecuniary Justice, and not that of moral Justice.

If I owe a person money, and cannot pay him, and he threatens to put me in prison, another person can take the debt upon himself, and pay it for me; but if I have committed a crime, every circumstance of the case is changed; moral Justice cannot take the innocent for the guilty, even if the innocent would offer itself. To suppose Justice to do this, is to destroy the principle of its existence, which is the thing itself; it is then no longer Justice, it is indiscriminate revenge.

This single reflection will show, that the doctrine of redemption is founded on a mere pecuniary idea corresponding to that of a debt which another person might pay; and as this pecuniary idea corresponds again with the system of second redemption, obtained through the means of money given to the Church for pardons, the probability is that the same persons fabricated both the one and the other of those theories; and that, in truth there is no such thing as redemption—that it is fabulous, and that man stands in the same relative condition with his Maker he ever did stand since man existed, and that it is his greatest consolation to think so.

Let him believe this, and he will live more consistently and morally than by any other system; it is by his being taught to contemplate himself as an outlaw, as an outcast, as a beggar, as a mumper, as one thrown, as it were, on a dunghill at an immense distance from his Creator, and who must make his approaches by creeping and cringing to intermediate beings, that he conceives either a contemptuous disregard for everything under the name of religion, or becomes indifferent, or turns what he calls devout. In the latter case, he consumes his life in grief, or the affectation of it; his prayers are reproaches; his humility is ingratitude; he calls himself a worm, and the fertile earth a dunghill; and all the blessings of life by the thankless name of vanities; he despises the choicest gift of God to man, the GIFT OF REASON; and having endeavored to force upon himself the belief of a system against which reason revolts, he ungratefully calls it human reason, as if man could give reason to himself.

Yet, with all this strange appearance of humility and this contempt for human reason, he ventures into the boldest presumptions; he finds fault with everything; his selfishness is never satisfied; his ingratitude is never at an end. He takes on himself to direct the Almighty what to do, even in the government of the universe; he prays dictatorially; when it is sunshine, he prays for rain, and when it is rain, he prays for sunshine; he follows the same idea in everything that he prays for; for what is the amount of all his prayers, but an attempt to make the Almighty change his mind, and act otherwise than he does? It is as if he were to say: Thou knowest not so well as I.

But some, perhaps will say: Are we to have no word of God—no revelation? I answer, Yes; there is a word of God; there is a revelation.

THE WORD OF GOD IS THE CREATION WE BEHOLD and it is in this word, which no human invention can counterfeit or alter, that God speaketh universally to man.

Human language is local and changeable, and is therefore incapable of being used as the means of unchangeable and universal information. The idea that God sent Jesus Christ to publish, as they say, the glad tidings to all nations, from one end of the earth unto the other, is consistent only with the ignorance of those who knew nothing of the extent of the world, and who believed, as those world-saviours believed, and continued to believe for several centuries (and that in contradiction to the discoveries of philosophers and the experience of navigators), that the earth was flat like a trencher, and that a man might walk to the end of it.

But how was Jesus Christ to make anything known to all nations? He could speak but one language; which was Hebrew and there are in the world several hundred languages. Scarcely any two nations speak the same language, or understand each other; and as to translations, every man who knows anything of languages knows that it is impossible to translate from one language into another, not only without losing a great part of the original, but frequently of mistaking the sense; and besides all this, the art of printing was wholly unknown at the time Christ lived.

It is always necessary that the means that are to accomplish any end be equal to the accomplishment of that end, or the end cannot be accomplished. It is in this that the difference between finite and infinite power and wisdom discovers itself. Man frequently fails in accomplishing his ends, from a natural inability of the power to the purpose, and frequently from the want of wisdom to apply power properly. But it is impossible for infinite power and wisdom to fail as man faileth. The means it useth are always equal to the end; but human language, more especially as there is not a universal language, is incapable of being used as a universal means of unchangeable and uniform information, and therefore it is not the means that God useth in manifesting himself universally to man.

It is only in the CREATION that all our ideas and conceptions of a word of God can unite. The Creation speaketh a universal language, independently of human speech or human language, multiplied and various as they may be. It is an ever-existing original, which every man can read. It cannot be forged; it cannot be counterfeited; it cannot be lost; it cannot be altered; it cannot be suppressed. It does not depend upon the will of man whether it shall be published or not; it publishes itself from one end of the earth to the other. It preaches to all nations and to all worlds; and this word of God reveals to man all that is necessary for man to know of God.

Do we want to contemplate his power? We see it in the immensity of the Creation. Do we want to contemplate his wisdom? We see it in the unchangeable order by which the incomprehensible whole is governed! Do we want to contemplate his munificence? We see it in the abundance with which he fills the earth. Do we want to contemplate his mercy? We see it in his not withholding that abundance even from the unthankful. In finè, do we want to know what God is? Search not the book called the Scripture, which any human hand might make, but the Scripture called the Creation.

The only idea man can affix to the name of God is that of a first cause, the cause of all things. And incomprehensible and difficult as it is for a man to conceive what a first cause is, he arrives at the belief of it from the tenfold greater difficulty of disbelieving it. It is difficult beyond description to conceive that space can have no end; but it is more difficult to conceive an end. It is difficult beyond the power of man to conceive an eternal duration of what we call time; but it is more impossible to conceive a time when there shall be no time.

In like manner of reasoning, everything we behold carries in itself the internal evidence that it did not make itself. Every man is an evidence to himself that he did not make himself; neither could his father make himself, nor his grandfather, nor any of his race; neither could any tree, plant, or animal make itself; and it is the conviction arising from this evidence that carries us on, as it were, by necessity to the belief of a first cause eternally existing, of a nature totally different to any material existence we know of, and by the power of which all things exist; and this first cause man calls God.

It is only by the exercise of reason that man can discover God. Take away that reason, and he would be incapable of understanding anything; and in this case it would be just as consistent to read even the book called the Bible to a horse as to a man. How then is it that those people pretend to reject reason?

Almost the only parts in the book called the Bible that convey to us any idea of God, are some chapters in Job, and the 19th Psalm; I recollect no other. Those parts are true deistical compositions, for they treat of the Deity through his works. They take the book of Creation as the word of God, they refer to no other book, and all the inferences they make are drawn from that volume.

I insert in this place the 19th Psalm, as paraphrased into English verse by Addison. I recollect not the prose, and where I write this I have not the opportunity of seeing it.

> "The spacious firmament on high,
> With all the blue ethereal sky,
> And spangled heavens, a shining frame,
> Their great original proclaim.
> The unwearied sun, from day to day,
> Does his Creator's power display;
> And publishes to every land
> The work of an Almighty hand.
>
> "Soon as the evening shades prevail,
> The moon takes up the wondrous tale,
> And nightly to the list'ning earth
> Repeats the story of her birth;
> Whilst all the stars that round her burn,
> And all the planets, in their turn,
> Confirm the tidings as they roll,
> And spread the truth from pole to pole.
>
> "What though in solemn silence all
> Move round this dark terrestrial ball?
> What though no real voice, or sound,
> Amidst their radiant orbs be found
> In reason's ear they all rejoice
> And utter forth a glorious voice,
> Forever singing, as they shine,
> THE HAND THAT MADE US IS DIVINE."

What more does man want to know, than that the hand or power that made these things is divine, is omnipotent? Let him believe this with the force it is impossible to repel, if he permits his reason to act, and his rule of moral life will follow of course.

The allusions in Job have, all of them, the same tendency with this Psalm; that of deducing or proving a truth that would be otherwise unknown, from truths already known.

I recollect not enough of the passages in Job to insert them correctly; but there is one that occurs to me that is applicable to the subject I am speaking upon. "Canst thou by searching find out God? Canst thou find out the Almighty to perfection?"

I know not how the printers have pointed this passage, for I keep no Bible; but it contains two distinct questions that admit of distinct answers.

First,—Canst thou by searching find out God? Yes; because, in the first place, I know I did not make myself, and yet I have existence; and by searching into the nature of other things, I find that no other thing could make itself; and yet millions of other things exist; therefore it is, that I know, by positive conclusion resulting from this search, that there is a power superior to all those things, and that power is God.

Secondly,–Canst thou find out the Almighty to perfection? No; not only because the power and wisdom He has manifested in the structure of the Creation that I behold is to me incomprehensible, but because even this manifestation, great as it is, is probably but a small display of that immensity of power and wisdom by which millions of other worlds, to me invisible by their distance, were created and continue to exist.

It is evident that both of these questions were put to the reason of the person to whom they are supposed to have been addressed; and it is only by admitting the first question to be answered affirmatively, that the second could follow. It would have been unnecessary and even absurd, to have put a second question, more difficult than the first, if the first question had been answered negatively. The two questions have different objects; the first refers to the existence of God, the second to his attributes; reason can discover the one, but it falls infinitely short in discovering the whole of the other.

I recollect not a single passage in all the writings ascribed to the men called apostles, that conveys any idea of what God is. Those writings are chiefly controversial; and the subjects they dwell upon, that of a man dying in agony on a cross, is better suited to the gloomy genius of a monk in a cell, by whom it is not impossible they were written, than to any man breathing the open air of the Creation. The only passage that occurs to me, that has any reference to the works of God, by which only his power and wisdom can be known, is related to have been spoken by Jesus Christ, as a remedy against distrustful care. "Behold the lilies of the field, they toil not, neither do they spin." This, however, is far inferior to the allusions in Job and in the 19th Psalm; but it is similar in idea, and the modesty of the imagery is correspondent to the modesty of the man.

As to the Christian system of faith, it appears to me as a species of Atheism–a sort of religious denial of God. It professes to believe in a man rather than in God. It is a compound made up chiefly of Manism with but little Deism, and is as near to Atheism as twilight is to darkness. It introduces between man and his Maker an opaque body, which it calls a Redeemer, as the moon introduces her opaque self between the earth and the sun, and it produces by this means a religious, or an irreligious, eclipse of light. It has put the whole orbit of reason into shade.

The effect of this obscurity has been that of turning everything upside down, and representing it in reverse, and among the revolutions it has thus magically produced, it has made a revolution in theology.

That which is now called natural philosophy, embracing the whole circle of science, of which astronomy occupies the chief place, is the study of the works of God, and of the power and wisdom of God in his works, and is the true theology.

As to the theology that is now studied in its place, it is the study of human opinions and of human fancies concerning God. It is not the study of God himself in the works that he has made, but in the works or writings that man has made; and it is not among the least of the mischiefs that the Christian system has done to the world, that it has abandoned the original and beautiful system of theology, like a beautiful innocent, to distress and reproach, to make room for the hag of superstition.

The Book of Job and the 19th Psalm, which even the Church admits to be more ancient than the chronological order in which they stand in the book called the Bible, are theological orations conformable to the original system of theology. The internal evidence of those orations proves to a demonstration that the study and contemplation of the works of creation, and of the power and wisdom of God, revealed and manifested in those works, made a great part of the religious devotion of the times in which they were written; and it was this devotional study and contemplation that led to the discovery of the principles upon which what are now called sciences are established; and it is to the discovery of these principles that almost all the arts that contribute to the convenience of human life owe their existence. Every principal art has some science for its parent, though the person who mechanically performs the work does not always, and but very seldom, perceive the connection.

It is a fraud of the Christian system to call the sciences human inventions; it is only the application of them that is human. Every science has for its basis a system of principles as fixed and unalterable as those by which the universe is regulated and governed. Man cannot make principles, he can only discover them.

For example: Every person who looks at an almanac sees an account when an eclipse will take place, and he sees also that it never fails to take place according to the account there given. This shows that man is acquainted with the laws by which the heavenly bodies move. But it would be something worse than ignorance, were any Church on earth to say that those laws are a human invention. It would also be ignorance, or something worse, to say that the scientific principles by the aid of which man is enabled to calculate and foreknow when an eclipse will take place, are a human invention. Man cannot invent any thing that is eternal and immutable; and the scientific principles he employs for this purpose must be, and are of necessity, as eternal and immutable as the laws by which the heavenly bodies move, or they could not be used as they are to ascertain the time when, and the manner how, an eclipse will take place.

The scientific principles that man employs to obtain the foreknowledge of an eclipse, or of anything else relating to the motion of the heavenly bodies, are contained chiefly in that part of science that is called trigonometry, or the properties of a triangle, which, when applied to the study of the heavenly bodies, is called astronomy; when applied to direct the course of a ship on the ocean, it is called navigation; when applied to the construction of figures drawn by a rule and compass, it is called geometry; when applied to the construction of plans of edifices, it is called architecture; when applied to the measurement of any portion of the surface of the earth, it is called land-surveying. In finè, it is the soul of science; it is an eternal truth; it contains the mathematical demonstration of which man speaks, and the extent of its uses are unknown.

It may be said that man can make or draw a triangle, and therefore a triangle is a human invention.

But the triangle, when drawn, is no other than the image of the principle; it is a delineation to the eye, and from thence to the mind, of a principle that would otherwise be imperceptible. The triangle does not make the principle, any more than a candle taken into a room that was dark makes the chairs and tables that before were invisible. All the properties of a triangle exist independently of the figure, and existed before any triangle was drawn or thought of by man. Man had no more to do in the formation of those properties or principles, than he had to do in making the laws by which the heavenly bodies move; and therefore the one must have the same Divine origin as the other.

In the same manner, as it may be said, that man can make a triangle, so also, may it be said, he can make the mechanical instrument called a lever; but the principle by which the lever acts is a thing distinct from the instrument, and would exist if the instrument did not; it attaches itself to the instrument after it is made; the instrument, therefore, cannot act otherwise than it does act; neither can all the efforts of human invention make it act otherwise; that which, in all such cases, man calls the effect is no other than the principle itself rendered perceptible to the senses.

Since, then, man cannot make principles, from whence did he gain a knowledge of them, so as to be able to apply them, not only to things on earth, but to ascertain the motion of bodies so immensely distant from him as all the heavenly bodies are? From whence, I ask, could he gain that knowledge, but from the study of the true theology?

It is the structure of the universe that has taught this knowledge to man. That structure is an ever-existing exhibition of every principle upon which every part of mathematical science is founded. The offspring of this science is mechanics; for mechanics is no other than the principles of science applied practically. The man who proportions the several parts of a mill, uses the same scientific principles as if he had the power of constructing a universe; but as he cannot give to matter that invisible agency by which all the component parts of the immense machine of the universe have influence upon each other, and act in motional unison together, without any apparent contact, and to which man has given the name of attraction, gravitation, and repulsion, he supplies the place of that agency by the humble imitation of teeth and cogs. All the parts of man's microcosm must visibly touch; but could he gain a knowledge of that agency, so as to be able to apply it in practice, we might then say that another canonical book of the Word of God had been discovered.

If man could alter the properties of the lever, so also could he alter the properties of the triangle: for a lever (taking that sort of lever which is called a steelyard, for the sake of explanation) forms, when in motion, a triangle. The line it descends from (one point of that line being in the fulcrum), the line it descends to, and the chord of the arc which the end of the lever describes in the air, are the three sides of a triangle. The other arm of the lever describes also a triangle; and the corresponding sides of those two triangles, calculated scientifically, or measured geometrically, and also the sines, tangents, and secants generated from the angles, and geometrically measured, have the same proportions to each other, as the different weights have that will balance each other on the lever, leaving the weight of the lever out of the case.

It may also be said, that man can make a wheel and axis; that he can put wheels of different magnitudes together, and produce a mill. Still the case comes back to the same point, which is, that he did not make the principle that gives the wheels those powers. This principle is as unalterable as in the former case or rather it is the same principle under a different appearance to the eye.

The power that two wheels of different magnitudes have upon each other, is in the same proportion as if the semi-diameter of the two wheels were joined together and made into that kind of lever I have described, suspended at the part where the semi-diameters join; for the two wheels, scientifically considered, are no other than the two circles generated by the motion of the compound lever.

It is from the study of the true theology that all our knowledge of science is derived, and it is from that knowledge that all the arts have originated.

The Almighty Lecturer, by displaying the principles of science in the structure of the universe, has invited man to study and to imitation. It is as if He had said to the inhabitants of this globe that we call ours, "I have made an earth for man to dwell upon, and I have rendered the starry heavens visible, to teach him science and the arts. He can now provide for his own comfort, AND LEARN FROM MY MUNIFICENCE TO ALL, TO BE KIND TO EACH OTHER."

Of what use is it, unless it be to teach man something, that his eye is endowed with the power of beholding to an incomprehensible distance, an immensity of worlds revolving in the ocean of space? Or of what use is it that this immensity of worlds is visible to man? What has man to do with the Pleiades, with Orion, with Sirius, with the star he calls the North Star, with the moving orbs he has named Saturn, Jupiter, Mars, Venus, and Mercury, if no uses are to follow from their being visible? A less power of vision would have been sufficient for man, if the immensity he now possesses were given only to waste itself, as it were, on an immense desert of space glittering with shows.

It is only by contemplating what he calls the starry heavens, as the book and school of science, that he discovers any use in their being visible to him, or any advantage resulting from his immensity of vision. But when be contemplates the subject in this light, he sees an additional motive for saying, that nothing was made in vain; for in vain would be this power of vision if it taught man nothing.

As the Christian system of faith has made a revolution in theology, so also bas it made a revolution in the state of learning. That which is now called learning, was not learning originally. Learning does not consist, as the schools now make it consist, in the knowledge of languages, but in the knowledge of things to which language gives names.

The Greeks were a learned people, but learning with them did not consist in speaking Greek, any more than in a Roman's speaking Latin, or a Frenchman's speaking French, or an Englishman's speaking English. From what we know of the Greeks, it does not appear that they knew or studied any language but their own, and this was one cause of their becoming so learned: it afforded them more time to apply themselves to better studies. The schools of the Greeks were schools of science and philosophy, and not of languages; and it is in the knowledge of the things that science and philosophy teach, that learning consists.

Almost all the scientific learning that now exists came to us from the Greeks, or the people who spoke the Greek language. It, therefore, became necessary for the people of other nations who spoke a different language that some among them should learn the Greek language, in order that the learning the Greeks had, might be made known in those nations, by translating the Greek books of science and philosophy into the mother tongue of each nation.

The study, therefore, of the Greek language (and in the same manner for the Latin) was no other than the drudgery business of a linguist; and the language thus obtained, was no other than the means, or as it were the tools, employed to obtain the learning the Greeks had. It made no part of the learning itself, and was so distinct from it, as to make it exceedingly probable that the persons who had studied Greek sufficiently to translate those works, such, for instance as Euclid's Elements, did not understand any of the learning the works contained.

As there is now nothing new to be learned from the dead languages, all the useful books being already translated, the languages are become useless, and the time expended in teaching and in learning them is wasted. So far as the study of languages may contribute to the progress and communication of knowledge, (for it has nothing to do with the creation of knowledge), it is only in the living languages that new knowledge is to be found; and certain it is that, in general, a youth will learn more of a living language in one year, than of a dead language in seven, and it is but seldom that the teacher knows much of it himself. The difficulty of learning the dead languages does not arise from any superior abstruseness in the languages themselves, but in their being dead, and the pronunciation entirely lost. It would be the same thing with any other language when it becomes dead. The best Greek linguist that now exists does not understand Greek so well as a Grecian plowman did, or a Grecian milkmaid; and the same for the Latin, compared with a plowman or a milkmaid of the Romans; it would therefore be advantageous to the state of learning to abolish the study of the dead languages, and to make learning consist, as it originally did, in scientific knowledge.

The apology that is sometimes made for continuing to teach the dead languages is, that they are taught at a time when a child is not capable of exerting any other mental faculty than that of memory; but that is altogether erroneous. The human mind has a natural disposition to scientific knowledge, and to the things connected with it. The first and favourite amusement of a child, even before it begins to play, is that of imitating the works of man. It builds houses with cards or sticks; it navigates the little ocean of a bowl of water with a paper boat, or dams the stream of a gutter and contrives something which it calls a mill; and it interests itself in the fate of its works with a care that resembles affection. It afterwards goes to school, where its genius is killed by the barren study of a dead language, and the philosopher is lost in the linguist.

But the apology that is now made for continuing to teach the dead languages, could not be the cause, at first, of cutting down learning to the narrow and humble sphere of linguistry; the cause, therefore, must be sought for elsewhere. In all researches of this kind, the best evidence that can be produced, is the internal evidence the thing carries with itself, and the evidence of circumstances that unites with it; both of which, in this case, are not difficult to be discovered.

Putting then aside, as a matter of distinct consideration, the outrage offered to the moral justice of God by supposing him to make the innocent suffer for the guilty, and also the loose morality and low contrivance of supposing him to change himself into the shape of a man, in order to make an excuse to himself for not executing his supposed sentence upon Adam—putting, I say, those things aside as a matter of distinct consideration, it is certain that what is called the Christian system of faith, including in it the whimsical account of the creation—the strange story of Eve—the snake, and the apple—the amphibious idea of a man-god—the corporeal idea of the death of a god—the mythological idea of a family of gods, and the Christian system of arithmetic, that three are one, and one is three, are all irreconcilable, not only to the divine gift of reason that God, has given to man, but to the knowledge that man gains of the power and wisdom of God by the aid of the sciences and by studying the structure of the universe that God has made.

The setters-up, therefore, and the advocates of the Christian system of faith could not but foresee that the continually progressive knowledge that man would gain, by the aid of science, of the power and wisdom of God, manifested in the structure of the universe and in all the works of Creation, would militate against, and call into question, the truth of their system of faith; and therefore it became necessary to their purpose to cut learning down to a size less dangerous to their project, and this they effected by restricting the idea of learning to the dead study of dead languages.

They not only rejected the study of science out of the Christian schools, but they persecuted it, and it is only within about the last two centuries that the study has been revived. So late as 1610, Galileo, a Florentine, discovered and introduced the use of telescopes, and by applying them to observe the motions and appearances of the heavenly bodies, afforded additional means for ascertaining the true structure of the universe. Instead of being esteemed for these discoveries, he was sentenced to renounce them, or the opinions resulting from them, as a damnable heresy. And, prior to that time, Virgilius was condemned to be burned for asserting the antipodes, or in other words that the earth was a globe, and habitable in every part where there was land; yet the truth of this is now too well known even to be told.

If the belief of errors not morally bad did no mischief, it would make no part of the moral duty of man to oppose and remove them. There was no moral ill in believing the earth was flat like a trencher, any more than there was moral virtue in believing it was round like a globe; neither was there any moral ill in believing that the Creator made no other world than this, any more than there was moral virtue in believing that he made millions, and that the infinity of space is filled with worlds. But when a system of religion is made to grow out of a supposed system of creation that is not true, and to unite itself therewith in a manner almost inseparable therefrom, the case assumes an entirely different ground. It is then that errors not morally bad become fraught with the same mischiefs as if they were. It is then that the truth, though otherwise indifferent itself, becomes an essential by becoming the criterion that either confirms by corresponding evidence, or denies by contradictory evidence, the reality of the religion itself. In this view of the case it is the moral duty of man to obtain every possible evidence that the structure of the heavens, or any other part of creation affords, with respect to systems of religion. But this, the supporters or partisans of the Christian system, as if dreading the result, incessantly opposed, and not only rejected the sciences, but persecuted the professors. Had Newton or Descartes lived three or four hundred years ago, and pursued their studies as they did, it is most probable they would not have lived to finish them; and had Franklin drawn lightning from the clouds at the same time, it would have been at the hazard of expiring for it in flames.

Later times have laid all the blame upon the Goths and Vandals; but, however unwilling the partisans of the Christian system may be to believe or to acknowledge it, it is nevertheless true, that the age of ignorance commenced with the Christian system. There was more knowledge in the world before that period than for many centuries afterwards; and as to religious knowledge, the Christian system, as already said was only another species of mythology, and the mythology to which it succeeded was a corruption of an ancient system of theism.*

*It is impossible for us now to know at what time the heathen mythology began; but it is certain, from the internal evidence that it carries, that it did not begin in the same state or condition in which it ended. All the gods of that mythology, except Saturn, were of modern invention. The supposed reign of Saturn was prior to that which is called the heathen mythology, and was so far a species of theism, that it admitted the belief of only one God. Saturn is supposed to have abdicated the govemment in favor of his three sons and one daughter, Jupiter, Pluto, Neptune, and Juno; after this, thousands of other Gods and demi-gods were imaginarily created, and the calendar of gods increased as fast as the calendar of saints and the calendar of courts have increased since. All the corruptions that have taken place, in theology and in religion, have been produced by admitting of what man calls revealed religion. The Mythologists pretended to more revealed religion than the Christians do. They had their oracles and their priests, who were supposed to receive and deliver the word of God verbally, on almost all occasions. Since, then, all corruptions, down from Moloch to modem predestinarianism, and the human sacrifices of the heathens to the Christian sacrifice of the Creator, have been produced by admitting of what is called revealed religion, the most effectual means to prevent all such evils and impositions is not to admit of any other revelation than that which is manifested in the book of creation, and to contemplate the creation as the only true and real word of God that ever did or ever will exist; and everything else called the word of God, is fable and imposition.

It is owing to this long interregnum of science, and to no other cause, that we have now to look back through a vast chasm of many hundred years to the respectable characters we call the ancients. Had the progression of knowledge gone on proportionably with the stock that before existed, that chasm would have been filled up with characters rising superior in knowledge to each other; and those ancients we now so much admire would have appeared respectably in the background of the scene. But the Christian system laid all waste; and if we take our stand about the beginning of the sixteenth century, we look back through that long chasm, to the times of the ancients, as over a vast sandy desert, in which not a shrub appears to intercept the vision to the fertile hills beyond.

It is an inconsistency scarcely possible to be credited, that any thing should exist, under the name of a religion, that held it to be irreligious to study and contemplate the structure of the universe that God has made. But the fact is too well established to be denied. The event that served more than any other to break the first link in this long chain of despotic ignorance is that known by the name of the Reformation by Luther. From that time, though it does not appear to have made any part of the intention of Luther, or of those who are called reformers, the sciences began to revive, and liberality, their natural associate, began to appear. This was the only public good the Reformation did; for with respect to religious good, it might as well not have taken place. The mythology still continued the same, and a multiplicity of National Popes grew out of the downfall of the Pope of Christendom.

Having thus shown from the internal evidence of things the cause that produced a change in the state of learning, and the motive for substituting the study of the dead languages in the place of the sciences, I proceed, in addition to the several observations already made in the former part of this work, to compare, or rather to confront, the evidence that the structure of the universe affords with the Christian system of religion; but, as I cannot begin this part better than by referring to the ideas that occurred to me at an early part of life, and which I doubt not have occurred in some degree to almost every other person at one time or other, I shall state what those ideas were, and add thereto such other matter as shall arise out of the subject, giving to the whole, by way of preface, a short introduction.

My father being of the Quaker profession, it was my good fortune to have an exceedingly good moral education, and a tolerable stock of useful learning. Though I went to the grammar school,* I did not learn Latin, not only because I had no inclination to learn languages, but because of the objection the Quakers have against the books in which the language is taught. But this did not prevent me from being acquainted with the subjects of all the Latin books used in the school.

*The same school, Thetford In Norfolk that the present Counsellor Mingay went to and under the same master.

The natural bent of my mind was to science. I had some turn, and I believe some talent for poetry; but this I rather repressed than encouraged, as leading too much into the field of imagination. As soon as I was able I purchased a pair of globes, and attended the philosophical lectures of Martin and Ferguson, and became afterwards acquainted with Dr. Bevis, of the society called the Royal Society, then living in the Temple, and an excellent astronomer.

I had no disposition for what was called politics. It presented to my mind no other idea than is contained in the word Jockeyship. When therefore I turned my thoughts toward matters of government, I had to form a system for myself that accorded with the moral and philosophic principles in which I had been educated. I saw, or at least I thought I saw, a vast scene opening itself to the world in the affairs of America, and it appeared to me that unless the Americans changed the plan they were then pursuing with respect to the government of England, and declared themselves independent, they would not only involve themselves in a multiplicity of new difficulties, but shut out the prospect that was then offering itself to mankind through their means. It was from these motives that I published the work known by the name of Common Sense, which is the first work I ever did publish; and so far as I can judge of myself, I believe I should never have been known in the world as an author, on any subject whatever, had it not been for the affairs of America. I wrote Common Sense the latter end of the year 1775, and published it the first of January, 1776. Independence was declared the fourth of July following.

Any person who has made observations on the state and progress of the human mind, by observing his own, can not but have observed that there are two distinct classes of what are called thoughts–those that we produce in ourselves by reflection and the act of thinking, and those that bolt into the mind of their own accord. I have always made it a rule to treat those voluntary visitors with civility, taking care to examine, as well as I was able, if they were worth entertaining, and it is from them I have acquired almost all the knowledge that I have. As to the learning that any person gains from school education, it serves only, like a small capital, to put him in the way of beginning learning for himself afterward. Every person of learning is finally his own teacher, the reason of which is that principles, being of a distinct quality to circumstances, cannot be impressed upon the memory; their place of mental residence is the understanding and they are never so lasting as when they begin by conception. Thus much for the introductory part.

From the time I was capable of conceiving an idea and acting upon it by reflection, I either doubted the truth of the Christian system or thought it to be a strange affair; I scarcely knew which it was, but I well remember, when about seven or eight years of age, hearing a sermon read by a relation of mine, who was a great devotee of the Church, upon the subject of what is called redemption by the death of the Son of God. After the sermon was ended, I went into the garden, and as I was going down the garden steps (for I perfectly recollect the spot) I revolted at the recollection of what I had heard, and thought to myself that it was making God Almighty act like a passionate man, that killed his son when he could not revenge himself any other way, and as I was sure a man would be hanged that did such a thing, I could not see for what purpose they preached such sermons. This was not one of those kind of thoughts that had anything in it of childish levity; it was to me a serious reflection, arising from the idea I had that God was too good to do such an action, and also too almighty to be under any necessity of doing it. I believe in the same manner to this moment; and I moreover believe, that any system of religion that has anything in it that shocks the mind of a child, cannot be a true system.

It seems as if parents of the Christian profession were ashamed to tell their children anything about the principles of their religion. They sometimes instruct them in morals, and talk to them of the goodness of what they call Providence, for the Christian mythology has five deities–there is God the Father, God the Son, God the Holy Ghost, the God Providence, and the Goddess Nature. But the Christian story of God the Father putting his son to death, or employing people to do it (for that is the plain language of the story) cannot be told by a parent to a child; and to tell him that it was done to make mankind happier and better is making the story still worse–as if mankind could be improved by the example of murder; and to tell him that all this is a mystery is only making an excuse for the incredibility of it.

How different is this to the pure and simple profession of Deism! The true Deist has but one Deity, and his religion consists in contemplating the power, wisdom, and benignity of the Deity in his works, and in endeavouring to imitate him in everything moral, scientifical, and mechanical.

The religion that approaches the nearest of all others to true Deism, in the moral and benign part thereof, is that professed by the Quakers; but they have contracted themselves too much, by leaving the works of God out of their system. Though I reverence their philanthropy, I cannot help smiling at the conceit, that if the taste of a Quaker could have been consulted at the creation, what a silent and drab-colored creation it would have been! Not a flower would have blossomed its gayeties, nor a bird been permitted to sing. Quitting these reflections, I proceed to other matters. After I had made myself master of the use of the globes, and of the orrery,* and conceived an idea of the infinity of space, and of the eternal divisibility of matter, and obtained at least a general knowledge of what was called natural philosophy, I began to compare, or, as I have before said, to confront, the internal evidence those things afford with the Christian system of faith.

*As this book may fall into the bands of persons who do not know what an orrery is, it is for their information I add this note, as the name gives no idea of the uses of the thing. The orrery has its name from the person who invented it. It is a machinery of clock-work, representing the universe in miniature, and in which the revolution of the earth round itself and round the sun, the revolution of the moon round the earth, the revolution of the planets round the sun, their relative distances from the sun, as the centre of the whole system, their relative distances from each other, and their different magnitudes, are represented as they really exist in what we call the heavens.

Though it is not a direct article of the Christian system that this world that we inhabit is the whole of the habitable creation, yet it is so worked up therewith, from what is called the Mosaic account of the Creation, the story of Eve and the apple, and the counterpart of that story, the death of the Son of God, that to believe otherwise, that is, to believe that God created a plurality of worlds, at least as numerous as what we call stars, renders the Christian system of faith at once little and ridiculous, and scatters it in the mind like feathers in the air. The two beliefs cannot be held together in the same mind, and he who thinks that be believes both, has thought but little of either.

Though the belief of a plurality of worlds was familiar to the ancients, it is only within the last three centuries that the extent and dimensions of this globe that we inhabit have been ascertained. Several vessels, following the tract of the ocean, have sailed entirely round the world, as a man may march in a circle, and come round by the contrary side of the circle to the spot he set out from. The circular dimensions of our world, in the widest part, as a man would measure the widest round of an apple, or a ball, is only twenty-five thousand and twenty English miles, reckoning sixty-nine miles and a half to an equatorial degree, and may be sailed round in the space of about three years.*

*Allowing a ship to sail, on an average, three miles in an hour, she would sail entirely round the world in less than one year, if she could sail in a direct circle; but she is obliged to follow the course of the ocean.

A world of this extent may, at first thought, appear to us to be great; but if we compare it with the immensity of space in which it is suspended, like a bubble or a balloon in the air, it is infinitely less in proportion than the smallest grain of sand is to the size of the world, or the finest particle of dew to the whole ocean, and is therefore but small; and, as will be hereafter shown, is only one of a system of worlds of which the universal creation is composed.

It is not difficult to gain some faint idea of the immensity of space in which this and all the other worlds are suspended, if we follow a progression of ideas. When we think of the size or dimensions of a room, our ideas limit themselves to the walls, and there they stop; but when our eye or our imagination darts into space, that is, when it looks upward into what we call the open air, we cannot conceive any walls or boundaries it can have, and if for the sake of resting our ideas, we suppose a boundary, the question immediately renews itself, and asks, what is beyond that boundary? and in the same manner, what is beyond the next boundary? and so on till the fatigued imagination returns and says, There is no end. Certainly, then, the Creator was not pent for room when he made this world no larger than it is, and we have to seek the reason in something else.

If we take a survey of our own world, or rather of this, of which the Creator has given us the use as our portion in the immense system of creation, we find every part of it–the earth, the waters, and the air that surround it–filled and, as it were crowded with life, down from the largest animals that we know of to the smallest insects the naked eye can behold, and from thence to others still smaller, and totally invisible without the assistance of the microscope. Every tree, every plant, every leaf, serves not only as a habitation but as a world to some numerous race, till animal existence becomes so exceedingly refined that the effluvia of a blade of grass would be food for thousands.

Since, then, no part of our earth is left unoccupied, why is it to be supposed that the immensity of space is a naked void, lying in eternal waste? There is room for millions of worlds as large or larger than ours, and each of them millions of miles apart from each other.

Having now arrived at this point, if we carry our ideas only one thought further, we shall see, perhaps, the true reason, at least a very good reason for our happiness, why the

Creator, instead of making one immense world extending over an immense quantity of space, has preferred dividing that quantity of matter into several distinct and separate worlds, which we call planets, of which our earth is one. But before I explain my ideas upon this subject, it is necessary (not for the sake of those that already know, but for those who do not) to show what the system of the universe is.

That part of the universe that is called the solar system (meaning the system of worlds to which our earth belongs, and of which Sol, or in English language, the Sun, is the centre) consists, besides the Sun, of six distinct orbs, or planets, or worlds, besides the secondary called the satellites or moons, of which our earth has one that attends her in her annual revolution round the Sun, in like manner as the other satellites or moons attend the planets or worlds to which they severally belong, as may be seen by the assistance of the telescope.

The Sun is the centre round which those six worlds or planets revolve at different distances therefrom, and in circles concentric to each other. Each world keeps constantly in nearly the same track round the Sun, and continues, at the same time, turning round itself in nearly an upright position, as a top turns round itself when it is spinning on the ground, and leans a little sideways.

It is this leaning of the earth (23.5 degrees) that occasions summer and winter, and the different length of days and nights. If the earth turned round itself in a position perpendicular to the plane or level of the circle it moves in a round the Sun, as a top turns round when it stands erect on the ground, the days and nights would be always of the same length, twelve hours day and twelve hours night, and the season would be uniformly the same throughout the year.

Every time that a planet (our earth for example) turns round itself, it makes what we call day and night; and every time it goes entirely round the Sun it makes what we call a year; consequently our world turns three hundred and sixty-five times round itself, in going once round the Sun.*

> *Those who supposed that the sun went round the earth every 24 hours made the same mistake in idea that a cook would do in fact, that should make the fire go round the meat, instead of the meat turning round itself toward the fire.

The names that the ancients gave to those six worlds, and which are still called by the same names, are Mercury, Venus, this world that we call ours, Mars, Jupiter, and Saturn. They appear larger to the eye than the stars, being many million miles nearer to our earth than any of the stars are. The planet Venus is that which is called the evening star, and sometimes the morning star, as she happens to set after or rise before the Sun, which in either case is never more than three hours.

The Sun as before said, being the centre, the planet or world nearest the Sun is Mercury; his distance from the Sun is thirty-four million miles, and he moves round in a circle always at that distance from the Sun, as a top may be supposed to spin round in the track in which a horse goes in a mill. The second world is Venus; she is fifty-seven million miles distant from the Sun, and consequently moves round in a circle much greater than that of Mercury. The third world is this that we inhabit, and which is eighty-eight million miles distant from the Sun, and consequently moves round in a circle greater than that of Venus. The fourth world is Mars; he is distant from the Sun one hundred and thirty-four million miles, and consequently moves round in a circle greater than that of our earth. The fifth is Jupiter; he is distant from the Sun five hundred and fifty-seven million miles, and consequently moves round in a circle greater than that of Mars. The sixth world is Saturn; he is distant from the Sun seven hundred and sixty-three million miles, and consequently moves round in a circle that surrounds the circles, or orbits, of all the other worlds or planets.

The space, therefore, in the air, or in the immensity of space, that our solar system takes up for the several worlds to perform their revolutions in round the Sun, is of the extent in a straight line of the whole diameter of the orbit or circle, in which Saturn moves round the Sun, which being double his distance from the Sun, is fifteen hundred and twenty-six million miles, and its circular extent is nearly five thousand million, and its globular contents is almost three thousand five hundred million times three thousand five hundred million square miles.*

*If it should be asked, how can man know these things? I have one plain answer to give, which is, that man knows how to calculate an eclipse, and also how to calculate to a minute of time when the planet Venus, in making her revolutions round the sun, will come in a straight line between our earth and the sun, and will appear to us about the size of a large pea passing across the face of the sun. This happens but twice in about a hundred years, at the distance of about eight years from each other, and has happened twice in our time, both of which were foreknown by calculation. It can also be known when they will happen again for a thousand years to come, or to any other portion of time. As therefore, man could not be able to do these things if he did not understand the solar system, and the manner in which the revolutions of the several planets or worlds are performed, the fact of calculating an eclipse, or a transit of Venus, is a proof in point that the knowledge exists; and as to a few thousand, or even a few million miles, more or less, it makes scarcely any sensible difference in such immense distances.

But this, immense as it is, is only one system of worlds. Beyond this, at a vast distance into space, far beyond all power of calculation, are the stars called the fixed stars. They are called fixed, because they have no revolutionary motion, as the six worlds or planets have that I have been describing. Those fixed stars continue always at the same distance from each other, and always in the same place, as the Sun does in the centre of our system. The probability, therefore, is, that each of those fixed stars is also a Sun, round which another system of worlds or planets, though too remote for us to discover, performs its revolutions, as our system of worlds does round our central Sun.

By this easy progression of ideas, the immensity of space will appear to us to be filled with systems of worlds, and that no part of space lies at waste, any more than any part of our globe of earth and water is left unoccupied.

Having thus endeavoured to convey, in a familiar and easy manner, some idea of the structure of the universe, I return to explain what I before alluded to, namely, the great benefits arising to man in consequence of the Creator having made a plurality of worlds, such as our system is, consisting of a central Sun and six worlds, besides satellites, in preference to that of creating one world only of a vast extent.

It is an idea I have never lost sight of, that all our knowledge of science is derived from the revolutions (exhibited to our eye and from thence to our understanding) which those several planets or worlds of which our system is composed make in their circuit round the Sun.

Had, then, the quantity of matter which these six worlds contain been blended into one solitary globe, the consequence to us would have been, that either no revolutionary motion would have existed, or not a sufficiency of it to give us the ideas and the knowledge of science we now have; and it is from the sciences that all the mechanical arts that contribute so much to our earthly felicity and comfort are derived.

As, therefore, the Creator made nothing in vain, so also must it be believed that he organized the structure of the universe in the most advantageous manner for the benefit of man; and as we see, and from experience feel, the benefits we derive from the structure of the universe formed as it is, which benefits we should not have had the opportunity of enjoying, if the structure, so far as relates to our system, had been a solitary globe—we can discover at least one reason why a plurality of worlds has been made, and that reason calls forth the devotional gratitude of man, as well as his admiration.

But it is not to us, the inhabitants of this globe, only, that the benefits arising from a plurality of worlds are limited. The inhabitants of each of the worlds of which our system is composed enjoy the same opportunities of knowledge as we do. They behold the revolutionary motions of our earth, as we behold theirs. All the planets revolve in sight of each other, and, therefore, the same universal school of science presents itself to all.

Neither does the knowledge stop here. The system of worlds next to us exhibits, in its revolutions, the same principles and school of science to the inhabitants of their system, as our system does to us, and in like manner throughout the immensity of space.

Our ideas, not only of the almightiness of the Creator, but of his wisdom and his beneficence, become enlarged in proportion as we contemplate the extent and the structure of the universe. The solitary idea of a solitary world, rolling or at rest in the immense ocean of space, gives place to the cheerful idea of a society of worlds, so happily contrived as to administer, even by their motion, instruction to man. We see our own earth filled with abundance, but we forget to consider how much of that abundance is owing to the scientific knowledge the vast machinery of the universe has unfolded.

But, in the midst of those reflections, what are we to think of the Christian system of faith, that forms itself upon the idea of only one world, and that of no greater extent, as is before shown, than twenty-five thousand miles. An extent which a man walking at the rate of three miles an hour, for twelve hours in the day, could he keep on in a circular direction, would walk entirely round in less than two years. Alas! what is this to the mighty ocean of space, and the almighty power of the Creator?

From whence, then, could arise the solitary and strange conceit that the Almighty, who had millions of worlds equally dependent on his protection, should quit the care of all the rest, and come to die in our world, because, they say, one man and one woman had eaten an apple? And, on the other hand, are we to suppose that every world in the boundless creation had an Eve, an apple, a serpent, and a redeemer? In this case, the person who is irreverently called the Son of God, and sometimes God himself, would have nothing else to do than to travel from world to world, in an endless succession of deaths, with scarcely a momentary interval of life.

It has been by rejecting the evidence that the word or works of God in the creation affords to our senses, and the action of our reason upon that evidence, that so many wild and whimsical systems of faith and of religion, have been fabricated and set up. There may be many systems of religion that, so far from being morally bad, are in many respects morally good; but there can be but ONE that is true; and that one necessarily must, as it ever will, be in all things consistent with the ever-existing word of God that we behold in his works. But such is the strange construction of the Christian system of faith that every evidence the Heavens affords to man either directly contradicts it or renders it absurd.

It is possible to believe, and I always feel pleasure in encouraging myself to believe it, that there have been men in the world who persuade themselves that what is called a pious fraud might, at least under particular circumstances, be productive of some good. But the fraud being once established, could not afterwards be explained, for it is with a pious fraud as with a bad action, it begets a calamitous necessity of going on.

The persons who first preached the Christian system of faith, and in some measure combined with it the morality preached by Jesus Christ, might persuade themselves that it was better than the heathen mythology that then prevailed. From the first preachers the fraud went on to the second, and to the third, till the idea of its being a pious fraud became lost in the belief of its being true; and that belief became again encouraged by the interest of those who made a livelihood by preaching it.

But though such a belief might by such means be rendered almost general among the laity, it is next to impossible to account for the continual persecution carried on by the Church, for several hundred years, against the sciences and against the professors of science, if the Church had not some record or tradition that it was originally no other than a pious fraud, or did not foresee that it could not be maintained against the evidence that the structure of the universe afforded.

Having thus shown the irreconcileable inconsistencies between the real word of God existing in the universe, and that which is called the Word of God, as shown to us in a printed book that any man might make, I proceed to speak of the three principal means that have been employed in all ages, and perhaps in all countries, to impose upon mankind.

Those three means are Mystery, Miracle, and Prophecy, The first two are incompatible with true religion, and the third ought always to be suspected.

With respect to mystery, everything we behold is, in one sense, a mystery to us. Our own existence is a mystery; the whole vegetable world is a mystery. We cannot account how it is that an acorn, when put into the ground, is made to develop itself and become an oak. We know not how it is that the seed we sow unfolds and multiplies itself, and returns to us such an abundant interest for so small a capital.

The fact, however, as distinct from the operating cause, is not a mystery, because we see it, and we know also the means we are to use, which is no other than putting the seed in the ground. We know, therefore, as much as is necessary for us to know; and that part of the operation that we do not know, and which, if we did, we could not perform, the Creator takes upon himself and performs it for us. We are, therefore, better off than if we had been let into the secret, and left to do it for ourselves.

But though every created thing is, in this sense, a mystery, the word mystery cannot be applied to moral truth, any more than obscurity can be applied to light. The God in whom we believe is a God of moral truth, and not a God of mystery or obscurity. Mystery is the antagonist of truth. It is a fog of human invention, that obscures truth, and represents it in distortion. Truth never envelops itself in mystery, and the mystery in which it is at any time enveloped is the work of its antagonist, and never of itself.

Religion, therefore, being the belief of a God, and the practice of moral truth, cannot have connection with mystery. The belief of a God, so far from having any thing of mystery in it, is of all beliefs the most easy, because it arises to us, as is before observed, out of necessity. And the practice of moral truth, or, in other words, a practical imitation of the moral goodness of God, is no other than our acting toward each other as he acts benignly toward all. We cannot serve God in the manner we serve those who cannot do without such service; and, therefore, the only idea we can have of serving God, is that of contributing to the happiness of the living creation that God has made. This cannot be done by retiring ourselves from the society of the world and spending a recluse life in selfish devotion.

The very nature and design of religion, if I may so express it, prove even to demonstration that it must be free from every thing of mystery, and unencumbered with everything that is mysterious. Religion, considered as a duty, is incumbent upon every living soul alike, and, therefore, must be on a level to the understanding and comprehension of all. Man does not learn religion as he learns the secrets and mysteries of a trade. He learns the theory of religion by reflection. It arises out of the action of his own mind upon the things which he sees, or upon what he may happen to hear or to read, and the practice joins itself thereto.

When men, whether from policy or pious fraud, set up systems of religion incompatible with the word or works of God in the creation, and not only above, but repugnant to human comprehension, they were under the necessity of inventing or adopting a word that should serve as a bar to all questions, inquiries and speculations. The word mystery answered this purpose, and thus it has happened that religion, which is in itself without mystery, has been corrupted into a fog of mysteries.

As mystery answered all general purposes, miracle followed as an occasional auxiliary. The former served to bewilder the mind, the latter to puzzle the senses. The one was the lingo, the other the legerdemain.

But before going further into this subject, it will be proper to inquire what is to be understood by a miracle.

In the same sense that everything may be said to be a mystery, so also may it be said that everything is a miracle, and that no one thing is a greater miracle than another. The elephant, though larger, is not a greater miracle than a mite, nor a mountain a greater miracle than an atom. To an almighty power, it is no more difficult to make the one than the other, and no more difficult to make a millions of worlds than to make one. Everything, therefore, is a miracle, in one sense, whilst in the other sense, there is no such thing as a miracle. It is a miracle when compared to our power and to our comprehension; if not a miracle compared to the power that performs it; but as nothing in this description conveys the idea that is affixed to the word miracle, it is necessary to carry the inquiry further.

Mankind have conceived to themselves certain laws, by which what they call nature is supposed to act; and that a miracle is something contrary to the operation and effect of those laws; but unless we know the whole extent of those laws, and of what are commonly called the powers of nature, we are not able to judge whether any thing that may appear to us wonderful or miraculous be within, or be beyond, or be contrary to, her natural power of acting.

The ascension of a man several miles high into the air would have everything in it that constitutes the idea of a miracle, if it were not known that a species of air can be generated, several times lighter than the common atmospheric air, and yet possess elasticity enough to prevent the balloon in which that light air is enclosed from being compressed into as many times less bulk, by the common air that surrounds it. In like manner, extracting flashes or sparks of fire from the human body, as visible as from a steel struck with a flint, and causing iron or steel to move without any visible agent, would also give the idea of a miracle, if we were not acquainted with electricity and magnetism. So also would many other experiments in natural philosophy, to those who are not acquainted with the subject. The restoring persons to life who are to appearance dead as is practised upon drowned persons, would also be a miracle, if it were not known that animation is capable of being suspended without being extinct.

Besides these, there are performances be slight-of-hand, and by persons acting in concert, that have a miraculous appearance, which when known are thought nothing of. And besides these, there are mechanical and optical deceptions. There is now an exhibition in Paris of ghosts or spectres, which, though it is not imposed upon the spectators as a fact, has an astonishing appearance. As, therefore, we know not the extent to which either nature or art can go, there is no criterion to determine what a miracle is, and mankind, in giving credit to appearances, under the idea of their being miracles, are subject to be continually imposed upon.

Since, then, appearances are so capable of deceiving, and things not real have a strong resemblance to things that are, nothing can be more inconsistent than to suppose that the Almighty would make use of means such as are called miracles, that would subject the person who performed them to the suspicion of being an impostor, and the person who related them to be suspected of lying, and the doctrine intended to be supported thereby to be suspected as a fabulous invention.

Of all the modes of evidence that ever were invented to obtain belief to any system or opinion to which the name of religion has been given, that of miracle, however successful the imposition may have been, is the most inconsistent. For, in the first place, whenever recourse is had to show, for the purpose of procuring that belief, (for a miracle, under any idea of the word, is a show), it implies a lameness or weakness in the doctrine that is preached. And, in the second place, it is degrading the Almighty into the character of a showman, playing tricks to amuse and make the people stare and wonder. It is also the most equivocal sort of evidence that can be set up; for the belief is not to depend upon the thing called a miracle, but upon the credit of the reporter who says that he saw it; and, therefore, the thing, were it true, would have no better chance of being believed than if it were a lie.

Suppose I were to say, that when I sat down to write this book, a hand presented itself in the air, took up the pen, and wrote every word that is herein written; would anybody believe me? Certainly they would not. Would they believe me a whit the more if the thing had been a fact? Certainly they would not. Since, then, a real miracle, were it to happen, would be subject to the same fate as the falsehood, the inconsistency becomes the greater of supposing the Almighty would make use of means that would not answer the purpose for which they were intended, even if they were real.

If we are to suppose a miracle to be something so entirely out of the course of what is called nature, that she must go out of that course to accomplish it, and we see an account given of such a miracle by the person who said he saw it, it raises a question in the mind very easily decided, which is, is it more probable that nature should go out of her course, or that a man should tell a lie? We have never seen, in our time, nature go out of her course; but we have good reason to believe that millions of lies have been told in the same time; it is therefore, at least millions to one, that the reporter of a miracle tells a lie.

The story of the whale swallowing Jonah, though a whale is large enough to do it, borders greatly on the marvellous; but it would have approached nearer to the idea of a miracle, if Jonah had swallowed the whale. In this, which may serve for all cases of miracles, the matter would decide itself, as before stated, namely, is it more probable that a man should have swallowed a whale or told a lie?

But suppose that Jonah had really swallowed the whale, and gone with it in his belly to Nineveh, and to convince the people that it was true, had cast it up in their sight, of the full length and size of a whale, would they not have believed him to have been the devil, instead of a prophet? Or if the whale had carried Jonah to Nineveh, and cast him up in the same public manner, would they not have believed the whale to have been the devil, and Jonah one of his imps?

The most extraordinary of all the things called miracles, related in the New Testament, is that of the devil flying away with Jesus Christ, and carrying him to the top of a high mountain, and to the top of the highest pinnacle of the temple, and showing him and promising to him all the kingdoms of the World. How happened it that he did not discover America, or is it only with kingdoms that his sooty highness has any interest?

I have too much respect for the moral character of Christ to believe that he told this whale of a miracle himself; neither is it easy to account for what purpose it could have been fabricated, unless it were to impose upon the connoisseurs of Queen Anne's farthings and collectors of relics and antiquities; or to render the belief of miracles ridiculous, by outdoing miracles, as Don Quixote outdid chivalry; or to embarrass the belief of miracles, by making it doubtful by what power, whether of God or of the devil, anything called a miracle was performed. It requires, however, a great deal of faith in the devil to believe this miracle.

In every point of view in which those things called miracles can be placed and considered, the reality of them is improbable and their existence unnecessary. They would not, as before observed, answer any useful purpose, even if they were true; for it is more difficult to obtain belief to a miracle, than to a principle evidently moral without any miracle. Moral principle speaks universally for itself. Miracle could be but a thing of the moment, and seen but by a few; after this it requires a transfer of faith from God to man to believe a miracle upon man's report. Instead, therefore, of admitting the recitals of miracles as evidence of any system of religion being true, they ought to be considered as symptoms of its being fabulous. It is necessary to the full and upright character of truth that it rejects the crutch, and it is consistent with the character of fable to seek the aid that truth rejects. Thus much for mystery and miracle.

As mystery and miracle took charge of the past and the present, prophecy took charge of the future and rounded the tenses of faith. It was not sufficient to know what had been done, but what would be done. The supposed prophet was the supposed historian of times to come; and if he happened, in shooting with a long bow of a thousand years, to strike within a thousand miles of a mark, the ingenuity of posterity could make it point-blank; and if he happened to be directly wrong, it was only to suppose, as in the case of Jonah and Nineveh, that God had repented himself and changed his mind. What a fool do fabulous systems make of man!

It has been shown, in a former part of this work, that the original meaning of the words prophet and prophesying has been changed, and that a prophet, in the sense of the word as now used, is a creature of modern invention;

and it is owing to this change in the meaning of the words, that the flights and metaphors of the Jewish poets, and phrases and expressions now rendered obscure by our not being acquainted with the local circumstances to which they applied at the time they were used, have been erected into prophecies, and made to bend to explanations at the will and whimsical conceits of sectaries, expounders, and commentators. Everything unintelligible was prophetical, and everything insignificant was typical. A blunder would have served for a prophecy, and a dish-clout for a type.

If by a prophet we are to suppose a man to whom the Almighty communicated some event that would take place in the future, either there were such men or there were not. If there were, it is consistent to believe that the event so communicated would be told in terms that could be understood, and not related in such a loose and obscure manner as to be out of the comprehension of those that heard it, and so equivocal as to fit almost any circumstance that might happen afterward. It is conceiving very irreverently of the Almighty, to suppose he would deal in this jesting manner with mankind, yet all the things called prophecies in the book called the Bible come under this description.

But it is with prophecy as it is with miracle; it could not answer the purpose even if it were real. Those to whom a prophecy should be told, could not tell whether the man prophesied or lied, or whether it had been revealed to him, or whether he conceited it; and if the thing that he prophesied, or intended to prophesy, should happen, or something like it, among the multitude of things that are daily happening, nobody could again know whether he foreknew it, or guessed at it, or whether it was accidental. A prophet, therefore, is a character useless and unnecessary; and the safe side of the case is to guard against being imposed upon by not giving credit to such relations.

Upon the whole, mystery, miracle, and prophecy are appendages that belong to fabulous and not to true religion. They are the means by which so many Lo, heres! and Lo, theres! have been spread about the world, and religion been made into a trade. The success of one impostor gave encouragement to another, and the quieting salvo of doing some good by keeping up a pious fraud protected them from remorse.

Having now extended the subject to a greater length than I first intended, I shall bring it to a close by abstracting a summary from the whole.

First—That the idea or belief of a word of God existing in print, or in writing, or in speech, is inconsistent in itself for the reasons already assigned. These reasons, among many others, are the want of a universal language; the mutability of language; the errors to which translations are subject; the possibility of totally suppressing such a word; the probability of altering it, or of fabricating the whole, and imposing it upon the world.

Secondly—That the Creation we behold is the real and ever-existing word of God, in which we cannot be deceived. It proclaimeth his power, it demonstrates his wisdom, it manifests his goodness and beneficence.

Thirdly—That the moral duty of man consists in imitating the moral goodness and beneficence of God manifested in the creation toward all his creatures. That seeing, as we daily do, the goodness of God to all men, it is an example calling upon all men to practise the same toward each other; and, consequently, that everything of persecution and revenge between man and man, and everything of cruelty to animals, is a violation of moral duty.

I trouble not myself about the manner of future existence. I content myself with believing, even to positive conviction, that the Power that gave me existence is able to continue it, in any form and manner he pleases, either with or without this body; and it appears more probable to me that I shall continue to exist hereafter, than that I should have had existence, as I now have, before that existence began.

It is certain that, in one point, all nations of the earth and all religions agree–all believe in a God; the things in which they disagree, are the redundancies annexed to that belief; and therefore, if ever an universal religion should prevail, it will not be believing anything new, but in getting rid of redundancies, and believing as man believed at first. Adam, if ever there was such a man, was created a Deist; but in the meantime, let every man follow, as he has a right to do, the religion and worship he prefers.

CRITICAL EYE

For Discussion

a. Paine claims "My own mind is my own church." What exactly does he mean? Is this assertion important?

b. Many viewed Paine's work as following early eighteenth century British Deism. What does this approach outline? Do you think it is an appropriate way to approach religion, or is it, as many claimed, blasphemy?

Re-approaching the Reading

Many claim that religion is the foundation of any civilized society; as such, how does Paine's approach to religion speak to his juxtaposition of "common sense" and spirituality?

Writing Assignment

Researching Paine's life, how does the treatment he received–social expulsion, prison, not allowing his body to be buried on American soil–speak to religious indignation? Are Americans overly-religious and, as a result, intolerant, or have we truly evolved into a country where a person can worship however they choose without fear of repercussion?

TIERNEY SNEED

WHEN IT COMES TO SAME-SEX MARRIAGE, BOTH SIDES CLAIM POPE FRANCIS

San Francisco Archbishop Salvatore Cordileone's planned participation in a rally to protest same-sex marriage should not come as a surprise, considering his long history of outspoken advocacy that marriage should be between one man and one woman–a key tenet of the Catholic faith.

He chairs the subcommittee for the Promotion and Defense of Marriage of the U.S. Conference of Catholic Bishops. He was a key fundraiser to get California's Proposition 8–which banned same-sex marriage–on the state's ballot in 2008. He has signed the Manhattan Declaration, pledging to to defy the law in the name of maintaining marriage as a union of one man and one woman, and on a Catholic radio show he once said, "The ultimate attack of the Evil One is the attack on marriage."

Nevertheless, his plans to take the stage at Thursday's March on Marriage in Washington, which will also feature politicians such as former Arkansas Gov. Mike Huckabee and former Pennsylvania Sen. Rick Santorum, has riled same-sex marriage activists and even some in the faith community.

The Human Rights Campaign blasted Cordileone for agreeing to appear alongside controversial activists like Bishop Harry Jackson, an evangelical minister who has called the movement to legalize same-sex marriage a "satanic plot" comparable to "the times of Hitler," evangelical leader Jim Garlow who said same-sex marriage would bring about enslavement, and Heritage Foundation fellow Ryan Anderson who compared homosexuality to alcoholism and pedophilia. California religious leaders and public officials wrote Cordileone an open letter urging him to cancel his plans, given the opinions fellow attendees have expressed. The social justice-oriented Christian group Faithful America posted an online petition also urging Cordileone to forgo the rally, gathering tens of thousands of signatures.

Framing many of the criticisms of his participation is the accusation that his presence among such firebrands runs counter to the rhetoric being offered by Pope Francis when it comes to talking about LGBT people. When asked about gay priests last July, the pope made headlines by saying, "Who am I to judge?" He echoed that language in September, saying, "When God looks at a gay person, does he endorse the existence of this person with love, or reject and condemn this person? We must always consider the person." He has also suggested that the church could "look at the different cases and evaluate them in their variety," when it came to the matter of civil unions.

"Pope Francis has powerfully inspired countless Catholics and other Christians to a new vision for how the church can be compassionate," says Michael Sherrard, executive director of Faithful America. "Unfortunately too many–not all, but too many–of the bishops in the United States and their conservative activist allies have really flouted what Pope Francis has had to say about gay and lesbian people."

To be clear, the church has not changed its position in opposing same-sex marriage. In a joint encyclical with his predecessor Pope Benedict XVI, Pope Francis condemned same-sex marriage, a stance he has reiterated since. Earlier this month, the pope urged married couples not to try to raise cats and dogs in the place of children, which was read by some as a signal of the importance of procreation in marriage, one of the main arguments pushed by those opposing same-sex marriage.

Yet the softening of his tone is being seen as an olive branch to Catholics who support LGBT rights and same-sex marriage–including 50 percent of U.S. Catholics who regularly attend Mass, and 72 percent of those who self-identified as infrequent Mass-attendees, per a survey by Univision. For this shift in approach, he has attracted the praise of LGBT activists, and the gay publication *The Advocate* hailed Pope Francis as its person of the year in 2013.

"The pope has taken the church in a completely new direction when it comes to their messages and their treatment of LGBT people," says Charles Joughin, an HRC spokesman. "It's just shocking that the archbishop would align himself in a public way with these people who clearly hold such differing values than Pope Francis, who is effectively Archbishop Cordileone's boss."

Cordileone was not available to comment, but Christine Mugridge, director of communications for the Archdiocese of San Francisco, defended his plans to attend the rally.

Cordileone's work "is intimately connected to the Catholic understanding that Pope Francis speaks about. There is nothing derogatory in the stances that the archbishop takes," she says.

"He is speaking in defense of the religious understanding of what marriage is, and then for the promotion of it. He is accepting opportunities on behalf of the Holy Father as his emissary in the Archdiocese of San Francisco, and he is obliged to defend the Catholic teaching on that."

Likewise, Chris Plant–regional director of National Organization for Marriage, a group leading the opposition to same-sex marriage that is organizing the rally–says Pope Francis's tone is in line with the approach he sees his organization taking on the issue. "He is focusing on the fact that our dialogue ought to be civil," Plant says. "We absolutely ask for it to be a civil."

As to why then NOM had invited same-sex marriage opponents known to make contentious remarks, Plant says, "What faith leaders chose to say from their pulpits is in their purview."

He adds, "All the people who say things for a living do say wrong things occasionally ... I acknowledge that people on both sides have said the darndest things."

While softening his rhetoric when talking about LGBT people, Pope Francis has also been promoting other issues of the church's concern.

"I think he wants to move a little bit beyond the culture wars, at least certainly key issues in the culture wars," says Rev. Thomas P. Rausch, a Jesuit priest and a professor of Catholic theology at Loyola Marymount University in Los Angeles. "He can't simply change the church's teachings–the whole church has to be involved in that. But he can change the way that the church is perceived in terms of the range of issues it addresses. And I suspect that is what he wants to do."

In September, the pope said if the church focuses too much of its attention toward divisive social debates like abortion, gay marriage and the use of contraceptive methods, that it could bring the institution down "like a house of cards."

Nevertheless, participants at this week's U.S. Conference of Catholic Bishops (of which Cordileone was an attendee) expressed a commitment to continue the emphasis on abortion, same-sex marriage, and contraceptives in the document the bishops publish every four years to guide church teaching on public policy in the United States.

"All of this is illustrative of a really serious rift in the Catholic Church and the failure of the following through on the promise of Vatican II," says Jay Corrin, a sociology professor who teaches on religion and politics at Boston University. "Vatican II was an attempt to open the church up and bring it into accord with the major social changes that were all part of the process of modernity itself," he says. Conservative church leaders, he contends, stymied those efforts in the years after Vatican II. "What we see with Francis is a willingness to entertain the social and economic traditions of the church."

Those issues have included immigration, human trafficking and economic inequality, all of which Pope Francis has highlighted from nearly the start of his papacy in March 2013. On the latter point, his criticism of trickle-down economics put him at odds with some Catholic politicians who push for austerity measures, and had conservative pundits labeling him a Marxist.

But LGBT rights are poised to dominate the headlines in months to come, with same-sex marriage being legalized on the state level at a speed neither side was anticipating, and activists in both camps agreeing on one thing: sooner or later they would like to see the Supreme Court rule on same-sex marriage once and for all. With both sides claiming Pope Francis as their own, or at least using him to lob criticisms at their opponents, it appears that his efforts to distance the church from the heated debate surrounding same-sex marriage has had the opposite effect. It put him right in the center of a tug of war:

"He is a very popular figure, so everyone is going to try make it look like he's on their side," Rausch says.

CRITICAL EYE

For Discussion

a. Given our understanding of religious doctrines and expectations, why are the new pope's assertions so shocking?

Re-approaching the Reading

As you see it, why is Pope Frances commenting on the LGBTQ community and its relationship to the Catholic Church? What is gained by being less critical or absolute about a community that has long been shunned by most religious leadership around the globe?

Writing Assignment

How is the quest for LGBTQ rights the new civil rights movement of the 21st century?

THE BOOK OF GENESIS

THE GREAT FLOOD

Sons of God, Daughters of Men

1 And it came to pass, when men began to multiply on the face of the earth, and daughters were born unto them,

2 That the sons of God saw the daughters of men that they were fair; and they took them wives of all which they chose.

3 And the LORD said, My spirit shall not always strive with man, for that he also is flesh: yet his days shall be an hundred and twenty years.

4 There were giants in the earth in those days; and also after that, when the sons of God came in unto the daughters of men, and they bare children to them, the same became mighty men which were of old, men of renown.

5 And GOD saw that the wickedness of man was great in the earth, and that every imagination of the thoughts of his heart was only evil continually.

6 And it repented the LORD that he had made man on the earth, and it grieved him at his heart.

7 And the LORD said, I will destroy man whom I have created from the face of the earth; both man, and beast, and the creeping thing, and the fowls of the air; for it repenteth me that I have made them.

Noah, Shem, Ham, and Japheth

8 But Noah found grace in the eyes of the LORD.

9 These are the generations of Noah: Noah was a just man and perfect in his generations, and Noah walked with God.

10 And Noah begat three sons, Shem, Ham, and Japheth.

11 The earth also was corrupt before God, and the earth was filled with violence.

12 And God looked upon the earth, and, behold, it was corrupt; for all flesh had corrupted his way upon the earth.

13 And God said unto Noah, The end of all flesh is come before me; for the earth is filled with violence through them; and, behold, I will destroy them with the earth.

Cubit, Pitch, and Gopher Wood

14 Make thee an ark of gopher wood; rooms shalt thou make in the ark, and shalt pitch it within and without with pitch.

15 And this is the fashion which thou shalt make it of The length of the ark shall be three hundred cubits, the breadth of it fifty cubits, and the height of it thirty cubits.

16 A window shalt thou make to the ark, and in a cubit shalt thou finish it above; and the door of the ark shalt thou set in the side

thereof; with lower, second, and third stories shalt thou make it.

17 And, behold, I, even I, do bring a flood of waters upon the earth, to destroy all flesh, wherein is the breath of life, from under heaven; and every thing that is in the earth shall die.

18 But with thee will I establish covenant; and thou shalt come into the ark, thou, and thy sons, and wife, and thy sons' wives with thee.

19 And of every living thing of all flesh, two of every sort shalt thou bring into the ark, to keep them alive with thee; they shall be male and female.

20 Of fowls after their kind, and of cattle after their kind, of every creeping thing of the earth after his kind, two of every sort shall come unto thee to keep them alive.

21 And take thou unto thee of all food that is eaten, and thou shalt gather it to thee; and it shall be for food for thee, and for them.

22 Thus did Noah; according to all that God commanded him, so did he.

The Deluge

1 And the LORD said unto Noah, Come thou and all thy house into the ark; for thee have I seen righteous before me in this generation.

2 Of every clean beast thou shalt take to thee by sevens, the male and his female: and of beasts that are not clean by two, the male and his female.

3 Of fowls also of the air by sevens, the male and the female; to keep seed alive upon the face of all the earth.

4 For yet seven days, and I will cause it to rain upon the earth forty days and forty nights; and every living substance that I have made will I destroy from off the face of the earth.

5 And Noah did according unto all that the LORD commanded him.

6 And Noah was six hundred years old when the flood of waters was upon the earth.

7 And Noah went in, and his sons, and his wife, and his sons' wives with him, into the ark, because of the waters of the flood.

8 Of clean beasts, and of beasts that are not clean, and of fowls, and of every thing that creepeth upon the earth,

9 There went in two and two unto Noah into the ark, the male and the female, as God had commanded Noah.

10 And it came to pass after seven days, that the waters of the flood were upon the earth.

11 In the six hundredth year of Noah's life, in the second month, the seventeenth day of the month, the same day were all the fountains of the great deep broken up, and the windows of heaven were opened.

12 And the rain was upon the earth forty days and forty nights.

13 In the selfsame day entered Noah, and Shem, and Ham, and Japheth, the sons of Noah, and Noah's wife, and the three wives of his sons with them, into the ark;

14 They, and every beast after his kind, and all the cattle after their kind, and every creeping thing that creepeth upon the earth after his kind, and every fowl after his kind, every bird of every sort.

15 And they went in unto Noah into the ark, two and two of all flesh, wherein is the breath of life.

16 And they that went in, went in male and female of all flesh, as God had commanded him: and the LORD shut him in.

17 And the flood was forty days upon the earth; and the waters increased, and bare up the ark, and it was lift up above the earth.

18 And the waters prevailed, and were increased greatly upon the earth; and the ark went upon the face of the waters.

19 And the waters prevailed exceedingly upon the earth; and all the high hills, that were under the whole heaven, were covered.

20 Fifteen cubits upward did the waters prevail; and the mountains were covered.

21 And all flesh died that moved upon the earth, both of fowl, and of cattle, and of beast, and of every creeping thing that creepeth upon the earth, and every man:

22 All in whose nostrils was the breath of life, of all that was in the dry land, died.

23 And every living substance was destroyed which was upon the face of the ground, both man, and cattle, and the creeping things, and the fowl of the heaven; and they were destroyed from the earth: and Noah only remained alive, and they that were with him in the ark,

24 And the waters prevailed upon the earth an hundred and fifty days.

Waters Assuaged

1 And God remembered Noah, and every living thing, and all the cattle that was with him in the ark: and God made a wind to pass over the earth, and the waters assuaged;

2 The fountains also of the deep and the windows of heaven were stopped, and the rain from heaven was restrained;

3 And the waters returned from off the earth continually: and after the end of the hundred and fifty days the waters were abated.

An Ark in Mountains of Ararat

4 And the ark rested in the seventh month, on the seventeenth day of the month, upon the mountains of Ararat.

5 And the waters decreased continually until the tenth month: in the tenth month, on the first day of the month, were the tops of the mountains seen.

6 And it came to pass at the end of forty days, that Noah opened the window of the ark which he had made:

7 And he sent forth a raven, which went forth to and fro, until the waters were dried up from off the earth.

8 Also he sent forth a dove from him, to see if the waters were abated from off the face of the ground;

9 But the dove found no rest for the sole of her foot, and she returned unto him into the ark, for the waters were on the face of the whole earth: then he put forth his hand, and took her, and pulled, her in unto him into the ark.

10 And he stayed yet other seven days; and again he sent forth the dove out of the ark;

11 And the dove came in to him in the evening, and, lo, in her mouth was an olive leaf pluckt off: so Noah knew that the waters were abated from off the earth.

12 And he stayed yet another seven days; and. sent forth the dove; which returned not again unto him any more.

13 And it came to pass in the six hundreth and first year, in the first month, the first day of the month, the waters were dried up from off the earth: and Noah removed the covering of the ark, and looked, and, behold, the face of the ground was dry.

The Replenishing of the Earth

14 And in the second month, on the seven and twentieth day of the month, was the earth dried.

15 And God spake unto Noah, saying,

16 Go forth of the ark, thou, and thy wife, and thy sons, and thy sons' wives with thee.

17 Bring forth with thee every living thing that is with thee, of all flesh, both of fowl, and of cattle, and of every creeping thing that creepeth upon the earth; that they may breed abundantly in the earth; and be fruitful, and multiply upon the earth.

18 And Noah went forth, and his sons, and his wife, and his sons' wives with him:

19 Every beast, every creeping thing, and every fowl, and whatsoever creepeth upon the earth, after their kinds, went forth out of the ark.

20 And Noah builded an altar unto the LORD; and took of every clean beast, and of every clean fowl, and offered burnt offerings on the altar.

21 And the LORD smelled a sweet savour; and the LORD said in his heart, I will not again curse the ground any more for man's sake; for the imagination of man's heart is evil from his youth; neither will I again smite any more every thing living, as I have done.

22 While the earth remaineth, seedtime and harvest, and cold and heat, and summer and winter, and day and night shall not cease.

Death of Noah

1 And God blessed Noah and his sons, and said unto them, Be fruitful, and multiply, and replenish the earth.

2 And the fear of you and the dread of you shall be upon every beast of the earth, and every fowl of the air, upon all that moveth upon the earth, and upon all the fishes of the sea; into your hand are they delivered.

3 Every moving thing that liveth shall be meat for you; even as the green herb have I given you all things.

4 But flesh with the life thereof, which is the blood thereof, shall ye not eat.

5 And surely your blood of your lives will I require; at the hand of every beast will I require it, and at the hand of man; at the hand of every man's brother will I require the life of man.

6 Who so sheddeth man's blood, by man shall his blood be shed: for in the image of God made he man.

7 And you, be ye fruitful, and multiply; bring forth abundantly in the earth, and multiply therein.

8 And God spake unto Noah, and to his sons with him, saying,

9 And I, behold, I establish my covenant with you, and with your seed after you;

10 And with every living creature that is with you, of the fowl, of The cattle, and of every beast of the earth with you; from all that go out of the ark, to every beast of the earth.

11 And I will establish my covenant with you; neither shall all flesh be cut off any more by the waters of a flood; neither shall there any more be a flood to destroy the earth.

12 And God said, This is the token of the covenant which I make between me and you and every living creature that is with you, for perpetual generations:

13 I do set my bow in the cloud, and it shall be for a token of a covenant between me and the earth.

14 And it shall come to pass, when I bring a cloud over the earth, that the bow shall be seen in the cloud:

15 And I will remember my covenant, which is between me and you and every living creature of all flesh; and the waters shall no more become a flood to destroy all flesh.

16 And the bow shall be in the cloud; and I will look upon it, that I may remember the everlasting covenant between God and every living creature of all flesh that is upon the earth.

17 And God said unto Noah, This is the token of the covenant, which I have established between Me and all flesh that is upon the earth.

18 And the sons of Noah, that went forth of the ark, were Shem, and Ham, and Japheth: and Ham is the Noah: and of them was the whole earth overspread.

CRITICAL EYE

For Discussion

a. Consider the stories of Mallam Sile and Noah. How do these men use their respective faiths to get them through trying times?

b. In this excerpt, God seems to echo the exact same sentiment expressed by many of the writers in this anthology; namely, that mankind is wicked. If God has little to no faith in humanity, how can we?

c. At the end of the text, God assures Noah that He will never again destroy the planet Earth and its inhabitants. If so, why then are so many people predicting and waiting for the end of the world?

Re-approaching the Reading

Examine this excerpt from the book of *Genesis* alongside of Twain's "The Lowest Animal" and Aesop's "A Lion and Other Animals Go Hunting." Although written at different points in our global history, each seems to argue against humanity's ability to treat each other with respect and kindness. How is this true? Be specific.

Writing Assignment

If all of mankind is wicked, why is that God relies upon one man to help save humankind?

RALPH WALDO EMERSON

DIVINITY SCHOOL ADDRESS

Delivered before the Senior Class in Divinity College, Cambridge, Sunday Evening, July 15, 1838

In this refulgent summer, it has been a luxury to draw the breath of life. The grass grows, the buds burst, the meadow is spotted with fire and gold in the tint of flowers. The air is full of birds, and sweet with the breath of the pine, the balm-of-Gilead, and the new hay. Night brings no gloom to the heart with its welcome shade. Through the transparent darkness the stars pour their almost spiritual rays. Man under them seems a young child, and his huge globe a toy. The cool night bathes the world as with a river, and prepares his eyes again for the crimson dawn. The mystery of nature was never displayed more happily. The corn and the wine have been freely dealt to all creatures, and the never-broken silence with which the old bounty goes forward, has not yielded yet one word of explanation. One is constrained to respect the perfection of this world, in which our senses converse. How wide; how rich; what invitation from every property it gives to every faculty of man! In its fruitful soils; in its navigable sea; in its mountains of metal and stone; in its forests of all woods; in its animals; in its chemical ingredients; in the powers and path of light, heat, attraction, and life, it is well worth the pith and heart of great men to subdue and enjoy it. The planters, the mechanics, the inventors, the astronomers, the builders of cities, and the captains, history delights to honor.

But when the mind opens, and reveals the laws which traverse the universe, and make things what they are, then shrinks the great world at once into a mere illustration and fable of this mind. What am I? and What is? asks the human spirit with a curiosity new-kindled, but never to be quenched. Behold these outrunning laws, which our imperfect apprehension can see tend this way and that, but not come full circle. Behold these infinite relations, so like, so unlike; many, yet one. I would study, I would know, I would admire forever. These works of thought have been the entertainments of the human spirit in all ages.

A more secret, sweet, and overpowering beauty appears to man when his heart and mind open to the sentiment of virtue. Then he is instructed in what is above him. He learns that his being is without bound; that, to the good, to the perfect, he is born, low as he now lies in evil and weakness. That which he venerates is still his own, though he has not realized it yet. *He ought*. He knows the sense of that grand word, though his analysis fails entirely to render account of it. When in innocency, or when by intellectual perception, he attains to say, – `I love the Right; Truth is beautiful within and without, forevermore. Virtue, I am thine: save me: use me: thee will I serve, day and night, in great, in small, that I may be not virtuous, but virtue;' – then is the end of the creation answered, and God is well pleased.

The sentiment of virtue is a reverence and delight in the presence of certain divine laws.

It perceives that this homely game of life we play, covers, under what seem foolish details, principles that astonish. The child amidst his baubles, is learning the action of light, motion, gravity, muscular force; and in the game of human life, love, fear, justice, appetite, man, and God, interact. These laws refuse to be adequately stated. They will not be written out on paper, or spoken by the tongue. They elude our persevering thought; yet we read them hourly in each other's faces, in each other's actions, in our own remorse. The moral traits which are all globed into every virtuous act and thought, – in speech, we must sever, and describe or suggest by painful enumeration of many particulars. Yet, as this sentiment is the essence of all religion, let me guide your eye to the precise objects of the sentiment, by an enumeration of some of those classes of facts in which this element is conspicuous.

The intuition of the moral sentiment is an insight of the perfection of the laws of the soul. These laws execute themselves. They are out of time, out of space, and not subject to circumstance. Thus; in the soul of man there is a justice whose retributions are instant and entire. He who does a good deed, is instantly ennobled. He who does a mean deed, is by the action itself contracted. He who puts off impurity, thereby puts on purity. If a man is at heart just, then in so far is he God; the safety of God, the immortality of God, the majesty of God do enter into that man with justice. If a man dissemble, deceive, he deceives himself, and goes out of acquaintance with his own being. A man in the view of absolute goodness, adores, with total humility. Every step so downward, is a step upward. The man who renounces himself, comes to himself.

See how this rapid intrinsic energy worketh everywhere, righting wrongs, correcting appearances, and bringing up facts to a harmony with thoughts. Its operation in life, though slow to the senses, is, at last, as sure as in the soul. By it, a man is made the Providence to himself, dispensing good to his goodness, and evil to his sin. Character is always known. Thefts never enrich; alms never impoverish; murder will speak out of stone walls. The least admixture of a lie, – for example, the taint of vanity, the least attempt to make a good impression, a favorable appearance, – will instantly vitiate the effect. But speak the truth, and all nature and all spirits help you with unexpected furtherance. Speak the truth, and all things alive or brute are vouchers, and the very roots of the grass underground there, do seem to stir and move to bear you witness. See again the perfection of the Law as it applies itself to the affections, and becomes the law of society. As we are, so we associate. The good, by affinity, seek the good; the vile, by affinity, the vile. Thus of their own volition, souls proceed into heaven, into hell.

These facts have always suggested to man the sublime creed, that the world is not the product of manifold power, but of one will, of one mind; and that one mind is everywhere active, in each ray of the star, in each wavelet of the pool; and whatever opposes that will, is everywhere balked and baffled, because things are made so, and not otherwise. Good is positive. Evil is merely privative, not absolute: it is like cold, which is the privation of heat. All evil is so much death or nonentity. Benevolence is absolute and real. So much benevolence as a man hath, so much life hath he. For all things proceed out of this same spirit, which is differently named love, justice, temperance, in its different applications, just as the ocean receives different names on the several shores which it washes. All things proceed out of the same spirit, and all things conspire with it. Whilst a man seeks good ends, he is strong by the whole strength of nature. In so far as he roves from these ends, he bereaves himself of power, of auxiliaries; his being shrinks out of all remote channels, he becomes less and less, a mote, a point, until absolute badness is absolute death.

The perception of this law of laws awakens in the mind a sentiment which we call the religious sentiment, and which makes our highest happiness. Wonderful is its power to charm and to command. It is a mountain air. It is the embalmer of the world. It is myrrh and storax, and chlorine and rosemary. It makes the sky and the hills sublime, and the silent song of the stars is it. By it, is the universe made safe and habitable, not by science or power. Thought may work cold and intransitive in things, and find no end or unity; but the dawn of the sentiment of virtue on the heart, gives and is the assurance that Law is sovereign over all natures; and the worlds, time, space, eternity, do seem to break out into joy.

This sentiment is divine and deifying. It is the beatitude of man. It makes him illimitable. Through it, the soul first knows itself. It corrects the capital mistake of the infant man, who seeks to be great by following the great, and hopes to derive advantages *from another*, – by showing the fountain of all good to be in himself, and that he, equally with every man, is an inlet into the deeps of Reason. When he says, "I ought;" when love warms him; when he chooses, warned from on high, the good and great deed; then, deep melodies wander through his soul from Supreme Wisdom. Then he can worship, and be enlarged by his worship; for he can never go behind this sentiment. In the sublimest flights of the soul, rectitude is never surmounted, love is never outgrown.

This sentiment lies at the foundation of society, and successively creates all forms of worship. The principle of veneration never dies out. Man fallen into superstition, into sensuality, is never quite without the visions of the moral sentiment. In like manner, all the expressions of this sentiment are sacred and permanent in proportion to their purity. The expressions of this sentiment affect us more than all other compositions. The sentences of the oldest time, which ejaculate this piety, are still fresh and fragrant. This thought dwelled always deepest in the minds of men in the devout and contemplative East; not alone in Palestine, where it reached its purest expression, but in Egypt, in Persia, in India, in China. Europe has always owed to oriental genius, its divine impulses. What these holy bards said, all sane men found agreeable and true. And the unique impression of Jesus upon mankind, whose name is not so much written as ploughed into the history of this world, is proof of the subtle virtue of this infusion.

Meantime, whilst the doors of the temple stand open, night and day, before every man, and the oracles of this truth cease never, it is guarded by one stern condition; this, namely; it is an intuition. It cannot be received at second hand. Truly speaking, it is not instruction, but provocation, that I can receive from another soul. What he announces, I must find true in me, or wholly reject; and on his word, or as his second, be he who he may, I can accept nothing. On the contrary, the absence of this primary faith is the presence of degradation. As is the flood so is the ebb. Let this faith depart, and the very words it spake, and the things it made, become false and hurtful. Then falls the church, the state, art, letters, life. The doctrine of the divine nature being forgotten, a sickness infects and dwarfs the constitution. Once man was all; now he is an appendage, a nuisance. And because the indwelling Supreme Spirit cannot wholly be got rid of, the doctrine of it suffers this perversion, that the divine nature is attributed to one or two persons, and denied to all the rest, and denied with fury. The doctrine of inspiration is lost; the base doctrine of the majority of voices, usurps the place of the doctrine of the soul. Miracles, prophecy, poetry; the ideal life, the holy life, exist as ancient history merely; they are not in the belief, nor in the aspiration of society; but, when suggested, seem ridiculous. Life is comic or pitiful, as soon as the high ends of being fade out of sight, and man becomes near-sighted, and can only attend to what addresses the senses.

These general views, which, whilst they are general, none will contest, find abundant illustration in the history of religion, and especially in the history of the Christian church. In that, all of us have had our birth and nurture. The truth contained in that, you, my young friends, are now setting forth to teach. As the Cultus, or established worship of the civilized world, it has great historical interest for us. Of its blessed words, which have been the consolation of humanity, you need not that I should speak. I shall endeavor to discharge my duty to you, on this occasion, by pointing out two errors in its administration, which daily appear more gross from the point of view we have just now taken.

Jesus Christ belonged to the true race of prophets. He saw with open eye the mystery of the soul. Drawn by its severe harmony, ravished with its beauty, he lived in it, and had his being there. Alone in all history, he estimated the greatness of man. One man was true to what is in you and me. He saw that God incarnates himself in man, and evermore goes forth anew to take possession of his world. He said, in this jubilee of sublime emotion, `I am divine. Through me, God acts; through me, speaks. Would you see God, see me; or, see thee, when thou also thinkest as I now think.' But what a distortion did his doctrine and memory suffer in the same, in the next, and the following ages! There is no doctrine of the Reason which will bear to be taught by the Understanding. The understanding caught this high chant from the poet's lips, and said, in the next age, `This was Jehovah come down out of heaven. I will kill you, if you say he was a man.' The idioms of his language, and the figures of his rhetoric, have usurped the place of his truth; and churches are not built on his principles, but on his tropes. Christianity became a Mythus, as the poetic teaching of Greece and of Egypt, before. He spoke of miracles; for he felt that man's life was a miracle, and all that man doth, and he knew that this daily miracle shines, as the character ascends. But the word Miracle, as pronounced by Christian churches, gives a false impression; it is Monster. It is not one with the blowing clover and the falling rain.

He felt respect for Moses and the prophets; but no unfit tenderness at postponing their initial revelations, to the hour and the man that now is; to the eternal revelation in the heart. Thus was he a true man. Having seen that the law in us is commanding, he would not suffer it to be commanded. Boldly, with hand, and heart, and life, he declared it was God. Thus is he, as I think, the only soul in history who has appreciated the worth of a man.

1. In this point of view we become very sensible of the first defect of historical Christianity. Historical Christianity has fallen into the error that corrupts all attempts to communicate religion. As it appears to us, and as it has appeared for ages, it is not the doctrine of the soul, but an exaggeration of the personal, the positive, the ritual. It has dwelt, it dwells, with noxious exaggeration about the *person* of Jesus. The soul knows no persons. It invites every man to expand to the full circle of the universe, and will have no preferences but those of spontaneous love. But by this eastern monarchy of a Christianity, which indolence and fear have built, the friend of man is made the injurer of man. The manner in which his name is surrounded with expressions, which were once sallies of admiration and love, but are now petrified into official titles, kills all generous sympathy and liking. All who hear me, feel, that the language that describes Christ to Europe and America, is not the style of friendship and enthusiasm to a good and noble heart, but is appropriated and formal, – paints a demigod, as the Orientals or the Greeks would describe Osiris or Apollo. Ac-

cept the injurious impositions of our early catachetical instruction, and even honesty and self-denial were but splendid sins, if they did not wear the Christian name. One would rather be

`A pagan, suckled in a creed outworn,'

than to be defrauded of his manly right in coming into nature, and finding not names and places, not land and professions, but even virtue and truth foreclosed and monopolized. You shall not be a man even. You shall not own the world; you shall not dare, and live after the infinite Law that is in you, and in company with the infinite Beauty which heaven and earth reflect to you in all lovely forms; but you must subordinate your nature to Christ's nature; you must accept our interpretations; and take his portrait as the vulgar draw it.

That is always best which gives me to myself. The sublime is excited in me by the great stoical doctrine, Obey thyself. That which shows God in me, fortifies me. That which shows God out of me, makes me a wart and a wen. There is no longer a necessary reason for my being. Already the long shadows of untimely oblivion creep over me, and I shall decease forever.

The divine bards are the friends of my virtue, of my intellect of my strength. They admonish me, that the gleams which flash across my mind, are not mine, but God's; that they had the like, and were not disobedient to the heavenly vision. So I love them. Noble provocations go out from them, inviting me to resist evil; to subdue the world; and to Be. And thus by his holy thoughts, Jesus serves us, and thus only. To aim to convert a man by miracles, is a profanation of the soul. A true conversion, a true Christ, is now, as always, to be made, by the reception of beautiful sentiments. It is true that a great and rich soul, like his, falling among the simple, does so preponderate, that, as his did, it names the world. The world seems to them to exist for him, and they have not yet drunk so deeply of his sense, as to see that only by coming again to themselves, or to God in themselves, can they grow forevermore. It is a low benefit to give me something; it is a high benefit to enable me to do somewhat of myself. The time is coming when all men will see, that the gift of God to the soul is not a vaunting, overpowering, excluding sanctity, but a sweet, natural goodness, a goodness like thine and mine, and that so invites thine and mine to be and to grow.

The injustice of the vulgar tone of preaching is not less flagrant to Jesus, than to the souls which it profanes. The preachers do not see that they make his gospel not glad, and shear him of the locks of beauty and the attributes of heaven. When I see a majestic Epaminondas, or Washington; when I see among my contemporaries, a true orator, an upright judge, a dear friend; when I vibrate to the melody and fancy of a poem; I see beauty that is to be desired. And so lovely, and with yet more entire consent of my human being, sounds in my ear the severe music of the bards that have sung of the true God in all ages. Now do not degrade the life and dialogues of Christ out of the circle of this charm, by insulation and peculiarity. Let them lie as they befel, alive and warm, part of human life, and of the landscape, and of the cheerful day.

2. The second defect of the traditionary and limited way of using the mind of Christ is a consequence of the first; this, namely; that the Moral Nature, that Law of laws, whose revelations introduce greatness, – yea, God himself, into the open soul, is not explored as the fountain of the established teaching in society. Men have come to speak of the revelation as somewhat long ago given and done, as if God were dead. The injury to faith throttles

the preacher; and the goodliest of institutions becomes an uncertain and inarticulate voice.

It is very certain that it is the effect of conversation with the beauty of the soul, to beget a desire and need to impart to others the same knowledge and love. If utterance is denied, the thought lies like a burden on the man. Always the seer is a sayer. Somehow his dream is told: somehow he publishes it with solemn joy: sometimes with pencil on canvas; sometimes with chisel on stone; sometimes in towers and aisles of granite, his soul's worship is builded; sometimes in anthems of indefinite music; but clearest and most permanent, in words.

The man enamored of this excellency, becomes its priest or poet. The office is coeval with the world. But observe the condition, the spiritual limitation of the office. The spirit only can teach. Not any profane man, not any sensual, not any liar, not any slave can teach, but only he can give, who has; he only can create, who is. The man on whom the soul descends, through whom the soul speaks, alone can teach. Courage, piety, love, wisdom, can teach; and every man can open his door to these angels, and they shall bring him the gift of tongues. But the man who aims to speak as books enable, as synods use, as the fashion guides, and as interest commands, babbles. Let him hush.

To this holy office, you propose to devote yourselves. I wish you may feel your call in throbs of desire and hope. The office is the first in the world. It is of that reality, that it cannot suffer the deduction of any falsehood. And it is my duty to say to you, that the need was never greater of new revelation than now. From the views I have already expressed, you will infer the sad conviction, which I share, I believe, with numbers, of the universal decay and now almost death of faith in society. The soul is not preached. The Church seems to totter to its fall, almost all life extinct. On this occasion, any complaisance would be criminal, which told you, whose hope and commission it is to preach the faith of Christ, that the faith of Christ is preached.

It is time that this ill-suppressed murmur of all thoughtful men against the famine of our churches; this moaning of the heart because it is bereaved of the consolation, the hope, the grandeur, that come alone out of the culture of the moral nature; should be heard through the sleep of indolence, and over the din of routine. This great and perpetual office of the preacher is not discharged. Preaching is the expression of the moral sentiment in application to the duties of life. In how many churches, by how many prophets, tell me, is man made sensible that he is an infinite Soul; that the earth and heavens are passing into his mind; that he is drinking forever the soul of God? Where now sounds the persuasion, that by its very melody imparadises my heart, and so affirms its own origin in heaven? Where shall I hear words such as in elder ages drew men to leave all and follow, — father and mother, house and land, wife and child? Where shall I hear these august laws of moral being so pronounced, as to fill my ear, and I feel ennobled by the offer of my uttermost action and passion? The test of the true faith, certainly, should be its power to charm and command the soul, as the laws of nature control the activity of the hands, — so commanding that we find pleasure and honor in obeying. The faith should blend with the light of rising and of setting suns, with the flying cloud, the singing bird, and the breath of flowers. But now the priest's Sabbath has lost the splendor of nature; it is unlovely; we are glad when it is done; we can make, we do make, even sitting in our pews, a far better, holier, sweeter, for ourselves.

Whenever the pulpit is usurped by a formalist, then is the worshipper defrauded and disconsolate. We shrink as soon as the prayers begin, which do not uplift, but smite and offend us. We are fain to wrap our cloaks about us, and secure, as best we can, a solitude that hears not. I once heard a preacher who sorely tempted me to say, I would go to church no more. Men go, thought I, where they are wont to go, else had no soul entered the temple in the afternoon. A snow storm was falling around us. The snow storm was real; the preacher merely spectral; and the eye felt the sad contrast in looking at him, and then out of the window behind him, into the beautiful meteor of the snow. He had lived in vain. He had no one word intimating that he had laughed or wept, was married or in love, had been commended, or cheated, or chagrined. If he had ever lived and acted, we were none the wiser for it. The capital secret of his profession, namely, to convert life into truth, he had not learned. Not one fact in all his experience, had he yet imported into his doctrine. This man had ploughed, and planted, and talked, and bought, and sold; he had read books; he had eaten and drunken; his head aches; his heart throbs; he smiles and suffers; yet was there not a surmise, a hint, in all the discourse, that he had ever lived at all. Not a line did he draw out of real history. The true preacher can be known by this, that he deals out to the people his life, – life passed through the fire of thought. But of the bad preacher, it could not be told from his sermon, what age of the world he fell in; whether he had a father or a child; whether he was a freeholder or a pauper; whether he was a citizen or a countryman; or any other fact of his biography. It seemed strange that the people should come to church. It seemed as if their houses were very unentertaining, that they should prefer this thoughtless clamor. It shows that there is a commanding attraction in the moral sentiment, that can lend a faint tint of light to dulness and ignorance, coming in its name and place. The good hearer is sure he has been touched sometimes; is sure there is somewhat to be reached, and some word that can reach it. When he listens to these vain words, he comforts himself by their relation to his remembrance of better hours, and so they clatter and echo unchallenged.

I am not ignorant that when we preach unworthily, it is not always quite in vain. There is a good ear, in some men, that draws supplies to virtue out of very indifferent nutriment. There is poetic truth concealed in all the common-places of prayer and of sermons, and though foolishly spoken, they may be wisely heard; for, each is some select expression that broke out in a moment of piety from some stricken or jubilant soul, and its excellency made it remembered. The prayers and even the dogmas of our church, are like the zodiac of Denderah, and the astronomical monuments of the Hindoos, wholly insulated from anything now extant in the life and business of the people. They mark the height to which the waters once rose. But this docility is a check upon the mischief from the good and devout. In a large portion of the community, the religious service gives rise to quite other thoughts and emotions. We need not chide the negligent servant. We are struck with pity, rather, at the swift retribution of his sloth. Alas for the unhappy man that is called to stand in the pulpit, and *not* give bread of life. Everything that befalls, accuses him. Would he ask contributions for the missions, foreign or domestic? Instantly his face is suffused with shame, to propose to his parish, that they should send money a hundred or a thousand miles, to furnish such poor fare as they have at home, and would do well to go the hundred or the thousand miles to escape. Would he urge people to a godly way of living; – and can he ask a fellow-creature to come to Sabbath meetings, when he and they all know what is the poor uttermost they can hope for therein? Will he invite them privately to the Lord's Supper? He dares not. If no heart warm this rite, the hollow, dry, creaking formality is too plain, than that he can face a man of wit and energy, and put the invitation without terror. In the street, what has he to say to the bold village blasphemer? The village blasphemer sees fear in the face, form, and gait of the minister.

Let me not taint the sincerity of this plea by any oversight of the claims of good men. I know and honor the purity and strict conscience of numbers of the clergy. What life the public worship retains, it owes to the scattered company of pious men, who minister here and there in the churches, and who, sometimes accepting with too great tenderness the tenet of the elders, have not accepted from others, but from their own heart, the genuine impulses of virtue, and so still command our love and awe, to the sanctity of character. Moreover, the exceptions are not so much to be found in a few eminent preachers, as in the better hours, the truer inspirations of all, – nay, in the sincere moments of every man. But with whatever exception, it is still true, that tradition characterizes the preaching of this country; that it comes out of the memory, and not out of the soul; that it aims at what is usual, and not at what is necessary and eternal; that thus, historical Christianity destroys the power of preaching, by withdrawing it from the exploration of the moral nature of man, where the sublime is, where are the resources of astonishment and power. What a cruel injustice it is to that Law, the joy of the whole earth, which alone can make thought dear and rich; that Law whose fatal sureness the astronomical orbits poorly emulate, that it is travestied and depreciated, that it is behooted and behowled, and not a trait, not a word of it articulated. The pulpit in losing sight of this Law, loses its reason, and gropes after it knows not what. And for want of this culture, the soul of the community is sick and faithless. It wants nothing so much as a stern, high, stoical, Christian discipline, to make it know itself and the divinity that speaks through it. Now man is ashamed of himself; he skulks and sneaks through the world, to be tolerated, to be pitied, and scarcely in a thousand years does any man dare to be wise and good, and so draw after him the tears and blessings of his kind.

Certainly there have been periods when, from the inactivity of the intellect on certain truths, a greater faith was possible in names and persons. The Puritans in England and America, found in the Christ of the Catholic Church, and in the dogmas inherited from Rome, scope for their austere piety, and their longings for civil freedom. But their creed is passing away, and none arises in its room. I think no man can go with his thoughts about him, into one of our churches, without feeling, that what hold the public worship had on men is gone, or going. It has lost its grasp on the affection of the good, and the fear of the bad. In the country, neighborhoods, half parishes are *signing off*, – to use the local term. It is already beginning to indicate character and religion to withdraw from the religious meetings. I have heard a devout person, who prized the Sabbath, say in bitterness of heart, "On Sundays, it seems wicked to go to church." And the motive, that holds the best there, is now only a hope and a waiting. What was once a mere circumstance, that the best and the worst men in the parish, the poor and the rich, the learned and the ignorant, young and old, should meet one day as fellows in one house, in sign of an equal right in the soul, – has come to be a paramount motive for going thither.

My friends, in these two errors, I think, I find the causes of a decaying church and a wasting unbelief. And what greater calamity can fall upon a nation, than the loss of worship? Then all things go to decay. Genius leaves the temple, to haunt the senate, or the market. Literature becomes frivolous. Science is cold. The eye of youth is not lighted by the hope of other worlds, and age is without honor. Society lives to trifles, and when men die, we do not mention them.

And now, my brothers, you will ask, What in these desponding days can be done by us? The remedy is already declared in the ground of our complaint of the Church. We have contrasted the Church with the Soul. In the soul, then, let the redemption be sought. Wherever a man comes, there comes revolution. The old is for slaves. When a man comes, all books are legible, all things transparent, all religions are forms. He is religious. Man is the wonderworker. He is seen amid miracles. All men bless and curse. He saith yea and nay, only. The stationariness of religion; the assumption that the age of inspiration is past, that the Bible is closed; the fear of degrading the character of Jesus by representing him as a man; indicate with sufficient clearness the falsehood of our theology. It is the office of a true teacher to show us that God is, not was; that He speaketh, not spake. The true Christianity, – a faith like Christ's in the infinitude of man, – is lost. None believeth in the soul of man, but only in some man or person old and departed. Ah me! no man goeth alone. All men go in flocks to this saint or that poet, avoiding the God who seeth in secret. They cannot see in secret; they love to be blind in public. They think society wiser than their soul, and know not that one soul, and their soul, is wiser than the whole world. See how nations and races flit by on the sea of time, and leave no ripple to tell where they floated or sunk, and one good soul shall make the name of Moses, or of Zeno, or of Zoroaster, reverend forever. None assayeth the stern ambition to be the Self of the nation, and of nature, but each would be an easy secondary to some Christian scheme, or sectarian connection, or some eminent man. Once leave your own knowledge of God, your own sentiment, and take secondary knowledge, as St. Paul's, or George Fox's, or Swedenborg's, and you get wide from God with every year this secondary form lasts, and if, as now, for centuries, – the chasm yawns to that breadth, that men can scarcely be convinced there is in them anything divine.

Let me admonish you, first of all, to go alone; to refuse the good models, even those which are sacred in the imagination of men, and dare to love God without mediator or veil. Friends enough you shall find who will hold up to your emulation Wesleys and Oberlins, Saints and Prophets. Thank God for these good men, but say, `I also am a man.' Imitation cannot go above its model. The imitator dooms himself to hopeless mediocrity. The inventor did it, because it was natural to him, and so in him it has a charm. In the imitator, something else is natural, and he bereaves himself of his own beauty, to come short of another man's.

Yourself a newborn bard of the Holy Ghost, – cast behind you all conformity, and acquaint men at first hand with Deity. Look to it first and only, that fashion, custom, authority, pleasure, and money, are nothing to you, – are not bandages over your eyes, that you cannot see, – but live with the privilege of the immeasurable mind. Not too anxious to visit periodically all families and each family in your parish connection, – when you meet one of these men or women, be to them a divine man; be to them thought and virtue; let their timid aspirations find in you a friend; let their trampled instincts be genially tempted out in your atmosphere; let their doubts know that you have doubted, and their wonder feel that you have wondered. By trusting your own heart, you shall gain more confidence in other men. For all our penny-wisdom, for all our soul-destroying slavery to habit, it is not to be doubted, that all men have sublime thoughts; that all men value the few real hours of life; they love to be heard; they love to be caught up into the vision of principles. We mark with light in the memory the few interviews we have had, in the dreary years of routine and of sin, with souls that made our souls wiser; that spoke what we thought; that told us what we knew; that gave us leave to be what we inly were. Discharge to men the priestly office, and, present or absent, you shall be followed with their love as by an angel.

And, to this end, let us not aim at common degrees of merit. Can we not leave, to such as love it, the virtue that glitters for the commendation of society, and ourselves pierce the deep solitudes of absolute ability and worth? We easily come up to the standard of goodness in society. Society's praise can be cheaply secured, and almost all men are content with those easy merits; but the instant effect of conversing with God, will be, to put them away. There are persons who are not actors, not speakers, but influences; persons too great for fame, for display; who disdain eloquence; to whom all we call art and artist, seems too nearly allied to show and by-ends, to the exaggeration of the finite and selfish, and loss of the universal. The orators, the poets, the commanders encroach on us only as fair women do, by our allowance and homage. Slight them by preoccupation of mind, slight them, as you can well afford to do, by high and universal aims, and they instantly feel that you have right, and that it is in lower places that they must shine. They also feel your right; for they with you are open to the influx of the all-knowing Spirit, which annihilates before its broad noon the little shades and gradations of intelligence in the compositions we call wiser and wisest.

In such high communion, let us study the grand strokes of rectitude: a bold benevolence, an independence of friends, so that not the unjust wishes of those who love us, shall impair our freedom, but we shall resist for truth's sake the freest flow of kindness, and appeal to sympathies far in advance; and, – what is the highest form in which we know this beautiful element, – a certain solidity of merit, that has nothing to do with opinion, and which is so essentially and manifestly virtue, that it is taken for granted, that the right, the brave, the generous step will be taken by it, and nobody thinks of commending it. You would compliment a coxcomb doing a good act, but you would not praise an angel. The silence that accepts merit as the most natural thing in the world, is the highest applause. Such souls, when they appear, are the Imperial Guard of Virtue, the perpetual reserve, the dictators of fortune. One needs not praise their courage, – they are the heart and soul of nature. O my friends, there are resources in us on which we have not drawn. There are men who rise refreshed on hearing a threat; men to whom a crisis which intimidates and paralyzes the majority, – demanding not the faculties of prudence and thrift, but comprehension, immovableness, the readiness of sacrifice, – comes graceful and beloved as a bride. Napoleon said of Massena, that he was not himself until the battle began to go against him; then, when the dead began to fall in ranks around him, awoke his powers of combination, and he put on terror and victory as a robe. So it is in rugged crises, in unweariable endurance, and in aims which put sympathy out of question, that the angel is shown. But these are heights that we can scarce remember and look up to, without contrition and shame. Let us thank God that such things exist.

And now let us do what we can to rekindle the smouldering, nigh quenched fire on the altar. The evils of the church that now is are manifest. The question returns, What shall we do? I confess, all attempts to project and establish a Cultus with new rites and forms, seem to me vain. Faith makes us, and not we it, and faith makes its own forms. All attempts to contrive a system are as cold as the new worship introduced by the French to the goddess of Reason, – to-day, pasteboard and fillagree, and ending to-morrow in madness and murder. Rather let the breath of new life be breathed by you through the forms already existing. For, if once you are alive, you shall find they shall become plastic and new. The remedy to their deformity is, first, soul, and second, soul, and evermore, soul. A whole popedom of forms, one pulsation of virtue can uplift and vivify. Two inestimable advantages Christianity has given us; first; the Sabbath, the jubilee of the whole world; whose light dawns welcome alike into the closet of the philosopher, into the garret of toil, and into prison cells, and everywhere suggests, even to the vile, the dignity of spiritual being. Let it stand forevermore, a temple, which new love, new faith, new sight shall restore to more than its first splendor to mankind. And secondly, the institution of preaching, – the speech of man to men, – essentially the most flexible of all organs, of all forms. What hinders that now, everywhere, in pulpits, in lecture-rooms, in houses, in fields, wherever the invitation of men or your own occasions lead you, you speak the very truth, as your life and conscience teach it, and cheer the waiting, fainting hearts of men with new hope and new revelation?

I look for the hour when that supreme Beauty, which ravished the souls of those eastern men, and chiefly of those Hebrews, and through their lips spoke oracles to all time, shall speak in the West also. The Hebrew and Greek Scriptures contain immortal sentences, that have been bread of life to millions. But they have no epical integrity; are fragmentary; are not shown in their order to the intellect. I look for the new Teacher, that shall follow so far those shining laws, that he shall see them come full circle; shall see their rounding complete grace; shall see the world to be the mirror of the soul; shall see the identity of the law of gravitation with purity of heart; and shall show that the Ought, that Duty, is one thing with Science, with Beauty, and with Joy.

CRITICAL EYE

For Discussion

a. Emerson argues that the individual must embrace the power of "intuition" because from that humanity will discover what he calls "the sentiment of virtue." When he discusses the "laws of the soul," what is he talking about? And how do these positions differ from Unitarian beliefs?

b. When he says "The soul knows no person," and that Jesus should not be elevated over others, what is he trying to get the reader to understand? Is this simply blasphemy, or is Emerson trying to get people to be more than they thought they could be?

Re-approaching the Reading

Emerson says that "Man is God" to the degree that he is inwardly virtuous. Is he claiming that "Man" is the World creator? He goes on to claim that human beings must recognize the divine virtue that speaks through each person and that when the human soul is elevated, we can actually decide for ourselves if we will go to heaven or hell. Is this true? Ridiculous? Explain.

Writing Assignment

If there is nothing predetermined about the ultimate fate of the soul–if goodness is real, while evil, the absence of goodness, is not–then where does personal responsibility begin? If Emerson is right, what exactly does God control? And if we agree with Emerson, what does that say about the universal sense of "Faith" that all religions insist upon? Looking at this essay alongside "Self-Reliance" and Paine's "The Age of Reason," discuss what it means to believe in God while questioning religion and religious doctrines.

Fork in the Road

If you don't know where you are going, any road will lead you nowhere.
Henry Kissinger

Life is one big road with lots of signs. So when you are riding through the ruts, don't complicate your mind. Flee from hate, mischief and jealousy. Don't bury your thoughts, put your vision to reality. Wake up and live!
Bob Marley

There are only two mistakes one can make along the road to truth: not going all the way and not starting.
The Buddha

The wonderful thing about life is that it continues to provide us with opportunities to experience something new about ourselves. If we are lucky, these revelations are interesting and help us to transform into new and better versions of ourselves. In the end, fork-in-the-road moments are needed. Without them, we remain stagnant. It is, therefore, important that we stand before the proverbial mirror and ask the age-old question: "Who am I?"

Undeniably, "Who am I?" "What should I do with my life?" and "How did I get to this point?" are the most often asked self-queries that beg to be addressed. And, as we go through life wondering, hoping for more, we find ourselves pondering the prolific utterance that Jack Nicholson's movie made famous, "Is this as good as it gets?"

The average preteen has already discovered that life is tough, and that it, all too frequently, is unfair. If you ask teenagers about love, marriage, or adulthood in general, they will explain to you that one day they plan to get married, get a good job, have children, buy a home, and become productive members of their communities. If you talk with them further, these same young, maturing people will explain how they anticipate being unhappy with their chosen careers, that marriage and children are "hard work," and that some level of misery is to be expected.

Apparently, living our lives is a paved road filled with potholes, sometimes even landmines that appear primed to explode. As a result, we find ourselves going through life desperately trying to figure out how to make sense of our socioeconomic status, our complex home environments, love, death, education, work, and, yes, even where and how to vacation—all the while looking for that path that will shine a light into our shaded eyes. So many of us hope for a better way of being. So many of us want to break a cycle and rise up, evolve, and display that we are better than before—stronger, smarter, capable of leaping where we once stumbled. So many of us look at the way the world divides those who succeed from those who never see "new" or "better" leaving us moored to a fixed post. Summed up, so many of us want things to change. Yet, at some point, many of us trip over the "fork"—the opening pathway that signals that a new day, be it cognizant recognition or physical transformation, is offering a new opportunity; the one that, when recognized, will change everything.

Clearly, one point remains a constant: No matter how you slice it, the proverbial "fork in the road" and the choices one makes upon it end up being character definers. As you read these selected works, you will note the following: Some people do not like what they find out about themselves; others welcome the challenge, and may find that those around them—whom they consider "constant"—fail them at every turn.

SIR ARTHUR CONAN DOYLE

From the Novel

A STUDY IN SCARLET

Chapter I. Mr. Sherlock Holmes.

IN the year 1878 I took my degree of Doctor of Medicine of the University of London, and proceeded to Netley to go through the course prescribed for surgeons in the army. Having completed my studies there, I was duly attached to the Fifth Northumberland Fusiliers as Assistant Surgeon. The regiment was stationed in India at the time, and before I could join it, the second Afghan war had broken out. On landing at Bombay, I learned that my corps had advanced through the passes, and was already deep in the enemy's country. I followed, however, with many other officers who were in the same situation as myself, and succeeded in reaching Candahar in safety, where I found my regiment, and at once entered upon my new duties.

The campaign brought honours and promotion to many, but for me it had nothing but misfortune and disaster. I was removed from my brigade and attached to the Berkshires, with whom I served at the fatal battle of Maiwand. There I was struck on the shoulder by a Jezail bullet, which shattered the bone and grazed the subclavian artery. I should have fallen into the hands of the murderous Ghazis had it not been for the devotion and courage shown by Murray, my orderly, who threw me across a pack-horse, and succeeded in bringing me safely to the British lines.

Worn with pain, and weak from the prolonged hardships which I had undergone, I was removed, with a great train of wounded sufferers, to the base hospital at Peshawar. Here I rallied, and had already improved so far as to be able to walk about the wards, and even to bask a little upon the verandah, when I was struck down by enteric fever, that curse of our Indian possessions. For months my life was despaired of, and when at last I came to myself and became convalescent, I was so weak and emaciated that a medical board determined that not a day should be lost in sending me back to England. I was dispatched, accordingly, in the troopship "Orontes," and landed a month later on Portsmouth jetty, with my health irretrievably ruined, but with permission from a paternal government to spend the next nine months in attempting to improve it.

I had neither kith nor kin in England, and was therefore as free as air–or as free as an income of eleven shillings and sixpence a day will permit a man to be. Under such circumstances, I naturally gravitated to London, that great cesspool into which all the loungers and idlers of the Empire are irresistibly drained. There I stayed for some time at a private hotel in the Strand, leading a comfortless, meaningless existence, and spending such money as I had, considerably more freely than I ought. So alarming did the state of my finances become, that I soon realized that I must either leave the metropolis and rusticate somewhere in the country, or that I must make a complete alteration in my style of living. Choosing the latter alternative, I began by making up my mind to leave the hotel, and to take up my quarters in some less pretentious and less expensive domicile.

On the very day that I had come to this conclusion, I was standing at the Criterion Bar, when some one tapped me on the shoulder, and turning round I recognized young Stamford, who had been a dresser under me at Barts. The sight of a friendly face in the great wilderness of London is a pleasant thing indeed to a lonely man. In old days Stamford had never been a particular crony of mine, but now I hailed him with enthusiasm, and he, in his turn, appeared to be delighted to see me. In the exuberance of my joy, I asked him to lunch with me at the Holborn, and we started off together in a hansom.

"Whatever have you been doing with yourself, Watson?" he asked in undisguised wonder, as we rattled through the crowded London streets. "You are as thin as a lath and as brown as a nut."

I gave him a short sketch of my adventures, and had hardly concluded it by the time that we reached our destination.

"Poor devil!" he said, commiseratingly, after he had listened to my misfortunes. "What are you up to now?"

"Looking for lodgings." I answered. "Trying to solve the problem as to whether it is possible to get comfortable rooms at a reasonable price."

"That's a strange thing," remarked my companion; "you are the second man to-day that has used that expression to me."

"And who was the first?" I asked.

"A fellow who is working at the chemical laboratory up at the hospital. He was bemoaning himself this morning because he could not get someone to go halves with him in some nice rooms which he had found, and which were too much for his purse."

"By Jove!" I cried, "if he really wants someone to share the rooms and the expense, I am the very man for him. I should prefer having a partner to being alone."

Young Stamford looked rather strangely at me over his wine-glass. "You don't know Sherlock Holmes yet," he said; "perhaps you would not care for him as a constant companion."

"Why, what is there against him?"

"Oh, I didn't say there was anything against him. He is a little queer in his ideas–an enthusiast in some branches of science. As far as I know he is a decent fellow enough."

"A medical student, I suppose?" said I.

"No–I have no idea what he intends to go in for. I believe he is well up in anatomy, and he is a first-class chemist; but, as far as I know, he has never taken out any systematic medical classes. His studies are very desultory and eccentric, but he has amassed a lot of out-of-the way knowledge which would astonish his professors."

"Did you never ask him what he was going in for?" I asked.

"No; he is not a man that it is easy to draw out, though he can be communicative enough when the fancy seizes him."

"I should like to meet him," I said. "If I am to lodge with anyone, I should prefer a man of studious and quiet habits. I am not strong enough yet to stand much noise or excitement. I had enough of both in Afghanistan to last me for the remainder of my natural existence. How could I meet this friend of yours?"

"He is sure to be at the laboratory," returned my companion. "He either avoids the place for weeks, or else he works there from morning to night. If you like, we shall drive round together after luncheon."

"Certainly," I answered, and the conversation drifted away into other channels.

As we made our way to the hospital after leaving the Holborn, Stamford gave me a few more particulars about the gentleman whom I proposed to take as a fellow-lodger.

"You mustn't blame me if you don't get on with him," he said; "I know nothing more of him than I have learned from meeting him occasionally in the laboratory. You proposed this arrangement, so you must not hold me responsible."

"If we don't get on it will be easy to part company," I answered. "It seems to me, Stamford," I added, looking hard at my companion, "that you have some reason for washing your hands of the matter. Is this fellow's temper so formidable, or what is it? Don't be mealy-mouthed about it."

"It is not easy to express the inexpressible," he answered with a laugh. "Holmes is a little too scientific for my tastes–it approaches to cold-bloodedness. I could imagine his giving a friend a little pinch of the latest vegetable alkaloid, not out of malevolence, you understand, but simply out of a spirit of inquiry in order to have an accurate idea of the effects. To do him justice, I think that he would take it himself with the same readiness. He appears to have a passion for definite and exact knowledge."

"Very right too."

"Yes, but it may be pushed to excess. When it comes to beating the subjects in the dissecting-rooms with a stick, it is certainly taking rather a bizarre shape."

"Beating the subjects!"

"Yes, to verify how far bruises may be produced after death. I saw him at it with my own eyes."

"And yet you say he is not a medical student?"

"No. Heaven knows what the objects of his studies are. But here we are, and you must form your own impressions about him." As he spoke, we turned down a narrow lane and passed through a small side-door, which opened into a wing of the great hospital. It was familiar ground to me, and I needed no guiding as we ascended the bleak stone staircase and made our way down the long corridor with its vista of whitewashed wall and dun-coloured doors. Near the further end a low arched passage branched away from it and led to the chemical laboratory.

This was a lofty chamber, lined and littered with countless bottles. Broad, low tables were scattered about, which bristled with retorts, test-tubes, and little Bunsen lamps, with their blue flickering flames. There was only one student in the room, who was bending over a distant table absorbed in his work. At the sound of our steps he glanced round and sprang to his feet with a cry of pleasure. "I've found it! I've found it," he shouted to my companion, running towards us with a test-tube in his hand. "I have found a re-agent which is precipitated by hoemoglobin,[4] and by nothing else." Had he discovered a gold mine, greater delight could not have shone upon his features.

"Dr. Watson, Mr. Sherlock Holmes," said Stamford, introducing us.

"How are you?" he said cordially, gripping my hand with a strength for which I should hardly have given him credit. "You have been in Afghanistan, I perceive."

"How on earth did you know that?" I asked in astonishment.

"Never mind," said he, chuckling to himself. "The question now is about hoemoglobin. No doubt you see the significance of this discovery of mine?"

"It is interesting, chemically, no doubt," I answered, "but practically—"

"Why, man, it is the most practical medico-legal discovery for years. Don't you see that it gives us an infallible test for blood stains. Come over here now!" He seized me by the coat-sleeve in his eagerness, and drew me over to the table at which he had been working. "Let us have some fresh blood," he said, digging a long bodkin into his finger, and drawing off the resulting drop of blood in a chemical pipette. "Now, I add this small quantity of blood to a litre of water. You perceive that the resulting mixture has the appearance of pure water. The proportion of blood cannot be more than one in a million. I have no doubt, however, that we shall be able to obtain the characteristic reaction." As he spoke, he threw into the vessel a few white crystals, and then added some drops of a transparent fluid. In an instant the contents assumed a dull mahogany colour, and a brownish dust was precipitated to the bottom of the glass jar.

"Ha! ha!" he cried, clapping his hands, and looking as delighted as a child with a new toy. "What do you think of that?"

"It seems to be a very delicate test," I remarked.

"Beautiful! beautiful! The old Guiacum test was very clumsy and uncertain. So is the microscopic examination for blood corpuscles. The latter is valueless if the stains are a few hours old. Now, this appears to act as well whether the blood is old or new. Had this test been invented, there are hundreds of men now walking the earth who would long ago have paid the penalty of their crimes."

"Indeed!" I murmured.

"Criminal cases are continually hinging upon that one point. A man is suspected of a crime months perhaps after it has been committed. His linen or clothes are examined, and brownish stains discovered upon them. Are they blood stains, or mud stains, or rust stains, or fruit stains, or what are they? That is a question which has puzzled many an expert, and why? Because there was no reliable test. Now we have the Sherlock Holmes' test, and there will no longer be any difficulty."

His eyes fairly glittered as he spoke, and he put his hand over his heart and bowed as if to some applauding crowd conjured up by his imagination.

"You are to be congratulated," I remarked, considerably surprised at his enthusiasm.

"There was the case of Von Bischoff at Frankfort last year. He would certainly have been hung had this test been in existence. Then there was Mason of Bradford, and the notorious Muller, and Lefevre of Montpellier, and Samson of new Orleans. I could name a score of cases in which it would have been decisive."

"You seem to be a walking calendar of crime," said Stamford with a laugh. "You might start a paper on those lines. Call it the 'Police News of the Past.'"

"Very interesting reading it might be made, too," remarked Sherlock Holmes, sticking a small piece of plaster over the prick on his finger. "I have to be careful," he continued, turning to me with a smile, "for I dabble with poisons a good deal." He held out his hand as he spoke, and I noticed that it was all mottled over with similar pieces of plaster, and discoloured with strong acids.

"We came here on business," said Stamford, sitting down on a high three-legged stool, and pushing another one in my direction with his foot. "My friend here wants to take diggings, and as you were complaining that you could get no one to go halves with you, I thought that I had better bring you together."

Sherlock Holmes seemed delighted at the idea of sharing his rooms with me. "I have my eye on a suite in Baker Street," he said, "which would suit us down to the ground. You don't mind the smell of strong tobacco, I hope?"

"I always smoke 'ship's' myself," I answered.

"That's good enough. I generally have chemicals about, and occasionally do experiments. Would that annoy you?"

"By no means."

"Let me see—what are my other shortcomings. I get in the dumps at times, and don't open my mouth for days on end. You must not think I am sulky when I do that. Just let me alone, and I'll soon be right. What have you to confess now? It's just as well for two fellows to know the worst of one another before they begin to live together."

I laughed at this cross-examination. "I keep a bull pup," I said, "and I object to rows because my nerves are shaken, and I get up at all sorts of ungodly hours, and I am extremely lazy. I have another set of vices when I'm well, but those are the principal ones at present."

"Do you include violin-playing in your category of rows?" he asked, anxiously.

"It depends on the player," I answered. "A well-played violin is a treat for the gods—a badly-played one—"

"Oh, that's all right," he cried, with a merry laugh. "I think we may consider the thing as settled—that is, if the rooms are agreeable to you."

"When shall we see them?"

"Call for me here at noon to-morrow, and we'll go together and settle everything," he answered.

"All right—noon exactly," said I, shaking his hand.

We left him working among his chemicals, and we walked together towards my hotel.

"By the way," I asked suddenly, stopping and turning upon Stamford, "how the deuce did he know that I had come from Afghanistan?"

My companion smiled an enigmatical smile. "That's just his little peculiarity," he said. "A good many people have wanted to know how he finds things out."

"Oh! a mystery is it?" I cried, rubbing my hands. "This is very piquant. I am much obliged to you for bringing us together. 'The proper study of mankind is man,' you know."

"You must study him, then," Stamford said, as he bade me good-bye. "You'll find him a knotty problem, though. I'll wager he learns more about you than you about him. Good-bye."

"Good-bye," I answered, and strolled on to my hotel, considerably interested in my new acquaintance.

Chapter II. The Science of Deduction.

WE met next day as he had arranged, and inspected the rooms at No. 221B, Baker Street, of which he had spoken at our meeting. They consisted of a couple of comfortable bed-rooms and a single large airy sitting-room, cheerfully furnished, and illuminated by two broad windows. So desirable in every way were the apartments, and so moderate did the terms seem when divided between us, that the bargain was concluded upon the spot, and we at once entered into possession. That very evening I moved my things round from the hotel, and on the following morning Sherlock Holmes followed me with several boxes and portmanteaus. For a day or two we were busily employed in unpacking and laying out our property to the best advantage. That done, we gradually began to settle down and to accommodate ourselves to our new surroundings.

Holmes was certainly not a difficult man to live with. He was quiet in his ways, and his habits were regular. It was rare for him to be up after ten at night, and he had invariably breakfasted and gone out before I rose in the morning. Sometimes he spent his day at the chemical laboratory, sometimes in the dissecting-rooms, and occasionally in long walks, which appeared to take him into the lowest portions of the City. Nothing could exceed his energy when the working fit was upon him; but now and again a reaction would seize him, and for days on end he would lie upon the sofa in the sitting-room, hardly uttering a word or moving a muscle from morning to night. On these occasions I have noticed such a dreamy, vacant expression in his eyes, that I might have suspected him of being addicted to the use of some narcotic, had not the temperance and cleanliness of his whole life forbidden such a notion.

As the weeks went by, my interest in him and my curiosity as to his aims in life, gradually deepened and increased. His very person and appearance were such as to strike the attention of the most casual observer. In height he was rather over six feet, and so excessively lean that he seemed to be considerably taller. His eyes were sharp and piercing, save during those intervals of torpor to which I have alluded; and his thin, hawk-like nose gave his whole expression an air of alertness and decision. His chin, too, had the prominence and squareness which mark the man of determination. His hands were invariably blotted with ink and stained with chemicals, yet he was possessed of extraordinary delicacy of touch, as I frequently had occasion to observe when I watched him manipulating his fragile philosophical instruments.

The reader may set me down as a hopeless busybody, when I confess how much this man stimulated my curiosity, and how often I endeavoured to break through the reticence which he showed on all that concerned himself. Before pronouncing judgment, however, be it remembered, how objectless was my life, and how little there was to engage my attention. My health forbade me from venturing out unless the weather was exceptionally genial, and I had no friends who would call upon me and break the monotony of my daily existence. Under these circumstances, I eagerly hailed the little mystery which hung around my companion, and spent much of my time in endeavouring to unravel it.

He was not studying medicine. He had himself, in reply to a question, confirmed Stamford's opinion upon that point. Neither did he appear to have pursued any course of reading which might fit him for a degree in science or any other recognized portal which would give him an entrance into the learned world. Yet his zeal for certain studies was remarkable, and within eccentric limits his knowledge was so extraordinarily ample and minute that his observations have fairly astounded me. Surely no man would work so hard or attain such precise information unless he had some definite end in view. Desultory readers are seldom remarkable for the exactness of their learning. No man burdens his mind with small matters unless he has some very good reason for doing so.

His ignorance was as remarkable as his knowledge. Of contemporary literature, philosophy and politics he appeared to know next to nothing. Upon my quoting Thomas Carlyle, he inquired in the naivest way who he might be and what he had done. My surprise reached a climax, however, when I found incidentally that he was ignorant of the Copernican Theory and of the composition of the Solar System. That any civilized human being in this nineteenth century should not be aware that the earth travelled round the sun appeared to be to me such an extraordinary fact that I could hardly realize it.

"You appear to be astonished," he said, smiling at my expression of surprise. "Now that I do know it I shall do my best to forget it."

"To forget it!"

"You see," he explained, "I consider that a man's brain originally is like a little empty attic, and you have to stock it with such furniture as you choose. A fool takes in all the lumber of every sort that he comes across, so that the knowledge which might be useful to him gets crowded out, or at best is jumbled up with a lot of other things so that he has a difficulty in laying his hands upon it. Now the skilful workman is very careful indeed as to what he takes into his brain-attic. He will have nothing but the tools which may help him in doing his work, but of these he has a large assortment, and all in the most perfect order. It is a mistake to think that that little room has elastic walls and can distend to any extent. Depend upon it there comes a time when for every addition of knowledge you forget something that you knew before. It is of the highest importance, therefore, not to have useless facts elbowing out the useful ones."

"But the Solar System!" I protested.

"What the deuce is it to me?" he interrupted impatiently; "you say that we go round the sun. If we went round the moon it would not make a pennyworth of difference to me or to my work."

I was on the point of asking him what that work might be, but something in his manner showed me that the question would be an unwelcome one. I pondered over our short conversation, however, and endeavoured to draw my deductions from it. He said that he would acquire no knowledge which did not bear upon his object. Therefore all the knowledge which he possessed was such as would be useful to him. I enumerated in my own mind all the various points upon which he had shown me that he was exceptionally well-informed. I even took a pencil and jotted them down. I could not help smiling at the document when I had completed it. It ran in this way–

SHERLOCK HOLMES–his limits.

1. Knowledge of Literature.–Nil.
2. Philosophy.–Nil.
3. Astronomy.–Nil.
4. Politics.–Feeble.
5. Botany.–Variable. Well up in belladonna, opium, and poisons generally. Knows nothing of practical gardening.
6. Geology.–Practical, but limited. Tells at a glance different soils from each other. After walks has shown me splashes upon his trousers, and told me by their colour and consistence in what part of London he had received them.
7. Chemistry.–Profound.
8. Anatomy.–Accurate, but unsystematic.
9. Sensational Literature.–Immense. He appears to know every detail of every horror perpetrated in the century.
10. Plays the violin well.
11. Is an expert singlestick player, boxer, and swordsman.
12. Has a good practical knowledge of British law.

When I had got so far in my list I threw it into the fire in despair. "If I can only find what the fellow is driving at by reconciling all these accomplishments, and discovering a calling which needs them all," I said to myself, "I may as well give up the attempt at once."

I see that I have alluded above to his powers upon the violin. These were very remarkable, but as eccentric as all his other accomplishments. That he could play pieces, and difficult pieces, I knew well, because at my request he has played me some of Mendelssohn's Lieder, and other favourites. When left to himself, however, he would seldom produce any music or attempt any recognized air. Leaning back in his arm-chair of an evening, he would close his eyes and scrape carelessly at the fiddle which was thrown across his knee. Sometimes the chords were sonorous and melancholy. Occasionally they were fantastic and cheerful. Clearly they reflected the thoughts which possessed him, but whether the music aided those thoughts, or whether the playing was simply the result of a whim or fancy was more than I could determine. I might have rebelled against these exasperating solos had it not been that he usually terminated them by playing in quick succession a whole series of my favourite airs as a slight compensation for the trial upon my patience.

During the first week or so we had no callers, and I had begun to think that my companion was as friendless a man as I was myself. Presently, however, I found that he had many acquaintances, and those in the most different classes of society. There was one little sallow rat-faced, dark-eyed fellow who was introduced to me as Mr. Lestrade, and who came three or four times in a single week. One morning a young girl called, fashionably dressed, and stayed for half an hour or more. The same afternoon brought a grey-headed, seedy visitor, looking like a Jew pedlar, who appeared to me to be much excited, and who was closely followed by a slip-shod elderly woman. On another occasion an old white-haired gentleman had an interview with my companion; and on another a railway porter in his velveteen uniform. When any of these nondescript individuals put in an appearance, Sherlock Holmes used to beg for the use of the sitting-room, and I would retire to my bed-room. He always apologized to me for putting me to this inconvenience. "I have to use this room as a place of business," he said, "and these people are my clients." Again I had an opportunity of asking him a point blank question, and again my delicacy prevented me from forcing another man to confide in me. I imagined at the time that he had some strong reason for not alluding to it, but he soon dispelled the idea by coming round to the subject of his own accord.

It was upon the 4th of March, as I have good reason to remember, that I rose somewhat earlier than usual, and found that Sherlock Holmes had not yet finished his breakfast. The landlady had become so accustomed to my late habits that my place had not been laid nor my coffee prepared. With the unreasonable petulance of mankind I rang the bell and gave a curt intimation that I was ready. Then I picked up a magazine from the table and attempted to while away the time with it, while my companion munched silently at his toast. One of the articles had a pencil mark at the heading, and I naturally began to run my eye through it.

Its somewhat ambitious title was "The Book of Life," and it attempted to show how much an observant man might learn by an accurate and systematic examination of all that came in his way. It struck me as being a remarkable mixture of shrewdness and of absurdity. The reasoning was close and intense, but the deductions appeared to me to be far-fetched and exaggerated. The writer claimed by a momentary expression, a twitch of a muscle or a glance of an eye, to fathom a man's inmost thoughts. Deceit, according to him, was an impossibility in the case of one trained to observation and analysis. His conclusions were as infallible as so many propositions of

Euclid. So startling would his results appear to the uninitiated that until they learned the processes by which he had arrived at them they might well consider him as a necromancer.

"From a drop of water," said the writer, "a logician could infer the possibility of an Atlantic or a Niagara without having seen or heard of one or the other. So all life is a great chain, the nature of which is known whenever we are shown a single link of it. Like all other arts, the Science of Deduction and Analysis is one which can only be acquired by long and patient study nor is life long enough to allow any mortal to attain the highest possible perfection in it. Before turning to those moral and mental aspects of the matter which present the greatest difficulties, let the enquirer begin by mastering more elementary problems. Let him, on meeting a fellow-mortal, learn at a glance to distinguish the history of the man, and the trade or profession to which he belongs. Puerile as such an exercise may seem, it sharpens the faculties of observation, and teaches one where to look and what to look for. By a man's finger nails, by his coat-sleeve, by his boot, by his trouser knees, by the callosities of his forefinger and thumb, by his expression, by his shirt cuffs—by each of these things a man's calling is plainly revealed. That all united should fail to enlighten the competent enquirer in any case is almost inconceivable."

"What ineffable twaddle!" I cried, slapping the magazine down on the table, "I never read such rubbish in my life."

"What is it?" asked Sherlock Holmes.

"Why, this article," I said, pointing at it with my egg spoon as I sat down to my breakfast. "I see that you have read it since you have marked it. I don't deny that it is smartly written. It irritates me though. It is evidently the theory of some arm-chair lounger who evolves all these neat little paradoxes in the seclusion of his own study. It is not practical. I should like to see him clapped down in a third class carriage on the Underground, and asked to give the trades of all his fellow-travellers. I would lay a thousand to one against him."

"You would lose your money," Sherlock Holmes remarked calmly. "As for the article I wrote it myself."

"You!"

"Yes, I have a turn both for observation and for deduction. The theories which I have expressed there, and which appear to you to be so chimerical are really extremely practical—so practical that I depend upon them for my bread and cheese."

"And how?" I asked involuntarily.

"Well, I have a trade of my own. I suppose I am the only one in the world. I'm a consulting detective, if you can understand what that is. Here in London we have lots of Government detectives and lots of private ones. When these fellows are at fault they come to me, and I manage to put them on the right scent. They lay all the evidence before me, and I am generally able, by the help of my knowledge of the history of crime, to set them straight. There is a strong family resemblance about misdeeds, and if you have all the details of a thousand at your finger ends, it is odd if you can't unravel the thousand and first. Lestrade is a well-known detective. He got himself into a fog recently over a forgery case, and that was what brought him here."

"And these other people?"

"They are mostly sent on by private inquiry agencies. They are all people who are in trouble about something, and want a little enlightening. I listen to their story, they listen to my comments, and then I pocket my fee."

"But do you mean to say," I said, "that without leaving your room you can unravel some knot which other men can make nothing of, although they have seen every detail for themselves?"

"Quite so. I have a kind of intuition that way. Now and again a case turns up which is a little more complex. Then I have to bustle about and see things with my own eyes. You see I have a lot of special knowledge which I apply to the problem, and which facilitates matters wonderfully. Those rules of deduction laid down in that article which aroused your scorn, are invaluable to me in practical work. Observation with me is second nature. You appeared to be surprised when I told you, on our first meeting, that you had come from Afghanistan."

"You were told, no doubt."

"Nothing of the sort. I knew you came from Afghanistan. From long habit the train of thoughts ran so swiftly through my mind, that I arrived at the conclusion without being conscious of intermediate steps. There were such steps, however. The train of reasoning ran, 'Here is a gentleman of a medical type, but with the air of a military man. Clearly an army doctor, then. He has just come from the tropics, for his face is dark, and that is not the natural tint of his skin, for his wrists are fair. He has undergone hardship and sickness, as his haggard face says clearly. His left arm has been injured. He holds it in a stiff and unnatural manner. Where in the tropics could an English army doctor have seen much hardship and got his arm wounded? Clearly in Afghanistan.' The whole train of thought did not occupy a second. I then remarked that you came from Afghanistan, and you were astonished."

"It is simple enough as you explain it," I said, smiling. "You remind me of Edgar Allen Poe's Dupin. I had no idea that such individuals did exist outside of stories."

Sherlock Holmes rose and lit his pipe. "No doubt you think that you are complimenting me in comparing me to Dupin," he observed. "Now, in my opinion, Dupin was a very inferior fellow. That trick of his of breaking in on his friends' thoughts with an apropos remark after a quarter of an hour's silence is really very showy and superficial. He had some analytical genius, no doubt; but he was by no means such a phenomenon as Poe appeared to imagine."

"Have you read Gaboriau's works?" I asked. "Does Lecoq come up to your idea of a detective?"

Sherlock Holmes sniffed sardonically. "Lecoq was a miserable bungler," he said, in an angry voice; "he had only one thing to recommend him, and that was his energy. That book made me positively ill. The question was how to identify an unknown prisoner. I could have done it in twenty-four hours. Lecoq took six months or so. It might be made a text-book for detectives to teach them what to avoid."

I felt rather indignant at having two characters whom I had admired treated in this cavalier style. I walked over to the window, and stood looking out into the busy street. "This fellow may be very clever," I said to myself, "but he is certainly very conceited."

"There are no crimes and no criminals in these days," he said, querulously. "What is the use of having brains in our profession. I know well that I have it in me to make my name famous. No man lives or has ever lived who has brought the same amount of study and of natural talent to the detection of crime which I have done. And what is the result? There is no crime to detect, or, at most, some bungling villany with a motive so transparent that even a Scotland Yard official can see through it."

I was still annoyed at his bumptious style of conversation. I thought it best to change the topic.

"I wonder what that fellow is looking for?" I asked, pointing to a stalwart, plainly-dressed individual who was walking slowly down the other side of the street, looking anxiously at the numbers. He had a large blue envelope in his hand, and was evidently the bearer of a message.

"You mean the retired sergeant of Marines," said Sherlock Holmes.

"Brag and bounce!" thought I to myself. "He knows that I cannot verify his guess."

The thought had hardly passed through my mind when the man whom we were watching caught sight of the number on our door, and ran rapidly across the roadway. We heard a loud knock, a deep voice below, and heavy steps ascending the stair.

"For Mr. Sherlock Holmes," he said, stepping into the room and handing my friend the letter.

Here was an opportunity of taking the conceit out of him. He little thought of this when he made that random shot. "May I ask, my lad," I said, in the blandest voice, "what your trade may be?"

"Commissionaire, sir," he said, gruffly. "Uniform away for repairs."

"And you were?" I asked, with a slightly malicious glance at my companion.

"A sergeant, sir, Royal Marine Light Infantry, sir. No answer? Right, sir."

He clicked his heels together, raised his hand in a salute, and was gone.

Chapter III. The Lauriston Garden Mystery

I CONFESS that I was considerably startled by this fresh proof of the practical nature of my companion's theories. My respect for his powers of analysis increased wondrously. There still remained some lurking suspicion in my mind, however, that the whole thing was a pre-arranged episode, intended to dazzle me, though what earthly object he could have in taking me in was past my comprehension. When I looked at him he had finished reading the note, and his eyes had assumed the vacant, lack-lustre expression which showed mental abstraction.

"How in the world did you deduce that?" I asked.

"Deduce what?" said he, petulantly.

"Why, that he was a retired sergeant of Marines."

"I have no time for trifles," he answered, brusquely; then with a smile, "Excuse my rudeness. You broke the thread of my thoughts; but perhaps it is as well. So you actually were not able to see that that man was a sergeant of Marines?"

"No, indeed."

"It was easier to know it than to explain why I knew it. If you were asked to prove that two and two made four, you might find some difficulty, and yet you are quite sure of the fact. Even across the street I could see a great blue anchor tattooed on the back of the fellow's hand. That smacked of the sea. He had a military carriage, however, and regulation side whiskers. There we have the marine. He was a man with some amount of self-importance and a certain air of command. You must have observed the way in which he held his head and swung his cane. A steady, respectable, middle-aged man, too, on the face of him–all facts which led me to believe that he had been a sergeant."

"Wonderful!" I ejaculated.

"Commonplace," said Holmes, though I thought from his expression that he was pleased at my evident surprise and admiration. "I said just now that there were no criminals. It appears that I am wrong–look at this!" He threw me over the note which the commissionaire had brought.

"Why," I cried, as I cast my eye over it, "this is terrible!"

"It does seem to be a little out of the common," he remarked, calmly. "Would you mind reading it to me aloud?"

This is the letter which I read to him—

"MY DEAR MR. SHERLOCK HOLMES,–

"There has been a bad business during the night at 3, Lauriston Gardens, off the Brixton Road. Our man on the beat saw a light there about two in the morning, and as the house was an empty one, suspected that something was amiss. He found the door open, and in the front room, which is bare of furniture, discovered the body of a gentleman, well dressed, and having cards in his pocket bearing the name of 'Enoch J. Drebber, Cleveland, Ohio, U.S.A.' There had been no robbery, nor is there any evidence as to how the man met his death. There are marks of blood in the room, but there is no wound upon his person. We are at a loss as to how he came into the empty house; indeed, the whole affair is a puzzler. If you can come round to the house any time before twelve, you will find me there. I have left everything in status quo until I hear from you. If you are unable to come I shall give you fuller details, and would esteem it a great kindness if you would favour me with your opinion. Yours faithfully,

"TOBIAS GREGSON."

"Gregson is the smartest of the Scotland Yarders," my friend remarked; "he and Lestrade are the pick of a bad lot. They are both quick and energetic, but conventional–shockingly so. They have their knives into one another, too. They are as jealous as a pair of professional beauties. There will be some fun over this case if they are both put upon the scent."

I was amazed at the calm way in which he rippled on. "Surely there is not a moment to be lost," I cried, "shall I go and order you a cab?"

"I'm not sure about whether I shall go. I am the most incurably lazy devil that ever stood in shoe leather–that is, when the fit is on me, for I can be spry enough at times."

"Why, it is just such a chance as you have been longing for."

"My dear fellow, what does it matter to me. Supposing I unravel the whole matter, you may be sure that Gregson, Lestrade, and Co. will pocket all the credit. That comes of being an unofficial personage."

"But he begs you to help him."

"Yes. He knows that I am his superior, and acknowledges it to me; but he would cut his tongue out before he would own it to any third person. However, we may as well go and have a look. I shall work it out on my own hook. I may have a laugh at them if I have nothing else. Come on!"

He hustled on his overcoat, and bustled about in a way that showed that an energetic fit had superseded the apathetic one.

"Get your hat," he said.

"You wish me to come?"

"Yes, if you have nothing better to do." A minute later we were both in a hansom, driving furiously for the Brixton Road.

It was a foggy, cloudy morning, and a dun-coloured veil hung over the house-tops, looking like the reflection of the mud-coloured streets beneath. My companion was in the best of spirits, and prattled away about Cremona fiddles, and the difference between a Stradivarius and an Amati. As for myself, I was silent, for the dull weather and the melancholy business upon which we were engaged, depressed my spirits.

"You don't seem to give much thought to the matter in hand," I said at last, interrupting Holmes' musical disquisition.

"No data yet," he answered. "It is a capital mistake to theorize before you have all the evidence. It biases the judgment."

"You will have your data soon," I remarked, pointing with my finger; "this is the Brixton Road, and that is the house, if I am not very much mistaken."

"So it is. Stop, driver, stop!" We were still a hundred yards or so from it, but he insisted upon our alighting, and we finished our journey upon foot.

Number 3, Lauriston Gardens wore an ill-omened and minatory look. It was one of four which stood back some little way from the street, two being occupied and two empty. The latter looked out with three tiers of vacant melancholy windows, which were blank and dreary, save that here and there a "To Let" card had developed like a cataract upon the bleared panes. A small garden sprinkled over with a scattered eruption of sickly plants separated each of these houses from the street, and was traversed by a narrow pathway, yellowish in colour, and consisting apparently of a mixture of clay and of gravel. The whole place was very sloppy from the rain which had fallen through the night. The garden was bounded by a three-foot brick wall with a fringe of wood rails upon the top, and against this wall was leaning a stalwart police constable, surrounded by a small knot of loafers, who craned their necks and strained their eyes in the vain hope of catching some glimpse of the proceedings within.

I had imagined that Sherlock Holmes would at once have hurried into the house and plunged into a study of the mystery. Nothing appeared to be further from his intention. With an air of nonchalance which, under the circumstances, seemed to me to border upon affectation, he lounged up and down the pavement, and gazed vacantly at the ground, the sky, the opposite houses and the line of railings. Having finished his scrutiny, he proceeded slowly down the path, or rather down the fringe of grass which flanked the path, keeping his eyes riveted upon the ground. Twice he stopped, and once I saw him smile, and heard him utter an exclamation of satisfaction. There were many marks of footsteps upon the wet clayey soil, but since the police had been coming and going over it, I was unable to see how my companion could hope to learn anything from it. Still I had had such extraordinary evidence of the quickness of his perceptive faculties, that I had no doubt that he could see a great deal which was hidden from me.

At the door of the house we were met by a tall, white-faced, flaxen-haired man, with a notebook in his hand, who rushed forward and wrung my companion's hand with effusion. "It is indeed kind of you to come," he said, "I have had everything left untouched."

"Except that!" my friend answered, pointing at the pathway. "If a herd of buffaloes had passed along there could not be a greater mess. No doubt, however, you had drawn your own conclusions, Gregson, before you permitted this."

"I have had so much to do inside the house," the detective said evasively. "My colleague, Mr. Lestrade, is here. I had relied upon him to look after this."

Holmes glanced at me and raised his eyebrows sardonically. "With two such men as yourself and Lestrade upon the ground, there will not be much for a third party to find out," he said.

Gregson rubbed his hands in a self-satisfied way. "I think we have done all that can be done," he answered; "it's a queer case though, and I knew your taste for such things."

"You did not come here in a cab?" asked Sherlock Holmes.

"No, sir."

"Nor Lestrade?"

"No, sir."

"Then let us go and look at the room." With which inconsequent remark he strode on into the house, followed by Gregson, whose features expressed his astonishment.

A short passage, bare planked and dusty, led to the kitchen and offices. Two doors opened out of it to the left and to the right. One of these had obviously been closed for many weeks. The other belonged to the dining-room, which was the apartment in which the mysterious affair had occurred. Holmes walked in, and I followed him with that subdued feeling at my heart which the presence of death inspires.

It was a large square room, looking all the larger from the absence of all furniture. A vulgar flaring paper adorned the walls, but it was blotched in places with mildew, and here and there great strips had become detached and hung down, exposing the yellow plaster beneath. Opposite the door was a showy fireplace, surmounted by a mantelpiece of imitation white marble. On one corner of this was stuck the stump of a red wax candle. The solitary window was so dirty that the light was hazy and uncertain, giving a dull grey tinge to everything, which was intensified by the thick layer of dust which coated the whole apartment.

All these details I observed afterwards. At present my attention was centred upon the single grim motionless figure which lay stretched upon the boards, with vacant sightless eyes staring up at the discoloured ceiling. It was that of a man about forty-three or forty-four years of age, middle-sized, broad shouldered, with crisp curling black hair, and a short stubbly beard. He was dressed in a heavy broadcloth frock coat and waistcoat, with light-coloured trousers, and immaculate collar and cuffs. A top hat, well brushed and trim, was placed upon the floor beside him. His hands were clenched and his arms thrown abroad, while his lower limbs were interlocked as though his death struggle had been a grievous one. On his rigid face there stood an expression of horror, and as it seemed to me, of hatred, such as I have never seen upon human features. This malignant and terrible contortion, combined with the low forehead, blunt nose, and prognathous jaw gave the dead man a singularly simious and ape-like appearance, which was increased by his writhing, unnatural posture. I have seen death in many forms, but never has it appeared to me in a more fearsome aspect than in that dark grimy apartment, which looked out upon one of the main arteries of suburban London.

Lestrade, lean and ferret-like as ever, was standing by the doorway, and greeted my companion and myself.

"This case will make a stir, sir," he remarked. "It beats anything I have seen, and I am no chicken."

"There is no clue?" said Gregson.

"None at all," chimed in Lestrade.

Sherlock Holmes approached the body, and, kneeling down, examined it intently. "You are sure that there is no wound?" he asked, pointing to numerous gouts and splashes of blood which lay all round.

"Positive!" cried both detectives.

"Then, of course, this blood belongs to a second individual–presumably the murderer, if murder has been committed. It reminds me of the circumstances attendant on the death of Van Jansen, in Utrecht, in the year '34. Do you remember the case, Gregson?"

"No, sir."

"Read it up–you really should. There is nothing new under the sun. It has all been done before."

As he spoke, his nimble fingers were flying here, there, and everywhere, feeling, pressing, unbuttoning, examining, while his eyes wore the same far-away expression which I have already remarked upon. So swiftly was the examination made, that one would hardly have guessed the minuteness with which it was conducted. Finally, he sniffed the dead man's lips, and then glanced at the soles of his patent leather boots.

"He has not been moved at all?" he asked.

"No more than was necessary for the purposes of our examination."

"You can take him to the mortuary now," he said. "There is nothing more to be learned."

Gregson had a stretcher and four men at hand. At his call they entered the room, and the stranger was lifted and carried out. As they raised him, a ring tinkled down and rolled across the floor. Lestrade grabbed it up and stared at it with mystified eyes.

"There's been a woman here," he cried. "It's a woman's wedding-ring."

He held it out, as he spoke, upon the palm of his hand. We all gathered round him and gazed at it. There could be no doubt that that circlet of plain gold had once adorned the finger of a bride.

"This complicates matters," said Gregson. "Heaven knows, they were complicated enough before."

"You're sure it doesn't simplify them?" observed Holmes. "There's nothing to be learned by staring at it. What did you find in his pockets?"

"We have it all here," said Gregson, pointing to a litter of objects upon one of the bottom steps of the stairs. "A gold watch, No. 97163, by Barraud, of London. Gold Albert chain, very heavy and solid. Gold ring, with masonic device. Gold pin—bull-dog's head, with rubies as eyes. Russian leather card-case, with cards of Enoch J. Drebber of Cleveland, corresponding with the E. J. D. upon the linen. No purse, but loose money to the extent of seven pounds thirteen. Pocket edition of Boccaccio's 'Decameron,' with name of Joseph Stangerson upon the fly-leaf. Two letters—one addressed to E. J. Drebber and one to Joseph Stangerson."

"At what address?"

"American Exchange, Strand—to be left till called for. They are both from the Guion Steamship Company, and refer to the sailing of their boats from Liverpool. It is clear that this unfortunate man was about to return to New York."

"Have you made any inquiries as to this man, Stangerson?"

"I did it at once, sir," said Gregson. "I have had advertisements sent to all the newspapers, and one of my men has gone to the American Exchange, but he has not returned yet."

"Have you sent to Cleveland?"

"We telegraphed this morning."

"How did you word your inquiries?"

"We simply detailed the circumstances, and said that we should be glad of any information which could help us."

"You did not ask for particulars on any point which appeared to you to be crucial?"

"I asked about Stangerson."

"Nothing else? Is there no circumstance on which this whole case appears to hinge? Will you not telegraph again?"

"I have said all I have to say," said Gregson, in an offended voice.

Sherlock Holmes chuckled to himself, and appeared to be about to make some remark, when Lestrade, who had been in the front room while we were holding this conversation in the hall, reappeared upon the scene, rubbing his hands in a pompous and self-satisfied manner.

"Mr. Gregson," he said, "I have just made a discovery of the highest importance, and one which would have been overlooked had I not made a careful examination of the walls."

The little man's eyes sparkled as he spoke, and he was evidently in a state of suppressed exultation at having scored a point against his colleague.

"Come here," he said, bustling back into the room, the atmosphere of which felt clearer since the removal of its ghastly inmate. "Now, stand there!"

He struck a match on his boot and held it up against the wall.

"Look at that!" he said, triumphantly.

I have remarked that the paper had fallen away in parts. In this particular corner of the room a large piece had peeled off, leaving a yellow square of coarse plastering. Across this bare space there was scrawled in blood-red letters a single word–

RACHE.

"What do you think of that?" cried the detective, with the air of a showman exhibiting his show. "This was overlooked because it was in the darkest corner of the room, and no one thought of looking there. The murderer has written it with his or her own blood. See this smear where it has trickled down the wall! That disposes of the idea of suicide anyhow. Why was that corner chosen to write it on? I will tell you. See that candle on the mantelpiece. It was lit at the time, and if it was lit this corner would be the brightest instead of the darkest portion of the wall."

"And what does it mean now that you have found it?" asked Gregson in a depreciatory voice.

"Mean? Why, it means that the writer was going to put the female name Rachel, but was disturbed before he or she had time to finish. You mark my words, when this case comes to be cleared up you will find that a woman named Rachel has something to do with it. It's all very well for you to laugh, Mr. Sherlock Holmes. You may be very smart and clever, but the old hound is the best, when all is said and done."

"I really beg your pardon!" said my companion, who had ruffled the little man's temper by bursting into an explosion of laughter. "You certainly have the credit of being the first of us to find this out, and, as you say, it bears every mark of having been written by the other participant in last night's mystery. I have not had time to examine this room yet, but with your permission I shall do so now."

As he spoke, he whipped a tape measure and a large round magnifying glass from his pocket. With these two implements he trotted noiselessly about the room, sometimes stopping, occasionally kneeling, and once lying flat upon his face. So engrossed was he with his occupation that he appeared to have forgotten our presence, for he chattered away to himself under his breath the whole time, keeping up a running fire of exclamations, groans, whistles, and little cries suggestive of encouragement and of hope. As I watched him I was irresistibly reminded of a pure-blooded well-trained foxhound as it dashes backwards and forwards through the covert, whining in its eagerness, until it comes across the lost scent. For twenty minutes or more he continued his researches, measuring with the most exact care the distance between marks which were entirely invisible to me, and occasionally applying his tape to the walls in an equally incomprehensible manner. In one place he gathered up very carefully a little pile of grey dust from the floor, and packed it away in an envelope. Finally, he examined with his glass the word upon the wall, going over every letter of it with the most minute exactness. This done, he appeared to be satisfied, for he replaced his tape and his glass in his pocket.

"They say that genius is an infinite capacity for taking pains," he remarked with a smile. "It's a very bad definition, but it does apply to detective work."

Gregson and Lestrade had watched the manoeuvres of their amateur companion with considerable curiosity and some contempt. They evidently failed to appreciate the fact, which I had begun to realize, that Sherlock Holmes' smallest actions were all directed towards some definite and practical end.

"What do you think of it, sir?" they both asked.

"It would be robbing you of the credit of the case if I was to presume to help you," remarked my friend. "You are doing so well now that it would be a pity for anyone to interfere." There was a world of sarcasm in his voice as he spoke. "If you will let me know how your investigations go," he continued, "I shall be happy to give you any help I can. In the meantime I should like to speak to the constable who found the body. Can you give me his name and address?"

Lestrade glanced at his note-book. "John Rance," he said. "He is off duty now. You will find him at 46, Audley Court, Kennington Park Gate."

Holmes took a note of the address.

"Come along, Doctor," he said; "we shall go and look him up. I'll tell you one thing which may help you in the case," he continued, turning to the two detectives. "There has been murder done, and the murderer was a man. He was more than six feet high, was in the prime of life, had small feet for his height, wore coarse, square-toed boots and smoked a Trichinopoly cigar. He came here with his victim in a four-wheeled cab, which was drawn by a horse with three old shoes and one new one on his off fore leg. In all probability the murderer had a florid face, and the finger-nails of his right hand were remarkably long. These are only a few indications, but they may assist you."

Lestrade and Gregson glanced at each other with an incredulous smile.

"If this man was murdered, how was it done?" asked the former.

"Poison," said Sherlock Holmes curtly, and strode off. "One other thing, Lestrade," he added, turning round at the door: "'Rache,' is the German for 'revenge;' so don't lose your time looking for Miss Rachel."

With which Parthian shot he walked away, leaving the two rivals open-mouthed behind him.

Chapter IV. What John Rance Had To Tell.

IT was one o'clock when we left No. 3, Lauriston Gardens. Sherlock Holmes led me to the nearest telegraph office, whence he dispatched a long telegram. He then hailed a cab, and ordered the driver to take us to the address given us by Lestrade.

"There is nothing like first hand evidence," he remarked; "as a matter of fact, my mind is entirely made up upon the case, but still we may as well learn all that is to be learned."

"You amaze me, Holmes," said I. "Surely you are not as sure as you pretend to be of all those particulars which you gave."

"There's no room for a mistake," he answered. "The very first thing which I observed on arriving there was that a cab had made two ruts with its wheels close to the curb. Now, up to last night, we have had no rain for a week, so that those wheels which left such a deep impression must have been there during the night. There were the marks of the horse's hoofs, too, the outline of one of which was far more clearly cut than that of the other three, showing that that was a new shoe. Since the cab was there after the rain began, and was not there at any time during the morning—I have Gregson's word for that—it follows that it must have been there during the night, and, therefore, that it brought those two individuals to the house."

"That seems simple enough," said I; "but how about the other man's height?"

"Why, the height of a man, in nine cases out of ten, can be told from the length of his stride. It is a simple calculation enough, though there is no use my boring you with figures. I had this fellow's stride both on the clay outside and on the dust within. Then I had a way of checking my calculation. When a man writes on a wall, his instinct leads him to write about the level of his own eyes. Now that writing was just over six feet from the ground. It was child's play."

"And his age?" I asked.

"Well, if a man can stride four and a-half feet without the smallest effort, he can't be quite in the sere and yellow. That was the breadth of a puddle on the garden walk which he had evidently walked across. Patent-leather boots had gone round, and Square-toes had hopped over. There is no mystery about it at all. I am simply applying to ordinary life a few of those precepts of observation and deduction which I advocated in that article. Is there anything else that puzzles you?"

"The finger nails and the Trichinopoly," I suggested.

"The writing on the wall was done with a man's forefinger dipped in blood. My glass allowed me to observe that the plaster was slightly scratched in doing it, which would not have been the case if the man's nail had been trimmed. I gathered up some scattered ash from the floor. It was dark in colour and flakey—such an ash as is only made by a Trichinopoly. I have made a special study of cigar ashes—in fact, I have written a monograph upon the subject. I flatter myself that I can distinguish at a glance the ash of any known brand, either of cigar or of tobacco. It is just in such details that the skilled detective differs from the Gregson and Lestrade type."

"And the florid face?" I asked.

"Ah, that was a more daring shot, though I have no doubt that I was right. You must not ask me that at the present state of the affair."

I passed my hand over my brow. "My head is in a whirl," I remarked; "the more one thinks of it the more mysterious it grows. How came these two men—if there were two men—into an empty house? What has become of the cabman who drove them? How could one man compel another to take poison? Where did the blood come from? What was the object of the murderer, since robbery had no part in it? How came the woman's ring there? Above all, why should the second man write up the German word RACHE before decamping? I confess that I cannot see any possible way of reconciling all these facts."

My companion smiled approvingly.

"You sum up the difficulties of the situation succinctly and well," he said. "There is much that is still obscure, though I have quite made up my mind on the main facts. As to poor Lestrade's discovery it was simply a blind intended to put the police upon a wrong track, by suggesting Socialism and secret societies. It was not done by a German. The A, if you noticed, was printed somewhat after the German fashion. Now, a real German invariably prints in the Latin character, so that we may safely say that this was not written by one, but by a clumsy imitator who overdid his part. It was simply a ruse to divert inquiry into a wrong channel. I'm not going to tell you much more of the case, Doctor. You know a conjuror gets no credit when once he has explained his trick, and if I show you too much of my method of working, you will come to the conclusion that I am a very ordinary individual after all."

"I shall never do that," I answered; "you have brought detection as near an exact science as it ever will be brought in this world."

My companion flushed up with pleasure at my words, and the earnest way in which I uttered them. I had already observed that he was as sensitive to flattery on the score of his art as any girl could be of her beauty.

"I'll tell you one other thing," he said. "Patent leathers and Square-toes came in the same cab, and they walked down the pathway together as friendly as possible–arm-in-arm, in all probability. When they got inside they walked up and down the room–or rather, Patent-leathers stood still while Square-toes walked up and down. I could read all that in the dust; and I could read that as he walked he grew more and more excited. That is shown by the increased length of his strides. He was talking all the while, and working himself up, no doubt, into a fury. Then the tragedy occurred. I've told you all I know myself now, for the rest is mere surmise and conjecture. We have a good working basis, however, on which to start. We must hurry up, for I want to go to Halle's concert to hear Norman Neruda this afternoon."

This conversation had occurred while our cab had been threading its way through a long succession of dingy streets and dreary by-ways. In the dingiest and dreariest of them our driver suddenly came to a stand. "That's Audley Court in there," he said, pointing to a narrow slit in the line of dead-coloured brick. "You'll find me here when you come back."

Audley Court was not an attractive locality. The narrow passage led us into a quadrangle paved with flags and lined by sordid dwellings. We picked our way among groups of dirty children, and through lines of discoloured linen, until we came to Number 46, the door of which was decorated with a small slip of brass on which the name Rance was engraved. On enquiry we found that the constable was in bed, and we were shown into a little front parlour to await his coming.

He appeared presently, looking a little irritable at being disturbed in his slumbers. "I made my report at the office," he said.

Holmes took a half-sovereign from his pocket and played with it pensively. "We thought that we should like to hear it all from your own lips," he said.

"I shall be most happy to tell you anything I can," the constable answered with his eyes upon the little golden disk.

"Just let us hear it all in your own way as it occurred."

Rance sat down on the horsehair sofa, and knitted his brows as though determined not to omit anything in his narrative.

"I'll tell it ye from the beginning," he said. "My time is from ten at night to six in the morning. At eleven there was a fight at the 'White Hart'; but bar that all was quiet enough on the beat. At one o'clock it began to rain, and I met Harry Murcher–him who has the Holland Grove beat–and we stood together at the corner of Henrietta Street a-talkin'. Presently–maybe about two or a little after–I thought I would take a look round and see that all was right down the Brixton Road. It was precious dirty and lonely. Not a soul did I meet all the way down, though a cab or two went past me. I was a strollin' down, thinkin' between ourselves how uncommon handy a four of gin hot would be, when suddenly the glint of a light caught my eye in the window of that same house. Now, I knew that them two houses in Lauriston Gardens was empty on account of him that owns them who won't have the drains seed to, though the very last tenant what lived in one of them died o' typhoid fever. I was knocked all in a heap therefore at seeing a light in the window, and I suspected as something was wrong. When I got to the door—"

"You stopped, and then walked back to the garden gate," my companion interrupted. "What did you do that for?"

Rance gave a violent jump, and stared at Sherlock Holmes with the utmost amazement upon his features.

"Why, that's true, sir," he said; "though how you come to know it, Heaven only knows. Ye see, when I got up to the door it was so still and so lonesome, that I thought I'd be none the worse for some one with me. I ain't afeared of anything on this side o' the grave; but I thought that maybe it was him that died o' the typhoid inspecting the drains what killed him. The thought gave me a kind o' turn, and I walked back to the gate to see if I could see Murcher's lantern, but there wasn't no sign of him nor of anyone else."

"There was no one in the street?"

"Not a livin' soul, sir, nor as much as a dog. Then I pulled myself together and went back and pushed the door open. All was quiet inside, so I went into the room where the light was a-burnin'. There was a candle flickerin' on the mantelpiece–a red wax one–and by its light I saw—"

"Yes, I know all that you saw. You walked round the room several times, and you knelt down by the body, and then you walked through and tried the kitchen door, and then—"

John Rance sprang to his feet with a frightened face and suspicion in his eyes. "Where was you hid to see all that?" he cried. "It seems to me that you knows a deal more than you should."

Holmes laughed and threw his card across the table to the constable. "Don't get arresting me for the murder," he said. "I am one of the hounds and not the wolf; Mr. Gregson or Mr. Lestrade will answer for that. Go on, though. What did you do next?"

Rance resumed his seat, without however losing his mystified expression. "I went back to the gate and sounded my whistle. That brought Murcher and two more to the spot."

"Was the street empty then?"

"Well, it was, as far as anybody that could be of any good goes."

"What do you mean?"

The constable's features broadened into a grin. "I've seen many a drunk chap in my time," he said, "but never anyone so cryin' drunk as that cove. He was at the gate when I came out, a-leanin' up agin the railings, and a-singin' at the pitch o' his lungs about Columbine's New-fangled Banner, or some such stuff. He couldn't stand, far less help."

"What sort of a man was he?" asked Sherlock Holmes.

John Rance appeared to be somewhat irritated at this digression. "He was an uncommon drunk sort o' man," he said. "He'd ha' found hisself in the station if we hadn't been so took up."

"His face–his dress–didn't you notice them?" Holmes broke in impatiently.

"I should think I did notice them, seeing that I had to prop him up–me and Murcher between us. He was a long chap, with a red face, the lower part muffled round—"

"That will do," cried Holmes. "What became of him?"

"We'd enough to do without lookin' after him," the policeman said, in an aggrieved voice. "I'll wager he found his way home all right."

"How was he dressed?"

"A brown overcoat."

"Had he a whip in his hand?"

"A whip—no."

"He must have left it behind," muttered my companion. "You didn't happen to see or hear a cab after that?"

"No."

"There's a half-sovereign for you," my companion said, standing up and taking his hat. "I am afraid, Rance, that you will never rise in the force. That head of yours should be for use as well as ornament. You might have gained your sergeant's stripes last night. The man whom you held in your hands is the man who holds the clue of this mystery, and whom we are seeking. There is no use of arguing about it now; I tell you that it is so. Come along, Doctor."

We started off for the cab together, leaving our informant incredulous, but obviously uncomfortable.

"The blundering fool," Holmes said, bitterly, as we drove back to our lodgings. "Just to think of his having such an incomparable bit of good luck, and not taking advantage of it."

"I am rather in the dark still. It is true that the description of this man tallies with your idea of the second party in this mystery. But why should he come back to the house after leaving it? That is not the way of criminals."

"The ring, man, the ring: that was what he came back for. If we have no other way of catching him, we can always bait our line with the ring. I shall have him, Doctor—I'll lay you two to one that I have him. I must thank you for it all. I might not have gone but for you, and so have missed the finest study I ever came across: a study in scarlet, eh? Why shouldn't we use a little art jargon. There's the scarlet thread of murder running through the colourless skein of life, and our duty is to unravel it, and isolate it, and expose every inch of it. And now for lunch, and then for Norman Neruda. Her attack and her bowing are splendid. What's that little thing of Chopin's she plays so magnificently: Tra-la-la-lira-lira-lay."

Leaning back in the cab, this amateur bloodhound carolled away like a lark while I meditated upon the many-sidedness of the human mind.

Chapter V. Our Advertisement Brings a Visitor.

OUR morning's exertions had been too much for my weak health, and I was tired out in the afternoon. After Holmes' departure for the concert, I lay down upon the sofa and endeavoured to get a couple of hours' sleep. It was a useless attempt. My mind had been too much excited by all that had occurred, and the strangest fancies and surmises crowded into it. Every time that I closed my eyes I saw before me the distorted baboon-like countenance of the murdered man. So sinister was the impression which that face had produced upon me that I found it difficult to feel anything but gratitude for him who had removed its owner from the world. If ever human features bespoke vice of the most malignant type, they were certainly those of Enoch J. Drebber, of Cleveland. Still I recognized that justice must be done, and that the depravity of the victim was no condonment in the eyes of the law.

The more I thought of it the more extraordinary did my companion's hypothesis, that the man had been poisoned, appear. I remembered how he had sniffed his lips, and had no doubt that he had detected something which had given rise to the idea. Then, again, if not poison, what had caused the man's death, since there was neither wound nor marks of strangulation? But, on the other hand, whose blood was that which lay so thickly upon the floor? There were no signs of a struggle, nor had the victim any weapon with which he might have wounded an antagonist. As long as all these questions were unsolved, I felt that sleep would be no easy matter, either for Holmes or myself. His quiet self-confident manner convinced me that he had already formed a theory which explained all the facts, though what it was I could not for an instant conjecture.

He was very late in returning–so late, that I knew that the concert could not have detained him all the time. Dinner was on the table before he appeared.

"It was magnificent," he said, as he took his seat. "Do you remember what Darwin says about music? He claims that the power of producing and appreciating it existed among the human race long before the power of speech was arrived at. Perhaps that is why we are so subtly influenced by it. There are vague memories in our souls of those misty centuries when the world was in its childhood."

"That's rather a broad idea," I remarked.

"One's ideas must be as broad as Nature if they are to interpret Nature," he answered. "What's the matter? You're not looking quite yourself. This Brixton Road affair has upset you."

"To tell the truth, it has," I said. "I ought to be more case-hardened after my Afghan experiences. I saw my own comrades hacked to pieces at Maiwand without losing my nerve."

"I can understand. There is a mystery about this which stimulates the imagination; where there is no imagination there is no horror. Have you seen the evening paper?"

"No."

"It gives a fairly good account of the affair. It does not mention the fact that when the man was raised up, a woman's wedding ring fell upon the floor. It is just as well it does not."

"Why?"

"Look at this advertisement," he answered. "I had one sent to every paper this morning immediately after the affair."

He threw the paper across to me and I glanced at the place indicated. It was the first announcement in the "Found" column. "In Brixton Road, this morning," it ran, "a plain gold wedding ring, found in the roadway between the 'White Hart' Tavern and Holland Grove. Apply Dr. Watson, 221B, Baker Street, between eight and nine this evening."

"Excuse my using your name," he said. "If I used my own some of these dunderheads would recognize it, and want to meddle in the affair."

"That is all right," I answered. "But supposing anyone applies, I have no ring."

"Oh yes, you have," said he, handing me one. "This will do very well. It is almost a facsimile."

"And who do you expect will answer this advertisement."

"Why, the man in the brown coat–our florid friend with the square toes. If he does not come himself he will send an accomplice."

"Would he not consider it as too dangerous?"

"Not at all. If my view of the case is correct, and I have every reason to believe that it is, this man would rather risk anything than lose the ring. According to my notion he dropped it while stooping over Drebber's body, and did not miss it at the time. After leaving the house he discovered his loss and hurried back, but found the police already in possession, owing to his own folly in leaving the candle burning. He had to pretend to be drunk in order to allay the suspicions which might have been aroused by his appearance at the gate. Now put yourself in that man's place. On thinking the matter over, it must have occurred to him that it was possible that he had lost the ring in the road after leaving the house. What would he do, then? He would eagerly look out for the evening papers in the hope of seeing it among the articles found. His eye, of course, would light upon this. He would be overjoyed. Why should he fear a trap? There would be no reason in his eyes why the finding of the ring should be connected with the murder. He would come. He will come. You shall see him within an hour?"

"And then?" I asked.

"Oh, you can leave me to deal with him then. Have you any arms?"

"I have my old service revolver and a few cartridges."

"You had better clean it and load it. He will be a desperate man, and though I shall take him unawares, it is as well to be ready for anything."

I went to my bedroom and followed his advice. When I returned with the pistol the table had been cleared, and Holmes was engaged in his favourite occupation of scraping upon his violin.

"The plot thickens," he said, as I entered; "I have just had an answer to my American telegram. My view of the case is the correct one."

"And that is?" I asked eagerly.

"My fiddle would be the better for new strings," he remarked. "Put your pistol in your pocket. When the fellow comes speak to him in an ordinary way. Leave the rest to me. Don't frighten him by looking at him too hard."

"It is eight o'clock now," I said, glancing at my watch.

"Yes. He will probably be here in a few minutes. Open the door slightly. That will do. Now put the key on the inside. Thank you! This is a queer old book I picked up at a stall yesterday–'De Jure inter Gentes'–published in Latin at Liege in the Lowlands, in 1642. Charles' head was still firm on his shoulders when this little brown-backed volume was struck off."

"Who is the printer?"

"Philippe de Croy, whoever he may have been. On the fly-leaf, in very faded ink, is written 'Ex libris Guliolmi Whyte.' I wonder who William Whyte was. Some pragmatical seventeenth century lawyer, I suppose. His writing has a legal twist about it. Here comes our man, I think."

As he spoke there was a sharp ring at the bell. Sherlock Holmes rose softly and moved his chair in the direction of the door. We heard the servant pass along the hall, and the sharp click of the latch as she opened it.

"Does Dr. Watson live here?" asked a clear but rather harsh voice. We could not hear the servant's reply, but the door closed, and some one began to ascend the stairs. The footfall was an uncertain and shuffling one. A look of surprise passed over the face of my companion as he listened to it. It came slowly along the passage, and there was a feeble tap at the door.

"Come in," I cried.

At my summons, instead of the man of violence whom we expected, a very old and wrinkled woman hobbled into the apartment. She appeared to be dazzled by the sudden blaze of light, and after dropping a curtsey, she stood blinking at us with her bleared eyes and fumbling in her pocket with nervous, shaky fingers. I glanced at my companion, and his face had assumed such a disconsolate expression that it was all I could do to keep my countenance.

The old crone drew out an evening paper, and pointed at our advertisement. "It's this as has brought me, good gentlemen," she said, dropping another curtsey; "a gold wedding ring in the Brixton Road. It belongs to my girl Sally, as was married only this time twelvemonth, which her husband is steward aboard a Union boat, and what he'd say if he come 'ome and found her without her ring is more than I can think, he being short enough at the best o' times, but more especially when he has the drink. If it please you, she went to the circus last night along with—"

"Is that her ring?" I asked.

"The Lord be thanked!" cried the old woman; "Sally will be a glad woman this night. That's the ring."

"And what may your address be?" I inquired, taking up a pencil.

"13, Duncan Street, Houndsditch. A weary way from here."

"The Brixton Road does not lie between any circus and Houndsditch," said Sherlock Holmes sharply.

The old woman faced round and looked keenly at him from her little red-rimmed eyes. "The gentleman asked me for my address," she said. "Sally lives in lodgings at 3, Mayfield Place, Peckham."

"And your name is—?"

"My name is Sawyer–her's is Dennis, which Tom Dennis married her–and a smart, clean lad, too, as long as he's at sea, and no steward in the company more thought of; but when on shore, what with the women and what with liquor shops—"

"Here is your ring, Mrs. Sawyer," I interrupted, in obedience to a sign from my companion; "it clearly belongs to your daughter, and I am glad to be able to restore it to the rightful owner."

With many mumbled blessings and protestations of gratitude the old crone packed it away in her pocket, and shuffled off down the stairs. Sherlock Holmes sprang to his feet the moment that she was gone and rushed into his room. He returned in a few seconds enveloped in an ulster and a cravat. "I'll follow her," he said, hurriedly; "she must be an accomplice, and will lead me to him. Wait up for me." The hall door had hardly slammed behind our visitor before Holmes had descended the stair. Looking through the window I could see her walking feebly along the other side, while her pursuer dogged her some little distance behind. "Either his whole theory is incorrect," I thought to myself, "or else he will be led now to the heart of the mystery." There was no need for him to ask me to wait up for him, for I felt that sleep was impossible until I heard the result of his adventure.

It was close upon nine when he set out. I had no idea how long he might be, but I sat stolidly puffing at my pipe and skipping over the pages of Henri Murger's "Vie de Bohème." Ten o'clock passed, and I heard the footsteps of the maid as they pattered off to bed. Eleven, and the more stately tread of the landlady passed my door, bound for the same destination. It was close upon twelve before I heard the sharp sound of his latch-key. The instant he entered I saw by his face that he had not been successful. Amusement and chagrin seemed to be struggling for the mastery, until the former suddenly carried the day, and he burst into a hearty laugh.

"I wouldn't have the Scotland Yarders know it for the world," he cried, dropping into his chair; "I have chaffed them so much that they would never have let me hear the end of it. I can afford to laugh, because I know that I will be even with them in the long run."

"What is it then?" I asked.

"Oh, I don't mind telling a story against myself. That creature had gone a little way when she began to limp and show every sign of being foot-sore. Presently she came to a halt, and hailed a four-wheeler which was passing. I managed to be close to her so as to hear the address, but I need not have been so anxious, for she sang it out loud enough to be heard at the other side of the street, 'Drive to 13, Duncan Street, Houndsditch,' she cried. This begins to look genuine, I thought, and having seen her safely inside, I perched myself behind. That's an art which every detective should be an expert at. Well, away we rattled, and never drew rein until we reached the street in question. I hopped off before we came to the door, and strolled down the street in an easy, lounging way. I saw the cab pull up. The driver jumped down, and I saw him open the door and stand expectantly. Nothing came out though. When I reached him he was groping about frantically in the empty cab, and giving vent to the finest assorted collection of oaths that ever I listened to. There was no sign or trace of his passenger, and I fear it will be some time before he gets his fare. On inquiring at Number 13 we found that the house belonged to a respectable paperhanger, named Keswick, and that no one of the name either of Sawyer or Dennis had ever been heard of there."

"You don't mean to say," I cried, in amazement, "that that tottering, feeble old woman was able to get out of the cab while it was in motion, without either you or the driver seeing her?"

"Old woman be damned!" said Sherlock Holmes, sharply. "We were the old women to be so taken in. It must have been a young man, and an active one, too, besides being an incomparable actor. The get-up was inimitable. He saw that he was followed, no doubt, and used this means of giving me the slip. It shows that the man we are after is not as lonely as I imagined he was, but has friends who are ready to risk something for him. Now, Doctor, you are looking done-up. Take my advice and turn in."

I was certainly feeling very weary, so I obeyed his injunction. I left Holmes seated in front of the smouldering fire, and long into the watches of the night I heard the low, melancholy wailings of his violin, and knew that he was still pondering over the strange problem which he had set himself to unravel.

Chapter VI. Tobias Gregson Shows What He Can Do.

THE papers next day were full of the "Brixton Mystery," as they termed it. Each had a long account of the affair, and some had leaders upon it in addition. There was some information in them which was new to me. I still retain in my scrap-book numerous clippings and extracts bearing upon the case. Here is a condensation of a few of them:—

The *Daily Telegraph* remarked that in the history of crime there had seldom been a tragedy which presented stranger features. The German name of the victim, the absence of all other motive, and the sinister inscription on the wall, all pointed to its perpetration by political refugees and revolutionists. The Socialists had many branches in America, and the deceased had, no doubt, infringed their unwritten laws, and been tracked down by them. After alluding airily to the Vehmgericht, aqua tofana, Carbonari, the Marchioness de Brinvilliers, the Darwinian theory, the principles of Malthus, and the Ratcliff Highway murders, the article concluded by admonishing the Government and advocating a closer watch over foreigners in England.

The *Standard* commented upon the fact that lawless outrages of the sort usually occurred under a Liberal Administration. They arose from the unsettling of the minds of the masses, and the consequent weakening of all authority.

The deceased was an American gentleman who had been residing for some weeks in the Metropolis. He had stayed at the boarding-house of Madame Charpentier, in Torquay Terrace, Camberwell. He was accompanied in his travels by his private secretary, Mr. Joseph Stangerson. The two bade adieu to their landlady upon Tuesday, the 4th inst., and departed to Euston Station with the avowed intention of catching the Liverpool express. They were afterwards seen together upon the platform. Nothing more is known of them until Mr. Drebber's body was, as recorded, discovered in an empty house in the Brixton Road, many miles from Euston. How he came there, or how he met his fate, are questions which are still involved in mystery. Nothing is known of the whereabouts of Stangerson. We are glad to learn that Mr. Lestrade and Mr. Gregson, of Scotland Yard, are both engaged upon the case, and it is confidently anticipated that these well-known officers will speedily throw light upon the matter.

The *Daily News* observed that there was no doubt as to the crime being a political one. The despotism and hatred of Liberalism which animated the Continental Governments had had the effect of driving to our shores a number of men who might have made excellent citizens were they not soured by the recollection of all that they had undergone. Among these men there was a stringent code of honour, any infringement of which was punished by death. Every effort should be made to find the secretary, Stangerson, and to ascertain some particulars of the habits of the deceased. A great step had been gained by the discovery of the address of the house at which he had boarded—a result which was entirely due to the acuteness and energy of Mr. Gregson of Scotland Yard.

Sherlock Holmes and I read these notices over together at breakfast, and they appeared to afford him considerable amusement.

"I told you that, whatever happened, Lestrade and Gregson would be sure to score."

"That depends on how it turns out."

"Oh, bless you, it doesn't matter in the least. If the man is caught, it will be *on account* of their exertions; if he escapes, it will be *in spite* of their exertions. It's heads I win and tails you lose. Whatever they do, they will have followers. 'Un sot trouve toujours un plus sot qui l'admire.'"

"What on earth is this?" I cried, for at this moment there came the pattering of many steps in the hall and on the stairs, accompanied by audible expressions of disgust upon the part of our landlady.

"It's the Baker Street division of the detective police force," said my companion, gravely; and as he spoke there rushed into the room half a dozen of the dirtiest and most ragged street Arabs that ever I clapped eyes on.

"'Tention!" cried Holmes, in a sharp tone, and the six dirty little scoundrels stood in a line like so many disreputable statuettes. "In future you shall send up Wiggins alone to report, and the rest of you must wait in the street. Have you found it, Wiggins?"

"No, sir, we hain't," said one of the youths.

"I hardly expected you would. You must keep on until you do. Here are your wages." He handed each of them a shilling.

"Now, off you go, and come back with a better report next time."

He waved his hand, and they scampered away downstairs like so many rats, and we heard their shrill voices next moment in the street.

"There's more work to be got out of one of those little beggars than out of a dozen of the force," Holmes remarked. "The mere sight of an official-looking person seals men's lips. These youngsters, however, go everywhere and hear everything. They are as sharp as needles, too; all they want is organisation."

"Is it on this Brixton case that you are employing them?" I asked.

"Yes; there is a point which I wish to ascertain. It is merely a matter of time. Hullo! we are going to hear some news now with a vengeance! Here is Gregson coming down the road with beatitude written upon every feature of his face. Bound for us, I know. Yes, he is stopping. There he is!"

There was a violent peal at the bell, and in a few seconds the fair-haired detective came up the stairs, three steps at a time, and burst into our sitting-room.

"My dear fellow," he cried, wringing Holmes' unresponsive hand, "congratulate me! I have made the whole thing as clear as day."

A shade of anxiety seemed to me to cross my companion's expressive face.

"Do you mean that you are on the right track?" he asked.

"The right track! Why, sir, we have the man under lock and key."

"And his name is?"

"Arthur Charpentier, sub-lieutenant in Her Majesty's navy," cried Gregson, pompously, rubbing his fat hands and inflating his chest.

Sherlock Holmes gave a sigh of relief, and relaxed into a smile.

"Take a seat, and try one of these cigars," he said. "We are anxious to know how you managed it. Will you have some whiskey and water?"

"I don't mind if I do," the detective answered. "The tremendous exertions which I have gone through during the last day or two have worn me out. Not so much bodily exertion, you understand, as the strain upon the mind. You will appreciate that, Mr. Sherlock Holmes, for we are both brain-workers."

"You do me too much honour," said Holmes, gravely. "Let us hear how you arrived at this most gratifying result."

The detective seated himself in the arm-chair, and puffed complacently at his cigar. Then suddenly he slapped his thigh in a paroxysm of amusement.

"The fun of it is," he cried, "that that fool Lestrade, who thinks himself so smart, has gone off upon the wrong track altogether. He is after the secretary Stangerson, who had no more to do with the crime than the babe unborn. I have no doubt that he has caught him by this time."

The idea tickled Gregson so much that he laughed until he choked.

"And how did you get your clue?"

"Ah, I'll tell you all about it. Of course, Doctor Watson, this is strictly between ourselves. The first difficulty which we had to contend with was the finding of this American's antecedents. Some people would have waited until their advertisements were answered, or until parties came forward and volunteered information. That is not Tobias Gregson's way of going to work. You remember the hat beside the dead man?"

"Yes," said Holmes; "by John Underwood and Sons, 129, Camberwell Road."

Gregson looked quite crest-fallen.

"I had no idea that you noticed that," he said. "Have you been there?"

"No."

"Ha!" cried Gregson, in a relieved voice; "you should never neglect a chance, however small it may seem."

"To a great mind, nothing is little," remarked Holmes, sententiously.

"Well, I went to Underwood, and asked him if he had sold a hat of that size and description.

He looked over his books, and came on it at once. He had sent the hat to a Mr. Drebber, residing at Charpentier's Boarding Establishment, Torquay Terrace. Thus I got at his address."

"Smart—very smart!" murmured Sherlock Holmes.

"I next called upon Madame Charpentier," continued the detective. "I found her very pale and distressed. Her daughter was in the room, too—an uncommonly fine girl she is, too; she was looking red about the eyes and her lips trembled as I spoke to her. That didn't escape my notice. I began to smell a rat. You know the feeling, Mr. Sherlock Holmes, when you come upon the right scent—a kind of thrill in your nerves. 'Have you heard of the mysterious death of your late boarder Mr. Enoch J. Drebber, of Cleveland?' I asked.

"The mother nodded. She didn't seem able to get out a word. The daughter burst into tears. I felt more than ever that these people knew something of the matter.

"'At what o'clock did Mr. Drebber leave your house for the train?' I asked.

"'At eight o'clock,' she said, gulping in her throat to keep down her agitation. 'His secretary, Mr. Stangerson, said that there were two trains—one at 9.15 and one at 11. He was to catch the first.

"'And was that the last which you saw of him?'

"A terrible change came over the woman's face as I asked the question. Her features turned perfectly livid. It was some seconds before she could get out the single word 'Yes'—and when it did come it was in a husky unnatural tone.

"There was silence for a moment, and then the daughter spoke in a calm clear voice.

"'No good can ever come of falsehood, mother,' she said. 'Let us be frank with this gentleman. We *did* see Mr. Drebber again.'

"'God forgive you!' cried Madame Charpentier, throwing up her hands and sinking back in her chair. 'You have murdered your brother.'

"'Arthur would rather that we spoke the truth,' the girl answered firmly.

"'You had best tell me all about it now,' I said. 'Half-confidences are worse than none. Besides, you do not know how much we know of it.'

"'On your head be it, Alice!' cried her mother; and then, turning to me, 'I will tell you all, sir. Do not imagine that my agitation on behalf of my son arises from any fear lest he should have had a hand in this terrible affair. He is utterly innocent of it. My dread is, however, that in your eyes and in the eyes of others he may appear to be compromised. That however is surely impossible. His high character, his profession, his antecedents would all forbid it.'

"'Your best way is to make a clean breast of the facts,' I answered. 'Depend upon it, if your son is innocent he will be none the worse.'

"'Perhaps, Alice, you had better leave us together,' she said, and her daughter withdrew. 'Now, sir,' she continued, 'I had no intention of telling you all this, but since my poor daughter has disclosed it I have no alternative. Having once decided to speak, I will tell you all without omitting any particular.'

"'It is your wisest course,' said I.

"'Mr. Drebber has been with us nearly three weeks. He and his secretary, Mr. Stangerson, had been travelling on the Continent. I noticed a "Copenhagen" label upon each of their trunks, showing that that had been their last stopping place. Stangerson was a quiet reserved man, but his employer, I am sorry to say, was far otherwise. He was coarse in his habits and brutish in his ways. The very night of his arrival he became very much the worse for drink, and, indeed, after twelve o'clock in the day he could hardly ever be said to be sober. His manners towards the maid-servants were disgustingly free and familiar. Worst of all, he speedily assumed the same attitude towards my daughter, Alice, and spoke to her more than once in a way which, fortunately, she is too innocent to understand. On one occasion he actually seized her in his arms and embraced her–an outrage which caused his own secretary to reproach him for his unmanly conduct.'

"'But why did you stand all this,' I asked. 'I suppose that you can get rid of your boarders when you wish.'

"Mrs. Charpentier blushed at my pertinent question. 'Would to God that I had given him notice on the very day that he came,' she said. 'But it was a sore temptation. They were paying a pound a day each–fourteen pounds a week, and this is the slack season. I am a widow, and my boy in the Navy has cost me much. I grudged to lose the money. I acted for the best. This last was too much, however, and I gave him notice to leave on account of it. That was the reason of his going.'

"'Well?'

"'My heart grew light when I saw him drive away. My son is on leave just now, but I did not tell him anything of all this, for his temper is violent, and he is passionately fond of his sister. When I closed the door behind them a load seemed to be lifted from my mind. Alas, in less than an hour there was a ring at the bell, and I learned that Mr. Drebber had returned. He was much excited, and evidently the worse for drink. He forced his way into the room, where I was sitting with my daughter, and made some incoherent remark about having missed his train. He then turned to Alice, and before my very face, proposed to her that she should fly with him. "You are of age," he said, "and there is no law to stop you. I have money enough and to spare. Never mind the old girl here, but come along with me now straight away. You shall live like a princess." Poor Alice was so frightened that she shrunk away from him, but he caught her by the wrist and endeavoured to draw her towards the door. I screamed, and at that moment my son Arthur came into the room. What happened then I do not know. I heard oaths and the confused sounds of a scuffle. I was too terrified to raise my head. When I did look up I saw Arthur standing in the doorway laughing, with a stick in his hand. "I don't think that fine fellow will trouble us again," he said. "I will just go after him and see what he does with himself." With those words he took his hat and started off down the street. The next morning we heard of Mr. Drebber's mysterious death.'

"This statement came from Mrs. Charpentier's lips with many gasps and pauses. At times she spoke so low that I could hardly catch the words. I made shorthand notes of all that she said, however, so that there should be no possibility of a mistake."

"It's quite exciting," said Sherlock Holmes, with a yawn. "What happened next?"

"When Mrs. Charpentier paused," the detective continued, "I saw that the whole case hung upon one point. Fixing her with my eye in a way which I always found effective with women, I asked her at what hour her son returned.

"'I do not know,' she answered.

"'Not know?'

"'No; he has a latch-key, and he let himself in.'

"'After you went to bed?'

"'Yes.'

"'When did you go to bed?'

"'About eleven.'

"'So your son was gone at least two hours?'

"'Yes.'

"'Possibly four or five?'

"'Yes.'

"'What was he doing during that time?'

"'I do not know,' she answered, turning white to her very lips.

"Of course after that there was nothing more to be done. I found out where Lieutenant Charpentier was, took two officers with me, and arrested him. When I touched him on the shoulder and warned him to come quietly with us, he answered us as bold as brass, 'I suppose you are arresting me for being concerned in the death of that scoundrel Drebber,' he said. We had said nothing to him about it, so that his alluding to it had a most suspicious aspect."

"Very," said Holmes.

"He still carried the heavy stick which the mother described him as having with him when he followed Drebber. It was a stout oak cudgel."

"What is your theory, then?"

"Well, my theory is that he followed Drebber as far as the Brixton Road. When there, a fresh altercation arose between them, in the course of which Drebber received a blow from the stick, in the pit of the stomach, perhaps, which killed him without leaving any mark. The night was so wet that no one was about, so Charpentier dragged the body of his victim into the empty house. As to the candle, and the blood, and the writing on the wall, and the ring, they may all be so many tricks to throw the police on to the wrong scent."

"Well done!" said Holmes in an encouraging voice. "Really, Gregson, you are getting along. We shall make something of you yet."

"I flatter myself that I have managed it rather neatly," the detective answered proudly. "The young man volunteered a statement, in which he said that after following Drebber some time, the latter perceived him, and took a cab in order to get away from him. On his way home he met an old shipmate, and took a long walk with him. On being asked where this old shipmate lived, he was unable to give any satisfactory reply. I think the whole case fits together uncommonly well. What amuses me is to think of Lestrade, who had started off upon the wrong scent. I am afraid he won't make much of. Why, by Jove, here's the very man himself!

It was indeed Lestrade, who had ascended the stairs while we were talking, and who now entered the room. The assurance and jauntiness which generally marked his demeanour and dress were, however, wanting. His face was disturbed and troubled, while his clothes were disarranged and untidy. He had evidently come with the intention of consulting with Sherlock Holmes, for on perceiving his colleague he appeared to be embarrassed and put out. He stood in the centre of the room, fumbling nervously with his hat and uncertain what to do. "This is a most extraordinary case," he said at last—"a most incomprehensible affair."

"Ah, you find it so, Mr. Lestrade!" cried Gregson, triumphantly. "I thought you would come to that conclusion. Have you managed to find the Secretary, Mr. Joseph Stangerson?"

"The Secretary, Mr. Joseph Stangerson," said Lestrade gravely, "was murdered at Halliday's Private Hotel about six o'clock this morning."

Chapter VII. Light In The Darkness.

THE intelligence with which Lestrade greeted us was so momentous and so unexpected, that we were all three fairly dumfoundered. Gregson sprang out of his chair and upset the remainder of his whiskey and water. I stared in silence at Sherlock Holmes, whose lips were compressed and his brows drawn down over his eyes.

"Stangerson too!" he muttered. "The plot thickens."

"It was quite thick enough before," grumbled Lestrade, taking a chair. "I seem to have dropped into a sort of council of war."

"Are you–are you sure of this piece of intelligence?" stammered Gregson.

"I have just come from his room," said Lestrade. "I was the first to discover what had occurred."

"We have been hearing Gregson's view of the matter," Holmes observed. "Would you mind letting us know what you have seen and done?"

"I have no objection," Lestrade answered, seating himself. "I freely confess that I was of the opinion that Stangerson was concerned in the death of Drebber. This fresh development has shown me that I was completely mistaken. Full of the one idea, I set myself to find out what had become of the Secretary. They had been seen together at Euston Station about half-past eight on the evening of the third. At two in the morning Drebber had been found in the Brixton Road. The question which confronted me was to find out how Stangerson had been employed between 8.30 and the time of the crime, and what had become of him afterwards. I telegraphed to Liverpool, giving a description of the man, and warning them to keep a watch upon the American boats. I then set to work calling upon all the hotels and lodging-houses in the vicinity of Euston. You see, I argued that if Drebber and his companion had become separated, the natural course for the latter would be to put up somewhere in the vicinity for the night, and then to hang about the station again next morning."

"They would be likely to agree on some meeting-place beforehand," remarked Holmes.

"So it proved. I spent the whole of yesterday evening in making enquiries entirely without avail. This morning I began very early, and at eight o'clock I reached Halliday's Private Hotel, in Little George Street. On my enquiry as to whether a Mr. Stangerson was living there, they at once answered me in the affirmative.

"'No doubt you are the gentleman whom he was expecting,' they said. 'He has been waiting for a gentleman for two days.'

"'Where is he now?' I asked.

"'He is upstairs in bed. He wished to be called at nine.'

"'I will go up and see him at once,' I said.

"It seemed to me that my sudden appearance might shake his nerves and lead him to say something unguarded. The Boots volunteered to show me the room: it was on the second floor, and there was a small corridor leading up to it. The Boots pointed out the door to me, and was about to go downstairs again when I saw something that made me feel sickish, in spite of my twenty years' experience. From under the door there curled a little red ribbon of blood, which had meandered across the passage and formed a little pool along the skirting at the other side. I gave a cry, which brought the Boots back. He nearly fainted when he saw it. The door was locked on the inside, but we put our shoulders to it, and knocked it in. The window of the room was open, and beside the window, all huddled up, lay the body of a man in his nightdress. He was quite dead, and had been for some time, for his limbs were rigid and cold. When we turned him over, the Boots recognized him at once as being the same gentleman who had engaged the room under the name of Joseph Stangerson. The cause of death was a deep stab in the left side, which must have penetrated the heart. And now comes the strangest part of the affair. What do you suppose was above the murdered man?"

I felt a creeping of the flesh, and a presentiment of coming horror, even before Sherlock Holmes answered.

"The word RACHE, written in letters of blood," he said.

"That was it," said Lestrade, in an awe-struck voice; and we were all silent for a while.

There was something so methodical and so incomprehensible about the deeds of this unknown assassin, that it imparted a fresh ghastliness to his crimes. My nerves, which were steady enough on the field of battle tingled as I thought of it.

"The man was seen," continued Lestrade. "A milk boy, passing on his way to the dairy, happened to walk down the lane which leads from the mews at the back of the hotel. He noticed that a ladder, which usually lay there, was raised against one of the windows of the second floor, which was wide open. After passing, he looked back and saw a man descend the ladder. He came down so quietly and openly that the boy imagined him to be some carpenter or joiner at work in the hotel. He took no particular notice of him, beyond thinking in his own mind that it was early for him to be at work. He has an impression that the man was tall, had a reddish face, and was dressed in a long, brownish coat. He must have stayed in the room some little time after the murder, for we found blood-stained water in the basin, where he had washed his hands, and marks on the sheets where he had deliberately wiped his knife."

I glanced at Holmes on hearing the description of the murderer, which tallied so exactly with his own. There was, however, no trace of exultation or satisfaction upon his face.

"Did you find nothing in the room which could furnish a clue to the murderer?" he asked.

"Nothing. Stangerson had Drebber's purse in his pocket, but it seems that this was usual, as he did all the paying. There was eighty odd pounds in it, but nothing had been taken. Whatever the motives of these extraordinary crimes, robbery is certainly not one of them. There were no papers or memoranda in the murdered man's pocket, except a single telegram, dated from Cleveland about a month ago, and containing the words, 'J. H. is in Europe.' There was no name appended to this message."

"And there was nothing else?" Holmes asked.

"Nothing of any importance. The man's novel, with which he had read himself to sleep was lying upon the bed, and his pipe was on a chair beside him. There was a glass of water on the table, and on the window-sill a small chip ointment box containing a couple of pills."

Sherlock Holmes sprang from his chair with an exclamation of delight.

"The last link," he cried, exultantly. "My case is complete."

The two detectives stared at him in amazement.

"I have now in my hands," my companion said, confidently, "all the threads which have formed such a tangle. There are, of course, details to be filled in, but I am as certain of all the main facts, from the time that Drebber parted from Stangerson at the station, up to the discovery of the body of the latter, as if I had seen them with my own eyes. I will give you a proof of my knowledge. Could you lay your hand upon those pills?"

"I have them," said Lestrade, producing a small white box; "I took them and the purse and the telegram, intending to have them put in a place of safety at the Police Station. It was the merest chance my taking these pills, for I am bound to say that I do not attach any importance to them."

"Give them here," said Holmes. "Now, Doctor," turning to me, "are those ordinary pills?"

They certainly were not. They were of a pearly grey colour, small, round, and almost transparent against the light. "From their lightness and transparency, I should imagine that they are soluble in water," I remarked.

"Precisely so," answered Holmes. "Now would you mind going down and fetching that poor little devil of a terrier which has been bad so long, and which the landlady wanted you to put out of its pain yesterday."

I went downstairs and carried the dog upstair in my arms. It's laboured breathing and glazing eye showed that it was not far from its end. Indeed, its snow-white muzzle proclaimed that it had already exceeded the usual term of canine existence. I placed it upon a cushion on the rug.

"I will now cut one of these pills in two," said Holmes, and drawing his penknife he suited the action to the word. "One half we return into the box for future purposes. The other half I will place in this wine glass, in which is a teaspoonful of water. You perceive that our friend, the Doctor, is right, and that it readily dissolves."

"This may be very interesting," said Lestrade, in the injured tone of one who suspects that he is being laughed at, "I cannot see, however, what it has to do with the death of Mr. Joseph Stangerson."

"Patience, my friend, patience! You will find in time that it has everything to do with it. I shall now add a little milk to make the mixture palatable, and on presenting it to the dog we find that he laps it up readily enough."

As he spoke he turned the contents of the wine glass into a saucer and placed it in front of the terrier, who speedily licked it dry. Sherlock Holmes' earnest demeanour had so far convinced us that we all sat in silence, watching the animal intently, and expecting some startling effect. None such appeared, however. The dog continued to lie stretched upon tho cushion, breathing in a laboured way, but apparently neither the better nor the worse for its draught.

Holmes had taken out his watch, and as minute followed minute without result, an expression of the utmost chagrin and disappointment appeared upon his features. He gnawed his lip, drummed his fingers upon the table, and showed every other symptom of acute impatience. So great was his emotion, that I felt sincerely sorry for him, while the two detectives smiled derisively, by no means displeased at this check which he had met.

"It can't be a coincidence," he cried, at last springing from his chair and pacing wildly up and down the room; "it is impossible that it should be a mere coincidence. The very pills which I suspected in the case of Drebber are actually found after the death of Stangerson. And yet they are inert. What can it mean? Surely my whole chain of reasoning cannot have been false. It is impossible! And yet this wretched dog is none the worse. Ah, I have it! I have it!" With a perfect shriek of delight he rushed to the box, cut the other pill in two, dissolved it, added milk, and presented it to the terrier. The unfortunate creature's tongue seemed hardly to have been moistened in it before it gave a convulsive shiver in every limb, and lay as rigid and lifeless as if it had been struck by lightning.

Sherlock Holmes drew a long breath, and wiped the perspiration from his forehead. "I should have more faith," he said; "I ought to know by this time that when a fact appears to be opposed to a long train of deductions, it invariably proves to be capable of bearing some other interpretation. Of the two pills in that box one was of the most deadly poison, and the other was entirely harmless. I ought to have known that before ever I saw the box at all."

This last statement appeared to me to be so startling, that I could hardly believe that he was in his sober senses. There was the dead dog, however, to prove that his conjecture had been correct. It seemed to me that the mists in my own mind were gradually clearing away, and I began to have a dim, vague perception of the truth.

"All this seems strange to you," continued Holmes, "because you failed at the beginning of the inquiry to grasp the importance of the single real clue which was presented to you. I had the good fortune to seize upon that, and everything which has occurred since then has served to confirm my original supposition, and, indeed, was the logical sequence of it. Hence things which have perplexed you and made the case more obscure, have served to enlighten me and to strengthen my conclusions. It is a mistake to confound strangeness with mystery. The most commonplace crime is often the most mysterious because it presents no new or special features from which deductions may be drawn. This murder would have been infinitely more difficult to unravel had the body of the victim been simply found lying in the roadway without any of those *outré* and sensational accompaniments which have rendered it remarkable. These strange details, far from making the case more difficult, have really had the effect of making it less so.»

Mr. Gregson, who had listened to this address with considerable impatience, could contain himself no longer. "Look here, Mr. Sherlock Holmes," he said, "we are all ready to acknowledge that you are a smart man, and that you have your own methods of working. We want something more than mere theory and preaching now, though. It is a case of taking the man. I have made my case out, and it seems I was wrong. Young Charpentier could not have been engaged in this second affair. Lestrade went after his man, Stangerson, and it appears that he was wrong too. You have thrown out hints here, and hints there, and seem to know more than we do, but the time has come when we feel that we have a right to ask you straight how much you do know of the business. Can you name the man who did it?"

"I cannot help feeling that Gregson is right, sir," remarked Lestrade. "We have both tried, and we have both failed. You have remarked more than once since I have been in the room that you had all the evidence which you require. Surely you will not withhold it any longer."

"Any delay in arresting the assassin," I observed, "might give him time to perpetrate some fresh atrocity."

Thus pressed by us all, Holmes showed signs of irresolution. He continued to walk up and down the room with his head sunk on his chest and his brows drawn down, as was his habit when lost in thought.

"There will be no more murders," he said at last, stopping abruptly and facing us. "You can put that consideration out of the question. You have asked me if I know the name of the assassin. I do. The mere knowing of his name is a small thing, however, compared with the power of laying our hands upon him. This I expect very shortly to do. I have good hopes of managing it through my own arrangements; but it is a thing which needs delicate handling, for we have a shrewd and desperate man to deal with, who is supported, as I have had occasion to prove, by another who is as clever as himself. As long as this man has no idea that anyone can have a clue there is some chance of securing him; but if he had the slightest suspicion, he would change his name, and vanish in an instant among the four million inhabitants of this great city. Without meaning to hurt either of your feelings, I am bound to say that I consider these men to be more than a match for the official force, and that is why I have not asked your assistance. If I fail I shall, of course, incur all the blame due to this omission; but that I am prepared for. At present I am ready to promise that the instant that I can communicate with you without endangering my own combinations, I shall do so."

Gregson and Lestrade seemed to be far from satisfied by this assurance, or by the depreciating allusion to the detective police.

The former had flushed up to the roots of his flaxen hair, while the other's beady eyes glistened with curiosity and resentment. Neither of them had time to speak, however, before there was a tap at the door, and the spokesman of the street Arabs, young Wiggins, introduced his insignificant and unsavoury person.

"Please, sir," he said, touching his forelock, "I have the cab downstairs."

"Good boy," said Holmes, blandly. "Why don't you introduce this pattern at Scotland Yard?" he continued, taking a pair of steel handcuffs from a drawer. "See how beautifully the spring works. They fasten in an instant."

"The old pattern is good enough," remarked Lestrade, "if we can only find the man to put them on."

"Very good, very good," said Holmes, smiling. "The cabman may as well help me with my boxes. Just ask him to step up, Wiggins."

I was surprised to find my companion speaking as though he were about to set out on a journey, since he had not said anything to me about it. There was a small portmanteau in the room, and this he pulled out and began to strap. He was busily engaged at it when the cabman entered the room.

"Just give me a help with this buckle, cabman," he said, kneeling over his task, and never turning his head.

The fellow came forward with a somewhat sullen, defiant air, and put down his hands to assist. At that instant there was a sharp click, the jangling of metal, and Sherlock Holmes sprang to his feet again.

"Gentlemen," he cried, with flashing eyes, "let me introduce you to Mr. Jefferson Hope, the murderer of Enoch Drebber and of Joseph Stangerson."

The whole thing occurred in a moment—so quickly that I had no time to realize it. I have a vivid recollection of that instant, of Holmes' triumphant expression and the ring of his voice, of the cabman's dazed, savage face, as he glared at the glittering handcuffs, which had appeared as if by magic upon his wrists. For a second or two we might have been a group of statues. Then, with an inarticulate roar of fury, the prisoner wrenched himself free from Holmes's grasp, and hurled himself through the window. Woodwork and glass gave way before him; but before he got quite through, Gregson, Lestrade, and Holmes sprang upon him like so many staghounds. He was dragged back into the room, and then commenced a terrific conflict. So powerful and so fierce was he, that the four of us were shaken off again and again. He appeared to have the convulsive strength of a man in an epileptic fit. His face and hands were terribly mangled by his passage through the glass, but loss of blood had no effect in diminishing his resistance. It was not until Lestrade succeeded in getting his hand inside his neckcloth and half-strangling him that we made him realize that his struggles were of no avail; and even then we felt no security until we had pinioned his feet as well as his hands. That done, we rose to our feet breathless and panting.

"We have his cab," said Sherlock Holmes. "It will serve to take him to Scotland Yard. And now, gentlemen," he continued, with a pleasant smile, "we have reached the end of our little mystery. You are very welcome to put any questions that you like to me now, and there is no danger that I will refuse to answer them."

CRITICAL EYE

For Discussion

a. Why is Dr. Watson thrilled to dedicate himself to Holmes and a lifelong pursuit of endless danger?

b. Why does Watson find it so difficult to acclimate after the war?

Re-approaching the Reading

Sherlock Holmes was such an appealing character that, over time, people began to believe that he was a real man. What is it about Holmes and his adventures that have made him larger than the page?

Writing Assignment

Detective fiction as a genre deals with the search for truth. What is it about the genius, an individual who can perceive what the average person cannot, that forces them to intercede in the face of deception?

FREDERICK DOUGLASS

From the Autobiography

NARRATIVE OF THE LIFE OF FREDERICK DOUGLASS, AN AMERICAN SLAVE

CHAPTER I

I was born in Tuckahoe, near Hillsborough, and about twelve miles from Easton, in Talbot county, Maryland. I have no accurate knowledge of my age, never having seen any authentic record containing it. By far the larger part of the slaves know as little of their age as horses know of theirs, and it is the wish of most masters within my knowledge to keep their slaves thus ignorant. I do not remember to have ever met a slave who could tell of his birthday. They seldom come nearer to it than planting-time, harvest-time, cherry-time, spring-time, or fall-time. A want of information concerning my own was a source of unhappiness to me even during childhood. The white children could tell their ages. I could not tell why I ought to be deprived of the same privilege. I was not allowed to make any inquiries of my master concerning it. He deemed all such inquiries on the part of a slave improper and impertinent, and evidence of a restless spirit. The nearest estimate I can give makes me now between twenty-seven and twenty-eight years of age. I come to this, from hearing my master say, some time during 1835, I was about seventeen years old.

My mother was named Harriet Bailey. She was the daughter of Isaac and Betsey Bailey, both colored, and quite dark. My mother was of a darker complexion than either my grandmother or grandfather.

My father was a white man. He was admitted to be such by all I ever heard speak of my parentage. The opinion was also whispered that my master was my father; but of the correctness of this opinion, I know nothing; the means of knowing was withheld from me. My mother and I were separated when I was but an infant–before I knew her as my mother. It is a common custom, in the part of Maryland from which I ran away, to part children from their mothers at a very early age. Frequently, before the child has reached its twelfth month, its mother is taken from it, and hired out on some farm a considerable distance off, and the child is placed under the care of an old woman, too old for field labor. For what this separation is done, I do not know, unless it be to hinder the development of the child's affection toward its mother, and to blunt and destroy the natural affection of the mother for the child. This is the inevitable result.

I never saw my mother, to know her as such, more than four or five times in my life; and each of these times was very short in duration, and at night. She was hired by a Mr. Stewart, who lived about twelve miles from my home. She made her journeys to see me in the night, travelling the whole distance on foot, after the performance of her day's work. She was a field hand, and a whipping is the penalty of not being in the field at sunrise, unless a slave has special permission from his or her master to the contrary–a permission which they seldom get, and one that gives to him that gives it the proud name of being a kind master. I do not recollect of ever seeing my mother by the light of day. She was with me in the night. She would lie down with me, and get me to sleep, but long before I waked she was gone. Very little communication ever took place between us. Death soon ended what little we could have while she lived, and with it her hardships and suffering. She died when I was about seven years old, on one of my master's farms, near Lee's Mill. I was not allowed to be present during her illness, at her death, or burial. She was gone long before I knew any thing about it. Never having enjoyed, to any considerable extent, her soothing presence, her tender and watchful care, I received the tidings of her death with much the same emotions I should have probably felt at the death of a stranger.

Called thus suddenly away, she left me without the slightest intimation of who my father was. The whisper that my master was my father, may or may not be true; and, true or false, it is of but little consequence to my purpose whilst the fact remains, in all its glaring odiousness, that slaveholders have ordained, and by law established, that the children of slave women shall in all cases follow the condition of their mothers; and this is done too obviously to administer to their own lusts, and make a gratification of their wicked desires profitable as well as pleasurable; for by this cunning arrangement, the slaveholder, in cases not a few, sustains to his slaves the double relation of master and father.

I know of such cases; and it is worthy of remark that such slaves invariably suffer greater hardships, and have more to contend with, than others. They are, in the first place, a constant offence to their mistress. She is ever disposed to find fault with them; they can seldom do any thing to please her; she is never better pleased than when she sees them under the lash, especially when she suspects her husband of showing to his mulatto children favors which he withholds from his black slaves. The master is frequently compelled to sell this class of his slaves, out of deference to the feelings of his white wife; and, cruel as the deed may strike any one to be, for a man to sell his own children to human flesh-mongers, it is often the dictate of humanity for him to do so; for, unless he does this, he must not only whip them himself, but must stand by and see one white son tie up his brother, of but few shades darker complexion than himself, and ply the gory lash to his naked back; and if he lisp one word of disapproval, it is set down to his parental partiality, and only makes a bad matter worse, both for himself and the slave whom he would protect and defend.

Every year brings with it multitudes of this class of slaves. It was doubtless in consequence of a knowledge of this fact, that one great statesman of the south predicted the downfall of slavery by the inevitable laws of population. Whether this prophecy is ever fulfilled or not, it is nevertheless plain that a very different-looking class of people are springing up at the south, and are now held in slavery, from those originally brought to this country from Africa; and if their increase will do no other good, it will do away the force of the argument, that God cursed Ham, and therefore American slavery is right. If the lineal descendants of Ham are alone to be scripturally enslaved, it is certain that slavery at the south must soon become unscriptural; for thousands are ushered into the world, annually, who, like myself, owe their existence to white fathers, and those fathers most frequently their own masters.

I have had two masters. My first master's name was Anthony. I do not remember his first name. He was generally called Captain Anthony–a title which, I presume, he acquired by sailing a craft on the Chesapeake Bay. He was not considered a rich slaveholder. He owned two or three farms, and about thirty slaves. His farms and slaves were under the care of an overseer. The overseer's name was Plummer. Mr. Plummer was a miserable drunkard, a profane swearer, and a savage monster. He always went armed with a cowskin and a heavy cudgel. I have known him to cut and slash the women's heads so horribly, that even master would be enraged at his cruelty, and would threaten to whip him if he did not mind himself. Master, however, was not a humane slaveholder. It required extraordinary barbarity on the part of an overseer to affect him. He was a cruel man, hardened by a long life of slaveholding. He would at times seem to take great pleasure in whipping a slave. I have often been awakened at the dawn of day by the most heart-rending shrieks of an own aunt of mine, whom he used to tie up to a joist, and whip upon her naked back till she was literally covered with blood. No words, no tears, no prayers, from his gory victim, seemed to move his iron heart from its bloody purpose. The louder she screamed, the harder he whipped; and where the blood ran fastest, there he whipped longest. He would whip her to make her scream, and whip her to make her hush; and not until overcome by fatigue, would he cease to swing the blood-clotted cowskin. I remember the first time I ever witnessed this horrible exhibition. I was quite a child, but I well remember it. I never shall forget it whilst I remember any thing. It was the first of a long series of such outrages, of which I was doomed to be a witness and a participant. It struck me with awful force. It was the blood-stained gate, the entrance to the hell of slavery, through which I was about to pass. It was a most terrible spectacle. I wish I could commit to paper the feelings with which I beheld it.

This occurrence took place very soon after I went to live with my old master, and under the following circumstances. Aunt Hester went out one night,—where or for what I do not know,—and happened to be absent when my master desired her presence. He had ordered her not to go out evenings, and warned her that she must never let him catch her in company with a young man, who was paying attention to her belonging to Colonel Lloyd. The young man's name was Ned Roberts, generally called Lloyd's Ned. Why master was so careful of her, may be safely left to conjecture. She was a woman of noble form, and of graceful proportions, having very few equals, and fewer superiors, in personal appearance, among the colored or white women of our neighborhood.

Aunt Hester had not only disobeyed his orders in going out, but had been found in company with Lloyd's Ned; which circumstance, I found, from what he said while whipping her, was the chief offence. Had he been a man of pure morals himself, he might have been thought interested in protecting the innocence of my aunt; but those who knew him will not suspect him of any such virtue. Before he commenced whipping Aunt Hester, he took her into the kitchen, and stripped her from neck to waist, leaving her neck, shoulders, and back, entirely naked. He then told her to cross her hands, calling her at the same time a d—d b—h. After crossing her hands, he tied them with a strong rope, and led her to a stool under a large hook in the joist, put in for the purpose. He made her get upon the stool, and tied her hands to the hook. She now stood fair for his infernal purpose. Her arms were stretched up at their full length, so that she stood upon the ends of her toes. He then said to her, "Now, you d—d b—h, I'll learn you how to disobey my orders!" and after rolling up his sleeves, he commenced to lay on the heavy cowskin, and soon the warm, red blood (amid heart-rending shrieks from her, and horrid oaths from him) came dripping to the floor. I was so terrified and horror-stricken at the sight, that I hid myself in a closet, and dared not venture out till long after the bloody transaction was over. I expected it would be my turn next. It was all new to me. I had never seen any thing like it before. I had always lived with my grandmother on the outskirts of the plantation, where she was put to raise the children of the younger women. I had therefore been, until now, out of the way of the bloody scenes that often occurred on the plantation.

CHAPTER II

My master's family consisted of two sons, Andrew and Richard; one daughter, Lucretia, and her husband, Captain Thomas Auld. They lived in one house, upon the home plantation of Colonel Edward Lloyd. My master was Colonel Lloyd's clerk and superintendent. He was what might be called the overseer of the overseers. I spent two years of childhood on this plantation in my old master's family. It was here that I witnessed the bloody transaction recorded in the first chapter; and as I received my first impressions of slavery on this plantation, I will give some description of it, and of slavery as it there existed. The plantation is about twelve miles north of Easton, in Talbot county, and is situated on the border of Miles River. The principal products raised upon it were tobacco, corn, and wheat. These were raised in great abundance; so that, with the products of this and the other farms belonging to him, he was able to keep in almost constant employment a large sloop, in carrying them to market at Baltimore. This sloop was named Sally Lloyd, in honor of one of the colonel's daughters. My master's son-in-law, Captain Auld, was master of the vessel; she was otherwise manned by the colonel's own slaves. Their names were Peter, Isaac, Rich, and Jake. These were esteemed very highly by the other slaves, and looked upon as the privileged ones of the plantation; for it was no small affair, in the eyes of the slaves, to be allowed to see Baltimore.

Colonel Lloyd kept from three to four hundred slaves on his home plantation, and owned a large number more on the neighboring farms belonging to him. The names of the farms nearest to the home plantation were Wye Town and New Design. "Wye Town" was under the overseership of a man named Noah Willis. New Design was under the overseership of a Mr. Townsend. The overseers of these, and all the rest of the farms, numbering over twenty, received advice and direction from the managers of the home plantation. This was the great business place. It was the seat of government for the whole twenty farms. All disputes among the overseers were settled here. If a slave was convicted of any high misdemeanor, became unmanageable, or evinced a determination to run away, he was brought immediately here, severely whipped, put on board the sloop, carried to Baltimore, and sold to Austin Woolfolk, or some other slave-trader, as a warning to the slaves remaining.

Here, too, the slaves of all the other farms received their monthly allowance of food, and their yearly clothing. The men and women slaves received, as their monthly allowance of food, eight pounds of pork, or its equivalent in fish, and one bushel of corn meal. Their yearly clothing consisted of two coarse linen shirts, one pair of linen trousers, like the shirts, one jacket, one pair of trousers for winter, made of coarse negro cloth, one pair of stockings, and one pair of shoes; the whole of which could not have cost more than seven dollars. The allowance of the slave children was given to their mothers, or the old women having the care of them. The children unable to work in the field had neither shoes, stockings, jackets, nor trousers, given to them; their clothing consisted of two coarse linen shirts per year. When these failed them, they went naked until the next allowance-day. Children from seven to ten years old, of both sexes, almost naked, might be seen at all seasons of the year.

There were no beds given the slaves, unless one coarse blanket be considered such, and none but the men and women had these. This, however, is not considered a very great privation. They find less difficulty from the want of beds, than from the want of time to sleep; for when their day's work in the field is done, the most of them having their washing, mending, and cooking to do, and having few or none of the ordinary facilities for doing either of these, very many of their sleeping hours are consumed in preparing for the field the coming day; and when this is done, old and young, male and female, married and single, drop down side by side, on one common bed,–the cold, damp floor,–each covering himself or herself with their miserable blankets; and here they sleep till they are summoned to the field by the driver's horn. At the sound of this, all must rise, and be off to the field. There must be no halting; every one must be at his or her post; and woe betides them who hear not this morning summons to the field; for if they are not awakened by the sense of hearing, they are by the sense of feeling: no age nor sex finds any favor. Mr. Severe, the overseer, used to stand by the door of the quarter, armed with a large hickory stick and heavy cowskin, ready to whip any one who was so unfortunate as not to hear, or, from any other cause, was prevented from being ready to start for the field at the sound of the horn.

Mr. Severe was rightly named: he was a cruel man. I have seen him whip a woman, causing the blood to run half an hour at the time; and this, too, in the midst of her crying children, pleading for their mother's release. He seemed to take pleasure in manifesting his fiendish barbarity. Added to his cruelty, he was a profane swearer. It was enough to chill the blood and stiffen the hair of an ordinary man to hear him talk. Scarce a sentence escaped him but that was commenced or concluded by some horrid oath. The field was the place to witness his cruelty and profanity. His presence made it both the field of blood and of blasphemy. From the rising till the going down of the sun, he was cursing, raving, cutting, and slashing among the slaves of the field, in the most frightful manner. His career was short. He died very soon after I went to Colonel Lloyd's; and he died as he lived, uttering, with his dying groans, bitter curses and horrid oaths. His death was regarded by the slaves as the result of a merciful providence.

Mr. Severe's place was filled by a Mr. Hopkins. He was a very different man. He was less cruel, less profane, and made less noise, than Mr. Severe. His course was characterized by no extraordinary demonstrations of cruelty. He whipped, but seemed to take no pleasure in it. He was called by the slaves a good overseer.

The home plantation of Colonel Lloyd wore the appearance of a country village. All the mechanical operations for all the farms were performed here. The shoemaking and mending, the blacksmithing, cartwrighting, coopering, weaving, and grain-grinding, were all performed by the slaves on the home plantation. The whole place wore a business-like aspect very unlike the neighboring farms. The number of houses, too, conspired to give it advantage over the neighboring farms. It was called by the slaves the *Great House Farm.* Few privileges were esteemed higher, by the slaves of the out-farms, than that of being selected to do errands at the Great House Farm. It was associated in their minds with greatness. A representative could not be prouder of his election to a seat in the American Congress, than a slave on one of the out-farms would be of his election to do errands at the Great House Farm. They regarded it as evidence of great confidence reposed in them by their overseers; and it was on this account, as well as a constant desire to be out of the field from under the driver's lash, that they esteemed it a high privilege, one worth careful living for. He was called the smartest and most trusty fellow, who had this honor conferred upon him the most frequently. The competitors for this office sought as diligently to please their overseers, as the office-seekers in the political parties seek to please and deceive the people. The same traits of character might be seen in Colonel Lloyd's slaves, as are seen in the slaves of the political parties.

The slaves selected to go to the Great House Farm, for the monthly allowance for themselves and their fellow-slaves, were peculiarly enthusiastic. While on their way, they would make the dense old woods, for miles around, reverberate with their wild songs, revealing at once the highest joy and the deepest sadness. They would compose and sing as they went along, consulting neither time nor tune. The thought that came up, came out–if not in the word, in the sound;–and as frequently in the one as in the other. They would sometimes sing the most pathetic sentiment in the most rapturous tone, and the most rapturous sentiment in the most pathetic tone. Into all of their songs they would manage to weave something of the Great House Farm. Especially would they do this, when leaving home. They would then sing most exultingly the following words:–

"I am going away to the Great House Farm!
O, yea! O, yea! O!"

This they would sing, as a chorus, to words which to many would seem unmeaning jargon, but which, nevertheless, were full of meaning to themselves. I have sometimes thought that the mere hearing of those songs would do more to impress some minds with the horrible character of slavery, than the reading of whole volumes of philosophy on the subject could do.

I did not, when a slave, understand the deep meaning of those rude and apparently incoherent songs. I was myself within the circle; so that I neither saw nor heard as those without might see and hear. They told a tale of woe which was then altogether beyond my feeble comprehension; they were tones loud, long, and deep; they breathed the prayer and complaint of souls boiling over with the bitterest anguish. Every tone was a testimony against slavery, and a prayer to God for deliverance from chains. The hearing of those wild notes always depressed my spirit, and filled me with ineffable sadness. I have frequently found myself in tears while hearing them. The mere recurrence to those songs, even now, afflicts me; and while I am writing these lines, an expression of feeling has already found its way down my cheek. To those songs I trace my first glimmering conception of the dehumanizing character of slavery. I can never get rid of that conception. Those songs still follow me, to deepen my hatred of slavery, and quicken my sympathies for my brethren in bonds. If any one wishes to be impressed with the soul-killing effects of slavery, let him go to Colonel Lloyd's plantation, and, on allowance-day, place himself in the deep pine woods, and there let him, in silence, analyze the sounds that shall pass through the chambers of his soul,–and if he is not thus impressed, it will only be because "there is no flesh in his obdurate heart."

I have often been utterly astonished, since I came to the north, to find persons who could speak of the singing, among slaves, as evidence of their contentment and happiness. It is impossible to conceive of a greater mistake. Slaves sing most when they are most unhappy. The songs of the slave represent the sorrows of his heart; and he is relieved by them, only as an aching heart is relieved by its tears. At least, such is my experience. I have often sung to drown my sorrow, but seldom to express my happiness. Crying for joy, and singing for joy, were alike uncommon to me while in the jaws of slavery. The singing of a man cast away upon a desolate island might be as appropriately considered as evidence of contentment and happiness, as the singing of a slave; the songs of the one and of the other are prompted by the same emotion.

Critical Eye

For Discussion

a. Douglass doesn't exaggerate about the horrors he experienced as a slave. Instead, his recollections are meant to portray the institution of slavery as a systemic and purposeful dismantling of African identity—one destined to have a long-term impact on the African-American community. How does he accomplish this? Was he right?

Re-approaching the Reading

For many African Americans, gospel music is one of the great strengths of the Black community. This musical genre is historical, cultural, and a means of social interaction. In short, this uplifting music speaks to the survival of a people. Douglass, however, sees it differently. In his estimation, the "negro spiritual" does little more than reflect the allowed pain and suffering of a brutalized people. How are both representations true?

Writing Assignment

If we hold men to a specific standard—one where they are expected to protect and provide for those deemed weaker—how emasculating is it for Douglass to watch the women around him being abused and mistreated?

BHARATI MUKHERJEE

A FATHER

One Wednesday morning in mid-May Mr. Bhowmick woke up as he usually did at 5:43 A.M., checked his Rolex against the alarm clock's digital readout, punched down the alarm (set for 5:45), then nudged his wife awake. She worked as a claims investigator for an insurance company that had an office in a nearby shopping mall. She didn't really have to leave the house until 8:30, but she liked to get up early and cook him a big breakfast. Mr. Bhowmick had to drive a long way to work. He was a naturally dutiful, cautious man, and he set the alarm clock early enough to accommodate a margin for accidents.

While his wife, in a pink nylon negligee she had paid for with her own MasterCard card, made him a new version of French toast from a clipping ("Eggs-cellent Recipes!") Scotchtaped to the inside of a kitchen cupboard, Mr. Bhowmick brushed his teeth. He brushed, he gurgled with the loud, hawking noises that he and his brother had been taught as children to make in order to flush clean not merely teeth but also tongue and palate.

After that he showered, then, back in the bedroom again, he recited prayers in Sanskrit to Kali, the patron goddess of his family, the goddess of wrath and vengeance. In the pokey flat of his childhood in Ranchi, Bihar, his mother had given over a whole bedroom to her collection of gods and goddesses. Mr. Bhowmick couldn't be that extravagant in Detroit. His daughter, twenty-six and an electrical engineer, slept in the other of the two bedrooms in his apartment. But he had done his best. He had taken Woodworking I and II at a nearby recreation center and built a grotto for the goddess. Kali-Mata was eight inches tall, made of metal and painted a glistening black so that the metal glowed like the oiled, black skin of a peasant woman. And though Kali-Mata was totally nude except for a tiny gilt crown and a garland strung together from sinners' chopped off heads, she looked warm, cozy, *pleased,* in her makeshift wooden shrine in Detroit. Mr. Bhowmick had gathered quite a crowd of admiring, fellow woodworkers in those final weeks of decoration.

"Hurry it up with the prayers," his wife shouted from the kitchen. She was an agnostic, a believer in ambition, not grace. She frequently complained that his prayers had gotten so long that soon he wouldn't have time to go to work, play duplicate bridge with the Ghosals, or play the tabla in the Bengali Association's one Sunday per month musical soirees. Lately she'd begun to drain him in a wholly new way. He wasn't praying, she nagged; he was shutting her out of his life. There'd be no peace in the house until she hid Kali-Mata in a suitcase.

She nagged, and he threatened to beat her with his shoe as his father had threatened his mother: it was the thrust and volley of marriage. There was no question of actually taking off a shoe and applying it to his wife's body. She was bigger than he was. And, secretly, he admired her for having the nerve, the agnosticism, which as a college boy in backward Bihar he too had claimed.

"I have time," he shot at her. He was still wrapped in a damp terry towel.

"You have time for everything but domestic life."

It was the fault of the shopping mall that his wife had started to buy pop psychology paperbacks. These paperbacks preached that for couples who could sit down and talk about their "relationship," life would be sweet again. His engineer daughter was on his wife's side. She accused him of holding things in.

"Face it, Dad," she said. "You have an affect deficit."

But surely everyone had feelings they didn't want to talk about or talk over. He definitely did not want to blurt out anything about the sick-in-the-guts sensations that came over him most mornings and that he couldn't bubble down with Alka-Seltzer or smother with Gas-X. The women in his family were smarter than him. They were cheerful, outgoing, more American somehow.

How could he tell these bright, mocking women that in the 5:43 A.M. darkness, he sensed invisible presences: gods and snakes frolicked in the master bedroom, little white sparks of cosmic static crackled up the legs of his pajamas. Something was out there in the dark, something that could invent accidents and coincidences to remind mortals that even in Detroit they were no more than mortal. His wife would label this paranoia and dismiss it. Paranoia, premonition: whatever it was, it had begun to undermine his composure.

Take this morning. Mr. Bhowmick had woken up from a pleasant dream about a man taking a Club Med vacation, and the postdream satisfaction had lasted through the shower, but when he'd come back to the shrine in the bedroom, he'd noticed all at once how scarlet and saucy was the tongue that Kali-Mata stuck out at the world. Surely he had not lavished such alarming detail, such admonitory colors on that flap of flesh.

Watch out, ambulatory sinners. Be careful out there, the goddess warned him, and not with the affection of Sergeant Esterhaus, either.

"French toast must be eaten hot-hot," his wife nagged. "Otherwise they'll taste like rubber."

Mr. Bhowmick laid the trousers of a two-trouser suit he had bought on sale that winter against his favorite tweed jacket. The navy stripes in the trousers and the small, navy tweed flecks in the jacket looked quite good together. So what if the Chief Engineer had already started wearing summer cottons?

"I am coming, I am coming," he shouted back. "You want me to eat hot-hot, you start the frying only when I am sitting down. You didn't learn anything from Mother in Ranchi?"

"Mother cooked French toast from fancy recipes? I mean French Sandwich Toast with complicated filling?"

He came into the room to give her his testiest look. "You don't know the meaning of complicated cookery. And mother had to get the coal fire of the *chula* going first."

His daughter was already at the table. "Why don't you break down and buy her a microwave oven? That's what I mean about sitting down and talking things out." She had finished her orange juice. She took a plastic measure of Slim-Fast out of its can and poured the powder into a glass of skim milk. "It's ridiculous."

Babli was not the child he would have chosen as his only heir. She was brighter certainly than the sons and daughters of the other Bengalis he knew in Detroit, and she had been the only female student in most of her classes at Georgia Tech, but as she sat there in her beige linen business suit, her thick chin dropping into a polka-dotted cravat, he regretted again that she was not the child of his dreams. Babli would be able to help him out moneywise if something happened to him, something so bad that even his pension plans and his insurance policies and his money market schemes wouldn't be enough. But Babli could never comfort him. She wasn't womanly or tender the way that unmarried girls had been in the wistful days of his adolescence. She could sing Hindi film songs, mimicking exactly the high, artificial voice of Lata Mungeshkar, and she had taken two years of dance lessons at Sona Devi's Dance Academy in Southfield, but these accomplishments didn't add up to real femininity. Not the kind that had given him palpitations in Ranchi.

Mr. Bhowmick did his best with his wife's French toast. In spite of its filling of marshmallows, apricot jam and maple syrup, it tasted rubbery. He drank two cups of Darjeeling tea, said, "Well, I'm off," and took off.

All might have gone well if Mr. Bhowmick hadn't fussed longer than usual about putting his briefcase and his trenchcoat in the backseat. He got in behind the wheel of his Oldsmobile, fixed his seatbelt and was just about to turn the key in the ignition when his neighbor, Al Stazniak, who was starting up his Buick Skylark, sneezed. A sneeze at the start of a journey brings bad luck. Al Stazniak's sneeze was fierce, made up of five short bursts, too loud to be ignored.

Be careful out there! Mr. Bhowmick could see the goddess's scarlet little tongue tip wagging at him.

He was a modern man, an intelligent man. Otherwise he couldn't have had the options in life that he did have. He couldn't have given up a good job with perks in Bombay and found a better job with General Motors in Detroit. But Mr. Bhowmick was also a prudent enough man to know that some abiding truth lies bunkered within each wanton Hindu superstition. A sneeze was more than a sneeze. The heedless are carried off in ambulances. He had choices to make. He could ignore the sneeze, and so challenge the world unseen by men. Perhaps Al Stazniak had hay fever. For a sneeze to be a potent omen, surely it had to be unprovoked and terrifying, a thunderclap cleaving the summer skies. Or he could admit the smallness of mortals, undo the fate of the universe by starting over, and go back inside the apartment, sit for a second on the sofa, then restart his trip.

Al Stazniak rolled down his window. "Everything okay?"

Mr. Bhowmick nodded shyly. They weren't really friends in the way neighbors can sometimes be. They talked as they parked or pulled out of their adjacent parking stalls. For all Mr. Bhowmick knew, Al Stazniak had no legs. He had never seen the man out of his Skylark.

He let the Buick back out first. Everything was okay, yes, please. All the same he undid his seatbelt. Compromise, adaptability, call it what you will. A dozen times a day he made these small trade-offs between new-world reasonableness and old-world beliefs.

While he was sitting in his parked car, his wife's ride came by. For fifty dollars a month, she was picked up and dropped off by a hard up, newly divorced woman who worked at a florist's shop in the same mall. His wife came out the front door in brown K-Mart pants and a burgundy windbreaker. She waved to him, then slipped into the passenger seat of the florist's rusty Japanese car.

He was a metallurgist. He knew about rust and ways of preventing it, secret ways, thus far unknown to the Japanese.

Babli's fiery red Mitsubishi was still in the lot. She wouldn't leave for work for another eight minutes. He didn't want her to know he'd been undone by a sneeze. Babli wasn't tolerant of superstitions. She played New Wave music in her tapedeck. If asked about Hinduism, all she'd ever said to her American friends was that "it's neat." Mr. Bhowmick had heard her on the phone years before. The cosmos balanced on the head of a snake was like a beachball balanced on the snout of a circus seal. "This Hindu myth stuff," he'd heard her say, "is like a series of super graphics."

He'd forgiven her. He could probably forgive her anything. It was her way of surviving high school in a city that was both native to her, and alien.

There was no question of going back where he'd come from. He hated Ranchi. Ranchi was no place for dreamers. All through his teenage years, Mr. Bhowmick had dreamed of success abroad. What form that success would take he had left vague. Success had meant to him escape from the constant plotting and bitterness that wore out India's middle class.

Babli should have come out of the apartment and driven off to work by now. Mr. Bhowmick decided to take a risk, to dash inside and pretend he'd left his briefcase on the coffee table.

When he entered the living room, he noticed Babli's spring coat and large vinyl pocketbook on the sofa. She was probably sorting through the junk jewelry on her dresser to give her business suit a lift. She read hints about dressing in women's magazines and applied them to her person with seriousness. If his luck held, he could sit on the sofa, say a quick prayer and get back to the car without her catching on.

It surprised him that she didn't shout out from her bedroom, "Who's there?" What if he had been a rapist?

Then he heard Babli in the bathroom. He heard unladylike squawking noises. She was throwing up, A squawk, a spitting, then the horrible gurgle of a waterfall.

A revelation came to Mr. Bhowmick. A woman vomiting in the privacy of the bathroom could mean many things. She was coming down with the flu. She was nervous about a meeting. But Mr. Bhowmick knew at once that his daughter, his untender, unloving daughter whom he couldn't love and hadn't tried to love, was not, in the larger world of Detroit, unloved. Sinners are everywhere, even in the bosom of an upright, unambitious family like the Bhowmicks. It was the goddess sticking out her tongue at him.

The father sat heavily on the sofa, shrinking from contact with her coat and pocketbook. His brisk, bright engineer daughter was pregnant. Someone had taken time to make love to her. Someone had thought her tender, feminine. Someone even now was perhaps mooning over her. The idea excited him. It was so grotesque and wondrous. At twenty-six Babli had found the man of her dreams; whereas at twenty-six Mr. Bhowmick had given up on truth, beauty and poetry and exchanged them for two years at Carnegie Tech.

Mr. Bhowmick's tweed-jacketed body sagged against the sofa cushions. Babli would abort, of course. He knew his Babli. It was the only possible option if she didn't want to bring shame to the Bhowmick family. All the same, he could see a chubby baby boy on the rug, crawling to his granddaddy. Shame like that was easier to hide in Ranchi. There was always a barren womb sanctified by marriage that could claim sudden fructifying by the goddess

Parvati. Babli would do what she wanted. She was headstrong and independent and he was afraid of her.

Babli staggered out of the bathroom. Damp stains ruined her linen suit. It was the first time he had seen his daughter look ridiculous, quite unprofessional. She didn't come into the living room to investigate the noises he'd made. He glimpsed her shoeless stockinged feet flip-flop on collapsed arches down the hall to her bedroom.

"Are you all right?" Mr. Bhowmick asked, standing in the hall. "Do you need Sinutab?"

She wheeled around. "What're you doing here?"

He was the one who should be angry. "I'm feeling poorly too," he said. "I'm taking the day off."

"I feel fine, "Babli said.

Within fifteen minutes Babli had changed her clothes and left. Mr. Bhowmick had the apartment to himself all day. All day for praising or cursing the life that had brought him along with its other surprises an illegitimate grandchild.

It was his wife that he blamed. Coming to America to live had been his wife's idea. After the wedding, the young Bhowmicks had spent two years in Pittsburgh on his student visa, then gone back home to Ranchi for nine years. Nine crushing years. Then the job in Bombay had come through. All during those nine years his wife had screamed and wept. She was a woman of wild, progressive ideas–she'd called them her "American" ideas–and she'd been martyred by her neighbors for them. American *memsahib. Markin mem, Markin mem.* In bazaars the beggar boys had trailed her and hooted. She'd done provocative things. She'd hired a *chamar* woman who by caste rules was forbidden to cook for higher caste families, especially for widowed mothers of decent men. This had caused a blowup in the neighborhood. She'd made other, lesser errors. While other wives shopped and cooked every day, his wife had cooked the whole week's menu on weekends.

"What's the point of having a refrigerator, then?" She'd been scornful of the Ranchi women.

His mother, an old-fashioned widow, had accused her of trying to kill her by poisoning. "You are in such a hurry? You want to get rid of me quick-quick so you can go back to the States?"

Family life had been turbulent.

He had kept aloof, inwardly siding with his mother. He did not love his wife now, and he had not loved her then. In any case, he had not defended her. He felt some affection, and he felt guilty for having shunned her during those unhappy years. But he had thought of it then as revenge. He had wanted to marry a beautiful woman. Not being a young man of means, only a young man with prospects, he had had no right to yearn for pure beauty. He cursed his fate and after a while, settled for a barrister's daughter, a plain girl with a wide, flat plank of a body and myopic eyes. The barrister had sweetened the deal by throwing in an all-expenses-paid two years' study at Carnegie Tech to which Mr. Bhowmick had been admitted. Those two years had changed his wife from pliant girl to an ambitious woman. She wanted America, nothing less.

It was his wife who had forced him to apply for permanent resident status in the U.S. even though he had a good job in Ranchi as a government engineer. The putting together of documents for the immigrant visa had been a long and humbling process. He had had to explain to a chilly clerk in the Embassy that, like most Indians of his generation, he had no birth certificate. He had to swear out affidavits, suffer through police checks, bribe orderlies whose job it was to move his dossier from desk to desk. The decision, the clerk had advised him, would take months, maybe years. He hadn't dared hope that merit might be rewarded. Merit could collapse under bad luck. It was for grace that he prayed.

While the immigration papers were being processed, he had found the job in Bombay. So he'd moved his mother in with his younger brother's family, and left his hometown for good. Life in Bombay had been lighthearted, almost fulfilling. His wife had thrown herself into charity work with the same energy that had offended the Ranchi women. He was happy to be in a big city at last. Bombay was the Rio de Janeiro of the East; he'd read that in a travel brochure. He drove out to Nariman Point at least once a week to admire the necklace of municipal lights, toss coconut shells into the dark ocean, drink beer at the Oberoi-Sheraton where overseas Indian girls in designer jeans beckoned him in sly ways. His nights were full. He played duplicate bridge, went to the movies, took his wife to Bingo nights at his club. In Detroit he was a lonelier man.

Then the green card had come through. For him, for his wife, and for the daughter who had been born to them in Bombay. He sold what he could sell, and put in his brother's informal trust what he couldn't to save on taxes. Then he had left for America, and one more start.

All through the week, Mr. Bhowmick watched his daughter. He kept furtive notes on how many times she rushed to the bathroom and made hawking, wrenching noises, how many times she stayed late at the office, calling her mother to say she'd be taking in a movie and pizza afterwards with friends.

He had to tell her that he knew. And he probably didn't have much time. She shouldn't be on Slim-Fast in her condition. He had to talk things over with her. But what would he say to her? What position could he take? He had to choose between public shame for the family, and murder.

For three more weeks he watched her and kept his silence. Babli wore shifts to the office instead of business suits, and he liked her better in those garments. Perhaps she was dressing for her young man, not from necessity. Her skin was pale and blotchy by turn. At breakfast her fingers looked stiff, and she had trouble with silverware.

Two Saturdays running, he lost badly at duplicate bridge. His wife scolded him. He had made silly mistakes. When was Babli meeting this man? Where? He must be American; Mr. Bhowmick prayed only that he was white. He pictured his grandson crawling to him, and the grandson was always fat and brown and buttery-skinned, like the infant Krishna. An American son-in-law was a terrifying notion. Why was she not mentioning men, at least, preparing the way for the major announcement? He listened sharply for men's names, rehearsed little lines like, "Hello, Bob, I'm Babli's old man," with a cracked little laugh. Bob, Jack, Jimmy, Tom. But no names surfaced. When she went out for pizza and a movie it was with the familiar set of Indian girls and their strange, unpopular, American friends, all without men. Mr. Bhowmick tried to be reasonable. Maybe she had already gotten married and was keeping it secret. "Well, Bob, you and Babli sure had Mrs. Bhowmick and me going there, heh-heh," he mumbled one night with the Sahas and Ghosals, over cards. "Pardon?" asked Pronob Saha. Mr. Bhowmick dropped two tricks, and his wife glared. "Such stupid blunders," she fumed on the drive back. A new truth was dawning; there would be no marriage for Babli. Her young man probably was not so young and not so available. He must be already married. She must have yielded to passion or been raped in the office. His wife seemed to have noticed nothing. Was he a murderer, or a conspirator? He kept his secret from his wife; his daughter kept her decision to herself.

Nights, Mr. Bhowmick pretended to sleep, but as soon as his wife began her snoring–not real snores so much as loud, gaspy gulpings for breath–he turned on his side and prayed to Kali-Mata.

In July, when Babli's belly had begun to push up against the waistless dress she'd bought herself, Mr. Bhowmick came out of the shower one weekend morning and found the two women screaming at each other. His wife had a rolling pin in one hand. His daughter held up a *National Geographic* as a shield for her head. The crazy look that had been in his wife's eyes when she'd shooed away beggar kids was in her eyes again.

"Stop it!" His own boldness overwhelmed him. "Shut up! Babli's pregnant so what? It's your fault, you made us come to the States."

Girls like Babli were caught between rules, that's the point he wished to make. They were too smart, too impulsive for a backward place like Ranchi, but not tough nor smart enough for sex-crazy places like Detroit.

"My fault?" his wife cried. "I told her to do hanky-panky with boys? I told her to shame us like this?"

She got in one blow with the rolling pin. The second glanced off Babli's shoulder and fell on his arm which he had stuck out for his grandson's sake.

"I'm calling the police," Babli shouted. She was out of the rolling pin's range "This is brutality. You can't do this to me."

"Shut up! Shut your mouth, foolish woman." He wrenched the weapon from his wife's fist. He made a show of taking off his shoe to beat his wife on the face.

"What do you know? You don't know anything." She let herself down slowly on a dining chair. Her hair, curled overnight, stood in wild whorls around her head. "Nothing."

"And you do!" He laughed. He remembered her tormentors, and laughed again. He had begun to enjoy himself. Now *he* was the one with the crazy, progressive ideas.

"Your daughter is pregnant, yes," she said, "any fool knows that. But ask her the name of the father. Go, ask."

He stared at his daughter who gazed straight ahead, eyes burning with hate, jaw clenched with fury.

"Babli?"

"Who needs a man?" she hissed. "The father of my baby is a bottle and a syringe. Men louse up your lives. I just want a baby. Oh, don't worry–he's a certified fit donor. No diseases, college graduate, above average, and he made the easiest twenty-five dollars of his life–"

"Like animals," his wife said. For the first time he heard horror in her voice. His daughter grinned at him. He saw her tongue, thick and red, squirming behind her row of perfect teeth.

"Yes, yes, yes," she screamed, "like livestock. Just like animals. You should be happy–that's what marriage is all about, isn't it? Matching bloodlines, matching horoscopes, matching castes, matching, matching, matching . . ." and it was difficult to know if she was laughing or singing, or mocking and like a madwoman.

Mr. Bhowmick lifted the rolling pin high above his head and brought it down hard on the dome of Babli's stomach. In the end, it was his wife who called the police.

CRITICAL EYE

For Discussion

a. In what way(s) is the father's traditional role in his home being undermined? Is this a bad thing? Shouldn't the women in his family be allowed to take advantage of the freedoms granted by their new homeland?

b. The father believes that his wife and daughter have become more American. Why is this a problem for him? What does he believe has been lost culturally? Is there really something wrong, or is this merely a culture clash?

c. Why is the father moved to violence at the end of the story? What is he *really* angry about?

Re-approaching the Reading

How is this story about the difficulties immigrants experience once they arrive in America? How are their traditions challenged? What are they expected to surrender?

Writing Assignment

As much as this is a story about the father's moment of truth, in what ways is this story about the daughter taking her life into her own hands? Is this defining moment traumatic for most parents? If so, why? Also, once independent, do children owe their parents their future? In short, because they gave us life, do we owe our parents our futures?

DAVID SEDARIS

GO CAROLINA

ANYONE WHO WATCHES EVEN THE SLIGHTEST amount of TV is familiar with the scene: An agent knocks on the door of some seemingly ordinary home or office. The door opens, and the person holding the knob is asked to identify himself. The agent then says, "I'm going to ask you to come with me."

They're always remarkably calm, these agents. If asked "Why do I need to go anywhere with you?" they'll straighten their shirt cuffs or idly brush stray hairs from the sleeves of their sport coats and say, "Oh, I think we both know why."

The suspect then chooses between doing things the hard way and doing things the easy way, and the scene ends with either gunfire or the gentlemanly application of handcuffs. Occasionally it's a case of mistaken identity, but most often the suspect knows exactly why he's being taken. It seems he's been expecting this to happen. The anticipation has ruled his life, and now, finally, the wait is over. You're sometimes led to believe that this person is actually relieved, but I've never bought it. Though it probably has its moments, the average day spent in hiding is bound to beat the average day spent in prison. When it comes time to decide who gets the bottom bunk, I think anyone would agree that there's a lot to be said for doing things the hard way.

The agent came for me during a geography lesson. She entered the room and nodded at my fifth-grade teacher, who stood frowning at a map of Europe. What would needle me later was the realization that this had all been prearranged. My capture had been scheduled to go down at exactly 2:30 on a Thursday afternoon. The agent would be wearing a dung-colored blazer over a red knit turtleneck, her heels sensibly low in case the suspect should attempt a quick getaway.

"David," the teacher said, "this is Miss Samson, and she'd like you to go with her now."

No one else had been called, so why me? I ran down a list of recent crimes, looking for a conviction that might stick. Setting fire to a reportedly flameproof Halloween costume, stealing a set of barbecue tongs from an unguarded patio, altering the word on a list of rules posted on the gymnasium door; never did it occur to me that I might be innocent.

"You might want to take your books with you," the teacher said. "And your jacket. You probably won't be back before the bell rings."

Though she seemed old at the time, the agent was most likely fresh out of college. She walked beside me and asked what appeared to be an innocent and unrelated question: "So, which do you like better, State or Carolina?"

She was referring to the athletic rivalry between the Triangle area's two largest universities. Those who cared about such things tended to express their allegiance by wearing either Tar Heel powder blue, or Wolf Pack red, two colors that managed to look good on no one. The question of team preference was common in our part of North Carolina, and the answer supposedly spoke volumes about the kind of person you either were or hoped to become. I had no interest in football or basketball but had learned it was best to pretend otherwise. If a boy didn't care for barbecued chicken or potato chips, people would accept it as a matter of personal taste, saying, "Oh well, I guess it takes all kinds." You could turn up your nose at the president or Coke or even God, but there were names for boys who didn't like sports. When the subject came up, I found it best to ask which team my questioner preferred. Then I'd say, "Really? Me, too!"

Asked by the agent which team I supported, I took my cue from her red turtleneck and told her that I was for State. "Definitely State. State all the way."

It was an answer I would regret for years to come.

"State, did you say?" the agent asked.

"Yes, State. They're the greatest."

"I see." She led me through an unmarked door near the principal's office, into a small, windowless room furnished with two facing desks. It was the kind of room where you'd grill someone until they snapped, the kind frequently painted so as to cover the bloodstains. She gestured toward what was to become my regular seat, then continued her line of questioning.

"And what exactly are they, State and Carolina?"

"Colleges? Universities?"

She opened a file on her desk, saying, "Yes, you're right. Your answers are correct, but you're saying them incorrectly. You're telling me that they're colleg*eth* and univeriti*eth,* when actually they're college *s* and univer*sitie s*. You're giving me a *th* sound instead of a nice clear *s*. "Can you hear the di*s*tinction between the two different *s*ound*s*?"

I nodded.

"May I plea*se* have an actual an*s*wer?"

"Uh-huh."

" 'Uh-huh' i*s* not a word."

"Okay."

"Okay what?"

"Okay," I said. "Sure, I can hear it."

"You can hear what, the di*s*tinction? The contra*s*t?"

"Yeah, that."

It was the first battle of my war against the letter *s,* and I was determined to dig my foxhole before the sun went down. According to Agent Samson, a *s*tate *c*ertified *s*peech therapi*s*t," my *s* was sibilate, meaning that I lisped.

This was not news to me.

"Our goal i*s* to work together until eventually you can *s*peak correctly," Agent Samson said. She made a great show of enunciating her own sparkling *s*'s, and the effect was profoundly irritating. "I'm trying to help you, but the longer you play the*s*e little game*s* the longer thi*s* i*s* going to take."

The woman spoke with a heavy western North Carolina accent, which I used to discredit her authority. Here was a person for whom the word *pen* had two syllables. Her people undoubtedly drank from clay jugs and hollered for Paw when the vittles were ready – so who was she to advise me on anything? Over the coming years I would find a crack in each of the therapists sent to train what Miss Samson now defined as my lazy tongue. "That*'s* it*s* problem," she said. "It*'s* ju*s*t plain lazy."

My sisters Amy and Gretchen were, at the time, undergoing therapy for their lazy eyes, while my older sister, Lisa, had been born with a lazy leg that had refused to grow at the same rate as its twin. She'd worn a corrective brace for the first two years of her life, and wherever she roamed she left a trail of scratch marks in the soft pine floor. I liked the idea that a part of one's body might be thought of as lazy – not thoughtless or hostile, just unwilling to extend itself for the betterment of the team. My father often accused my mother of having a lazy mind, while she in turn accused him of having a lazy index finger, unable to dial the phone when he knew damn well he was going to be late.

My therapy sessions were scheduled for every Thursday at 2:30, and with the exception of my mother, I discussed them with no one. The word *therapy* suggested a profound failure on my part. Mental patients had therapy. Normal people did not. I didn't see my sessions as the sort of thing that one would want to advertise, but as my teacher liked to say, "I guess it takes all kinds." Whereas my goal was to keep it a secret, hers was to inform the entire class. If I got up from my seat at 2:30, she'd say, "Sit back down, David. You've still got five minutes before your speech therapy session." If I remained seated until 2:30, she'd say, "David, don't forget you have a speech therapy session at two-thirty." On the days I was absent, I imagined she addressed the room, saying, "David's not here today but if he were, he'd have a speech therapy session at two-thirty."

My sessions varied from week to week. Sometimes I'd spend the half hour parroting whatever Agent Samson had to say. We'd occasionally pass the time examining charts on tongue position or reading childish *s*-laden texts recounting the adventures of seals or settlers named Sassy or Samuel. On the worst of days she'd haul out a tape recorder and show me just how much progress I was failing to make.

"My *s*peech therapi*s*t*'s* name i*s* Mi*ss* Chri*s*-*s*y *S*am*s*on." She'd hand me the microphone and lean back with her arms crossed. "Go ahead, *s*ay it. I want you to hear what you *s*ound like."

She was in love with the sound of her own name and seemed to view my speech impediment as a personal assault. If I wanted to spend the rest of my life as David Thedarith, then so be it. She, however, was going to be called Mi*ss* Chri*ss*y *S*am*s*on. Had her name included no *s*'s, she probably would have bypassed a career in therapy and devoted herself to yanking out healthy molars or performing unwanted clitoridectomies on the schoolgirls of Africa. Such was her personality.

"Oh, come on," my mother would say. "I'm sure she's not *that* bad. Give her a break. The girl's just trying to do her job."

I was a few minutes early one week and entered the office to find Agent Samson doing her job on Garth Barclay, a slight, kittenish boy I'd met back in the fourth grade. "You may wait outside in the hallway until it i*s* your turn," she told me. A week or two later my session was interrupted by mincing Steve Bixler, who popped his head in the door and announced that his parents were taking him out of town for a long weekend, meaning that he would miss his regular Friday session. "Thorry about that," he said.

I started keeping watch over the speech therapy door, taking note of who came and went. Had I seen one popular student leaving the office, I could have believed my mother and viewed my lisp as the sort of thing that might happen to anyone. Unfortunately, I saw no popular students. Chuck Coggins, Sam Shelton, Louis Delucca: obviously, there was some connection between a sibilate *s* and a complete lack of interest in the State versus Carolina issue.

None of the therapy students were girls. They were all boys like me who kept movie star scrapbooks and made their own curtains. "You don't want to be doing that," the men in our families would say. "That's a girl thing." Baking scones and cupcakes for the school janitors, watching *Guiding Light* with our mothers, collecting rose petals for use in a fragrant potpourri: anything worth doing turned out to be a girl thing. In order to enjoy ourselves, we learned to be duplicitous. Our stacks of *Cosmopolitan* were topped with an unread issue of *Boy's Life* or *Sports Illustrated*, and our decoupage projects were concealed beneath the sporting equipment we never asked for but always received. When asked what we wanted to be when we grew up, we hid the truth and listed who we wanted to sleep with when we grew up. "A policeman or a fireman or one of those guys who works with high-tension wires." Symptoms were feigned, and our mothers wrote notes excusing our absences on the day of the intramural softball tournament. Brian had a stomach virus or Ted suffered from that twenty-four-hour bug that seemed to be going around.

One of the*s*e day*s* I'm going to have to hang a *s*ign on that door," Agent Samson used to say. She was probably thinking along the lines of SPEECH THERAPY LAB, though a more appropriate marker would have read FUTURE HOMOSEXUALS OF AMERICA. We knocked ourselves out trying to fit in but were ultimately betrayed by our tongues. At the beginning of the school year, while we were congratulating ourselves on successfully passing for normal, Agent Samson was taking names as our assembled teachers raised their hands, saying, "I've got one in my homeroom," and "There are two in my fourth-period math class." Were they also able to spot the future drunks and depressives? Did they hope that by eliminating our lisps, they might set us on a different path, or were they trying to prepare us for future stage and choral careers?

Miss Samson instructed me, when forming an *s*, to position the tip of my tongue against the rear of my top teeth, right up against the gum line. The effect produced a sound not unlike that of a tire releasing air. It was awkward and strange-sounding, and elicited much more attention than the original lisp. I failed to see the hissy *s* as a solution to the problem and continued to talk normally, at least at home, where my lazy tongue fell upon equally lazy ears. At school, where every teacher was a potential spy, I tried to avoid an *s*ound whenever possible. "Yes," became "correct," or a military "affirmative." "Please," became "with your kind permission," and questions were pleaded rather than asked. After a few weeks of what she called "endless pestering" and what I called "repeated badgering," my mother bought me a pocket thesaurus, which provided me with *s*-free alternatives to just about everything. I consulted the book both at home in my room and at the daily learning academy other people called our school. Agent Samson was not amused when I began referring to her as an articulation coach, but the majority of my teachers were delighted. "What a nice vocabulary," they said. "My goodness, such big words!"

Plurals presented a considerable problem, but I worked around them as best I could; "rivers," for example, became either "a river or two" or "many a river." Possessives were a similar headache, and it was easier to say nothing than to announce that the left-hand and the right-hand glove of Janet had fallen to the floor. After all the compliments I had received on my improved vocabulary, it seemed prudent to lie low and keep my mouth shut. I didn't want anyone thinking I was trying to be a pet of the teacher.

When I first began my speech therapy, I worried that the Agent Samson plan might work for everyone but me, that the other boys might strengthen their lazy tongues, turn their lives around, and leave me stranded. Luckily my fears were never realized. Despite the woman's best efforts, no one seemed to make any significant improvement. The only difference was that we were all a little quieter. Thanks to Agent Samson's tape recorder, I, along with the others, now had a clear sense of what I actually sounded like. There was the lisp, of course, but more troubling was my voice itself, with its excitable tone and high, girlish pitch. I'd hear myself ordering lunch in the cafeteria, and the sound would turn my stomach. How could anyone stand to listen to me? Whereas those around me might grow up to be lawyers or movie stars, my only option was to take a vow of silence and become a monk. My former classmates would call the abbey, wondering how I was doing, and the priest would answer the phone. "You can't talk to him!" he'd say. "Why, Brother David hasn't spoken to anyone in thirty-five years!"

"Oh, relax," my mother said. "Your voice will change eventually."

"And what if it doesn't?"

She shuddered. "Don't be so morbid."

It turned out that Agent Samson was something along the lines of a circuit-court speech therapist. She spent four months at our school and then moved on to another. Our last meeting was held the day before school let out for Christmas. My classrooms were all decorated, the halls – everything but her office, which remained as bare as ever. I was expecting a regular half hour of Sassy the seal and was delighted to find her packing up her tape recorder.

"I thought that thi*s* afternoon we might let loo*s*e and have a party, you and I. How doe*s* that *s*ound?" She reached into her desk drawer and withdrew a festive tin of cookies. "Here, have one. I made them my*s*elf from *s*cratch and, boy, was it a me*ss*! Do you ever make cookie*s*?"

I lied, saying that no, I never had.

"Well, it'*s* hard work," she said. "E*s*pecially if you don't have a mixer."

It was unlike Agent Samson to speak so casually, and awkward to sit in the hot little room, pretending to have a normal conversation. "*S*o," she said, "what are your plan*s* for the holiday*s*?"

"Well, I usually remain here and, you know, open a gift from my family."

"Only one?" she asked.

"Maybe eight or ten."

"Never *s*ix or *s*even?"

"Rarely," I said.

"And what do you do on De*c*ember thirty-fir*s*t, New Year'*s* Eve?"

"On the final day of the year we take down the pine tree in our living room and eat marine life."

"You're pretty good at avoiding those *s*'s," she said. "I have to hand it to you, you're tougher than most."

I thought she would continue trying to trip me up, but instead she talked about her own holiday plans. "It's pretty hard with my fiancé in Vietnam," she said. "Last year we went up to see his folks in Roanoke, but this year

I'll spend Christmas with my grandmother outside of Asheville. My parent still will come, and we'll all try our best to have a good time. I'll eat some turkey and go to church, and then, the next day, a friend and I will drive down to Jacksonville to watch Florida play Tennessee in the Gator Bowl."

I couldn't imagine anything worse than driving down to Florida to watch a football game, but I pretended to be impressed. "Wow, that ought to be eventful."

"I was in Memphis last year when N C State whooped Georgia fourteen to seven in the Liberty Bowl," she said. "And next year, I don't care who's playing, but I want to be sitting front-row center at the Tangerine Bowl. Have you ever been to Orlando? It's a super fun place. If my future husband can find a job in his field, we're hoping to move down there within a year or two. Me living in Florida. I bet that would make you happy, wouldn't it?"

I didn't quite know how to respond. Who was this college bowl fanatic with no mixer and a fiancé in Vietnam, and why had she taken so long to reveal herself? Here I'd thought of her as a cold-blooded agent when she was really nothing but a slightly dopey, inexperienced speech teacher. She wasn't a bad person, Miss Samson, but her timing was off. She should have acted friendly at the beginning of the year instead of waiting until now, when all I could do was feel sorry for her.

"I tried my best to work with you and the others, but sometimes a person's best just isn't good enough."

She took another cookie and turned it over in her hands. "I really wanted to prove myself and make a difference in people's lives, but it's hard to do your job when you're met with so much resistance. My students don't like me, and I guess that's just the way it is. What can I say? As a speech teacher, I'm a complete failure."

She moved her hands toward her face, and I worried that she might start to cry. "Hey, look," I said. "I'm thorry."

"Ha-ha," she said. "I got you." She laughed much more than she needed to and was still at it when she signed the form recommending me for the following year's speech therapy program. "Thorry, indeed. You've got some work ahead of you, mister."

I related the story to my mother, who got a huge kick out of it. "You've got to admit that you really are a sucker," she said.

I agreed but, because none of my speech classes ever made a difference, I still prefer to use the word *chump*.

CRITICAL EYE

For Discussion

a. In looking at the world from the perspective of young David, one thing is clear: he is distrustful of teachers and other academic authority figures. Is this a sentiment you agree with? Do most students believe that the adults within the academy are less than helpful and are out to get them?

b. David believes that his speech therapy sessions had nothing to do with him having a "lazy tongue" and everything to do with his sexual orientation. Do you agree? Was his speech therapist attempting to "normalize" him?

c. Can you make the argument that the speech therapist was just doing her job and that she had no ulterior motives?

Re-approaching the Reading

Perhaps the greatest offense was not the speech therapy lessons but, rather, that young David was singled out in front of the other students. How is this process dangerous for young people, especially when we consider that it takes very little to become a target of bullying these days?

Writing Assignment

There are two relationships present within the story: student-teacher and mother-son. How do these relationships mirror each other? How do these women see David? What do they want from him?

MONIQUE FERRELL

GO BROOKLYN!

This story begins with a whimper and ends with a bang–literally and figuratively on both accounts. I had come into Manhattan with a camera crew to visit the law offices of Mason, Furman, & Shaw. It was an all-purpose, high-end firm that handled everything from divorces to murder cases.

Traditionally, the law firm had always been an "all-boys" club, but it had just added two new partners: Corrin Thomas and Madelyn Schwartz. Corrin was Black and bi-sexual. She had jet-black dreadlocks that hung to the middle of her back and was also tall with a runway model's body and looks to match. Madelyn, another tall beauty, had a head full of "I should be doing hair care commercials" blonde hair. She had piercing green eyes that I'm sure contributed to her many wins. Not because she used them to mesmerize but, instead, to intimidate and confuse juries and witnesses. While undeniably attractive, this woman seemed to be so much more, at least initially, than a "dumb blonde." The firm had hit the jackpot when they lured them from the competition. By adding these two ladies, they were firmly embracing political correctness and kissing every left-wing liberal in the mouth. The senior partners had covered almost every base. Women. Sexual Orientation. Race. I wondered if the men in charge had longed for one of them to develop a degenerative limp so they could corner the disability niche. A winning firm with those kinds of demographics would be unstoppable. Maybe the partners would pay someone to bust one of their kneecaps.

In the courtroom, Corrin and Madelyn were quite dangerous and were often referred to as the Tiger Lady and the Shark Woman respectively. I liked what I'd heard about them, their professionalism, and their antics in the courtroom. Surprise witnesses. The ability to break the opposition's witnesses. The ability to find just the right evidence at just the right time. They were both legal wunderkinds. So great were each at their jobs that when they once battled each other, the judge had to declare a mistrial because the jury was hung. Articulate. Savvy. Smart. Beautiful. Sexy. Isn't that what we want in our lawyers? What keeps us glued to our television sets watching ill-written one hour law dramas? Corrin and Madlyn had it all, and they were the only undefeated women lawyers in the city. Mason, Furman, & Shaw wanted them, and they got them. Believe me, they paid dearly to get them. It cost a very high six figures a piece just to sign them.

I thought a story on these two would fit in nicely on my current affairs news program, *The Issue At Hand.* Corrine and Madelyn were serving as co-counsel on a murder case. A well-known football player had been accused of murdering his ex-fiancé. The collective brain matter of the country was dulled by the feeling that we had all been here before. At the time, my show was the highest rated program on the highest rated news channel on cable television. So, I wasn't doing too badly myself. Some critics were heralding me as the "new" Oprah Winfrey, and, at only thirty-four years old, it was a moniker I was willing to take on.

I was a poor kid from the projects whose mother and father struggled to send me to the best schools and to ballet class twice a week to, as they called it, "keep me out of trouble, off my back, and from having some deadbeat nigga's baby." My parents are a hoot, but they meant well. They had seen too many of the young girls in our neighborhood succumb to the kinds of clichés that are the norm in "the hood."

And because of their commitment to me, I did them proud. With a Bachelor's and a Master's degree in Communications, I worked my way up from gopher and coffee getter to the host of my own number one show. I guess that's what peaked my interest in Corrin and Madelyn. Initially, they appeared to be women after my own heart–go-getters. And, halleluiah, the gender had come far, but we still had a long way to go as women. I wanted to be a part of that and help other women along the way if I could, no matter where they hailed from on the planet. So I thought it was my duty as a fellow go-getting woman to promote Corrine and Madelyn.

The news van pulled up in front of the office building on Friday at 1:00 P.M. sharp with time to spare for our 2:00 P.M. interview. This would give my camera people enough time to set up and me a chance to review my notes. As we headed toward the building, I noticed a young Hispanic woman de-boarding a city bus–briefcase and shopping bag in hand. She raced to the building's gold and brass doors looking harried and talking to herself. Once inside the building, we found her waiting at the elevator. When the elevator doors closed behind us, she pressed her floor and, noticing the cameras, asked, "Has something happened somewhere in the building?"

"No," I said, "I'm here to interview Corrin Thomas and Madelyn Schwartz."

"My goodness," she said with recognition in her eyes. "You're Desiree Mandel. You're here for Corrin and Madelyn? I'm their assistant, Bethany. They didn't tell me you were coming."

While I could tell that she was a bit astonished to see someone from television in her office space, I was sure I also detected the fact that she was a bit pissed off because no one had told her I was coming.

"Listen, why don't you get yourself settled in? It looks like you're coming back from lunch. Take a few minutes, and then let them know we're here."

She looked relieved. Hurt and relieved. The doors opened on the fiftieth floor, and Bethany led us to a lavish waiting area. She placed her briefcase behind her desk and took a shopping bag from Ellington's with her and walked into a huge meeting room where two women, clearly the women of the hour, could be seen and heard discussing what had to be a case.

"Corrin. Madelyn. Desiree Mandel is here to interview you. Oh, and Madelyn, here is your blouse."

Okay. Strike one.

Did these heffas send their assistant out to pick up a personal item?

I've been told by people over the years that I have a sixth sense. Sometimes, I can tell when a story is a dud or when a source is being less than truthful. In my personal life, I can tell by the first date if the guy is a dud or is being less than truthful–which was probably why I hadn't had a date in six months. My parents could never keep the Christmas gifts hidden, so they took to buying them on Christmas Eve. I could also read someone's character instantly. My nose twitched. Really, it did. The twitch was imperceptible to those who didn't know me well, but it was there nonetheless–a slight movement at the end of my button nose.

Both women bounced out of the office well-dressed and full of smiles. I despised them instantly. I'd been in the news game for a very long time. I could spot a good story and a bad one. This was a bad one. I hated to think it, but I was sure that these were two of the biggest bitches on planet Earth. And I had the strangest feeling that they each tortured Bethany in special ways every day. How do you not tell your assistant–who is usually the right hand in any office–that a camera crew is coming? How do you send that same assistant out to buy your damn blouse during her lunch break? They looked shocked to see her back so soon. And then it suddenly dawned on me; they hadn't *wanted* her there to greet me.

With much pomp and circumstance, they thanked me for coming. Then they told me how happy they were to meet me and asked Bethany to show us into the conference room where we could set up.

By the time the interview was over, I hated these women with everything within me. They weren't *real* women. They were two sets of breasts with sharp teeth and long claws. They fawned over each other in the interview–each heaping phony praise on the other. Puffing up their respective chests with answers that, if you listened closely, seemed to say, "Enough about me, what do think about me?"

Madelyn actually said, "It's really important for us to be here. Just think of all the opportunities we're able to give other women. Like our assistant, Bethany. She's a minority. To some, what prospects are there for her in the legal field that don't involve finger-printing and a mug shot? I mean, I hate to say it, but that's how some people see things. They don't see that she's a capable, bright woman. They may just see her Dominican face and hear her accent." Once finished, she flipped her hair over her shoulders and giggled like a five-year-old cheerleader in knee socks. Traditional dingbat move.

"Yes, this is so true," chimed in Corrin with an above-it-all and dismissive edge in her voice, all the while talking with her hands. "We still have some very serious Civil Rights issues at hand in this country. I think working here enables Bethany to see the possibilities of her life and reminds her to stay focused. We're trying to coax her into going to law school."

Wellfuckme. Yes, that's what they actually said about that very intelligent woman that my crew and I encountered on the elevator, who spoke perfect English, had no visible accent, and was not Dominican. I ought to know because I'm half Black and half Dominican, and I know my own people.

The tip of my nose was on fire.

After my time with them, I went on to interview the male partners of the firm. It was a welcome relief. They stuck to the situation at hand, being rather frank about the importance of having Corrin and Madelyn in the firm as partners. They were even honest about the fact that some of their clients were concerned about having two relatively young women in the firm. Because, as they said, women get married. Have babies. Change their priorities. In other words, men get married, have babies, never change their priorities and, most of all, they don't have periods. Horace Mason, son of founding father Davis Mason, damn near floated out of his seat every time he mentioned Madelyn's name. No question about what was going on there. Same old game. I guess casting couches were in law offices, too. A token Negro and a Dingbat. As smart as they were in the courtroom, they were nothing more than clichés. And mean-spirited at that.

After wrapping up the interview, I said my goodbyes and made my way to the bathroom. I wanted to fill a sink with cold water and dunk my head in. Once there, I looked into the mirror and shook my head at my reflection. I was already thinking of ways to edit this piece so that these very important women didn't come off looking like the assholes they were. Yeah, they probably deserved to be outed, but men have been protecting each other for generations–wasn't it our turn? I ran my fingers through my shoulder length twists and exhaled. Then I heard it.

Whimpering. Someone was crying.

"Excuse me, is someone in here?" I asked.

The far end stall door opened and out walked Bethany.

"I'm sorry Ms. Mandel. I'm so embarrassed. And I know it's unprofessional to cry at work, but I'm just a little overwhelmed today. I have a lot on my mind."

"I bet you do, Mija," I said with a smirk.

I checked every stall in the bathroom and then handed her a paper towel.

"Toma. And stop apologizing. I know what's going on here. I'm not a reporter for nothing."

"Where are you from?" she asked.

"From here. My father is Black and my mother is from the D.R. What about you? *They* seem to think you're Dominican."

"They think I'm Dominican?" she laughed loudly. "Of course they do. I'm Puerto Rican, first generation New Yorican. And my Spanish is horrible."

"Why are you in here crying?" As if I didn't already know.

"I just feel trapped. I feel like I'm never going to be the one in the office with the big cases. I just don't feel like anyone sees me. Hell, I don't even see me any more. When I leave here, I have to go to law school at night. I work like an unappreciated dog here all day. I work like a dog at school. Home is a mess. I'm just so tired, and I'm very embarrassed to be breaking down and telling you this."

"And I bet they don't make it any easier, huh?"

She didn't answer. Still protective of the lady barracudas even though they had each shown her no loyalty or respect at all. That's what happens when you're powerless; you tend to protect those who hold your future in their hands.

"Listen, Bethany, whatever you discuss with me stays within the walls of this bathroom. I know integrity is not something that many reporters have anymore, but I do. Hear what I am saying. There are 365 days in the year, which means that it is statistically impossible for you to be wrong every single one of them. Sometimes it is not you; it *is* them. Get away from these people before they kill everything that is good and strong in you."

With that, I reached into my bag and pulled out my business card.

"Call me on Monday. We have a legal department over at the station. I'm sure we can use you. Sometimes, it's who you know. Tu sabes? Knowing people seems to work around here, just ask Madelyn."

Her eyes opened wide as saucers. How had I known? Was I going to reveal it on the show? She just stood there amazed that her life had just turned on a dime. It's like that sometimes.

My own life was about to make a sudden change, and I didn't even know it.

"You're right," I said, turning to leave. "It's bad to be around people who don't see you, but you're wrong about one thing–I see you. I see you very clearly."

Once downstairs, we loaded the van and discussed bar options. We all desperately needed to get drunk to wash ourselves clean of the Tiger Lady and the Shark Woman. I turned to look at the corner where I'd seen Bethany exit her bus and hoped against hope that she'd never have to take a bus to run someone else's errands again.

Suddenly, for the second time that day, something on a city bus caught my attention.

The poster on the side of the just-arriving bus was an advertisement for an upcoming movie for a rap artist called Big Ru. The film was called *Bullet Proof.* I'd heard of the artist before. I'd even heard some of his lyrics and, as usual, I was not impressed. Moreover, I was insulted as a Black woman and as a Black person. Hell, I was insulted as a human being who walked the earth. To say I hated rap music was an understatement. These artists, if you can call them that, embarrassed me–giving me a cultural shame that I couldn't even begin to define.

But this so-called artist was special. Everyone knew him as Big Ru.

But if my eyes were not deceiving me, the man on the bus was Darnel Quincy, and, if I had my way, he was going to be in big trouble on live, national television.

The tip of my nose was on fire.

I boarded the van, cylinders clicking, already working on what I knew would be my next story and what I hoped would change the face of Hip Hop music–maybe even bring it to its knees.

Two weeks later, the story about Corrin and Madelyn aired making them look like the brilliant minds they *thought* they were. They each sent me flowers, long-winded individual *thank you* notes, and invitations to dinner with the other partners. They even seemed to forgive the fact that I'd stolen Bethany. So, I had made some powerful friends.

I was already wrapped up in my next story. I had my assistants Matt and Gloria digging up every piece of information on Big Ru, or as I knew him to be called, Darnel Quincy, that they could find. His record company, *Body Blow Records,* created a bio on Ru, a pseudonym for their constructed bad boy Alvin Jenkins, which rivaled any fairytale on the market. They had to create a life for Ru because no actual birth certificate existed. How the media had neglected to research this man thoroughly was beyond me. But how shocked could I really be? This is the madness that we had descended into as a once honorable profession. We no longer pushed stories that celebrated profound world-changing ideas or brilliant discoveries. Instead, we focused on barely researched stories that reflected our chaotic and loud drift towards mediocrity.

According to *Body Blow,* Big Ru was from the mean streets of Bed-Stuy Brooklyn. His father was doing life in prison for armed bank robbery and for killing two guards and a civilian when Ru was five. His mother was killed while turning tricks in an alley in the Bronx's Hunts Point area when he was nine. Apparently, his mother became a prostitute to support herself and Ru in his father's absence. Once an orphan, Ru's grandparents took him in, where they raised him to the best of their ability in the Paul Gleeson Housing Projects on Laurleton Street–notoriously one of the worst neighborhoods and housing developments in Brooklyn. To support himself and to protect his aging grandparents, who worked at a paper factory by the Brooklyn docks, Ru began establishing himself as a major contender in the drug game. He was merciless to those who stole from him and was determined to rule all of Brooklyn's drug trade. And then came that fateful night during his seventeenth year.

According to legend, and I do mean legend, it was a deal gone bad. Ru was supposedly set up by his nemesis, a guy named Black from a rivaling neighborhood. It was to be a swap of money and drugs, but, instead, Ru and his crew were met by handguns and semi-automatics in an abandoned building. Most of his "boys" were killed–including his nemesis–and Ru, always strapped, pulled out his gat and busted a cap in those mother. . . . I'm being facetious, but isn't that always how the cliché goes?

So he fights his way out, takes a bullet in the leg and one in the hand. He turns a corner, trying to get home and hears someone behind him. Now, here is where the street fiction comes into play–the ghetto scuttlebutt that Matt and Gloria helped me dig up. Scared and injured after the shootout, Ru turns and fires without looking and hits a boy. A ten-year-old named Darius Mead. It is then that Ru throws the gun in the sewer and, despite the fact that he hears police cars coming around the corner, he stays with the little boy, who cannot or will not say who shot him. Ru tells the cops they were both shot by the same assailant. The police, with no gun in sight, could not pin the crime on him. But, they find the drugs, and he does a nickel in a New York State prison. The child survives the gun wound and never tells the truth. Supposedly, another reason why no one could tie him to the events of that fated evening was that Ru was a background boss. A mastermind, if you will. He let his minions do his work, and, therefore, people never knew just who the top dog really was.

Clark Kent. Superman.

Back to the *Body Blow Records* biographical account. While in jail, apparently Ru has a dream. In it, his grandfather comes to him and tells him to, and I am quoting here, "Get out of his own way." He also tells him "There are all kinds of ways to make people rue the day they met you. Not all of it has to do with bloodshed."

The next eventful day behind bars, he receives word that his grandfather died the previous night from heart failure, and Ru decides to leave his life of crime behind. He also takes his grandfather's words to heart and becomes Big Ru, as in rue the day. And, poof, just like that, a Hip Hop legend was born. And who can refute the story? Everyone from the neighborhood, so-called enemies and friends alike, are dead. And the low level drug dealers who remained all wanted to attest to the fact that they both *knew* and *rolled* with Big Ru.

Welcomed by today's angry, confused, disenfranchised youth–Black, White, and everything in between–Ru became the poet of his generation. He was welcomed because everyone believed that he came up from the streets, made it, and proved his manhood.

As I read the bio *Body Blow* sent along with the notes Matt and Gloria put together, I almost peed my pants.

"Oh, what a hunk of bullshit!" I said to the papers in my hand.

"What, Des?" Matt asked with a jump. He often sat in my office while I read the research he'd help me gather. If there was something wrong or missing, he wanted to be there to explain it or to fix it.

Poor Matt. He wanted more than anything to be a reporter and was convinced that somehow he was failing me at every turn. The kid had a great mind. He was a Dean's List sophomore at one of the leading universities in the city and was interning with me. He had an eye for news, and he could write.

I didn't answer him. I just kept reading.

"Lies. Lies. Lies. Damn, how had I missed this? How long has Big Ru been putting out music?" I looked at Gloria.

"Five years now. His last two albums have all but skyrocketed him off the planet. This guy *is* Hip Hop, Desiree. And, this movie he's in, *Bullet Proof,* is about to change everything. This man is about to become *the* wealthiest rap artist ever. And he's barely thirty."

Gloria Liu was a senior researcher for the *Issue At Hand* and was next in line to become the producer of my show. The media business was about as cutthroat as everything else, but Gloria didn't take any shit and she knew her field and how to work with reporters. At 110 pounds soaking wet, and the ripe statuesque height of 4′10, this was no easy task. But she was good at her job. She was also good at training Matt. He worshiped her and thought she was brilliant.

"Okay, people," I said, snapping out of my trance. "Here's our next story."

"You want to do a story on Big Ru?"

"Yes, Matt, I do. And let me tell you why . . ."

I don't think I'd ever been so smug, but this was a big one. And, with that, I reached into my desk and pulled out my own file on Big Ru complete with interviews I'd been conducting for about two weeks. I had been calling all of my old high school friends and teachers. I even took a walk down to a precinct in good old Brooklyn and asked them about an old case involving a fourteen-year-old-boy named Darnel Quincy. And, while I was there, I asked about a notorious dealer from Bed-Stuy and his antics and found that the reason no cop or FBI or DEA agent ever came knocking at Big Ru's mansion was because they didn't know who or what the hell he was talking about. A journalist is nothing without good sources. And, once again, mine at the Public Records office located two sets of birth certificates and social security numbers that could be traced back to Darnel Quincy.

I was able to obtain college transcripts and old college identification cards. And then I pulled out my high school year book and, with a shit eating grin, I opened it to a picture of a fourteen-year-old boy dressed in his catholic school uniform. He was smiling and was surrounded by his chess teammates. The trophy, off to the side and awaiting a winner, was extravagant and taller than either of the players who, locked in a heated chess battle, were framed forever in the photo. Above him, the high school newspaper headline read, "King Me." It was The New York City High School Chess Championship, and Darnel Quincy was about to make a chess move that has yet to be bested in the subsequent years. It was probably the last day he was ever really happy.

Matt and Gloria looked at the picture.

"Who is the cute kid?" Gloria asked.

I reached into the folder and pulled out a color copy of Darnel Quincy's college I.D. "They look kinda the same. They related?" Matt asked.

And then I picked up an enlarged color photo for the cover art of Big Ru's latest album.

"He's had his nose done. That's because it was broken when he was fourteen. He's dyed his hair. He was a redhead like his mother. He's also had something done to his eyes. Reconstructive surgery. I'm sure he's had to have quite a bit of it done over the years due to his injuries. But, this my friends . . ."

". . . is fucken' Big Ru," Gloria gasped. "The chess geek is fucken' Big Ru!" As it often did whenever she got excited, I could hear a smidgen of her Chinese accent come out.

"This is a big deal. The 'slap dem bitches,' 'I'm from the hood,' 'I did time in jail,' big-time gangsta went to Catholic School? He's Catholic? And a dirty nerdy chess player, too?"

"Yep."

"But," said Matt "the Catholic Church reveres the Virgin Mary. He talks about women like, well, like they're animals. I've never seen a woman with her clothes on in his videos. At best, this is interesting. It's trippy. All rap artists lie about their reps. Not to ruin the moment for you, boss, but what's the big deal? Sure, it'll hurt him, maybe even ruin his career.

Get us some extra ratings. But it won't get us an Emmy or snagged by a bigger network or change the face of Hip Hop all that much."

"Oh, but wait. There is indeed more." And then I let it all fly . . .

When I was done, they both sat in silence with their mouths open. They could not believe that I knew this man when he was a boy—before something, a moment in time, changed his life. That's all we are, when you come to think of it, a series of moments that can maim or strengthen us. He chose his path, and now I was about to change mine.

"Are we really going to do this, Desiree?" Matt said. The Hip Hop community is going to crucify you. You'll get everything journalists dream of, but some people are going to call you a sell-out—and this may just destroy the Hip Hop industry. Or make some artists do even worse shit to prove just how *hard* they are."

"A sell-out to what, Matt? A music that hates women—women that look like me? A music that turned Black men into animals and makes it so that you—my young brown friend—can't even walk down the street without someone thinking you're a criminal? Do you think the world out there sees you, Matt? Or do you think they see a 'ghetto nigga' from one of these videos? No, it's time. Right is right. Wrong is wrong. Somebody has got to stand up. And as far as toppling *the industry,* the industry, if you can call it that, needs to be cleaned up! It, like The Black Television Network, is a disgrace to the Black people it pretends to serve and has created little more than a pimp/whore relationship between them and all of us. And, for the record, fuck an Emmy. I'm sick of that being the moment of glory for so-called journalists. I smelled a story and went after it! I did the research. I looked at a simple poster on the side of a city bus and found the story of the year because I have an eidetic memory and great journalistic savvy—that's the job. Whatever happened to getting the story? Whatever happened to finding the truth? Speaking to the cultural consciousness of our nation? We're so goddamned scared of the truth that we lie every time the camera comes on, or we love pushing someone else's lie. No sir, not me."

"I'll make the call." Having said that, Gloria picked up the phone and called the big wigs at *Body Blow Records* to ask Big Ru's people for an interview. Given the release of his new movie and its soundtrack and the status of my show, how could they say no?

When we were done, it was after 6:00 P.M. on a Friday. I asked Matt and Gloria if they wanted to get drinks and dinner. We went to *Solstice* across the street. I'd been drinking a lot lately. I knew something was coming. It was literally one of those days when you could feel your future shifting. It was like those damn stairs at Hogwarts in those *Harry Potter* books. They moved without telling you, taking you off somewhere into a new distance. And that's how I felt, like the ground was shifting beneath me. But I wasn't quite sure where I was going or how I was going to feel once I got there.

The next ten days were a haze of activity. We checked and re-checked with the legal department to make sure our asses were covered and to make sure that all of our facts were solid. After all, you can't bring down a label, slit the throat of an entire genre of music, and destroy an artist without expecting some serious repercussions.

I asked that Bethany be assigned to check each and every legal aspect of the pending show. She was happy to and was flourishing in the legal wing of my network. Because she was extra grateful to me, she went above and beyond to make sure my ass was covered. If this went as I knew it would, Matt and Gloria would be promoted, and I would start getting offers from other networks. And, of course, more money, too.

It all came together. Big Ru's company wanted him on my show. It was the imagery of it all that made their mouths water. What a coup it was going to be: the new major player in Hip Hop, fresh from prison and the ghetto, with a bevy of number one hits and a soon-to-be released movie face-to-face with the new Belle of cable news—a *sister,* at that. Even better, a half and half sister. Hip Hop spoke to both the Black and Latino youth of our country, didn't it? We shall overcome. Black is beautiful. Latino is Lovely. You can get some, too, White folks. And so could every other racial group in the middle. Up with the people. Malcolm, Martin and Mandela would have been so proud.

One of the great advantages of doing what I was going to do is that my show airs live. There would be no second takes. No editing. His first response would be his only one, and everyone who was watching would see every stutter and stammer. They'd see the tick around his eyes and mouth as I revealed every lie he'd ever told.

The night before the show, I lay in bed unable to sleep. While I date occasionally, and have had my share of serious relationships, the most recent, which lasted for three years, had ended because his job moved to France and I wouldn't go with him. I'm not one of those women who feels that she has to give it all up for love. There is nothing cute or romantic about sacrificing everything you've worked for just so you can have a man in your bed. Logically, it didn't make sense. And, I knew, that just as I'd loved him, I would love someone else.

Let's face it, not only am I a feminist, but I'm also a womanist, and I am not impressed by men. Neither do I feel them to be a necessary component of a woman's life, any more than I believe that we are necessary to men. I believe that relationships complement us. They do not complete us. And, if we allow ourselves to be defined by who we have in our beds, we miss the larger picture of who we are and what we have to offer—what we're born to do.

But I must admit, that night, I gave in to every feminine stereotype there was, because I wanted a man in my bed. I wanted to be held.

Instead, I was alone. Wide awake. Wondering.

I was doing the right thing, wasn't I? This wasn't a gimmick, was it? I wasn't doing to Darnell what Corrin and Madelyn had done to Bethany, was I? Wouldn't everybody see that I was trying to right an egregious wrong that people had learned to live with? There wasn't an ounce of cruelty in my intentions, but, rather, I just wanted the madness and the validation of that madness to stop. The end result would be good for Black people—it had to be. There are two million people in prison in this country, and over a million of them are Black. And, big frigging surprise, the majority of their crimes are drug related. And *this* fool was standing before the entire world glorifying all of this. What was worse was that he was speaking to and about a world he could never lay claim to—feeding an already helpless generation more crooked fodder for their needy veins. Rap music wasn't the cause of all of the evil that befell Black folk, but it damn sure wasn't helping. Perhaps pulling the plug on a destructive industry would free the captives so that they could get down to the work of saving their own lives. Right?

I rose the next morning after only three hours sleep. I told myself that I was just nervous because of the weight of what I was about to do. Perhaps, I thought to myself, I'd been experiencing a little racial guilt. Wasn't I selling out a Black man, a brother, for the infamous, omnipresent Man? What right did I have?

But, the other side of me, the woman in me, growing more furious by the minute, was tired of men using women as the ass rag of their world. I was tired of being inundated with catcalls on the street, the possibility of being sexually assaulted just *because.* I was tired of being paid less, of being challenged at every turn because men still didn't think we had the intestinal fortitude to defend ourselves. And, finally, music–which should have been a bastion of fair play– had been turned into a haven of misogyny and sexism. We were making these men rich beyond all imagination and allowing them to lie and beef up their reputations by way of keeping us on our backs.

Well, I wasn't a turtle. I wasn't going to lie defenseless and tuck my head inside while hoping no one would see me and run me over on the road. I'd thrown the gauntlet down– and it was going to stay there.

Big Ru arrived promptly at 7:00 P.M. He came with his manager, a White man named Skip Peterson of all things, and his album producer, Kevin Davis. He was also White. Creepy factoids: Most of the labels that produce Hip Hop are owned by White men, and most Hip Hop music is bought by White men. So, the influence and capital of the music are held by those who don't live the set of circumstances discussed in the music. They do not hail from the race and culture they profit from. Additionally, those at the forefront who perform the music are often soon parted from their money, do not seem to comprehend or care about the cultural damage they inflict on the national conscience, and are unaware of the sick cyclical nature of it all.

The three men waited in the green room after we made our introductions. Big Ru showed no signs of recognizing me. But, why would he? Darnel had spent most of his life avoiding the eyes of others–especially after that fateful day.

He was about six feet tall and had clearly been working out quite a bit. He still had those hazel eyes that almost turned green when the light hit them at a certain angle. He wore a T-shirt advertising his new movie and a pair of jeans low on his waist. He also wore a white baseball cap that read simply in bright bold, black letters: MINE. I should have paid attention to that.

The first twenty-five minutes of the program went off without a hitch. Correspondents from the field gave their reports and segued into their pre-recorded interviews. Then the real fun began. We came back from commercial, and I introduced the world to Big Ru and a little boy named Darnel Quincy.

"Good evening and welcome back to *The Issue At Hand.* Tonight, I am pleased to have the leading Hip Hop artist of all time, Big Ru. Now, should I call you Big Ru or Ru?"

"Ru is fine." He smiled revealing two rows of perfectly white, even teeth. I'd heard that ladies loved his smile and his dimples. It's easy to have a smile like that when your teeth are not your own, I thought.

"Okay, so I'll start with the obvious. One of the major and most compelling things about you, which seems to make you speak to both genders and transcend color lines, is that people seem to appreciate your rise from poverty."

"Yeah, I mean people, my fans, see me as the real deal. Maybe they look at me and think if he did it, maybe I can, too."

"But, what's so compelling about your story? It's certainly no different or any more painful than most people's. Why you?"

His face twitched.

"I think people are into me because I spit the truth. And, I turned it all around. I showed them that the world didn't break me. I broke the world."

"And, just how did you do that?"

He leaned forward in his chair and smiled. Using his hands to help articulate his reply.

"Are you kidding? I sell mad records. There are artists who have been around longer than me and I've outsold them. I'm rich. *Real* rich.

I took my people wit' me up from the ghetto. And now I'm going to be a movie star. I have changed the face of Hip Hop–again. And, I did it better."

"True, but some would argue that you've done all of that on the backs of *your* people, women, and by lying."

"I hear that all of the time. Why? Because I say nigga? Ooh, can I say that on television?"

"You just did. But, you're all about keeping it real. So let's dispense with the P.C. use of the N-word. Yes, you say nigger."

"Nigga."

"Oh stop. You know the words are the same. Let's not insult each other's intelligence. I've listened to your album, and you actually say nigger or 'nigga,' over the course of 14 songs, 213 times. Don't you think that's overkill? I say this because, as you've pointed out, you are a major contender in music..."

"*THE* contender."

"Okay, *THE* contender. Doesn't that mean you are very influential? That you are allowing and perpetuating racism, demeaning your own people, and encouraging others who are not Black to use the word? What, if anything, is your social responsibility? Or, is it just about selling albums?"

SILENCE

"So," he said, leaning forward. "This is going to be one of those interviews?"

"Meaning?"

"Meaning, you're one of those women."

"Meaning?"

"Your one of dem Feminazis. You take the music too literally and get all upset when no one is talking about *you* specifically."

"Oh, Mr. Ru–please. Don't tell me you're going to be one of those artists?"

"Meaning?" He said with a smile. Thinking I was the mouse in his cat's game.

"Meaning you are filled with double-talk and become condescending when you've painted yourself into a corner."

He smiled. All teeth now. He looked over at his manager. Not for support but, as if to say, "do you believe this bitch?"

"You see Ru, *I* am from Bed-Stuy. *I* am a child of the projects. I've got as much nerve as you think you have–and maybe a bit more. So, when you say I'm a Feminazi, I take great umbrage, because whatever you say about *any* women, you say about me. Unfortunately, we live in a society that does not always make the distinction between who *you* call a "bitch" and a "ho" and me. We have outrageous statistics when it comes to violence against women. So when you talk about smacking bitches and keeping them in their place, you *have* to be talking about me and informing men about how to respond to me."

"It's just a form of expression. It means to keep your situation straight and in order. In essence, you run things–nobody else."

"And you keep your house in order by smacking a woman and busting a cap?

"Again, you're being too literal."

"But aren't you? This is the life you're 'up from.' The majority of Blacks and Hispanics who listen to you are living through what you say you've come 'up from.' Aren't you validating their experiences of violence, or of being violated? And, since the majority of your records–hell, most rap records–are bought by White middleclass men, aren't you perpetuating a stereotype of Black men?

"I've done all that? Are *you* serious?"

"*Are you?* Your last album went diamond. If you never sell another album again, you'll never have to worry about money. Your image and those you portray in videos are cast around the globe. People in Africa and the Ukraine know who you are. You are a man of influence. I have never once heard you rap, 'pick up a book and go to college.' And you know why you don't? Because there is more money in being you."

"Because no one wants to hear that bull," he snapped and then, just as quickly, collected himself. "The world is a real place and things happen to people. People want to hear how you struggle up through that sh...stuff to make a better life."

"And, the way to do that is kill, sell dope, and smack women?"

"Sometimes. Sometimes there are no other options. It isn't pretty, but you have to tell the truth."

"The truth? That's an insult!"

"When did the truth ever become an insult?"

"The truth isn't an insult. *Pretending* to tell the truth is. Truth is relative, and the merit of what it reveals is all in the telling and the teller. No one has the right to kidnap a generation's future based upon a lie. As I've said, I'm from where you *say* you are from. I've seen what you *say* you've lived through, and it was never my truth. I wouldn't let it be. But, since you are all about truth and, believe me, the truth is very important to me, why don't you tell your fans *your* real truth? Don't you think that would help them?"

I have always believed that in a moment of crisis, backed into a corner, forced to trip over the lies you've told, you become who you really are. In Ru's case, who he *really was,* was a well-educated, articulate young man. And, everyone who was watching or listening could hear his roughneck, ebonic speech leave his verbiage.

Gloria and Matt were pacing back and forth behind the cameras. This was the moment. Ru's manager and producer knew that something was up.

"What do you mean? You are acting as if I am still a part of *that* life. Can't I be judged for who I am now? And how on earth have I become a kidnapper of a generation? Now I'm evil incarnate?"

"You are absolutely correct; I am doing my absolute best to judge everything about you. And, I'd be careful about all of the fancy talk, Darnel. Your true level of education is beginning to show."

"I'm sorry, who?"

First, he nervously shifted from side to side in his chair. And then he leaned forward. I didn't take my eyes off of him. I didn't move. I've heard that some animals turn and run when confronted by a predator. Some bury their heads in the dirt adopting the "if I can't see them, they can't see me" strategy. Others choose the stand-off, locking themselves in an eye-to-eye confrontation. For them it becomes a matter of waiting to see who makes the first move and then responding accordingly. This mode of defense was about drawing first blood and living to tell the story.

I continued.

"Darnel. Darnel Quincy. That is your real name, is it not? You are Darnel Quincy?"

Darnel's manager, Skip, took a seat in one of the studio folding chairs while his producer nudged him, miming, "What's wrong?"

But Ru was no fool. The first rule of a lie is to keep it going until the other player reveals his or her hand. Maybe, I *didn't* know everything. So what, I knew his *real* legal name. I couldn't know everything. That his parents had changed his name after the incident or that the other name was constructed by the record company. He wasn't the same. His face was different. He was older. He'd successfully assumed another personality with a fraudulent name, Social

Security number, birthday, and bio twice in one lifetime. I couldn't know everything unless I was there. But, the trouble for Big Ru, alias James Clark before college and Alvin Jenkins pre Big Ru, was that I had been there. I was a witness, and he didn't recognize me.

He played his hand.

"Suddenly we've gone from an interview to an interrogation?"

"Answer the question, or let's move on. Are you Darnel Quincy? Are you this young boy?"

And behind us, on the big full-screen monitor there sat pictures of Darnel at his chess match, Darnel as James Clark on his college I.D. card, and at his college graduation from Billford University–one of the top colleges in this country.

"You see, my question is, why is this little boy, this man, nothing to rap about? Why is Ru more of a celebration than this boy and his story? Ru is an invention. It's the same tired, redundant, irresponsible M.O. But, this boy, he has a survival story."

Darnel leaned back in his chair. He seemed neither defeated nor afraid. Actually, he seemed relieved.

"You sure you wanna go here, Miss Reporter Lady? I mean you're from the mean streets, but are you ready for me?"

It was at this point that I should have realized that Ru had left Darnel behind. He had nothing else available to him except the man he'd constructed out of the ashes of his life.

I continued.

"Is it true that you are really Darnel Quincy? That your parents were, are, quite wealthy? At one time they were both lawyers for the *top* law firm in this state. If I am correct, and I am pretty sure that I am, you grew up in the Heights section of Brooklyn where your family owned a brownstone worth well over a million dollars. Your street bio says that you were born and raised in 'the hood' and that your father is in jail and your mother, a prostitute, is deceased. But, in truth, your father is a White man named Evan Quincy. And your mother is very much alive, isn't she? My investigation also unearthed that you haven't spoken to your family since you've taken on this persona. I can see how they would want to distance themselves from you and you from them. Apparently, your father didn't much get you when you were a child, and I'm sure he's rather disgusted by you now. How could he, *they,* claim you now? How could they explain you to their colleagues and wealthy friends? They barely survived the scandal of your childhood."

I turned once again to the screen, pointing to the pictures of the young Darnel. The youthful face was both different and the same from the man who sat before me. The adult face, changed in so many ways by the skillful hand of a cosmetic surgeon, could not completely erase what the finger of God had both molded and etched while Darnel grew in his mother's womb. We are who we are. Anyone looking at the photos of the teenage boy and the so-called artist who sat before me had to see the truth.

I continued.

"Is it true that *this* boy went to a Catholic high school in Brooklyn, and that he was sweet, kind, a chess champion? Many called you a borderline genius. And, because he wasn't cool, wasn't entirely comfortable with the Black kids or the White kids but, was instead, just your run-of the-mill American nerd, he was often bullied and beaten up? Wasn't he a science and math geek? A loner who felt more comfortable with his teachers than his peers because those who were too ignorant to understand or comprehend his beauty or intellect mistreated him?

Is it true that these same bullies dragged this beautiful boy into a bathroom, and, as mobs often do, things got way out of hand and he was beaten unmercifully? Causing him to receive reconstructive surgery, especially around his nose and mouth?"

Still nothing.

"Isn't it true, Darnel, that your school underestimated just how brutal and sadistic this particular group of bullies was? That because the victimized students were so terrified of retaliation, those young tyrants literally ruled your high school unbeknownst to the administration and faculty? And isn't it true, Darnel, that to further humiliate that beautiful little boy that they sodomized him? That they made him perform oral sex on all five of them before they left him in a pool of his own blood to be found by another student? Is it true that the school was sued, lost all funding, and was subsequently closed because no one could believe that the caretakers of our children could be that oblivious? Didn't you and your parents go into hiding for a time because of the scandal and, also, to give you time to heal? Isn't it true that you've changed your name at least twice? Once before you entered college and once again before you became Ru? Do you even know who you are anymore?"

He didn't move.

"Maybe I'm wrong. Maybe Ru is real. Maybe he is Darnel's rage. I understand how rap music became appealing to you. It was the opposite of everything you used to be—everything that you believed led to your abuse and subsequent victimization. It was strong where you were weak. Irreverent where you had always been a follower of rules. Vengeance in the face of your weakness. I was there, Darnel. I went to your school. My family scrimped and saved to send me there, but I was there. Three years ahead of you. I want you to tell me, Darnel, what does truth mean to you now?"

"Well, Miss Reporter Lady, it means this," he said, pulling out a gun.

Gloria screamed and sent someone for security.

"Ru, man, don't do this!" his agent yelled.

Ru turned to the camera man and hissed, "If you shut off one camera, or leave this room, this bitch is dead."

"Leave it on," I said. "I am not scared. I'm not scared of Darnel at all."

And I wasn't. Neither was Darnel. The truth was that both of us, in our own way, were truly exhausted. Darnel was tired of carrying around three extra identities. It couldn't have been easy running away from a self that beheld the worst of everything imaginable. And then covering that same self up with another identity constructed to pretend it all away. And finally, in a last ditch effort to kill the darkness of his own soul, making a bigger and badder self that was, hopefully, mightier than every bully in the world.

Me? Maybe I was just sick and tired of being sick and tired. Maybe I'd lost all of my convictions. Maybe I didn't believe in "the truth" anymore. Perhaps all of that grandstanding in my office about the truth and change was subterfuge and bullshit. Here I was unearthing Darnel's secrets while I let the world believe a lie about Corrin and Madelyn. And it wasn't the first time I'd done it either—sculpted an impression for my viewers. I guess I just had this vision of the world, about how it *should* be, and about how it *should* feel about itself. I wanted to make that vision a reality because it seemed best. The truth is, I was beginning to lose my faith in people. We weren't making good choices anymore. We wanted "things" over the humanity of our own souls. We were being led by and emulating silly celebutants. Our children, barely able to read, comprehend science, or compute mathematical equations were the most uninspired entitled brats who believed that their parents owed them nothing less than everything. Every single economist, scientist, and poll taker had attested to the fact that as a nation we were getting dumber and fatter and, even worse, greedier.

And how do you lead a nation like that? How do you reason with them five days a week for ninety minutes? Well, sometimes you have to lie to them. Sometimes, you have to tell them the truth, but sometimes, more often than not, you have to shock the hell out of them to get them to listen or take a good hard look at themselves. In that moment with Darnel, I understood why all of our nation's presidents go almost completely gray after only a short time in office. Someone pulls them into a quiet space outside of the Oval Office and tells them what they're up against–and then they realize what they'll have to do in order to really do the job–and it scares the fuck out of them.

And that's what I'd been doing. What I was doing with Darnel. Someone had to see what we were doing to ourselves. How what we say and listen to matters. How our own ignorance and unwillingness to see had pushed this man to the brink because his supposed manhood had been challenged and we were never going to allow him to forget it. And because we weren't going to forget, he would never heal. I wanted everyone to see that all of this began with bullying. While Darnel's bullies were a bunch of rich, tyrannical sociopaths who did a few years in juvenile detention and then had their records sealed, we were all facing our own tyrants each and every day. Some of them were the drivers of our politics. Others were our bosses, spouses–hell even the unknown passersby on the street. But the bullies alone didn't hold all of the cards. It's the ill-fated maneuvers that we make in order to deal with them, or our ignoring them altogether that causes the most harm. I guess that's the point I was trying to make. Together, Darnel and I were about to find out which one of us had chosen the best option.

Darnel had not moved from his seat.

"*This* bitch is bold, huh?" he said to no one in particular. "Oh, I'm sorry," he continued, "I forgot how much you hate *that* word."

He was laughing now. That sound you emit from your throat when that fine thread between sanity and going over the deep end is all but frayed. He rose to his feet, placing the barrel of the gun to my forehead, and then, just as quickly, he stepped back and looked at me.

"Don't worry about me, Darnel. I'm a big girl. As an *actual* child of the streets, I've seen a gun before. I've seen what they can do, and I've seen them in the hands of angrier and more violent men than you."

I was pretty cocky for someone whose life was in imminent danger, no? Darnel attempted to remedy the insolence. He slapped me with his free hand. Matt yelled out for him not to hurt me. Gloria, dumbstruck, covered both sides of her face with her hands.

Ru's people did their best to calm him down. I heard my producer asking how in the hell he'd gotten a gun into the building. Everyone was afraid. But, no one left me. No one hit the deck. Everyone stayed. I'd like to believe that I'd earned the loyalty–that they cared for me as opposed to being afraid that he'd shoot each and every one of them in the back if they tried to flee to safety.

"I have to say, one day I knew this would all come out. My mother always said 'everything always comes out in the wash.' What, nothing else to say, Reporter Lady?"

I could taste the blood in my mouth. I'd bitten my lip and could feel my cheek begin to swell. I rose to face him.

"So, what do you want Darnel? What do you wish to accomplish here, and with a gun at that? They are never going to let you get out of this building. It's over. All of it."

"It's all over because you are a nosey bitch!" he screamed.

He lurched forward as if to strike me again. I stepped back and took a defensive posture.

"Darnel, if you hit me again, I'm going to make you shoot me."

There was that insolence again. When in the corner, become who you really are. And I was a fighter. If this was it, I was going to leave the world kicking and screaming.

"Oh, and she's a tough bitch, too. You think you got me all figured out? You gonna make some money offa me, Reporter Lady? Get yourself some big old ratings–maybe be a bigger star than me?"

"Oh, please, you think this is about ratings?"

I was screaming now and was losing all sense of the danger I was in.

"You think I give a shit about some damn ratings? I did this because I am sick of you! I'm sick of people like you! You keep touching the world in all of these dark and dangerous ways, and you don't give a damn about the mayhem you leave behind. I get it, something bad happened to you, and it should never have happened. But, you could have found a way to deal with it. The way millions of girls and women are told to do and made to do every god-damned day! But no, you had to create a whole other way of living in the world. You could have been a real man and told your story in a million different ways, but, instead, you've got millions of people bobbing their heads to a bunch of nonsense. You could have really made a difference–said something important . . ."

"What the fuck have I got to say, lady? Who the fuck would have listened to me then, and who gone listen to me now? You took my shit. You stripped me of my manhood. Again! Men act! I'm not a man. Do you know what happened to me in that bathroom? Bitch, you're standing here feeding me and them nothing but bullshit."

He turned to face the main camera.

"Put that shit on me, man," he said to one of the cameramen. "This society only respects a man when he's attached to money and power. Ain't that right, America? And please, let's not pretend we don't expect men to lead with a mighty hand. We don't respect a man unless he's willing to smack someone in the mouth. We don't want to know anything about little boys getting raped in bathrooms or men getting attacked in jails, right? 'Cuz then he's some kind of fag, right? Do you know my father could barely look at me after it happened? He was always disappointed in me, thought I was small and weak because I liked to read. Because I was smart. He saw all of that as a weakness. I didn't like sports. I didn't like fighting. So what, that made me fucking unlovable? Do you know he actually asked my mother why I hadn't fought back? Five against one, and he wanted to know why I hadn't fought. And you gone stand here and judge me, too? I had a right to do whatever I needed to forget. So what now, Reporter Lady? What am I supposed to do now? You gone get me therapy?"

He pointed at Skip and Davis.

"They took a chance on me. To them, I was just some suburban kid who could flow. And they invested in that. They saw something special in me," he said pounding his chest. "They made me into something. I didn't have to remember nothing about my childhood; all I had to do was make my music. So what if they made some shit up to get me some street cred? You can't sell my kind of music without none. I wasn't hurting anyone."

"Yes, you did. You hurt yourself. Look at you. You're standing here with a gun. You have three different personalities, and, in the end, you're still that little boy that no one bothered to protect. What do you need a gun for, Darnel? You aren't Ru. You don't have any enemies. You haven't been to jail. *Your* life isn't real. Everybody has got their *something* Darnel. We all get bad news, have the blues, and have a set of bad memories. You aren't better than anyone else, and you damned sure aren't entitled to any more happiness than anyone on the planet."

I turned to the screen and pointed to the newspaper clipping of him at the chess match.

"Look, Darnel, I was there when you won that trophy. Look at the screen, Darnel. I'm in the picture. I'm standing right behind you. When I think about that little boy, I don't remember the tragedy, I remember that moment. I remember his intellect. I remember a young Black kid who was bound for big things."

He stopped and looked. Suddenly, a brief smile covered his face. Just then the police entered with their guns drawn. Great, just what the situation needed, more guns. Darnel had a loaded gun on me. There were now no less than five guns trained on Darnel. I could hear more people with guns outside of the studio doors. Somewhere on the other side of the camera one of the viewers was probably cleaning a gun or using one to scratch his ass.

"Don't come up in here. So help me God! I will kill her. Stay back. I'm not done talking yet!"

"I'm okay," I said. I raised my hands as if to say "let's all just relax." I was trying to diffuse what I was certain was about to happen. "Please stop. Do not kill him. Please, I'm all right. He's not going to hurt me, and you don't need to hurt him. Right, Darnel? We're okay up here, right?"

"Put the gun down, son," one of the officers said. "No one has to get hurt here."

"Shut up, man." Darnel said. The gun was still fixed on me. "I got some shit to say. You leave that camera on."

The officers began clearing the studio. Isaac, the cameraman who always filmed my best side, agreed to stay. "I won't leave you," he mouthed. They had to drag Gloria and Matt out.

"Son, you don't want to hurt anyone. And you don't want to hurt anyone in front of all of your fans, do you?"

"Nigga, fuck you. I ain't your son."

And then he turned to the camera, speaking to a man he hadn't seen in years. He ain't my daddy, is he Pop?" he said meanly.

Turning back to the officer that had just addressed him, he said, "Man, don't try to con me. Half of my fans will cheer. The other half will move on to the next rapper. Ain't that right, Miss Reporter Lady? It's just a game. It's just a game. It was just a game all of those years ago, too. It started because someone grabbed my book bag. As usual, that's all they ever did. But this time. I got mad and hit back. You see, people only understand violence. But they had to teach me a lesson. There is a pecking order, and no one is supposed to step out of their place. I wasn't supposed to get strong."

"Darnel," I said "this isn't strength now. Ru is a lie. He lies to people. He exists because you couldn't live with what happened–something that was beyond your control. But you survived, you went to college. You . . ."

"But, I couldn't get the shit out of my mind. Don't you see? I couldn't get the shit out of my mind." He started slapping himself in the forehead with his free hand. "Darnel never grew up. He's still fourteen, laid out on a bathroom floor. He still has his mouth wired shut. His nose is still hanging off of his face. Do you know that those fuckers did juvey? Fuckenjuvey? And then they got out. And then their records were sealed. They went on and lived. They're men. Darnel isn't a man, but Ru is. Hip Hop is full of men—even if they have to pretend. No one fucks with them because of the threat of what they might do. You see, you think you know, but you don't know. And you don't know shit about being a Black man."

"Darnel. This is not being a Black man. You have been manipulating people into believing that you are a jailbird, a murderer, and a drug dealer—hoping that no one will notice that you're terrified. You were born into money, were well-educated, never hungry a day in your life, and you're a multimillionaire many times over. Your responsibility was to survive, live on, and help someone else. You sold your soul because you were too weak to live with the fact that you survived."

He shook his head and then looked me in the eyes.

"But, you didn't have the right to tell it!"

The gun began to shake in his hand. He began looking around. First at me, then at the monitor displaying the pictures, and then, finally, at the cops. He seemed stuck between worlds. He didn't know who he was anymore.

"That's enough, Darnell. Let's stop now. If you were going to shoot me, you would have done it already. I'll walk out of here with you. I won't leave your side, whatever happens. You were not born to be this, Darnel. You are not a killer. You are a chess player."

I had decided that we were both right.

And that we were both wrong.

He nodded at me. I was bridging the gap between us. The police kept screaming at me to sit down. I placed my hand on the gun.

I was reaching him.

"Put it down, Darnel. Tell the truth, and teach these people who call themselves your fans what it really means to be a man. Please. If you don't, who will?"

He didn't let go, but I sensed his resolve beginning to fade. Things would have been okay except one of the officers came too close to the stage. Darnel turned, and his eyes went wide. He didn't mean to, but he squeezed the trigger. It was an involuntary reflex. Even the camera saw that. And that's important because I want them to know that he—Darnel Quincy—did not shoot me on purpose. But I did get shot. And it was bad. And, then Darnel turned the gun on himself. And, the police officers—in their zest to stop him—shot him in the head.

We lay there in a heap, almost on top of each other, until the police closed in and separated our bleeding bodies. There was so much chaos. And so much blood. Walkie-talkies were buzzing all around me. I remember the EMS workers showing up. I remember saying, "don't let him die."

I remember an officer saying, "What did she believe would happen bringing someone like him in here?" I remember reaching out to touch Darnel as we lay side by side on our stretchers. He smiled at me through his oxygen mask. He looked so peaceful. We were being wheeled to the elevators. Matt and Gloria were at my side telling me to hold on. Darnel reached back for me.

We had said so much about truth and about who has the right to speak it. I guess I don't know what the truth is. But I know what beauty is. It's a Black man at peace. Hell, maybe it's any man at peace—unburdened of all of the trappings we heap upon them. My God, who will our little boys become if we do not let them cry?

As they wheeled him out, I remember seeing Darnel smile at me before closing his eyes for what I knew would be the very last time.

And, as for me, all the rest was silence.

Critical Eye

For Discussion

a. Our main character says that she is deeply concerned about how Black and Hispanic men and women are portrayed in the Hip Hop industry, but what gives her the right to speak for these groups?

b. By the end of the story, our main character admits that she lies to her viewers in order to push her own agenda. Is she right to do so? Must we lie to the citizens of the world in order to make them better people?

c. Whether or not you agree with the main character's deeds, can you argue that her behavior is justified?

Re-approaching the Reading

Consider this story alongside Craig's essay about Hip Hop. How are the authors' assertions about race and the Hip Hop music similar?

Writing Assignment

Consider the story from Darnel's perspective. Is he right? Why must he keep what happened to him as a child hidden? Why couldn't he "sell" his triumph over his childhood adversity? What are the consequences for him as a man after Desiree reveals his past?

MARY SHELLEY

From the Novel
FRANKENSTEIN

Chapter 16

"Cursed, cursed creator! Why did I live? Why, in that instant, did I not extinguish the spark of existence which you had so wantonly bestowed? I know not; despair had not yet taken possession of me; my feelings were those of rage and revenge. I could with pleasure have destroyed the cottage and its inhabitants and have glutted myself with their shrieks and misery.

"When night came I quitted my retreat and wandered in the wood; and now, no longer restrained by the fear of discovery, I gave vent to my anguish in fearful howlings. I was like a wild beast that had broken the toils, destroying the objects that obstructed me and ranging through the wood with a stag-like swiftness. Oh! What a miserable night I passed! The cold stars shone in mockery, and the bare trees waved their branches above me; now and then the sweet voice of a bird burst forth amidst the universal stillness. All, save I, were at rest or in enjoyment; I, like the arch-fiend, bore a hell within me, and finding myself unsympathized with, wished to tear up the trees, spread havoc and destruction around me, and then to have sat down and enjoyed the ruin.

"But this was a luxury of sensation that could not endure; I became fatigued with excess of bodily exertion and sank on the damp grass in the sick impotence of despair. There was none among the myriads of men that existed who would pity or assist me; and should I feel kindness towards my enemies? No; from that moment I declared everlasting war against the species, and more than all, against him who had formed me and sent me forth to this insupportable misery.

"The sun rose; I heard the voices of men and knew that it was impossible to return to my retreat during that day. Accordingly I hid myself in some thick underwood, determining to devote the ensuing hours to reflection on my situation.

"The pleasant sunshine and the pure air of day restored me to some degree of tranquillity; and when I considered what had passed at the cottage, I could not help believing that I had been too hasty in my conclusions. I had certainly acted imprudently. It was apparent that my conversation had interested the father in my behalf, and I was a fool in having exposed my person to the horror of his children. I ought to have familiarized the old De Lacey to me, and by degrees to have discovered myself to the rest of his family, when they should have been prepared for my approach. But I did not believe my errors to be irretrievable, and after much consideration I resolved to return to the cottage, seek the old man, and by my representations win him to my party.

"These thoughts calmed me, and in the afternoon I sank into a profound sleep; but the fever of my blood did not allow me to be visited by peaceful dreams. The horrible scene of the preceding day was forever acting before my eyes; the females were flying and the enraged Felix tearing me from his father's feet. I awoke exhausted, and finding that it was already night, I crept forth from my hiding-place, and went in search of food.

"When my hunger was appeased, I directed my steps towards the well-known path that conducted to the cottage. All there was at peace. I crept into my hovel and remained in silent expectation of the accustomed hour when the family arose. That hour passed, the sun mounted high in the heavens, but the cottagers did not appear. I trembled violently, apprehending some dreadful misfortune. The inside of the cottage was dark, and I heard no motion; I cannot describe the agony of this suspense.

"Presently two countrymen passed by, but pausing near the cottage, they entered into conversation, using violent gesticulations; but I did not understand what they said, as they spoke the language of the country, which differed from that of my protectors. Soon after, however, Felix approached with another man; I was surprised, as I knew that he had not quitted the cottage that morning, and waited anxiously to discover from his discourse the meaning of these unusual appearances.

"'Do you consider,' said his companion to him, 'that you will be obliged to pay three months' rent and to lose the produce of your garden? I do not wish to take any unfair advantage, and I beg therefore that you will take some days to consider of your determination.'

"'It is utterly useless,' replied Felix; 'we can never again inhabit your cottage. The life of my father is in the greatest danger, owing to the dreadful circumstance that I have related. My wife and my sister will never recover from their horror. I entreat you not to reason with me any more. Take possession of your tenement and let me fly from this place.'

"Felix trembled violently as he said this. He and his companion entered the cottage, in which they remained for a few minutes, and then departed. I never saw any of the family of De Lacey more.

"I continued for the remainder of the day in my hovel in a state of utter and stupid despair. My protectors had departed and had broken the only link that held me to the world. For the first time the feelings of revenge and hatred filled my bosom, and I did not strive to control them, but allowing myself to be borne away by the stream, I bent my mind towards injury and death. When I thought of my friends, of the mild voice of De Lacey, the gentle eyes of Agatha, and the exquisite beauty of the Arabian, these thoughts vanished and a gush of tears somewhat soothed me. But again when I reflected that they had spurned and deserted me, anger returned, a rage of anger, and unable to injure anything human, I turned my fury towards inanimate objects. As night advanced I placed a variety of combustibles around the cottage, and after having destroyed every vestige of cultivation in the garden, I waited with forced impatience until the moon had sunk to commence my operations.

"As the night advanced, a fierce wind arose from the woods and quickly dispersed the clouds that had loitered in the heavens; the blast tore along like a mighty avalanche and produced a kind of insanity in my spirits that burst all bounds of reason and reflection. I lighted the dry branch of a tree and danced with fury around the devoted cottage, my eyes still fixed on the western horizon, the edge of which the moon nearly touched. A part of its orb was at length hid, and I waved my brand; it sank, and with a loud scream I fired the straw, and heath, and bushes, which I had collected. The wind fanned the fire, and the cottage was quickly enveloped by the flames, which clung to it and licked it with their forked and destroying tongues.

"As soon as I was convinced that no assistance could save any part of the habitation, I quitted the scene and sought for refuge in the woods.

"And now, with the world before me, whither should I bend my steps? I resolved to fly far from the scene of my misfortunes; but to me, hated and despised, every country must be equally horrible. At length the thought of you crossed my mind. I learned from your papers that you were my father, my creator; and to whom could I apply with more fitness than to him who had given me life? Among the lessons that Felix had bestowed upon Safie, geography had not been omitted; I had learned from these the relative situations of the different countries of the earth. You had mentioned Geneva as the name of your native town, and towards this place I resolved to proceed.

"But how was I to direct myself? I knew that I must travel in a southwesterly direction to reach my destination, but the sun was my only guide. I did not know the names of the towns that I was to pass through, nor could I ask information from a single human being; but I did not despair. From you only could I hope for succour, although towards you I felt no sentiment but that of hatred. Unfeeling, heartless creator! You had endowed me with perceptions and passions and then cast me abroad an object for the scorn and horror of mankind. But on you only had I any claim for pity and redress, and from you I determined to seek that justice which I vainly attempted to gain from any other being that wore the human form.

"My travels were long and the sufferings I endured intense. It was late in autumn when I quitted the district where I had so long resided. I travelled only at night, fearful of encountering the visage of a human being. Nature decayed around me, and the sun became heatless; rain and snow poured around me; mighty rivers were frozen; the surface of the earth was hard and chill, and bare, and I found no shelter. Oh, earth! How often did I imprecate curses on the cause of my being! The mildness of my nature had fled, and all within me was turned to gall and bitterness. The nearer I approached to your habitation, the more deeply did I feel the spirit of revenge enkindled in my heart. Snow fell, and the waters were hardened, but I rested not. A few incidents now and then directed me, and I possessed a map of the country; but I often wandered wide from my path. The agony of my feelings allowed me no respite; no incident occurred from which my rage and misery could not extract its food; but a circumstance that happened when I arrived on the confines of Switzerland, when the sun had recovered its warmth and the earth again began to look green, confirmed in an especial manner the bitterness and horror of my feelings.

"I generally rested during the day and travelled only when I was secured by night from the view of man. One morning, however, finding that my path lay through a deep wood, I ventured to continue my journey after the sun had risen; the day, which was one of the first of spring, cheered even me by the loveliness of its sunshine and the balminess of the air. I felt emotions of gentleness and pleasure, that had long appeared dead, revive within me. Half surprised by the novelty of these sensations, I allowed myself to be borne away by them, and forgetting my solitude and deformity, dared to be happy. Soft tears again bedewed my cheeks, and I even raised my humid eyes with thankfulness towards the blessed sun, which bestowed such joy upon me.

"I continued to wind among the paths of the wood, until I came to its boundary, which was skirted by a deep and rapid river, into which many of the trees bent their branches, now budding with the fresh spring. Here I paused, not exactly knowing what path to pursue, when I heard the sound of voices, that induced me to conceal myself under the shade of a cypress. I was scarcely hid when a young girl came running towards the spot where I was concealed, laughing, as if she ran from someone in sport. She continued her course along the precipitous sides of the river, when suddenly her foot slipped, and she fell into the rapid stream. I rushed from my hiding-place and with extreme labour, from the force of the current, saved her and dragged her to shore. She was senseless, and I endeavoured by every means in my power to restore animation, when I was suddenly interrupted by the approach of a rustic, who was probably the person from whom she had playfully fled. On seeing me, he darted towards me, and tearing the girl from my arms, hastened towards the deeper parts of the wood. I followed speedily, I hardly knew why; but when the man saw me draw near, he aimed a gun, which he carried, at my body and fired. I sank to the ground, and my injurer, with increased swiftness, escaped into the wood.

"This was then the reward of my benevolence! I had saved a human being from destruction, and as a recompense I now writhed under the miserable pain of a wound which shattered the flesh and bone. The feelings of kindness and gentleness which I had entertained but a few moments before gave place to hellish rage and gnashing of teeth. Inflamed by pain, I vowed eternal hatred and vengeance to all mankind. But the agony of my wound overcame me; my pulses paused, and I fainted.

"For some weeks I led a miserable life in the woods, endeavouring to cure the wound which I had received. The ball had entered my shoulder, and I knew not whether it had remained there or passed through; at any rate I had no means of extracting it. My sufferings were augmented also by the oppressive sense of the injustice and ingratitude of their infliction. My daily vows rose for revenge—a deep and deadly revenge, such as would alone compensate for the outrages and anguish I had endured.

"After some weeks my wound healed, and I continued my journey. The labours I endured were no longer to be alleviated by the bright sun or gentle breezes of spring; all joy was but a mockery which insulted my desolate state and made me feel more painfully that I was not made for the enjoyment of pleasure.

"But my toils now drew near a close, and in two months from this time I reached the environs of Geneva.

"It was evening when I arrived, and I retired to a hiding-place among the fields that surround it to meditate in what manner I should apply to you. I was oppressed by fatigue and hunger and far too unhappy to enjoy the gentle breezes of evening or the prospect of the sun setting behind the stupendous mountains of Jura.

"At this time a slight sleep relieved me from the pain of reflection, which was disturbed by the approach of a beautiful child, who came running into the recess I had chosen, with all the sportiveness of infancy. Suddenly, as I gazed on him, an idea seized me that this little creature was unprejudiced and had lived too short a time to have imbibed a horror of deformity. If, therefore, I could seize him and educate him as my companion and friend, I should not be so desolate in this peopled earth.

"Urged by this impulse, I seized on the boy as he passed and drew him towards me. As soon as he beheld my form, he placed his hands before his eyes and uttered a shrill scream; I drew his hand forcibly from his face and said, 'Child, what is the meaning of this? I do not intend to hurt you; listen to me.'

"He struggled violently. 'Let me go,' he cried; 'monster! Ugly wretch! You wish to eat me and tear me to pieces. You are an ogre. Let me go, or I will tell my papa.'

"'Boy, you will never see your father again; you must come with me.'

"'Hideous monster! Let me go. My papa is a syndic–he is M. Frankenstein–he will punish you. You dare not keep me.'

"'Frankenstein! you belong then to my enemy–to him towards whom I have sworn eternal revenge; you shall be my first victim.'

"The child still struggled and loaded me with epithets which carried despair to my heart; I grasped his throat to silence him, and in a moment he lay dead at my feet.

"I gazed on my victim, and my heart swelled with exultation and hellish triumph; clapping my hands, I exclaimed, 'I too can create desolation; my enemy is not invulnerable; this death will carry despair to him, and a thousand other miseries shall torment and destroy him.'

"As I fixed my eyes on the child, I saw something glittering on his breast. I took it; it was a portrait of a most lovely woman. In spite of my malignity, it softened and attracted me. For a few moments I gazed with delight on her dark eyes, fringed by deep lashes, and her lovely lips; but presently my rage returned; I remembered that I was forever deprived of the delights that such beautiful creatures could bestow and that she whose resemblance I contemplated would, in regarding me, have changed that air of divine benignity to one expressive of disgust and affright.

"Can you wonder that such thoughts transported me with rage? I only wonder that at that moment, instead of venting my sensations in exclamations and agony, I did not rush among mankind and perish in the attempt to destroy them.

"While I was overcome by these feelings, I left the spot where I had committed the murder, and seeking a more secluded hiding-place, I entered a barn which had appeared to me to be empty. A woman was sleeping on some straw; she was young, not indeed so beautiful as her whose portrait I held, but of an agreeable aspect and blooming in the loveliness of youth and health. Here, I thought, is one of those whose joy-imparting smiles are bestowed on all but me. And then I bent over her and whispered, 'Awake, fairest, thy lover is near–he who would give his life but to obtain one look of affection from thine eyes; my beloved, awake!'

"The sleeper stirred; a thrill of terror ran through me. Should she indeed awake, and see me, and curse me, and denounce the murderer? Thus would she assuredly act if her darkened eyes opened and she beheld me. The thought was madness; it stirred the fiend within me–not I, but she, shall suffer; the murder I have committed because I am forever robbed of all that she could give me, she shall atone. The crime had its source in her; be hers the punishment! Thanks to the lessons of Felix and the sanguinary laws of man, I had learned now to work mischief. I bent over her and placed the portrait securely in one of the folds of her dress. She moved again, and I fled.

"For some days I haunted the spot where these scenes had taken place, sometimes wishing to see you, sometimes resolved to quit the world and its miseries forever. At length I wandered towards these mountains, and have ranged through their immense recesses, consumed by a burning passion which you alone can gratify. We may not part until you have promised to comply with my requisition. I am alone and miserable; man will not associate with me; but one as deformed and horrible as myself would not deny herself to me. My companion must be of the same species and have the same defects. This being you must create."

Chapter 17

The being finished speaking and fixed his looks upon me in the expectation of a reply. But I was bewildered, perplexed, and unable to arrange my ideas sufficiently to understand the full extent of his proposition. He continued,

"You must create a female for me with whom I can live in the interchange of those sympathies necessary for my being. This you alone can do, and I demand it of you as a right which you must not refuse to concede."

The latter part of his tale had kindled anew in me the anger that had died away while he narrated his peaceful life among the cottagers, and as he said this I could no longer suppress the rage that burned within me.

"I do refuse it," I replied; "and no torture shall ever extort a consent from me. You may render me the most miserable of men, but you shall never make me base in my own eyes. Shall I create another like yourself, whose joint wickedness might desolate the world. Begone! I have answered you; you may torture me, but I will never consent."

"You are in the wrong," replied the fiend; "and instead of threatening, I am content to reason with you. I am malicious because I am miserable. Am I not shunned and hated by all mankind? You, my creator, would tear me to pieces and triumph; remember that, and tell me why I should pity man more than he pities me? You would not call it murder if you could precipitate me into one of those ice-rifts and destroy my frame, the work of your own hands. Shall I respect man when he condemns me? Let him live with me in the interchange of kindness, and instead of injury I would bestow every benefit upon him with tears of gratitude at his acceptance. But that cannot be; the human senses are insurmountable barriers to our union. Yet mine shall not be the submission of abject slavery. I will revenge my injuries; if I cannot inspire love, I will cause fear, and chiefly towards you my arch-enemy, because my creator, do I swear inextinguishable hatred. Have a care; I will work at your destruction, nor finish until I desolate your heart, so that you shall curse the hour of your birth."

A fiendish rage animated him as he said this; his face was wrinkled into contortions too horrible for human eyes to behold; but presently he calmed himself and proceeded–

"I intended to reason. This passion is detrimental to me, for you do not reflect that YOU are the cause of its excess. If any being felt emotions of benevolence towards me, I should return them a hundred and a hundredfold; for that one creature's sake I would make peace with the whole kind! But I now indulge in dreams of bliss that cannot be realized. What I ask of you is reasonable and moderate; I demand a creature of another sex, but as hideous as myself; the gratification is small, but it is all that I can receive, and it shall content me. It is true, we shall be monsters, cut off from all the world; but on that account we shall be more attached to one another. Our lives will not be happy, but they will be harmless and free from the misery I now feel. Oh! My creator, make me happy; let me feel gratitude towards you for one benefit! Let me see that I excite the sympathy of some existing thing; do not deny me my request!"

I was moved. I shuddered when I thought of the possible consequences of my consent, but I felt that there was some justice in his argument. His tale and the feelings he now expressed proved him to be a creature of fine sensations, and did I not as his maker owe him all the portion of happiness that it was in my power to bestow? He saw my change of feeling and continued,

"If you consent, neither you nor any other human being shall ever see us again; I will go to the vast wilds of South America. My food is not that of man; I do not destroy the lamb and the kid to glut my appetite; acorns and berries afford me sufficient nourishment. My companion will be of the same nature as myself and will be content with the same fare. We shall make our bed of dried leaves; the sun will shine on us as on man and will ripen our food. The picture I present to you is peaceful and human, and you must feel that you could deny it only in the wantonness of power and cruelty. Pitiless as you have been towards me, I now see compassion in your eyes; let me seize the favourable moment and persuade you to promise what I so ardently desire."

"You propose," replied I, "to fly from the habitations of man, to dwell in those wilds where the beasts of the field will be your only companions. How can you, who long for the love and sympathy of man, persevere in this exile? You will return and again seek their kindness, and you will meet with their detestation; your evil passions will be renewed, and you will then have a companion to aid you in the task of destruction. This may not be; cease to argue the point, for I cannot consent."

"How inconstant are your feelings! But a moment ago you were moved by my representations, and why do you again harden yourself to my complaints? I swear to you, by the earth which I inhabit, and by you that made me, that with the companion you bestow I will quit the neighbourhood of man and dwell, as it may chance, in the most savage of places. My evil passions will have fled, for I shall meet with sympathy! My life will flow quietly away, and in my dying moments I shall not curse my maker."

His words had a strange effect upon me. I compassionated him and sometimes felt a wish to console him, but when I looked upon him, when I saw the filthy mass that moved and talked, my heart sickened and my feelings were altered to those of horror and hatred. I tried to stifle these sensations; I thought that as I could not sympathize with him, I had no right to withhold from him the small portion of happiness which was yet in my power to bestow.

"You swear," I said, "to be harmless; but have you not already shown a degree of malice that should reasonably make me distrust you? May not even this be a feint that will increase your triumph by affording a wider scope for your revenge?"

"How is this? I must not be trifled with, and I demand an answer. If I have no ties and no affections, hatred and vice must be my portion; the love of another will destroy the cause of my crimes, and I shall become a thing of whose existence everyone will be ignorant. My vices are the children of a forced solitude that I abhor, and my virtues will necessarily arise when I live in communion with an equal. I shall feel the affections of a sensitive being and become linked to the chain of existence and events from which I am now excluded."

I paused some time to reflect on all he had related and the various arguments which he had employed. I thought of the promise of virtues which he had displayed on the opening of his existence and the subsequent blight of all kindly feeling by the loathing and scorn which his protectors had manifested towards him. His power and threats were not omitted in my calculations; a creature who could exist in the ice caves of the glaciers and hide himself from pursuit among the ridges of inaccessible precipices was a being possessing faculties it would be vain to cope with. After a long pause of reflection I concluded that the justice due both to him and my fellow creatures demanded of me that I should comply with his request. Turning to him, therefore, I said,

"I consent to your demand, on your solemn oath to quit Europe forever, and every other place in the neighbourhood of man, as soon as I shall deliver into your hands a female who will accompany you in your exile."

"I swear," he cried, "by the sun, and by the blue sky of heaven, and by the fire of love that burns my heart, that if you grant my prayer, while they exist you shall never behold me again. Depart to your home and commence your labours; I shall watch their progress with unutterable anxiety; and fear not but that when you are ready I shall appear."

Saying this, he suddenly quitted me, fearful, perhaps, of any change in my sentiments. I saw him descend the mountain with greater speed than the flight of an eagle, and quickly lost among the undulations of the sea of ice.

CRITICAL EYE

For Discussion

a. Why does Victor Frankenstein create "the monster"? What is he looking for? Why does he refuse to make his creation a mate?

b. In many ways, Frankenstein is very much like a parent who is deeply disappointed in the way his/her child turned out. How is this true?

Re-approaching the Reading

How is the "monster" similar to real-life disenfranchised people who simply want to be valued and loved? Why do communities often refuse to see "different" people as being capable of possessing intellect and humanity?

Writing Topic

In what way is Shelly's text stating that we are responsible for what we create: our children, wars, illness, poverty, each other, hatred—essentially everything?

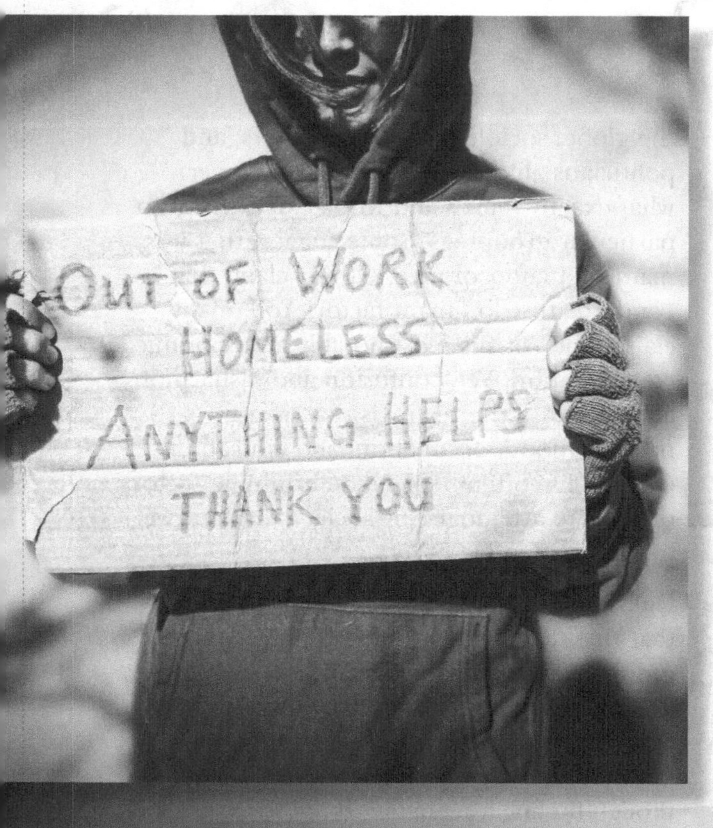

CHAPTER 5

Class and the Culture of Power

Two people can form a community by excluding a third.
Jean Paul Sartre

Power acquired by violence is only a usurpation, and lasts only as long as the force who prevails over those who obey.
Denis Diderot

We learn how to do it at a very early age: place things and people into categories. Perhaps our school years are when we first learn to make distinctions between the cool people and the nerds, our regular friends and our besties, the stylish clothes that will garner much-wanted attention and the simple clothes that will place us on the fringes of the popular world and inner circles we wish to inhabit. We learned when we were young that the world is made up of two kinds of people: those who matter and those who don't. And if, for some reason, you're in the middle, you better make sure you make it to the "right" side of the equation.

It is of little wonder that by the time we make it to adulthood we have all but mastered classifying, segregating, and disenfranchising people. What's terrifying is that we don't seem to care.

To socially classify a group of people is an idea as old as the development of civilization itself. Since the dawn of human beings, mankind has always compared itself to those forms of nature it could most readily relate with–ultimately deeming itself the dominant species. The obvious luxury of this positioning–of recognizing the species of humankind as being number one–is that those who are beneath humans on the measuring stick are often susceptible to the whims of humans as king of the world.

With this understanding, the differentiating of humanity was inevitable. Undeniably, differentiating the "haves" and the "have-nots" has been the main platform for establishing social difference–of distinguishing a society's vision of what we have come to call "Class." When it comes to Class, individuals function in society based upon the stratification that accords their grouping status.

Scientists would argue that this separation is no different than the established hierarchy that other species employ. Yet, around the globe, sociologists, philosophers, and politicians alike have attempted to discern what exactly makes and who actually fits into particular groupings. Some suggest that it is mainly a matter of race. Others claim that gender is the dominant factor. And, many claim that Class is most notably an economic consideration. Yet, confusion and disharmony arise because the reality is that language, neighborhood, occupation, and education–even looks–often become determining factors of how we are judged by society and how we, in turn, will judge others.

Unlike the strong and domineering creatures that rule the jungle or the sea, humankind's grouping and separating is far more perplexing. The interesting thing about who fits and who does not–what determines Class and what should not be a consideration–is that even though finding a set definition of social Class is, at best, as obscure as it is convoluted, all agree that social differentiation is undeniable and inescapable. The following selections seek to explore these complexities and considerations surrounding Class.

NAOMI WOLF

THE MAKING OF A SLUT

So much of the debate over issues relating to women and sexuality today is stereotypical, grinding together false dualisms of good and evil, saints and villains. All too often we discuss important issues such as teen pregnancy and date rape with a lot of name-calling but with too little real-life experience providing a background against which to measure myths and distortions.

Because sexual awakening for girls and sexuality for women are almost always complex, contextual and nuanced, I felt a need to "unpack" the statistics and the polemics. As a writer, I have faith in the power of stories to get at truths that numbers and political screeds can't reach. So this is my effort to tell some of the stories that statistics can't and that polemics won't.

Many women of my mother's generation told their stories of sexual coming-of-age in the shadow of the repressive hypocrisy of the fifties, and of "finding themselves" by casting off that era's inhibitions. For a quarter century, their conclusions have shaped our discussions of sex, women, and freedom. Those conclusions no longer fit the experiences of the two generations that have grown into womanhood during and after the sexual and feminist revolutions—generations whose experiences are sometimes so very different from those of their mothers that in some ways their stories are harder to tell, and, consequently, harder to learn from.

It is still more difficult to lay claim to the personal experiences of the slut than to those of the virgin. Women's sexual past is still materially used against them. This can happen in a court of law, a place of business, a congressional hearing, or an intimate negotiation. When someone's past "catches up with her," that woman is scapegoated and separated from the "good girls." But the punishment aimed at her inhibits all of us, and can keep us from actions ranging from charging a supervisor with sexual harassment to running for school board office to fighting for custody of children. And, in the wake of the sexual revolution, the line between "good" and "bad" girls is always shifting, keeping us unsteady, as it is meant to do.

It will not be safe for us to live comfortably in our skins until we say: "You can no longer separate us out one from another. We are all 'bad' girls."

In any group of girls, someone has to be the slut.

In our group, Dinah became the slut. She found that role—or rather, it found her—and she did not deign to fight it. She put it on with dignity.

We were fourteen and a half; it was our eighth-grade year at our junior high. After school, before she became an outcast, I used to go over to Dinah's house in the Fillmore District almost every day.

She had the gift not only of inventing a more alluring world, but of extending it to others so they could see it too. When the two of us were alone, a glamour would descend on us. Dinah had a chewed-up collection of records of musicals, and for her these created an alternative world. Singing along with them, her pointed chin would lift upward as she sang, and her red-rimmed eyes would light up, and she would lose her tough scrapper quality. The headache-tight Lee jeans, the hair darkened with henna streaks, the pookah shell necklaces, the run-down hiking boots, would all disappear. She became Mary Martin in the South Seas or Auntie Mame loose on Manhattan.

But Dinah was the slut. She became the slut because of conditions so tangential that they could almost never have been, or could as easily have slipped the designation to someone else. She was poor; that is, poorer than the other white kids. And her body changed faster than many of the other girls'. Her breasts were large and high by seventh grade—but that visitation had come to other girls, too. It was how she decided to carry it that did her in.

She refused the good-girl slump, the binder held crosswise across her chest. She would not back down and rest her weight on her pelvis and ruin her line. Instead she flagrantly kept walking with her spine extended to her full height, her back slightly swayed. I understood what she was doing with her tailbone tucked under and her torso supple and erect like a figure on the prow of a ship, and her feet turned carefully out: she was being a star. She was thinking of the technique of stage movement that she was reading about in the books on drama, and trying always to imagine a fine filament connecting the top of her talented head to the heavens. She was walking always out to her public, graciously, for an encore. But there was no visual language in our world for a poor girl with big breasts walking tall except "slut."

By watching what happened to Dinah, we discovered that sex—for girls at least—was a game of musical chairs. It was very important to stay in the game, if always nervously moving; but finding yourself suddenly singled out was nothing short of fatal. And—just like that game—the rules that isolated one or another of us were arbitrary and capricious. One thing was certain: if you were targeted, no matter how randomly, whether you had moved not fast enough or too fast for the music, in some sure way your exclusion was your own fault.

Dinah was a spectacular dancer. On late afternoons, she could usually be found practicing steps alone in our school's shabby music room, head up, facing solemnly into the wall-length mirror. Dinah's kicks were higher and her splits deeper than those of any of the other girls over whom she towered in our class. She was more than disciplined with herself—she was almost brutal in the service of what she thought of, very levelly, as her art. There was a genre of teenage-girl novels in which a hardworking and usually orphaned ballet student pits her all to attain the great performance and accolades, and then a life of grace and ease. Dinah devoured these books.

It was no surprise that, when the call for cheerleader auditions went out, it provoked her competitive spirit. We were not the kind of girls to approach the cheerleader squad with straight faces. But the idea of a test—even more compellingly, a test of skill and charm—seduced us. Cheerleading was sexy, but for once it was a sexuality that was also absolutely safe for us.

The junior high school cheerleading squad would be chosen not by P.E. or drama teachers on the basis of physical skill, but rather, by a panel of regular subject teachers. These teachers thought of themselves as the conscience of the school. ("And," as one was overheard to say, "the cheerleaders represent the school.") They saw a heavily made-up girl, in her short red-leather jacket and midriff cropped T-shirt, leaning against a graffiti-stained wall every afternoon with the guys in the band, smoking; and they thought they knew all about Dinah.

For weeks, Dinah prepared. She believed in merit. In the try-out red plush outfit that she had sewn herself, she played the role of "wholesome cheerleader"—the only jarring note being the crease of metallic blue eye shadow that, against the dictates of Seventeen magazine, she insisted on applying daily. On the afternoon of the tryout, Dinah was tense. But her performance of the two cheers was, insofar as such a crude and bouncy set piece could be, a star turn. She held out her arms to the dark and silent auditorium seats, pom-poms lifted in an exuberant V, and then swooped them low.

The panel of teachers sat in the center of the pit, in the otherwise empty auditorium, their faces impassive.

Then the other girls and I tried out, sheepishly, in jeans. None of us were any better than pedestrian in contrast to Dinah. We went back outside to wait for the panel's decision.

A secretary posted a typewritten list outside the gym door. She avoided our eyes. All the new members of the team consisted of commonly acknowledged "popular" older girls. And me. In a mostly poor and working-class school, almost all of the chosen were daughters of the middle class. And—in a student population that was mostly Chinese, Japanese, Filipino, or African American—almost all were white. Dinah was not even an alternate.

I felt sick.

Dinah looked at the list on the door. She made her "Judy Garland chin-out struggling" face, then laughed at herself. "You," she said, "don't know what to say."

She shrugged her shoulders under her leather jacket. "It's that I hang out with the wrong group, that's all," she said. She looked past me to the hills above the playground, and assumed the ironic detachment she was so good at. "Well," she said crisply, lighting a Marlboro and then making one perfect French curl of smoke, "it can't be because they think I don't know how to dance."

We filed to the bus stop together in silence. We had been classified differently and we knew it. Our companionship was never exactly the same again.

The girl named head cheerleader, called "the cutest girl in ninth grade" and paragon of her church group, was no angel. But her parents were "nice" and her clothes were good. The popular girls whom the teachers approved of often conducted their sexual experiences after sneaking away from their parents' cabanas on the white-sand beaches of family vacations. Dinah went out with nineteen-year-old store clerk motorcycle rockers and lay around on foam mattresses in garages.

Dinah got called a slut because she was too poor and she was too proud of her body, and, by implication, she was too proud of her sexuality.

By the time we reached high school, Dinah had found a new gang. They were mostly guys, the rough kind of guys. Class considerations, which were like invisible, undeniable hands moving us over a school-sized chessboard, directed Dinah to a whole new group of girls. The whole school spread rumors that girls in that gang had mastered every technique in *The Sensuous Woman.*

Years later, another woman who as a girl was familiar with what was becoming Dinah's world, said that fellatio was the first genuine adult skill she ever mastered except driving, and that it made her feel just as powerful, just as valuable and free of her childhood helplessness. She spoke about the feeling among the girls in that subculture that sex was a performance for the benefit of boys.

Dinah's reputation worsened as we got older. But I also guess from having known her that during the same time in her life that her name became a fixture on the boys' bathroom walls, she was probably studying and trying to keep her family life together. According to the junior high and high school grapevine, when she heard about the graffiti in the bathrooms that talked about her blow jobs, she thought it was funny. At least, I heard she laughed. I believed it. She liked to shock the world that had repudiated her.

By our junior year in high school, her clothes tighter and her makeup heavier than ever, Dinah still seemed proud, and she still carried herself with that head-held-high, fuck-you regalness. I don't know for sure what she was thinking because I stopped knowing her–the result of that adolescent social dynamic, when class or race or gender pulls friends apart, that is so irrevocable. Class had declared her a slut by fourteen, while she was still technically a virgin, and kept her there, and kept me and my other wild little middle-class friends safe. As she passed us in the halls, her face grew more and more impassive with every year. That still haunts me.

From her story, and the stories of so many others, I knew that "keeping control of my desire was the only key to keeping myself and my emerging identity safe. So much depended on my taking the careful, balanced paces of a tightrope walker. Go–but DON'T JUMP!!! Go, but go slow, and keep watching. Yet part of me wanted above all else the experience of shutting my eyes and falling through the air.

I knew I was dangerous to myself the day that I let a boy walk me home from school and drew me into the overgrown alley that ran alongside the stone staircase up the hill to my house. He pushed the hair away from my forehead and then kissed my forehead, as if to make everything all right. He kissed down the side of my face to the corner of my mouth, too shy to look me in the eyes, but moving always closer to my lips. All I had to do was turn my face up toward him, and hold perfectly still. It was the easiest important thing I had ever done.

I knew that arching my neck just a little meant, "That's all right; go on." His hand lay against my clavicle and then against my chest above my collar. Finally, he slid just the tips of his fingers not even to my breast but to the skin between that lay just inside the line of my clothing. Through my closed eyes, the light went red. He withdrew his hand and watched my face. Even as the cold air rippled my shirt, his fingerprints were still burning.

He was watching to see if it was all right. It wasn't all right. I was capable of anything. I was capable of being Dinah.

Almost every society punishes its sluts in its own ways. It's just that right now, our own sometimes pretends it does not. The summer that I went back home to ask my friends about our girlhoods, there was a rash of sex industry films coming out of Hollywood. *Striptease* and *Showgirls* were following their predecessor, *Pretty Woman.* Teenage girls were reading about how Demi Moore worked out for hours each day to play a stripper; how she would go to the strip joints and hang with the dancers to "get it right."

As we drove through the hills above Marin, I asked a friend who had grown up with us what she thought about those films. Her opinion was better informed than most of ours was, for she had spent time as a stripper, and later as a professional mistress. She embodied the contradiction we live under: a college-educated, happily married, community-minded woman with curly black hair, a hip way of wearing her tailored clothes, a timid grin–indistinguishable from any of the rest of our tribe. But by the standards of the culture she had been a real whore, a true, dyed-in-the-wool, no-argument, verifiable slut.

She had gone all the way. The bad girl, the good girl—the dimorphism was a fantasy. They were both here in the car; in her, in myself, in us all.

As she drove, the carefree mood of two women in their early thirties thinking about girlhood in an open car, feet on the dashboard and reggae on the radio, evaporated. "Here is all I have to say about how they are glamorizing those images for girls, who are just sucking it in," she said. Her words became slow and deliberate. "When men think a woman is a whore, it's open . . . season . . . on her. They can say anything to her they want, they can do anything they want, they can be absolutely as crass and vile and violent and cruel and uncaring as the darkest part of their personality wants to be. And it's okay. They don't have to afford the woman one ounce of respect for being a human being. She's not a human being. She's a thing.

"Since the sexual revolution, there's a license, and there's terror, and we're living under . . . both."

Then the words came out in a torrent. "I was shocked. I was shocked. I thought that because of the progress that women have made in our society men would have a clue that prostitutes are human beings and that they don't deserve to be treated so poorly, but they don't. It's almost as if now they see sex workers as the only women that they can be so aggressive and cruel to. They can't get away with it in their jobs anymore, they can't get away with it in their marriages, but with sex workers, it's okay. That's what they're paid for! They're paid to be sexually harassed, they're paid to be assaulted. Women outside the sex industry won't put up with it anymore."

I was quiet. I was thinking: if all women, even nice women, can do what only whores used to do, but you can no longer treat all women who do such things like whores—that is, if feminism is succeeding at breaking down some of the penalties that used to be directed at nonprofessional, sexually licentious women—then society will all the more rigidly professionalize and demarcate the bad girl for sale, to whom anything can be done. My friend was explaining that "real" prostitutes used to bear the burden of the fact that nice girls had a limited repertoire; now they bear the burden of the fact that nice girls have gotten wild.

The feeling of foreboding that had hung over the word "slut" in my sexually libertine girlhood became clearer. The culture had said: Take it off. Take it all off. The culture had also said, of the raped girl, of the hitchhiker, of the dead girl: She was in the wrong place at the wrong time, doing the wrong thing.

Suddenly, as the soft round hills sped by, I saw flash before my eyes a photograph from one of the social histories I had been reading. It was of the nearly intact, mummified remains, dating from the first century a.d., of a fourteen-year-old German girl. Her long, shapely legs and slender feet were intact, and her right arm still clutched the garrote that had been used to twist the rope around her neck. Her lips were still in an O of surprise or pain, and a twisted rag was still securely bound against her eyes. At fourteen, the girl had been blindfolded, strangled, and drowned, most likely as retribution for "adultery"—for what we would call a teenage love affair.

Given these origins, it is no wonder that even today fourteen-year-old girls who notice, let alone act upon, desire have the heart-racing sense that they are doing something obscurely, but surely, dangerous. It is also in part because of this inheritance that a contemporary woman wakes up after a night of being erotically "out of control" feeling sure, on some primal level, that something punitive is bound to happen to her—and that if it doesn't, it should.

CRITICAL EYE

For Discussion

a. Why are women held to a different sexual standard than men?

b. Are mothers now, in our modern-day society, more capable of speaking to their daughters about their own sexual experiences and desires?

c. Wolf argues that we make life very dangerous for the "bad girl." How is this true?

Re-approaching the Reading

Imagine a world where all women embrace the title of "slut." How would such a feat affect gender relations in America?

Writing Assignment

Can you argue that so-called "bad girls" are actually living Emerson's idea of being nonconformists?

MARK TWAIN

THE LOWEST ANIMAL

I have been studying the traits and dispositions of the "lower animals" (so-called), and contrasting them with the traits and dispositions of man. I find the result humiliating to me. For it obliges me to renounce my allegiance to the Darwinian theory of the Ascent of Man from the Lower Animals; since it now seems plain to me that that theory ought to be vacated in favor of a new and truer one, this new and truer one to be named the Descent of Man from the Higher Animals.

In proceeding toward this unpleasant conclusion I have not guessed or speculated or conjectured, but have used what is commonly called the scientific method. That is to say, I have subjected every postulate that presented itself to the crucial test of actual experiment, and have adopted it or rejected it according to the result. Thus I verified and established each step of my course in its turn before advancing to the next. These experiments were made in the London Zoological Gardens, and covered many months of painstaking and fatiguing work.

Before particularizing any of the experiments, I wish to state one or two things which seem to more properly belong in this place than further along. This in the interest of clearness. The massed experiments established to my satisfaction certain generalizations, to wit:

1. That the human race is of one distinct species. It exhibits slight variations–in color, stature, mental caliber, and so on–due to climate, environment, and so forth: but it is a species by itself, and not to be confounded with any other.
2. That the quadrupeds are a distinct family, also. This family exhibits variations–in color, size, food preferences and so on; but it is a family by itself.
3. That the other families–the birds, the fishes, the insects, the reptiles, etc.–are more or less distinct, also. They are in the procession. They are links in the chain which stretches down from the higher animals to man at the bottom.

Some of my experiments were quite curious. In the course of my reading I had come across a case where, many years ago, some hunters on our Great Plains organized a buffalo hunt for the entertainment of an English earl–that, and to provide some fresh meat for his larder. They had charming sport. They killed seventy-two of those great animals: and ate part of one of them and left the seventy-one to rot. In order to determine the difference between an anaconda and an earl–if any–I caused seven young calves to be turned into the anaconda's cage. The grateful reptile immediately crushed one of them and swallowed it. Then lay back satisfied. It showed no further interest in the calves, and no disposition to harm them. I tried this experiment with other anacondas: always with the same result. The fact stood proven that the difference between an earl and an anaconda is that the earl is cruel and the anaconda isn't; and that the earl wantonly destroys what he has no use for, but the anaconda doesn't. This seemed to suggest that the anaconda was not descended from the earl. It also seemed to suggest that the earl was descended from the anaconda, and had lost a good deal in the transition.

I was aware that many men who have accumulated more millions of money than they can ever use have shown a rabid hunger for more, and have not scrupled to cheat the ignorant and the helpless out of their poor servings in order to partially appease that appetite. I furnished a hundred different kinds of wild and tame animals the opportunity to accumulate vast stores of food, but none of them would do it. The squirrels and bees and certain birds made accumulations, but stopped when they had gathered a winter's supply, and could not be persuaded to add to it either honestly or by chicane. In order to bolster up a tottering reputation the ant pretended to store up supplies, but I was not deceived. I know the ant. These experiments convinced me that there is this difference between man and the higher animals: he is avaricious and miserly, they are not.

In the course of my experiments I convinced myself that among the animals man is the only one that harbors insults and injuries, broods over them, waits till a chance offers, then takes revenge. The passion of revenge is unknown to the higher animals.

Roosters keep harems, but it is by consent of their concubines: therefore no wrong is done. Men keep harems, but it is by brute force, privileged by atrocious laws which the other sex is allowed no hand in making. In this matter man occupies a far lower place than the rooster.

Cats are loose in their morals, but not consciously so. Man, in his descent from the cat, has brought the cat's looseness with him but has left the unconsciousness behind—the saving grace which excuses the cat. The cat is innocent, man is not.

Indecency, vulgarity, obscenity—these are strictly confined to man: he invented them. Among the higher animals there is no trace of them. They hide nothing; they are not ashamed. Man, with his soiled mind, covers himself. He will not even enter a drawing room with his breast and back naked, so alive are he and his mates to indecent suggestion. Man is "The Animal that Laughs." But so does the monkey, as Mr. Darwin pointed out; and so does the Australian bird that is called the laughing jackass. No—Man is the Animal that Blushes. He is the only one that does it—or has occasion to.

At the head of this article we see how "three monks were burnt to death" a few days ago, and a prior "put to death with atrocious cruelty." Do we inquire into the details? No; or we should find out that the prior was subjected to unprintable multilations. Man—when he is a North American Indian—gouges out his prisoner's eyes; when he is King John, with a nephew to render untroublesome, he uses a red-hot iron; when he is a religious zealot dealing with heretics in the Middle Ages, he skins his captive alive and scatters salt on his back; in the first Richard's time he shuts up a multitude of Jew families in a tower and sets fire to it; in Columbus's time he captures a family of Spanish Jews and—but *that* is not printable; in our day in England a man is fined ten shillings for beating his mother nearly to death with a chair, and another man is fined forty shillings for having four pheasant eggs in his possession without being able to satisfactorily explain how he got them. Of all the animals, man is the only one that is cruel. He is the only one that inflicts pain for the pleasure of doing it. It is a trait that is not known to the higher animals. The cat plays with the frightened mouse; but she has this excuse, that she does not know that the mouse is suffering. The cat is moderate—unhumanly moderate: she only scares the mouse, she does not hurl it; she doesn't dig out its eyes, or tear off its skin, or drive splinters under its nails—man-fashion; when she is done playing with it she makes a sudden meal of it and puts it out of its trouble. Man is the Cruel Animal. He is alone in that distinction.

The higher animals engage in individual fights, but never in organized masses. Man is the only animal that deals in that atrocity of atrocities. War. He is the only one that gathers his brethren about him and goes forth in cold blood and with calm pulse to exterminate his kind. He is the only animal that for sordid wages will march out, as the Hessians[1] did in our Revolution, and as the boyish Prince Napoleon did in the Zulu war, and help to slaughter strangers of his own species who have done him no harm and with whom he has no quarrel.

Man is the only animal that robs his helpless fellow of his country—takes possession of it and drives him out of it or destroys him. Man has done this in all the ages. There is not an acre of ground on the globe that is in possession of its rightful owner, or that has not been taken away from owner after owner, cycle after cycle, by force and bloodshed.

Man is the only Slave. And he is the only animal who enslaves. He has always been a slave in one form or another, and has always held other slaves in bondage under him in one way or another. In our day he is always some man's slave for wages, and does that man's work; and this slave has other slaves under him for minor wages, and they do *his* work. The higher animals are the only ones who exclusively do their own work and provide their own living.

Man is the only Patriot. He sets himself apart in his own country, under his own flag, and sneers at the other nations, and keeps multitudinous uniformed assassins on hand at heavy expense to grab slices of other people's countries, and keep *them* from grabbing slices of *his*. And in the intervals between campaigns he washes the blood off his hands and works for "the universal brotherhood of man"—with his mouth.

Man is the Religious Animal. He is the only Religious Animal. He is the only animal that has the True Religion—several of them. He is the only animal that loves his neighbor as himself, and cuts his throat if his theology isn't straight. He has made a graveyard of the globe in trying his honest best to smooth his brother's path to happiness and heaven. He was at it in the time of the Caesars, he was at it in Mahomet's time, he was at it in the time of the Inquisition, he was at it in France a couple of centuries, he was at it in England in Mary's day, he has been at it ever since he first saw the light, he is at it today in Crete—as per the telegrams quoted above—he will be at it somewhere else tomorrow. The higher animals have no religion. And we are told that they are going to be left out, in the Hereafter. I wonder why? It seems questionable taste.

Man is the Reasoning Animal. Such is the claim. I think it is open to dispute. Indeed, my experiments have proven to me that he is the Unreasoning Animal. Note his history, as sketched above. It seems plain to me that whatever he is he is *not* a reasoning animal. His record is the fantastic record of a maniac. I consider that the strongest count against his intelligence is the fact that with that record back of him he blandly sets himself up as the head animal of the lot: whereas by his own standards he is the bottom one.

In truth, man is incurably foolish. Simple things which the other animals easily learn, he is incapable of learning. Among my experiments was this. In an hour I taught a cat and a dog to be friends. I put them

[1]Hessians: the German auxillary soldiers brought over by the British to fight the Americans during the Revolutionary War.

in a cage. In another hour I taught them to be friends with a rabbit. In the course of two days I was able to add a fox, a goose, a squirrel and some doves. Finally a monkey. They lived together in peace; even affectionately.

Next, in another cage I confined an Irish Catholic from Tipperary, and as soon as he seemed tame I added a Scotch Presbyterian from Aberdeen. Next a Turk from Constantinople; a Greek Christian from Crete; an Armenian; a Methodist from the wilds of Arkansas; a Buddhist from China; a Brahman from Benares. Finally, a Salvation Army Colonel from Wapping. Then I stayed away two whole days. When I came back to note result, the cage of Higher Animals was all right, but in the other there was but a chaos of gory odds and ends of turbans and fezzes and plaids and bones and flesh—not a specimen left alive. These Reasoning Animals had disagreed on a theological detail and carried the matter to a Higher Court.

One is obliged to concede that in true loftiness of character, Man cannot claim to approach even the meanest of the Higher Animals. It is plain that he is constitutionally incapable of approaching that altitude; that he is constitutionally afflicted with a Defect which must make such approach forever impossible, for it is manifest that this defect is permanent in him, indestructible, ineradicable.

I find this Defect to be *the Moral Sense.* He is the only animal that has it. It is the secret of his degradation. It is the quality *which enables him to do wrong.* It has no other office. It is incapable of performing any other function. It could never have been intended to perform any other. Without it, man could do no wrong. He would rise at once to the level of the Higher Animals.

Since the Moral Sense has but the one office, the one capacity—to enable man to do wrong—it is plainly without value to him. It is as valueless to him as is disease. In fact, it manifestly is a disease. *Rabies* is bad, but it is not so bad as this disease. Rabies enables a man to do a thing which he could not do when in a healthy state: kill his neighbor with a poisonous bite. No one is the better man for having rabies. The Moral Sense enables a man to do wrong. It enables him to do wrong in a thousand ways. Rabies is an innocent disease, compared to the Moral Sense. No one, then, can be the better man for having the Moral Sense. What, now, do we find the Primal Curse to have been? Plainly what it was in the beginning: the infliction upon man of the Moral Sense; the ability to distinguish good from evil; and with it, necessarily, the ability to *do* evil; for there can be no evil act without the presence of consciousness of it in the doer of it.

And so I find that we have descended and degenerated, from some far ancestor—some microscopic atom wandering at its pleasure between the mighty horizons of a drop of water perchance—insect by insect, animal by animal, reptile by reptile, down the long highway of smirchless innocence, till we have reached the bottom stage of development—namable as the Human Being. Below us—nothing.

Critical Eye

For Discussion

a. What commentary is Twain making about mankind?

b. Is he making a distinction between men and women?

c. Throughout history, what has man done to prove the validity of Twain's essay?

d. Read Emerson's *Nature* (download) and examine how it addresses Twain's positions.

Re-approaching the Reading

Apply Twain's perspective to how man continues to treat endangered species.

Writing Assignment

Early American colonists believed in the notion of Manifest Destiny, which stressed the notion of the settlers being ordained by God to cultivate America and tame its inhabitants. The book of Genesis in the Old Testament stresses the right of Adam to have dominion over the Earth and the animals therein. In what way(s) do these biblical assessments subvert Twain's argument?

JHUMPA LAHIRI

INTERPRETER OF MALADIES

At the tea stall Mr. and Mrs. Das bickered about who should take Tina to the toilet. Eventually Mrs. Das relented when Mr. Das pointed out that he had given the girl her bath the night before. In the rearview mirror Mr. Kapasi watched as Mrs. Das emerged slowly from his bulky white Ambassador, dragging her shaved, largely bare legs across the back seat. She did not hold the little girl's hand as they walked to the rest room.

They were on their way to see the Sun Temple at Konarak. It was a dry, bright Saturday, the mid-July heat tempered by a steady ocean breeze, ideal weather for sightseeing. Ordinarily Mr. Kapasi would not have stopped so soon along the way, but less than five minutes after he'd picked up the family that morning in front of Hotel Sandy Villa, the little girl had complained. The first thing Mr. Kapasi had noticed when he saw Mr. and Mrs. Das, standing with their children under the portico of the hotel, was that they were very young, perhaps not even thirty. In addition to Tina they had two boys, Ronny and Bobby, who appeared very close in age and had teeth covered in a network of flashing silver wires. The family looked Indian but dressed as foreigners did, the children in stiff, brightly colored clothing and caps with translucent visors. Mr. Kapasi was accustomed to foreign tourists; he was assigned to them regularly because he could speak English. Yesterday he had driven an elderly couple from Scotland, both with spotted faces and fluffy white hair so thin it exposed their sunburnt scalps. In comparison, the tanned, youthful faces of Mr. and Mrs. Das were all the more striking. When he'd introduced himself, Mr. Kapasi had pressed his palms together in greeting, but Mr. Das squeezed hands like an American so that Mr. Kapasi felt it in his elbow. Mrs. Das, for her part, had flexed one side of her mouth, smiling dutifully at Mr. Kapasi, without displaying any interest in him.

As they waited at the tea stall, Ronny, who looked like the older of the two boys, clambered suddenly out of the back seat, intrigued by a goat tied to a stake in the ground.

"Don't touch it," Mr. Das said. He glanced up from his paperback tour book, which said "INDIA" in yellow letters and looked as if it had been published abroad. His voice, somehow tentative and a little shrill, sounded as though it had not yet settled into maturity.

"I want to give it a piece of gum," the boy called back as he trotted ahead.

Mr. Das stepped out of the car and stretched his legs by squatting briefly to the ground. A clean-shaven man, he looked exactly like a magnified version of Ronny. He had a sapphire blue visor, and was dressed in shorts, sneakers, and a T-shirt. The camera slung around his neck, with an impressive telephoto lens and numerous buttons and markings, was the only complicated thing he wore. He frowned, watching as Ronny rushed toward the goat, but appeared to have no intention of intervening. "Bobby, make sure that your brother doesn't do anything stupid."

"I don't feel like it," Bobby said, not moving. He was sitting in the front seat beside Mr. Kapasi, studying a picture of the elephant god taped to the glove compartment.

"No need to worry," Mr. Kapasi said. "They are quite tame." Mr. Kapasi was forty-six years old, with receding hair that had gone completely silver, but his butterscotch complexion and his unlined brow, which he treated in spare moments to dabs of lotus-oil balm, made it easy to imagine what he must have looked like at an earlier age. He wore gray trousers and a matching jacket-style shirt, tapered at the waist, with short sleeves and a large pointed collar, made of a thin but durable synthetic material. He had specified both the cut and the fabric to his tailor–it was his preferred uniform for giving tours because it did not get crushed during his long hours behind the wheel. Through the windshield he watched as Ronny circled around the goat, touched it quickly on its side, then trotted back to the car.

"You left India as a child?" Mr. Kapasi asked when Mr. Das had settled once again into the passenger seat.

"Oh, Mina and I were both born in America," Mr. Das announced with an air of sudden confidence. "Born and raised. Our parents live here now, in Assansol. They retired. We visit them every couple years." He turned to watch as the little girl ran toward the car, the wide purple bows of her sundress flopping on her narrow brown shoulders. She was holding to her chest a doll with yellow hair that looked as it it had been chopped, as a punitive measure, with pair of dull scissors. "This is Tina's first trip to India, isn't it, Tina?"

"I don't have to go to the bathroom anymore," Tina announced.

"Where's Mina?" Mr. Das asked.

Mr. Kapasi found it strange that Mr. Das should refer to his wife by her first name when speaking to the little girl. Tina pointed to where Mrs. Das was purchasing something from one of the shirtless men who worked at the tea stall. Mr. Kapasi heard one of the shirtless men sing a phrase from a popular Hindi love song as Mrs. Das walked back to the car, but she did not appear to understand the words of the song, for she did not express irritation, or embarrassment, or react in any other way to the man's declarations.

He observed her. She wore a red-and-white-checkered skirt that stopped above her knees, slip-on shoes with a square wooden heel, and a close-fitting blouse styled like a man's undershirt. The blouse was decorated at chest-level with a calico appliqué in the shape of a strawberry. She was a short woman, with small hands like paws, her frosty pink fingernails painted to match her lips, and was slightly plump in her figure. Her hair, shorn only a little longer than her husband's, was parted far to one side. She was wearing large dark brown sunglasses with a pinkish tint to them, and carried a big straw bag, almost as big as her torso, shaped like a bowl, with a water bottle poking out of it. She walked slowly, carrying some puffed rice tossed with peanuts and chili peppers in a large packet made from newspapers. Mr. Kapasi turned to Mr. Das.

"Where in America do you live?"

"New Brunswick, New Jersey."

"Next to New York?"

"Exactly. I teach middle school there."

"What subject?"

"Science. In fact, every year I take my students on a trip to the Museum of Natural History in New York City. In a way we have a lot in common, you could say, you and I. How long have you been a tour guide, Mr. Kapasi?"

"Five years."

Mrs. Das reached the car. "How long's the trip?" she asked, shutting the door,

"About two and a half hours," Mr. Kapasi replied.

At this Mrs. Das gave an impatient sigh, as if she had been traveling her whole life without pause. She fanned herself with a folded Bombay film magazine written in English.

"I thought that the Sun Temple is only eighteen miles north of Puri," Mr. Das said, tapping on the tour book.

"The roads to Konarak are poor. Actually it is a distance of fifty-two miles," Mr. Kapasi explained.

Mr. Das nodded, readjusting the camera strap where it had begun to chafe the back of his neck.

Before starting the ignition. Mr. Kapasi reached back to make sure the cranklike locks on the inside of each of the back doors were secured. As soon as the car began to move the little girl began to play with the lock on her side, clicking it with some effort forward and backward, but Mrs. Das said nothing to stop her. She sat a bit slouched at one end of the back seat, not offering her puffed rice to anyone. Ronny and Tina sat on either side of her, both snapping bright green gum.

"Look," Bobby said as the car began to gather speed. He pointed with his finger to the tall trees that lined the road. "Look."

"Monkeys!" Ronny shrieked. "Wow!"

They were seated in groups along the branches, with shining black faces, silver bodies, horizontal eyebrows, and crested heads. Their long gray tails dangled like a series of ropes among the leaves. A few scratched themselves with black leathery hands, or swung their feet, staring as the car passed.

"We call them the hanuman," Mr. Kapasi said. "They are quite common in the area."

As soon as he spoke, one of the monkeys leaped into the middle of the road, causing Mr. Kapasi to brake suddenly. Another bounced onto the hood of the car, then sprang away. Mr. Kapasi beeped his horn. The children began to get excited, sucking in their breath and covering their faces partly with their hands. They had never seen monkeys outside of a zoo, Mr. Das explained. He asked Mr. Kapasi to stop the car so that he could take a picture.

While Mr. Das adjusted his telephoto lens, Mrs. Das reached into her straw bag and pulled out a bottle of colorless nail polish, which she proceeded to stroke on the tip of her index finger.

The little girl stuck out a hand. "Mine too. Mommy, do mine too."

"Leave me alone," Mrs. Das said, blowing on her nail and turning her body slightly. "You're making me mess up."

The little girl occupied herself by buttoning and unbuttoning a pinafore on the doll's plastic body.

"All set," Mr. Das said, replacing the lens cap.

The car rattled considerably as it raced along the dusty road, causing them all to pop up from their seats every now and then, but Mrs. Das continued to polish her nails. Mr. Kapasi eased up on the accelerator, hoping to produce a smoother ride. When he reached for the gearshift the boy in front accommodated him by swinging his hairless knees out of the way. Mr. Kapasi noted that this boy was slightly paler than than other children. "Daddy, why is the driver sitting on the wrong side in this car, too?" the boy asked.

"They all do that here, dummy," Ronny said.

"Don't call your brother a dummy," Mr. Das said. He turned to Mr. Kapasi. "In America, you know . . . it confuses them."

"Oh yes, I am well aware," Mr. Kapasi said. As delicately as he could, he shifted gears again, accelerating as they approached a hill in the road. "I see it on *Dallas,*° the steering wheels are on the left-hand side."

"What's *Dallas?*" Tina asked, hanging her now naked doll on the seat behind Mr. Kapasi.

"It went off the air," Mr. Das explained. "It's a television show."

They were all like siblings, Mr. Kapasi thought as they passed a row of date trees. Mr. and Mrs. Das behaved like an older brother and sister, not parents. It seemed that they were in charge of the children only for the day; it was hard to believe they were regularly responsible for anything other than themselves. Mr. Das tapped on his lens cap, and his tour book, dragging his thumbnail occasionally across the pages so that they made a scraping sound. Mrs. Das continued to polish her nails. She had still not removed her sunglasses. Every now and then Tina renewed her plea that she wanted her nails done, too, and so at one point Mrs. Das flicked a drop of polish on the little girl's finger before depositing the bottle back inside her straw bag.

"Isn't this an air-conditioned car?" she asked, still blowing on her hand. The window on Tina's side was broken and could not be rolled down.

"Quit complaining," Mr. Das said. "It isn't so hot."

"I told you to get a car with air-conditioning," Mrs. Das continued. "Why do you do this, Raj, just to save a few stupid rupees. What are you saving us, fifty cents?"

Their accents sounded just like the ones Mr. Kapasi heard on American television programs, though not like the ones on *Dallas.*

"Doesn't it get tiresome, Mr. Kapasi, showing people the same thing every day?" Mr. Das asked, rolling down his own window all the way. "Hey, do you mind stopping the car? I just want to get a shot of this guy."

Mr. Kapasi pulled over to the side of the road as Mr. Das took a picture of a barefoot man, his head wrapped in a dirty turban, seated on top of a cart of grain sacks pulled by a pair of bullocks. Both the man and the bullocks were emaciated. In the back seat Mrs. Das gazed out another window, at the sky, where nearly transparent clouds passed quickly in front of one another.

"I look forward to it, actually," Mr. Kapasi said as they continued on their way. "The Sun Temple is one of my favorite places. In that way it is a reward for me. I give tours on Fridays and Saturdays only. I have another job during the week."

"Oh? Where?" Mr. Das asked.

"I work in a doctor's office."

"You're a doctor?"

"I am not a doctor. I work with one. As an interpreter."

"What does a doctor need an interpreter for?"

"He has a number of Gujarati patients. My father was Gujarati, but many people do not speak Gujarati in this area, including the doctor. And so the doctor asked me to work in his office, interpreting what the patients say."

"Interesting. I've never heard of anything like that," Mr. Das said.

Mr. Kapasi shrugged. "It is a job like any other."

"But so romantic," Mrs. Das said dreamily, breaking her extended silence. She lifted her pinkish brown sunglasses and arranged them on top of her head like a tiara. For the first time, her eyes met Mr. Kapasi's in the rearview mirror: pale, a bit small, their gaze fixed but drowsy.

Mr. Das craned to look at her. "What's so romantic about it?"

"I don't know. Something." She shrugged, knitting her brows together for an instant. "Would you like a piece of gum, Mr. Kapasi?" she asked brightly. She reached into her straw bag and handed him a small square wrapped in green-and-striped paper. As soon as Mr. Kapasi put the gum in his mouth a thick sweet liquid burst onto his tongue.

"Tell us more about your job, Mr. Kapasi," Mrs. Das said.

"What would you like to know, madame?"

"I don't know," she shrugged, munching on some puffed rice and licking the mustard oil from the corners of her mouth. "Tell us a typical situation." She settled back in her seat, her head tilted in a patch of sun, and closed her eyes. "I want to picture what happens."

"Very well. The other day a man came in with a pain in his throat."

"Did he smoke cigarettes?"

"No. It was very curious. He complained that he felt as if there were long pieces of straw stuck in his throat. When I told the doctor he was able to prescribe the proper medication."

"That's so neat."

"Yes," Mr. Kapasi agreed after some hesitation.

"So these patients are totally dependent on you," Mrs. Das said. She spoke slowly, as if she were thinking aloud. "In a way, more dependent on you than the doctor."

"How do you mean? How could it be?"

"Well, for example, you could tell the doctor that the pain felt like a burning, not straw. The patient would never know what you had told the doctor, and the doctor wouldn't know that you had told the wrong thing. It's a big responsibility."

"Yes, a big responsibility you have there, Mr. Kapasi," Mr. Das agreed.

Mr. Kapasi had never thought of his job in such complimentary terms. To him it was a thankless occupation. He found nothing noble in interpreting people's maladies, assiduously translating the symptoms of so many swollen bones, countless cramps of bellies and bowels, spots on people's palms that changed color, shape, or size. The doctor, nearly half his age, had an affinity for bell-bottom trousers and made humorless jokes about the Congress party. Together they worked in a stale little infirmary where Mr. Kapasi's smartly tailored clothes clung to him in the heat, in spite of the blackened blades of a ceiling fan churning over their heads.

The job was a sign of his failings. In his youth he'd been a devoted scholar of foreign languages, the owner of an impressive collection of dictionaries. He had dreamed of being an interpreter for diplomats and dignitaries, resolving conflicts between people and nations, settling disputes of which he alone could understand both sides. He was a self-educated man. In a series of notebooks, in the evenings before his parents settled his marriage, he has listed the common etymologies of words, and at one point in his life he was confident that he could converse, if given the opportunity, in English, French, Russian, Portuguese, and Italian, not to mention Hindi, Bengali, Orissi, and Gujarati. Now only a handful of European phrases remained in his memory, scattered words for things like saucers and chairs. English was the only non-Indian language he spoke fluently anymore. Mr. Kapasi knew it was not a remarkable talent. Sometimes he feared that his children knew better English than he did, just from watching television. Still, it came in handy for the tours.

He had taken the job as an interpreter after his first son, at the age of seven, contracted typhoid–that was how he had first made the acquaintance of the doctor. At the time

Mr. Kapasi had been teaching English in a grammar school, and he bartered his skills as an interpreter to pay the increasingly exorbitant medical bills. In the end the boy had died one evening in his mother's arms, his limbs burning with fever, but then there was the funeral to pay for, and the other children who were born soon enough, and the newer, bigger house, and the good schools and tutors, and the fine shoes and the television, and the countless other ways he tried to console his wife and to keep her from crying in her sleep, and so when the doctor offered to pay him twice as much as he earned at the grammar school, he accepted. Mr. Kapasi knew that his wife had little regard for his career as an interpreter. He knew it reminded her of the son she'd lost, and that she resented the other lives he helped, in his own small way, to save. If ever she referred to his position, she used the phrase "doctor's assistant," as if the process of interpretation were equal to taking someone's temperature, or changing a bedpan. She never asked him about the patients who came to the doctor's office, or said that his job was a big responsibility.

For this reason it flattered Mr. Kapasi that Mrs. Das was so intrigued by his job. Unlike his wife, she had reminded him of its intellectual challenges. She had also used the word "romantic." She did not behave in a romantic way toward her husband, and yet she had used the word to describe him. He wondered if Mr. and Mrs. Das were a bad match, just as he and his wife were. Perhaps they, too, had little in common apart from three children and a decade of their lives. The signs he recognized from his own marriage were there—the bickering, the indifference, the protracted silences. Her sudden interest in him, an interest she did not express in either her husband or her children, was mildly intoxicating. When Mr. Kapasi thought once again about how she had said "romantic," the feeling of intoxication grew.

He began to check his reflection in the rearview mirror as he drove, feeling grateful that he had chosen the gray suit that morning and not the brown one, which tended to sag a little in the knees. From time to time he glanced through the mirror at Mrs. Das. In addition to glancing at her face he glanced at the strawberry between her breasts, and the golden brown hollow in her throat. He decided to tell Mrs. Das about another patient, and another: the young woman who had complained of a sensation of raindrops in her spine, the gentleman whose birthmark had begun to sprout hairs. Mrs. Das listened attentively, stroking her hair with a small plastic brush that resembled an oval bed of nails, asking more questions, for yet another example. The children were quiet, intent on spotting more monkeys in the trees, and Mr. Das was absorbed by his tour book, so it seemed like a private conversation between Mr. Kapasi and Mrs. Das. In this manner the next half hour passed, and when they stopped for lunch at a roadside restaurant that sold fritters and omelette sandwiches, usually something Mr. Kapasi looked forward to on his tours so that he could sit in peace and enjoy some hot tea, he was disappointed. As the Das family settled together under a magenta umbrella fringed with white and orange tassels, and placed their orders with one of the waiters who marched about in tricornered caps, Mr. Kapasi reluctantly headed toward a neighboring table.

"Mr. Kapasi, wait. There's room here," Mrs. Das called out. She gathered Tina onto her lap, insisting that he accompany them. And so, together, they had bottled mango juice and sandwiches and plates of onions and potatoes deep-fried in graham-flour batter. After finishing two omelette sandwiches Mr. Das took more pictures of the group as they ate.

"How much longer?" he asked Mr. Kapasi as he paused to load a new roll of film in the camera.

"About half an hour more."

By now the children had gotten up from the table to look at more monkeys perched in a nearby tree, so there was a considerable space between Mrs. Das and Mr. Kapasi. Mr. Das placed the camera to his face and squeezed one eye shut, his tongue exposed at one corner of his mouth. "This looks funny. Mina, you need to lean in closer to Mr. Kapasi."

She did. He could smell a scent on her skin, like a mixture of whiskey and rosewater. He worried suddenly that she could smell his perspiration, which he knew had collected beneath the synthetic material of his shirt. He polished off his mango juice in one gulp and smoothed his silver hair with his hands. A bit of the juice dripped onto his chin. He wondered if Mrs. Das had noticed.

She had not. "What's your address, Mr. Kapasi?" she inquired, fishing for something inside her straw bag.

"You would like my address?"

"So we can send you copies," she said. "Of the pictures." She handed him a scrap of paper which she had hastily ripped from a page of her film magazine. The blank portion was limited, for the narrow strip was crowded by lines of text and a tiny picture of a hero and heroine embracing under a eucalyptus tree.

The paper curled as Mr. Kapasi wrote his address in clear, careful letters. She would write to him, asking about his days interpreting at the doctor's office, and he would respond eloquently, choosing only the most entertaining anecdotes, ones that would make her laugh out loud as she read them in her house in New Jersey. In time she would reveal the disappointment of her marriage, and he his. In this way their friendship would grow, and flourish. He would possess a picture of the two of them, eating fried onions under a magenta umbrella, which he would keep, he decided, safely tucked between the pages of his Russian grammar. As his mind raced, Mr. Kapasi experienced a mild and pleasant shock. It was similar to a feeling he used to experience long ago when, after months of translating with the aid of a dictionary, he would finally read a passage from a French novel, or an Italian sonnet, and understand the words, one after another, unencumbered by his own efforts. In those moments Mr. Kapasi used to believe that all was right with the world, that all struggles were rewarded, that all of life's mistakes made sense in the end. The promise that he would hear from Mrs. Das now filled him with the same belief.

When he finished writing his address Mr. Kapasi handed her the paper, but as soon as he did so he worried that he had either misspelled his name, or accidentally reversed the numbers of his postal code. He dreaded the possibility of a lost letter, the photograph never reaching him, hovering somewhere in Orissa, close but ultimately unattainable. He thought of asking for the slip of paper again, just to make sure he had written his address accurately, but Mrs. Das had already dropped it into the jumble of her bag.

They reached Konarak at two-thirty. The temple, made of sandstone, was a massive pyramid-like structure in the shape of a chariot. It was dedicated to the great master of life, the sun, which struck three sides of the edifice as it made its journey each day across the sky. Twenty-four giant wheels were carved on the north and south sides of the plinth. The whole thing was drawn by a team of seven horses, speeding as if through the heavens. As they approached, Mr. Kapasi explained that the temple had been built between A.D. 1243 and 1255, with the efforts of twelve hundred artisans, by the great ruler of the Ganga dynasty, King Narasimhadeva the First, to commemorate his victory against the Muslin army.

"It says the temple occupies about a hundred and seventy acres of land," Mr. Das said, reading from his book.

"It's like a desert," Ronny said, his eyes wandering across the sand that stretched on all sides beyond the temple.

"The Chandrabhaga River once flowed one mile north of here. It is dry now," Mr. Kapasi said, turning off the engine.

They got out and walked toward the temple, posing first for pictures by the pair of lions that flanked the steps. Mr. Kapasi led them next to one of the wheels of the chariot, higher than any human being, nine feet in diameter.

"'The wheels are supposed to symbolize the wheel of life,'" Mr. Das read. "'They depict the cycle of creation, preservation, and achievement of realization.' Cool." He turned the page of his book. "'Each wheel is divided into eight thick and thin spokes, dividing the day into eight equal parts. The rims are carved with designs of birds and animals, whereas the medallions in the spokes are carved with women in luxurious poses, largely erotic in nature.'"

What he referred to were the countless friezes of entwined naked bodies, making love in various positions, women clinging to the necks of men, their knees wrapped eternally around their lovers' thighs. In addition to these were assorted scenes from daily life, of hunting and trading, of deer being killed with bows and arrows and marching warriors holding swords in their hands.

It was no longer possible to enter the temple, for it had filled with rubble years ago, but they admired the exterior, as did all the tourists Mr. Kapasi brought there, slowly strolling along each of its sides. Mr. Das trailed behind, taking pictures. The children ran ahead, pointing to figures of naked people, intrigued in particular by the Nagamithunas, the half-human, half-serpentine couples who were said, Mr. Kapasi told them, to live in the deepest waters of the sea. Mr. Kapasi was pleased that they liked the temple, pleased especially that it appealed to Mrs. Das. She stopped every three or four paces, staring silently at the carved lovers, and the processions of elephants, and the topless female musicians beating on two-sided drums.

Though Mr. Kapasi had been to the temple countless times, it occurred to him, as he, too, gazed at the topless women, that he had never seen his own wife fully naked. Even when they had made love she kept the panels of her blouse hooked together, the string of her petticoat knotted around her waist. He had never admired the backs of his wife's legs the way he now admired those of Mrs. Das, walking as if for his benefit alone. He had, of course, seen plenty of bare limbs before, belonging to the American and European ladies who took his tours. But Mrs. Das was different, Unlike the other women, who had an interest only in the temple, and kept their noses buried in a guidebook, or their eyes behind the lens of a camera, Mrs. Das had taken an interest in him.

Mr. Kapasi was anxious to be alone with her, to continue their private conversation, yet he felt nervous to walk at her side. She was lost behind her sunglasses, ignoring her husband's requests that she pose for another picture, walking past her children as if they were strangers. Worried that he might disturb her, Mr. Kapasi walked ahead, to admire, as he always did, the three life-sized bronze avatars of Surya, the sun god, each emerging from its own niche on the temple facade to greet the sun at dawn, noon, and evening. They wore elaborate headdresses, their languid, elongated eyes closed, their bare chests draped with carved chains and amulets. Hibiscus petals, offerings from previous visitors, were strewn at their gray-green feet. The last statue, on the northern wall of the temple, was Mr. Kapasi's favorite. This Surya had a tired expression, weary after a hard day of work, sitting astride a horse with folded legs. Even his horse's eyes were drowsy.

Around his body were smaller sculptures of women in pairs, their hips thrust to one side.

"Who's that?" Mrs. Das asked. He was startled to see that she was standing beside him.

"He is the Astachala-Surya," Mr. Kapasi said. "The setting sun."

"So in a couple of hours the sun will set right here?" She slipped a foot out of one of her square-heeled shoes, rubbed her toes on the back of her other leg.

"That is correct."

She raised her sunglasses for a moment, then put them back on again. "Neat."

Mr. Kapasi was not certain exactly what the word suggested, but he had a feeling it was a favorable response. He hoped that Mrs. Das had understood Surya's beauty, his power. Perhaps they would discuss it further in their letters. He would explain things to her, things about India, and she would explain things to him about America. In its own way this correspondence would fulfill his dream, of serving as an interpreter between nations. He looked at her straw bag, delighted that his address lay nestled among its contents. When he pictured her so many thousands of miles away he plummeted, so much so that he had an overwhelming urge to wrap his arms around her, to freeze with her, even for an instant, in an embrace witnessed by his favorite Surya. But Mrs. Das had already started walking.

"When do you return to America?" he asked, trying to sound placid.

"In ten days."

He calculated: A week to settle in, a week to develop the pictures, a few days to compose her letter, two weeks to get to India by air. According to his schedule, allowing room for delays, he would hear from Mrs. Das in approximately six weeks' time.

The family was silent as Mr. Kapasi drove them back, a little past four-thirty, to Hotel Sandy Villa. The children had bought miniature granite versions of the chariot's wheels at a souvenir stand, and they turned them round in their hands. Mr. Das continued to read his book. Mrs. Das untangled Tina's hair with her brush and divided it into two little ponytails.

Mr. Kapasi was beginning to dread the thought of dropping them off. He was not prepared to begin his six-week wait to her from Mrs. Das. As he stole glances at her in the rearview mirror, wrapping elastic bands around Tina's hair, he wondered how he might make the tour last a little longer. Ordinarily he sped back to Puri using a shortcut, eager to return home, scrub his feet and hands with sandalwood soap, and enjoy the evening newspaper and a cup of tea that his wife would serve him in silence. The though of that silence, something to which he'd long been resigned, now oppressed him. It was then that he suggested visiting the hills and Udayagiri and Khandagiri, where a number of monastic dwellings were hewn out of the ground, facing one another across a defile. It was some miles away, but well worth seeing, Mr. Kapasi told them.

"Oh yeah, there's something mentioned about it in this book," Mr. Das said. "Built by a Jain king or something."

"Shall we go then?" Mr. Kapasi asked. He paused at a turn in the road. "It's to the left."

Mr. Das turned to look at Mrs. Das. Both of them shrugged.

"Left, left," the children chanted.

Mr. Kapasi turned the wheel, almost delirious with relief. He did not know what he would do or say to Mrs. Das once they arrived at the hills. Perhaps he would tell her what a pleasing smile she had. Perhaps he would compliment her strawberry shirt, which he found irresistibly becoming. Perhaps, when

Mr. Das was busy taking a picture, he would take her hand.

He did not have to worry. When they got to the hills, divided by a steep path thick with trees, Mrs. Das refused to get out of the car. All along the path, dozens of monkeys were seated on stones, as well as on the branches of the trees. Their hind legs were stretched out in front and raised to shoulder level, their arms resting on their knees.

"My legs are tired," she said, sinking low in her seat. "I'll stay here."

"Why did you have to wear those stupid shoes?" Mr. Das said. "You won't be in the pictures."

"Pretend I'm there."

"But we could use one of these pictures for our Christmas card this year. We didn't get one of all five of us at the Sun Temple. Mr. Kapasi could take it."

"I'm not coming. Anyway, those monkeys give me the creeps."

"But they're harmless," Mr. Das said. He turned to Mr. Kapasi. "Aren't they?"

"They are more hungry than dangerous," Mr. Kapasi said. "Do not provoke them with food, and they will not bother you."

Mr. Das headed up the defile with the children, the boys at his side, the little girl on his shoulders. Mr. Kapasi watched as they crossed paths with a Japanese man and woman, the only other tourists there, who paused for a final photograph, then stepped into a nearby car and drove away. As the car disappeared out of view some of the monkeys called out, emitting soft whooping sounds, and then walked on their flat black hands and feet up the path. At one point a group of them formed a little ring around Mr. Das and the children. Tina screamed in delight. Ronny ran in circles around his father. Bobby bent down and picked up a fat stick on the ground. When he extended it, one of the monkeys approached him and snatched it, then briefly beat the ground.

"I'll join them," Mr. Kapasi said, unlocking the door on his side. "There is much to explain about the caves."

"No. Stay a minute," Mrs. Das said. She got out of the back seat and slipped in beside Mr. Kapasi. "Raj has his dumb book anyway." Together, through the windshield, Mrs. Das and Mr. Kapasi watched as Bobby and the monkey passed the stick back and forth between them.

"A brave little boy," Mr. Kapasi commented.

"It's not so surprising," Mrs. Das said.

"No?"

"He's not his."

"I beg your pardon?"

"Raj's. He's not Raj's son."

Mr. Kapasi felt a prickle on his skin. He reached into his shirt pocket for the small tin of lotus-oil balm he carried with him at all times, and applied it to three spots on his forehead. He knew that Mrs. Das was watching him, but he did not turn to face her. Instead he watched as the figures of Mr. Das and the children grew smaller, climbing up the steep path, pausing every now and then for a picture, surrounded by a growing number of monkeys.

"Are you surprised?" The way she put it made him choose his words with care.

"It's not the type of thing one assumes," Mr. Kapasi replied slowly. He put the tin of lotus-oil balm back in his pocket.

"No, of course not. And no one knows, of course. No one at all. I've kept it a secret for eight whole years." She looked at Mr. Kapasi, tilting her chin as if to gain a fresh perspective. "But now I've told you."

Mr. Kapasi nodded. He felt suddenly parched, and his forehead was warm and slightly numb from the balm. He considered asking Mrs. Das for a sip of water, then decided against it.

"We met when we were very young," she said. She reached into her straw bag in search of something, then pulled out a packet of puffed rice. "Want some?"

"No, thank you."

She put a fistful in her mouth, sank into the seat a little, and looked away from Mr. Kapasi, out the window on her side of the car. "We married when we were still in college. We were in high school when he proposed. We went to the same college, of course. Back then we couldn't stand the thought of being separated, not for a day, not for a minute. Our parents were best friends who lived in the same town. My entire life I saw him every weekend, either at our house or theirs. We were sent upstairs to play together while our parents joked about our marriage. Imagine! They never caught us at anything, though in a way I think it was all more or less a setup. The things we did those Friday and Saturday nights, while our parents sat downstairs drinking tea . . . I could tell you stories, Mr. Kapasi."

As a result of spending all her time in college with Raj, she continued, she did not make many close friends. There was no one to confide in about him at the end of a difficult day, or to share a passing thought or a worry. Her parents now lived on the other side of the world, but she had never been very close to them, anyway. After marrying so young she was overwhelmed by it all, having a child so quickly, and nursing, and warming up bottles of milk and testing their temperature against her wrist while Raj was at work, dressed in sweaters and corduroy pants, teaching his students about rocks and dinosaurs. Raj never looked cross or harried, or plump as she had become after the first baby.

Always tired, she declined invitations from her one or two college girlfriends, to have lunch or shop in Manhattan. Eventually the friends stopped calling her, so that she was left at home all day with the baby, surrounded by toys that made her trip when she walked or wince when she sat, always cross and tired. Only occasionally did they go out after Ronny was born, and even more rarely did they entertain. Raj didn't mind; he looked forward to coming home from teaching and watching television and bouncing Ronny on his knee. She had been outraged when Raj told her that a Punjabi friend, someone whom she had once met but did not remember, would be staying with them for a week for some job interviews in the New Brunswick area.

Bobby was conceived in the afternoon, on a sofa littered with rubber teething toys, after the friend learned that a London pharmaceutical company had hired him, while Ronny cried to be freed from his playpen. She made no protest when the friend touched the small of her back as she was about to make a pot of coffee, then pulled her against his crisp navy suit. He made love to her swiftly, in silence, with an expertise she had never known, without the meaningful expressions and smiles Raj always insisted on afterward. The next day Raj drove the friend to JFK. He was married now, to a Punjabi girl, and they lived in London still, and every year they exchanged Christmas cards with Raj and Mina, each couple tucking photos of their families into the envelopes. He did not know that he was Bobby's father. He never would.

"I beg your pardon, Mrs. Das, but why have you told me this information?" Mr. Kapasi asked when she had finally finished speaking, and had turned to face him once again.

"For God's sake, stop calling me Mrs. Das. I'm twenty-eight. You probably have children my age."

"Not quite." It disturbed Mr. Kapasi to learn that she thought of him as a parent. The feeling he had had toward her, that had made him check his reflection in the rearview mirror as they drove, evaporated a little.

"I told you because of your talents." She put the packet of puffed rice back into her bag without folding over the top.

"I don't understand," Mr. Kapasi said.

"Don't you see? For eight years I haven't been able to express this to anybody, not friends, certainly not to Raj. He doesn't even suspect it. He thinks I'm still in love with him. Well, don't you have anything to say?"

"About what?"

"About what I've just told you. About my secret, and about how terrible it makes me feel. I feel terrible looking at my children, and at Raj, always terrible. I have terrible urges, Mr. Kapasi, to throw things away. One day I had the urge to throw everything I own out the window, the television, the children, everything. Don't you think it's unhealthy?"

He was silent.

"Mr. Kapasi, don't you have anything to say? I thought that was your job."

"My job is to give tours, Mrs. Das."

"Not that. Your other job. As an interpreter."

"But we do not face a language barrier. What need is there for an interpreter?"

"That's not what I mean. I would never have told you otherwise. Don't you realize what it means for me to tell you?"

"What does it mean?"

"It means that I'm tired of feeling so terrible all the time. Eight years, Mr. Kapasi, I've been in pain eight years. I was hoping you could help me feel better, say the right thing. Suggest some kind of remedy."

He looked at her, in her red plaid skirt and strawberry T-shirt, a woman not yet thirty, who loved neither her husband nor her children, who had already fallen out of love with life. Her confession depressed him, depressed him all the more when he thought of Mr. Das at the top of the path, Tina clinging to his shoulders, taking pictures of ancient monastic cells cut into the hills to show his students in America, unsuspecting and unaware that one of his sons was not his own. Mr. Kapasi felt insulted that Mrs. Das should ask him to interpret her common, trivial little secret. She did not resemble the patients in the doctor's office, those who came glassy-eyed and desperate, unable to sleep or breathe or urinate with ease, unable, above all, to give words to their pains. Still, Mr. Kapasi believed it was his duty to assist Mrs. Das. Perhaps he ought to tell her to confess the truth to Mr. Das. He would explain that honesty was the best policy. Honesty, surely, would help her feel better, as she'd put it. Perhaps he would offer to preside over the discussion, as a mediator. He decided to begin with the most obvious question, to get to the heart of the matter, and so he asked, "Is it really pain you feel, Mrs. Das, or is it guilt?"

She turned to him and glared, mustard oil thick on her frosty pink lips. She opened her mouth to say something, but as she glared at Mr. Kapasi some certain knowledge seemed to pass before her eyes, and she stopped. It crushed him; he knew at that moment that he was not even important enough to be properly insulted. She opened the car door and began walking up the path, wobbling a little on her square wooden heels, reaching into her straw bag to eat handfuls of puffed rice. It fell through her fingers, leaving a zigzagging trail, causing a monkey to leap down from a tree and devour the little white grains. In search of more, the monkey began to follow Mrs. Das. Others joined him, so that she was soon being followed by about half a dozen of them, their velvety tails dragging behind.

Mr. Kapasi stepped out of the car. He wanted to holler, to alert her in some way, but he worried that if she knew they were behind her, she would grow nervous. Perhaps she would lose her balance. Perhaps they would pull at her bag or her hair. He began to jog up the path, taking a fallen branch in his hand to scare away the monkeys. Mrs. Das continued walking, oblivious, trailing grains of puffed rice. Near the top of the incline, before a group of cells fronted by a row of squat stone pillars, Mr. Das was kneeling on the ground focusing the lens of his camera. The children stood under the arcade, now hiding, now emerging from view.

"Wait for me," Mrs. Das called out. "I'm coming."

Tina jumped up and down. "Here comes Mommy!"

"Great," Mr. Das said without looking up. "Just in time. We'll get Mr. Kapasi to take a picture of the five of us."

Mr. Kapasi quickened his pace, waving his branch so that the monkeys scampered away, distracted, in another direction.

"Where's Bobby?" Mrs. Das asked when she stopped.

Mr. Das looked up from the camera. "I don't know. Ronny, where's Bobby?"

Ronny shrugged, "I thought he was right here."

"Where is he?" Mrs. Das repeated sharply. "What's wrong with all of you?"

They began calling his name, wandering up and down the path a bit. Because they were calling, they did not initially hear the boy's screams. When they found him, a little farther down the path under a tree, he was surrounded by a group of monkeys, over a dozen of them, pulling at his T-shirt with their long black fingers. The puffed rice Mrs. Das had spilled was scattered at his feet, raked over by the monkeys' hands. The boy was silent, his body frozen, swift tears running down his startled face. His bare legs were dusty and red with welts from where one of the monkeys struck him repeatedly with the stick he had given to it earlier.

"Daddy, the monkey's hurting Bobby," Tina said.

Mr. Das wiped his palms on the front of his shorts. In his nervousness he accidentally pressed the shutter on his camera; the whirring noise of the advancing film excited the monkeys, and the one with the stick began to beat Bobby more intently. "What are we supposed to do? What if they start attacking?"

"Mr. Kapasi," Mrs. Das shrieked, noticing him standing to one side. "Do something, for God's sake, do something!"

Mr. Kapasi took his branch and shooed them away, hissing at the ones that remained, stomping his feet to scare them. The animals retreated slowly, with a measured gait, obedient but unintimidated. Mr. Kapasi gathered Bobby in his arms and brought him back to where his parents and siblings were standing. As he carried him he was tempted to whisper a secret into the boy's ear. But Bobby was stunned, and shivering with fright, his legs bleeding slightly where the stick had broken the skin. When Mr. Kapasi delivered him to his parents, Mrs. Das brushed some dirt off the boy's T-shirt and put the visor on him the right way. Mrs. Das reached into her straw bag to find a bandage which she taped over the cut on his knee. Ronny offered his brother a fresh piece of gum. "He's fine. Just a little scared, right, Bobby?" Mr. Das said, patting the top of his head.

"God, let's get out of here," Mrs. Das said. She folded her arms across the strawberry on her chest. "This place gives me the creeps."

"Yeah. Back to the hotel, definitely," Mr. Das agreed.

"Poor Bobby," Mrs. Das said. "Come here a second. Let Mommy fix your hair." Again she reached into her straw bag, this time for her hairbrush, and began to run it around the edges of the translucent visor. When she whipped out the hairbrush, the slip of paper with Mr. Kapasi's address on it fluttered away in the wind. No one but Mr. Kapasi noticed. He watched as it rose, carried higher and higher by the breeze, into the trees where the monkeys now sat, solemnly observing the scene below. Mr. Kapasi observed it too, knowing that this was the picture of the Das family he would preserve forever in his mind.

CRITICAL EYE

For Discussion

a. How is it that all of the individuals in the story share the same ethnic identity but are so drastically different? What has informed their adult lives?

b. Discuss the metaphorical meaning of the phrase "interpreter of maladies."

c. How is this story about the life of an unfulfilled woman?

Re-approaching the Reading

Examine the main character in the film *Fight Club* and the woman from Lahiri's text. What do these two have in common, and how do both explore the notion of the need for confession?

Writing Assignment

Is this story an allusion to how adults often feel that their lives have been wasted?

HENRY DAVID THOREAU

ON THE DUTY OF CIVIL DISOBEDIENCE

I heartily accept the motto, "That government is best which governs least"; and I should like to see it acted up to more rapidly and systematically. Carried out, it finally amounts to this, which also I believe–"That government is best which governs not at all"; and when men are prepared for it, that will be the kind of government which they will have. Government is at best but an expedient; but most governments are usually, and all governments are sometimes, inexpedient. The objections which have been brought against a standing army, and they are many and weighty, and deserve to prevail, may also at last be brought against a standing government. The standing army is only an arm of the standing government. The government itself, which is only the mode which the people have chosen to execute their will, is equally liable to be abused and perverted before the people can act through it. Witness the present Mexican war, the work of comparatively a few individuals using the standing government as their tool; for in the outset, the people would not have consented to this measure.

This American government–what is it but a tradition, though a recent one, endeavoring to transmit itself unimpaired to posterity, but each instant losing some of its integrity? It has not the vitality and force of a single living man; for a single man can bend it to his will. It is a sort of wooden gun to the people themselves. But it is not the less necessary for this; for the people must have some complicated machinery or other, and hear its din, to satisfy that idea of government which they have. Governments show thus how successfully men can be imposed upon, even impose on themselves, for their own advantage. It is excellent, we must all allow. Yet this government never of itself furthered any enterprise, but by the alacrity with which it got out of its way. *It* does not keep the country free. *It* does not settle the West. *It* does not educate. The character inherent in the American people has done all that has been accomplished; and it would have done somewhat more, if the government had not sometimes got in its way. For government is an expedient, by which men would fain succeed in letting one another alone; and, as has been said, when it is most expedient, the governed are most let alone by it. Trade and commerce, if they were not made of india-rubber, would never manage to bounce over obstacles which legislators are continually putting in their way; and if one were to judge these men wholly by the effects of their actions and not partly by their intentions, they would deserve to be classed and punished with those mischievious persons who put obstructions on the railroads.

But, to speak practically and as a citizen, unlike those who call themselves no-government men, I ask for, not *at once* no government, but at once a better government. Let every man make known what kind of government would command his respect, and that will be one step toward obtaining it.

After all, the practical reason why, when the power is once in the hands of the people, a majority are permitted, and for a long period continue, to rule is not because they are most likely to be in the right, nor because this seems fairest to the minority, but because they are physically the strongest. But a government in which the majority rule in all cases can not be based on justice, even as far as men understand it. Can there not be a government in which the majorities do not virtually decide right and wrong, but conscience?—in which majorities decide only those questions to which the rule of expediency is applicable? Must the citizen ever for a moment, or in the least degree, resign his conscience to the legislator? Why has every man a conscience then? I think that we should be men first, and subjects afterward. It is not desirable to cultivate a respect for the law, so much as for the right. The only obligation which I have a right to assume is to do at any time what I think right. It is truly enough said that a corporation has no conscience; but a corporation of conscientious men is a corporation *with* a conscience. Law never made men a whit more just; and, by means of their respect for it, even the well-disposed are daily made the agents on injustice. A common and natural result of an undue respect for the law is, that you may see a file of soldiers, colonel, captain, corporal, privates, powder-monkeys, and all, marching in admirable order over hill and dale to the wars, against their wills, ay, against their common sense and consciences, which makes it very steep marching indeed, and produces a palpitation of the heart. They have no doubt that it is a damnable business in which they are concerned; they are all peaceably inclined. Now, what are they? Men at all? or small movable forts and magazines, at the service of some unscrupulous man in power? Visit the Navy Yard, and behold a marine, such a man as an American government can make, or such as it can make a man with its black arts—a mere shadow and reminiscence of humanity, a man laid out alive and standing, and already, as one may say, buried under arms with funeral accompaniment, though it may be,

"Not a drum was heard, not a funeral note,
As his corse to the rampart we hurried;
Not a soldier discharged his farewell shot
O'er the grave where our hero was buried."

The mass of men serve the state thus, not as men mainly, but as machines, with their bodies. They are the standing army, and the militia, jailers, constables, posse comitatus, etc. In most cases there is no free exercise whatever of the judgement or of the moral sense; but they put themselves on a level with wood and earth and stones; and wooden men can perhaps be manufactured that will serve the purpose as well. Such command no more respect than men of straw or a lump of dirt. They have the same sort of worth only as horses and dogs. Yet such as these even are commonly esteemed good citizens. Others—as most legislators, politicians, lawyers, ministers, and office-holders—serve the state chiefly with their heads; and, as they rarely make any moral distinctions, they are as likely to serve the devil, without *intending* it, as God. A very few—as heroes, patriots, martyrs, reformers in the great sense, and *men*—serve the state with their consciences also, and so necessarily resist it for the most part; and they are commonly treated as enemies by it. A wise man will only be useful as a man, and will not submit to be "clay," and "stop a hole to keep the wind away," but leave that office to his dust at least:

"I am too high born to be propertied,
To be a second at control,
Or useful serving-man and instrument
To any sovereign state throughout the world."

He who gives himself entirely to his fellow men appears to them useless and selfish; but he who gives himself partially to them is pronounced a benefactor and philanthropist.

How does it become a man to behave toward the American government today? I answer, that he cannot without disgrace be associated with it. I cannot for an instant recognize that political organization as *my* government which is the *slave's* government also.

All men recognize the right of revolution; that is, the right to refuse allegiance to, and to resist, the government, when its tyranny or its inefficiency are great and unendurable. But almost all say that such is not the case now. But such was the case, they think, in the Revolution of '75. If one were to tell me that this was a bad government because it taxed certain foreign commodities brought to its ports, it is most probable that I should not make an ado about it, for I can do without them. All machines have their friction; and possibly this does enough good to counter-balance the evil. At any rate, it is a great evil to make a stir about it. But when the friction comes to have its machine, and oppression and robbery are organized, I say, let us not have such a machine any longer. In other words, when a sixth of the population of a nation which has undertaken to be the refuge of liberty are slaves, and a whole country is unjustly overrun and conquered by a foreign army, and subjected to military law, I think that it is not too soon for honest men to rebel and revolutionize. What makes this duty the more urgent is that fact that the country so overrun is not our own, but ours is the invading army.

Paley, a common authority with many on moral questions, in his chapter on the "Duty of Submission to Civil Government," resolves all civil obligation into expediency; and he proceeds to say that "so long as the interest of the whole society requires it, that is, so long as the established government cannot be resisted or changed without public inconvenience, it is the will of God . . . that the established government be obeyed–and no longer. This principle being admitted, the justice of every particular case of resistance is reduced to a computation of the quantity of the danger and grievance on the one side, and of the probability and expense of redressing it on the other." Of this, he says, every man shall judge for himself. But Paley appears never to have contemplated those cases to which the rule of expediency does not apply, in which a people, as well as an individual, must do justice, cost what it may. If I have unjustly wrested a plank from a drowning man, I must restore it to him though I drown myself. This, according to Paley, would be inconvenient. But he that would save his life, in such a case, shall lose it. This people must cease to hold slaves, and to make war on Mexico, though it cost them their existence as a people.

In their practice, nations agree with Paley; but does anyone think that Massachusetts does exactly what is right at the present crisis?

"A drab of stat,
a cloth-o'-silver slut,
To have her train borne up,
and her soul trail in the dirt."

Practically speaking, the opponents to a reform in Massachusetts are not a hundred thousand politicians at the South, but a hundred thousand merchants and farmers here, who are more interested in commerce and agriculture than they are in humanity, and are not prepared to do justice to the slave and to Mexico, *cost what it may*. I quarrel not with far-off foes, but with those who, near at home, co-operate with, and do the bidding of, those far away, and without whom the latter would be harmless. We are accustomed to say, that the mass of men are unprepared; but improvement is slow, because the few are not as materially wiser or better than the many.

It is not so important that many should be good as you, as that there be some absolute goodness somewhere; for that will leaven the whole lump. There are thousands who are *in opinion* opposed to slavery and to the war, who yet in effect do nothing to put an end to them; who, esteeming themselves children of Washington and Franklin, sit down with their hands in their pockets, and say that they know not what to do, and do nothing; who even postpone the question of freedom to the question of free trade, and quietly read the prices-current along with the latest advices from Mexico, after dinner, and, it may be, fall asleep over them both. What is the price-current of an honest man and patriot today? They hesitate, and they regret, and sometimes they petition; but they do nothing in earnest and with effect. They will wait, well disposed, for other to remedy the evil, that they may no longer have it to regret. At most, they give up only a cheap vote, and a feeble countenance and Godspeed, to the right, as it goes by them. There are nine hundred and ninety-nine patrons of virtue to one virtuous man. But it is easier to deal with the real possessor of a thing than with the temporary guardian of it.

All voting is a sort of gaming, like checkers or backgammon, with a slight moral tinge to it, a playing with right and wrong, with moral questions; and betting naturally accompanies it. The character of the voters is not staked. I cast my vote, perchance, as I think right; but I am not vitally concerned that that right should prevail. I am willing to leave it to the majority. Its obligation, therefore, never exceeds that of expediency. Even *voting for the right* is *doing* nothing for it. It is only expressing to men feebly your desire that it should prevail. A wise man will not leave the right to the mercy of chance, nor wish it to prevail through the power of the majority. There is but little virtue in the action of masses of men. When the majority shall at length vote for the abolition of slavery, it will be because they are indifferent to slavery, or because there is but little slavery left to be abolished by their vote. *They* will then be the only slaves. Only *his* vote can hasten the abolition of slavery who asserts his own freedom by his vote.

I hear of a convention to be held at Baltimore, or elsewhere, for the selection of a candidate for the Presidency, made up chiefly of editors, and men who are politicians by profession; but I think, what is it to any independent, intelligent, and respectable man what decision they may come to? Shall we not have the advantage of this wisdom and honesty, nevertheless? Can we not count upon some independent votes? Are there not many individuals in the country who do not attend conventions? But no: I find that the respectable man, so called, has immediately drifted from his position, and despairs of his country, when his country has more reasons to despair of him. He forthwith adopts one of the candidates thus selected as the only *available* one, thus proving that he is himself *available* for any purposes of the demagogue. His vote is of no more worth than that of any unprincipled foreigner or hireling native, who may have been bought. O for a man who is a man, and, as my neighbor says, has a bone in his back which you cannot pass your hand through! Our statistics are at fault: the population has been returned too large. How many *men* are there to a square thousand miles in the country? Hardly one. Does not America offer any inducement for men to settle here? The American has dwindled into an Odd Fellow—one who may be known by the development of his organ of gregariousness, and a manifest lack of intellect and cheerful self-reliance; whose first and chief concern, on coming into the world, is to see that the almshouses are in good repair; and, before yet he has lawfully donned the virile garb, to collect a fund to the support of the widows and orphans that may be; who, in short, ventures to live only by the aid of the Mutual Insurance company, which has promised to bury him decently.

It is not a man's duty, as a matter of course, to devote himself to the eradication of any, even to most enormous wrong; he may still properly have other concerns to engage him; but it is his duty, at least, to wash his hands of it, and, if he gives it no thought longer, not to give it practically his support. If I devote myself to other pursuits and contemplations, I must first see, at least, that I do not pursue them sitting upon another man's shoulders. I must get off him first, that he may pursue his contemplations too. See what gross inconsistency is tolerated. I have heard some of my townsmen say, "I should like to have them order me out to help put down an insurrection of the slaves, or to march to Mexico—see if I would go"; and yet these very men have each, directly by their allegiance, and so indirectly, at least, by their money, furnished a substitute. The soldier is applauded who refuses to serve in an unjust war by those who do not refuse to sustain the unjust government which makes the war; is applauded by those whose own act and authority he disregards and sets at naught; as if the state were penitent to that degree that it hired one to scourge it while it sinned, but not to that degree that it left off sinning for a moment. Thus, under the name of Order and Civil Government, we are all made at last to pay homage to and support our own meanness. After the first blush of sin comes its indifference; and from immoral it becomes, as it were, unmoral, and not quite unnecessary to that life which we have made.

The broadest and most prevalent error requires the most disinterested virtue to sustain it. The slight reproach to which the virtue of patriotism is commonly liable, the noble are most likely to incur. Those who, while they disapprove of the character and measures of a government, yield to it their allegiance and support are undoubtedly its most conscientious supporters, and so frequently the most serious obstacles to reform. Some are petitioning the State to dissolve the Union, to disregard the requisitions of the President. Why do they not dissolve it themselves—the union between themselves and the State—and refuse to pay their quota into its treasury? Do not they stand in same relation to the State that the State does to the Union? And have not the same reasons prevented the State from resisting the Union which have prevented them from resisting the State?

How can a man be satisfied to entertain an opinion merely, and enjoy *it*? Is there any enjoyment in it, if his opinion is that he is aggrieved? If you are cheated out of a single dollar by your neighbor, you do not rest satisfied with knowing you are cheated, or with saying that you are cheated, or even with petitioning him to pay you your due; but you take effectual steps at once to obtain the full amount, and see to it that you are never cheated again. Action from principle, the perception and the performance of right, changes things and relations; it is essentially revolutionary, and does not consist wholly with anything which was. It not only divided States and churches, it divides families; ay, it divides the *individual*, separating the diabolical in him from the divine.

Unjust laws exist: shall we be content to obey them, or shall we endeavor to amend them, and obey them until we have succeeded, or shall we transgress them at once? Men, generally, under such a government as this, think that they ought to wait until they have persuaded the majority to alter them. They think that, if they should resist, the remedy would be worse than the evil. But it is the fault of the government itself that the remedy is worse than the evil. *It* makes it worse. Why is it not more apt to anticipate and provide for reform? Why does it not cherish its wise minority? Why does it cry and resist before it is hurt? Why does it not encourage its citizens to put out its faults, and *do* better than it would have them? Why does it always crucify Christ and excommunicate Copernicus and Luther, and pronounce Washington and Franklin rebels?

One would think, that a deliberate and practical denial of its authority was the only offense never contemplated by its government; else, why has it not assigned its definite, its suitable and proportionate, penalty? If a man who has no property refuses but once to earn nine shillings for the State, he is put in prison for a period unlimited by any law that I know, and determined only by the discretion of those who put him there; but if he should steal ninety times nine shillings from the State, he is soon permitted to go at large again.

If the injustice is part of the necessary friction of the machine of government, let it go, let it go: perchance it will wear smooth–certainly the machine will wear out. If the injustice has a spring, or a pulley, or a rope, or a crank, exclusively for itself, then perhaps you may consider whether the remedy will not be worse than the evil; but if it is of such a nature that it requires you to be the agent of injustice to another, then I say, break the law. Let your life be a counter-friction to stop the machine. What I have to do is to see, at any rate, that I do not lend myself to the wrong which I condemn.

As for adopting the ways of the State has provided for remedying the evil, I know not of such ways. They take too much time, and a man's life will be gone. I have other affairs to attend to. I came into this world, not chiefly to make this a good place to live in, but to live in it, be it good or bad. A man has not everything to do, but something; and because he cannot do *everything*, it is not necessary that he should be doing *something* wrong. It is not my business to be petitioning the Governor or the Legislature any more than it is theirs to petition me; and if they should not hear my petition, what should I do then? But in this case the State has provided no way: its very Constitution is the evil. This may seem to be harsh and stubborn and unconcilliatory; but it is to treat with the utmost kindness and consideration the only spirit that can appreciate or deserves it. So is all change for the better, like birth and death, which convulse the body.

Critical Eye

For Discussion

a. Is Thoreau correct, does the government actually hinder its citizens? How so?

b. The author argues that citizens owe their allegiance to each other and not the government that rules over them. Is this notion true?

Re-approaching the Reading

This essay was originally published under the title "Resistance to Civil Government." In short, Thoreau is positing that a single individual can and should attempt to bend the government to his/her will. Is this realistic or naïve thinking on the author's part?

Writing Topic

Consider our current American government and the social issues that are now at the forefront: marriage equality, raising the minimum wage, reproductive rights, the right to die, immigration, and nationwide healthcare coverage. Given Thoreau's argument, how have average individuals—the solitary "citizen"—impacted government rule and decision making?

FYODOR DOSTOYEVSKY

From the Novel
NOTES FROM THE UNDERGROUND

Part Two: Chapter I.

AT THAT TIME I was only twenty-four. My life was even then gloomy, ill-regulated, and as solitary as that of a savage. I made friends with no one and positively avoided talking, and buried myself more and more in my hole. At work in the office I never looked at anyone, and was perfectly well aware that my companions looked upon me, not only as a queer fellow, but even looked upon me–I always fancied this–with a sort of loathing. I sometimes wondered why it was that nobody except me fancied that he was looked upon with aversion? One of the clerks had a most repulsive, pock-marked face, which looked positively villainous. I believe I should not have dared to look at anyone with such an unsightly countenance. Another had such a very dirty old uniform that there was an unpleasant odour in his proximity. Yet not one of these gentlemen showed the slightest self-consciousness–either about their clothes or their countenance or their character in any way. Neither of them ever imagined that they were looked at with repulsion; if they had imagined it they would not have minded–so long as their superiors did not look at them in that way. It is clear to me now that, owing to my unbounded vanity and to the high standard I set for myself, I often looked at myself with furious discontent, which verged on loathing, and so I inwardly attributed the same feeling to everyone. I hated my face, for instance: I thought it disgusting, and even suspected that there was something base in my expression, and so every day when I turned up at the office I tried to behave as independently as possible, and to assume a lofty expression, so that I might not be suspected of being abject. "My face may be ugly," I thought, "but let it be lofty, expressive, and, above all, EXTREMELY intelligent." But I was positively and painfully certain that it was impossible for my countenance ever to express those qualities. And what was worst of all, I thought it actually stupid looking, and I would have been quite satisfied if I could have looked intelligent. In fact, I would even have put up with looking base if, at the same time, my face could have been thought strikingly intelligent.

Of course, I hated my fellow clerks one and all, and I despised them all, yet at the same time I was, as it were, afraid of them. In fact, it happened at times that I thought more highly of them than of myself. It somehow happened quite suddenly that I alternated between despising them and thinking them superior to myself. A cultivated and decent man cannot be vain without setting a fearfully high standard for himself, and without despising and almost hating himself at certain moments. But whether I despised them or thought them superior I dropped my eyes almost every time I met anyone. I even made experiments whether I could face so and so's looking at me, and I was always the first to drop my eyes. This worried me to distraction. I had a sickly dread, too, of being ridiculous, and so had a slavish passion for the conventional in everything external. I loved to fall into the common rut, and had a whole-hearted terror of any kind of eccentricity in myself. But how could I live up to it? I was morbidly sensitive as a man of our age should be. They were all stupid, and as like one another as so many sheep. Perhaps I was the only one in the office who fancied that I was a coward and a slave, and I fancied it just because I was more highly developed. But it was not only that I fancied it, it really was so.

I was a coward and a slave. I say this without the slightest embarrassment. Every decent man of our age must be a coward and a slave. That is his normal condition. Of that I am firmly persuaded. He is made and constructed to that very end. And not only at the present time owing to some casual circumstances, but always, at all times, a decent man is bound to be a coward and a slave. It is the law of nature for all decent people all over the earth. If anyone of them happens to be valiant about something, he need not be comforted nor carried away by that; he would show the white feather just the same before something else. That is how it invariably and inevitably ends. Only donkeys and mules are valiant, and they only till they are pushed up to the wall. It is not worth while to pay attention to them for they really are of no consequence.

Another circumstance, too, worried me in those days: that there was no one like me and I was unlike anyone else. "I am alone and they are EVERYONE," I thought—and pondered.

From that it is evident that I was still a youngster.

The very opposite sometimes happened. It was loathsome sometimes to go to the office; things reached such a point that I often came home ill.

But all at once, A PROPOS of nothing, there would come a phase of scepticism and indifference (everything happened in phases to me), and I would laugh myself at my intolerance and fastidiousness, I would reproach myself with being ROMANTIC. At one time I was unwilling to speak to anyone, while at other times I would not only talk, but go to the length of contemplating making friends with them. All my fastidiousness would suddenly, for no rhyme or reason, vanish. Who knows, perhaps I never had really had it, and it had simply been affected, and got out of books. I have not decided that question even now. Once I quite made friends with them, visited their homes, played preference, drank vodka, talked of promotions .... But here let me make a digression.

We Russians, speaking generally, have never had those foolish transcendental "romantics"—German, and still more French—on whom nothing produces any effect; if there were an earthquake, if all France perished at the barricades, they would still be the same, they would not even have the decency to affect a change, but would still go on singing their transcendental songs to the hour of their death, because they are fools. We, in Russia, have no fools; that is well known. That is what distinguishes us from foreign lands. Consequently these transcendental natures are not found amongst us in their pure form. The idea that they are is due to our "realistic" journalists and critics of that day, always on the look out for Kostanzhoglos and Uncle Pyotr Ivanitchs and foolishly accepting them as our ideal; they have slandered our romantics, taking them for the same transcendental sort as in Germany or France. On the contrary, the characteristics of our "romantics" are absolutely and directly opposed to the transcendental European type, and no European standard can be applied to them. (Allow me to make use of this word "romantic"—an old-fashioned and much respected word which has done good service and is familiar to all.) The characteristics of our romantic are to understand everything, TO SEE EVERYTHING

AND TO SEE IT OFTEN INCOMPARABLY MORE CLEARLY THAN OUR MOST REALISTIC MINDS SEE IT; to refuse to accept anyone or anything, but at the same time not to despise anything; to give way, to yield, from policy; never to lose sight of a useful practical object (such as rent-free quarters at the government expense, pensions, decorations), to keep their eye on that object through all the enthusiasms and volumes of lyrical poems, and at the same time to preserve "the sublime and the beautiful" inviolate within them to the hour of their death, and to preserve themselves also, incidentally, like some precious jewel wrapped in cotton wool if only for the benefit of "the sublime and the beautiful." Our "romantic" is a man of great breadth and the greatest rogue of all our rogues, I assure you .... I can assure you from experience, indeed. Of course, that is, if he is intelligent. But what am I saying! The romantic is always intelligent, and I only meant to observe that although we have had foolish romantics they don't count, and they were only so because in the flower of their youth they degenerated into Germans, and to preserve their precious jewel more comfortably, settled somewhere out there—by preference in Weimar or the Black Forest.

I, for instance, genuinely despised my official work and did not openly abuse it simply because I was in it myself and got a salary for it. Anyway, take note, I did not openly abuse it. Our romantic would rather go out of his mind—a thing, however, which very rarely happens—than take to open abuse, unless he had some other career in view; and he is never kicked out. At most, they would take him to the lunatic asylum as "the King of Spain" if he should go very mad. But it is only the thin, fair people who go out of their minds in Russia. Innumerable "romantics" attain later in life to considerable rank in the service. Their many-sidedness is remarkable! And what a faculty they have for the most contradictory sensations! I was comforted by this thought even in those days, and I am of the same opinion now. That is why there are so many "broad natures" among us who never lose their ideal even in the depths of degradation; and though they never stir a finger for their ideal, though they are arrant thieves and knaves, yet they tearfully cherish their first ideal and are extraordinarily honest at heart. Yes, it is only among us that the most incorrigible rogue can be absolutely and loftily honest at heart without in the least ceasing to be a rogue. I repeat, our romantics, frequently, become such accomplished rascals (I use the term "rascals" affectionately), suddenly display such a sense of reality and practical knowledge that their bewildered superiors and the public generally can only ejaculate in amazement.

Their many-sidedness is really amazing, and goodness knows what it may develop into later on, and what the future has in store for us. It is not a poor material! I do not say this from any foolish or boastful patriotism.

But I feel sure that you are again imagining that I am joking. Or perhaps it's just the contrary and you are convinced that I really think so. Anyway, gentlemen, I shall welcome both views as an honour and a special favour.

And do forgive my digression.

I did not, of course, maintain friendly relations with my comrades and soon was at loggerheads with them, and in my youth and inexperience I even gave up bowing to them, as though I had cut off all relations. That, however, only happened to me once. As a rule, I was always alone.

In the first place I spent most of my time at home, reading. I tried to stifle all that was continually seething within me by means of external impressions. And the only external means I had was reading. Reading, of course, was a great help—exciting me, giving me pleasure and pain. But at times it bored me fearfully. One longed for movement in spite of everything, and I plunged all at once into dark, underground, loathsome vice of the pettiest kind. My wretched passions were acute, smarting, from my continual, sickly irritability I had hysterical impulses, with tears and convulsions. I had no resource except reading, that is, there was nothing in my surroundings which I could respect and which attracted me. I was overwhelmed with depression, too; I had an hysterical craving for incongruity and for contrast, and so I took to vice. I have not said all this to justify myself .... But, no! I am lying. I did want to justify myself. I make that little observation for my own benefit, gentlemen. I don't want to lie. I vowed to myself I would not.

And so, furtively, timidly, in solitude, at night, I indulged in filthy vice, with a feeling of shame which never deserted me, even at the most loathsome moments, and which at such moments nearly made me curse.

Already even then I had my underground world in my soul. I was fearfully afraid of being seen, of being met, of being recognised. I visited various obscure haunts.

One night as I was passing a tavern I saw through a lighted window some gentlemen fighting with billiard cues, and saw one of them thrown out of the window. At other times I should have felt very much disgusted, but I was in such a mood at the time, that I actually envied the gentleman thrown out of the window—and I envied him so much that I even went into the tavern and into the billiard-room. "Perhaps," I thought, "I'll have a fight, too, and they'll throw me out of the window."

I was not drunk—but what is one to do—depression will drive a man to such a pitch of hysteria? But nothing happened. It seemed that I was not even equal to being thrown out of the window and I went away without having my fight.

An officer put me in my place from the first moment.

I was standing by the billiard-table and in my ignorance blocking up the way, and he wanted to pass; he took me by the shoulders and without a word—without a warning or explanation—moved me from where I was standing to another spot and passed by as though he had not noticed me. I could have forgiven blows, but I could not forgive his having moved me without noticing me.

Devil knows what I would have given for a real regular quarrel—a more decent, a more LITERARY one, so to speak. I had been treated like a fly. This officer was over six foot, while I was a spindly little fellow. But the quarrel was in my hands. I had only to protest and I certainly would have been thrown out of the window. But I changed my mind and preferred to beat a resentful retreat.

I went out of the tavern straight home, confused and troubled, and the next night I went out again with the same lewd intentions, still more furtively, abjectly and miserably than before, as it were, with tears in my eyes—but still I did go out again. Don't imagine, though, it was coward-ice made me slink away from the officer; I never have been a coward at heart, though I have always been a coward in action. Don't be in a hurry to laugh—I assure you I can explain it all.

Oh, if only that officer had been one of the sort who would consent to fight a duel! But no, he was one of those gentlemen (alas, long extinct!) who preferred fighting with cues or, like Gogol's Lieutenant Pirogov, appealing to the police. They did not fight duels and would have thought a duel with a civilian like me an utterly unseemly procedure in any case—and they looked upon the duel altogether as something impossible, something free-thinking and French. But they were quite ready to bully, especially when they were over six foot.

I did not slink away through cowardice, but through an unbounded vanity. I was afraid not of his six foot, not of getting a sound thrashing and being thrown out of the window; I should have had physical courage enough, I assure you; but I had not the moral courage. What I was afraid of was that everyone present, from the insolent marker down to the lowest little stinking, pimply clerk in a greasy collar, would jeer at me and fail to understand when I began to protest and to address them in literary language. For of the point of honour–not of honour, but of the point of honour (POINT D'HONNEUR)–one cannot speak among us except in literary language. You can't allude to the "point of honour" in ordinary language.

I was fully convinced (the sense of reality, in spite of all my romanticism!) that they would all simply split their sides with laughter, and that the officer would not simply beat me, that is, without insulting me, but would certainly prod me in the back with his knee, kick me round the billiard-table, and only then perhaps have pity and drop me out of the window.

Of course, this trivial incident could not with me end in that. I often met that officer afterwards in the street and noticed him very carefully. I am not quite sure whether he recognised me, I imagine not; I judge from certain signs. But I–I stared at him with spite and hatred and so it went on ... for several years! My resentment grew even deeper with years. At first I began making stealthy inquiries about this officer. It was difficult for me to do so, for I knew no one. But one day I heard someone shout his surname in the street as I was following him at a distance, as though I were tied to him–and so I learnt his surname. Another time I followed him to his flat, and for ten kopecks learned from the porter where he lived, on which storey, whether he lived alone or with others, and so on–in fact, everything one could learn from a porter. One morning, though I had never tried my hand with the pen, it suddenly occurred to me to write a satire on this officer in the form of a novel which would unmask his villainy. I wrote the novel with relish. I did unmask his villainy, I even exaggerated it; at first I so altered his surname that it could easily be recognised, but on second thoughts I changed it, and sent the story to the OTETCHESTVENNIYA ZAPISKI. But at that time such attacks were not the fashion and my story was not printed. That was a great vexation to me.

Sometimes I was positively choked with resentment. At last I determined to challenge my enemy to a duel. I composed a splendid, charming letter to him, imploring him to apologise to me, and hinting rather plainly at a duel in case of refusal. The letter was so composed that if the officer had had the least understanding of the sublime and the beautiful he would certainly have flung himself on my neck and have offered me his friendship. And how fine that would have been! How we should have got on together! "He could have shielded me with his higher rank, while I could have improved his mind with my culture, and, well ... my ideas, and all sorts of things might have happened." Only fancy, this was two years after his insult to me, and my challenge would have been a ridiculous anachronism, in spite of all the ingenuity of my letter in disguising and explaining away the anachronism. But, thank God (to this day I thank the Almighty with tears in my eyes) I did not send the letter to him. Cold shivers run down my back when I think of what might have happened if I had sent it.

And all at once I revenged myself in the simplest way, by a stroke of genius! A brilliant thought suddenly dawned upon me. Sometimes on holidays I used to stroll along the sunny side of the Nevsky about four o'clock in the afternoon. Though it was hardly a stroll so much as a series of innumerable miseries, humiliations and resentments; but no doubt that was just what I wanted. I used to wriggle along in a most unseemly fashion, like an eel, continually moving aside to make way for generals, for officers of the guards and the hussars, or for ladies. At such minutes there used to be a convulsive twinge at my heart, and I used to feel hot all down my back at the mere thought of the wretchedness of my attire, of the wretchedness and abjectness of my little scurrying figure. This was a regular martyrdom, a continual, intolerable humiliation at the thought, which passed into an incessant and direct sensation, that I was a mere fly in the eyes of all this world, a nasty, disgusting fly—more intelligent, more highly developed, more refined in feeling than any of them, of course—but a fly that was continually making way for everyone, insulted and injured by everyone.

Why I inflicted this torture upon myself, why I went to the Nevsky, I don't know. I felt simply drawn there at every possible opportunity.

Already then I began to experience a rush of the enjoyment of which I spoke in the first chapter. After my affair with the officer I felt even more drawn there than before: it was on the Nevsky that I met him most frequently, there I could admire him. He, too, went there chiefly on holidays, He, too, turned out of his path for generals and persons of high rank, and he too, wriggled between them like an eel; but people, like me, or even better dressed than me, he simply walked over; he made straight for them as though there was nothing but empty space before him, and never, under any circumstances, turned aside. I gloated over my resentment watching him and ... always resentfully made way for him. It exasperated me that even in the street I could not be on an even footing with him.

"Why must you invariably be the first to move aside?" I kept asking myself in hysterical rage, waking up sometimes at three o'clock in the morning. "Why is it you and not he? There's no regulation about it; there's no written law. Let the making way be equal as it usually is when refined people meet; he moves half-way and you move half-way; you pass with mutual respect."

But that never happened, and I always moved aside, while he did not even notice my making way for him. And lo and behold a bright idea dawned upon me! "What," I thought, "if I meet him and don't move on one side? What if I don't move aside on purpose, even if I knock up against him? How would that be?" This audacious idea took such a hold on me that it gave me no peace. I was dreaming of it continually, horribly, and I purposely went more frequently to the Nevsky in order to picture more vividly how I should do it when I did do it. I was delighted. This intention seemed to me more and more practical and possible.

"Of course I shall not really push him," I thought, already more good-natured in my joy. "I will simply not turn aside, will run up against him, not very violently, but just shouldering each other—just as much as decency permits. I will push against him just as much as he pushes against me." At last I made up my mind completely. But my preparations took a great deal of time. To begin with, when I carried out my plan I should need to be looking rather more decent, and so I had to think of my get-up. "In case of emergency, if, for instance, there were any sort of public scandal (and the public there is of the most RECHERCHE: the Countess walks there; Prince D. walks there; all the literary world is there), I must be well dressed; that inspires respect and of itself puts us on an equal footing in the eyes of the society."

With this object I asked for some of my salary in advance, and bought at Tchurkin's a pair of black gloves and a decent hat. Black gloves seemed to me both more dignified and BON TON than the lemon-coloured ones which I had contemplated at first. "The colour is too gaudy, it looks as though one were trying to be conspicuous," and I did not take the lemon-coloured ones. I had got ready long beforehand a good shirt, with white bone studs; my overcoat was the only thing that held me back. The coat in itself was a very good one, it kept me warm; but it was wadded and it had a raccoon collar which was the height of vulgarity. I had to change the collar at any sacrifice, and to have a beaver one like an officer's. For this purpose I began visiting the Gostiny Dvor and after several attempts I pitched upon a piece of cheap German beaver. Though these German beavers soon grow shabby and look wretched, yet at first they look exceedingly well, and I only needed it for the occasion. I asked the price; even so, it was too expensive. After thinking it over thoroughly I decided to sell my raccoon collar. The rest of the money–a considerable sum for me, I decided to borrow from Anton Antonitch Syetotchkin, my immediate superior, an unassuming person, though grave and judicious. He never lent money to anyone, but I had, on entering the service, been specially recommended to him by an important personage who had got me my berth. I was horribly worried. To borrow from Anton Antonitch seemed to me monstrous and shameful. I did not sleep for two or three nights. Indeed, I did not sleep well at that time, I was in a fever; I had a vague sinking at my heart or else a sudden throbbing, throbbing, throbbing! Anton Antonitch was surprised at first, then he frowned, then he reflected, and did after all lend me the money, receiving from me a written authorisation to take from my salary a fortnight later the sum that he had lent me.

In this way everything was at last ready. The handsome beaver replaced the mean-looking raccoon, and I began by degrees to get to work. It would never have done to act offhand, at random; the plan had to be carried out skilfully, by degrees. But I must confess that after many efforts I began to despair: we simply could not run into each other. I made every preparation, I was quite determined–it seemed as though we should run into one another directly–and before I knew what I was doing I had stepped aside for him again and he had passed without noticing me. I even prayed as I approached him that God would grant me determination. One time I had made up my mind thoroughly, but it ended in my stumbling and falling at his feet because at the very last instant when I was six inches from him my courage failed me. He very calmly stepped over me, while I flew on one side like a ball. That night I was ill again, feverish and delirious.

And suddenly it ended most happily. The night before I had made up my mind not to carry out my fatal plan and to abandon it all, and with that object I went to the Nevsky for the last time, just to see how I would abandon it all. Suddenly, three paces from my enemy, I unexpectedly made up my mind–I closed my eyes, and we ran full tilt, shoulder to shoulder, against one another! I did not budge an inch and passed him on a perfectly equal footing! He did not even look round and pretended not to notice it; but he was only pretending, I am convinced of that. I am convinced of that to this day! Of course, I got the worst of it–he was stronger, but that was not the point. The point was that I had attained my object, I had kept up my dignity, I had not yielded a step, and had put myself publicly on an equal social footing with him. I returned home feeling that I was fully avenged for everything. I was delighted. I was triumphant and sang Italian arias. Of course, I will not describe to you what happened to me three days later; if you have read my first chapter you can guess for yourself. The officer was afterwards transferred; I have not seen him now for fourteen years. What is the dear fellow doing now? Whom is he walking over?

Critical Eye

For Discussion

a. When we meet our main character, he is already filled with self-loathing. Although he is used to feeling this way about himself, when the officer treats him as a nonentity, it is particularly offensive. Why is this?

b. We normally associate bullying with something that is done by children at school or on a playground. In this story, however, we find a world filled with adults who treat each other just as unkindly. What does this say about the distinctions between awkward puberty and unfulfilled adulthood?

Re-approaching the Reading

Our main character, when hatching his vengeance plan, determines to build himself up by changing his appearance. In doing so, he makes this encounter a tale about social Class systems as well as one about manhood. Explain.

Writing Assignment

Challenging his rival on the street makes the main character very happy. He regains his dignity and feels very much like a true man. He later finds out that the officer has been transferred elsewhere, reducing the moment on the street to a futile effort that yields very little. As a result, our main character learns that life is unfair and serves to further humiliate the already injured. How is this true?

AESOP

A LION AND OTHER ANIMALS GO HUNTING

A lion, an ass, a jackal, and a wolf went hunting one day, and every one was to share and share alike in what they took. They plucked down a stag, and cut him up into four parts, but as they were beginning to divide shares, the lion said, "Hands off. *This* quarter is mine, by privilege of my rank, as King of Beasts. *This* quarter is mine because I frightened the stag with my roar. *This* quarter is mine because I delivered the first blow. As for *this* quarter, well, take it who dares." So the mouths of the allies were shut, and they went away, quiet as fishes.

Moral: There is no partnership with those who have the power.

Critical Eye

For Discussion

a. Does the lion's final statement speak to the historical posturing of the bully?

b. Provide current or historical evidence that presents a nation or governing body as a bully.

c. Thinking in terms of gender, race, and politics, who is generally seen as the bully?

d. Does historical evidence exist in which the "other," or those presumed to be powerless, assumed power and, subsequently, took on the persona of the bully?

Re-approaching the Reading

Look at the relationships between the animals in terms of political domination. How will the lion's behavior affect those deemed lesser? Be sure to juxtapose the story with issues of domination from our larger global society.

Writing Assignment

Using Aseop's tale as a platform, argue that the notion of the bully is a myth and that those in power are entitled to lead and set the gender, social, political, and cultural standards for those deemed weaker.

AL ANGELORO

COMIC BOOKS: HOW I LEARNED TO LOVE READING AND HATE THE CENSORS

When I was in the third grade at P.S. 97, in Bensonhurst Brooklyn, my parents purchased a set of encyclopedias from a door-to-door salesman. I'm not sure why, since they were used mainly as doorstops, until I got my Lionel electric trains. It was a wonderful train set and the locomotive even spouted white smoke as it went around the large piece of plywood it was mounted on in the cellar. Missing were the colorful tunnels pictured on the box it came in, so I found one more use for the encyclopedias: they made great tunnels for my puffing locomotive. It seems that nobody even thought of reading them when they had so many other uses.

At that time, I was very happy in public school, and it was there that I learned to read, thanks to Mrs. Colton. She had us kids working in groups and reading aloud from our third-grade reader to applause. She made reading a fun thing to do.

Then came doom #1: I was taken out of P.S. 97 and put into a Catholic school, ran by a bunch of violent, fiercely anti-intellectual women dressed in penguin outfits. We were only to read the approved topics which were all religious and displayed the Vatican's approval. Stumble on a "holy" word when reading aloud and you were hit with a stick, slapped in the face, or locked in the closet until the bell rang. In short, they tried very hard to instill a fear of reading and were, for the most part, successful. Humiliation goes a long way.

Then, a day of revelation when I discovered William Gaines's E.C. Comics (Entertaining Comics) series, featuring "Tales from the Crypt" and "The Old Witch," among its many intriguing titles. I discovered, in comic-book form, writers like Ray Bradbury, Fritz Lieber, Richard Matheson, Edgar Alan Poe, H.P. Lovecraft, and Harlan Ellison. It seemed that nobody knew how to categorize these guys: Science Fiction? Horror? Along with exceptional artwork, social commentary and contemporary issues like racial inequality and poverty were often themes in these comic books.

It was in these comics that I first read Ray Bradbury's "Dandelion Wine," "The Illustrated Man," "Something Wicked This Way Comes," even hints at what would become "Fahrenheit 451" and his future screenplay for Moby Dick.

Then there was the *Classic Comics* series where I discovered "Leather Stocking Tales," "The Prisoner of Zenda," "A Tale Of Two Cities," and other great novels in this wonderful art form. I would run to the Library to take out the novels, and this is what made me the voracious reader that I am today.

I then had my first introduction to censorship, a clear view of its simplistic folly, and the inevitable backlash that followed. My First Amendment rights as a child were taken away, giving proof to George Carlin's thesis that we don't have "rights," we have privileges, and privileges can be taken away when it's deemed necessary for the good of the nation.

Enter doom #2: the Devil. His name was Dr. Frederic Wertham, a psychiatrist, and his best-selling book, "Seduction of the Innocent." In great detail, he showed America that comic books were the root causes of juvenile delinquency and the obvious cure was to heavily censor and/or eliminate comic books entirely. Poverty, poor schools, segregation, broken-homes; all the U.S.A. had to do to cure these social ills was to blame comic books. The government and their religious allies convinced people that the causes of juvenile delinquency, sexual acting out, homosexuality, and the mixing of the races were to be found in comic books. There were congressional outcries and, believe it or not, hearings before the Senate Subcommittee on Juvenile Delinquency, in 1954. Get rid of comic books and the youth of America would be dancing to the "Star Spangled Banner" at their chaperoned (no mixing of the races) parties. (Many of these comics portrayed black and white people as equal.) Some politicians and clergymen held public comic-book-burning parties, while being led in prayer. These are the same kinds of people who had public burnings of Rhythm and Blues (read Black) phonograph records. Nothing really changes. In an era when homosexuality was actually a crime in some states, and was nationally condemned as a sick aberration, Dr. Wertham showed us that Batman and Robin were gay. He focused on how the artist drew their non-flaccid genitals to make his point. He saw covert images of female nudity concealed in the drawings of muscles and in some cases in tree-bark. Citing as further proof of the danger of comic books, Dr. Wertham said that 95% of children in reform school read comics. Superhero creator Stan Lee derides Wertham as having "said things that impressed the public and it was like shouting fire in a theater, but there was little scientific validity to it. And yet because he had the name doctor, people took what he said seriously, and it started a whole crusade against comics." Wonder Woman was a lesbian, and, although they gave her a seldom-seen boyfriend, the damage was done. Wertham said that her strength and independence was proof that she was a lesbian. In actuality, her creator, William Moulton Marston, denied she was a lesbian, saying she was really into bondage, hence her golden lasso. Shamelessly citing Nietzche, characters like Captain Marvel, Wonder Woman, Superman, and even Superduck were condemned as Nazi propaganda. It was observed that Superduck's girlfriend Luanna was indecent because she wore a short, tight skirt. She was a duck; a godamn duck. "This is really a claim of comics endorsing bestiality," said these seriously deranged experts. I don't know of anyone who was moved to have sex with a duck. (Although why Bobby Black was arrested in Prospect Park still remains a mystery and rumors still persist.)

So, in the face of "censorship," a word that nobody would admit to, or even use, The Comics Industry agreed to police themselves and brought forth the insipid "Comics Code." The code was designed specifically to prevent publication of the E.C. type of horror, reality, and crime comic books. The result was the silly and boring "Archie" comics with storylines having no relation to young life in America. The E.C.s went out of business (distributors refused to distribute to newsstands), and E.C. nearly went bankrupt. In 1955, and out of these ashes, *Mad Magazine* was born with a satirical look at life in America and the rest of the world. MAD paved the way for *The National Lampoon,* which itself morphed from their musical *The Lemmings* into *Saturday Night*

Live. This censorship exploded in their faces with the wonderfully insane, graphically violent, and sometimes pornographic genre known as "Comix." Here, the counter reaction was fierce and gave us artists like R. Crumb, Gilbert Shelton's "Fabulous Furry Freak Brothers" deliberately mirroring the stereotypes of the censors (lazy, on welfare, drug users and sellers), and many others. A reaction to the pathetic and simplistic censorship of the 1950s.

Out of these U.S. Senate hearings came strong anticensorship words by Federal Judge John M. Woolsey, who wrote about the First Amendment rights of children:

> Entertaining reading has never harmed anyone. It is only with the normal person that the law is concerned. Our American children are for the most part normal children. They are bright children, but those who want to prohibit comic magazines seem to see dirty, sneaky, perfected monsters who use the comics as a blueprint for action. Perverted little monsters are few and far between. They don't read comics. What are we afraid of? Are we afraid of our own children? Do we forget that they are citizens too and entitled to select what to read or do? Do you think our children are so evil, so simple minded, that it takes a story of a murder to set them to murder, a story of robbery to set them to robbery?"

Thanks to comic books, and fantasy, I was freed to discern the abstract from the literal and this was of course a danger to the youth of America. Still, to this day, it's the comics and cartoons like *The Simpsons, Family Guy, and American Dad* (he works for the C.I.A.) that dare to deal with the controversial. No sitcom that I know of ever dealt seriously with being gay, gay marriage, stem cell research, the teaching of "creationist science" as an equal to evolution, or legalizing marijuana, with animated characters smoking right in front of you. Jesus and Buddah regularly appear in *Family Guy*. There are growing complaints about this, and I worry that these cartoons will go the way of the E.C. Comics. It happened in the 1930s and 1940s when Betty Boop cartoons were seen as dangerous to America. Betty's boyfriend Bimbo is not human, they often pat each other's butts, she dresses provocatively, often had trouble keeping her clothes on, and presented black artists like jazz singer Cab Calloway. Her view from outer space of the earth during the Great Depression showing a giant "For Sale" sign stuck in the middle of the American continent, was banned. TV's Reverend Jerry Falwell accused "The Teletubbies" of covertly trying to convert children to homosexuality. He's not alone in demanding that animated programs like *Family Guy* et al. should be heavily censored. They will always be out there.

Keeping comic books alive as a serious genre are people like Art Spiegelman who won a Pulitzer for "Maus," his comic-book rendition of his father's experiences in the Holocaust. The Jews were mice and the Germans were cats–and British comic-book writer Neil Gaiman has been included in many a Ph.D. thesis.

CRITICAL EYE

For Discussion

a. We normally think of censorship as something that happens to adults. How does the author make the argument that children experience censorship, too? And when it happens, is he saying that it is no less damaging for a child—perhaps even more so?

b. It can be argued that by outlining the so-called offenses within comic books, the censors actually highlighted these "offenses" for comic book readers. How is this true?

c. Much of our early days are defined by what we learn in school. What did our author learn? What impact did school and educators have on him? How did the educational system fail him and also fail to provide him an outlet for his natural self?

Re-approaching the Reading

Compare this essay to the one by David Sedaris. What are the similarities? Both young male students suffered a form of academic hazing or humiliation at the hands of their teachers. How was their hazing similar? What were the results? What does this type of "instruction" do to a young mind?

Writing Assignment

The author derides the implementation of censorship—especially in institutions of learning. Examine our world today. Does censorship exist? Are there things we can't read, do, or say? What are these censorable offenses? Is some societal censorship acceptable?

Race and Racial Matters

Kindness and compassion toward all living things is a mark of a civilized society. Conversely, cruelty, whether it is directed against human beings or against animals, is not the exclusive province of any one culture or community of people. Racism, economic deprival, dog fighting and cock fighting, bull fighting and rodeos are cut from the same fabric: violence. Only when we have become nonviolent toward all life will we have learned to live well ourselves.
Cesar Chavez

In 2008, the United States of America took a bold step when the country elected its first Black president. In many ways, American citizens hoped that this moment signaled a sea change in the discussion about race, racial matters, and racism in America. Unfortunately, it did not. Instead, President Barack H. Obama's election revealed that the nation was still racially polarized and that there was little to no "post" in our discussion about skin color. In short, we still use skin color as a defining tool and as a mechanism to weed out those who are not like us, to uphold prejudices, or to establish kinship–which is an odd thing to do since we are ALL human, despite our varying racial backgrounds.

Humans are essentially comprised of ethnic, cultural, and regional groupings that we generally oversimplify by lumping into what we call "races" of people. Actually,

Homosapiens are all of one race–the human race. Yet, we still continue–based on skin color and language, cultural and religious affiliations, social mandates and values–to separate ourselves to the extent of judgment and, too often, violent segregation. These problems with those who are "other" in our worlds frequently result in blaming and, more tragically, self-incrimination. As a result, these so-called racial conflicts continue to flare up and burn out of control. But, when examined from a position of personal intuitiveness, these moments of narrow-mindedness seem to be, moreso, issues of how we see ourselves– those flawed reflections we cast in the mirror.

Perceived differences have represented the largest gap among humankind. Historically, the world has demonstrated little tolerance for difference, making so-called matters of race the most debated issue since the evolution of our species. That said, how do we move forward in a world that, currently, seems as ethnically intolerant as at any point in history? Moreover, how do we learn to embrace ourselves and our neighbors when the diverse images of our reflective lives continue to be attacked and subjugated to the point of self-hatred and confusion?

What seems most perplexing about the issue of race is that, in fact, there is an issue of "race." Somehow, we do not look at our fellow humans and see our own humanity. Perhaps what we must do is not examine the areas where racism is a threat or problem, but, instead, excise the very roots of difference, in order to define, combat, and eliminate one of, if not the, largest quandary to ever impact our world. The following selections allow readers to consider who they are in relation to the skin color that defines them and further question how and why these notions of race and racial matters color their views of the world.

DEAN OBEIDALLAH

Do Palestinians Really Exist?

We're not all terrorists, we're not "cockroaches," and we're certainly not an "invented" people. What you don't know about Palestinians.

Palestine. My late father, Abdul Musa Obeidallah, was born there in the 1930s. When I say Palestine, that's not a political statement. It's just a statement of fact. When he was born, there was no state of Israel. There was no Hamas. No PLO. There were just people of different faiths living together on the same small piece of land called Palestine.

And to be honest, but for the Palestinian-Israeli conflict, I doubt you would've heard much about Palestinians. My father, like the seven generations of Obeidallahs born before him in his sleepy farming town of Battir, didn't harbor grand dreams or bold plans. They lived a simple life of growing fruits, vegetables, and lots of olive trees. (Palestinians love olives!) Their biggest battles weren't with other people, but with the elements.

Most of my Palestinian ancestors lived and died within a few miles of where they were born. That would likely have been my father's path as well. But as we are all keenly aware, fate had far different plans.

I share this story because I think that lost in the current Gaza conflict is the story of the Palestinians as a people. Instead, they've been continually defined as being the "bad" part of the Israeli-Palestinian conflict. They've been broadly labeled as terrorists or seen as acceptable losses. Some Israeli leaders have alleged Palestinians don't exist, or called them "cockroaches," "crocodiles," or a "cancer."

As you might imagine, being Palestinian is unique. When you tell someone you're of Palestinian heritage, it's not just an ethnicity, it's a conversation starter. In fact, just saying the word Palestine inflames some. People will tell me to my face that there has never been a Palestine and there are no such thing as Palestinians. To them, I guess Palestinians are simply holograms.

When I ask these people what the land where Israel is now located was called before 1948, they tend to stammer or offer some convoluted response. The answer is simply Palestine. Not a big deal, really.

Indeed, the United Nations debate in 1947 over the creation of the state of Israel was described in terms of the "question of Palestine." The U.N. even explained in its official summary that "It is recognized that Palestine is the common country of both indigenous Arabs and Jews, that both these peoples have had an historic association with it," adding that "Palestinian citizens, as well as Arabs and Jews who, not holding Palestinian citizenship, reside in Palestine." It's hard to hold legal citizenship of a place that doesn't exist.

Nowadays, few disagree there is a Palestinian people. After all, there are more than 5 million Palestinians in the West Bank, Gaza, and Israel alone. Of course, that didn't stop Newt Gingrich from commenting during his failed 2012 run for president that the Palestinians are an "invented" people. Here, I thought for years my father had been a cook, but apparently he was an inventor. If Gingrich—who was simply parroting his then-benefactor Sheldon Adelson's views—had engaged in the most basic of research, he would have found that most historians mark the beginning of the Palestinian Arab nationalist movement as happening in 1824, when the Arabs there rebelled against Ottoman rule.

The Palestinians, along with Israelis, have been through a lot, to say the least, since 1948, when Israel was created and the boundaries of Palestine were revised by way of UN Resolution 181. That moment immediately changed the destiny of countless Palestinians who until then had been living a humble life.

As most know, a war immediately erupted, resulting in hundreds of thousands of Palestinians being driven from their home or fleeing. Ironically, this war was waged by the surrounding Arab nations—Egypt, Jordan, etc.—which claimed they were doing it for the Palestinian people. But when Palestinian refugees sought to move into these Arab countries after the war, they often were met with horrible discrimination. In some instances, they would not be able to obtain government benefits, were not hired because of their ethnicity, or worse, were fired from a job because a citizen of that country wanted it.

To this day, many are relegated to overcrowded refugee camps, which still exist in the occupied territories as well as in Lebanon and Jordan, which is home to 22 refugee camps and millions of registered refugees per the United Nations Relief and Works Agency (UNRWA). I've visited some of these refugee camps in the West Bank, and the Sabra and Shatila refugee camp in Lebanon. The Palestinians there don't live in tents, as we see with the more recent Syrian refugee crisis. It's more akin to overcrowded ghettos where dreams are deferred on a daily basis.

That's the life of millions of Palestinians. They have survived upon the "kindness of strangers." You see, there's nothing that truly links Arabs across the region. Moroccans don't have much in common with those in Dubai. Egyptians view themselves as leaders of the Arab world, while many in Lebanon, which is relatively close to Egypt in terms of kilometers, see themselves as more European than Arab. But sympathy for the Palestinians, on varying levels, is one issue that unites them.

My forebears didn't flee their homes in Battir during the 1948 war. Since then, they have been under Jordanian rule and then Israeli after the 1967 war. They have endured intifadas and an often cruel military occupation. My grandmother's land outside Bethlehem was even confiscated by Israeli settlers, who made it part of a Jewish-only settlement. Not because she did anything wrong but simply because she was the wrong religion.

In the 1950s, my father, along with many other Palestinians, immigrated to America in search of a better life. I've often wondered what would've become of me if I had been born in the West Bank instead of New Jersey. Would I have been able to go to college and law school? Would I have a job? Would I even be alive?

When I think back to growing up in New Jersey, I realize it was a far different time for Palestinians than today. Then we were generally unknown, almost exotic. Sure, the PLO was starting to grab headlines with its deplorable terrorist attacks, but the overwhelmingly negative images we currently see associated with Palestinians had not yet taken hold.

In fact, when I was about 9 years old in the late 1970s, my teacher asked about the ethnicity of each student so she could pin it on a map of the world. When she came to me, she was stumped–she didn't know much about Palestinians, and of course she couldn't find it on the map since it wasn't there. Thankfully for her I'm also half Sicilian, and she found that easily, since most of my classmates were Italian.

Later that night, I relayed that story to my father and asked him: "Where is Palestine?" He paused for a moment as he gathered his thoughts. He then touched his heart and head and responded: "In here."

I wonder what my response will be if I have children and one day they ask: "Where is Palestine?" Will I be able to take out a map and simply point it out, like most people do when they are asked about their heritage? Or will my only option be mimicking my late father's answer? What's most painful to me is not that those are my two options but that I feel powerless to change which answer I will be able to offer.

CRITICAL EYE

For Discussion

a. Without asking the reader to "take a side," the author is attempting to place a human face on himself and his people. Does he accomplish this task?

b. If you knew nothing of the Palestinian people before reading this article, determine whether or not your knowledge/understanding of the people has increased.

Re-approaching the Reading

In what ways is this article about family and Identity?

Writing Assignment

Author Elie Wiesel writes a lot about his life as a Jewish man and Jewish history and culture. Research the man and his writings and consider these findings alongside Dean Obeidallah's article. What is similar about how both men feel about their cultural history?

WOODEN LEG

YOUNG MEN, GO OUT AND FIGHT THEM

The gold rush of 1874, which lured thousands of white prospectors into the Black Hills of South Dakota, was a crucial factor in provoking a major confrontation between the United States and the Plains Indians. To the powerful Sioux nation these mountains were sacred terrain, and also properly protected by the Fort Laramie Treaty of 1868, signed by the Sioux and the United States government. It was Lieutenant Colonel George Armstrong Custer who originally violated that treaty. In July 1874, ostensibly to locate a site for a new fort, but covertly to hunt for mineral resources, Custer led the expedition into the Black Hills and reported that there was gold "from the grassroots down."

So it was poetic justice that in late June 1876 Custer's small command should blunder into the largest gathering of Plains Indian fighters ever assembled–an estimated twelve to fifteen thousand Indians, with at least four thousand fighting men, drawn from the Teton, Santee and Yankton Sioux, Assiniboine, Cheyenne, Arapaho, and Gros Ventre, camped together along three miles of the bank of the Little Big Horn River in central Montana. Under the leadership of the Sioux war chiefs Sitting Bull and Crazy Horse and the Cheyenne headman Two Moons, the natives comprised die-hard hostiles and recent reservation runaways come together momentarily as a united front.

Here is one warrior's memory of the tumultuous day of "many soldiers falling into camp," the battle of the Little Big Horn. Wooden Leg, the narrator, was about eighteen years old when Custer disastrously divided his Seventh Cavalry forces, ignored warnings from his Crow scouts, and was cut down along with all 225 of his officers and men. The battle was a freakish victory for the Indians, stunning the victors along with the vanquished. The tribes did not have sufficient unity or ammunition to follow it up with a broader offensive. Their forces quickly scattered, with Sitting Bull and his followers hiding out in Canada until 1881.

In my sleep I dreamed that a great crowd of people were making lots of noise. Something in the noise startled me. I found myself wide awake, sitting up and listening. My brother too awakened, and we both jumped to our feet. A great commotion was going on among the camps. We heard shooting. We hurried out from the trees so we might see as well as hear.

The shooting was somewhere at the upper part of the camp circles. It looked as if all of the Indians there were running away toward

"Young Men, Go Out and Fight Them" from *Wooden Leg: A Warrior Who Fought Custer.* Interpreted by Thomas B. Marquis. Published by the University of Nebraska Press.

the hills to the westward or down toward the village. Women were screaming and men were letting out war cries. Through it all we could hear old men calling: "Soldiers are here! Young men, go out and fight them."

We ran to our camp and to our home lodge. Everybody there was excited. Women were hurriedly making up little packs for flight. Some were going off northward or across the river without any packs. Children were hunting for their mothers. Mothers were anxiously trying to find their children. I got my lariat and my six-shooter. I hastened on down toward where had been our horse herd. . . .

My father had caught my favorite horse from the herd brought in by the boys and Bald Eagle. I quickly emptied out my war bag and set myself at getting ready to go into battle. I jerked off my ordinary clothing. I jerked on a pair of new breeches that had been given to me by an Uncpapa Sioux. I had a good cloth shirt, and I put it on. My old moccasins were kicked off and a pair of beaded moccasins substituted for them.

My father strapped a blanket upon my horse and arranged the rawhide lariat into a bridle. He stood holding my mount. "Hurry," he urged me.

The air was so full of dust I could not see where to go. But it was not, needful that I see that far. I kept my horse headed in the direction of movement by the crowd of Indians on horseback. I was led out around and far beyond the Uncpapa camp circle. Many hundreds of Indians on horseback were dashing to and fro in front of a body of soldiers. The soldiers were on the level valley ground and were shooting with rifles. Not many bullets were being sent back at them, but thousands of arrows were falling among them. I went on with a throng of Sioux until we got beyond and behind the white men. By this time, though, they had mounted their horses and were hiding themselves in the timber. . . .

Suddenly the hidden soldiers came tearing out on horseback, from the woods. I was around on that side where they came out. I whirled my horse and lashed it into a dash to escape from them. All others of my companions did the same. But soon we discovered they were not following us. They were running away from us. They were going as fast as their tired horses could carry them across an open valley space and toward the river. We stopped, looked a moment, and then we whipped our ponies into swift pursuit. A great throng of Sioux also were coming after them. A distant position put them among the leaders in the chase. The soldier horses moved slowly, as if they were very tired. Ours were lively. We gained rapidly on them.

I fired four shots with my six-shooter. I do not know whether or not any of my bullets did harm. I saw a Sioux put an arrow into the back of a soldier's head. Another arrow went into his shoulder. He tumbled from his horse to the ground. Others fell dead either from arrows or from stabbings or jabbings or from blows by the stone war clubs of the Sioux. Horses limped or staggered or sprawled out dead or dying.

Our war cries and war songs were mingled with many jeering calls, such as: "You are only boys. You ought not to be fighting. We whipped you on the Rosebud. You should have brought more Crows or Shoshones with you to do your fighting."

Little Bird and I were after one certain soldier. Little Bird was wearing a trailing warbonnet. He was at the right and I was at the left of the fleeing man. We were lashing him and his horse with our pony whips. It seemed not brave to shoot him. Besides, I did not want to waste my bullets. He pointed back his revolver, though, and sent a bullet into

Little Bird's thigh. Immediately I whacked the white man fighter on his head with the heavy elk-horn handle of my pony whip. The blow dazed him. I seized the rifle strapped on his back. I wrenched it and dragged the looping strap over his head. As I was getting possession of this weapon, he fell to the ground. I did not harm him further. I do not know what became of him. The jam of oncoming Indians swept me on. . . .

I returned to the west side of the river. Lots of Indians were hunting around there for dead soldiers or for wounded ones to kill. I joined in this search. I got some tobacco from the pockets of one dead man. I got also a belt having in it a few cartridges. All of the weapons and clothing and all other possessions were being taken from the bodies. The warriors were doing this. No old people nor women were there. They all had run away to the hill benches to the westward.

I went to a dead horse, to see what might be found there. Leather bags were on them, behind the saddles. I rummaged into one of these bags. I found there two pasteboard boxes. I broke open one of them. "Oh, cartridges!"

There were twenty of them in each box, forty in all. Thirty of them were used to fill up the vacant places in my belt. The remaining ten I wrapped into a piece of cloth and dropped them down into my own little kit bag. Now I need not be so careful in expending ammunition. Now I felt very brave. . . .

The shots quit coming from the soldiers. Warriors who had crept close to them began to call out that all of the white men were dead. All of the Indians then jumped up and rushed forward. All of the boys and old men on their horses came tearing into the crowd. The air was full of dust and smoke. Everybody was greatly excited. It looked like thousands of dogs might look if all of them were mixed together in a fight. All of the Indians were saying these soldiers also went crazy and killed themselves. I do not know. I could not see them. But I believe they did so. . . .

I took one scalp. As I went walking and leading my horse among the dead, I observed one face that interested me. The dead man had a long beard growing from both sides of his face and extending several inches below the chin. He had also a full mustache. All of the beard hair was of a light, yellow color, as I now recall it. Most of the soldiers had beards growing, in different lengths, but this was the longest one I saw among them. I think the dead man may have been thirty or more years old. "Here is a new kind of scalp," I said to a companion. I skinned one side of the face and half of the chin, so as to keep the long beard yet on the part removed. I got an arrow shaft and tied the strange scalp to the end of it. . . .

I waved my scalp as I rode among our people. The first person I met who took special interest in me was my mother's mother. She was living in a little willow dome lodge of her own. "What is that?" she asked me when I flourished the scalp stick toward her. I told her. "I give it to you," I said, and I held it out to her. She screamed and shrank away. "Take it," I urged. "It will be good medicine for you." Then I went on to tell her about my having killed the Crow or Shoshone at the first right up the river, about my getting the two guns, about my knocking in the head two soldiers in the river, about what I had done in the next fight on the hill where all of the soldiers had been killed. We talked about my soldier clothing. She said I looked good dressed that way. I had thought so too, but neither the coat nor the breeches fit me well. The arms and legs were too short for me. Finally she decided she would take the scalp. She went then into her own little lodge. . . .

There was no dancing nor celebrating of any kind in any of the camps that night. Too many people were in mourning, among all of the Sioux as well as among the Cheyennes. Too many Cheyenne and Sioux women had gashed their arms and legs, in token of their grief. The people generally were praying, not cheering. There was much noise and confusion, but this was from other causes. Young men were going out to fight the first soldiers now hiding themselves on the hill across the river from where had been the first fighting during the morning. . . .

I did not go back that afternoon nor that night to help in fighting the first soldiers. Late in the night, though, I went as a scout. Five young men of the Cheyennes were appointed to guard our camp while other people slept. These were Big Nose, Yellow Horse, Little Shield, Horse Road and Wooden Leg. One or other of us was out somewhere looking over the country all the time. Two of us went once over to the place where the soldiers were hidden. We got upon hill points higher than they were. We could look down among them. We could have shot among them, but we did not do this. We just saw that they yet were there.

Five other young men took our duties in the last part of the night. I was glad to be relieved. I did not go to my family group for rest. I let loose my horse and dropped myself down upon a thick pad of grassy sod.

WOODEN LEG, *Northern Cheyenne*

Critical Eye

For Discussion

a. Why does war seem to be such a necessary component of every society?

b. Why was the resistance to the colonists of such grave importance to the tribal peoples, even though their battles, in many cases, were futile?

Re-approaching the Reading

Some people say that the conquering of "weaker" peoples is a part of human nature. Keeping this in mind, discuss the rights of the settlers to the native lands.

Writing Assignment

Many ethnic groups in the United States, such as the Irish and Blacks, have undergone some form of harsh treatment at the hands of those perceived to be stronger or more superior. Have we resolved our differences or, racially speaking, are we worse off than at any time in American history?

TAHIRA NAQVI

BRAVE WE ARE

"Mom, Ammi," he asks, the little boy Kasim who is my son, who has near-black eyes and whose buck teeth give him a Bugs Bunny look when his mouth is open, as it is now, in query. "What does hybrid mean?"

"Hybrid?" I'm watching the water in the pot very closely; the tiny bubbles quivering restlessly on its surface indicate it's about to come to boil. Poised over the pot, clutching a batch of straw-colored Prince spaghetti, is my hand, suspended, warm from the steam and waiting for the moment when the bubbles will suddenly and turbulently come to life.

I'm not fussy about brands, especially where spaghetti is concerned (it's all pasta, after all), but I wish there was one which would fit snugly at the outset into my largest pot. As things stand now, the strands bend uncomfortably, contort, embroiling themselves in something of a struggle within the confines of the pot once they've been dropped into the boiling water. Someday of course, I will have a pot large enough to accommodate all possible lengths and varieties.

"Yeah, hybrid. Do you know what it means?"

The note of restive insistence in his voice compels me to tear my gaze away from the water. Kasim's face looks darker now than when he left for school this morning. Perhaps running up the steep driveway with the March wind lashing against his lean nine-year-old frame has forced the blood to rush to his face. Flushed, his face reminds me he's still only a child, 'only ten, just a baby,' as my mother often says when I sometimes take him to task in her presence, arguing with him as if he were a man behaving like a child.

A new spelling word? Such a difficult word for a fourth-grader. "Are you studying plants?"

"No, but can you tell me what it means?" Impatient, so impatient, so like the water that's hissing and tumbling in the pot, demanding immediate attention. He slides against the kitchen counter and hums, his fingers beating an indecipherable rhythm on the Formica, his eyes raised above mine, below mine, behind me, to the window outside which white, lavender and gray have mingled to become a muddied brown. Just as he reaches for the cookie jar I quickly throw in the spaghetti.

"Well, that's a hard word. Let me see." Helplessly I watch as he breaks off a Stella Doro biscuit in his mouth and crumbs disperse in a steady fall-out, over the counter, on the kitchen tile, some getting caught in his blue-and-green striped sweater, like flies in a spider's web. "It's a sort of mixture, a combination of different sorts of things," I say wisely, with the absolute knowledge that 'things' is susceptible to misinterpretation. I rack my brain for a good example. If I don't hurry up with one he's going to move away with the notion that his mother doesn't know what hybrid means.

"Brave We Are" from *Dying in a Strange Country* (Tsar, 2001), reprinted by permission of Tsar Publications.

"You mean if you mix orange juice with lemonade it's going to become hybrid juice?" The idea has proved ticklish, he smiles, crumbs from the Stella Doro dangling on the sides of his face; they obviously don't bother him as much as they bother me. I lean forward and rub a hand around his mouth just as he lunges toward the cookie jar again. He squirms and recoils at the touch of my ministering hand. Another biscuit is retrieved. I turn down the heat under the spaghetti to medium and start chopping onions.

Today I'm making spaghetti the way my mother makes it in Lahore, like pulao, the way I used to make it after I got married and was just learning to cook for a husband who had selective tastes in food. That was about the only thing I could make then so I worked hard to embellish and innovate. There, we call it noodles, although it's unmistakably spaghetti, with no tomato sauce or meatballs in or anywhere near it, no cheese either, and no one has heard of mozzarella or romano. The idea of cheese with our recipe would surprise the people in Lahore; even the ones with the most adventurous palates will cringe.

"Well, that too." And why not? My eyes smart from the sharpness of the onions, tears fill my eyes and spill over my cheeks. I turn away from the chopping board. "The word is used when you breed two different kinds of plants or animals, it's called cross-breeding." I snaffle. This gets harder. I know his knowledge of breeding is limited and 'cross' isn't going to help at all.

"*What's cross-what you may call it?*"

An example. One that will put the seal on hybrid forever. So he can boast his mother knows everything.

I wipe my watering eyes with a paper napkin and turn to the onions again. These, chopped thinly, are for the ground beef which will be cooked with small green peas, cubed potatoes and cut-leaf spinach and will be spiced with coriander, garlic, cumin, a touch of turmeric and half-inch long bristly strands of fresh ginger root. I'll throw the beef into the spaghetti when it's done and my husband and I alone will eat what I make. My children like spaghetti the way it should be, the way it is in America.

Moisture runs down my cheeks and my eyes smart. I place the knife down on the chopping board, tear out another sheet from the roll of Bounty towels on my right and rub my eyes and nose with it, my attention driven to the stark, brown limbs of trees outside as I wipe my face. The kitchen window that I now face as I do innumerable times during the day, faithfully reflects the movements of time and seasons of the small town in Connecticut where we live, compelling the spirit to buoyancy or, when the tones on its canvas are achromatous and dark, to melancholy, to sadness. Today, the sun is visible again and the white of the snow is distinguishable from the lavender of the bare, thin, stalky birches, unhealthy because we haven't tended them well. Sharply the sun cuts shadows on the clean, uncluttered snow.

Why does snow in February always remind me of February in Lahore? Incongruent, disparate, the seasons have so little in common. March is spring, grass so thick your foot settles into it, roses that bloom firm, their curves fleshy, the colors like undisturbed paint on an artist's palette, the air timberous, weaving in and out of swishing tree branches with the *sar, sar, sar* of a string instrument. Why do I turn to Eileen, my cleaning lady, and say, "Eileen, do you know it's spring in Lahore?" She looks up from the pot she's scrubbing in the kitchen sink with a good-humored smile. "No kidding? Really?" she asks, as if she didn't already know, as if she hadn't already heard it from me before.

An example, yes. "Now take an apple. A farmer can cross-breed a Macintosh apple with a Golden Yellow and get something which is a little bit like both. That will be a hybrid apple." I look closely at the boy's face for some signs of comprehension.

"You mean the apple's going to have a new name, like Macintosh Yellow?" he asks, his forehead creased thoughtfully.

"Yes." Relieved, I return to the onions, making a mental note to check the spaghetti soon, which, languorously swelled now, will have to be taken off from the stove and drained.

"But what about animals? You said there's *cross what you may call it* in animals too." He sprawls against the counter, up and down, right and left, like a gymnast.

"Yes there is. A cow from one family may be bred with a steer from another family and they'll end up with a calf that's a bit like the two of them." I wash my hands and he skips on the floor, dance-like steps, his arms raised.

"But man's an animal too, teacher says. Do people also cross . . . *umm* . . . breed?"

He's humming again. I know the tune now; "*Suzie Q/ Suzie Q/ I love you/O Suzie Q!*" It's from a song on his older brother Haider's tape, a catchy tune, sort of stays with you and you can't stop humming it. Both Haider and my younger son, Asghar, were amused when I showed an interest in the song. What do I know about music, their kind of music? Once, nearly two years ago, I tried to bribe Haider to memorize a ghazal by the poet Ghalib. The greatest Urdu poet of the subcontinent, I said passionately, the most complex. Egged on by the fifty dollars I was offering, he mastered the first verse by listening to a tape of ghazals sung by Mehdi Hasan.

> *Yeh naa thi hamari qismet ke visal-e-yaar ho*
> *Agar aurjeete rehte yehi intizar hota*
>
> "It was not fated that I should meet my beloved,
> Life will merely prolong the waiting"

Then, unable to sustain his interest, despite the now thirty-dollar a verse rate, Haider abandoned the project.

"The words are too hard," he complained when I protested, somewhat angrily. "The music's easy, but I can't keep up with the lyrics."

And I would have given him the money too. Actually I had decided to give him all of it after he had moved on to the second verse.

"Does that mean Mary is also hybrid?" Kasim's voice crashes into my thoughts of Suzie Q with a loud boom.

I lower the heat under the spaghetti—so what if it's a bit overdone. The yellow-white strands jump at each other in frantic embraces, hurried, as if there's no time to be lost.

"Mary? What are you talking about?" I know exactly what he's talking about. His vagueness passes through the sieve in my head and comes out as clarity. I fill in any blanks, uncannily, never ceasing to be surprised at the way this peculiar magic works.

"You know, Mary Khan, Dr. Khan's daughter? She's in my class Mom, you know her."

Yes, I know Mary well. Her full name is Marium. Her father, Amjad Khan and my husband, Ali, were together in the same medical school in Lahore, they graduated the same year, they completed residencies together at the same hospital in New York, where Amjad met and married Helen, a nurse. Helen is English. She's a few years older than I, very tall, almost a half-inch taller than Amjad, and has sleek, golden hair. We're good friends, Helen and I, and at least once a week we meet for lunch at a restaurant, an activity we decided to call 'sampling restaurants for later.' Over salmon lasagna or papadi chat and dosa or tandoori chicken she'll tell me how difficult Amjad is when it comes to their children, how upset he is that their son has taken it upon himself to date without his father's consent or approval.

I'll shake my head and try to explain that Amjad might have dated *her,* but like a good Muslim father, he can't accept that his son can have girlfriends. "Wait till Mary is older," I say with my hand on Helen's arm, "the Muslim father in him will drop all his masks." Together we do what most women do quite unabashedly: spend a great deal of time talking about husbands.

When Mary was born Amjad said, "We're going to call her Marium, it's a name everyone knows." Familiar and convenient is what he meant, since it's tri-religious. That doesn't sound right, but if we can say bisexual, surely we can say tri-religious too. Why not? After all Islam, Christianity and Judaism all profess a claim to this name. However, before the child was quite one 'Marium' was shortened permanently to Mary.

Kasim is at the breakfast table now, some of his earlier energy dissipated. A small piece of biscuit lies forlornly before him on the table and he fusses with it slowly, obviously unwilling to pop the last bit in his mouth, content just to play with it.

"You know, her mother's English and her father's Pakistani like Dad, and she's got blue eyes and black hair."

"Yes, she does have lovely blue eyes and they look so pretty with her dark hair." I grapple with something to blunt the sharpness of his next question which I anticipate and I know I cannot repel.

"Well, then she's hybrid too, isn't she?" He's looking straight at me. His eyes are bright with the defiance of someone who knows he's scored a point.

Brave we are, we who answer questions that spill forth artlessly from the mouths of nine-year-old purists, questions that can neither be waved nor dismissed with flippant ambiguity. Vigilant and alert, we must be ready with our answers.

"Technically speaking she is, I mean, wait, you can say she is." I lift a hand and stop him before he says more. "But we don't use the word for people." The firmness in my voice sounds forced. "Don't say anything to her, okay?"

"Why? Is it a swear?"

"No!" I hasten with denial. "Of course not. It's just a word we don't use for people, that's all. Understand?"

"But what do you call them then?" He persists. "Mary's like the apple, isn't she? Isn't she? Her name's Mary Khan, isn't it?"

"Yes, Kas, it is. But there's nothing wrong with that name, a name's a name." Kasim looks contemplative. I know he's saying to himself, *Mom doesn't really know, but Mary's a hybrid, she's got blue eyes and black hair.*

"She's a person Kasim, not an apple. Anyway, you didn't tell me where you heard that word. Is it on your spelling list for this week?"

"No, Mrs. Davis was reading us something about plants in the *Weekly Reader.* It's not homework." He shrugs, abandons the Stella Doro and humming, leaves the kitchen.

"Get to homework now," I call after him, wondering if there's an equivalent of 'hybrid' in Urdu, a whole word, not one or two strung together in a phrase to mean the same thing. Offhand I can't think of one.

Without meaning to I throw some oregano into the boiling spaghetti. I shouldn't have done that. How's oregano going to taste in the company of coriander and cumin? Well, no matter, it's too late anyway.

After I've drained the spaghetti I will take some out for the meat mixture, saving the rest for my children. Then I'll add to our portion, my husband's and mine, the beef and vegetable mixture and turn everything over ever so gently, making sure that the spaghetti isn't squelched. The strands must remain smooth, elusive, separate.

CRITICAL EYE

For Discussion

a. Can you make the argument that issues of race are very difficult for parents to discuss with their children?

b. Is it necessary for a child from a mixed background to choose a race?

c. In your opinion, why is the mother uncomfortable?

d. What do you think about the mother's responses to her child's questions about the notion of a "hybrid"?

Re-approaching the Reading

Consider how the story would change if the mother were to simply tell her child that race should never be an issue when determining one's worth.

Writing Assignment

Imagine a world where everyone has a mixed background. Would we then finally be rid of racial intolerance?

STEVEN ERLANGER

Amid Tears, Flickering Candles and Flowers, a Shaken Norway Mourns

OSLO—Sunday was a day of remembrance and self-examination for Norway, a small country shaken by the massacre of at least 93 of its people, many of them children, by one of its own.

The royal family and average citizens alike, some traveling long distances, came to a memorial service for the dead in the Oslo Cathedral. Long lines of people of all ages and colors waited patiently and quietly, some of them crying, to lay flowers or light candles at the spreading blanket of bouquets in front of the cathedral. Someone propped up a radio on a post so those waiting could listen to the service inside.

At the same time, the Norwegian police and security services faced numerous questions about their slow response to the reports of shooting on the island of Utoya, where the country's governing Labor Party was holding its annual political summer camp, considered Norway's nursery school for future leaders. The police took an hour to arrive on the island after the first reports, and officials said that it was hard to find boats and that their helicopters were only capable of surveillance, not of shooting down the killer.

Anders Behring Breivik, 32, the only suspect arrested, admits to the shootings on Utoya and the fatal bombing of government offices in Oslo, his lawyer, Geir Lippestad, told Norwegian news media, but rejects "criminal responsibility." Mr. Lippestad said that Mr. Breivik insists that he acted alone, and alone wrote his mammoth manifesto—rambling from a hostile historical look at Islam to recipes (and price lists) for bomb manufacture to his family's pressure on him to date.

"He has said that he believed the actions were atrocious, but that in his head they were necessary," the lawyer said. "He wanted a change in society and, from his perspective, he needed to force through a revolution. He wished to attack society and the structure of society."

He also clearly wants to leave a legacy and thinks he will create some kind of mass following, said Tore Bjorgo, one of Norway's most respected scholars of right-wing extremism. "He had this strange idea that he will provoke a mass following, despite the violence, which is why I put it in a Christian frame," said Mr. Bjorgo, a professor at the Norwegian Police University College.

Mr. Breivik, who has cooperated with the police, has asked for an open hearing in the City Court of Oslo on Monday morning, when the police will seek to detain him for another four weeks on suspicion of terrorism—longer if necessary for the investigation—before the prosecution brings formal charges.

Some speculated that Mr. Breivik is seeking another public platform for his anti-immigrant, anti-Muslim ideas, which center around the conservation of cultural and Christian values in the face of what he sees as a continuing effort by Islam to conquer Europe since the Ottomans were stopped at the gates of Vienna in 1683. His manifesto, called "2083—A European Declaration of Independence," seemed intended to reflect the 400th anniversary of the siege.

Mr. Breivik was said by analysts to have been an occasional commenter on a blog, Gates of Vienna, which is topped by these words: "At the siege of Vienna in 1683 Islam seemed poised to overrun Christian Europe. We are in a new phase of a very old war."

According to the police, when he surrendered, Mr. Breivik was carrying an automatic rifle and a pistol and he still retained "a considerable amount of ammunition." Doctors have said that he was apparently using dumdum bullets, expanding rounds designed to inflict the deadliest wounds possible in unarmored victims.

With no death penalty and the longest prison term possible in Norway set at 21 years, some Norwegians wondered how best to punish Mr. Breivik.

Hedda Felin, a political scientist and human resources manager, said that giving Mr. Breivik an open platform "was more of a reward than a punishment." He said in his manifesto that he considered killing Norway's top journalists at their yearly meeting, she said, for not listening to him and his arguments.

"He wants an open trial to be listened to, so journalists will now write about his ideas," Ms. Felin said. "A real punishment would be not to write about him at all."

There were church services all over Norway on Sunday. At the Oslo Cathedral, King Harald V and Queen Sonja of Norway were both in tears, and they were hardly alone. Prime Minister Jens Stoltenberg, who knew many of the dead, said, "We are crying with you, we feel for you." The brief period since the killings "feels like an eternity—hours and days and nights filled with shock and angst and weeping," he said.

"Each and every one of those who has left us is a tragedy," Mr. Stoltenberg added. "Together, it is a national tragedy."

Outside, among the mourners, Tured Mong, a pensioner, said she drove 40 miles with her husband to bring flowers from her garden and a candle she wanted to light. "I only want to lay them down here," Ms. Mong said. "I am sorry for all the parents waiting to find some news who don't know about their children." She added: "I wanted to bring the flowers and light a candle. It's very hard to just sit and watch the TV. I feel like I'm doing something."

Another mourner, Evy Andersen, from Oslo, brought a sunflower from her garden. "I have a niece who has been to this camp twice, and she has many friends who are missing," she said. "She is wondering about them. I did this for her and for myself."

Ms. Andersen said there would be useful introspection for a country that thinks of itself as favored and far from the world's worst problems. "We've been in such a favorable position, we've forgotten a bit about the others among us," she said. "We're a bit spoiled."

Borge Wilhemsen, a Labor Party activist, said he drove for five hours to be at the memorial service, along with his 6-year-old daughter.

"You can't take them away from everything," he said, referring to his daughter. "They have to learn that life is sometimes hard. I have not told her everything. I told her that there were two big accidents."

Mr. Wilhemsen said he knew a number of those killed at the island camp. Some of them were as young as 12, he said.

There were also many mourners who were immigrants or children of mixed race. Le Lemeo, a refugee from Vietnam 21 years ago, said: "Norway helped the Vietnamese people to come here. They were very welcoming." Mr. Le said he was a well-known sushi chef here. "I have a job and a family, and I wanted to come," he said. "It is very sad for all the young people."

Marina Heier, 15, is the product of a Norwegian mother and a South African father; she was born here and is a native Norwegian speaker as well as fluent in English. She, too, brought flowers from her garden. "It's important that everyone in Norway stands together," Marina said. "This is a reminder of the danger of hatred."

CRITICAL EYE

For Discussion

a. We often believe that issues of race and bigotry are specific to our own immediate part of the world. How does the Norwegian tragedy disprove that claim?

b. More often than not, this level of violence changes a people irrevocably. Given their law enforcement agency's slow response to the crime scene, what do you believe the people of Norway need to do differently? Will making these kinds of changes–in order to prepare for a more violent world–make this nation more like us?

Re-approaching the Reading

There is no death penalty in Norway, and the most that any one individual can spend in jail is 21 years. Is something wrong with this policy? Do they need to institute a death penalty policy immediately in order to bring Mr. Breivik to justice?

Writing Assignment

When individuals like Breivik commit these kinds of crimes, we often wonder just how sane the individual actually is. Is insanity ever a plausible excuse in the face of such depraved inhumanity? In order to deter them from committing these kinds of crimes, what should we do to punish them when these murderous individuals act out?

CHARLES CHESTNUT

AN EVENING VISIT

From the Novel *The House Behind the Cedars*

TOWARD evening of the same day, Warwick took his way down Front Street in the gathering dusk. By the time night had spread its mantle over the earth, he had reached the gate by which he had seen the girl of his morning walk enter the cedar-bordered garden. He stopped at the gate and glanced toward the house, which seemed dark and silent and deserted.

"It's more than likely," he thought, "that they are in the kitchen. I reckon I'd better try the back door."

But as he drew cautiously near the corner, he saw a man's figure outlined in the yellow light streaming from the open door of a small house between Front Street and the cooper shop. Wishing, for reasons of his own, to avoid observation, Warwick did not turn the corner, but walked on down Front Street until he reached a point from which he could see, at a long angle, a ray of light proceeding from the kitchen window of the house behind the cedars.

"They are there," he muttered with a sigh of relief, for he had feared they might be away. "I suspect I'll have to go to the front door, after all. No one can see me through the trees."

He retraced his steps to the front gate, which he essayed to open. There was apparently some defect in the latch, for it refused to work. Warwick remembered the trick, and with a slight sense of amusement, pushed his foot under the gate and gave it a hitch to the left, after which it opened readily enough. He walked softly up the sanded path, tiptoed up the steps and across the piazza, and rapped at the front door, not too loudly, lest this too might attract the attention of the man across the street. There was no response to his rap. He put his ear to the door and heard voices within, and the muffled sound of footsteps. After a moment he rapped again, a little louder than before.

There was an instant cessation of the sounds within. He rapped a third time, to satisfy any lingering doubt in the minds of those who he felt sure were listening in some trepidation. A moment later a ray of light streamed through the keyhole.

"Who's there?" a woman's voice inquired somewhat sharply.

"A gentleman," answered Warwick, not holding it yet time to reveal himself. "Does Mis' Molly Walden live here?"

"Yes," was the guarded answer. "I'm Mis' Walden. What's yo'r business?"

"I have a message to you from your son John."

A key clicked in the lock. The door opened, and the elder of the two women Warwick had seen upon the piazza stood in the doorway, peering curiously and with signs of great excitement into the face of the stranger.

"You've got a message from my son, you say?" she asked with tremulous agitation. "Is he sick, or in trouble?"

From *The House Behind the Cedars* by Charles Chestnut, Houghton Mifflin 1990.

"No. He's well and doing well, and sends his love to you, and hopes you've not forgotten him."

"Fergot him? No, God knows I ain't fergot him! But come in, sir, an' tell me somethin' mo' about him."

Warwick went in, and as the woman closed the door after him, he threw a glance round the room. On the wall, over the mantelpiece, hung a steel engraving of General Jackson at the battle of New Orleans, and, on the opposite wall, a framed fashion-plate from "Godey's Lady's Book." In the middle of the room an octagonal centre-table with a single leg, terminating in three sprawling feet, held a collection of curiously shaped sea-shells. There was a great haircloth sofa, somewhat the worse for wear, and a well-filled bookcase. The screen standing before the fireplace was covered with Confederate bank-notes of various denominations and designs, in which the heads of Jefferson Davis and other Confederate leaders were conspicuous.

> "Imperious Cæsar, dead, and turned to clay,
> Might stop a hole to keep the wind away,"

murmured the young man, as his eye fell upon this specimen of decorative art.

The woman showed her visitor to a seat. She then sat down facing him and looked at him closely. "When did you last see my son?" she asked.

"I've never met your son," he replied.

Her face fell. "Then the message comes through you from somebody else?"

"No, directly from your son."

She scanned his face with a puzzled look. This bearded young gentleman, who spoke so politely and was dressed so well, surely—no, it could not be! and yet—

Warwick was smiling at her through a mist of tears. An electric spark of sympathy flashed between them. They rose as if moved by one impulse, and were clasped in each other's arms.

"John, my John! It *is* John!"

"Mother—my dear old mother!"

"I didn't think," she sobbed, "that I'd ever see you again."

He smoothed her hair and kissed her. "And are you glad to see me, mother?"

"Am I glad to see you? It's like the dead comin' to life. I thought I'd lost you forever, John, my son, my darlin' boy!" she answered, hugging him strenuously.

"I couldn't live without seeing you, mother," he said. He meant it, too, or thought he did, although he had not seen her for ten years.

"You've grown so tall, John, and are such a fine gentleman! And you *are* a gentleman now, John, ain't you—sure enough? Nobody knows the old story?"

"Well, mother, I've taken a man's chance in life, and have tried to make the most of it; and I haven't felt under any obligation to spoil it by raking up old stories that are best forgotten. There are the dear old books: have they been read since I went away?"

"No, honey, there's be'n nobody to read 'em, excep' Rena, an' she don't take to books quite like you did. But I've kep' 'em dusted clean, an' kep' the moths an' the bugs out; for I hoped you'd come back some day, an' knowed you'd like to find 'em all in their places, jus' like you left 'em."

"That's mighty nice of you, mother. You could have done no more if you had loved them for themselves. But where is Rena? I saw her on the street to-day, but she didn't know me from Adam; nor did I guess it was she until she opened the gate and came into the yard."

"I've be'n so glad to see you that I'd fergot about her," answered the mother. "Rena, oh, Rena!"

The girl was not far away; she had been standing in the next room, listening intently to every word of the conversation, and only kept from coming in by a certain constraint that made a brother whom she had not met for so many years seem almost as much a stranger as if he had not been connected with her by any tie.

"Yes, mamma," she answered, coming forward.

"Rena, child, here's yo'r brother John, who's come back to see us. Tell 'im howdy."

As she came forward, Warwick rose, put his arm around her waist, drew her toward him, and kissed her affectionately, to her evident embarrassment. She was a tall girl, but he towered above her in quite a protecting fashion; and she thought with a thrill how fine it would be to have such a brother as this in the town all the time. How proud she would be, if she could but walk up the street with such a brother by her side! She could then hold up her head before all the world, oblivious to the glance of pity or contempt. She felt a very pronounced respect for this tall gentleman who held her blushing face between his hands and looked steadily into her eyes.

"You're the little sister I used to read stories to, and whom I promised to come and see some day. Do you remember how you cried when I went away?"

"It seems but yesterday," she answered. "I've still got the dime you gave me."

He kissed her again, and then drew her down beside him on the sofa, where he sat enthroned between the two loving and excited women. No king could have received more sincere or delighted homage. He was a man, come into a household of women,—a man of whom they were proud, and to whom they looked up with fond reverence. For he was not only a son,—a brother—but he represented to them the world from which circumstances had shut them out, and to which distance lent even more than its usual enchantment; and they felt nearer to this far-off world because of the glory which Warwick reflected from it.

"You're a very pretty girl," said Warwick, regarding his sister thoughtfully. "I followed you down Front Street this morning, and scarcely took my eyes off you all the way; and yet I didn't know you, and scarcely saw your face. You improve on acquaintance; to-night, I find you handsomer still."

"Now, John," said his mother, expostulating mildly, "you'll spile her, if you don't min'."

The girl was beaming with gratified vanity. What woman would not find such praise sweet from almost any source, and how much more so from this great man, who, from his exalted station in the world, must surely know the things whereof he spoke! She believed every word of it; she knew it very well indeed, but wished to hear it repeated and itemized and emphasized.

"No, he won't, mamma," she asserted, "for he's flattering me. He talks as if I was some rich young lady, who lives on the Hill,"—the Hill was the aristocratic portion of the town,—"instead of a poor"—

"Instead of a poor young girl, who has the hill to climb," replied her brother, smoothing her hair with his hand. Her hair was long and smooth and glossy, with a wave like the ripple of a summer breeze upon the surface of still water. It was the girl's great pride, and had been sedulously cared for. "What lovely hair! It has just the wave that yours lacks, mother."

"Yes," was the regretful reply, "I've never be'n able to git that wave out. But her hair's be'n took good care of, an' there ain't nary gal in town that's got any finer."

"Don't worry about the wave, mother. It's just the fashionable ripple, and becomes her immensely. I think my little Albert favors his Aunt Rena somewhat."

"Your little Albert!" they cried. "You've got a child?"

"Oh, yes," he replied calmly, "a very fine baby boy."

They began to purr in proud contentment at this information, and made minute inquiries about the age and weight and eyes and nose and other important details of this precious infant. They inquired more coldly about the child's mother, of whom they spoke with greater warmth when they learned that she was dead. They hung breathless on Warwick's words as he related briefly the story of his life since he had left, years before, the house behind the cedars–how with a stout heart and an abounding hope he had gone out into a seemingly hostile world, and made fortune stand and deliver. His story had for the women the charm of an escape from captivity, with all the thrill of a pirate's tale. With the whole world before him, he had remained in the South, the land of his fathers, where, he conceived, he had an inalienable birthright. By some good chance he had escaped military service in the Confederate army, and, in default of older and more experienced men, had undertaken, during the rebellion, the management of a large estate, which had been left in the hands of women and slaves. He had filled the place so acceptably, and employed his leisure to such advantage, that at the close of the war he found himself–he was modest enough to think, too, in default of a better man–the husband of the orphan daughter of the gentleman who had owned the plantation, and who had lost his life upon the battlefield. Warwick's wife was of good family, and in a more settled condition of society it would not have been easy for a young man of no visible antecedents to win her hand. A year or two later, he had taken the oath of allegiance, and had been admitted to the South Carolina bar. Rich in his wife's right, he had been able to practice his profession upon a high plane, without the worry of sordid cares, and with marked success for one of his age.

"I suppose," he concluded, "that I have got along at the bar, as elsewhere, owing to the lack of better men. Many of the good lawyers were killed in the war, and most of the remainder were disqualified; while I had the advantage of being alive, and of never having been in arms against the government. People had to have lawyers, and they gave me their business in preference to the carpet-baggers. Fortune, you know, favors the available man."

His mother drank in with parted lips and glistening eyes the story of his adventures and the record of his successes. As Rena listened, the narrow walls that hemmed her in seemed to draw closer and closer, as though they must crush her. Her brother watched her keenly. He had been talking not only to inform the women, but with a deeper purpose, conceived since his morning walk, and deepened as he had followed, during his narrative, the changing expression of Rena's face and noted her intense interest in his story, her pride in his successes, and the occasional wistful look that indexed her self-pity so completely.

"An' I s'pose you're happy, John?" asked his mother.

"Well, mother, happiness is a relative term, and depends, I imagine, upon how nearly we think we get what we think we want. I have had my chance and haven't thrown it away, and I suppose I ought to be happy. But then, I have lost my wife, whom I loved very dearly, and who loved me just as much, and I'm troubled about my child."

"Why?" they demanded. "Is there anything the matter with him?"

"No, not exactly. He's well enough, as babies go, and has a good enough nurse, as nurses go. But the nurse is ignorant, and not always careful. A child needs some woman of its own blood to love it and look after it intelligently."

Mis' Molly's eyes were filled with tearful yearning. She would have given all the world to warm her son's child upon her bosom; but she knew this could not be.

"Did your wife leave any kin?" she asked with an effort.

"No near kin; she was an only child."

"You'll be gettin' married again," suggested his mother.

"No," he replied; "I think not."

Warwick was still reading his sister's face, and saw the spark of hope that gleamed in her expressive eye.

"If I had some relation of my own that I could take into the house with me," he said reflectively, "the child might be healthier and happier, and I should be much more at ease about him."

The mother looked from son to daughter with a dawning apprehension and a sudden pallor. When she saw the yearning in Rena's eyes, she threw herself at her son's feet.

"Oh, John," she cried despairingly, "don't take her away from me! Don't take her, John, darlin', for it'd break my heart to lose her!"

Rena's arms were round her mother's neck, and Rena's voice was sounding in her ears. "There, there, mamma! Never mind! I won't leave you, mamma—dear old mamma! Your Rena'll stay with you always, and never, never leave you."

John smoothed his mother's hair with a comforting touch, patted her withered cheek soothingly, lifted her tenderly to her place by his side, and put his arm about her.

"You love your children, mother?"

"They're all I've got," she sobbed, "an' they cos' me all I had. When the las' one's gone, I'll want to go too, for I'll be all alone in the world. Don't take Rena, John; for if you do, I'll never see her again, an' I can't bear to think of it. How would you like to lose yo'r one child?"

"Well, well, mother, we'll say no more about it. And now tell me all about yourself, and about the neighbors, and how you got through the war, and who's dead and who's married—and everything."

The change of subject restored in some degree Mis' Molly's equanimity, and with returning calmness came a sense of other responsibilities.

"Good gracious, Rena!" she exclaimed. "John's be'n in the house an hour, and ain't had nothin' to eat yet! Go in the kitchen an' spread a clean tablecloth, an' git out that 'tater pone, an' a pitcher o' that las' kag o' persimmon beer, an' let John take a bite an' a sip."

Warwick smiled at the mention of these homely dainties. "I thought of your sweet-potato pone at the hotel to-day, when I was at dinner, and wondered if you'd have some in the house. There was never any like yours; and I've forgotten the taste of persimmon beer entirely."

Rena left the room to carry out her hospitable commission. Warwick, taking advantage of her absence, returned after a while to the former subject.

"Of course, mother," he said calmly, "I wouldn't think of taking Rena away against your wishes. A mother's claim upon her child is a high and holy one. Of course she will have no chance here, where our story is known. The war has wrought great changes, has put the bottom rail on top, and all that—but it hasn't wiped *that* out. Nothing but death can remove that stain, if it does not follow us even beyond the grave. Here she must forever be—nobody! With me she might have got out into the world; with her beauty she might have made a good marriage; and, if I mistake not, she has sense as well as beauty."

"Yes," sighed the mother, "she's got good sense. She ain't as quick as you was, an' don't read as many books, but she's keerful an' painstakin', an' always tries to do what's right. She's be'n thinkin' about goin' away somewhere an' tryin' to git a school to teach, er somethin', sence the Yankees have started 'em everywhere for po' white folks an' niggers too. But I don't like fer her to go too fur."

"With such beauty and brains," continued Warwick, "she could leave this town and make a place for herself. The place is already made. She has only to step into my carriage–after perhaps a little preparation– and ride up the hill which I have had to climb so painfully. It would be a great pleasure to me to see her at the top.

But of course it is impossible–a mere idle dream. *Your* claim comes first; her duty chains her here."

"It would be so lonely without her," murmured the mother weakly, "an' I love her so–my las' one!"

"No doubt–no doubt," returned Warwick, with a sympathetic sigh; "of course you love her. It's not to be thought of for a moment. It's a pity that she couldn't have a chance here–but how could she! I had thought she might marry a gentleman, but I dare say she'll do as well as the rest of her friends–as well as Mary B., for instance, who married– Homer Pettifoot, did you say? Or maybe Billy Oxendine might do for her. As long as she has never known any better, she'll probably be as well satisfied as though she married a rich man, and lived in a fine house, and kept a carriage and servants, and moved with the best in the land."

The tortured mother could endure no more. The one thing she desired above all others was her daughter's happiness. Her own life had not been governed by the highest standards, but about her love for her beautiful daughter there was no taint of selfishness. The life her son had described had been to her always the ideal but unattainable life. Circumstances, some beyond her control, and others for which she was herself in a measure responsible, had put it forever and inconceivably beyond her reach. It had been conquered by her son. It beckoned to her daughter. The comparison of this free and noble life with the sordid existence of those around her broke down the last barrier of opposition.

"O Lord!" she moaned, "what shall I do with out her? It'll be lonely, John–so lonely!"

"You'll have your home, mother," said Warwick tenderly, accepting the implied surrender. "You'll have your friends and relatives, and the knowledge that your children are happy. I'll let you hear from us often, and no doubt you can see Rena now and then. But you must let her go, mother,– it would be a sin against her to refuse."

"She may go," replied the mother brokenly. "I'll not stand in her way–I've got sins enough to answer for already."

Warwick watched her pityingly. He had stirred her feelings to unwonted depths, and his sympathy went out to her. If she had sinned, she had been more sinned against than sinning, and it was not his part to judge her. He had yielded to a sentimental weakness in deciding upon this trip to Patesville. A matter of business had brought him within a day's journey of the town, and an over-mastering impulse had compelled him to seek the mother who had given him birth and the old town where he had spent the earlier years of his life. No one would have acknowledged sooner than he the folly of this visit. Men who have elected to govern their lives by principles of abstract right and reason, which happen, perhaps, to be at variance with what society considers equally right and reasonable, should, for fear of complications, be careful about descending from the lofty heights of logic to the common level of impulse and affection. Many years before, Warwick, when a lad of eighteen, had shaken the dust of the town from his feet, and with it, he fondly thought, the blight of his inheritance, and had achieved elsewhere a worthy career. But during all these years of absence he had cherished a tender feeling for his mother, and now again found himself in her house, amid the familiar surroundings of his childhood. His visit had brought joy to his mother's heart, and was now to bring its shrouded companion, sorrow. His mother had lived her life, for good or ill. A wider door was open to his sister—her mother must not bar the entrance.

"She may go," the mother repeated sadly, drying her tears. "I'll give her up for her good."

"The table's ready, mamma," said Rena, coming to the door.

The lunch was spread in the kitchen, a large unplastered room at the rear, with a wide fireplace at one end. Only yesterday, it seemed to Warwick, he had sprawled upon the hearth, turning sweet potatoes before the fire, or roasting groundpeas in the ashes; or, more often, reading, by the light of a blazing pine-knot or lump of resin, some volume from the bookcase in the hall. From Bulwer's novel, he had read the story of Warwick the Kingmaker, and upon leaving home had chosen it for his own. He was a new man, but he had the blood of an old race, and he would select for his own one of its worthy names. Overhead loomed the same smoky beams, decorated with what might have been, from all appearances, the same bunches of dried herbs, the same strings of onions and red peppers. Over in the same corner stood the same spinning-wheel, and through the open door of an adjoining room he saw the old loom, where in childhood he had more than once thrown the shuttle. The kitchen was different from the stately dining-room of the old colonial mansion where he now lived; but it was homelike, and it was familiar. The sight of it moved his heart, and he felt for the moment a sort of a blind anger against the fate which made it necessary that he should visit the home of his childhood, if at all, like a thief in the night. But he realized, after a moment, that the thought was pure sentiment, and that one who had gained so much ought not to complain if he must give up a little. He who would climb the heights of life must leave even the pleasantest valleys behind.

"Rena," asked her mother, "how'd you like to go an' pay yo'r brother John a visit? I guess I might spare you for a little while."

The girl's eyes lighted up. She would not have gone if her mother had wished her to stay, but she would always have regarded this as the lost opportunity of her life.

"Are you sure you don't care, mamma?" she asked, hoping and yet doubting.

"Oh, I'll manage to git along somehow or other. You can go an' stay till you git homesick, an' then John'll let you come back home."

But Mis' Molly believed that she would never come back, except, like her brother, under cover of the night. She must lose her daughter as well as her son, and this should be the penance for her sin. That her children must expiate as well the sins of their fathers, who had sinned so lightly, after the manner of men, neither she nor they could foresee, since they could not read the future.

The next boat by which Warwick could take his sister away left early in the morning of the next day but one. He went back to his hotel with the understanding that the morrow should be devoted to getting Rena ready for her departure, and that Warwick would visit the household again the following evening; for, as has been intimated, there were several reasons why there should be no open relations between the fine gentleman at the hotel and the women in the house behind the cedars, who, while superior in blood and breeding to the people of the neighborhood in which they lived, were yet under the shadow of some cloud which clearly shut them out from the better society of the town. Almost any resident could have given one or more of these reasons, of which any one would have been sufficient to most of them; and to some of them Warwick's mere presence in the town would have seemed a bold and daring thing.

CRITCAL EYE

For Discussion

a. How significant is it that Warwick has taken "a man's chance in life" to his success? Could his sister, Rena, have taken the same chance alone?

b. Why can't Warwick risk taking his mother into his White world, too? What does his leaving her behind signify?

c. The fact that Warwick has decided to pass as a White person has led him to great success, as he is now respected and revered by all persons. Has he made the right choice? Said differently, is being a part of the majority–the ruling class by birth–worth denouncing one's true heritage?

Re-approaching the Reading

Examine this story alongside of Nella Larsen's *Passing*. What are the similarities? Why are these characters struggling with the issue of race? Why is being something other than what they are so appealing and necessary?

Writing Assignment

Imagine a circumstance where you would denounce your ethnicity and leave behind your family and, for that matter, all that you know. For a chance at the best education and social status, would you walk away from everything and everyone? Or, can you imagine a circumstance where you would give up the advantages afforded one based on skin color, religion, or social grouping–realities that provide ethnic privilege at birth–and willingly become part of another group?

Gender, Sex, and Sexuality

"I was like, Am I gay? Am I straight? And I realized...I'm just slutty. Where's my parade?"
Margret Cho

When I fight, I want to break his will. I want to take his manhood. I want to rip out his heart and show it to him.
Mike Tyson

There are more women on the planet than there are men. Sex still sells—almost anything. The global discussion and sea change surrounding the LGBT community and Marriage Equality continues. And what does any of this mean? Nothing. We are still just as conflicted and divided about matters of sex, sexuality, and sexual orientation. We are no more settled about the roles, expectations, and responsibilities of the genders than our parents or grandparents were. In fact, everything has become much more complicated. We live in a world of rules and codes that dictate who and what we should be, which often stand in stark contrast to who we really are.

We live in a world of only two genders. As the 21st century progresses, societies continue to explore and define what a male's and female's roles should be. Within the confines of our respective cultures, we embrace, expect, and exclude members based on these expectations of whom and, just as importantly, what its members should represent. Understanding how people should behave and look, as well as who we should become as citizens of nations, or, for that matter, who we can be intimate with, are mandates—either codified in law or unsaid but understood—that allow us to not only embrace our partners and neighbors, but punish them as well. Understanding how powerful sex is, how personally and socially defining it is—within the confines of our homes, schools, and religions—remains one of the most influential issues our world continues to grapple with.

Perhaps what is most perplexing about the issue of gender is that, in many ways, we are still holding fast to stereotypes that stagnate our identities. Should we still, in the 21st century, be arguing that men were born to do one thing and women another? Are we at a point where one's sexuality or sexual orientation can be viewed separately and distinctly from what makes them male or female? Moreover, should we consider that our sexual stereotyping is placing lives in danger?

The works presented here should help navigate the global ramifications of gender, sex, and sexuality in an attempt to help readers determine whether the old adage holds any truth. In short, "have we really come a long way, baby?"

JAMES BALDWIN

From the Novel
GIOVANNI'S ROOM

The person who appeared, and whom I did not know very well, was a girl named Sue, blonde and rather puffy, with the quality, in spite of the fact that she was not pretty, of the girls who are selected each year to be Miss Rheingold. She wore her curly blond hair cut very short, she had small breasts and a big behind, and in order, no doubt, to indicate to the world how little she cared for appearance or sensuality, she almost always wore tight blue jeans. I think she came from Philadelphia and her family was very rich. Sometimes, when she was drunk, she reviled them, and, sometimes, drunk in another way, she extolled their virtues of thrift and fidelity. I was both dismayed and relieved to see her. The moment she appeared I began, mentally, to take off all her clothes.

'Sit down,' I said. 'Have a drink.'

'I'm glad to *see* you,' she cried, sitting down, and looking about for the waiter. 'You'd rather dropped out of sight. How've you been?'–abandoning her search for the waiter and leaning forward to me with a friendly grin.

'I've been fine,' I told her. 'And you?'

'Oh, *me!* Nothing ever happens to me.' And she turned down the corners of her rather predatory and also vulnerable mouth to indicate that she was both joking and not joking. 'I'm built like a brick stone wall.' We both laughed. She peered at me. 'They tell me you're living way out at the end of Paris, near the zoo.'

'I found a maid's room out there. Very cheap.'

'Are you living alone?'

I did not know whether she knew about Giovanni or not. I felt a hint of sweat on my forehead. 'Sort of,' I said.

'Sort of? What the hell does *that* mean? Do you have a monkey with you, or something?'

I grinned, 'No. But this French kid I know, he lives with his mistress, but they fight a lot and it's really *his* room so sometimes, when his mistress throws him out, he bunks with me for a couple of days.'

'Ah!' she sighed. '*Chagrin d'amour!*'

'He's having a good time,' I said. 'He loves it.' I looked at her. 'Aren't you?

'Stone walls,' she said, 'are impenetrable.'

The waiter arrived. 'Doesn't it,' I dared, 'depend on the weapon?'

'What are you buying me to drink?' she asked.

'What do you want?' We were both grinning. The waiter stood above us, manifesting a kind of surly *joie de vivre.*

'I believe I'll have'—she batted the eyelashes of her tight blue eyes—'*un ricard.* With a hell of a lot of ice.'

'*Deux ricards,*' I said to the waiter '*avec beaucoup de la glace.*'

'*Oui, monsieur.*' I was sure he despised us both. I thought of Giovanni and of how many times in an evening the phrase, *Oui, monsieur* fell from his lips. With this fleeting thought there came another, equally fleeting: a new sense of Giovanni, his private life and pain, and all that moved like a flood in him when we lay together at night.

'To continue,' I said.

'To continue?' She made her eyes very wide and blank. 'Where were we?' She was trying to be coquettish and she was trying to be hard-headed. I felt that I was doing something very cruel.

But I could not stop. 'We were talking about stone walls and how they could be entered.'

'I never knew,' she simpered, 'that you had any interest in stone walls.'

'There's a lot about me you don't know.' The waiter returned with our drinks. 'Don't you think discoveries are fun?'

She stared discontentedly at her drink. 'Frankly,' she said, turning toward me again, with those eyes, 'no.'

'Oh, you're much too young for that,' I said. '*Everything* should be a discovery.'

She was silent for a moment. She sipped her drink. 'I've made,' she said, finally, 'all the discoveries that I can stand.' But I watched the way her thighs moved against the cloth of her jeans.

'But you can't just go on being a brick stone wall forever.'

'I don't see why not,' she said. 'Nor do I see *how* not.'

'Baby,' I said, 'I'm making you a proposition.'

She picked up her glass again and sipped it, staring straight outward at the boulevard. 'And what's the proposition?'

'Invite me for a drink. *Chez toi.*'

'I don't believe,' she said, turning to me, 'that I've got anything in the house.'

'We can pick up something on the way,' I said.

She stared at me for a long time. I forced myself not to drop my eyes. 'I'm sure that I shouldn't,' she said at last.

'Why not?'

She made a small, helpless movement in the wicker chair. 'I don't know. I don't know what you want.'

I laughed. 'If you invite me home for a drink,' I said, 'I'll show you.'

'I think you're being impossible,' she said, and for the first time there was something genuine in her eyes and voice.

'Well,' I said, 'I think *you* are.' I looked at her with a smile which was, I hoped, both boyish and insistent. 'I don't know what I've said that's so impossible. I've put all my cards on the table. But you're still holding yours. I don't know why you should think a man's being impossible when he declares himself attracted to you.'

'Oh, please,' she said, and finished her drink, 'I'm sure it's just the summer sun.'

'The summer sun,' I said, 'has nothing to do with it.' And when she still made no answer, 'All you've got to do,' I said desperately, 'is decide whether we'll have another drink here or at your place.'

She snapped her fingers abruptly but did not succeed in appearing jaunty. 'Come along,' she said. 'I'm certain to regret it. But you really will have to buy something to drink. There *isn't* anything in the house. And that way,' she added, after a moment, 'I'll be sure to get something out of the deal.'

It was I, then, who felt a dreadful holding back. To avoid looking at her, I made a great show of getting the waiter. And he came, as surly as ever, and I paid him, and we rose and started walking towards the rue de Sèvres, where Sue had a small apartment.

Her apartment was dark and full of furniture. 'None of it is mine,' she said. 'It all belongs to the French lady of a certain age from whom I rented it, who is now in Monte Carlo for her nerves.' She was very nervous, too, and I saw that this nervousness could be, for a little while, a great help to me. I had bought a small bottle of cognac and I put it down on her marble-topped table and took her in my arms. For some reason I was terribly aware that it was after seven in the evening, that soon the sun would have disappeared from the river, that all the Paris night was about to begin, and that Giovanni was now at work.

She was very big and she was disquietingly fluid–fluid without, however, being able to flow. I felt a hardness and a constriction in her, a grave distrust, created already by too many men like me ever to be conquered now. What we were about to do would not be pretty.

And, as though she felt this, she moved away from me. 'Let's have a drink' she said. 'Unless, of course, you're in a hurry. I'll try not to keep you any longer than absolutely necessary.'

She smiled and I smiled, too. We were as close in that instant as we would ever get–like two thieves. 'Let's have several drinks.' I said.

'But not *too* many,' she said, and simpered again suggestively, like a broken-down movie queen facing the cruel cameras again after a long eclipse.

She took the cognac and disappeared into her corner of a kitchen. 'Make yourself comfortable,' she shouted out to me. 'Take off your shoes. Take off your socks. Look at my books–I often wonder what I'd do if there weren't any books in the world.'

I took off my shoes and lay back on her sofa. I tried not to think. But I was thinking that what I did with Giovanni could not possibly be more immoral than what I was about to do with Sue.

She came back with two great brandy snifters. She came close to me on the sofa and we touched glasses. We drank a little, she watching me all the while, and then I touched her breasts. Her lips parted and she put her glass down with extraordinary clumsiness and lay against me. It was a gesture of great despair and I knew that she was giving herself, not to me, but to that lover who would never come.

And I–I thought of many things, lying coupled with Sue in that dark place. I wondered if she had done anything to prevent herself from becoming pregnant; and the thought of a child belonging to Sue and me, of my being trapped that way–in the very act, so to speak, of trying to escape–almost precipitated a laughing jag. I wondered if her blue jeans had been thrown on top of the cigarette she had been smoking. I wondered if anyone else had a key to her apartment, if we could be heard through the inadequate walls, how much in a few moments, we would hate each other. I also approached Sue as though she were a job of work, a job which it was necessary to do in an unforgettable manner. Somewhere, at the very bottom of myself, I realized that I was doing something awful to her and it became a matter of my honor not to let this fact become too obvious. I tried to convey, through this grisly act of love, the intelligence, at least, that it was not her, not *her* flesh, that I despised–it would not be her I could not face when we became vertical again. Again, somewhere at the bottom of me,

I realized that my fears had been excessive and groundless and, in effect, a lie: it became clearer every instant that what I had been afraid of had nothing to do with my body. Sue was not Hella and she did not lessen my terror of what would happen when Hella came: she increased it, she made it more real than it had been before. At the same time, I realized that my performance with Sue was succeeding even too well, and I tried not to despise her for feeling so little what her laborer felt. I travelled through a network of Sue's cries, of Sue's tom-tom fists on my back, and judged by means of her thighs, by means of her legs, how soon I could be free. Then I thought, *The end is coming soon,* her sobs became even higher and harsher, I was terribly aware of the small of my back and the cold sweat there, I thought, *Well, let her have it for Christ sake, get it over with;* then it was ending and I hated her and me, then it was over, and the dark, tiny room rushed back. And I wanted only to get out of there.

She lay still for a long time. I felt the night outside and it was calling me. I leaned up at last and found a cigarette.

'Perhaps,' she said, 'we should finish our drinks.'

She sat up and switched on the lamp which stood beside her bed. I had been dreading this moment. But she saw nothing in my eyes–she stared at me as though I had made a long journey on a white charger all the way to her prison house. She lifted her glass.

'*À la votre,*' I said.

'*À la* votre?' She giggled. '*À la* tienne, *chéri!*' She leaned over and kissed me on the mouth. Then, for a moment, she felt something; she leaned back and stared at me, her eyes not quite tightening yet; and she said, lightly, 'Do you suppose we could do this again sometime?'

'I don't see why not,' I told her, trying to laugh. 'We carry our own equipment.'

She was silent. Then: 'Could we have supper together–tonight?'

'I'm sorry,' I said. 'I'm really sorry, Sue, but I've got a date.'

'Oh. Tomorrow, maybe?'

'Look, Sue. I hate to make dates. I'll just surprise you.'

She finished her drink. 'I doubt that,' she said.

She got up and walked away from me. 'I'll just put on some clothes and come down with you.'

She disappeared and I heard the water running. I sat there, still naked, but with my socks on, and poured myself another brandy. Now I was afraid to go out into that night which had seemed to be calling me only a few moments before.

When she came back she was wearing a dress and some real shoes, and she had sort of fluffed up her hair. I had to admit she looked better that way, really more like a girl, like a school-girl. I rose and started putting on my clothes. 'You look nice,' I said.

There was a great many things she wanted to say, but she forced herself to say nothing. I could scarcely bear to watch the struggle occurring in her face, it made me so ashamed. 'Maybe you'll be lonely again,' she said, finally. 'I guess I won't mind if you come looking for me.' She wore the strangest smile I had ever seen. It was pained and vindictive and humiliated, but she inexpertly smeared across this grimace a bright, girlish gaiety–as rigid as the skeleton beneath her flabby body. If fate ever allowed Sue to reach me, she would kill me with just that smile.

'Keep a candle,' I said, 'in the window'–and she opened her door and we passed out into the streets.

CRITICAL EYE

For Discussion

a. In what way is the character dealing with his own self-hatred as he tries to reach out for human contact?

b. Is this text condemning casual sex or revealing a kind of enlightenment that comes as a result of it?

Re-approaching the Reading

While it is merely implied in this section, the larger text reveals that the main character is a homosexual. How does that impact your reading of this section?

Writing Assignment

In what ways are we all leading two lives? Is it almost necessary to do so in order to protect ourselves from the scrutiny and abuse of others?

JUNOT DIAZ

FIESTA 1980

Mami's youngest sister–my tía Yrma–finally made it to the United States that year. She and tío Miguel got themselves an apartment in the Bronx, off the Grand Concourse and everybody decided that we should have a party. Actually, my pops decided, but everybody–meaning Mami, tía Yrma, tío Miguel and their neighbors–thought it a dope idea. On the afternoon of the party Papi came back from work around six. Right on time. We were all dressed by then, which was a smart move on our part. If Papi had walked in and caught us lounging around in our underwear, he would have kicked our asses something serious.

He didn't say nothing to nobody, not even my moms. He just pushed past her, held up his hand when she tried to talk to him and headed right into the shower. Rafa gave me the look and I gave it back to him; we both knew Papi had been with that Puerto Rican woman he was seeing and wanted to wash off the evidence quick.

Mami looked really nice that day. The United States had finally put some meat on her; she was no longer the same flaca who had arrived here three years before. She had cut her hair short and was wearing tons of cheap-ass jewelry which on her didn't look too lousy. She smelled like herself, like the wind through a tree. She always waited until the last possible minute to put on her perfume because she said it was a waste to spray it on early and then have to spray it on again once you got to the party.

We–meaning me, my brother, my little sister and Mami–waited for Papi to finish his shower. Mami seemed anxious, in her usual dispassionate way. Her hands adjusted the buckle of her belt over and over again. That morning, when she had gotten us up for school, Mami told us that she wanted to have a good time at the party. I want to dance, she said, but now, with the sun sliding out of the sky like spit off a wall, she seemed ready just to get this over with.

Rafa didn't much want to go to no party either, and me, I never wanted to go anywhere with my family. There was a baseball game in the parking lot outside and we could hear our friends, yelling, Hey, and, Cabrón, to one another. We heard the pop of a ball as it sailed over the cars, the clatter of an aluminum bat dropping to the concrete. Not that me or Rafa loved baseball; we just liked playing with the local kids, thrashing them at anything they were doing. By the sounds of the shouting, we both knew the game was close, either of us could have made a difference. Rafa frowned and when I frowned back, he put up his fist. Don't you mirror me, he said.

Don't you mirror me, I said.

He punched me—I would have hit him back but Papi marched into the living room with his towel around his waist, looking a lot smaller than he did when he was dressed. He had a few strands of hair around his nipples and a surly closed-mouth expression, like maybe he'd scalded his tongue or something.

Have they eaten? he asked Mami.

She nodded. I made you something.

You didn't let him eat, did you?

Ay, Dios mío, she said, letting her arms fall to her side.

Ay, Dios mío is right, Papi said.

I was never supposed to eat before our car trips, but earlier, when she had put out our dinner of rice, beans and sweet platanos, guess who had been the first one to clean his plate? You couldn't blame Mami really, she had been busy—cooking, getting ready, dressing my sister Madai. I should have reminded her not to feed me but I wasn't that sort of son.

Papi turned to me. Coño, muchacho, why did you eat?

Rafa had already started inching away from me. I'd once told him I considered him a low-down chickenshit for moving out of the way every time Papi was going to smack me.

Collateral damage, Rafa had said. Ever heard of it?

No.

Look it up.

Chickenshit or not, I didn't dare glance at him. Papi was old-fashioned; he expected your undivided attention when you were getting your ass whupped. You couldn't look him in the eye either—that wasn't allowed. Better to stare at his belly button, which was perfectly round and immaculate. Papi pulled me to my feet by my ear.

If you throw up—

I won't, I cried, tears in my eyes, more out of reflex than pain.

Ya, Ramón, ya. It's not his fault, Mami said.

They've known about this party forever. How did they think we were going to get there? Fly?

He finally let go of my ear and I sat back down. Madai was too scared to open her eyes. Being around Papi all her life had turned her into a major-league wuss. Anytime Papi raised his voice her lip would start trembling, like some specialized tuning fork. Rafa pretended that he had knuckles to crack and when I shoved him, he gave me a *Don't start* look. But even that little bit of recognition made me feel better.

I was the one who was always in trouble with my dad. It was like my God-given duty to piss him off, to do everything the way he hated. Our fights didn't bother me too much. I still wanted him to love me, something that never seemed strange or contradictory until years later, when he was out of our lives.

By the time my ear stopped stinging Papi was dressed and Mami was crossing each one of us, solemnly, like we were heading off to war. We said, in turn, Bendición, Mami, and she poked us in our five cardinal spots while saying, Que Dios te bendiga.

This was how all our trips began, the words that followed me every time I left the house.

None of us spoke until we were inside Papi's Volkswagen van. Brand-new, lime-green and bought to impress. Oh, we were impressed, but me, every time I was in that VW and Papi went above twenty miles an hour, I vomited. I'd never had trouble with cars before—that van was like my curse. Mami suspected it was the upholstery. In her mind, American things—appliances, mouthwash, funny-looking upholstery—all seemed to have an intrinsic badness about them. Papi was careful about taking me anywhere in the VW, but when he had to, I rode up front in Mami's usual seat so I could throw up out a window.

¿Cómo te sientas? Mami asked over my shoulder when Papi pulled onto the turnpike. She had her hand on the base of my neck. One thing about Mami, her palms never sweated.

I'm OK, I said, keeping my eyes straight ahead. I definitely didn't want to trade glances with Papi. He had this one look, furious and sharp, that always left me feeling bruised.

Toma. Mami handed me four mentas. She had thrown three out her window at the beginning of our trip, an offering to Eshú; the rest were for me.

I took one and sucked it slowly, my tongue knocking it up against my teeth. We passed Newark Airport without any incident. If Madai had been awake she would have cried because the planes flew so close to the cars.

How's he feeling? Papi asked.

Fine, I said. I glanced back at Rafa and he pretended like he didn't see me. That was the way he was, at school and at home. When I was in trouble, he didn't know me. Madai was solidly asleep, but even with her face all wrinkled up and drooling she looked cute, her hair all separated into twists.

I turned around and concentrated on the candy. Papi even started to joke that we might not have to scrub the van out tonight. He was beginning to loosen up, not checking his watch too much. Maybe he was thinking about that Puerto Rican woman or maybe he was just happy that we were all together. I could never tell. At the toll, he was feeling positive enough to actually get out of the van and search around under the basket for dropped coins. It was something he had once done to amuse Madai, but now it was habit. Cars behind us honked their horns and I slid down in my seat. Rafa didn't care; he grinned back at the other cars and waved. His actual job was to make sure no cops were coming. Mami shook Madai awake and as soon as she saw Papi stooping for a couple of quarters she let out this screech of delight that almost took off the top of my head.

That was the end of the good times. Just outside the Washington Bridge, I started feeling woozy. The smell of the upholstery got all up inside my head and I found myself with a mouthful of saliva. Mami's hand tensed on my shoulder and when I caught Papi's eye, he was like, No way. Don't do it.

The first time I got sick in the van Papi was taking me to the library, Rafa was with us and he couldn't believe I threw up. I was famous for my steel-lined stomach. A third-world childhood could give you that. Papi was worried enough that just as quick as Rafa could drop off the books we were on our way home. Mami fixed me one of her honey-and-onion concoctions and that made my stomach feel better. A week later we tried the library again and on this go-around I couldn't get the window open in time. When Papi got me home, he went and cleaned out the van himself, an expression of askho on his face. This was a big deal, since Papi almost never cleaned anything himself. He came back inside and found me sitting on the couch feeling like hell.

It's the car, he said to Mami. It's making him sick.

This time the damage was pretty minimal, nothing Papi couldn't wash off the door with a blast of the hose. He was pissed, though; he jammed his finger into my cheek, a nice solid thrust. That was the way he was with his punishments: imaginative. Earlier that year I'd written an essay in school called "My Father the Torturer," but the teacher made me write a new one. She thought I was kidding.

We drove the rest of the way to the Bronx in silence. We only stopped once, so I could brush my teeth. Mami had brought along my toothbrush and a tube of toothpaste and while every car known to man sped by us she stood outside with me so I wouldn't feel alone.

Tío Miguel was about seven feet tall and had his hair combed up and out, into a demi-fro. He gave me and Rafa big spleen-crushing hugs and then kissed Mami and finally ended up with Madai on his shoulder. The last time I'd seen Tío was at the airport, his first day in the United States. I remembered how he hadn't seemed all that troubled to be in another country.

He looked down at me. Carajo, Yunior, you look horrible!

He threw up, my brother explained.

I pushed Rafa. Thanks a lot, ass-face.

Hey, he said. Tío asked.

Tío clapped a bricklayer's hand on my shoulder. Everybody gets sick sometimes, he said. You should have seen me on the plane over here. Dios mio! He rolled his Asian-looking eyes for emphasis. I thought we were all going to die.

Everybody could tell he was lying. I smiled like he was making me feel better.

Do you want me to get you a drink? Tío asked. We got beer and rum.

Miguel, Mami said. He's young.

Young? Back in Santo Domingo, he'd be getting laid by now.

Mami thinned her lips, which took some doing.

Well, it's true, Tío said.

So, Mami, I said. When do I get to go visit the D.R.?

That's enough, Yunior.

It's the only pussy you'll ever get, Rafa said to me in English.

Not counting your girlfriend, of course.

Rafa smiled. He had to give me that one.

Papi came in from parking the van. He and Miguel gave each other the sort of handshakes that would have turned my fingers into Wonder bread.

Coño, compa'i, ¿cómo va todo? they said to each other.

Tía came out then, with an apron on and maybe the longest Lee Press-On Nails I've ever seen in my life. There was this one guru motherfucker in the *Guinness Book of World Records* who had longer nails, but I tell you, it was close. She gave everybody kisses, told me and Rafa how guapo we were—Rafa, of course, believed her—told Madai how bella she was, but when she got to Papi, she froze a little, like maybe she'd seen a wasp on the tip of his nose, but then kissed him all the same.

Mami told us to join the other kids in the living room. Tío said, Wait a minute, I want to show you the apartment. I was glad Tía said, Hold on, because from what I'd seen so far, the place had been furnished in Contemporary Dominican Tacky. The less I saw, the better. I mean, I liked plastic sofa covers but damn, Tío and Tía had taken it to another level. They had a disco ball hanging in the living room and the type of stucco ceilings that looked like stalactite heaven. The sofas all had golden tassels dangling from their edges. Tía came out of the kitchen with some people I didn't know and by the time she got done introducing everybody, only Papi and Mami were given the guided tour of the four-room third-floor apartment. Me and Rafa joined the kids in the living room. They'd already started eating. We were hungry, one of the girls explained, a pastelito in hand. The boy was about three years younger than me but the girl who'd spoken, Leti, was my age. She and another girl were on the sofa together and they were cute as hell.

Leti introduced them: the boy was her brother Wilquins and the other girl was her neighbor Mari. Leti had some serious tetas and I could tell that my brother was going to gun for her. His taste in girls was predictable. He sat down right between Leti and Mari and by the way they were smiling at him I knew he'd do fine. Neither of the girls gave me more than a cursory one-two, which didn't bother me. Sure, I liked girls but I was always too terrified to speak to them unless we were arguing or I was calling them stupidos, which was one of my favorite words that year. I turned to Wilquins and asked him what there was to do around here. Mari, who had the lowest voice I'd ever heard, said, He can't speak.

What does that mean?

He's mute.

I looked at Wilquins incredulously. He smiled and nodded, as if he'd won a prize or something.

Does he understand? I asked.

Of course he understands, Rafa said. He's not dumb.

I could tell Rafa had said that just to score points with the girls. Both of them nodded. Low-voice Mari said, He's the best student in his grade.

I thought, Not bad for a mute. I sat next to Wilquins. After about two seconds of TV Wilquins whipped out a bag of dominos and motioned to me. Did I want to play? Sure. Me and him played Rafa and Leti and we whupped their collective asses twice, which put Rafa in a real bad mood. He looked at me like maybe he wanted to take a swing, just one to make him feel better. Leti kept whispering into Rafa's ear, telling him it was OK.

In the kitchen I could hear my parents slipping into their usual modes. Papi's voice was loud and argumentative; you didn't have to be anywhere near him to catch his drift. And Mami, you had to put cups to your ears to hear hers. I went into the kitchen a few times—once so the tíos could show off how much bullshit I'd been able to cram in my head the last few years; another time for a bucket-sized cup of soda. Mami and Tía were frying tostones and the last of the pastelitos. She appeared happier now and the way her hands worked on our dinner you would think she had a life somewhere else making rare and precious things. She nudged Tía every now and then, shit they must have been doing all their lives. As soon as Mami saw me though, she gave me the eye. Don't stay long, that eye said. Don't piss your old man off.

Papi was too busy arguing about Elvis to notice me. Then somebody mentioned María Montez and Papi barked, María Montez? Let me tell *you* about María Montez, compa'i.

Maybe I was used to him. His voice—louder than most adults'—didn't bother me none, though the other kids shifted uneasily in their seats. Wilquins was about to raise the volume on the TV, but Rafa said, I wouldn't do that. Muteboy had balls, though. He did it anyway and then sat down. Wilquins's pop came into the living room a second later, a bottle of Presidente in hand. That dude must have had Spider-senses or something. Did you raise that? he asked Wilquins and Wilquins nodded.

Is this your house? his pops asked. He looked ready to beat Wilquins silly but he lowered the volume instead.

See, Rafa said. You nearly got your *ass kicked*.

I met the Puerto Rican woman right after Papi had gotten the van. He was taking me on short trips, trying to cure me of my vomiting. It wasn't really working but I looked forward to our trips, even though at the end of each one I'd be sick. These were the only times me and Papi did anything together. When we were alone he treated me much better, like maybe I was his son or something.

Before each drive Mami would cross me.

Bendición, Mami, I'd say.

She'd kiss my forehead. Que Dios te bendiga. And then she would give me a handful of mentas because she wanted me to be OK. Mami didn't think these excursions would cure anything, but the one time she had brought it up to Papi he had told her to shut up, what did she know about anything anyway?

Me and Papi didn't talk much. We just drove around our neighborhood. Occasionally he'd ask, How is it?

And I'd nod, no matter how I felt.

One day I was sick outside of Perth Amboy. Instead of taking me home he went the other way on Industrial Avenue, stopping a few minutes later in front of a light blue house I didn't recognize. It reminded me of the Easter eggs we colored at school, the ones we threw out the bus windows at other cars.

The Puerto Rican woman was there and she helped me clean up. She had dry papery hands and when she rubbed the towel on my chest, she did it hard, like I was a bumper she was waxing. She was very thin and had a cloud of brown hair rising above her narrow face and the sharpest blackest eyes you've ever seen.

He's cute, she said to Papi.

Not when he's throwing up, Papi said.

What's your name? she asked me. Are you Rafa?

I shook my head.

Then it's Yunior, right?

I nodded.

You're the smart one, she said, suddenly happy with herself. Maybe you want to see my books?

They weren't hers. I recognized them as ones my father must have left in her house. Papi was a voracious reader, couldn't even go cheating without a paperback in his pocket.

Why don't you go watch TV? Papi suggested. He was looking at her like she was the last piece of chicken on earth.

We got plenty of channels, she said. Use the remote if you want.

The two of them went upstairs and I was too scared of what was happening to poke around. I just sat there, ashamed, expecting something big and fiery to crash down on our heads. I watched a whole hour of the news before Papi came downstairs and said, Let's go.

About two hours later the women laid out the food and like always nobody but the kids thanked them. It must be some Dominican tradition or something. There was everything I liked—chicharrones, fried chicken, tostones, sancocho, rice, fried cheese, yuca, avocado, potato salad, a meteor-sized hunk of pernil, even a tossed salad which I could do without—but when I joined the other kids around the serving table, Papi said, Oh no you don't, and took the paper plate out of my hand. His fingers weren't gentle.

What's wrong now? Tía asked, handing me another plate.

He ain't eating, Papi said. Mami pretended to help Rafa with the pernil.

Why can't he eat?

Because I said so.

The adults who didn't know us made like they hadn't heard a thing and Tío just smiled sheepishly and told everybody to go ahead and eat. All the kids—about ten of them now—trooped back into the living room with their plates a-heaping and all the adults ducked into the kitchen and the dining room, where the radio was playing loud-ass bachatas. I was the only one without a plate. Papi stopped me before I could get away from him. He kept his voice nice and low so nobody else could hear him.

If you eat anything, I'm going to beat you. ¿Entiendes?

I nodded.

And if your brother gives you any food, I'll beat him too. Right here in front of everybody. ¿Entiendes?

I nodded again. I wanted to kill him and he must have sensed it because he gave my head a little shove.

All the kids watched me come in and sit down in front of the TV.

What's wrong with your dad? Leti asked.

He's a dick, I said.

Rafa shook his head. Don't say that shit in front of people.

Easy for you to be nice when you're eating, I said.

Hey, if I was a pukey little baby, I wouldn't get no food either.

I almost said something back but I concentrated on the TV. I wasn't going to start it. No fucking way. So I watched Bruce Lee beat Chuck Norris into the floor of the Colosseum and tried to pretend that there was no food anywhere in the house. It was Tía who finally saved me. She came into the living room and said, Since you ain't eating, Yunior, you can at least help me get some ice.

I didn't want to, but she mistook my reluctance for something else.

I already asked your father.

She held my hand while we walked; Tía didn't have any kids but I could tell she wanted them. She was the sort of relative who always remembered your birthday but who you only went to visit because you had to. We didn't get past the first-floor landing before she opened her pocketbook and handed me the first of three pastelitos she had smuggled out of the apartment.

Go ahead, she said. And as soon as you get inside make sure you brush your teeth.

Thanks a lot, Tía, I said.

Those pastelitos didn't stand a chance.

She sat next to me on the stairs and smoked her cigarette. All the way down on the first floor and we could still hear the music and the adults and the television. Tía looked a ton like Mami; the two of them were both short and light-skinned. Tía smiled a lot and that was what set them apart the most.

How is it at home, Yunior?

What do you mean?

How's it going in the apartment? Are you kids OK?

I knew an interrogation when I heard one, no matter how sugar-coated it was. I didn't say anything. Don't get me wrong, I loved my tía, but something told me to keep my mouth shut. Maybe it was family loyalty, maybe I just wanted to protect Mami or I was afraid that Papi would find out—it could have been anything really.

Is your mom all right?

I shrugged.

Have there been lots of fights?

None, I said. Too many shrugs would have been just as bad as an answer. Papi's at work too much.

Work, Tía said, like it was somebody's name she didn't like.

Me and Rafa, we didn't talk much about the Puerto Rican woman. When we ate dinner at her house, the few times Papi had taken us over there, we still acted like nothing was out of the ordinary. Pass the ketchup, man. No sweat, bro. The affair was like a hole in our living room floor, one we'd gotten so used to circumnavigating that we sometimes forgot it was there.

By midnight all the adults were crazy dancing. I was sitting outside Tía's bedroom—where Madai was sleeping—trying not to attract attention. Rafa had me guarding the door; he and Leti were in there too, with some of the other kids, getting busy no doubt. Wilquins had gone across the hall to bed so I had me and the roaches to mess around with.

Whenever I peered into the main room I saw about twenty moms and dads dancing and drinking beers. Every now and then somebody yelled, ¡Quisqueya! And then everybody else would yell and stomp their feet. From what I could see my parents seemed to be enjoying themselves.

Mami and Tía spent a lot of time side by side, whispering, and I kept expecting something to come of this, a brawl maybe. I'd never once been out with my family when it hadn't turned to shit. We weren't even theatrical or straight crazy like other families. We fought like sixth-graders, without any real dignity. I guess the whole night I'd been waiting for a blowup, something between Papi and Mami. This was how I always figured Papi would be exposed, out in public, where everybody would know.

You're a cheater!

But everything was calmer than usual. And Mami didn't look like she was about to say anything to Papi. The two of them danced every now and then but they never lasted more than a song before Mami joined Tía again in whatever conversation they were having.

I tried to imagine Mami before Papi. Maybe I was tired, or just sad, thinking about the way my family was. Maybe I already knew how it would all end up in a few years, Mami without Papi, and that was why I did it. Picturing her alone wasn't easy. It seemed like Papi had always been with her, even when we were waiting in Santo Domingo for him to send for us.

The only photograph our family had of Mami as a young woman, before she married Papi, was the one that somebody took of her at an election party that I found one day while rummaging for money to go to the arcade. Mami had it tucked into her immigration papers. In the photo, she's surrounded by laughing cousins I will never meet, who are all shiny from dancing, whose clothes are rumpled and loose. You can tell it's night and hot and that the mosquitos have been biting. She sits straight and even in a crowd she stands out, smiling quietly like maybe she's the one everybody's celebrating. You can't see her hands but I imagined they're knotting a straw or a bit of thread. This was the woman my father met a year later on the Malecón, the woman Mami thought she'd always be.

Mami must have caught me studying her because she stopped what she was doing and gave me a smile, maybe her first one of the night. Suddenly I wanted to go over and hug her, for no other reason than I loved her, but there were about eleven fat jiggling bodies between us. So I sat down on the tiled floor and waited.

I must have fallen asleep because the next thing I knew Rafa was kicking me and saying, Let's go. He looked like he'd been hitting those girls off; he was all smiles. I got to my feet in time to kiss Tía and Tío good-bye. Mami was holding the serving dish she had brought with her.

Where's Papi? I asked,

He's downstairs, bringing the van around. Mami leaned down to kiss me.

You were good today, she said.

And then Papi burst in and told us to get the hell downstairs before some pendejo cop gave him a ticket. More kisses, more handshakes and then we were gone.

I don't remember being out of sorts after I met the Puerto Rican woman, but I must have been because Mami only asked me questions when she thought something was wrong in my life. It took her about ten passes but finally she cornered me one afternoon when we were alone in the apartment. Our upstairs neighbors were beating the crap out of their kids, and me and her had been listening to it all afternoon. She put her hand on mine and said, Is everything OK, Yunior? Have you been fighting with your brother?

Me and Rafa had already talked. We'd been in the basement, where our parents couldn't hear us. He told me that yeah, he knew about her.

Papi's taken me there twice now, he said.

Why didn't you tell me? I asked.

What the hell was I going to say? *Hey, Yunior, guess what happened yesterday? I met Papi's sucia!*

I didn't say anything to Mami either. She watched me, very very closely. Later I would think, maybe if I had told her, she would have confronted him, would have done something, but who can know these things? I said I'd been having trouble in school and like that everything was back to normal between us. She put her hand on my shoulder and squeezed and that was that.

We were on the turnpike, just past Exit 11, when I started feeling it again. I sat up from leaning against Rafa. His fingers smelled and he'd gone to sleep almost as soon as he got into the van. Madai was out too but at least she wasn't snoring.

In the darkness, I saw that Papi had a hand on Mami's knee and that the two of them were quiet and still. They weren't slumped back or anything; they were both wide awake, bolted into their seats. I couldn't see either of their faces and no matter how hard I tried I could not imagine their expressions. Neither of them moved. Every now and then the van was filled with the bright rush of somebody else's headlights. Finally I said, Mami, and they both looked back, already knowing what was happening.

CRITICAL EYE

For Discussion

a. Why, in your opinion, does the father seem comfortable flaunting his secret in front of his sons?

b. Is the father's treatment of his children discipline or child abuse?

Re-approaching the Reading

Compare this story to Mukherjee's "A Father." What is similar about the authors' approach to discussing family and immigration?

Writing Assignment

Should a child still love and respect a parent, even after discovering something shameful about the adult who is supposed to stand as a shining example of how to live?

FRANCES A. ALTHAUS

FEMALE CIRCUMCISION: RITE OF PASSAGE OR VIOLATION OF RIGHTS?

Female circumcision, the partial or total cutting away of the external female genitalia, has been practiced for centuries in parts of Africa, generally as one element of a rite of passage preparing young girls for womanhood and marriage. Often performed without anesthetic under septic conditions by lay practitioners with little or no knowledge of human anatomy or medicine, female circumcision can cause death or permanent health problems as well as severe pain. Despite these grave risks, its practitioners look on it as an integral part of their cultural and ethnic identity, and some perceive it as a religious obligation.

Opponents of female genital cutting, however, emphasize that the practice is detrimental to women's health and well-being. Some consider female circumcision a ritualized form of child abuse and violence against women, a violation of human rights.

The debate over female circumcision is relatively recent. The practice was rarely spoken of in Africa and little known in the West until the second half of this century. In the 1950s and 1960s, however, African activists and medical practitioners brought the health consequences of female circumcision to the attention of international organizations such as the United Nations and the World Health Organization (WHO). Still, it was not until 1979 that any formal policy statement was made: A seminar organized by WHO in Khartoum to address traditional practices affecting the health of women and children issued recommendations that governments work to eliminate the practice.

During the following decade, the widespread silence surrounding female circumcision was broken. After African women's organizations met in Dakar, Senegal, in 1984 to discuss female circumcision and other detrimental cultural practices, the Inter African Committee Against Harmful Traditional Practices (IAC) was formed. With national committees in more than 20 countries, the IAC has been important in bringing the harmful effects of female circumcision to the attention of African governments. In addition, other African women's networks and organizations that had focused primarily on such issues as reproductive health, women's rights and legal justice became involved in working against the practice. Such groups as Mandalaeo Ya Wanawake in Kenya, NOW in Nigeria and New Woman in Egypt now include the elimination of female circumcision among their goals.

In part because these groups brought fresh perspectives to the issue, the emphasis in discussions of female circumcision shifted to encompass women's human and reproductive rights as well as their health. International consensus statements and treaties such as

Althaus FA, Female Circumcision: Rite of passage or violation of rights? *International Family Planning Perspectives,* 1997, 23 (3): 130–133.

the Convention to Eliminate All Forms of Discrimination Against Women, the Convention on the Rights of the Child and the African Charter on the Rights and Welfare of the Child began to include language applicable to female circumcision. These documents, however, did not directly mention the practice, focusing instead on broad categories such as detrimental practices, violence and rights violations.

With shifts in emphasis came new language: Although activists and clinicians continued to refer to female circumcision when working directly with women in the community, policy statements and other documents began to use the term "female genital mutilation." That term was used in the first international document to specifically address the practice, the Programme of Action adopted by the International Conference on Population and Development in Cairo in 1994. The Program refers to female genital mutilation as a "basic rights violation" and urges governments to "prohibit and urgently stop the practice . . . wherever it exists."

In the Platform of the Fourth World Conference on Women, held in Beijing in 1995, female genital mutilation was cited as both a threat to women's reproductive health and a violation of their human rights. In addition to making general recommendations, the Platform specifically called on governments to "enact and enforce legislation against the perpetrators of practices and acts of violence against women, such as female genital mutilation. . . ." Notably, the drive to include language specifically condemning female genital mutilation in the Platform was led by Africans.

Against this background of activity and changing emphasis, the plight of Fauziya Kassindja, a 17-year-old woman from Togo, focused public attention in the United States on female circumcision. More important, her case was instrumental in redefining the practice as gender-based violence that could be grounds for the granting of political asylum. Kassindja, who fled her homeland in October 1994 to avoid an arranged marriage and the genital cutting that would be part of the marriage rites, was placed in a detention center after arriving in the United States under a false passport and asking for asylum. She was released a year and a half later and granted asylum after intensive media coverage of her situation.

Prevalence

Female circumcision is currently practiced in at least 28 countries stretching across the center of Africa north of the equator; it is not found in southern Africa or in the Arabic-speaking nations of North Africa, with the exception of Egypt. Female circumcision occurs among Muslims, Christians, Animists and one Jewish sect, although no religion requires it.

The availability of reliable figures on the prevalence of female circumcision has increased greatly in recent years: National data have now been collected in the Demographic and Health Survey (DHS) program for six countries–the Central African Republic. Côte d'Ivoire, Egypt, Eritrea, Mali and Sudan. In these countries, from 43% to 97% of reproductive-age women have been circumcised. Within countries, prevalence may vary across ethnic groups; in Mali, for example, where the overall proportion of women who have undergone circumcision is 94%, only 17% of women of Tamachek ethnicity have been circumcised.

Estimates for other countries are generally based on local surveys or anecdotal information. The estimated proportion of women who have undergone circumcision in these countries ranges from 5% in Uganda and the Congo (formerly Zaire) to 98%

in Djibouti and Somalia. Both because of wide variations in prevalence across social and demographic subgroups and because of data limitations, these figures should be interpreted with caution.

Types of Circumcision

Although circumcision may be performed during infancy, during adolescence or even during a woman's first pregnancy, the procedure is usually carried out on girls between ages four and 12. In the countries for which DHS data are available, the median age at excision ranges from less than two months in Eritrea to about six years in Mali and almost 10 years in Egypt. The operation is generally performed by a traditional birth attendant or an *exciseuse,* an elder village woman.

There are three basic types of genital excision, although practices vary widely. In the first type, clitoridectomy, part or all of the clitoris is amputated, while in the second (often referred to as excision), both the clitoris and the labia minora are removed. Infibulation, the third type, is the most severe: After excision of the clitoris and the labia minora, the labia majora are cut or scraped away to create raw surfaces, which are held in contact until they heal, either by stitching the edges of the wound or by tying the legs together. As the wounds heal, scar tissue joins the labia and covers the urethra and most of the vaginal orifice, leaving an opening that may be as small as a matchstick for the passage of urine and menstrual blood.

The overall proportion of women who have undergone each type of circumcision is not known, although clitoridectomy appears to be by far the most common procedure. It is estimated that about 15% of all circumcised women have been infibulated, although an estimated 80–90% of all circumcisions in Djibouti, Somalia and the Sudan are of this type.

Consequences of Excision

In the conditions under which female circumcision is generally performed in Africa, even the less extensive types of genital cutting can lead to potentially fatal complications, such as hemorrhage, infection and shock. The inability to pass urine because of pain, swelling and inflammation following the operation may lead to urinary tract infection. A woman may suffer from abscesses and pain from damaged nerve endings long after the initial wound has healed.

Infibulation is particularly likely to cause long-term health problems. Because the urethral opening is covered, repeated urinary tract infections are common, and stones may form in the urethra and bladder because of obstruction and infection. If the opening is very small, menstrual flow may be blocked, leading to reproductive tract infections and lowered fertility or sterility. One early study estimated that 20–25% of cases of sterility in northern Sudan can be linked to infibulation.

Without deinfibulation before childbirth, obstructed labor may occur, causing life-threatening complications for both mother and infant. Because birthrates are high in many countries where infibulation is practiced, a woman's infibulation scar may be cut and resewn many times during her reproductive years.

In addition, the amputation of the clitoris and other sensitive tissue reduces a woman's ability to experience sexual pleasure. For infibulated women, the consummation of marriage is likely to be painful because of the small vaginal opening and the lack of elasticity in the scar tissue that forms it. Tearing and bleeding may occur, or the infibulation scar may have to be cut open to allow penetration.

Infibulation may make intercourse unsatisfying for men as well as women: In a study of 300 polygynous Sudanese men, each of whom had one wife who had been infibulated and one or more who had not, 266 expressed a definite sexual preference for the uninfibulated wife; in addition, 60 said they had married a second, uninfibulated wife because of the penetration difficulties they experienced with their first wife, whose scarred vaginal opening became progressively more inelastic after each birth. Under such conditions, marital dissolution may occur, especially if a woman's fertility is affected. In Sudan, for example, one study found that infibulated women are almost twice as likely as other women to have lower fertility and more than twice as likely to be divorced. Thus, a practice that is justified as making girls marriageable and safeguarding their fertility may actually increase the risk of marital dissolution and subfertility.

Given the medical complications and related consequences of female circumcision, why does the practice continue? First, it is unclear how frequently such problems occur, for few data exist and those that are available come from small studies or are based on self-reports. Second, in societies in which few women remain uncircumcised, problems arising from female circumcision are likely to be seen as a normal part of a woman's life and may not even be associated with circumcision. The most important reasons, however, probably lie in the social and economic conditions of women's lives.

Social Context

Female circumcision is an integral part of the societies that practice it, where patriarchal authority and control of female sexuality and fertility are givens. In communities where a person's place in society is determined by lineage traced through fathers, female circumcision reduces the uncertainty surrounding paternity by discouraging or preventing women's sexual activity outside of marriage. Although the societies that practice circumcision vary in many ways, most girls receive little education and are valued primarily for their future role as sources of labor and producers of children. In some communities, the prospective husband's family pays a brideprice to the family of the bride, giving his family the right to her labor and her children; she herself has no right to or control over either.

A girl's virginity may be considered essential to her family's ability to arrange her marriage and receive a brideprice, as well as to family honor. In Somalia, for example, a prospective husband's family may have the right to inspect the bride's body prior to marriage, and mothers regularly check their infibulated daughters to ensure that they are still "closed." In this context, parents see both infibulation and early marriage as means of ensuring that their daughter remains "pure" and thus worthy of the brideprice.

In many cultures, considerable social pressure is brought to bear on families who resist conforming to the tradition of female circumcision. In Man, a town in the interior of Côte d'Ivoire, a Yacouba girl who has not been circumcised is not considered marriageable. Among the Samburu of Kenya, who consider uncircumcised girls unclean, promiscuous and immature, girls are generally circumcised at age 14 or 15, usually just before they are married. A girl with a younger brother may undergo circumcision if she remains unmarried by her late teens, since custom dictates that a boy with an uncircumcised older sister may not be initiated into the warrior class.

Girls' desires to conform to peer norms may make them eager to undergo circumcision, since those who remain uncut may be teased and looked down on by their age mates. In addition, the ritual cutting is often embedded in ceremonies in which the girls are feted and showered with presents and their families are honored. A girl's wishes, in any case, are often irrelevant; it is her family–often the father or elder female relatives–who decide whether she will undergo circumcision. According to one Yacouba father, "[My daughter] has no choice. I decide. Her viewpoint is not important."

Indeed, girls have very little choice. Given their age and their lack of education and resources, they are dependent on their parents, and later on their husband, for the basic necessities of life. Those who resist may be cut by force. If they remain uncircumcised and their families are therefore unable to arrange a marriage, they may be cast out without any means of subsistence.

Because of their lack of choice and the powerful influence of tradition, many girls accept circumcision as a necessary, and even natural part of life, and adopt the rationales given for its existence. Of the five countries for which DHS data are available on women's opinions toward excision, the Central African Republic is the only one in which the majority favor discontinuation. A variety of justifications are given by DHS respondents who favor continuation of the practice, including preservation of virginity before marriage, fidelity after marriage, enhancement of the husband's sexual pleasure, enhancement of fertility, prevention of infant and child mortality, cleanliness and religious requirements, but tradition is by far the most commonly mentioned reason.

As these data show, women themselves are involved in perpetuating the practice of female genital cutting. Data on the attitudes of men have been collected only in Eritrea and Sudan. DHS data for Eritrea show that men are slightly more likely than women to favor discontinuation, and that men who believe the practice should be stopped are about twice as likely as their female counterparts to cite medical complications and lack of sexual satisfaction as reasons. In Sudan, a 1981 study found that men are somewhat more likely than women to believe female genital cutting should continue, but are less than half as likely as women to prefer infibulation.

Working for Change

Efforts to eliminate female circumcision have often been unsuccessful because opponents of the practice ignored its social and economic context. In some cases, external intervention has strengthened the resolve of communities to continue their genital cutting rituals as a way of resisting what they perceive as cultural imperialism.

During the era of colonial rule in Africa, some governments attempted to ban female circumcision and met with resistance. In Sudan, when a law banning infibulation was about to be proclaimed in 1946, many parents rushed to midwives to have their daughters infibulated in case it should become impossible later on. When some midwives were arrested for performing circumcision, anticolonial protests broke out. The British colonial government, fearing a massive nationalist revolt such as those that had occurred in Egypt and Kenya, eventually let the law go unenforced.

More recently, calls to action by Western feminists and human rights activists have provoked similar negative reactions. African women have perceived many of these efforts as condescending and derogatory toward their culture. In the words of one infibulated Somali woman. "If Somali women change, it will be a change done by us, among us. When they order us to stop, tell us what we must do, it is offensive to the black person or the Muslim person who believes in circumcision. To advise is good, but not to order."

In many Western publications dealing with female circumcision, one anthropologist observes, "African women are . . . depicted as aberrant, while intact Western women have their sexuality affirmed as the norm." Yet, as Nahid Toubia points out, Western women also subject themselves to medically unnecessary, hazardous procedures, such as cosmetic surgery and the insertion of breast implants, to increase their sexual desirability.

The strong reactions against depictions of cultures practicing female circumcision as savage, violent and abusive of women and children have led to new ways of approaching the issue. Some international organizations working against the practice are supporting local activist groups with funding, training and technical expertise rather than choosing direct involvement. Numerous projects have been mounted to eliminate female circumcision, although none have included rigorous evaluations to determine their success. The following approaches are typical:

- *Community education.* A nationwide study conducted in 1985–1986 by the National Association of Nigerian Nurses and Midwives found that female circumcision was practiced in all states and that in five of the then 11 states at least 90% of the women had been cut. In response to this information, the organization designed an eradication campaign with support from Population Action International and the Program for Appropriate Technology in Health. The project trained health workers to teach individuals about the harmful effects of female circumcision and to work through religious organizations, women's organizations and social clubs to mobilize communities against the practice.
- *Alternative rituals.* The organization Maendeleo Ya Wanawake carried out a pilot project in the Meru district of Kenya in 1996 to develop an alternative initiation ritual. Some 25 mother-daughter pairs participated in a six-day training session that included information on the consequences of female circumcision and how to defend the decision not to be cut. The session culminated in a coming-of-age celebration planned by the community, excluding circumcision but including gifts and special T-shirts for the initiates, skits, and "books of wisdom" prepared by the parents of each girl.
- *Drama.* In Burkina Faso, the director of a local theater group developed a play, based on the experience of his niece, on the consequences of female circumcision; the play is aimed particularly at men. A grant from the Research Action and Information Network for Bodily Integrity of Women (RAINBO) enabled him to videotape the play and show it throughout the region.

Prospects for the Future

The available data provide little evidence that the practice of female circumcision will decline substantially in the near future. The Central African Republic, where prevalence is moderate, is the only country in which steady decline seems to be occurring. Young women in Côte d'Ivoire, Egypt, Eritrea and Mali appear to be no less likely than older women to have undergone circumcision. In Sudan, the sole country for which longitudinal comparisons can be made, prevalence appears to have declined slightly, from 96% to 89%, between the 1978–1979 Sudan Fertility Survey and the 1989–1990 Sudan DHS. Nevertheless, the DHS data do not indicate any differences between younger and older women.

Despite the overall lack of change in the percentages of girls who undergo circumcision, changes in attitudes and practices seem to be occurring in some countries. In Eritrea, for example, women and men younger than 25 are much more likely than those in their 40s to believe that the tradition should be discontinued. In Sudan, where the great majority of women have traditionally been infibulated, there appears to be a small shift toward clitoridectomy.

Given the lack of enforcement of most laws against female circumcision, it is unclear whether a purely legal approach is effective in itself. While legislation may be enforceable in countries where only a small minority adhere to the practice, that is unlikely to be the case when the majority follow the tradition. As Toubia points out, "Clear policy declarations by government and professional bodies are essential to send a strong message of disapproval, but if the majority of the society is still convinced that female genital mutilation serves the common good, legal sanctions that incriminate practitioners and families may be counterproductive." In such countries, she suggests, public information campaigns and counseling of families about the effects of the practice on children may be more useful.

Substantial change is likely to occur only with improvements in the status of women in society. According to Rogaia Abusharaf, "To get married and have children, which on the surface fulfills gender expectations and the reproductive potential of females, is, in reality, a survival strategy in a society plagued with poverty, disease, and illiteracy. . . . The socio economic dependency of women on men affects their response to female circumcision."

This view is born out by the DHS data: In most countries, women with higher levels of education and those who have income of their own are less likely than other women to have been circumcised and are also less likely to have had their daughters circumcised. As Toubia comments, "this one violation of women's rights cannot [be abolished] without placing it firmly within the context of efforts to address the social and economic injustice women face the world over. If women are to be considered as equal and responsible members of society, no aspect of their physical, psychological or sexual integrity can be compromised."

CRITICAL EYE

For Discussion

a. If every cultural practice can be questioned and changed, what is the purpose of tradition?

b. How can female circumcision be justified/viewed as a rite of passage?

c. The statistics tell us that women and children are the most abused and poorest people on the planet. Given this certainty, if we, as a global society, rise to eliminate one evil that women face, won't another merely take its place?

Re-approaching the Reading

Should African nations that still practice female circumcision view western interference and judgment as offensive?

Writing Assignment

Overt sexism, racism, and discrimination against the disabled are practices that America has engaged in. In your opinion, what other American practices need to be questioned in order to create reform and change?

CARA DORRIS

MY FAKE LEVANTINE ROMANCE

Our first date was at the best hummusia in Israel. We sat hillside in a white stone building, while the hummus, soaked with olive oil and topped with pine nuts and Egyptian brown beans, melted in our mouths like clotted cream. We were a few miles from Jerusalem on a scorching desert afternoon, in the Arab village of Abu Ghosh, a town known not only for its hummus but also for its peaceful relationship with nearby Jewish settlements.

But its reputation for tranquillity was dwindling. The previous night, the police found 28 cars with slashed tires and graffiti etched across Abu Ghosh houses: "Arabs Go Home." It was suspected to be the work of right-wing Jewish extremists. As an intern for a local newspaper, I was there to cover the story. My phone's battery was dead, and I needed a photograph. Suddenly desperate, I tapped a tall, olive-skinned man on the shoulder.

He turned around and looked me up and down before dropping his phone into my palm. I crouched between two photographers and snapped a photo of the graffiti. Then I offered it back. He shook his head.

"Put in your number."

His name was Sami. I was drawn to his sharp features and charmingly broken English. I told him I was a Jew. He told me he was an Arab. Competing newspapers were already writing the story: the attacks would forever damage the relations between Jews and Arabs in the historically peaceful village. This was the backdrop for our stilted romance.

Afternoons when I wasn't working and Sami didn't have classes, he would come to Jerusalem. We would eat *murtabak* – Yemeni mutton-filled pancakes – and walk through the narrow alleyways of Mount Zion. In the evenings we would drink arak from the bottle and watch the sunset from the top of the Citadel, the daily light show splashing across the 3,000-year-old walls.

All the while, I was rejecting advances from Israeli men who seemed eager to date a blond American. They would ask for my number, reeking of cigarettes and cologne. I told them I was already in love.

Sami was visiting two, three times a week. He always paid when we went out, but he never kissed me. Everything I read on Yahoo! Answers indicated that this was not really a relationship.

Then he asked me to meet his parents.

I wore a floor-length, long-sleeved dress. We sat on the couch and drank Turkish coffee. His older sister had dark skin and startling green eyes, her head covered as she comforted a screaming baby. His father passed around a plate of watermelon, and his mother asked me what part of Russia I was from. I told her I was American.

Suddenly Sami put his arm over my shoulder and pecked me on the lips. His father beamed.

We performed this strange ritual once a week. The gatherings quickly progressed from afternoon coffee to elaborate dinners, but when his family was gone, he would pull away. I didn't ask why. I convinced myself these were cultural differences. Besides, it was nearing the end of the summer, and I would soon return to school. At least I would have enough Facebook photographs to suggest a summer fling.

The night before my flight home, Sami asked me to meet him at a bar I hadn't heard of. It was at the far end of an alleyway, and there was no sign on the door, just a barred window. The drink special gave it away: Toxic Diva. It was drag night in the holy city.

By midnight the club was filled. Sami smiled apologetically. He grabbed my hand, and we sat next to a gray-haired Orthodox man in a black suit and wide-brimmed hat, his hands taut and treed with veins. The man stared emptily at the drag queens who thrashed to disco music, red lights flashing. It was my last night in Jerusalem, and I was sitting between a man who did not want to touch me and one who, by Jewish law, could not.

I had spent all summer denying to myself that Sami was hiding something from me, never questioning my role as his accomplice. Now we were at a gay bar. Neither of us could hide.

Suddenly Sami offered to switch places with me. He turned to the man, offering his hand. They locked eyes. Upon being touched, the religious man jolted to life. His face softened, and he shook, holding so tightly his whole body seemed to quake. He would not let go.

But I had to.

CRITICAL EYE

For Discussion

a. Our characters live in a world that is complicated for many reasons. What are these complications, and can they ever be overcome?

Re-approaching the Reading

Consider this story alongside David Sedaris's "Go Carolina." Both males are dealing with the same issues. David believes the speech lessons are meant to single out or identify certain "kinds" of boys. Sami is using his relationship with his girlfriend to prevent him from being identified as a certain "kind" of young man. What are these two stories attempting to reveal to us about what happens to people who are different? What do "different" people fear?

Writing Assignment

Despite the growing changes in how the world receives members of the LGBTQ community, what kind of challenges does the LGBTQ community still face worldwide?

ELIZA HAYWOOD

FANTOMINA: OR, LOVE IN A MAZE

Being a Secret History of an Amour Between Two Persons of Condition

In love the victors from vanquished fly.
They fly that wound, and they pursue that die.
Waller

A young Lady of distinguished Birth, Beauty, Wit, and Spirit, happened to be in a Box one Night at the Playhouse; where, though there were a great Number of celebrated Toasts, she perceived several Gentlemen extremely pleased themselves with entertaining a Woman who sat in a Corner of the Pit, and, by her Air and Manner of receiving them, might easily be known to be one of those who come there for no other Purpose, than to create Acquaintance with as many as seem desirous of it. She could not help testifying her Contempt of Men, who, regardless either of the Play, or Circle, threw away their Time in such a Manner, to some Ladies that sat by her: But they, either less surprised by being more accustomed to such Sights, than she who had been bred for the most Part in the Country, or not of a Disposition to consider any Thing very deeply, took but little Notice of it. She still thought of it, however; and the longer she reflected on it, the greater was her Wonder, that Men, some of whom she knew were accounted to have Wit, should have Tastes so very Depraved.–This excited a Curiosity in her to know in what Manner these Creatures were address'd:–She was young, a Stranger to the World, and consequently to the Dangers of it; and having no Body in Town, at that Time, to whom she was oblig'd to be accountable for her Actions, did in every Thing as her Inclinations or Humours render'd most agreeable to her: Therefore thought it not in the least a Fault to put in practice a little Whim which came immediately into her Head, to dress herself as near as she could in the Fashion of those Women who make sale of their Favours, and set herself in the Way of being accosted as such a one, having at that Time no other Aim, than the Gratification of an innocent Curiosity.–She had no sooner design'd this Frolick, than she put it in Execution; and muffling her Hoods over her Face, went the next Night into the Gallery-Box, and practising as much as she had observ'd, at that Distance, the Behaviour of that Woman, was not long before she found her Disguise had answer'd the Ends she wore it for:–A Crowd of Purchasers of all Degrees and Capacities were in a Moment gather'd about her, each endeavouring to out-bid the other, in offering her a Price for her Embraces.–She listen'd to 'em all, and was not a little diverted in her Mind at the Disappointment she shou'd give to so many, each of which thought himself secure of gaining her.–She was told by 'em all, that she was the most lovely Woman in the World; and some cry'd, *Gad, she is mighty like my fine Lady Such-a-one,*–naming her own Name. She was naturally vain, and receiv'd no small Pleasure in hearing herself prais'd, tho' in the Person of another, and a suppos'd Prostitute; but she dispatch'd as soon as she cou'd all that had hitherto attack'd her, when she saw the accomplish'd *Beauplaisir* was making his Way thro' the Crowd as fast as he was able, to reach the Bench she sat on. She had often seen him in the Drawing-Room, had talk'd with him; but then her Quality and reputed Virtue kept him from using her with that Freedom she now expected he wou'd do, and had discover'd something in him, which had made her often think she shou'd not be displeas'd, if he wou'd abate some Part of his Reserve.–Now was the Time to have her Wishes answer'd:–He look'd in her Face, and fancy'd, as many others had done, that she very much resembled that Lady whom she really was; but the vast Disparity there appear'd between their Characters, prevented him from entertaining even the most distant Thought that they cou'd be the same.–He address'd her at first with the usual Salutations of her pretended Profession, as, *Are you engag'd, Madam?–Will you permit me to wait on you home after the Play?–By Heaven, you are a fine Girl!–How long have you us'd this House?*–And such like Questions; but perceiving she had a Turn of Wit, and a genteel Manner in her Raillery, beyond what is frequently to be found among those Wretches, who are for the most part Gentlewomen but by Necessity, few of 'em having had an Education suitable to what they affect to appear, he chang'd the Form of his Conversation, and shew'd her it was not because he understood no better, that he had made use of Expressions so little polite.–In fine, they were infinitely charm'd with each other: He was transported to find so much Beauty and Wit in a Woman, who he doubted not but on very easy Terms he might enjoy; and she found a vast deal of Pleasure in conversing with him in this free and unrestrain'd Manner. They pass'd their Time all the Play with an equal Satisfaction; but when it was over, she found herself involv'd in a Difficulty, which before never enter'd into her Head, but which she knew not well how to get over.–The Passion he profess'd for her, was not of that humble Nature which can be content with distant Adorations:–He resolv'd not to part from her without the Gratifications of those Desires she had inspir'd; and presuming on the Liberties which her suppos'd Function allow'd off, told her she must either go with him to some convenient House of his procuring, or permit him to wait on her to her own Lodgings.–Never had she been in such a *Dilemma:* Three or four Times did she open her Mouth to confess her real Quality; but the influence of her ill Stars prevented it, by putting an Excuse into her Head, which did the Business as well, and at the same Time did not take from her the Power of seeing and entertaining him a second Time with the same Freedom she had done this.–She told him, she was under Obligations to a Man who maintain'd her, and whom she durst not disappoint, having promis'd to meet him that Night at a House hard by.–This Story so like what those Ladies sometimes tell, was not at all suspected by *Beauplaisir;* and assuring her he wou'd be far from doing her a Prejudice, desir'd that in return for the Pain he shou'd suffer in being depriv'd of her Company that Night, that she wou'd order her Affairs, so as not to render him unhappy the next. She gave a solemn Promise to be in the same Box on the Morrow Evening; and they took Leave of each other; he to the Tavern to drown the Remembrance of his Disappointment; she in a Hackney-Chair hurry'd home to indulge Contemplation on the Frolick she had taken, designing nothing less on her first Reflections, than to keep the Promise she had made him, and hugging herself with Joy, that she had the good Luck to come off undiscover'd.

But these Cogitations were but of a short Continuance, they vanish'd with the Hurry of her Spirits, and were succeeded by others vastly different and ruinous:–All the Charms of *Beauplaisir* came fresh into her Mind; she languish'd, she almost dy'd for another Opportunity of conversing with him; and not all the Admonitions of her Discretion were effectual to oblige her to deny laying hold of that which offer'd itself the next Night.–She depended on the Strength of her Virtue, to bear her fate thro' Tryals more dangerous than she apprehended this to be, and never having been address'd by him as Lady, – was resolv'd to receive his Devoirs as a Town-Mistress, imagining a world of Satisfaction to herself in engaging him in the Character of such a one, and in observing the Surprise he would be in to find himself refused by a Woman, who he supposed granted her Favours without Exception.–Strange and unaccountable were the Whimsies she was possess'd of,–wild and incoherent her Desires,–unfix'd and undetermin'd her Resolutions, but in that of seeing *Beauplaisir* in the Manner she had lately done. As for her Proceedings with him, or how a second Time to escape him, without discovering who she was, she cou'd neither assure herself, nor whither or not in the last Extremity she wou'd do so.–Bent, however, on meeting him, whatever shou'd be the Consequence, she went out some Hours before the Time of going to the Playhouse, and took lodgings in a House not very far from it, intending, that if he shou'd insist on passing some Part of the Night with her, to carry him there, thinking she might with more Security to her Honour entertain him at a Place where she was Mistress, than at any of his own chusing.

The appointed Hour being arriv'd, she had the Satisfaction to find his Love in his Assiduity: He was there before her; and nothing cou'd be more tender than the Manner in which he accosted her: But from the first Moment she came in, to that of the Play being done, he continued to assure her no Consideration shou'd prevail with him to part from her again, as she had done the Night before; and she rejoic'd to think she had taken that Precaution of providing herself with a Lodging, to which she thought she might invite him, without running any Risque, either of her Virtue or Reputation.–Having told him she wou'd admit of his accompanying her home, he seem'd perfectly satisfy'd; and leading her to the Place, which was not above twenty Houses distant, wou'd have order'd a Collation to be brought after them. But she wou'd not permit it, telling him she was not one of those who suffer'd themselves to be treated at their own Lodgings; and as soon as she was come in, sent a Servant, belonging to the House, to provide a very handsome Supper, and Wine, and every Thing was serv'd to Table in a Manner which shew'd the Director neither wanted Money, nor was ignorant how it shou'd be laid out.

This Proceeding, though it did not take from him the Opinion that she was what she appeared to be, yet it gave him Thoughts of her, which he had not before.–He believ'd her a *Mistress,* but believ'd her to be one of a superior Rank, and began to imagine the Possession of her would be much more Expensive than at first he had expected: But not being of a Humour to grudge any Thing for his Pleasures, he gave himself no further Trouble, than what were occasioned by Fears of not having Money enough to reach her Price, about him.

Supper being over, which was intermixed with a vast deal of amorous Conversation, he began to explain himself more than he had done; and both by his Words and Behaviour let her know, he would not be denied that Happiness the Freedoms she allow'd had made him hope.–It was in vain; she would have retracted the Encouragement she had given:–In vain she endeavoured to delay, till the next Meeting, the fulfilling of his Wishes:–She had now gone too far to retreat:–*He* was bold;–he was resolute: *She* fearful,–confus'd, altogether unprepar'd to resist in such Encounters, and rendered more so, by the extreme Liking she had to him.–Shock'd, however, at the Apprehension of really losing her Honour, she struggled all she could, and was just going to reveal the whole Secret of her Name and Quality, when the Thoughts of the Liberty he had taken with her, and those he still continued to prosecute, prevented her, with representing the Danger of being expos'd, and the whole Affair made a Theme for publick Ridicule.–Thus much, indeed, she told him, that she was a Virgin, and had assumed this Manner of Behaviour only to engage him. But that he little regarded, or if he had, would have been far from obliging him to desist;–nay, in the present burning Eagerness of Desire, 'tis probable, that had he been acquainted both with who and what she really was, the Knowledge of her Birth would not have influenc'd him with Respect sufficient to have curb'd the wild Exuberance of his luxurious Wishes, or made him in that longing,–that impatient Moment, change the Form of his Addresses. In fine, she was undone; and he gain'd a Victory, so highly rapturous, that had he known over whom, scarce could he have triumphed more. Her Tears, however, and the Destraction she appeared in, after the ruinous Extasy was past, as it heighten'd his Wonder, so it abated his Satisfaction:–He could not imagine for what Reason a Woman, who, if she intended not to be a *Mistress,* had counterfeited the Part of one, and taken so much Pains to engage him, should lament a Consequence which she could not but expect, and till the last Test, seem'd inclinable to grant; and was both surpris'd and troubled at the Mystery.–He omitted nothing that he thought might make her easy; and still retaining an Opinion that the Hope of Interest had been the chief Motive which had led her to act in the Manner she had done, and believing that she might know so little of him, as to suppose, now she had nothing left to give, he might not make that Recompense she expected for her Favours: To put her out of that Pain, he pulled out of his Pocket a Purse of Gold, entreating her to accept of that as an Earnest of what he intended to do for her; assuring her, with ten thousand Protestations, that he would spare nothing, which his whole Estate could purchase, to procure her Content and Happiness. This Treatment made her quite forget the Part she had assum'd, and throwing it from her with an Air of Disdain, Is this a Reward *(said she)* for Condescensions, such as I have yeilded to?–Can all the Wealth you are possessed of, make a Reparation for my Loss of Honour?–Oh! no, I am undone beyond the Power of Heaven itself to help me!–She uttered many more such Exclamations; which the amaz'd *Beauplaisir* heard without being able to reply to, till by Degrees sinking from that Rage of Temper, her Eyes resumed their softning Glances, and guessing at the Consternation he was in, No, my dear *Beauplaisir, (added she,)* your Love alone can compensate for the Shame you have involved me in; be you sincere and constant, and I hereafter shall, perhaps, be satisfy'd with my Fate, and forgive myself the Folly that betray'd me to you.

Beauplaisir thought he could not have a better Opportunity than these Words gave him of enquiring who she was, and wherefore she had feigned herself to be of a Profession which he was now convinc'd she was not; and after he had made her a thousand Vows of an Affection, as inviolable and ardent as she could wish to find in him, entreated she would inform him by what Means his Happiness has been brought about, and also to whom he was indebted for the Bliss he had enjoy'd.–Some remains of yet unextinguished Modesty, and Sense of Shame, made her Blush exceedingly at this Demand; but recollecting herself in a little Time, she told him so much of the Truth, as to what related to the Frolick she had taken of satisfying her Curiosity in what Manner *Mistresses,* of the Sort she appeared to be, were treated by those who addressed them; but forbore discovering her true Name and Quality, for the Reasons she had done before, resolving, if he boasted of this Affair, he should not have it in his Power to touch her Character: She therefore said she was the Daughter of a Country Gentleman, who was come to town to buy Cloaths, and that she was call'd *Fantomina.* He had no Reason to distrust the Truth of this Story, and was therefore satisfy'd with it; but did not doubt by the Beginning of her Conduct, but that in the End she would be in Reality, the Thing she so artfully had counterfeited; and had good Nature enough to pity the Misfortunes he imagin'd would be her Lot: But to tell her so, or offer his Advice in that Point, was not his Business, as least, as yet.

They parted not till towards Morning; and she oblig'd him to a willing Vow of visiting her the next Day at Three in the Afternoon. It was too late for her to go home that Night, therefore contented herself with lying there. In the Morning she sent for the Woman of the House to come up to her; and easily perceiving, by her Manner, that she was a Woman who might be influenced by Gifts, made her a Present of a Couple of Broad Pieces, and desir'd her, that if the Gentleman, who had been there the night before, should ask any Questions concerning her, that he should be told, she was lately come out of the Country, had lodg'd there about a Fortnight, and that her Name was *Fantomina.* I shall *(also added she)* lie but seldom here; nor, indeed, ever come but in those Times when I expect to meet him: I would, therefore, have you order it so, that he may think I am but just gone out, if he should happen by any Accident to call when I am not here; for I would not, for the World, have him imagine I do not constantly lodge here. The Landlady assur'd her she would do every Thing as she desired, and gave her to understand she wanted not the Gift of Secrecy.

Every Thing being ordered at this Home for the Security of her Reputation, she repaired to the other, where she easily excused to an unsuspecting Aunt, with whom she boarded, her having been abroad all Night, saying, she went with a Gentleman and his Lady in a Barge, to a little Country Seat of theirs up the River, all of them designing to return the same Evening; but that one of the Bargemen happ'ning to be taken ill on the sudden, and no other Waterman to be got that Night, they were oblig'd to tarry till Morning. Thus did this Lady's Wit and Vivacity assist her in all, but where it was most needful.–She had Discernment to forsee, and avoid all those Ills which might attend the Loss of her *Reputation,* but was wholly blind to those of the Ruin of her *Virtue;* and having managed her Affairs so as to secure the one, grew perfectly easy with the Remembrance, she had forfeited the *other.*–The more she reflected on the Merits of *Beauplaisir,* the more she excused herself for what she had done; and the Prospect of that continued Bliss she expected to share with him, took from her all Remorse for having engaged in an Affair which promised her so much Satisfaction, and in which she found not the least Danger of Misfortune.–If he is really *(said she, to herself)* the faithful, the constant Lover he has sworn to be, how charming will be our Amour?–And if he should be false, grow satiated, like other Men, I shall but, at the worst, have the private Vexation of knowing I have lost him;–the Intreague being a Secret, my Disgrace will be so too:–I shall hear no Whispers as I pass,–She is Forsaken:–The odious Word *Forsaken* will never wound my Ears; nor will my Wrongs excite either the Mirth or Pity of the talking World:–It will not be even in the Power of my Undoer himself to triumph over me; and while he laughs at, and perhaps despises the fond, the yielding *Fantomina,* he will revere and esteem the virtuous, the reserv'd Lady.–In this Manner did she applaud her own Conduct, and exult with the

Imagination that she had more Prudence than all her Sex beside. And it must be confessed, indeed, that she preserved an OEconomy in the management of this Intreague, beyond what almost any Woman but herself ever did: In the first Place, by making no Person in the World a Confident in it; and in the next, in concealing from *Beauplaisir* himself the Knowledge who she was; for though she met him three or four Days in a Week, at the Lodging she had taken for that Purpose, yet as much as he employ'd her Time and Thoughts, she was never miss'd from any Assembly she had been accustomed to frequent.—The Business of her Love has engross'd her till Six in the Evening, and before Seven she has been dress'd in a different Habit, and in another Place.—Slippers, and a Nightgown loosely flowing, has been the Garb in which he has left the languishing *Fantomina;*—Lac'd, and adorn'd with all the Blaze of Jewels, has he, in less than an Hour after, beheld at the Royal Chapel, the Palace Gardens, Drawing-Room, Opera, or Play, the Haughty Awe-Inspiring Lady—A thousand Times has he stood amaz'd at the prodigious Likeness between his little Mistress, and this Court Beauty; but was still as far from imagining they were the same, as he was the first Hour he had accosted her in the Playhouse, though it is not impossible, but that her Resemblance to this celebrated Lady, might keep his Inclination alive something longer than otherwise they would have been; and that it was to the Thoughts of this (as he supposed) unenjoy'd Charmer, she ow'd in great measure the Vigour of his latter Caresses.

But he varied not so much from his Sex as to be able to prolong Desire, to any great Length after Possession: The rifled Charms of *Fantomina* soon lost their Poinancy, and grew tastless and insipid; and when the Season of the Year inviting the Company to the *Bath,* she offer'd to accompany him, he made an Excuse to go without her. She easily perceiv'd his Coldness, and the Reason why he pretended her going would be inconvenient, and endur'd as much from the Discovery as any of her Sex could do: She dissembled it, however, before him, and took her Leave of him with the Shew of no other Concern than his Absence occasion'd: But this she did to take from him all Suspicion of her following him, as she intended, and had already laid a Scheme for.—From her first finding out that he design'd to leave her behind, she plainly saw it was for no other Reason, than being tir'd of her Conversation, he was willing to be at liberty to pursue new Conquests; and wisely considering that Complaints, Tears, Swooning, and all the Extravagancies which Women make use of in such Cases, have little Prevailence over a Heart inclin'd to rove, and only serve to render those who practice them more contemptible, by robbing them of that Beauty which alone can bring back the fugitive Lover, she resolved to take another Course; and remembring the Height of Transport she enjoyed when the agreeable *Beauplaisir* kneel'd at her Feet, imploring her first Favours, she long'd to prove the same again. Not but a Woman of her Beauty and Accomplishments might have beheld a Thousand in that Condition *Beauplaisir* had been; but with her Sex's Modesty, she had not also thrown off another Virtue equally valuable, tho' generally unfortunate, *Constancy:* She loved *Beauplaisir;* it was only he whose Solicitations could give her Pleasure; and had she seen the whole Species despairing, dying for her sake, it might, perhaps, have been a Satisfaction to her Pride, but none to her more tender Inclination.—Her Design was once more to engage him, to hear him sigh, to see him languish, to feel the strenuous Pressures of his eager Arms, to be compelled, to be sweetly forc'd to what she wished with equal Ardour, was what she wanted, and what she had form'd a Stratagem to obtain, in which she promis'd herself Success.

She no sooner heard he had left the Town, than making a Pretence to her Aunt, that she was going to visit a Relation in the Country, went towards *Bath,* attended but by two Servants, who she found Reasons to quarrel with on the Road and discharg'd: Clothing herself in a Habit she had brought with her, she forsook the Coach, and went into a Wagon, in which Equipage she arriv'd at *Bath.* The Dress she was in, was a round-ear'd Cap, a short Red Petticoat, and a little Jacket of Grey Stuff; all the rest of her Accoutrements were answerable to these, and join'd with a broad Country Dialect, a rude unpolish'd Air, which she, having been bred in these Parts, knew very well how to imitate, with her Hair and Eye-brows black'd, made it impossible for her to be known, or taken for any other than what she seem'd. Thus disguis'd did she offer herself to Service in the House where *Beauplaisir* lodg'd, having made it her Business to find out immediately where he was. Notwithstanding this Metamorphosis she was still extremely pretty; and the Mistress of the House happening at that Time to want a Maid, was very glad of the Opportunity of taking her. She was presently receiv'd into the Family; and had a Post in it (such as she would have chose, had she been left at her Liberty,) that of making the Gentlemen's Beds, getting them their Breakfasts, and waiting on them in their Chambers. Fortune in this Exploit was extremely on her side; there were no others of the Male-Sex in the House, than an old Gentleman, who had lost the Use of his Limbs with the Rheumatism, and had come thither for the Benefit of the Waters, and her belov'd *Beauplaisir;* so that she was in no Apprehensions of any Amorous Violence, but where she wish'd to find it. Nor were her Designs disappointed: He was fir'd with the first Sight of her; and tho' he did not presently take any farther Notice of her, than giving her two or three hearty Kisses, yet she, who now understood that Language but too well, easily saw they were the Prelude to more substantial Joys.—Coming the next Morning to bring his Chocolate, as he had order'd, he catch'd her by the pretty Leg, which the Shortness of her Petticoat did not in the least oppose; then pulling her gently to him, ask'd her, how long she had been at Service?—How many Sweethearts she had? If she had ever been in Love? and many other such Questions, befitting one of the Degree she appear'd to be: All which she answer'd with such seeming Innocence, as more enflam'd the amorous Heart of him who talk'd to her. He compelled her to sit in his Lap; and gazing on her blushing Beauties, which, if possible, receiv'd Addition from her plain and rural Dress, he soon lost the Power of containing himself.—His wild Desires burst out in all his Words and Actions: he call'd her little Angel, Cherubim, swore he must enjoy her, though Death were to be the Consequence, devour'd her Lips, her Breasts with greedy Kisses, held to his burning Bosom her half-yielding, half-reluctant Body, nor suffered her to get loose, till he had ravaged all, and glutted each rapacious Sense with the sweet Beauties of the pretty *Celia,* for that was the Name she bore in this second Expedition.—Generous as Liberality itself to all who gave him Joy this way, he gave her a handsome Sum of Gold, which she durst not now refuse, for fear of creating some Mistrust, and losing the Heart she so lately had regain'd; therefore taking it with an humble Curtesy, and a well counterfeited Shew of Surprise and Joy, cry'd, O Law, Sir! what must I do for all this? He laughed at her Simplicity, and kissing her again, tho' less fervently than he had done before, bad her not be out of the Way when he came home at Night. She promis'd she would not, and very obediently kept her Word.

His Stay at *Bath* exceeded not a Month; but in that Time his suppos'd Country Lass had persecuted him so much with her Fondness, that in spite of the Eagerness with which he first enjoy'd her, he was at last grown more weary of her, than he had been of *Fantomina;* which she perceiving, would not be troublesome, but quitting her Service, remained privately in the Town till she heard he was on his Return; and in that Time provided herself of another Disguise to carry on a third Plot, which her inventing Brain had furnished her with, once more to renew his twice-decay'd Ardours. The Dress she had order'd to be made, was such as Widows wear in their first Mourning, which, together with the most afflicted and penitential Countenance that ever was seen, was no small Alteration to her who us'd to seem all Gaiety.—To add to this, her Hair, which she was accustom'd to wear very loose, both when *Fantomina* and *Celia,* was now ty'd back so straight, and her Pinners coming so very forward, that there was none of it to be seen. In fine, her Habit and her Air were so much chang'd, that she was not more difficult to be known in the rude Country *Girl,* than she was now in the sorrowful *Widow.*

She knew that *Beauplaisir* came alone in his Chariot to the *Bath,* and in the Time of her being Servant in the House where he lodg'd, heard nothing of any Body that was to accompany him to *London,* and hop'd he wou'd return in the same Manner he had gone: She therefore hir'd Horses and a Man to attend her to an Inn about ten Miles on this side *Bath,* where having discharg'd them, she waited till the Chariot should come by; which when it did, and she saw that he was alone in it, she call'd to him that drove it to stop a Moment, and going to the Door saluted the Master with these Words:

The Distress'd and Wretched, Sir, *(said she,)* never fail to excite Compassion in a generous Mind; and I hope I am not deceiv'd in my Opinion that yours is such:—You have the Appearance of a Gentleman, and cannot, when you hear my Story, refuse that Assistance which is in your Power to give to an unhappy Woman, who without it, may be rendered the most miserable of all created Beings.

It would not be very easy to represent the Surprise, so odd an Address created in the Mind of him to whom it was made.—She had not the Appearance of one who wanted Charity; and what other Favour she requir'd he cou'd not conceive: But telling her, she might command any Thing in his Power, gave her Encouragement to declare herself in this Manner: You may judge, *(resumed she,)* by the melancholy Garb I am in, that I have lately lost all that ought to be valuable to Womankind; but it is impossible for you to guess the Greatness of my Misfortune, unless you had known my Husband, who was Master of every Perfection to endear him to a Wife's Affections.—But, notwithstanding, I look on myself as the most unhappy of my Sex in out-living him, I must so far obey the Dictates of my Discretion, as to take care of the little Fortune he left behind him, which being in the hands of a Brother of his in *London,* will be all carried off to *Holland,* where he is going to settle; if I reach not the Town before he leaves it, I am undone for ever.—To which End I left Bristol, the Place where we liv'd, hoping to get a Place in the Stage at *Bath,* but they were all taken up before I came; and being, by a Hurt I got in a Fall, render'd incapable of travelling any long Journey on Horseback, I have no Way to go to *London,* and must be inevitably ruin'd in the Loss of all I have on Earth, without you have good Nature enough to admit me to take Part of your Chariot.

Here the feigned Widow ended her sorrowful Tale, which had been several Times interrupted by a Parenthesis of Sighs and Groans; and *Beauplaisir,* with a complaisant and tender Air, assur'd her of his Readiness to serve her in Things of much greater Consequence than what she desir'd of him; and told her, it would be an Impossibility of denying a Place in his Chariot to a Lady, who he could not behold without yielding one in his Heart. She answered the Compliments he made her but with Tears, which seem'd to stream in such abundance from her Eyes, that she could not keep her Handkerchief from her Face one Moment. Being come into the Chariot, *Beauplaisir* said a thousand handsome Things to perswade her from giving way to so violent a Grief, which, he told her, would not only be distructive to her Beauty, but likewise her Health. But all his Endeavours for Consolement appear'd ineffectual, and he began to think he should have but a dull Journey, in the Company of one who seem'd so obstinately devoted to the Memory of her dead Husband, that there was no getting a Word from her on any other Theme:–But bethinking himself of the celebrated Story of the *Ephesian* Matron, it came into his Head to make Tryal, she who seem'd equally susceptible of *Sorrow,* might not also be so too of *Love;* and having begun a Discourse on almost every other Topick, and finding her still incapable of answering, resolv'd to put it to the Proof, if this would have no more Effect to rouze her sleeping Spirits:–With a gay Air, therefore, though accompany'd with the greatest Modesty and Respect, he turned the Conversation, as though without Design, on that Joy-giving Passion, and soon discover'd that was indeed the Subject she was best pleas'd to be entertained with; for on his giving her a Hint to begin upon, never any Tongue run more voluble than hers, on the prodigious Power it had to influence the Souls of those posses'd of it, to Actions even the most distant from their Intentions, Principles, or Humours.– From that she pass'd to a Description of the Happiness of mutual Affection;–the unspeakable Extasy of those who meet with equal Ardency; and represented it in Colours so lively, and disclos'd by the Gestures with which her Words were accompany'd, and the Accent of her Voice so true a Feeling of what she said, that *Beauplaisir,* without being as stupid, as he was really the contrary, could not avoid perceiving there were Seeds of Fire, not yet extinguish'd, in this fair Widow's Soul, which wanted but the kindling Breath of tender Sighs to light into a Blaze.–He now thought himself as fortunate, as some Moments before he had the Reverse; and doubted not, but, that before they parted, he should find a Way to dry the Tears of this lovely Mourner, to the Satisfaction of them both. He did not, however, offer, as he had done to *Fantomina* and *Celia,* to urge his Passion directly to her, but by a thousand little softning Artifices, which he well knew how to use, gave her leave to guess he was enamour'd. When they came to the Inn where they were to lie, he declar'd himself somewhat more freely, and perceiving she did not resent it past Forgiveness, grew more encroaching still:–He now took the Liberty of kissing away her Tears, and catching the Sighs as they issued from her Lips; telling her if Grief was infectious, he was resolv'd to have his Share; protesting he would gladly exchange Passions with her, and be content to bear her Load of *Sorrow,* if she would as willingly ease the Burden of his *Love.*–She said little in answer to the strenuous Pressures with which at last he ventur'd to enfold her, but not thinking it Decent, for the Character she had assum'd, to yield so suddenly, and unable to deny both his and her own Inclinations, she counterfeited a fainting, and fell motionless upon his Breast.– He had no great Notion that she was in a real Fit, and the Room they supp'd in happening to have a Bed in it, he took her in his Arms and laid her on it, believing, that whatever her Distemper was, that was the most proper Place to convey her to.–He laid himself down by her, and endeavour'd to bring her to herself; and she was too grateful to her kind Physician at her returning Sense, to remove from the Posture he had put her in, without his Leave.

It may, perhaps, seem strange that *Beauplaisir* should in such near Intimacies continue still deceiv'd: I know there are Men who will swear it is an Impossibility, and that no Disguise could hinder them from knowing a Woman they had once enjoy'd. In answer to these Scruples, I can only say, that besides the Alteration which the Change of Dress made in her, she was so admirably skill'd in the Art of feigning, that she had the Power of putting on almost what Face she pleas'd, and knew so exactly how to form her Behaviour to the Character she represented, that all the Comedians at both Playhouses are infinitely short of her Performances: She could vary her very Glances, tune her Voice to Accents the most different imaginable from those in which she spoke when she appear'd herself.–These Aids from Nature, join'd to the Wiles of Art, and the Distance between the Places where the imagin'd *Fantomina* and *Celia* were, might very well prevent his having any Thought that they were the same, or that the fair *Widow* was either of them: It never so much as enter'd his Head, and though he did fancy he observed in the Face of the latter, Features which were not altogether unknown to him, yet he could not recollect when or where he had known them;–and being told by her, that from her Birth, she had never remov'd from *Bristol,* a Place where he never was, he rejected the Belief of having seen her, and suppos'd his Mind had been deluded by an Idea of some other, whom she might have a Resemblance of.

They pass'd the Time of their Journey in as much Happiness as the most luxurious Gratification of wild Desires could make them; and when they came to the End of it, parted not without a mutual Promise of seeing each other often.–He told her to what Place she should direct a Letter to him; and she assur'd him she would send to let him know where to come to her, as soon as she was fixed in Lodgings.

She kept her Promise; and charm'd with the Continuance of his eager Fondness, went not home, but into private Lodgings, whence she wrote to him to visit her the first Opportunity, and enquire for the Widow *Bloomer.*–She had no sooner dispatched this Billet, than she repair'd to the House where she had lodg'd as *Fantomina,* charging the People if *Beauplaisir* should come there, not to let him know she had been out of Town. From thence she wrote to him, in a different Hand, a long Letter of Complaint, that he had been so cruel in not sending one Letter to her all the Time he had been absent, entreated to see him, and concluded with subscribing herself his unalterably Affectionate *Fantomina.* She received in one Day Answers to both these. The first contain'd these Lines:

To the Charming Mrs. Bloomer,
It would be impossible, my Angel! for me to express the thousandth Part of that Infinity of Transport, the Sight of your dear Letter gave me.–Never was Woman form'd to charm like you: Never did any look like you,–write like you,–bless like you;–nor did ever Man adore as I do.–Since Yesterday we parted, I have seem'd a Body without a Soul; and had you not by this inspiring Billet, gave me new Life, I know not what by To-morrow I should have been.–I will be with you this Evening about Five:–O, 'tis an Age till then!–But the cursed Formalities of Duty oblige me to Dine with my Lord–who never rises from Table till that Hour;– therefore Adieu till then sweet lovely Mistress of the Soul and all the Faculties of

Your most faithful,
Beauplaisir.

The other was in this Manner:

To the Lovely Fantomina.
If you were half so sensible as you ought of your own Power of charming, you would be assur'd, that to be unfaithful or unkind to you, would be among the Things that are in their very Natures Impossibilities.–It was my Misfortune, not my Fault, that you were not persecuted every Post with

a Declaration of my unchanging Passion; but I had unluckily forgot the Name of the Woman at whose House you are, and knew not how to form a Direction that it might come safe to your Hands.–And, indeed, the Reflection how you might misconstrue my Silence, brought me to Town some Weeks sooner than I intended–If you knew how I have languish'd to renew those Blessings I am permitted to enjoy in your Society, you would rather pity than condemn

Your ever faithful,
Beauplaisir.

P.S. *I fear I cannot see you till To-morrow; some Business has unluckily fallen out that will engross my Hours till then.–Once more, my Dear,* Adieu.

Traytor! *(cry'd she,)* as soon as she had read them, 'tis thus our silly, fond, believing Sex are serv'd when they put Faith in Man: So had I been deceiv'd and cheated, had I like the rest believ'd, and sat down mourning in Absence, and vainly waiting recover'd Tendernesses.–How do some Women, *(continued she)* make their Life a Hell, burning in fruitless Expectations, and dreaming out their Days in Hopes and Fears, then wake at last to all the Horror of Dispair?–But I have outwitted even the most Subtle of the deceiving Kind, and while he thinks to fool me, is himself the only beguiled Person.

She made herself, most certainly, extremely happy in the Reflection on the Success of her Stratagems; and while the Knowledge of his Inconstancy and Levity of Nature kept her from having that real Tenderness for him she would else have had, she found the Means of gratifying the Inclination she had for his agreeable Person, in as full a Manner as she could wish. She had all the Sweets of Love, but as yet had tasted none of the Gall, and was in a State of Contentment, which might be envy'd by the more Delicate.

When the expected Hour arriv'd, she found that her Lover had lost no part of the Fervency with which he had parted from her; but when the next Day she receiv'd him as *Fantomina,* she perceiv'd a prodigious Difference; which led her again into Reflections on the Unaccountableness of Men's Fancies, who still prefer the last Conquest, only because it is the last.–Here was an evident Proof of it; for there could not be a Difference in Merit, because they were the same Person; but the Widow *Bloomer* was a more new Acquaintance than *Fantomina,* and therefore esteem'd more valuable. This, indeed, must be said of Beauplaisir, that he had a greater Share of good Nature than most of his Sex, who, for the most part, when they are weary of an Intreague, break it entirely off, without any Regard to the Despair of the abandon'd Nymph. Though he retain'd no more than a bare Pity and Complaisance for *Fantomina,* yet believing she lov'd him to an Excess, would not entirely forsake her, though the Continuance of his Visits was now become rather a Penance than a Pleasure.

The Widow *Bloomer* triumph'd some Time longer over the Heart of this Inconstant, but at length her Sway was at an End, and she sunk in this Character, to the same Degree of Tastelessness, as she had done before in that of *Fantomina* and *Celia.*–She presently perceiv'd it, but bore it as she had always done; it being but what she expected, she had prepar'd herself for it, and had another Project in *embrio,* which she soon ripen'd into Action. She did not, indeed, compleat it altogether so suddenly as she had done the others, by reason there must be Persons employ'd in it; and the Aversion she had to any *Confidents* in her Affairs, and the Caution with which she had hitherto acted, and which she was still determin'd to continue, made it very difficult for her to find a Way without breaking thro' that Resolution to compass what she wish'd.–She got over the Difficulty at last, however, by proceeding in a Manner, if possible, more extraordinary than all her former Behaviour:—Muffling herself up in her Hood one Day, she went into the Park about the Hour when there are a great many necessitous Gentlemen, who think themselves above doing what they call little Things for a Maintenance, walking in the *Mall,* to take a *Camelion* Treat, and fill their Stomachs with Air instead of Meat. Two of those, who by their Physiognomy she thought most proper for her Purpose, she beckon'd to come to her; and taking them into a Walk more remote from Company, began to communicate the Business she had with them in these Words: I am sensible, Gentlemen, *(said she,)* that, through the blindness of Fortune, and Partiality of the World, Merit frequently goes unrewarded, and that those of the best Pretentions meet with the least Encouragement:—I ask your Pardon, *(continued she,)* perceiving they seem'd surpris'd, if I am mistaken in the Notion, that you two may, perhaps, be of the Number of those who have Reason to complain of the Injustice of Fate; but if you are such as I take you for, have a Proposal to make you, which may be of some little Advantage to you. Neither of them made any immediate Answer, but appear'd bury'd in Consideration for some Moments. At length, We should, doubtless, Madam, *(said one of them,)* willingly come into any Measures to oblige you, provided they are such as may bring us into no Danger, either as to our Persons or Reputations. That which I require of you, *(resumed she,)* has nothing in it criminal: All that I desire is *Secrecy* in what you are intrusted, and to disguise yourselves in such a Manner as you cannot be known, if hereafter seen by the Person on whom you are to impose.—In fine, the Business is only an innocent Frolick, but if blaz'd abroad, might be taken for too great a Freedom in me:—Therefore, if you resolve to assist me, here are five Pieces to Drink my Health, and assure you, that I have not discours'd you on an Affair, I design not to proceed in; and when it is accomplish'd fifty more lie ready for your Acceptance. These Words, and, above all, the Money, which was a Sum which, 'tis probable, they had not seen of a long Time, made them immediately assent to all she desir'd, and press for the Beginning of their Employment: But things were not yet ripe for Execution; and she told them, that the next Day they should be let into the Secret, charging them to meet her in the same Place at an hour she appointed. 'Tis hard to say, which of these Parties went away best pleas'd; *they,* that Fortune had sent them so unexpected a Windfall; or *she,* that she had found Persons, who appeared so well qualified to serve her.

Indefatigable in the Pursuit of whatsoever her Humour was bent upon, she had no sooner left her new-engag'd Emissaries, than she went in search of a House for the compleating of her Project.—She pitch'd on one very large, and magnificently furnished, which she hir'd by the Week, giving them the Money beforehand, to prevent any Inquiries. The next Day she repaired to the Park, where she met the punctual 'Squires of low Degree; and ordering them to follow her to the House she had taken, told them they must condescend to appear like Servants, and gave each of them a very rich Livery. Then writing a Letter to *Beauplaisir,* in a Character vastly different from either of those she had made use of, as *Fantomina,* or the fair Widow *Bloomer,* order'd one of them to deliver it into his own Hands, to bring back an Answer, and to be careful that he sifted out nothing of the Truth.—I do not fear, *(said she,)* that you should discover to him who I am, because that is a Secret, of which you yourselves are ignorant; but I would have you be so careful in your Replies, that he may not think the Concealment springs from any other Reasons than your great Integrity to your Trust.—Seem therefore to know my whole Affairs; and let your refusing to make him Partaker in the Secret, appear to be only the Effect of your Zeal for my Interest and Reputation. Promises of entire Fidelity on the one side, and Reward on the other, being past, the Messenger made what haste he could to the House of *Beauplaisir;* and being there told where he might find him, perform'd exactly the Injunction that had been given him. But never Astonishment exceeding that which *Beauplaisir* felt at the reading this Billet, in which he found these Lines:

To the All-conquering Beauplaisir.

I imagine not that 'tis a new Thing to you, to be told, you are the greatest Charm in Nature to our Sex: I shall therefore, not to fill up my Letter with any impertinent Praises on your Wit or Person, only tell you, that I am infinite in Love with both, and if you have a Heart not too deeply engag'd, should think myself the happiest of my Sex in being capable of inspiring it with some Tenderness.–There is but one Thing in my Power to refuse you, which is the Knowledge of my Name, which believing the Sight of my Face will render no Secret, you must not take it ill that I conceal from you.–The Bearer of this is a Person I can trust; send by him your Answer; but endeavour not to dive into the Meaning of this Mystery, which will be impossible for you to unravel, and at the same Time very much disoblige me:–But that you may be in no Apprehensions of being impos'd on by a Woman unworthy of your Regard, I will venture to assure you, the first and greatest Men in the Kingdom, would think themselves blest to have that Influence over me you have, though unknown to yourself acquir'd.–But I need not go about to raise your Curiosity, by giving you any Idea of what my Person is; if you think fit to be satisfied, resolve to visit me To-morrow about Three in the Afternoon; and though my Face is hid, you shall not want sufficient Demonstration, that she who takes these unusual Measures to commence a Friendship with you, is neither Old, nor Deform'd. Till then I am,

Yours,

INCOGNITA.

He had scarce come to the Conclusion, before he ask'd the Person who brought it, from what Place he came;–the Name of the Lady he serv'd;–if she were a Wife, or Widow, and several other Questions directly opposite to the Directions of the Letter; but Silence would have avail'd him as much as did all those Testimonies of Curiosity: *No Italian Bravo,* employ'd in a Business of the like Nature, perform'd his Office with more Artifice; and the impatient Enquirer was convinc'd that nothing but doing as he was desir'd, could give him any Light into the Character of the Woman who declar'd so violent a Passion for him; and little fearing any Consequence which could ensue from such an Encounter, resolv'd to rest satisfy'd till he was inform'd of every Thing from herself, not imagining this *Incognita* varied so much from the Generality of her Sex, as to be able to refuse the Knowledge of any Thing to the Man she lov'd with that Transcendency of Passion she profess'd, and which his many Successes with the Ladies gave him Encouragement enough to believe. He therefore took Pen and Paper, and answer'd her Letter in terms tender enough for a Man who had never seen the Person to whom he wrote. The Words were as follows:

To the Obliging and Witty
Incognita.

Though to tell me I am happy enough to be lik'd by a Woman, such, as by your Manner of Writing, I imagine you to be, is an Honour which I can never sufficiently acknowledge, yet I know not how I am able to content myself with admiring the Wonders of your Wit alone: I am certain, a Soul like yours must shine in your Eyes with a Vivacity, which must bless all they look on.–I shall, however, endeavour to restrain myself in these Bounds you are pleas'd to set me, till by the Knowledge of my inviolable Fedility, I may be thought worthy of gazing on that Heaven I am now but to enjoy in Contemplation.–You need not doubt my glad Compliance with your obliging Summons: There is a Charm in your Lines, which gives too sweet an Idea of their lovely Author to be resisted.–I am all impatient for the blissful Moment, which is to throw me at your Feet, and give me an Opportunity of convincing you that I am,

Your everlasting Slave,

BEAUPLAISIR.

Nothing could be more pleas'd than she, to whom it was directed, at the Receipt of this Letter; but when she was told how inquisitive he had been concerning her Character and Circumstances, she could not forbear laughing heartily to think of the Tricks she had play'd him, and applauding her own Strength of Genius, and Force of Resolution, which by such unthought-of Ways could triumph over her Lover's Inconstancy, and render that very Temper, which to other Women is the greatest Curse, a Means to make herself more bless'd.–Had he been faithful to me, *(said she, to herself,)* either as *Fantomina,* or *Celia,* or the Widow *Bloomer,* the most violent Passion, if it does not change its Object, in Time will wither: Possession naturally abates the Vigour of Desire, and I should have had, at best, but a cold, insipid, husband-like Lover in my Arms; but by these Arts of passing on him as a new Mistress whenever the Ardour, which alone makes Love a Blessing, begins to diminish, for the former one, I have him always raving, wild, impatient, longing, dying.–O that all neglected Wives, and fond abandon'd Nymphs would take this Method!–Men would be caught in their own Snare, and have no Cause to scorn our easy, weeping, wailing Sex! Thus did she pride herself as if secure she never should have any Reason to repent the present Gaiety of her Humour. The Hour drawing near in which he was to come, she dress'd herself in as magnificent a Manner, as if she were to be that Night at a Ball at Court, endeavouring to repair the want of those Beauties which the Vizard should conceal, by setting forth the others with the greatest Care and Exactness. Her fine Shape, and Air, and Neck, appear'd to great Advantage; and by that which was to be seen of her, one might believe the rest to be perfectly agreeable. *Beauplaisir* was prodigiously charm'd, as well with her Appearance, as with the Manner she entertain'd him: But though he was wild with Impatience for the Sight of a Face which belong'd to so exquisite a Body, yet he would not immediately press for it, believing before he left her he should easily obtain that Satisfaction.–A noble Collation being over, he began to sue for the Performance of her Promise of granting every Thing he could ask, excepting the Sight of her Face, and Knowledge of her Name. It would have been a ridiculous Piece of Affection in her to have seem'd coy in complying with what she herself had been the first in desiring: She yielded without even a Shew of Reluctance: And if there be any true Felicity in an Armour such as theirs, both here enjoy'd it to the full. But not in the Height of all their mutual Raptures, could he prevail on her to satisfy his Curiosity with the Sight of her Face: She told him that she hop'd he knew so much of her, as might serve to convince him, she was not unworthy of his tenderest Regard; and if he cou'd not content himself with that which she was willing to reveal, and which was the Conditions of their meeting, dear as he was to her, she would rather part with him for ever, than consent to gratify an Inquisitiveness, which, in her Opinion, had no Business with his Love. It was in vain that he endeavour'd to make her sensible of her Mistake; and that this Restraint was the greatest Enemy imaginable to the Happiness of them both: She was not to be perswaded, and he was oblig'd to desist his Solicitations, though determin'd in his Mind to compass what he so ardently desir'd, before he left the House. He then turned the Discourse wholly on the Violence of the Passion he had for her; and express'd the greatest Discontent in the World at the Apprehensions of being separated;– swore he could dwell for ever in her Arms, and with such an undeniable Earnestness pressed to be permitted to tarry with her the whole Night, that had she been less charm'd with his renew'd Eagerness of Desire, she scarce would have had the Power of refusing him; but in granting this Request, she was not without a Thought that he had another Reason for making it besides the Extremity of his Passion, and had it immediately in her Head how to disappoint him.

The Hours of Repose being arriv'd, he begg'd she would retire to her Chamber; to which she consented, but oblig'd him to go to Bed first; which he did not much oppose, because he suppos'd she would not lie in her Mask, and doubted not but the Morning's Dawn would bring the wish'd Discovery.–The two imagin'd Servants usher'd him to his new Lodging; where he lay some Moments in all the Perplexity imaginable at the Oddness of this Adventure. But she suffer'd not these Cogitations to be of any long Continuance: She came, but came in the Dark; which being no more than he expected by the former Part of her Proceedings, he said nothing of; but as much Satisfaction as he found in her Embraces, nothing ever long'd for the Approach of Day with more Impatience than he did. At last it came; but how great was his Disappointment, when by the Noises he heard in the Street, the hurry of the Coaches, and the Cries of Penny-Merchants, he was convinc'd it was Night no where but with him? He was still in the same Darkness as before; for she had taken care to blind the Windows in such a manner, that not the least Chink was left to let in the Day.–He complain'd of her Behaviour in Terms that she would not have been able to resist yielding to, if she had not been certain it would have been the Ruin of her Passion:–She, therefore, answered him only as she had done before; and getting out of the Bed from him, flew out of the Room with too much Swiftness for him to have overtaken her, if he had attempted it. The Moment she left him, the two Attendants enter'd the Chamber, and plucking down the Implements which had skreen'd him from the Knowledge of that which he so much desir'd to find out, restored his Eyes once more to Day:–They attended to assist him in Dressing, brought him Tea, and by their Obsequiousness, let him see there was but one Thing which the Mistress of them would not gladly oblige him in.–He was so much out of Humour, however, at the Disappointment of his Curiosity, that he resolv'd never to make a second Visit.–Finding her in an outer Room, he made no Scruples of expressing the Sense he had of the little Trust she reposed in him, and at last plainly told her, he could not submit to receive Obligations from a Lady, who thought him uncapable of keeping a Secret, which she made no Difficulty of letting her Servants into.–He resented,–he once more entreated,–he said all that Man could do, to prevail on her to unfold the Mystery; but all his Adjurations were fruitless; and he went out of the House determin'd never to re-enter it, till she should pay the Price of his Company with the Discovery of her Face and Circumstances.–She suffer'd him to go with this Resolution, and doubted not but he would recede from it, when he reflected on the happy Moments they had pass'd together; but if he did not, she comforted herself with the Design of forming some other Stratagem, with which to impose on him a fourth Time.

She kept the House, and her Gentlemen-Equipage for about a Fortnight, in which Time she continu'd to write to him as *Fantomina* and the Widow *Bloomer,* and received the Visits he sometimes made to each; but his Behaviour to both was grown so cold, that she began to grow as weary of receiving his now insipid Caresses as he was of offering them: She was beginning to think in what Manner she should drop these two Characters, when the sudden Arrival of her Mother, who had been some Time in a foreign Country, oblig'd her to put an immediate Stop to the Course of her whimsical Adventures.–That Lady, who was severely virtuous, did not approve of many Things she had been told of the Conduct of her Daughter; and though it was not in the Power of any Person in the World to inform her of the Truth of what she had been guilty of, yet she heard enough to make her keep her afterwards in a Restraint, little agreeable to her Humour, and the Liberties to which she had been accustomed.

But this Confinement was not the greatest Part of the Trouble of this now afflicted Lady: She found the Consequences of her amorous Follies would be, without almost a Miracle, impossible to be concealed:–She was with Child; and though she would easily have found Means to have skreen'd even this from the Knowledge of the World, had she been at liberty to have acted with the same unquestionable Authority over herself, as she did before the coming of her Mother, yet now all her Invention was at a Loss for a Stratagem to impose on a Woman of her Penetration:–By eating little, lacing prodigious strait, and the Advantage of a great Hoop-Petticoat, however, her Bigness was not taken notice of, and, perhaps, she would not have been suspected till the Time of her going into the Country, where her Mother design'd to send her, and from whence she intended to make her escape to some Place where she might be delivered with Secrecy, if the Time of it had not happen'd much Sooner than she expected.–A Ball being at Court, the good Old Lady was willing she should partake of the Diversion of it as a Farewel to the Town.–It was there she was seiz'd with those Pangs, which none in her Condition are exempt from:–She could not conceal the sudden Rack which all at once invaded her; or had her Tongue been mute, her wildly rolling Eyes, the Distortion of her Features, and the Convulsions which shook her whole Frame, in spite of her, would have reveal'd she labour'd under some terrible Shock of Nature.–Every Body was surpris'd, every Body was concern'd, but few guessed at the Occasion.–Her Mother griev'd beyond Expression, doubted not but she was struct with the Hand of Death; and order'd her to be carried Home in a Chair, while herself follow'd in another.–A Physician was immediately sent for: But he was presently perceiving what was her Distemper, call'd the old Lady aside, and told her, it was not a Doctor of his Sex, but one of her own, her Daughter stood in need of.–Never was Astonishment and Horror greater than that which seiz'd the Soul of this afflicted Parent at these Words: She could not for a Time believe the Truth of what she heard; but he insisting on it, and conjuring her to send for a Midwife, she was at length convinc'd if it.–All the Pity and Tenderness she had been for some Moment before possess'd of, now vanish'd, and were succeeded by an adequate Shame and Indignation:–She flew to the Bed where her Daughter was lying, and telling her what she had been inform'd of, and which she was now far from doubting, commanded her to reveal the Name of the Person whose Insinuations had drawn her to this Dishonour.–It was a great while before she could be brought to confess any Thing, and much longer before she could be prevailed on to name the Man whom she so fatally had lov'd; but the Rack of Nature growing more fierce, and the enraged old Lady protesting no Help should be afforded her while she persisted in her Obstinacy, she, with great Difficulty and Hesitation in her Speech, at last pronounc'd the Name of *Beauplaisir.* She had no sooner satisfy'd her weeping Mother, than that sorrowful Lady sent Messengers at the same Time, for a Midwife, and for that Gentleman who had occasion'd the other's being wanted.–He happen'd by Accident to be at home, and immediately obey'd the Summons, though prodigiously surpris'd what Business a Lady so much a Stranger to him could have to impart.—But how much greater was his Amazement, when taking him into her Closet, she there acquainted him with her Daughter's Misfortune, of the Discovery she had made, and how far he was concern'd in it?—All the Idea one can form of wild Astonishment, was mean to what he felt:—He assur'd her, that the young Lady her Daughter was a Person who he had never, more than at a Distance, admir'd:—That he had indeed, spoke to her in publick Company, but that he never had a Thought which tended to her Dishonour.—His Denials, if possible, added to the Indignation she was before enflam'd with:—She had no longer Patience; and carrying him into the Chamber, where she was just deliver'd of a fine Girl, cry'd out, I will not be impos'd on: The Truth by one of you shall be reveal'd.—*Beauplaisir* being brought to the Bed side, was beginning to address himself to the Lady in it, to beg she would clear the Mistake her Mother was involv'd in; when she, covering herself with the Cloaths, and ready to die a second Time with the inward Agitations of her Soul, shriek'd out, Oh, I am undone!—I cannot live, and bear this Shame!—But the old Lady believing that now or never was the Time to dive into the Bottom of this Mystery, forcing her to rear her Head, told her, she should not hope to Escape the Scrutiny of a Parent she had dishonour'd in such a Manner, and pointing to *Beauplaisir,* Is this the Gentleman, *(said she,)* to whom you owe your Ruin? or have you deceiv'd me by a fictitious Tale? Oh! no, *(resum'd the trembling Creature,)* he is, indeed, the innocent Cause of my Undoing:—Promise me your Pardon, *(continued she,)* and I will relate the Means. Here she ceas'd, expecting what she would reply, which, on hearing *Beauplaisir* cry out, What mean you Madam? I your Undoing, who never harbour'd the least Design on you in my Life, she did in these Words, Though the Injury you have done your Family, *(said she,)* is of a Nature which cannot justly hope Forgiveness, yet be assur'd, I shall much sooner excuse you when satisfied of the Truth, than while I am kept in a Suspence, if possible, as vexatious as the Crime itself is to me. Encouraged by this she related the whole Truth. And 'tis difficult to determine, if *Beauplaisir,* or the Lady, were most surpris'd at what they heard; he, that he should have been blinded so often by her Artifices; or she, that so young a Creature should have the Skill to make use of them. Both sat for some Time in a profound Revery; till at length she broke it first in these Words: Pardon, Sir, *(said she,)* the Trouble I have given you: I must confess it was with a Design to oblige you to repair the supposed Injury you had done this unfortunate Girl, by marrying her, but now I know not what to say;—The Blame is wholly her's, and I have nothing to request further of you, than that you will not divulge the distracted Folly she has been guilty of.—He answered her in Terms perfectly polite; but made no Offer of that which, perhaps, she expected, though could not, now inform'd of her Daughter's Proceedings, demand. He assured her, however, that if she would commit the new-born Lady to his Care, he would discharge it faithfully. But neither of them would consent to that; and he took his Leave, full of Cogitations, more confus'd than ever he had known in his whole Life. He continued to visit there, to enquire after her Health every Day; but the old Lady perceiving there was nothing likely to ensue from these Civilities, but, perhaps, a Renewing of the Crime, she entreated him to refrain; and as soon as her Daughter was in a Condition, sent her to a Monastery in *France,* the Abbess of which had been her particular Friend. And thus ended an Intreague, which, considering the Time it lasted, was as full of Variety as any, perhaps, that many Ages has produced.

FINIS.

CRITICAL EYE

For Discussion

a. How practical is the experiment the main character engages in?

b. One of the implications of what the main character does is that she feels men are simplistic and can be fooled easily. How offensive or realistic are these claims?

c. Consider this piece alongside Wolf's "The Making of a Slut." Is Fantomina a "bad girl," or is she ahead of her time?

Re-approaching the Reading

From a male standpoint, could this text be viewed as sexist toward men?

Writing Assignment

How much of the main character's dilemma stems from the "dream" that women are sold about love and finding a "Prince Charming"?

CHAPTER 8

Manmade and Natural Disasters

Today, as never before, the fates of men are so intimately linked to one another that a disaster for one is a disaster for everybody.
Natalia Ginzburg

The world is beautiful. Seven continents. Life-bearing oceans and seas. An animal kingdom that defies the imagination. And then there is us, the scientists, artists, healers—the destructive brutes. In many ways, despite our unique understanding of the planet and our talents, we have made the world a mess. Point. Blank. Period. From the effects of global warming to gang warfare on the streets of Chicago, there isn't a section of our immediate world that isn't touched by some kind of perpetual cliffhanging moment, events brought on by the natural world that often seems hell bent on purging us from the planet, or, far more frightening, by the destructiveness of human folly.

In today's turbulent world, we live in constant fear. This unease is a result of our inability to control the environment under our very feet—one that, as time passes, continues to spiral out of control. For centuries, we have been afraid of those we deem different. Because of this, humanity has created a world of crime and violence–a world that is literally at war with itself. If there is a higher being, a creator–a God–then human beings are arguably our maker's most destructive mistake. We will slaughter each other for land and profit, for personal offenses and text-based judgments, for ethnic and cultural dissimilarities, as well as sexual hostility and so-called perversion. We attack each other. We hate and destroy. We are not above the complete decimation of species we deem weaker or less important than ourselves. We are cruel more than not, and our indifference towards destruction is the basis for the extinction of creatures we hunt for sport.

In the last decade, nature, which humans constantly tamper with, has finally become fed up. In recent years, the world community has suffered tremendously as water and wind rage across the globe. Hurricanes, Tsunami's, tornadoes, and flooding have devastated property and killed hundreds, thousands, in the blink of an eye. Cities and countries are still in disrepair–the result of natural disasters coupled with human neglect. People are displaced. The wetlands have been polluted. The polar ice caps are melting. All of this natural annihilation is happening while politicians argue over aide and, even more ridiculously, government and corporation culpability. Fascinatingly, many people in power even dismiss the notion that Global Warming exists.

This chapter will look at the devastation, both manmade and natural, that has slashed a path of destruction across the globe–damage that, if it continues at this rate, may possibly result in humanity's annihilation.

SIMON ROMERO

QUAKE ACCENTUATED CHASM THAT HAS DEFINED HAITI

PORT-AU-PRINCE, Haiti–The lights of the casino above this wrecked city beckoned as gamblers in freshly pressed clothes streamed to the roulette table and slot machines. In a restaurant nearby, diners quaffed Veuve Clicquot Ponsardin Champagne and ate New Zealand lamb chops at prices rivaling those in Manhattan.

A few yards away, hundreds of families displaced by the earthquake languished under tents and tarps, bathing themselves from buckets and relieving themselves in the street as barefoot children frolicked on pavement strewn with garbage.

This is the Pétionville district of Port-au-Prince, a hillside bastion of Haiti's well-heeled where a mangled sense of normalcy has taken hold after the earthquake in January. Business is bustling at the lavish boutiques, restaurants and nightclubs that have reopened in the breezy hills above the capital, while thousands of homeless and hungry people camp in the streets around them, sometimes literally on their doorstep.

"The rich people sometimes need to step over us to get inside," said Judith Pierre, 28, a maid who has lived for weeks in a tent with her two daughters in front of Magdoos, a chic Lebanese restaurant where diners relax in a garden and smoke flavored tobacco from hookahs. Chauffeurs for some of the customers inside lined up sport utility vehicles next to Ms. Pierre's tent on the sidewalk near the entrance.

Haiti has long had glaring inequality, with tiny pockets of wealth persisting amid extreme poverty, and Pétionville itself was economically mixed before the earthquake, with poor families living near the gated mansions and villas of the rich.

But the disaster has focused new attention on this gap, making for surreal contrasts along the streets above Port-au-Prince's central districts. People in tent camps reeking of sewage are living in areas where prosperous Haitians, foreign aid workers and diplomats come to spend their money and unwind. Often, just a gate and a private guard armed with a 12-gauge shotgun separate the newly homeless from establishments like Les Galeries Rivoli, a boutique where wealthy Haitians and foreigners shop for Raymond Weil watches and Izod shirts.

"There's nothing logical about what's going on right now," said Tatiana Wah, a Haitian planning expert at Columbia University who is living in Pétionville and working as an adviser to Haiti's government. Ms. Wah said the revelry at some nightclubs near her home, which are frequented by rich Haitians and foreigners, was now as loud–or louder–than before the earthquake.

The nongovernmental organizations "are flooding the local economy with their spending," she said, "but it's not clear if much of it is trickling down."

Aleksandr Dobrianskiy, the Ukrainian owner of the Bagheera casino here in the hills, smiled as customers flowed in one recent Saturday evening, drinking Cuba Libres and plunking tokens into slot machines.

He said business had never been better, attributing the uptick at his casino to the money coming into Haiti for relief projects. That spending is percolating through select areas of the economy, as some educated Haitians get jobs working with relief agencies and foreigners bring in cash from abroad, using it on housing, security, transportation and entertainment.

"Haiti's like a submarine that just hit the bottom of the sea," said Mr. Dobrianskiy, 39, who moved here a year ago and carries a semiautomatic Glock handgun for protection. "It's got nowhere to go but up."

Sometimes the worlds of haves and have-nots collide. Violent crime and kidnappings have been relatively low since the earthquake. But when two European relief workers from Doctors Without Borders were abducted outside the exclusive Plantation restaurant this month and held for five days, the episode served as a reminder of how Haiti's poverty could give rise to resentment and crime.

The breadth of Haiti's economic misery seemed incomprehensible to many before the quake, with almost 80 percent of the population living on less than $2 a day. A small elite in gated mansions here in Pétionville and other hillside districts wields vast economic power.

But with parts of Port-au-Prince now in ruins, tens of thousands of people displaced by the quake are camping directly in the bulwarks once associated with power and wealth, like Place St.-Pierre (across from the elegant Kinam Hotel) and the grounds of Prime Minister Jean-Max Bellerive's office.

The city's biggest tent camp, with more than 40,000 displaced people, sprawls over the hills of the Pétionville Club, a country club with a golf course that before the quake had its own Facebook page for former members. ("Had the best Citronade; I bet I drank thousands of them, no exaggeration," one reminiscence said.)

Pétionville's boutiques and restaurants stand in stark contrast to the parallel economic reality in the camp now at the Pétionville Club. Throughout its maze of tents, merchants sell dried fish and yams for a fraction of what the French cuisine costs in exclusive restaurants nearby like Quartier Latin or La Souvenance.

Manicurists in the camp do nails. A stylist in a hovel applies hair extensions. The camp even has its own Paradis Ciné, set up in a tent with space for as many as 30 people. It charges admission of about $1.50 for screenings of "2012," the end-of-times disaster movie known here as "Apocalypse."

"The people in the camp need their diversion, too," said Cined Milien, 22, the operator of Paradis Ciné.

Still, a ticket to see "Apocalypse" is a luxury out of the grasp of most people who lost their homes in the earthquake. Some of the well-off in Pétionville who have reopened their businesses have done so cautiously, aware of the misfortune that persists on their doorstep.

"It's kind of hard for people to dance and have fun," said Anastasia Chassagne, 27, the Florida-educated owner of a trendy bar in Pétionville. "I put music, but really low, so like the people walking outside the street don't hear, like, 'Hey, these people are having fun.' "

Not everyone in Pétionville has such qualms. Mr. Dobrianskiy, the casino entrepreneur, said he was pleased that Haiti's currency, the gourde, had recently strengthened against the dollar to a value higher than before the quake, in part because of the influx of money from abroad.

And on the floor above Mr. Dobrianskiy's casino, a nightclub called Barak, with blaring music and Miami-priced cocktails, caters to a different elite here: United Nations employees and foreigners working for aid groups. They mingle with dozens of suggestively clad Haitian women and a few moneyed Haitian men taking in the scene.

As hundreds of displaced families gathered under tents a few yards away, the music of Barak continued into the night. A bartender could not keep up with orders for Presidente beers.

"Those who are gone are gone and buried, and we can't do anything about that," said Michel Sejoure, 21, a Haitian enjoying a drink at Barak. Asked about the displaced-persons camp down the street, he said, "I would want to help but I don't have enough, and the government should be the ones that are actually helping these people out."

"But," he said over the booming music, "they're not."

CRITICAL EYE

For Discussion

a. The Island nation of Haiti was already struggling with issues of extreme poverty and political corruption prior to the earthquake. As you see it, who is most to blame for the country's slow recovery?

b. In many ways, the article highlights how the people of Haiti are attempting to return to some kind of normalcy in the face of decimation and loss. Why is this crucial? Would you argue that doing so prevents Haiti's citizens from slipping into the abyss of anarchy, violence, and chaos?

c. Once again, in the face of such a national catastrophe, the world opened its heart and its wallets to aid those who were in need. Keeping this is mind, has anything changed on the island nation?

Re-approaching the Reading

We have now had a massive earthquake in Haiti, a devastating hurricane in New Orleans, and crippling tsunami in Japan. As you see it, have our world leaders learned anything about how to respond to natural disasters?

Writing Assignment

Shockingly, the attention and scrutiny of the media highlighted how the factors of race and poverty are often linked in America. Has anything changed for the disenfranchised of New Orleans? Or, has the media simply moved on to its next big and sensationalized story? Has the same thing happened to Haiti?

JEEVAN VASAGAR

THE NIGHTWALKERS

Every evening, in war-torn northern Uganda, 40,000 children leave home and trek to the safety of special night shelters.

Mary Aciro has spent the day gathering sheaves of grass to feed the cattle, weeding the vegetable patch and helping her mother cook dinner over a charcoal fire: the life of any African girl in any African village. But as daylight begins to fade, Mary slips away from the family's tiny mud hut and strides down a sandy track into the nearest town. The adults in the town of Lacor in northern Uganda are going home for dinner on buses which spray plumes of dust over Mary's face and clothes as she walks. Mary, along with hundreds of other children, is going the other way. The children are dressed in rags and flip-flops; some carry sacks or rolled-up blankets on their shoulders. They scramble over grassy banks and hurry down the sun-scorched roadside on the way to the night shelters, which are guarded by government troops.

In any other country, a 14-year-old girl leaving her home and an anxious mother for the night would spell rebellion. Here, it's simply about survival. "We fear the rebels, we fear thugs and robbers who come at night to disturb us," says Mary as she walks with a swinging stride.

On a troubled continent, the war in this region stands out. It is Africa's longest-running civil war, and perhaps the only conflict in history where children are both the main victims and the principal aggressors. Mary and the other children walk to safety every night because they fear, with very good reason, abduction by the Lord's Resistance Army, a Christian fundamentalist rebel group which uses children as soldiers, porters and sexual slaves. The LRA carries out its raids at night, storming into villages from the surrounding bush, killing adults and forcing children to bludgeon their parents before marching them away to camps deep in the bush.

Mary's 15-year-old brother Geoffrey was abducted by the rebels; he was held for three months. "They made him carry heavy loads, beat him at times, he went without food," their mother Agnes says. Geoffrey only escaped when a government helicopter gunship strafed the rebels holding him. Mary's neighbour, a girl named Florence, was abducted too. She spent three years with the rebels: she was forced into sexual slavery and became pregnant.

Desperate to keep the child-snatchers from their doors, parents in northern Uganda began sending their children into nearby towns at night in 2002. Back then, children used to sleep on the pavements, curling up together for warmth. They came in vast numbers: 40,000 children across northern Uganda started walking into towns to sleep. Aid agencies set up shelters to give them somewhere safe to go, and it's one of these that Mary is heading for.

As she approaches Lacor town, she walks past bars lit by a single, bare lightbulb, where a few drinkers sit outside on white plastic chairs sipping fizzy drinks or local beers, past tiny shops whose wooden shelves are crammed with cooking oil, salt, soap powder and mobile phone top-up cards. As the shadows spread, the shopkeepers are bolting their thief-proof metal doors and stepping out on to the chipped concrete pavements.

Mary lives near the town and follows the main road, but some of the other children walk for hours to reach safety, following winding unlit paths between mango trees and thickets of scrub. When she reaches the shelter, it is already full of children, some of them barely toddlers, others in their late teens. The shelter is made up of stark concrete buildings, bare as a barn inside, as well as rows of giant white canvas tents propped up by wooden stakes. The children give them names such as Pope Paul II and Moon Star Hall.

Lillian Apiyo, 14, is already inside. "I come here for protection," she says, sitting on a concrete step. "I always get new friends from here. There is nowhere to stay at home." The children filter through the gates looking subdued, but a party atmosphere soon develops. A dozen or so children begin dancing, gyrating their hips and nodding their heads. At other shelters there is frenetic singing of hymns or motivational songs, accompanied by the beating of cowhide drums. In one camp, adult volunteers chant: "Who are you? Who are you?" as the children arrive, and they shriek back: "I'm a winner—a winner!"

At Mary's shelter, groups of boys are washing themselves beneath communal taps, their wet bodies glistening in the semi-darkness provided by the moon and a sprinkling of lightbulbs.

The children are not given anything to eat. The shelters are busy enough as it is, and if food were provided they would be overwhelmed. Adult wardens patrol with torches, breaking up the occasional fight over a blanket and checking on children who look scared or upset.

Often, children feel more looked after here than they do at home. "When I am here, I feel I am somebody," says Gabriel Oloya, who studies his schoolbooks in the dim light. "When I am at home I'm always upset. I feel lonely and so many thoughts come into my mind. Here I tend to forget such things." Gabriel is head of his family, responsible for the four younger brothers who walk with him to the shelter. "My parents are dead, killed by the rebels," he says.

Childhood is short in rural Africa—boys in their teens will herd cattle and girls of 10 must fetch water—but it is rare for children to be thrown so completely on their own resources as they are in this war-damaged society.

Gabriel receives food handouts from the UN. Together with his even smaller brothers, the skinny 15-year-old hauls bricks for a little money. "What worries me most is the absence of my parents," he says. "I have to be responsible for taking care of my brothers."

The children who come to the shelters crave affection. Many of them are cuckoos at home—orphans whose parents were murdered by the rebels and have been taken in by their extended family. Freed from the responsibility of caring for younger siblings, or working in vegetable gardens, they can be young again in the shelters. The girls comb and braid each other's hair while the boys spin bottle-tops or engage in play-fights.

Collins Ocen, a tiny 13-year-old who looks scarecrow-like in an oversized coat, ragged shorts and flip-flops, comes partly for the fun. "I like playing, sharing stories with others and bathing," he says.

Elsewhere, teenage hormones are going wild. A crowd of watching children gathers around the gaggle of dancers. In the villages, dances such as these were courtship rituals; a chance for teenage boys and girls to sneak glances at each other in a setting approved by their elders. In the shelter, the wardens keep boys and girls apart, but outside its metal gates young couples are cuddling in the semi-darkness.

This sort of thing does worry Mary's mother. "We can't follow our children up to the shelter," Agnes says. "Sometimes a girl says she has gone there, but she has gone to a boyfriend, and she becomes pregnant and drops out of school." But then there are more serious things to worry about than teenage boys in the night shelters; in this land of lost innocence the troops who are meant to guard the children have been known to press girls into prostitution, or shoot boys merely for leaving the huts at night.

Mary's shelter fills up quickly. There are soon more than 1,000 children here, more boys than girls, and the adults are busy making sure everyone has a place to sleep. The boys and girls sleep in separate dormitories, spreading mats or blankets they have brought from home across the bare floors. By 10pm they have settled down for the night and the lights go out. Some are already half-asleep; many are exhausted from the walk in. A few of the small ones are agitated; they seem to be having nightmares, and cuddle up against older brothers or sisters for comfort.

The Acholi and Lango tribes of northern Uganda were once peasant farmers, living in small, scattered villages amid their herds of long-horned cattle and fields of maize. But 19 years of war have warped everything: virtually the entire population of the north, some 1.5 million people, has been displaced into crowded, dusty encampments on the outskirts of the main towns. Families live pressed together in tiny mud huts with thatched roofs. There is little space to farm or keep their cattle. Despair has bred alcoholism and domestic violence; the horror of war is part and parcel of life. It is so common, in fact, to have lost both parents that children here talk about it in calm, steady voices.

As the older generation dies out, so does the hope of anyone here returning to a normal life. This is a culture with few written records, which relies on memories rather than maps to place the boundaries of farmland and the distance to the nearest stream. When their parents are gone, the children's link with their original villages will be broken for ever.

"Half of the population of people in the camps are under 15," says Father Carlos Rodriguez Soto, a Roman Catholic priest who has spent 18 years in Uganda. "[They] are losing memory of the original demarcation of their land. For me, the worst thing that may happen here is a situation where officially there is no war, but everybody remains in the camps."

The sun has not quite risen when the adult wardens rouse the children. There is laughter and the sound of scuffling from inside the tents as they get dressed and hurry outside, turning on the washing taps in the raw pre-dawn light.

The new day begins with a communal prayer, led by the adults. Some children raise their right hands in the air, a gesture common among the evangelical churches sweeping up souls in the most desperate corners of Africa. Some crouch down and cover their faces, a symbol, the adult wardens explain, of being "humble before God". Surveying this crowd of skinny children in second-hand rags, it is hard to imagine any group of people on earth more humble.

After the prayer, the children who have blankets roll them on to their shoulders, the older ones gather up younger brothers and sisters and they begin to slip out of the gates and stream on to the road. By 9am the sun will burn and sweat will drip from every forehead, but now it is gentle. It is a good time to walk home.

CRITICAL EYE

For Discussion

a. Research and statistics tell us that women and children are the poorest and most abused people on the planet. The plight of the Ugandan children is known worldwide. If we know that the world's children are often prey for the villains of our global community, why don't we do more to protect them?

b. How can the world community best help the nation of Uganda?

Re-approaching the Reading

Consider this article alongside of the one about Haiti. As they both relate to the citizens and how they move forward in the face of grave danger and tragedy, in what way(s) are they similar?

Writing Assignment

Compare the tragedies described in this article to Kristof's "Bring Back Our Girls." What commentary is being made about childhood? Why are these kidnappers so focused on destroying family connections and formal education?

RICHARD LLOYD PARRY

GHOSTS OF THE TSUNAMI

I met a priest in the north of Japan who exorcised the spirits of people who had drowned in the tsunami. The ghosts did not appear in large numbers until later in the year, but Reverend Kaneda's first case of possession came to him after less than a fortnight. He was chief priest at a Zen temple in the inland town of Kurihara. The earthquake on 11 March 2011 was the most violent that he, or anyone he knew, had ever experienced. The great wooden beams of the temple's halls had flexed and groaned with the strain. Power, water and telephone lines were fractured for days; deprived of electricity, people in Kurihara, thirty miles from the coast, had a dimmer idea of what was going on there than television viewers on the other side of the world. But it became clear enough, when first a handful of families, and then a mass of them, began arriving at Kaneda's temple with corpses to bury.

Nearly twenty thousand people had died at a stroke. In the space of a month, Kaneda performed funeral services for two hundred of them. More appalling than the scale of death was the spectacle of the bereaved survivors. 'They didn't cry,' Kaneda said to me a year later. 'There was no emotion at all. The loss was so profound and death had come so suddenly. They understood the facts of their situation individually – that they had lost their homes, lost their livelihoods and lost their families. They understood each piece, but they couldn't see it as a whole, and they couldn't understand what they should do, or sometimes even where they were. I couldn't really talk to them, to be honest. All I could do was stay with them, and read the sutras and conduct the ceremonies. That was the thing I could do.'

Amid this numbness and horror, Kaneda received a visit from a man he knew, a local builder whom I will call Takeshi Ono. Ono was ashamed of what had happened, and didn't want his real name to be published. 'He's such an innocent person,' Kaneda said to me. 'He takes everything at face value. You're from England, aren't you? He's like your Mr Bean.' I wouldn't have gone so far, because there was nothing ridiculous about Ono. He was a strong, stocky man in his late thirties, the kind of man most comfortable in blue overalls. But he had a dreamy ingenuousness that made the story he told all the more believable.

He had been at work on a house when the earthquake struck. He clung to the ground for as long as it lasted; even his lorry shook as if it was about to topple over. The drive home, along roads without traffic lights, was alarming, but the physical damage was remarkably slight: a few telegraph poles lolling at an angle, toppled garden walls. As the owner of a small building firm, no one was better equipped to deal with the practical

This article first appeared in the *London Review of Books*. Reprinted by permission.

inconveniences inflicted by an earthquake. Ono spent the next few days busying himself with camping stoves, generators and jerry cans, and paying little attention to the news.

But once television was restored it was impossible to be unaware of what had happened. Ono watched the endlessly replayed image of the explosive plume above the nuclear reactor, and the mobile phone films of the black wave crunching up ports, houses, shopping centres, cars and human figures. These were places he had known all his life, fishing towns and beaches just over the hills, an hour's drive away. And watching their destruction produced in Ono a feeling common at that time, even among those most directly affected by displacement and bereavement. Although what had happened was undeniable – the destruction of entire towns and villages, the extinction of a multitude – it was also impossible. Impossible and, in fact, absurd. Insupportable, soul-crushing, unfathomable – but also just silly.

'My life had returned to normal,' he told me. 'I had petrol, I had an electricity generator, no one I knew was dead or hurt. I hadn't seen the tsunami myself, not with my own eyes. So I felt as if I was in a kind of dream.'

Ten days after the disaster, Ono, his wife and his widowed mother drove over the mountains to see for themselves. They left in the morning in good spirits, stopped on the way to go shopping, and reached the coast in time for lunch. For most of the journey, the scene was familiar: brown rice fields, villages of wood and tile, bridges over wide slow rivers. Once they had climbed into the hills, they passed more and more emergency vehicles, not only those of the police and fire services, but military trucks of the Japan Self-Defence Forces. As the road descended towards the coast, their jaunty mood began to evaporate. Suddenly, before they understood where they were, they had entered the tsunami zone.

There was no advance warning, no marginal area of incremental damage. The wave had come in with full force, spent itself and stopped at a point as clearly defined as the reach of a high tide. Above it, nothing had been touched; below it, everything was changed.

No still photograph was capable of describing it. Even television images failed to encompass the panoramic quality of the disaster, the sense within the plain of destruction, of being surrounded by it on all sides. In describing the landscapes of war, we often speak of 'total' devastation. But even the most intense aerial bombing leaves walls and foundations of burned-out buildings, as well as parks and woods, roads and tracks, fields and cemeteries. The tsunami spared nothing, and achieved feats of surreal juxtaposition that no mere explosion could match. It plucked forests up by their roots and scattered them miles inland. It peeled the macadam off the roads and cast it hither and thither in buckled ribbons. It stripped houses to their foundations, and lifted cars, lorries, ships and corpses onto the tops of tall buildings.

At this point in Ono's narrative, he became reluctant to describe in detail what he did or where he went. 'I saw the rubble, I saw the sea,' he said. 'I saw buildings damaged by the tsunami. It wasn't just the things themselves, but the atmosphere. It was a place I used to go so often. It was such a shock to see it. And all the police and soldiers there. It's difficult to describe. It felt dangerous. My first feeling was that this is terrible. My next thought was: "Is it real?"'

Ono, his wife and his mother sat down for dinner as usual that evening. He remembered that he drank two small cans of beer with the meal. Afterwards, and for no obvious reason, he began calling friends on his mobile phone. 'I'd just ring and say, "Hi, how are you?" – that kind of thing,' he told me. 'It wasn't that I had much to say. I don't know why, but I was starting to feel very lonely.'

His wife had already left the house when he woke the next morning. Ono had no particular work of his own, and passed an idle day at home. His mother bustled in and out, but she seemed mysteriously upset, even angry. When his wife got back from her office, she was similarly tense. 'Is something wrong?' Ono asked.

'I'm divorcing you!' she replied.

'Divorce? But why? Why?'

And so his wife and mother described the events of the night before, after the round of needy phone calls. How he had jumped down on all fours and begun licking the tatami mats and futon, and squirmed on them like a beast. How at first they had nervously laughed at his tomfoolery, but then been silenced when he began snarling: 'You must die. You must die. Everyone must die. Everything must die and be lost.' In front of the house was an unsown field, and Ono had run out into it and rolled over and over in the mud, as if he was being tumbled by a wave, shouting: 'There, over there! They're all over there – look!' Then he had stood up and walked out into the field, calling, 'I'm coming to you. I'm coming over to that side,' before his wife physically wrestled him back into the house. The writhing and bellowing went on all night until, around five in the morning, Ono cried out, 'There's something on top of me,' collapsed, and fell asleep.

'My wife and my mother were so anxious and upset,' he said. 'Of course I told them how sorry I was. But I had no memory of what I did or why.'

It went on for three nights. The next evening, as darkness fell, he saw figures walking past the house: parents and children, a group of young friends, a grandfather and a child. 'They were covered in mud,' he said. 'They were no more than twenty feet away, and they stared at me, but I wasn't afraid. I just thought, "Why are they in those muddy things? Why don't they change their clothes? Perhaps their washing machine's broken." They were like people I might have known once, or seen before somewhere. The scene was flickering, like a film. But I felt perfectly normal, and I thought that they were just ordinary people.'

The next day, Ono was lethargic and inert. At night, he would lie down, sleep heavily for ten minutes, then wake up as lively and refreshed as if eight hours had passed. He staggered when he walked, glared at his wife and mother and even waved a knife. 'Drop dead!' he would snarl. 'Everyone else is dead, so die!'

After three days of pleading by his family, he went to Reverend Kaneda at the temple. 'His eyes were dull,' Kaneda said. 'Like a person with depression after taking their medication. I knew at a glance that something was wrong.' Ono recounted the visit to the coast, and his wife and mother described his behaviour in the days since. 'The Reverend was looking hard at me as I spoke,' Ono said, 'and in part of my mind I was saying, "Don't look at me like that, you bastard. I hate your guts! Why are you looking at me?"'

Kaneda took Ono by the hand and led him into the main hall of the temple. 'He told me to sit down. I was not myself. I still remember that strong feeling of resistance. But part of me was also relieved – I wanted to be helped, and to believe in the priest. The part of me that was still me wanted to be saved.'

Kaneda beat the temple drum as he chanted the Heart Sutra:

There are no eyes, no ears, no nose, no tongue,
no body, mind; no colour, sound, or smell;
no taste, no touch, no thing; no realm of sight,
no realm of thoughts; no ignorance, no end
to ignorance; no old age and no death;
no end to age and death; no suffering,
nor any cause of suffering, nor end
to suffering, no path, no wisdom and no
fulfilment.

Ono's wife told him that he pressed his hands together in prayer and that as the priest's recitation continued, they rose high above his head as if being pulled from above. The priest splashed him with holy water, and then suddenly he returned to his senses and found himself with wet hair and shirt, filled with a sensation of tranquillity and release. 'My head was light,' he said. 'In a moment, the thing that had been there had gone. I felt fine physically, but my nose was blocked, as if I'd come down with a heavy cold.'

Kaneda spoke to him sternly; they both understood what had happened. 'Ono told me that he'd walked along the beach in that devastated area, eating an ice cream,' the priest said. 'He even put up a sign in the car in the windscreen saying 'disaster relief', so that no one would stop him. He went there flippantly, without giving it any thought at all. I told him: "You fool. If you go to a place where many people have died, you must go with a feeling of respect. That's common sense. You have suffered a kind of punishment for what you did. Something got hold of you, perhaps the dead who cannot accept yet that they are dead. They have been trying to express their regret and their resentment through you."' Kaneda smiled as he remembered it. 'Mr Bean!' he said. 'He's so innocent and open. That's another reason they were able to possess him.'

Ono recognised all this, and more. It wasn't just the spirits of men and women that had possessed him, he saw now, but also animals – cats and dogs and other beasts which had drowned with their masters.

He thanked the priest, and drove home. His nose was streaming as if with catarrh, but what came out was not mucus, but a bright pink jelly like nothing he had seen before.

*

The wave penetrated no more than a few miles inland, but over the hills in Kurihara it transformed the life of Reverend Kaneda. He had inherited his temple as the son and grandson of the previous priests, and the task of dealing with the survivors of the tsunami had tested him in ways for which he was unprepared. It had been the greatest disaster of postwar Japan: no larger single loss of life had occurred since the bombing of Nagasaki in 1945. And yet the pain did not announce itself; it dug underground and burrowed deep. Once the immediate emergency had abated, once the bodies were cremated, the memorial services held and the homeless sheltered, Kaneda set about trying to gain entry into the dungeon of silence in which he saw so many of the survivors languishing.

He began travelling around the coast with a group of fellow priests, organising an event he called 'Café de Monku' – a bilingual pun. As well as being the Japanese pronunciation of the English word 'monk', *monku* means 'complaint'. 'We think it will take a long time to get back to a calm, quiet, ordinary life,' the flyer said. 'Why don't you come and join us – take a break and have a little moan? The monks will listen to your complaint – and have a *monku* of their own too.'

Under this pretext – a casual cup of tea and a friendly chat – people came to the temples and community centres where Café de Monku was held. Many lived in 'temporary residences', the grim prefabricated huts, freezing in winter and sweltering in summer, where those who could afford nothing better ended up. The priests listened sympathetically and made a point of not asking too many questions. 'People don't like to cry,' Kaneda said. 'They see it as selfish. Among those who are living in the temporary homes, there's hardly anyone who hasn't lost a member of their family. Everyone's in the same boat, so they don't like to seem self-indulgent. But when they start talking, and when you listen to them, and sense their gritted teeth and their suffering, all the suffering they can't and won't express, in time the tears come, and they flow without end.'

Haltingly, apologetically, then with increasing fluency, the survivors spoke of the terror of the wave, the pain of bereavement and their fears for the future. They also talked about encounters with the supernatural. They described sightings of ghostly strangers, friends and neighbours, and dead loved ones. They reported hauntings at home, at work, in offices and public places, on the beaches and in the ruined towns. The experiences ranged from eerie dreams and feelings of vague unease to cases, like that of Takeshi Ono, of outright possession.

A young man complained of pressure on his chest at night, as if some creature was straddling him as he slept. A teenage girl spoke of a fearful figure who squatted in her house. A middle-aged man hated to go out in the rain, because the eyes of the dead stared out at him from puddles.

A civil servant in Soma visited a devastated stretch of coast, and saw a solitary woman in a scarlet dress far from the nearest road or house, with no means of transport in sight. When he looked for her again she had disappeared.

A fire station in Tagajo received calls to places where all the houses had been destroyed by the tsunami. The crews went out to the ruins anyway and prayed for the spirits of those who had died – and the ghostly calls ceased.

A cab driver in the city of Sendai picked up a sad-faced man who asked to be taken to an address that no longer existed. Halfway through the journey, he looked into his mirror to see that the rear seat was empty. He drove on anyway, stopped in front of the levelled foundations of a destroyed house, and politely opened the door to allow the invisible passenger out at his former home.

At a refugee community in Onagawa, an old neighbour would appear in the living rooms of the temporary houses, and sit down for a cup of tea with their startled occupants. No one had the heart to tell her that she was dead; the cushion on which she had sat was wet with seawater.

Priests – Christian and Shinto, as well as Buddhist – found themselves called on repeatedly to quell unhappy spirits. A Buddhist monk wrote an article in a learned journal about 'the ghost problem', and academics at Tohoku University began to catalogue the stories. 'So many people are having these experiences,' Kaneda told me. 'It's impossible to identify who and where they all are. But there are countless such people, and I think that their number is going to increase. And all we do is treat the symptoms.'

*

When opinion polls put the question, 'How religious are you?', the Japanese rank among the most ungodly people in the world. It took a catastrophe for me to understand how misleading this self-assessment is. It is true that the organised religions, Buddhism and Shinto, have little influence on private or national life. But over the centuries both have been pressed into the service of the true faith of Japan: the cult of the ancestors.

I knew about the 'household altars', or *butsudan*, which are still seen in most homes and on which the memorial tablets of dead ancestors – the *ihai* – are displayed. The*butsudan* are black cabinets of lacquer and gilt, with openwork carvings of lions and birds; the *ihai* are upright tablets of black polished wood, vertically inscribed in gold. Offerings of flowers, incense, rice, fruit and drinks are placed before them; at the summer Festival of the Dead, families light candles and lanterns to welcome home the ancestral spirits. I had assumed that these picturesque practices were matters of symbolism and custom, attended to in the same way that people in the West will participate in a

Christian funeral without any literal belief in the words of the liturgy. But in Japan spiritual beliefs are regarded less as expressions of faith than as simple common sense, so lightly and casually worn that it is easy to miss them altogether. 'The dead are not as dead there as they are in our own society,' the religious scholar Herman Ooms writes. 'It has always made perfect sense in Japan as far back as history goes to treat the dead as more alive than we do ... even to the extent that death becomes a variant, not a negation of life.'

At the heart of ancestor worship is a contract. The food, drink, prayers and rituals offered by their descendants gratify the dead, who in turn bestow good fortune on the living. Families vary in how seriously they take these ceremonies, but even for the unobservant, the dead play a continuing part in domestic life. For much of the time, their status is something like that of beloved, deaf and slightly batty old folk who can't expect to be at the centre of the family but who are made to feel included on important occasions. Young people who have passed important entrance examinations, got a job or made a good marriage kneel before the *butsudan* to report their success. Victory or defeat in an important legal case, for example, will be shared with the ancestors in the same way.

When grief is raw the presence of the deceased is overwhelming. In households that lost children in the tsunami it became routine, after half an hour of tea and chat, to be asked if I would like to 'meet' the dead sons and daughters. I would be led to a shrine covered with framed photographs, toys, favourite drinks and snacks, letters, drawings and school exercise books. One mother had commissioned Photoshopped portraits of her children, showing them as they would have been had they lived: a boy who died in primary school smiling proudly in high school uniform, a teenage girl as she should have looked in a kimono at her coming of age ceremony. Here, every morning, she began the day by talking to her dead children, weeping love and apology, as unselfconsciously as if she were speaking over a long-distance telephone line.

The tsunami did appalling violence to the religion of the ancestors. Along with walls, roofs and people, the water carried away household altars, memorial tablets and family photographs. Cemetery vaults were ripped open and the bones of the dead scattered. Temples were destroyed, along with memorial books listing the names of ancestors over generations. 'The memorial tablets – it's difficult to exaggerate their importance,' Yozo Taniyama, a priest and friend of Reverend Kaneda, told me. 'When there's a fire or an earthquake, the *ihai* are the first thing many people will save, before money or documents. People died in the tsunami because they went home for the *ihai*. It's life – like saving your late father's life.'

When people die violently or prematurely, in anger or anguish, they are at risk of becoming *gaki*, 'hungry ghosts', who wander between worlds, propagating curses and mischief. There are rituals for placating unhappy spirits, but in the aftermath of the disaster few families were in a position to perform them. And then there were those ancestors whose descendants were entirely wiped out by the wave. Their comfort in the afterlife depended entirely on the reverence of living families, which had been permanently and irrevocably cut off: their situation was as helpless as that of orphaned children.

Thousands of spirits had passed from life to death; countless others were cut loose from their moorings in the afterlife. How could they all be cared for? Who was to honour the compact between the living and the dead? In such circumstances, how could there fail to be a swarm of ghosts?

*

Even before the tsunami struck its coast, nowhere in Japan was closer to the world of the dead than Tohoku, the northern part of the island of Honshu. In ancient times, it was a notorious frontier realm of barbarians, goblins and bitter cold. For modern Japanese, it remains a remote, marginal, faintly melancholy place, of thick dialects and quaint conservatism, the symbol of a rural tradition that, for city dwellers, is no more than a folk memory. Tohoku has bullet trains and smartphones and all the other 21st-century conveniences, but it also has secret Buddhist cults, a lively literature of supernatural tales and a sisterhood of blind shamanesses who gather once a year at a volcano called Osore-san, or 'Mt Fear', the traditional entrance to the underworld.

Masashi Hijikata, the closest thing you could find to a Tohoku nationalist, understood immediately that after the disaster hauntings would follow. 'We remembered the old ghost stories,' he said, 'and we told one another that there would be many new stories like that. Personally, I don't believe in the existence of spirits, but that's not the point. If people say they see ghosts, then that's fine – we can leave it at that.'

Hijikata was born in Hokkaido, Japan's northernmost island, but came to Sendai as a university student, and has the passion of the successful immigrant for his adopted home. When I met him he was running a small publishing company whose books and journals were exclusively on Tohoku subjects. Prominent among his authors was the academic Norio Akasaka, a stern critic of the policies of the central government towards the region. These had been starkly illuminated by the nuclear disaster in Fukushima: an industrial plant erected by Tokyo, supplying electricity to the capital, and now spitting radiation over people who had enjoyed none of its benefits. 'Before the war, it used to be said that Tohoku provided men as soldiers, women as prostitutes, and rice as tribute,' Akasaka wrote. 'I had thought that that kind of colonial situation had changed, but after the disaster I changed my thinking.'

Hijikata explained the politics of ghosts to me, as well as the opportunity and the risk they represented for the people of Tohoku. 'We realised that so many people were having experiences like this,' he said, 'but there were people taking advantage of them. Trying to sell them this and that, telling them: "This will give you relief."' He met a woman who had lost her son in the disaster, and who was troubled by a sense of being haunted. She went to the hospital: the doctor gave her anti-depressants. She went to the temple: the priest sold her an amulet, and told her to read the sutras. 'But all she wanted,' he said, 'was to see her son again. There are so many like her. They don't care if they are ghosts – they want to encounter ghosts.'

'Given all that, we thought we had to do something. Of course, there are some people who are experiencing trauma, and if your mental health is suffering then you need medical treatment. Other people will rely on the power of religion, and that is their choice. What we do is to create a place where people can accept the fact that they are witnessing the supernatural. We provide an alternative for helping people through the power of literature.'

Hijikata revived a literary form which had flourished in the feudal era: the *kaidan*, or 'weird tale'. *Kaidankai*, or 'weird tale parties', had been a popular summer pastime, when the delicious chill imparted by ghost stories served as a form of pre-industrial air conditioning. Hijikata's *kaidankai* were held in modern community centres and public halls. They would begin with a reading by one of his authors. Then members of the audience would share experiences of their own: students, housewives, working people, retirees. He organised *kaidan*-writing competitions, and published the best of them in an anthology. Among the winners was Ayane Suto, whom I met one afternoon at Hijikata's office.

She was a calm, neat young woman with black glasses and a fringe, who worked in Sendai at a care home for the disabled. The fishing port of Kesennuma, where she grew up, was one of the towns worst hit by the tsunami. Ayane's family home was beyond the reach of the wave, and her mother, sister and grandparents were untouched by it. But her father, a maritime engineer, worked in an office on the town's harbour front, and that evening he didn't come home.

'I thought about him all the time,' Ayane said. 'It was obvious something had happened. But I said to myself that he might just be injured – he might be lying in hospital somewhere. I knew that I should prepare for the worst. But I wasn't prepared at all.' She passed painful days in Sendai, trying to clear up the mess caused in her flat by the earthquake, thinking always of her father. Two weeks after the disaster, his body was found.

She arrived back at her family home just before the coffin was carried in. Friends and extended family had gathered, most of them casually dressed: everything black, everything formal, had been washed away. 'He hadn't drowned, as most people did,' Ayane said. 'He died of a blow to the chest from some big piece of rubble. In the coffin you could only see his face through a glass window. It had been a fortnight, and I was afraid that his body might have decayed. I looked through the window. I could see that he had a few cuts, and he was pale. But it was still the face of my father.' She wanted to touch his face for the last time, but the casket and its window had been sealed shut. On it lay a white flower, a single cut stem placed on the coffin's wood by the undertaker. There was nothing unusual about it. But to Ayane it was extraordinary. Ten days earlier, at the height of her hope and despair, in an effort to escape her anxiety, Ayane had gone to a big public bathhouse to soak in the hot spring water. When she came out, she retrieved her boots from the locker and felt an obstruction in the toe as she pulled them on. 'I could feel how cold it was,' she remembered, 'even through my socks. And it felt soft, fluffy.' She reached in, and removed a white flower, as fresh and flawless as if had just been cut.

A minor mystery: how could such an object have found its way into a boot inside a locked container? It faded from her mind, until that moment in front of her father's coffin, when the same flower presented itself again. 'The first time, I had the feeling that this might be a premonition of bad news,' Ayane said. 'Dad might not be alive any more, and this might be a sign of his death. But then I thought about it later, about the coolness of the flower, and the whiteness of the flower, and that feeling of softness against my toe. And I thought of that as the touch of my father, which I couldn't experience when he was in his coffin.'

Ayane knew that the flower was just a flower. She didn't believe in ghosts, or that her dead father had sent it to her as a sign – if such communication was possible, why would a loving parent express it in such obscure terms? 'I think it was a coincidence,' she said, 'and that I made something good of it. When people see ghosts, they are telling a story, a story which has been broken off. They dream of ghosts, because then the story carries on, or comes to a conclusion. And if that brings them comfort, that's a good thing.'

Committed to print as a *kaidan*, published in Hijikata's magazine, it took on greater significance. 'There were thousands of deaths, each of them different,' Ayane said. 'Most of them have never been told. My father's name was Tsutomu Suto. By writing about him, I share his death with others. Perhaps I save him in some way, and perhaps I save myself.'

*

Late last summer I went back to see Reverend Kaneda again. Two and a half years had passed since the disaster, and inland there was no visible evidence of it at all. The towns and cities of Tohoku were humming with the money being injected into the region for its reconstruction. A hundred thousand people still lived in prefabricated houses, but these upsetting places were tucked away out of sight of the casual visitor. None of the towns destroyed by the wave had been rebuilt, but they had been scoured of rubble. Coarse, tussocky grass had overgrown the coastal strip, and those ruins that were still visible looked more like neglected archaeological sites than places of continuing pain and despair.

I visited Kaneda in his temple, and sat in the room where he received visitors. Lined up on the tatami were dozens of small clay statues, which would be handed out to the patrons of Café de Monku. They were representations of Jizo, the bodhisattva associated with kindness and mercy, who consoles the living and the dead.

In this room, Kaneda told me, he recently met a 25-year-old woman whom I will call Rumiko Takahashi. She had telephoned him in June in a state of incoherent distress. She talked of killing herself; she shouted about things entering her. That evening, a car pulled up at the temple: Rumiko, her mother, sister and fiancé were inside. She was a nurse from Sendai – 'a very gentle person', Kaneda said, 'nothing peculiar or unusual about her at all'. Neither she, nor her family, had been hurt by the tsunami. But for weeks, her fiancé said, she had been complaining of something pushing into her from a place deep below, of dead presences 'pouring out' invisibly around her. Rumiko herself was slumped over the table. She stirred as Kaneda addressed the creature within her. 'I asked: "Who are you, and what do you want?"' he said. 'When it spoke, it didn't sound like her at all. It talked for three hours.'

It was the spirit of a young woman whose mother had divorced and remarried, and who found herself unloved and unwanted by her new family. She ran away and found work in the *mizu shobai,* or 'water trade', the night-time world of clubs, bars and prostitution. There she became more and more isolated and depressed, and fell under the influence of a morbid and manipulative man. Unknown to her family, unmourned by anyone, she killed herself. Since then, not a stick of incense had been lit in her memory.

Kaneda asked the spirit: 'Will you come with me? Do you want me to lead you to the light?' He took her to the main hall of the temple, where he recited the sutra and sprinkled holy water. By the time the prayers were done, at half past one in the morning, Rumiko had returned to herself, and she and her family went home.

Three days later she was back. She complained of great pain in her left leg; once again, she had the sensation of being stalked by an alien presence. The effort of keeping out the intruder was exhausting. 'That was the strain, the feeling that made her suicidal,' Kaneda said. 'I told her: "Don't worry – just let it in."' Rumiko's posture and voice immediately stiffened and deepened; Kaneda found himself talking to a gruff man with a peremptory manner of speech, a sailor of the old Imperial Navy who had died in action during the Second World War after his left leg had been gravely injured by a shell.

The priest spoke soothingly to the old veteran: he prayed and chanted, the interloper departed, and Rumiko was calm. But all of this was just a prologue. 'All the people who came,' Kaneda said, 'and each one of the stories they told had some connection with water.'

*

Over the course of last summer, Reverend Kaneda exorcised 25 spirits from Rumiko

Takahashi. They came and went at the rate of several a week. All of them, after the wartime sailor, were ghosts of the tsunami. For Kaneda, the days followed a relentless routine. The telephone call from Rumiko would come in the early evening; at nine o'clock her fiancé would pull up in front of the temple and carry her out of the car. As many as three spirits would appear in a single session. Kaneda talked to each personality in turn, sometimes over several hours: he established their circumstances, calmed their fears and politely but firmly enjoined them to follow him towards the light. Kaneda's wife would sit with Rumiko; sometimes other priests were present to join in with the prayers. In the early hours of the morning, Rumiko would be driven home. 'Each time she would feel better, and go back to Sendai, and go to work,' Kaneda told me. 'But then after a few days, she'd be overwhelmed again.' Out among the living, surrounded by the city, she would become conscious of the dead, a thousand importunate spirits pressing in on her and trying to get inside.

One of the first was a middle-aged man who, speaking through Rumiko, despairingly called the name of his daughter.

'Kaori!' said the voice. 'Kaori! I have to get to Kaori. Where are you, Kaori? I have to get to the school, there's a tsunami coming.'

The man's daughter had been at her school by the sea when the earthquake struck. He had rushed out of work and driven along the coast road to pick her up, when the water had overtaken him. His agitation was intense; he was impatient and suspicious of Kaneda.

The voice asked: 'Am I alive or not?'

'No,' Kaneda said. 'You are dead.'

'And how many people died?' the voice asked.

'Twenty thousand people died.'

'Twenty thousand? So many?'

Later, Kaneda asked him where he was.

'I'm at the bottom of the sea. It is very cold.'

'Come up from the sea to the world of light,' Kaneda said.

'But the light is so small,' the man replied. 'There are bodies all around me, and I can't reach it. And who are you anyway? Who are you to lead me to the world of light?'

The conversation went round and round for two hours. Eventually, Kaneda said: 'You are a father. You understand the anxieties of a parent. Consider this girl whose body you have used. She has a father and mother who are worried about her. Have you thought of that?'

There was a long pause, and the man said, 'You're right,' then moaned. Kaneda chanted the sutra. He paused from time to time when the voice uttered choked sounds, but they faded to mumbles and finally the man was gone.

Day after day, week after week, the spirits kept coming: men and women, young people and old, with accents rough and polished. They told their stories at length, but there was never enough specific detail – surnames, place names, addresses – to verify any individual account, and Kaneda felt no urge to. One man had survived the tsunami but killed himself after learning of the death of his two daughters. Another wanted to join the rest of his ancestors but couldn't find his way because his home and everything in it had been washed away. There was an old man who spoke in thick Tohoku dialect. He was desperately worried about his wife, who had survived and was living alone and uncared-for in one of the bleak metal huts. In a shoebox, she kept a white rope which she would contemplate and caress. He feared what she planned to use it for.

Kaneda reasoned and cajoled, prayed and chanted, and in the end each of the spirits gave way. But days or hours after one group of ghosts had been dismissed, more would stumble forward to take their place. One night in the temple, Rumiko announced: 'There are dogs all around me, it's loud! They are barking so loudly I can't bear it.' Then she said: 'No! I don't want it. I don't want to be a dog.' Finally she said: 'Give it rice and water to eat. I'm going to let it in.'

'She told us to seize hold of her,' Kaneda said, 'and when the dog entered her it had tremendous power. There were three men holding on to her, but they were not strong enough, and she threw them off. She was scratching the floor and roaring, a deep growl.' Later, after the chanting of the sutra, and the return to her peaceful self, Rumiko recounted the story of the dog. It had been the pet of an old couple who lived close to the Fukushima Dai-ichi nuclear power plant. When the radiation began to leak, its owners had fled in panic with all their neighbours. But they forgot to unchain the dog, which slowly died of thirst and hunger. Later, when it was much too late, the spirit of the animal observed men in white protective suits coming in and peering at its shrivelled corpse.

In time, Rumiko became able to exercise control over the spirits; she spoke of a container, which she could choose to open or close. A friend of Kaneda, who was present at one of the exorcisms, compared her to a chronically ill patient habituated to vomiting: what at first was disgusting became over time familiar and bearable. By August, she reported being able to brush the spirits away when they approached her. She was still conscious of their presence: they were no longer shoving and jostling her but skulking at the room's edge. The evening telephone calls and late-night visits became less and less frequent. Rumiko and her fiancé married and moved away from Sendai, and to his extreme relief Kaneda stopped hearing from her.

The effort of the exorcisms was too much. Friends were beginning to worry about him. 'I was overwhelmed,' he said. 'Over the months, I'd become accustomed to hearing the stories of survivors. But all of a sudden, I found myself listening to the voices of the dead.'

Most difficult to bear were the occasions when Rumiko was possessed by the personalities of children. 'When a child appeared,' Kaneda said, 'my wife took her hand. She said: "It's Mummy – it's Mummy here. It's all right, it's all all right. Let's go together."' The first to appear was a tiny nameless boy, too young to understand what was being said to him, or to do anything more than call for his mother over and over again. The second was a girl of seven or eight. She had been with her even younger brother when the tsunami struck, and tried to run away with him. But in the water, as they were both drowning, she had let go of his hand; now she was afraid that her mother would be angry. 'There's a black wave coming,' she said. 'I'm scared, Mummy. Mummy, I'm sorry, I'm sorry.'

The voice of the girl was terrified and confused. Her body was drifting helplessly in the cold water, and it was a long struggle to guide her upwards towards the light. 'She gripped my wife's hand tightly until she finally came to the gate of the world of light,' Kaneda recalled. 'Then she said: "Mum, I can go on my own now, you can let go."'

Afterwards, Mrs Kaneda tried to describe the moment when she released the hand of the young-woman-as-little-drowned-girl. The priest himself was weeping for her, and for the twenty thousand other stories of terror and extinction. But his wife was aware only of a huge energy dissipating. It made her remember the experience of childbirth, and the sense of power discharging at the end of pain as the newborn child finally enters the world.

CRITICAL EYE

For Discussion

a. What does the journalist want us to understand about the aftermath of the tsunami?

b. How does this article address the notion of honoring the dead verses mourning the dead? Is there a distinction?

Re-approaching the Reading

Throughout this book are readings about manmade and natural disasters, tragedies, and our historical responses to them as they occur. Manmade tragedies often occur because human beings are inherently flawed, and natural disasters are beyond our control–leaving us with no actual person to hold accountable. In your opinion, how does this article teach us that natural disasters leave us bereft in unimaginable ways that are almost always difficult to recover from?

Writing Assignment

Compare this article to Romero's article about the earthquake that devastated the island nation of Haiti. How are both nations attempting to excise ghosts?

ELI SASLOW

AFTER NEWTOWN SHOOTING, MOURNING PARENTS ENTER INTO THE LONELY QUIET

They had promised to try everything, so Mark Barden went down into the basement to begin another project in memory of Daniel. The families of Sandy Hook Elementary were collaborating on a Mother's Day card, which would be produced by a marketing firm and mailed to hundreds of politicians across the country. "A difference-maker," the organizers had called it. Maybe if Mark could find the most arresting photo of his 7-year-old son, people would be compelled to act.

It hardly mattered that what Mark and his wife, Jackie, really wanted was to ignore Mother's Day altogether, to stay in their pajamas with their two surviving children, turn off their phones and reward themselves for making it through another day with a glass of Irish whiskey neat.

"Our purpose now is to force people to remember," Mark said, so down he went into his office to sift through 1,700 photos of the family they had been.

The Bardens had already tried to change America's gun laws by studying the Second Amendment and meeting with President Obama in the Oval Office. They had spoken at tea party rallies, posed for People magazine and grieved on TV with Katie Couric. They had taken advice from a public relations firm, learning to say "magazine limits" and not "magazine bans," to say "gun responsibility" and never "gun control." When none of that worked, they had walked the halls of Congress with a bag of 200 glossy pictures and beseeched lawmakers to look at their son: his auburn hair curling at the ears, his front teeth sacrificed to a soccer collision, his arms wrapped around Ninja Cat, the stuffed animal that had traveled with him everywhere, including into the hearse and underground.

Almost six months now, and so little had gotten through. So maybe a Mother's Day card. Maybe that.

Mark turned on his computer and began looking for the right picture. "Something lighthearted," he said. "Something sweet." He had been sitting in the same chair Dec. 14, when he received an automated call about a Code Red Alert, and much of the basement had been preserved in that moment. Nobody had touched the foosball table, because Daniel had been the last to play. His books and toy trains sat in their familiar piles, gathering dust. The basement had always been Daniel's space, and some days Mark believed he could still smell him here, just in from playing outside, all grassy and muddy.

Now it was Daniel's face staring back at him on the computer screen, alit in an orange glow as he blew out seven candles on a birthday cake in September.

"Oh God. His last birthday," Mark said, rubbing his forehead, scanning to the next photo, knowing the chronology that came next.

Daniel dressed as an elf for Halloween. Daniel grinning after his hair was cut short on Dec. 4. Daniel in a video taken a week before his death, wearing reindeer horns and carrying cookies to the neighbor's house. "Bye, Dad," he was saying.

Next came a photo Mark had taken early that last morning. He and Daniel had been lying on the couch, half asleep, after the rest of the family had left for school. Daniel had noticed how the sunrise and the Christmas lights were reflecting on the window, like a red-and-orange kaleidoscope. "Wow," he had said. Mark had grabbed his camera and taken a picture of the window, and now he was searching that picture for a trace of Daniel's reflection in the glass, zooming in, running his fingers against the screen.

"He has to be in here," Mark said. Maybe he had taken another. He flipped to the next picture, but it was from four days later, of a police car parked in front of their house.

It sometimes felt to Mark in these moments like his grief was still deepening, like the worst was yet to come. After the gunfire, the funerals, the NRA protests and the congressional debates, they were finally coming into the lonely quiet. They were coming to the truth of what Newtown would become. Would it be the transformative moment in American gun policy that, in those first days, so many had promised? Or another Columbine, Virginia Tech, Gabby Giffords, Aurora–one more proper noun added to an ever-growing list? The FBI had closed its temporary Newtown office. Politicians in Washington were moving on to other issues. Scariest of all to Mark, he was starting to forget little things, too, losing pieces of Daniel to the recesses of his mind, so he had started a journal to log memories before they disappeared.

"I'm always one minute farther away from my life with Daniel," he had written one day. "The gulf keeps getting bigger."

He returned upstairs with four photos and brought them to Jackie in the living room. "For the Mother's Day card," he said. She looked at one that showed Daniel at 4, his freckled arms wrapped around her neck and his face buried into hers. She gasped. She touched her neck. "It physically hurts," she said, reaching for Mark. "Stomach, arms, legs, chest."

She had developed a habit in the last months of what her counselor called "defensive delusions," when she would imagine for a few hours that Daniel was away at a friend's house. Pretending helped her summon the energy to return a few e-mails or cook dinner, but the easiness of the mental game was starting to scare her. "Is it normal?" Jackie had asked the counselor at their last appointment. "Is this something other people do?"

"There is no normal," the counselor had said. "There are only hard days to get through."

So now, on this hard day, Jackie stared at the photo and considered whether to release another intimate moment to the world.

"Will it make a difference?" she asked Mark.

"I don't know," he said.

There were 26 of them in all – 26 victims, which meant 26 families left adrift, grasping for a way to continue on. Some found it in church, returning to the pews every Wednesday and Sunday with a Sandy Hook Bible group, lighting 26 candles each time they went. Others found it in the spiritual medium that contacted victims' families on Facebook, offering to facilitate a private seance and "connect them with the other side." Some started nonprofit foundations in their child's name or escaped back into jobs in Manhattan or ordered wine by the case or planted 26 trees or considered moving out of state or installed blackout curtains for privacy. One mother took a job sorting corporate donations to the Newtown community fund, organizing 26,000 bottles of "Sandy Hook Green" nail polish and 2,600 wool blankets, because the magnitude of the donations helped reaffirm the magnitude of her loss.

What the Bardens chose to believe in during those first days was cause and effect, order and logic. America's mental health system was broken, but they could fix it. Gun culture was extreme, but they could moderate it. This was the way they made sense of the world, which was why, less than a week after Daniel's death, Mark and Jackie met with a start-up advocacy organization called Sandy Hook Promise and offered to help.

They had never owned or fired a gun, so they took trips with Sandy Hook Promise and the parents of four other victims to California and New York, where they learned about the National Rifle Association and technological advances in gun safety. The governor of Connecticut sent them drafts of new legislation. Vice President Biden briefed them on congressional voting procedures. Four times this year, Mark and Jackie traveled to Washington with their photographs of Daniel and met with two dozen senators to discuss a bill requiring universal background checks on gun purchases. When the measure came up for a vote in April, all four of the Bardens watched from the gallery: the father, a professional jazz guitarist who rarely had the desire to play anymore; the wife, an elementary school reading teacher who couldn't imagine stepping back into a classroom; the eldest son, 13, fiddling with a Rubik's Cube to quiet his anxiety; the daughter, 11, suddenly afraid of big cities, and loud noises, and darkness, and strangers.

When the Senate vote failed, Mark was asked to introduce President Obama for a speech in the Rose Garden. "Let's go rip some bark off it," Obama told him. And yes, Mark was angry, too—angry enough that his hands balled into fists and trembled at the podium—but mostly he was unmoored. "So what does all of this add up to now?" he had asked a White House employee later that day, when the speeches ended.

Because if it amounted to nothing at all, what was the logic, the order, the meaning of their broken lives?

What was the meaning of the anger he felt lately while shopping at Costco, hoping one of the strangers in the aisles might be a gun nut who would recognize and approach him, so he had an excuse to shout back?

What was the meaning of the endless tributes? A song performed in concert for Daniel because he liked music. A 5K race for Daniel because he liked to run. A mud festival for Daniel because he liked mud. A Play Day for Daniel because he liked to play. Then there were the boxes of mementos that filled a room in their house, gifts created and mailed by strangers: magnets bearing Daniel's picture, paintings of him, wood carvings, wind chimes, T-shirts, pins and blankets stitched with a 10-foot image of his face. "To Our Angel," the packages read—or to "Dan," "Danny" or, weirdest of all, "Daniel Barden," so formal and unfamiliar, like the etching on a headstone.

And what was the meaning of their new nighttime routine? All four of them crammed into one room in a five-bedroom house, three on a queen bed and one on the futon so they could will one another through the night, Jackie up every few hours, Mark closing his eyes and thinking about Daniel, always hoping he might come to him in a dream, even though he never did.

And then it was morning.

Down the stairs into the kitchen came the son, James, carrying his backpack and soccer cleats, ready for the 6:20 bus to junior high. "How are you today?" Jackie asked him, as she did every morning. "Pretty good," he said, which was mostly true. He was starring on a competitive soccer team, working as a referee, playing bass in the school orchestra. "Can you believe these Barden kids?" one of Biden's aides had said a few months earlier, after spending a morning with James. So polite. So resilient. But sometimes Jackie watched him from the window while he played soccer alone in the yard, where he had always played with Daniel. She thought he looked lost. "Want to talk about it with someone?" she had asked him. "I guess," he had said, so now he was seeing a counselor who let him lie down in her office and work his Rubik's Cube.

Next down the stairs came the daughter, Natalie, Newtown's fifth-grade student of the month–a pianist and a violin player, a master of grade school hand-clapping games, a performer in the school musical. "Natalie is a social and academic marvel in my class," one teacher had written in Natalie's spring evaluation, not knowing that just getting her to class each morning had become a battle, because her newfound fear made her reluctant to leave home.

"I'm sick," she said now, rubbing her eyes. "I don't think I should go to school."

"Probably just allergies," Mark said. "You'll be fine."

"I should stay home," she said.

"How many times do we have to have this conversation?" Jackie said.

"I don't want to go."

"Please stop it," Jackie said.

"You're so lucky," Natalie said.

"Lucky?"

"You get to stay home."

"Do you even know what you're saying?" Jackie said, her voice louder now. "You think I'm home because I want to be? You think I wouldn't rather be going on with my life, going to work? Lucky? I'm not even having this conversation."

Jackie started to cry, and then Natalie started to cry. "I'm sorry," she said. "Oh sweet pea," Mark said, wrapping her into a hug, tearing up now, too. All three of them sat down for breakfast and then walked together to the bus stop. "Love you," Natalie told them, settling in a window seat next to a friend, beginning a clapping game against the window. The bus rolled up the hill, and Mark and Jackie walked back to the house. Just them now. Nobody left to come downstairs. They sat in the living room sipping coffee in silence.

It had always seemed to them that this was the perfect house, in the perfect neighborhood, in the perfect town. They had often wondered: How did they get so lucky that life delivered them here? Mark had given up a touring career in Nashville, and Jackie had decided she could drive 45 minutes each way to her teaching job in Pawling, N.Y. They had borrowed money from both sides of the family and bought an unpretentious country house on a dead-end road, with an acre of wooded land where the kids could play freeze tag and leave out leftover food for hungry raccoons.

But lately everything about the house reminded them of Daniel, comfort and affliction all at once. Up there, on the ceiling, was the sticky toy he had bought in a vending machine and accidentally thrown too high. In the kitchen was the blender Mark had used to make him a smoothie each afternoon, always with four gummy vitamins at the bottom of the glass, always, in Daniel's words, "the best one yet!" Out front was the dead-end road where he had waited for the school bus in a sprinter's crouch each morning, so he could run alongside it for a block before climbing on board. Out back was the wooden play structure where he had knocked his head and bled for the first time, which sometimes made Mark and Jackie wonder about the last time. Had it been quick? Had he been scared? Had anybody held him?

"Let's get out of here," Mark said. "Let's go get breakfast."

"Someplace new," Jackie agreed.

They drove nine miles outside of town to a small diner that a friend had once recommended. They had never been before. There were no memories here. A waitress led them to a booth by the window and handed over menus. "Perfect," Mark said. The coffee tasted good. The restaurant was empty. They were the first customers of the day. The campy decor reminded Mark of a place he had liked in Nashville. "Pretty fun vibe," he said. "I'm thinking about treating myself to the eggs Benedict," Jackie said. "Yum," Mark said.

Now another car pulled into the restaurant lot, carrying the second customers of the day, and out of all the people in central Connecticut, and all of the possible places and times for them to eat, these were two whom the Bardens recognized: a mother and her young son, who had been Daniel's classmate in kindergarten.

"Do you remember the Bardens?" the mother asked her son, bringing him over to their booth.

"Hi!" the boy said, sitting down at the table next to them.

"Let's let them enjoy their breakfast," the mother told her son, sensing the awkwardness of the moment, pointing him to another table in the corner of the restaurant. She turned back to the Bardens: "I'm sorry. He's excited. It's his birthday."

"Oh wow," Jackie said.

"So nice," Mark said.

"Seven," the mother said, following her son to the other table.

"Should we leave?" Jackie said, whispering to Mark, once the mother was out of earshot. "Would it be easier?"

"It might be," Mark said.

But instead they sat at the table and watched as the waiter brought the boy a gigantic waffle covered in powdered sugar, berries and whipped cream. They watched as the waiter stuck a candle into the center of that waffle, and as the mother sang "Happy Birthday" and took a picture with her phone. They watched as the boy swept his fingers through the whipped cream, smearing it across his mouth and face while his mother laughed. "You're so silly," she said.

This boy, who had ended up in the other first-grade class at Sandy Hook Elementary.

This boy, who had hidden in the other bathroom.

"Oh God," Jackie said, shoulders trembling, questions and doubts tumbling out as she tried to catch her breath. "Why did we wait to enroll him in school?" she said. "He could have started a year earlier. He could have been in second grade. He was old enough."

"We were thinking about what was best for him," Mark said, knowing the cycle that was starting, the blame, the need for absolution. "We wanted him to be one of the oldest."

"So he would be a leader and not a follower," Jackie said, nodding.

"So he would be confident," Mark said.

"So he wouldn't be last to get his driver's license," she said.

They sat at the booth and thought about Daniel at 16. The coffee had gone cold. The eggs sat on their plates. The boy and his mother stood up to leave, walking past their table. "We had to eat in a hurry today," the mother said. She explained that her son's name and birth date were going to be read over the loudspeaker during the morning announcements at school, and he wanted to be there in time to hear it.

"Take care," the mother told them.

"Bye!" the boy said, and Mark and Jackie watched as he ran to the parking lot.

A few days later, Mark and Jackie decided to go to Delaware."Who even cares about Delaware?" Natalie had asked as they began to pack, and so they had explained to their daughter what political advisers had explained to them: that momentum for gun laws had stalled in Washington, and that the best remaining chance was to build momentum state by state, one incremental law at a time.

In Delaware that meant House Bill 58, championed by Democratic Gov. Jack Markell, who had called it "a historic and sweeping measure." But when Mark began researching the bill on his computer in the days before the trip, what he mostly noticed was the addendum of exceptions. The bill proposed to make it illegal to possess high-capacity magazines of 10 bullets or more in the country's second-smallest state–unless you only possessed those magazines at your house, which was okay; or on private property, which was also okay; or at a shooting range, which was fine; or if you were carrying a high-capacity magazine separately from a firearm, which would still be permitted; or if you were law enforcement or retired law enforcement or active military or a licensed firearms dealer, in which cases you were exempt. First-time violators would face a misdemeanor charge and a $75 fine. "Like a traffic ticket," Mark told Jackie.

The NRA had dispatched two lobbyists to the state Capitol in opposition of the bill. Markell did not want to schedule a vote until he knew he had the 21 votes necessary to pass it, and he was still three or four short.

"Your heartfelt, personal stories might still help us make history," one of the governor's aides had written in an e-mail invitation to Sandy Hook families.

At the moment, it was the only history there was to make, and the best invitation they had, so Mark and Jackie traveled with a group that included a public relations specialist, the director of Sandy Hook Promise and the parents of two other victims: Nicole Hockley, mother of Dylan; and Nelba Marquez-Greene, mother of Ana. They took a car to a train to another car to a hotel located alongside a commercial highway on the outskirts of Dover. "What brings you to Delaware?" asked a cheery 18-year-old at the front desk, and for a few seconds the parents stared back at him in awkward silence. "Life, I guess," Mark said, finally. "Bad luck," Hockley said, with a slight smile. "Is this personal travel or business?" the hotel employee said, looking at his computer. "Both. It is personal business travel," Mark said, and the parents laughed.

They went to the Capitol the next morning for a meeting with the governor's staff to discuss their trip. "Basically, we want to make sure to maximize this visit," the lieutenant governor told them, explaining that there would be a news conference, a lunch with lawmakers and dinner at the governor's residence. One of the governor's aides handed out head shots of all 41 state lawmakers, divided into who was a soft no or a soft yes. The parents' mission, he explained, was to walk the halls of the Capitol and give their children's photos to anyone who would take them. A survivor of the Virginia Tech shooting already had come to Delaware to lobby. Gabby Giffords's husband already had come. "We think you all are the extra difference," the aide said.

He said a last-minute opportunity had arisen for the parents to be recognized during a moment of silence on the House floor. Were they interested?

"We don't love those," Hockley said. "It is a little like being the exhibit in a museum."

"I understand," the staffer said. "We just want every one of these lawmakers to see you. We want them to feel your loss and understand what's at stake."

"Will they read off the victims' names?" Mark asked, dreading that.

"Yes."

"And the ages?" he asked, dreading that, too.

"Yes."

Mark looked across the table at Hockley. She grimaced and shrugged. He looked over at Jackie. She nodded.

"Okay then," Mark said.

They were led to seats in the House chamber, where a junior lawmaker recited the Pledge of Allegiance. "Today we have some special guests," she said, and 41 lawmakers turned to look. "Will our guests please stand?" she said, and the parents stood. "Please come up here," she said, and they did that, too. The room went quiet as she began reading the names.

Daniel Barden. Seven. Dylan Hockley. Six. Ana Marquez-Greene. Six. Six. Six. Six. Seven. Six. How long could one minute last? Mark looked at the lawmakers and tried to pick out the three who already had refused to meet with the Newtown parents. Could he barge into their offices? Wait at their cars? Jackie counted the seconds in her head—"breathe, breathe," she told herself—believing she was holding it together until a lawmaker handed her a box of tissues. Hockley saw the tissues and thought about how she rarely cried anymore except for alone at night, unconscious in her sleep, awakening to a damp pillow. Marquez-Greene listened to the names and pictured her daughter dressed for school that last day: pudgy cheeks, curly hair and a T-shirt decorated with a sequined purple peace sign—a peace Marquez-Greene was still promising to deliver to her daughter every night when she prayed to her memory and whispered, "Love wins."

The gavel banged. The moment of silence ended. The parents sat back in their chairs.

"Next is a motion to recognize National Nurses Week," the House speaker said. "All in favor?"

"Aye!"

"A motion to recognize women's clubs for the important role they play."

"Aye!"

"A motion to honor a champion among us, one of our own, the winner of the state peach pie eating contest . . ."

"Aye!"

"A motion to recognize another special guest, here on her vacation, the mother of one of our lawmakers . . ."

"Let's go," Mark said, standing up in the middle of the session, motioning for the other parents to follow. They walked upstairs into a private conference room. "This gets more surreal every day," Hockley said. "Crazy," Mark said. How was it, they wondered, that government could roll through its inconsequential daily agenda but then stall for months on an issue like gun control? They had seen polls that showed 80 percent of Delaware residents favored a ban on high-capacity magazines. Ninety percent of Americans wanted universal background checks. But in the months since the shooting in Newtown, only a handful of states with already-stringent gun laws had managed to pass stricter laws. Most states had done nothing, and the U.S. Senate had postponed another vote.

"Some of those lawmakers in there didn't want to look at us," Mark said.

"Just squirming," Hockley said.

"It's exhausting," Jackie said, rubbing her eyes.

They drove back to the hotel, where the same teenage employee was waiting for them at the front desk. "How'd it go today?" he asked. He explained that some of the hotel staff had been watching the local TV news, and they had learned the exact nature of this group's personal business. One of the employees, a bartender in the restaurant, had stayed up all night creating a tribute. She had scoured the Internet for pictures of Dylan Hockley and Daniel Barden and placed a rushed order for customized frames. "Please follow me to the bar," the front desk employee said now. The parents walked with him into a corner of the restaurant that was dark except for the glow of 26 candles, which had been placed on a table next to framed photos of their children. "Our Angel Dylan," one frame read. "Our Angel Daniel," read the other. The table was secluded behind velvet rope, and the bartender came over with a bottle of whiskey.

"Please sit," the bartender said, and the only thing the parents could think to do was to thank her, fill their glasses and drink fast before going upstairs to bed.

They were tired. They missed the kids. They were ready to go home. But there was still more to do. Before the parents left Delaware, they had a news conference with the governor.

They met with him privately first in a hallway at the Capitol. "Thank you for being here," he said. The parents handed him pictures of their children, and he studied each one for a long minute, repeating their names out loud. "Dylan." "Ana." "Daniel." He touched the pictures to his chest and nodded at the parents. "Look, the courage that you have shown to be here today ...well, what can I even say?" he told them.

The parents followed him into his office, which two assistants had staged for the news conference. "It's a casual and not a heavy," one of the press assistants had told the parents, explaining how they would sit with the governor and answer questions while the media taped B-roll. The governor sat at the head of the coffee table. Jackie and Mark held hands on a couch under a chandelier. Hockley and Marquez-Greene sat across from them. Fifteen cameras and 12 reporters crowded into the room. "A good turnout for a small market," the governor's press secretary said, motioning for another staffer to close the door.

"Okay. We're on," the press secretary said, nodding to the governor.

He looked up at the row of cameras. He held up the victims' pictures. He repeated their names. He touched the photos to his chest. "Look, the courage that you have shown to be here today ... well, what can I say?" he told the parents again.

Jackie sat on the couch while the governor kept talking and thought about the first time her family had discussed guns, two days after Daniel's death. Natalie had suggested something that Mark and Jackie thought was simple and beautiful: Why not collect all the guns and bury them at the bottom of the ocean, where they would rot and decay? They had encouraged her to write a letter to the president about her idea, which she had done: "My name is Natalie Barden and I wanted to tell the president that only police officers and the military should get guns," she had written.

But the past five months had taught Mark and Jackie that simplicity and innocence didn't work in politics. Neither did rage or brokenness. Their grief was only effective if it was resolute, polite, purposeful and factual. The uncertain path between a raw, four-minute massacre and U.S. policy was a months-long grind that consisted of marketing campaigns, fundraisers and public relations consultants. In the parents' briefing book for the Delaware trip, a press aide had provided a list of possible talking points, the same suggestions parents had been given in Illinois, New York, New Jersey and Connecticut.

"We are not anti-gun. We are not for gun control. We are for gun responsibility and for gun safety laws," one suggestion read.

"I am here today to honor my child's memory," read another.

"The Sandy Hook shooter used 30-round magazines. He fired 154 bullets in four minutes, murdering 20 children and six adults," read one more.

Now, at this latest news conference, the governor finished his introduction and a reporter raised his hand to ask a question. "This one is for the parents," he said. "How would a high-capacity ban prevent something like the carnage at Sandy Hook?"

Carnage? Mark squeezed Jackie's hand. She stared down at the floor. He looked up at the cameras.

"The bills on the table here make good, common sense," he said.

"This is not about banning or confiscation," Hockley said.

"We are here to honor our children," Marquez-Greene said.

"Our shooter used high-capacity magazines to fire 154 bullets," Hockley said.

"Please know, this is not about gun control but gun responsibility," Mark said, as the governor nodded in affirmation.

"So polished," the press secretary told Mark afterward, squeezing his shoulder, and it was true. He never lost his temper. He always made eye contact. He spoke in anecdotes that were moving and hopeful.

But sometimes the story Mark really wanted to share was the unpolished one, the one that never seemed right for a news conference, or a vigil, or a meet and greet, or the Oval Office, or a TV interview, or a moment of silence, or a Mother's Day card. Sometimes what he really wanted to tell them was what it was like in his house on another unbearable morning, like the one a few days earlier.

All of them awake again in the same room.

James to the bus.

Natalie to the bus.

And then it was upon them, the worst hour of the day, from 7:30 to 8:30 a.m., when Daniel had been alone with them in the house waiting for his bus. They had tried many ways of passing that hour: out to breakfast, back in bed, walking or hiring a trainer to meet them at the gym. A few times they had decided to wait for Daniel's bus themselves, standing at the end of the driveway and climbing the four steps to hug Mr. Wheeler, the longtime bus driver who had loved Daniel and delivered a eulogy about how the boy raced his school bus, running sideways and backward in the grass, tripping and tumbling with his green backpack.

On this particular morning, the Bardens saw their next-door neighbor on the sidewalk at 7:30 and invited her in for coffee. She was a mother of three, including a second-grade girl who had been one of Daniel's best friends. Before his death, the neighbor had come for coffee often, but lately the Bardens found it easier to see her less.

"Come visit," Mark said.

"Are you sure?" the neighbor asked.

"It will be good," Jackie said. "We've been trying to talk more about Daniel."

So the neighbor came inside, poured coffee and started to tell stories they all knew. About how her daughter and Daniel had shared so many secrets, games they played for hours in the driveway and refused to tell anyone else about. About how Daniel had excused himself from a pizza party at her house five nights before his death, because the adults were watching "National Lampoon's Christmas Vacation" in the living room, and Daniel, an old soul and a rule follower, had said: "This language probably isn't appropriate for me."

Then she started telling another story, one the Bardens had never heard before, one about that day. The neighbor said her second-grade daughter had lost her glasses while scrambling to hide in her classroom during the chaos of the shooting. The girl had clung to her teacher's leg on the way out of the school, unable to see anything, and she had still been clinging to that leg when her mother found her alive at the firehouse an hour later. She had brought her daughter home and, later that night, tried to tell her about Daniel. But her daughter had screamed not to say his name, that his name was now one of their secrets. She had sat by the window in her room and looked across the woods to Daniel's room, as she always did, and she had sobbed because she couldn't see it without her glasses.

"She loved him," the neighbor was saying now.

"Oh God," Jackie said. "It's too much. Please stop."

"I'm sorry," the neighbor said, reaching for a box of tissues. "I, I ... I shouldn't have."

"It's okay," Mark said, but now his mind was back inside the school that morning, where it sometimes went. Jackie's imagination walked Daniel to the door of his classroom and no farther. She wanted to protect herself from the details, so she had left the box containing Daniel's clothes from that day untouched and unlooked at in the attic, where state troopers had deposited it a few weeks after his death. Mark, however, felt compelled to know. For seven years, two months and 17 days, he had known every detail of Daniel's life—the teeth that were just beginning to come in, the way his hands moved as they played "Jingle Bells" that morning on the piano—so it seemed necessary that he should also know every detail of its end. He had asked law enforcement officers to give him a tour of the school, which was still an active crime scene, and he had gone there one Friday morning while Jackie stayed home. The officers had walked him through the attack, all four minutes and 154 rounds, and because of that Mark could precisely picture the shooter, with his Bushmaster rifle, his earplugs and his olive green vest, firing six holes into the glass front door. He could hear the shouting over the intercom in the main office, where the principal had been shot, and he could hear the shooter's footsteps on the linoleum hallway as he walked by one first-grade classroom and into the next, Daniel's. He could see the substitute teacher scrambling to move the children into the corner, where there was a small bathroom. He could see all 15 of them huddled in there, squeezed together, and somewhere in that pile he could see Daniel.

Mark could see himself that morning, too, rushing out of the house at 10, knowing only that shots had been fired at Sandy Hook and parents would be reunited with their children at the firehouse. Jackie had started driving from Pawling, calling and texting him again and again. "Do you have him?" "DO YOU HAVE HIM YET?" A priest had announced that the principal had been killed, and Mark had wondered: "How will we explain this to Daniel?" Then the same priest had said 20 children were also dead, and there was shrieking and vomiting in the firehouse, and Mark had imagined Daniel running alone in the woods behind the school. He was fast. He had escaped.

Then the governor was in front of them, and he was saying, "No more survivors," and a state trooper was driving Mark and Jackie home. Mark was sitting in the passenger seat, dazed and quiet and looking over at the state trooper, who had begun to weep.

"I should have waited with you at the school until the end," the neighbor said now, in the kitchen.

"No," Mark said. "You had to get your daughter home."

"Oh dear God," the neighbor said.

"I feel sick," Jackie said, standing up and then sitting back down.

The neighbor looked at the clock and saw it was almost 8:30, time to walk her daughter to the bus. "I have to go," she said, hugging the Bardens, leaving them at the kitchen table. Jackie poured more coffee. Mark checked his phone messages. Jackie walked outside to get the mail and brought it into the living room. Mark opened a package from Minnesota that contained a Sherpa blanket and a note that read: "We will never forget."

The school bus came. The school bus went.

"What do you want to do?" Mark asked, and in that moment, the answer to both of them was clear.

"What can we do?" Jackie said.

"Nothing," Mark said, and he sank down next to her on the couch.

CRITICAL EYE

For Discussion

a. How does this particular examination of the Newtown shootings differ from other kinds of daily news coverage?

b. In light of everything that has happened to the Bardens, how do they view the world now?

c. What does this article reveal to us about our government and its response to nationwide traumas?

Re-approaching the Reading

Imagine that this tragedy happened in a nation like Canada, England, or France? Would the government responses to the tragedy be different? How so? How can news reporting be non-exploitative in situations like these?

Writing Assignment

Compare this article to "Amid Tears, Flickering Candles and Flowers, A Shaken Norway Mourns" by Steven Erlanger. What's similar about the two pieces? What is dissimilar? How do the journalists want the readers to feel? How successful are their journalistic methods?

NICHOLAS KRISTOF

'BRING BACK OUR GIRLS'

DOZENS of heavily armed terrorists rolled into the sleepy little town one night in a convoy of trucks, buses and vans. They made their way to the girls' boarding school.

The high school girls, asleep in their dormitory, awoke to gunfire. The attackers stormed the school, set it on fire, and, residents said, then herded several hundred terrified girls into the vehicles–and drove off and vanished.

That was April 15 in northern Nigeria. The girls were kidnapped by an extremist Muslim group called Boko Haram, whose name in the Hausa language means "Western education is a sin."

These girls, ages 15 to 18 and Christians and Muslims alike, knew the risks of seeking an education, and schools in the area had closed in March for fear of terror attacks. But this school had reopened so that the girls–the stars of their families and villages–could take their final exams. They were expected to move on to become teachers, doctors, lawyers.

Instead, they reportedly are being auctioned off for $12 each to become "wives" of militants. About 50 girls escaped, but the police say that 276 are still missing – and the Nigerian government has done next to nothing to recover the girls.

"We are now asking for world power countries to intervene," the desperate father of a missing 18-year-old girl, Ayesha, told me by phone. He said that the parents had given up on Nigerian government officials–"they are just saying lies"–and pleaded for international pressure on Nigeria to rescue the girls.

The parents pursued the kidnappers, carrying bows and arrows to confront militants armed with AK-47s, but finally had to turn back. The father, who asked not to be named for fear of retribution, said that the parents are now praying to God for the United States and United Nations to help get their daughters back.

While there has been a major international search for the missing people on Malaysian flight MH370, and nonstop news coverage, there has been no meaningful search for the even greater number of missing schoolgirls.

I spoke by telephone with Secretary of State John Kerry, who is visiting Africa, and asked him whether the United States can nudge Nigerian authorities to do more to find the girls.

"We're really pushing them ... about the situation with the girls," Kerry said. "Oh, God! Yes, absolutely." He described it as "not just an act of terrorism. It's a massive human trafficking moment and grotesque."

I asked whether the United States could use satellites or intelligence assets to try to locate the girls. "We're engaged and cooperating," he said, declining to discuss details. Kerry also emphasized the broader effort to disrupt Boko Haram and its financial flows, while supporting the training of Nigerian authorities to respond to terror attacks without violating human rights. "We're upping the game with them," he said.

In hopes of viral pressure on Nigerian authorities to try to recover the girls, campaigns have started on the White House website, on Change.org and on Facebook to demand: "Bring Back Our Girls." All this may or may not help, but it's worth trying.

The attack in Nigeria is part of a global backlash against girls' education by extremists. The Pakistani Taliban shot Malala Yousafzai in the head at age 15 because she advocated for girls' education. Extremists threw acid in the faces of girls walking to school in Afghanistan. And in Nigeria, militants destroyed 50 schools last year alone.

If the girls aren't rescued, "no parent will allow their female child to go to school," Hadiza Bala Usman, who has led protests in Nigeria on behalf of the missing girls, warned in a telephone interview.

Northern Nigeria is a deeply conservative area, and if the schoolgirls are recovered, it may be difficult for them to marry because of suspicions that they are no longer virgins.

While the Nigerian military has shown little interest in rescuing the girls, it has, in the last few years, presided over a brutal counterinsurgency in response to Boko Haram bombings. There is viciousness on both sides.

The best tool to fight extremism is education, especially of girls—and that means ensuring that it is safe to study. The greatest threat to militancy in the long run comes not from drones but from girls with schoolbooks.

"These abducted schoolgirls are my sisters," Malala told me in an email from Britain, where she is recovering from the Taliban attack, "and I call on the international community and the government of Nigeria to take action and save my sisters." She added: "It should be our duty to speak up for our brothers and sisters in Nigeria who are in a very difficult situation."

Malala's right. More than 200 teenage girls have just been enslaved because they had the brains and guts to seek to become teachers or doctors. They deserve a serious international effort to rescue them.

Critical Eye

For Discussion

a. Why does the abduction of the Nigerian schoolgirls deserve an international response?

b. Why are we especially "moved" as human beings when evil befalls children?

Re-approaching the Reading

Compare this article to "The Nightwalkers" by Jeevan Vasagar. What's similar about the treatment of the children within these African nations? What do these articles reveal to us about the devaluation of children and teenagers?

Writing Assignment

Whether it is the Ebola crisis, high rates of HIV and AIDS infection, mass violence, war, or the mistreatment of and violence against children, there is clearly something amiss within certain countries on the African continent. In your opinion, what international social, political, and gender issues have led to the aforementioned crises? What, if anything, can be done to combat these issues?

Index

A

academic authority, 280–286
Adventures of Huckleberry Finn (Twain), 75–79
African identity, institution of slavery and, 265–271
"After Newtown Shooting, Mourning Parents Enter Into the Lonely Quiet" (Saslow), 463–474
"Age of Reason, The" (Paine), 171–205
Ali, Mohammed Naseehu, 162–170
Althaus, Frances A., 412–419
"Amid Tears, Flickering Candles and Flowers, a Shaken Norway Mourns" (Erlanger), 381–384
Angeloro, Al, 360–363
authority, 280–286

B

"bad girl" social construct, 317–322
Baldwin, James, 397–401
Barden family, 463–474
Bible, 210–214
Bidpai, 39–40
biracial children, 376–380, 385–393
birth control, 41–46
"blasphemy," religion and, 171–205
Boko Haram, 475–477
"Brave We Are" (Naqvi), 376–380
Breivik, Anders Behring, 381–384
"Bring Back Our Girls" (Kristof), 475–477
"British Deism," religion and, 171–205
bullying, 350–357, 358–359

C

Cambridge, University of, 215–226
"Camel and His Friends, The" (Bidpai), 39–40
censorship, 360–363
Chestnut, Charles, 385–393
choices, making. *see* "fork-in-the-road moments"
circumcision, of females, 412–419
civility, loss of, 140–153
civil rights
    LGBTQ rights and religion, 206–209
    social responsibility and, 47–56
class and culture of power, 315–363
    "A Lion and Other Animals Go Hunting" (Aesop), 358–359

"Comic Books: How I Learned to Love Reading and Hate the Censors" (Angeloro), 360–363
"Interpreter of Maladies" (Lahiri), 328–342
Notes from the Underground (Dostoyevsky), 350–357
"On the Duty of Civil Disobedience" (Thoreau), 343–349
overview, 315–316
social responsibility and, 19–38
"The Lowest Animal" (Twain), 323–327
"The Making of a Slut" (Wolf), 317–322
colonialism, 140–153
"Comic Books: How I Learned to Love Reading and Hate the Censors" (Angeloro), 360–363
Craig, Todd, 47–56
creating, responsibility and, 305–314
Custer, George Armstrong, 371–375

D

death and violence, 67–153
Adventures of Huckleberry Finn (Twain), 75–79
"Lynch Law in America" (Wells-Barnett), 80–86
overview, 67–68
Paradise (Morrison), 69–74
"Three California Teens Arrested for Rape that Allegedly Drove Teen Girl to Suicide, Parents Demand Justice" (Walsh), 137–139
The Tragedy of Macbeth (Shakespeare), 87–136
The War of the Worlds (Wells), 140–153
detective fiction. *see Study in Scarlet, A* (Doyle)
Diaz, Junot, 402–411
disasters. *see* manmade and natural disasters
"Divinity School Address" (Emerson), 215–226
"Do Palestinians Really Exist?" (Obeidallah), 367–370
Dorris, Cara, 420–422
Dostoyevsky, Fyodor, 350–357
Douglass, Frederick, 265–271
Doyle, Sir Arthur Conan, 229–264

E

ego. *see Tragedy of Macbeth, The* (Shakespeare)
Emerson, Ralph Waldo
"Divinity School Address," 215–226
"Self-Reliance," 3–18
Erlanger, Steven, 381–384
ethnicity
ethnic identity and class, 328–342
Hip Hop portrayal of, 287–305
"Evening Visit, An" (Chestnut), 385–393

F

faith. *see* religion, faith, and spirituality
"Fantomina: Or, Love in a Maze" (Haywood), 423–440
"Father, A" (Mukherjee), 272–279
"Female Circumcision: Rite of Passage or Violation of Rights?" (Althaus), 412–419
Ferrell, Monique, 287–305
"Fiesta 1980" (Diaz), 402–411
"fork-in-the-road moments," 227–314
"A Father" (Mukherjee), 272–279
Frankenstein (Shelley), 305–314
"Go Brooklyn!" (Ferrell), 287–305
"Go Carolina" (Sedaris), 280–286
Narrative of the Life of Frederick Douglass, An American Slave (Douglass), 265–271
overview, 227–228
A Study in Scarlet (Doyle), 229–264
Francis (Pope), 206–209
Frankenstein (Shelley), 305–314
friendship, 19–38

G

gender, sex, and sexuality, 393–440
"Fantomina: Or, Love in a Maze" (Haywood), 423–440
"Female Circumcision: Rite of Passage or Violation of Rights?" (Althaus), 412–419
"Fiesta 1980" (Diaz), 402–411
gender roles, 393–394
gender roles and fatherhood, 272–279
Giovannia's Room (Baldwin), 397–401
"My Fake Levantine Romance" (Dorris), 420–422
overview, 393–394

respect and, 170
sexual standards for females and males, 317–322
slavery and, 265–271
Genesis, 210–214
genital mutilation, 412–419
"Ghosts of the Tsunami" (Parry), 451–462
Giovanni's Room (Baldwin), 397–401
"Go Brooklyn!" (Ferrell), 287–305
"Go Carolina" (Sedaris), 280–286
government, allegiance and, 343–349
"Great Flood, The" (Book of Genesis), 210–214

H

Haiti, earthquake in, 443–446
Haywood, Eliza, 423–440
Hip Hop, 47–56, 287–305
Hosseini, Khaled, 19–38
House Behind the Cedars, The (Chestnut). *see* "Evening Visit, An" (Chestnut)

I

immigrants, fatherhood and, 272–279
imperialism, 140–153
indigenous population, of Alaska, 157–161
"inner genius," 3–18
Inter African Committee Against Harmful Traditional Practices (IAC), 412
"Interpreter of Maladies" (Lahiri), 328–342
interracial relations, 385–393

J

Japan, tsunami in, 451–462

K

Kite Runner, The (Hosseini), 19–38
Kristof, Nicholas, 475–477

L

Lahiri, Jhumpa, 328–342
LGBTQ issues
religion and, 206–209
same-sex desire and, 397–401
sexual desire and, 420–422
"Lion and Other Animals Go Hunting, A" (Aesop), 358–359
Little Big Horn, battle of, 371–375
"Lowest Animal, The" (Twain), 323–327
lynching, 80–86

M

"Making of a Slut, The" (Wolf), 317–322
male frailty. *see Tragedy of Macbeth, The* (Shakespeare)
"Mallam Sile" (Ali), 162–170
manmade and natural disasters, 441–477
"After Newtown Shooting, Mourning Parents Enter Into the Lonely Quiet" (Saslow), 463–474
"Bring Back Our Girls" (Kristof), 475–477
"Ghosts of the Tsunami" (Parry), 451–462
overview, 441–442
"Quake Accentuated Chasm That Has Defined Haiti" (Romero), 443–446
"The Nightwalkers" (Vasagar), 447–450
mob mentality, 75–79
Morrison, Toni, 69–74
music, Hip Hop, 47–56, 287–305
"My Fake Levantine Romance" (Dorris), 420–422

N

Naqvi, Tahira, 376–380
Narrative of the Life of Frederick Douglass, An American Slave (Douglass), 265–271
natural disasters. *see* manmade and natural disasters
Newtown (Connecticut), shootings in, 463–474
Nigeria, Boko Haram kidnappings in, 475–477
"Nightwalkers, The" (Vasagar), 447–450
Noah (Biblical character), 210–214
Norway, shootings at, 381–384
Notes from the Underground (Dostoyevsky), 350–357

O

Obeidallah, Dean, 367–370
"On the Duty of Civil Disobedience" (Thoreau), 343–349
"Open Season 2014": The Birth of Civil Rights Lost (Craig), 47–56
"others," 366

P

Paine, Thomas, 171–205
Palestinians, 367–370
Paradise (Morrison), 69–74
Parry, Richard Lloyd, 451–462
Parsons, Rehtaeh, 137–139
political representation, spirituality and, 157–161
Pott, Audrie, 137–139
power. *see* class and culture of power

Q

"Quake Accentuated Chasm That Has Defined Haiti" (Romero), 443–446

R

race and racial matters, 365–393
 "Amid Tears, Flickering Candles and Flowers, a Shaken Norway Mourns" (Erlanger), 381–384
 "An Evening Visit" (Chestnut), 385–393
 "Brave We Are" (Naqvi), 376–380
 "Do Palestinians Really Exist?" (Obeidallah), 367–370
 Hip Hop portrayal of, 287–305
 overview, 365–366
 racism and lynching, 80–86
 "Young Men, Go Out and Fight Them" (Wooden Leg), 371–375
rape, 137–139
religion, faith, and spirituality, 155–226
 "Divinity School Address" (Emerson), 215–226
 "Mallam Sile" (Ali), 162–170
 overview, 155–156
 "The Age of Reason" (Paine), 171–205
 "The Great Flood" (Book of Genesis), 210–214
 "When Global Warming Kills Your God" (Weymouth), 157–161
 "When It Comes to Same-Sex Marriage, Both Sides Claim Pope Francis" (Sneed), 206–209
respect, gender roles and, 170
"Ride, The" (Williams), 57–65
Romero, Simon, 443–446

S

same-sex marriage, religion and, 206–209
Sanger, Margaret, 41–46
Saslow, Eli, 463–474
Sedaris, David, 280–286
"Self-Reliance" (Emerson), 3–18
self-sacrifice, 39–40
Shakespeare, William, 87–136
Shelley, Mary, 305–314
Sioux nation, 371–375
slavery, 265–271, 447–450
Sneed, Tierney, 206–209
social Darwinism, 140–153
social responsibility, 1–65
 "Open Season 2014": The Birth of Civil Rights Lost (Craig), 47–56
 overview, 1–2
 "Self-Reliance" (Emerson), 3–18
 "The Camel and His Friends" (Bidpai), 39–40
 The Kite Runner (Hosseini), 19–38
 "The Ride" (Williams), 57–65
 "The Turbid Ebb and Flow of Mystery" (Sanger), 41–46
specieism, 323–327
spirituality. *see* religion, faith, and spirituality
Study in Scarlet, A (Doyle), 229–264
suicide, 137–139

T

Thoreau, Henry David, 343–349
Tragedy of Macbeth, The (Shakespeare), 87–136
"Turbid Ebb and Flow of Mystery, The" (Sanger), 41–46
Twain, Mark
 Adventures of Huckleberry Finn, 75–79
 "The Lowest Animal," 323–327

U

Uganda, child slaves in, 447–450
University of Cambridge, Emerson's address to, 215–226
Utoya (Norway), shootings at, 381–384

V

Vasagar, Jeevan, 447–450
violence
  social responsibility and, 57–65 (*see also* death and violence)
  against women, 69–74

W

Walsh, Michael, 137–139
War of the Worlds, The (Wells), 140–153
Wells, H. G., 140–153
Wells-Barnett, Ida B., 80–86
Weymouth, Adam, 157–161
"When Global Warming Kills Your God" (Weymouth), 157–161
"When It Comes to Same-Sex Marriage, Both Sides Claim Pope Francis" (Sneed), 206–209
Williams, JL, 57–65
Wolf, Naomi, 317–322
women, violence against, 69–74
Wooden Leg, 371–375
World Health Organization (WHO), 412

Y

"Young Men, Go Out and Fight Them" (Wooden Leg), 371–375
Yup'ik people, 157–161

CPSIA information can be obtained at www.ICGtesting.com
Printed in the USA
LVOW01s1307020215

425068LV00001B/1/P